The SURFING Yearbook

Margo, by Sean Davey.

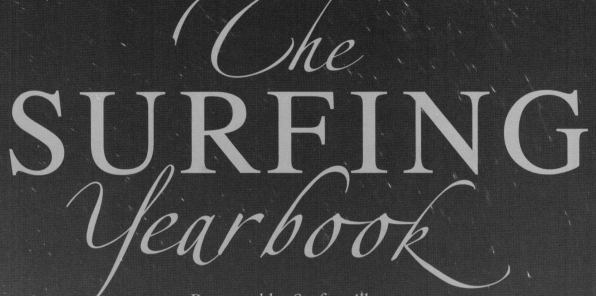

The SURFING Yearbook

Presented by Surfersvillage

First Edition

GIBBS SMITH
TO ENRICH AND INSPIRE HUMANKIND
Salt Lake City | Charleston | Santa Fe | Santa Barbara

First Edition

13 12 11 10 09   5 4 3 2 1

Text © 2009 Surfersvillage unless otherwise noted
Photographs © 2009 as noted througout

Published by
Gibbs Smith
P.O. Box 667
Layton, Utah 84041

Orders: 1.800.835.4993
www.gibbs-smith.com

Designed by Kurt Wahlner
Almanac icon designed by Allison Reich
Contents photo MickeySmith.com
Printed and bound in Australia

Gibbs Smith books are printed on either recycled, 100%
post-consumer waste, FSC-certified papers or on paper
produced from a 100% certified sustainable forest/
controlled wood source.

ISBN 13: 978-1-4236-0558-4

ISBN 10: 1-4236-0558-6

ISSN 1947-4296

Contents

S L A T E R

KELLY SLATER 9X ASP WORLD CHAMPION

 www.quiksilver-europe.com

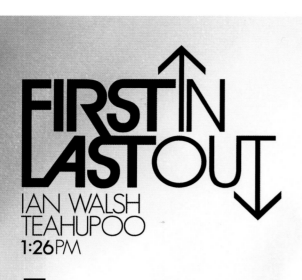

FIRST IN
LAST OUT
IAN WALSH
TEAHUPOO
1:26PM
—

"A WAVE THAT
POWERFUL, THAT BIG...
IT'S ADDICTIVE"
IAN WALSH
*

O'NEILL

NATHAN FLETCHER / JOEL TUDOR / TIMMY REYES / KALANI CHAPMAN / SHEA LOPEZ / DANE_PAT_TANNER GUDAUSKAS
JASON RATBOY COLLINS / JOHN JOHN_NATHAN_IVAN FLORENCE / REEF MCINTOSH / JOSH MULCOY / MIKE GLEASON
TYLER_RUSSEL SMITH / KAI BORG GARCIA / ALEX KNOST / ANDREW DOHENY

GIRLS : KARINA PETRONI / ERICA HOSSEINI / SAGE ERICKSON / LEILA HURST / ALEX FLORENCE

FOR BEFORE AND AFTER SURFING. VANSSURF.COM

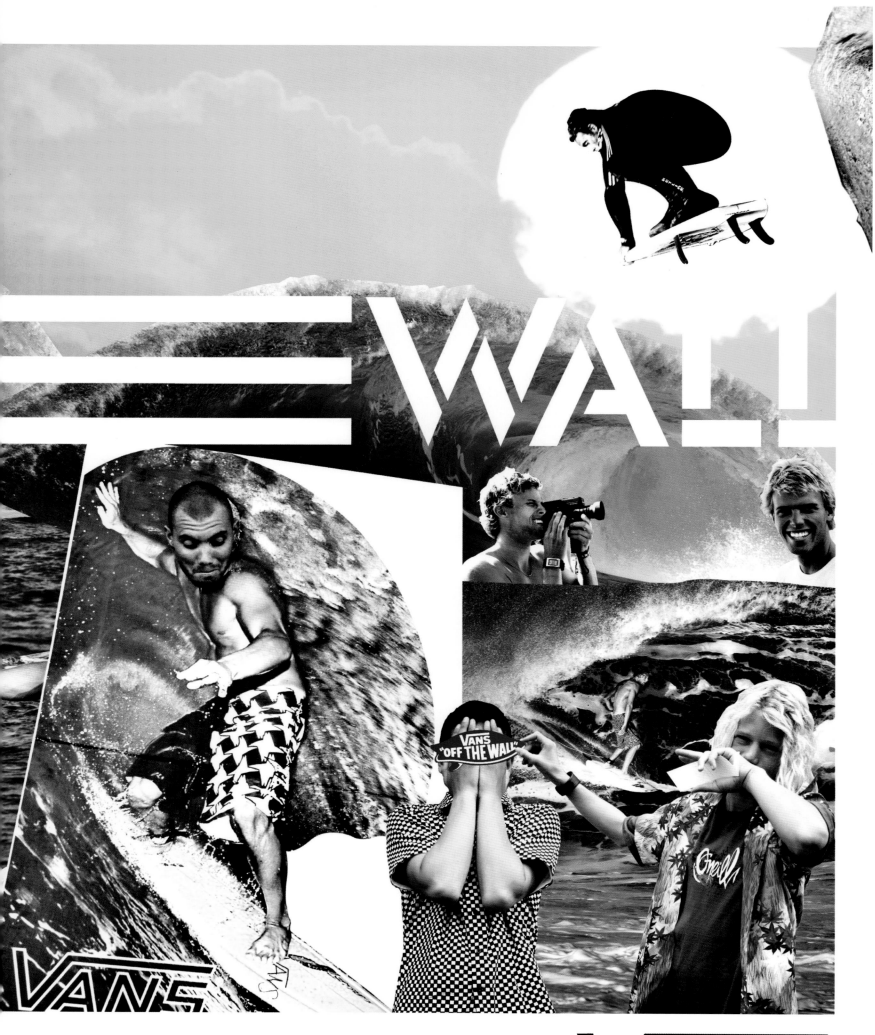

Tim Boal

FREEFREEFREEFREEFREEF REEF REEF REEF REEF **REEF**

to control your destiny ...

europe.reef.com

The Best

FEATURED BOATS: (this pic) the iconic *Indies Trader I*, and over the page, the mighty *Indies Trader III*.

In the

Maldives

...the sunny side of life

www.visitmaldives.com

Chaaya ISLAND DHONVELI

Pasta Point

Atoll Adventures @ Chaaya Island Dhonveli
....the Maldives premier surfing tour.

Atoll Travel

www.atolltravel.com
Email: info@atolltravel.com

WaterWays

www.waterwaystravel.com
Email: waterways@waterwaystravel.com

Jaymes Triglone
Dawn sessions, picture by Smithy
05:30 am. on Sunday, 20 May 2007
at Whale Beach, Australia

www.sharkenergy.com

Introduction

I f the year began ominously, with giant swells testing
surfers at Belharra in the Atlantic and Cortes Bank in the
Pacific, it ended considerably more ominously, with the
global financial crisis finally taking its toll on the surfing
industry, threaten-ing everyone from cottage industry shapers
to the giant corporations. But if there was any consolation to be
had, it was in the fact that surfing remained surfing, unassailed
by, if not immune from, the ebbs and flows of fortune in these
troubled times.

While the excrement connected with the overhead cooling
device all over the world, surfers continued to ride waves
that were increasingly protected by a greater awareness of
the necessity to save our playgrounds, and they rode them on
a variety of surfcraft that reflected a new appreciation of the
many facets of our surfing culture, from its Polynesian roots to
its greener future.

At the same time, we were inspired by some of the finest
competitive surfing performances ever, led from the front by
King Kelly, who took the first event on the Dream Tour and
never looked back, crushing his opposition to secure six wins
on his way to a record ninth world title. The youngest surfer
to win a world title, the oldest, the most tour victories, the
longest run of successive titles . . . the statistics have become
almost meaningless as the Slater machine has powered through
the second half of a most remarkable career, a career that
may not be over yet. Perhaps of even greater interest than the
Slater statistics is the impact that his dominance has had on
his contemporaries. It is almost 30 years since Mark Richards
began a run of four consecutive world titles that broke the hearts
and spirits of contenders such as Cheyne Horan. Now Slater has
pushed Andy Irons out of the limelight and effectively relegated
greats like Taj Burrow and Joel Parkinson to supporting roles.
It is fitting, therefore, that Mark Richards should be the one to
explore the Slater legacy in this, our first *Surfing Yearbook*.

As the year began, it seemed that Australia's new title
twins, Mick Fanning and Stephanie Gilmore, were going to
travel everywhere by helicopter, courtesy of their over-excited
sponsor, Rip Curl. But while Mick soon fell to earth, Steph
proved she had the mettle to come from behind and snatch
a second women's ASP title, outfoxing a late run by Layne
Beachley, who had earlier drawn the curtain on a glorious
career in which seven world titles made her the second most
successful surfer in history. Steph pressed her claim as a future
legend, while Layne bowed out with great dignity, at the top of
her game and anointing her successor.

Meanwhile, the International Surfing Association (ISA),
surfing's other global engine room, had its busiest year on
record, staging three world championships while moving ever
closer to its goal of surfing being accepted as an Olympic sport.

Interestingly, because of the necessity to provide surfable waves at the Olympic host cities, this goal has become part of a broader movement to bring surfing to the masses by creating wave stadiums wherever they are likely to be profitable. With high-quality wave-making machinery in place in several beach theme parks around the world, it seems likely that, whether the purists like it or not, in the future many, perhaps a majority of, people will experience artificial surfing rather than the real thing. But in terms of experiential buzz, it beats surfing the Web.

Speaking of which, through its increasingly sophisticated network of news, commerce and forecasting, real surfing has become an important presence on the Web, and through live Webcasts, major surfing events have finally found the audience they need to survive and even thrive. For all that, however, there is a growing resistance to the "know before you go" concept of Webcams, which, many say, multiply the crowd factor at better-known breaks.

These issues and many more are canvassed in this first *Surfing Yearbook*, along with a week-by-week almanac that offers a light and easy-to-read take on events that relate to surfing around the world, plus the most comprehensive compendium of competition results ever presented in print. It's an ambitious volume you have before you, and one we hope will become an annual contribution to the positive representation of our sport and culture around the world.

If you are a surfer, or you have surfers in your family or circle of friends, you will understand what we are trying to achieve with *The Surfing Yearbook*, but if you are new to surfing, a brief primer might be helpful.

Originally the sport of Polynesian nobility, surfing made its first migration, to the Hawaiian Islands in about 400 AD, and by 1000 AD, the Hawaiians had progressed to stand-up surfboards. By the time of its colonization, Hawaii had embraced surfing as a sport that helped define its culture and its sense of identity. But all that was taken away when the nineteenth- century Calvinists became their moral guardians and declared that surfing was too much fun. After decades under wraps, however, surfing re-emerged, in part because of its discovery by popular writers such as Mark Twain and Jack London.

When California tourism and industry boosters sponsored the Irish/ Hawaiian George Freeth to perform exhibitions in southern California in the early years of the twentieth century, the sport took off in the western world's most potent social laboratory. Meanwhile, the Hawaiian Olympic swimming champion Duke Kahanamoku introduced surfing to Australia in 1915 and soon after became the first surfing superstar. By the outbreak of World War II, there were significant (although quite different) surfing cultures in California and Australia, as well as in Hawaii. After the war, when young men had experienced the thrill of travel and adventure, the sport exploded, and by the late 1950s, the surfboard had evolved from a stylized piece of wood to a finely tuned instrument.

Along with the birth of the surfboard industry (followed within the decade by surfwear) came the emergence of the surf contest, fathered by the Makaha carnival sponsored by service clubs in Hawaii from the early '50s. The Makaha event became the unofficial world championships until the establishment, in 1964, of an official version. A decade later, surfing, like tennis and golf, embraced the concept of a pro tour, which was formalized in 1976, with Australian Peter Townend winning the first world pro title. These days, the Association of Surfing Professionals manages the men's and women's "dream tours" and strong qualifying and junior series. Amateur surfing took a back seat for some years, until the emergence of a strong and unified International Surfing Association, which now oversees the direction of national governing bodies all over the world. We are proud to have the support of, and contributions from, both of surfing's international governing bodies.

In 2008, we could boast a $10 billion industry and a strong and healthy competitive surfing structure that encouraged the development of the sport at all levels in many parts of the world. In 2009, our goal will be to ensure that the hard work of so many people over so many years is protected and that we build on all the opportunities that uncertain times present.

And if all else fails, we can just go surfing!

Finally, and on a personal note, I feel quite honored to have been appointed by Surfersvillage founder Bruce Boal to head up the editorial team on this project; but, of course, it has been very much a team effort, and this will be acknowledged elsewhere. For here and now, let me just doff my cap to Captain Bruce for keeping on course through fair seas and foul.

— **Phil Jarratt**

Kelly Slater and Phil Jarratt, Bakio, Spain. Photo Jackie Jarratt.

Tim Boal, 2008 ASP European Champion, & 2009 World Tour rookie. Photo Alex Laurel/Reef.

WEEK 1
JANUARY 1–7

● AUSTRALIA

As huge swells batter Sydney's northern beaches on New Year's morning, 10-year-old James Grant takes up a position on the balcony of his parents' North Narrabeen apartment to watch for his heroes competing in the Billabong Pro Junior. Suddenly the keen-eyed grom notices a lone surfer in distress in pounding waves. James drops his binoculars and sprints 400 meters to the lifeguard tower to raise the alert. The surfer was soon pulled from the break. Nice one, James!

As the swells continue to smash the east coast, 16-year-old Matthew Brown breaks his leash while surfing Snapper Rocks in Queensland and is swept 7 kilometers north before being rescued.

● HAWAII

Just two weeks after its debut, the *New York Times* weighs in to the debate over the controversial Hawaii Superferry, which can take 866 passengers and 286 cars between Honolulu and Maui. Opponents of the ferry are claiming that it is an environmental and social hazard, threatening the lives of calving humpback whales as it slices through the water at speed, and the lifestyles of outer island residents as it dumps thousands of itinerants in pick-ups each week.

Ten-year-old lifesaver James Grant. Photo Newspix/Carlos Furtado.

● CALIFORNIA

Former world longboard champion Joel Tudor places second in the Brazilian Jiu-Jitsu No-Gi World Championships in Los Angeles.

● UK

Developers in Cornwall claim a boom year ahead, thanks to the growth of the Newquay-based 42 million pound local surfing industry. Stuart Brereton, land director for the Acorn Property Group, says young, well-to-do people were keen to invest not just in bricks and mortar but in the surf lifestyle. "It's all about the sea, the buzz of surfing,"

he says. Acorn is one of several development groups building or planning massive apartment complexes along the coast, while many of the traditional chintzy hotels are being converted into studio flats, known in developer-speak as "surf-pods."

● MEXICO

A spate of rapes, carjacking and armed robberies is having a serious impact on surfing-related tourism in northern Baja California, according to San Diego surfers. Lori Hoffman, a San Diego nurse, says she was sexually assaulted in front of her boyfriend, surf instructor Pat Weber, at a campground

200 miles south of the border. Weber was forced to kneel at gunpoint while the attack took place. Baja tourism officials acknowledge that visitation is down as much as 30 percent in the worst areas.

● AUSTRALIA

In Sydney for a free performance, Beach Boys legend Brian Wilson admits he has been afraid of surfing ever since an early attempt ended in near-disaster. Asked if he will be taking advantage of Sydney's monster swell, he says, "No way. I tried it one time and my board almost hit me in the head. That was the end of Brian Wilson the surfer."

WEEK 2
JANUARY 8–14

● CALIFORNIA

While the Quiksilver in Memory of Eddie Aikau remains on hold as an anticipated huge swell fails to fully materialize, the Mavericks Contest gets a green light to run in solid 25 feet plus surf at Half Moon Bay, south of San Francisco. A huge crowd watches from the cliffs, on the big screen at San Francisco's AT&T Park or on-line at MySpace.com as San Clemente's Greg Long takes the title from defending champion Grant "Twiggy" Baker of South Africa. With the swell already beginning to back off, the finalists agree to share the prize money equally.

Wave of the Week

● CALIFORNIA

Possibly the biggest wave ever ridden—estimated to be between 75 and 85 feet—was surfed at Cortes Bank on January 5 by Mike "Snips" Parsons and photographed by Rob Brown. Snips and Brad Gerlach, Greg Long and Grant Baker had to act fast to take advantage of a window of clean swell between huge storms.

● FRANCE

Consolation prize WOTW goes to Vincent Lartizen from Hossegor, who took this Belharra drop on January 4.

Mike Parsons, Billabong XXL Global Big Wave Awards. Photo Robert Brown/BillabongXXL.com.

Vincent Lartizen, Billabong XXL Global Big Wave Awards. Photo Greg Rabejac/BillabongXXL.com.

Winner Greg Long. Photo maverickssurf.com.

Pregnant former world champ Chelsea Georgeson Hedges. Photo Swilly.

Matt Argyle. Photo Will Comer.

Denis Callinan.

● AUSTRALIA

The Roxy Surf Festival kicks off at Philip Island, Victoria, without former title-holder Chelsea Georgeson Hedges, who has announced her first pregnancy, with she and shaper husband Jason expecting a baby in June. Reigning world women's champ Steph Gilmore also misses the event owing to sponsor commitments.

● BRITAIN

As the popularity of stand-up paddle surfing continues to grow around the world, paddlers in the UK establish the British Stand Up Paddle Surfing Association, announcing a five-event UK tour to be held across the '08 summer. Meanwhile, in Florida, the stand-up paddle skateboard makes its debut. The Kahuna Big Stick is said to be perfect for sidewalk paddling. Go figure.

● AUSTRALIA

Historian Mark Maddox puts the cat amongst the pigeons with his bold assertion that the legendary Duke Kahanamoku was not the first person to ride a surfboard in Australia. "The story of the Duke being the first . . . is a romantic myth," he says, launching his book, the catchily titled *100 Years: A Celebration of Surf Lifesaving at North Steyne*. Maddox claims that, in fact, the Duke was forced to stage his famous 1914 exhibition at Freshwater Beach because of the large crowd of boardriders in the water at North Steyne. Serious surfing historians, like Malcolm Gault-Williams, are skeptical of the claims.

WEEK 3
JANUARY 15–21

● AUSTRALIA

Gold Coast surfers are mourning the passing of surfing solicitor Denis Callinan, who died January 16 of complications following a heart attack in December. The charismatic 53-year-old Burleigh Heads surfer was known as an absolute charger in the waves, and a tireless worker for charity on the land. "Only last month he helped raise $100,000 for cancer kids," said best mate Rabbit Bartholomew. Back in the '80s, Dennis founded Surfers Against Nuclear Destruction (later Surfers Against Nature's Destruction) and remained president of the eco-activist group until his death.

● CALIFORNIA

US bookmaker BetUs enters the fast-growing world of betting on the results of the ASP World Tour, offering highly competitive odds on which surfer will win the world title and each event on the tour. Not to be outdone, South African bookmaker Black Pearl Betting also fields the tour. Surfers can compare the odds on offer at surfing-odds.com.

● BRITAIN

Two-meter waves will break in front of a disused dock on London's River Thames, if surfer/entrepreneur Steve Jones can get his Venture Xtreme at Silvertown Quays to fly. Jones says he is on track to have the 20-million-pound project operational by 2011, offering urban surfers the "quintessential California surf lifestyle," complete with palm trees, fire pits and barbeques. (June gloom shouldn't be a problem either!) Punters will pay 30 pounds for an hour's session, with at least 10 waves guaranteed.

● EUROPE

Belgian surf nuts Toni Vanderwalle and Bart Van Vooren kick off the 25th birthday celebrations for their D'Light company, distributors of O'Neill products. The partners, possibly Europe's best-traveled surfers as well as savvy businessmen, plan a few birthday surf trips as well as cake-cutting parties.

● CALIFORNIA

California governor Arnold Schwarzenegger comes out in support of the controversial proposed 241 toll road extension right on top of the iconic Trestles surf break. "We're absolutely taken aback by this," says Surfrider Foundation CEO Jim Moriarty. "For the governor to take this unprecedented step of interfering with the workings of an independent commission . . . is entirely inappropriate." Schwarzenegger's support for the road, which would affect

Lower Trestles. Photo ASP Karen © Covered Images.

more than 60 percent of the San Onofre State Beach Park, comes just a week after his unveiling of a plan to close down 48 California state parks.

● HAWAII

Former world longboard champion Bonga Perkins takes out the first ever stand-up paddle surfing event on Oahu's North Shore. With 18- to 20-foot

Bonga Perkins. Photo Allen Mozo.

monster westerly peaks hitting Sunset Beach, Bonga shows his class in taking down an international field of big wave riders and paddlers to win the Paddle Core Fitness Pro.

Bustin' poster. Courtesy Fresh & Smoked Films.

Inspired by Gisele. Photo Associated Press/Evolution Surf.

WEEK 4
JANUARY 22–28

● CALIFORNIA

The long-awaited surf documentary *Bustin' Down The Door* premiers at the Santa Barbara Film Festival, with a sellout crowd filling the 2,200-seat Arlington Theater. The festival has so many ticket requests it has to program further screenings. Producer Shaun Tomson, the 1977 world champion, gathers fellow world champions Rabbit Bartholomew, Peter Townend and Mark Richards around him for a post-movie discussion of the North Shore seasons more than 30 years ago that revolutionized pro surfing.

● HAWAII

The waiting period for the 36th annual Pipeline Bodysurfing Classic starts January 27, with a good swell predicted to arrive in time for the one-day event to be decided. Hawaii's Steve Kapela defends his 2006 title (due to permit

conflicts, the event was not held in 2007) against such bodysurfing greats as Mike Stewart, Mark Cunningham, Todd Sells and Keith Malloy.

● ASIA

A sudden tropical downpour does not dampen the spirits of more than 40,000 Malaysian surfing fans at the Quiksilver Revolution 2.0 surf, skate and music show at Kuala Lumpur's Sunway Lagoon wave pool. Two-time world aerial champion Josh Kerr of Australia thrills the crowd with huge airs against the night sky, while fellow Aussie Troy Brooks lands several of his patented "superman" moves.

● CALIFORNIA

Evolution Surf launches its "Surf Celebrity Exclusive Editions" surfboard range, which includes boards "designed and inspired" by superspunk celebs like Cameron Diaz, Gisele Bundchen and Tyra Banks. The garish celebrity specials retail between $2,800 and $4,500.

WEEK 5
JANUARY 29–FEBRUARY 4

● BRITAIN

When surfing brothers Rob and Mart Drake-Knight both became seriously ill from surfing in polluted European waters, they decided to go into business spreading the word about saving the planet. The result is Isle of Wight–based Rapanui Clothing, an organic

Photo www.rapanuiclothing.com.

and sustainable company powered by renewable energy and using only natural fabrics. The brothers, both in their early twenties, claim that Rapanui is possibly the greenest clothing company in the world. Mart's studies in renewable energy engineering gave him an insight into what could be achieved, and now their sustainable bamboo, organic and convergence cotton garments are selling so well that Rapanui has imposed an "earth tax" on itself, with 5 percent of profits being donated to conservation charities.

● CALIFORNIA

Surfwear giant Quiksilver appoints investment bank JP Morgan to help offload its troubled ski and snowboard brand, Rossignol. Quiksilver acquired the venerable French snow company in 2005, but it has underperformed ever since. Quiksilver wrote down the carrying value of Rossignol by $166 million in the 2007 financial year.

An all-star cast is on hand at Mavericks February 1 for one of the best swells of the season. Big wave chargers Greg Long, Garrett McNamara, Jamie Mitchell, Grant Washburn and Carlos Burle are all seem in the lineup braving the freezing conditions, but the star of the day is Hawaii's 15-year-old Jon-Jon Florence, who becomes the youngest surfer to paddle into a Mavs monster.

James Watson, Mavericks. Photo Eric Akiskalian/Towsurfer.com.

Aritz Aranburu. Photo Aquashot/Aspeurope.com.

Whale activists Dave Rastovich and Hannah Fraser. Photo Global Surf Industries.

● EUROPE

Aritz Aranburu from Zarautz, Spain, becomes the first Basque and Spanish surfer to qualify for the ASP's World Championship Tour, after almost a decade of climbing the ladder through junior, regional and then ASP Europe events. After just two years on the WQS tour full time, Aritz won the European Pro Tour championship in 2007 on his way to qualifying for the World Tour at just 22. He becomes one of Europe's "Fantastic Four" on the ASP World Tour.

WEEK 6
FEBRUARY 5–11

● CALIFORNIA

The International Surfing Association calls for global standardization of surf schools and a global educational standard for instructors. The ISA, which introduced a register of surf schools around the world in 2007, listing only those that met minimum safety standards and practices, wants all surf schools to operate through a coaching accreditation scheme. Already it has Surfing New Zealand, Surfing Australia, AIP Japan, CBS Brazil, Austrian Surfing and Viareggio Surf School in Italy as "official presenters."

● HAWAII

ASP tour surfer Fred Patacchia explains just what was going on when he hit the beach in the middle of the final of the Monster Energy Pro WQS event at Pipeline and swapped his surfboard for a pretty pink bodyboard. Cornered on the issue by the ASP tour website, Freddy fesses up. "Pancho Sullivan had us all combo'ed halfway through the final. Conditions weren't that good and I could see there was no way I could win, so I decided to pay Pancho a compliment and just call it a day. But when I reached the beach, the Hawaiians started yelling at me to get back out

there. Then they started yelling, "Take the bodyboard!" So I grabbed this pink thing that a guy had been riding earlier and paddled out, got one wave on it and took my worst wipeout of the day. It was all in fun, seemed like a good idea at the time . . . but Pinky won't be coming on tour with me."

● EUROPE

Patagonia, Inc., is awarded "Ecobrand of the Year at the Volvo Eco-Design Forum, part of the ISPO trade show in Munich, Germany. The award recognizes the California-based brand's efforts and initiatives to lower its impact on the environment. The judges note that in 2008, 74 percent of Patagonia's products contain an e-fiber and 53 percent are recyclable.

Irish/English tow team Al Mennie and Duncan Scott are nominated for the Billabong XXL Big Wave Awards following an epic season on the Irish west coast. In December 2007, the pair rode waves 55 to 60 feet high, the biggest waves ever recorded by Ireland's Marine Institute. The nomination is the first for either Irish or UK surfers and is testament to the commitment of the duo, who this season surfed Aileens at minus nine degrees centigrade with snow on the beach!

Fred Patacchia and Pinky. Photo ASP Towner © Covered Images.

● AUSTRALIA

Japanese Yakuza gangsters launch a campaign of intimidation to force a media blackout on negative publicity about the country's killing of whales and dolphins. Australian surfer/activist Dave Rastovich, who led a hugely publicized raid on the dolphin killing fields in Japan in late 2007, said the Japanese surf industry was feeling the heat. "Goons for the fishing industry are visiting surf stores and threatening people with financial punishment," says Rasta.

Duncan Scott, Aileens, Ireland. Photo Aaron Pearce.

Commitment. Photo Aaron Pearce.

WEEK 7
FEBRUARY 12–18

CALIFORNIA
● Surfing rabbi Yom Tov Glaser jets in from Jerusalem to play music and spread Hasidic wisdom amongst students at his alma mater University of

Surfing rabbi Yom Tov Glaser and Kelly Slater. Photo John D. Goodman.

California Santa Barbara. But the party-loving rabbi also finds time to catch a few waves at Rincon and hang out with Kelly Slater and Jack Johnson.

SOUTH AFRICA
● Surfing sensation Jordy Smith is crowned surfer of the year for the second year in a row at the South African Surfing Awards in Durban. The young power surfer is now South Africa's great hope on the World Championship Tour. Pioneer surfer Frenchy Fredericks and shaper Spider Murphy are inducted into the Hall of Fame.

Kirra from the air. Photo Reward Developments Australia Pty Ltd.

Lennox from the air. Photo Above Photography.

CALIFORNIA
● Quiksilver announces that company president Bernard Mariette has resigned "to pursue other interests." This follows the appointment of JP Morgan to help off-load struggling snow subsidiary Rossignol. Mariette, architect of the 2005 purchase, is said to be putting together an acquisition plan for Rossignol.

AUSTRALIA
● Business leaders in Kirra, once the home of the Gold Coast's deepest barrels, launch the Kirra Business Group (KBG) to fight for the restoration of the famous wave, alongside the recently formed Kirra Point Committee. Since the movement of sand destroyed

the point break a few years back, the movement of surfers to the Snapper Rocks Superbank has pretty much destroyed business. KBG spokesperson John Rankin says the group will form relationships with government and environmental interests to explore ways of bringing back the wave and the people.

● Meanwhile, a couple of hours south on another of Australia's fabled surf breaks, Lennox Head, has become the country's largest surfing reserve. The new reserve declared by the New South Wales government covers some 400 hectares and stretches 7.5 kilometers along the coast.

WEEK 8
FEBRUARY 19–25

CALIFORNIA
● The long-awaited history of the Gotcha brand, *Goin' Big: Gotcha and the Evolution of Modern Surf Style,* is published. In the style of 2006's Quiksilver history, the Gotcha book is big and brassy, with more than 150 pages of advertising and product design. Gotcha, founded by Michael Tomson and Joel Cooper at the beginning of the '80s, had by the end of the decade become the benchmark for surf style's reach into the broader marketplace. The book celebrates the brand's audacious decade at the top.

Cover of Goin' Big. *Courtesy of Gotcha.*

AUSTRALIA
● The atmosphere is electric at the Gold Coast Convention Center as local heroes Mick Fanning and Steph Gilmore arrive by helicopter to be crowned world champions. Fanning receives his first title after six years on the tour, while Gilmore makes history by claiming the title in her maiden year. Also receiving accolades are men's runner-up Taj Burrow, rookie of the year Jeremy Flores and most improved surfer Bede Durbidge. Brazil's Phil Rajzman is crowned men's longboarding champ and California's Jen Smith takes the women's, Pablo Paulino of Brazil and Sally Fitzgibbons of Australia take the junior crowns, South African Jordy Smith takes the WQS title and Mark Occhilupo is a popular winner of the coveted Peter Whittaker Award for his contribution to surfing.

Jordy Smith. Photo Al Nicoll.

Coolangatta's world champs, Fanning and Gilmore. Photo ASP Kirstin © Covered Images.

Chris Brown at Shark Park. Photo Greg Huglin.

Debbie and Yesseia. Photo Shifisurfshots.

Noosa opening ceremony. Photo Steve Robertson.

CALIFORNIA

● Nine unprovoked shark attacks are confirmed to have taken place on the Pacific Coast of the USA in 2007, the Shark Research Committee reports. Five of the nine attacks were on surfers, two on swimmers and one each on a kayaker and a paddleboarder. Great whites were positively identified in four of the nine attacks.

As California's big wave season nears an end, veteran surf photographer Greg Huglin reveals a big score at Shark Park in February, almost two years to the day since his crew last surfed the mysto tow-in break. Although smaller than the previous session, the team surfs glassy 15-to-18-foot waves by themselves all day.

INDONESIA

● Indonesia holds its breath as a powerful 7.2 Richter-reading earthquake hits Bengkulu Province, Sumatra, sparking tsunami warnings. Although the quake causes widespread panic, there are no reported casualties and a tsunami does not eventuate.

WEEK 9
FEBRUARY 26–MARCH 3

CALIFORNIA

● Known for setting the standard for power hacks and rail gouges in the water, WCT veteran Taylor Knox has taken on the task of setting new standards on land. Instead of whining about high prices at the pump, Knox has stepped up and converted his diesel-powered Ford F-250 truck into a veggie oil–powered machine. With financial help from sponsor Rip Curl, the crew at Grease Not Gas did the conversion for approximately $3,700. "It's incredible," says Knox. "I've got a tank that holds 73 gallons of veggie oil and I hardly ever have to fill it. When I do, I go to the Hill Street Café in Oceanside, transfer their unwanted grease into my tank and I'm good to go."

COSTA RICA

● In a weekend of intense competition at Costa Rica's Circuito Nacional de Surf event at Playa Nosara, 17-year-old Debbie Zec pips 27-year-old Yesseia Alfaro for the title Miss Surf Organic and Natural. Debbie, who apparently also had to surf, will now go into the national finals of the, ah, event, organized (need we say more) by Reef.

AUSTRALIA

● Australian surfing pioneer Mark Warren is honored as the 2008 inductee into Hall of Fame at the Australian Surfing Awards held at Coolangatta.

Seventies pro pioneer, '80s coach and media star, '90s ASP tour representative and finally Quiksilver media director, Warren has never stopped giving back to surfing, but he reflected on how much the sport had given him. "Surfing is the gift that keeps on giving. I get as big a thrill now out of a good wave as I did when I was a kid."

● Under leaden skies and with the tiniest of swells hitting the fabled First Point, the GSI Noosa Festival of Surfing gets underway with a traditional Hawaiian opening ceremony led by Makaha waterman Brian Keaulana, and a "Feet of Fame" induction ceremony honoring local legends Bob McTavish and Hayden Kenny. The biggest surf festival in Noosa in years, the GSI runs for over a week with longboarding pro-am events complemented by a waterman spectacular, including paddle marathons, stand-up paddle and tandem, a four-day surf expo in a tent village, and Australia's first "surf summit," featuring industry leaders and a dozen current and former world surfing champions.

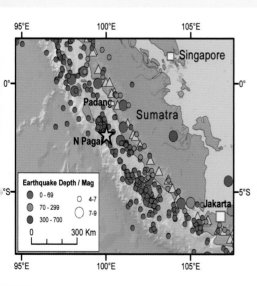

Earthquake epicenter in Southern Mentawais. Map courtesy National Earthquake Information Center, US Geological Survey.

Noosa paddle-out. Photo Steve Robertson.

Mark Warren. Photo Steve Robertson.

*Kelly Slater claims it. Photo ASP Kirstin ©
Covered Images.*

WEEK 10
MARCH 4–10

AUSTRALIA
● More surfing history in the making? Eight-time-world champion Kelly Slater, who finished third in 2007 after a late run at the prize, starts the 2008 ASP World Tour season in the best possible fashion with a stunning win at the Quiksilver Pro Gold Coast. Slater beats reigning champion Mick Fanning at the latter's home break, Snapper Rocks, to go 5-4 in front in their clashes and forge a significant psychological advantage over the new champion. It's early days on the 11-stop 2008 tour, but already the pundits are saying that Slater has fire in his eyes.

IRELAND
● Coat and tie are mandatory, lads, at the second annual Legends Dinner Dance in Tramore, Ireland, this year apparently honoring the legendary Joe Roddy, although the press release is unclear. But leave your jeans and tee shirts at home, that much IS clear! The craic will again be on at the Grand Hotel in Tramore and the entire Irish surfing tribe will be there!

JAMAICA
● Shades of *Cool Running*? The Jamaican team is gearing up for the ISA World Masters Championships set to go down in Punta Rocas, Peru. Finishing a creditable ninth and beating such major surf countries as Brazil and Spain in the inaugural event in 2007, the Jamaican masters, grand masters and kahunas are neoprened up for the cold water, cashed up with good sponsorship and raring to go, says JSA president Billy Wilmot.

FLORIDA
● The Space Coast's favorite son may still be the phenomenal Kelly Slater, but new Satellite Beach phenom Adam Wickwire is on the way with a local finance company launching him into fiscal space with this trademark lip bash.

Billy Wilmot in training. Photo Jamaica Surfing Association.

It might not be a surfing first—there's been a Kelly Slater card for a couple of years—but it's no mean feat to get your moves immortalized in plastic, and Adam is suitably stoked, according to his on-the-ball manager Mitch Varnes, who has been successfully boosting East Coast talent for a generation.

INDONESIA
● Tourism authorities in Sumatra issue a "notification letter" to all surf resort and boat charter operators, outlining new and more stringent legislation covering procedures, taxes and tariffs. The beginning of the end for the cowboy operators? Informed insiders welcome the clarifications but say the battle is far from over.

AUSTRALIA
● After being skunked for waves most of the week, the GSI Noosa Festival of Surfing hits pay dirt for the final weekend, with classic First Point providing a suitable climax to the event's most successful year.

WEEK 11
MARCH 11–17

FLORIDA
● Despite an increasingly difficult economy, Surf Expo trade show reports a successful January show, with 15,000 attendance, equaling the previous year. Surf Expo director Lori Kisner says the show had proven that the surf industry was resilient in tough times, with retailers coming out in force to "feel the verve and vibe" as well as write paper.

Space Coast Credit Union Adam Wickwire Debit Card.

CALIFORNIA
● Nvohk (pronounced "invoke," how cute) launches in Los Angeles as the world's first user-owned surf lifestyle brand. For just $50, members get to design logos, product, advertising campaigns, you name it. Only 5,000 people can become members, so sign up today . . . or maybe it's "capped at 40,000", depending which part of the blurb you read. Anyway, nvohk is all about saving the planet and giving power back to the punter . . . or something like that.

AUSTRALIA
● A marine biologist is captured by the British tabloid media touching a great white shark off the coast of Australia. According to London's *Mirror* newspaper and website, the shark had been lured to the boat with chunks of bait as part of a test of Shark Shield products, electronic devices designed to keep sharks away from surfers. So why did the marine biologist feel the need to

Alan Atkins winning One Design. Photo Steve Robertson.

New Pier bomb for Graeme Bird. Photo Mike van Heerden/ActivPix.

Memorial stones. Photo Shawn Alladio.

reach out and touch? Ask yourself, you would if you could, wouldn't you?

SOUTH AFRICA

● Cyclone Jokwe tracks north from Mozambique and delivers another classic east swell for Durban, with booming six- to eight-foot sets rocking New Pier as Thursday, March 13 dawns. Jason Ribbink, Wok Wright, Twiggy Baker and Davey Weare are among those on hand to enjoy.

FRANCE

● Meanwhile in Europe a spectacular Atlantic storm smashes France, Spain and southern England, killing two people and sinking and sending aground several vessels. Wave buoys record 58-foot waves off the west coast of Ireland and 45 feet off Brittany later the same day. French tow teams are in readiness for Belharra, but the swell subsides as quickly as it arrived.

CALIFORNIA

● Memorial stones now adorn the footpath leading to the point at Mav-

ericks, commemorating the lives of Mark Foo, Jay Moriarity and Peter Davi. The legendary Hawaiian big wave rider Foo was lost at Mavericks during a paddle-in session, while Mavericks regulars Moriarity and Davi died in subsequent surfing accidents.

WEEK 12
MARCH 18–24

CALIFORNIA

● Jazz-loving kneelo Dan Young announces his candidacy for county supervisor in Santa Cruz on a platform of re-enfranchising the surf community. President of the Santa Cruz Jazz Festival and a board member of the Santa Cruz Surfing Club, Dan promises a swinging campaign.

PUNTA DE LOBOS, PICHILEMU CHILE
WORLD CUP TOW-IN SURFING CHAMPIONSHIP
AND BIG WAVE SURFING CONTEST

Rider: Ramon Navarro ~ Photo: EscobarPhoto.com   Holding period: April 15, 2008 - October 31, 2008

APT World Tour Tow-In Surfing Circuit 2008/2009

EscobarPhoto.com.

CHILE

● The Association of Professional Towsurfers announces the first stop on the 2008 pro tour as Pichilemu, Chile, with a holding period from mid-April to mid-July. The preferred break, Punta de Lobos, is Chile's longest and most powerful left and has been ridden by local chargers Ramon Navarro, Diego Medina and Christian Merrello at more than 50 feet. The $35,000 invitational will feature most of the leading tow teams in the world, including Mike Parsons and Brad Gerlach of California, Carlos Burle and Eraldo Gueiros of Brazil, Makua Rothman and Ikaika Kalama of Hawaii, and Ross Clarke Jones of Australia and Ian Walsh of Hawaii.

AUSTRALIA

● World champion Mick Fanning is presented with a team jersey by Australian Rules footballers

Mark McVeigh and Andrew Welsh of the Essendon Bombers. The footie stars are surfers too and stoked to meet the champ, but not as stoked as footie-mad Fanning, currently number two in the rankings and looking to get back on top at the Rip Curl Bells Pro.

● Former world champion Sunny Garcia is one of the headliners at Western Australia's Drug Aware Pro Margaret River WQS as his comeback attempt kicks into high gear. Garcia, 38, was

Mark McVeigh, Andrew Welsh and Mick Fanning at Bells. Photo ASP Kirstin © Covered Images.

Storms rock Europe. Photo Mike Newman/Ocean-Image.com.

Slater victorious. Photo ASP Robertson © Covered Images.

Good craic in Ireland. Photo www.mickeysmith.co.uk.

Sunny on the comeback trail. Photo ASP Tostee © Covered Images.

the 2000 world champion but since then he has suffered setback upon setback, including jail time for tax evasion. Now, at an age when most top line surfers are contemplating retirement, Sunny is frothing at the prospect of requalifying for the 2009 ASP World Tour, and Margaret River's Hawaiian-style power offers him a great chance to help his cause.

WEEK 13
MARCH 25–31

CALIFORNIA
● Malibu surf shop proprietor, explosives expert, sometimes firefighter and one-time sheriff Jefferson "Zuma Jay" Wagner unveils a campaign to win a seat on the Malibu City Council, joining several other surf identities seeking election to public office. Zuma tells lo-

cal surfwriter Ben Marcus the focus of his campaign will be "the pier, water quality and density."

FRANCE
● The head of cycling equipment group Look International says he is interested in buying Rossignol, the iconic French snow brand and troubled subsidiary of Quiksilver. CEO Dominique Bergin says that "Rossignol is a nice brand . . . and Look, with its carbon technology, can bring a lot of know-how to it. Quiksilver's stock price rallies on the news.

INDONESIA
● SurfAid International reaches another milestone with the completion of stage two of its Malaria Free Mentawai program, delivering mosquito nets and malaria education to 53,000 people on three of the four Mentawai Islands off Sumatra's west coast. SurfAid CEO Dr. Dave Jenkins says the milestone has been reached in just 12 months, despite delays when the malaria teams were diverted to emergency work after two major earthquakes in the region. SurfAid, centred on one of the world's great remote surfing locations, is supported by a broad cross-section of the surf industry around the world.

AUSTRALIA
● Two down, nine to go. The remarkable "comeback" of Kelly Slater continues as he miraculously defeats Bede

Durbidge to take out the Rip Curl Pro at Bells Beach, making him undefeated in two events of an 11-event tour. In taking his 36th tour victory, Slater comes from behind with three minutes to go, finding a winning wave at Rincon Point, which hadn't appeared to be breaking.

IRELAND
● Irish surfing documentary *Sea Fever* opens to critical acclaim across Ireland and the UK. The film, which covers surfing in Ireland from the 1950s, culminates with a spectacular sequence of tow-in surfing at 50-foot Aileens, off the Cliffs of Moher. "Spectacular waves," says the Irish Examiner.

WEEK 14
APRIL 1–7

AUSTRALIA
● Global Surf Industries announces a sponsorship of fast-growing nonprofit Surfing Mums, Inc. GSI CEO Mark Kelly says that the group is the perfect embodiment of his company mantra, "life is better when you surf." Founded in Byron Bay in 2006, Surfing Mums now has 10 groups under its banner around Australia and one in New Zealand. Founder Vanessa Thompson says the idea of the group is to provide a support system to enable mums who surf to get back into the water as often as possible.

● History is set to be made at Margaret River when the first father-and-daughter team surf in the same event. Former top pro Dave Macaulay, 44, and daughter Laura, 16, will line up together in a field of 250 professional surfers taking part in the Drug Aware Pro. Laura has secured a wildcard entry into the event, while Dad, twice ranked number three in the world, has to fight his way through the trials.

INDONESIA
● What an opportunity! WavePark Mentawai resort is looking for a chef on a six-month contract to cover the surf season. The kitchen already has two prep chefs and the ordering system is in place, so all you have to do is

Laura and Dave Macaulay. Photo SROSurf.

Zuma Jay rinses off after fighting the Malibu fires. Photo Bill Parr.

Surfing Mums at Byron Bay. Photo Kat Cobley/surfingmums.com.

Gabe Davies surfs Mullaghmore for the film Waveriders. *www.waveridersthemovie.com. Photo www.mickeysmith.co.uk.*

Dane Patterson. Photo Barry Tuck/Quiksilver.

rustle up the grub a couple of times a day and get barreled the rest. Do I hear the stampeding of feet? Three hundred bucks a month for beer, the Park covers the rest. Just get yourself there!

AUSTRALIA

● A teenage boy tells lifesavers the sea turned red after his 16-year-old friend was fatally attacked by a large shark while surfing at Ballina near Byron Bay. The boy, from Wollongbar, west of Ballina, died after being bitten on the legs and body while bodyboarding at popular Lighthouse Beach.

ENGLAND

● Veteran Europe pro Gabe Davies has been appointed patron of the British Surfing Museum. Museum founder Pete Robinson says Gabe, a legendary and fearless big wave rider whose tow-in exploits in Ireland have been hugely promoted, had great credentials to promote the museum, which plans to have a permanent home in Cornwall by 2010.

WEEK 15
APRIL 8–14

CALIFORNIA

● Surf betting website Surfing-Odds.com has eight-time world champion Kelly Slater at short odds of 2.3 to 1 to win a ninth world title, just two events into the 2008 tour. Going into the Billabong Pro Teahupoo, Slater has a longer price of 4.5 on that event, but the oddsmakers believe that he is a shoo-in for another title unless he suffers a major injury.

SOUTH AFRICA

● Quiksilver South Africa marketing manager Dane Patterson is seriously injured in a freak accident at Dairy

Beach. Patterson, a skilled and highly competitive surfer, does a "face plant" on a shallow sandbank and suffers displaced vertebrae in his neck, the classic "broken neck" injury. Friend Dane Logie drags him from the water and he is airlifted to hospital by helicopter. With surgery required to fuse the vertebrae, Patterson is expected to make a full recovery but be out of the water for up to a year.

ENGLAND

● Plastic litter on the beaches of Britain has reached record levels, endangering dolphins, whales and seabirds, according to an environmental survey. The survey, conducted by the Marine Conservation Society, revealed that litter levels had increased by 126 percent since its first survey in 1994. Nearly 4,000 volunteers took part in the survey of 354 beaches in September 2007, removing more than 350,000 pieces of litter.

CALIFORNIA

● In front of more than 2,000 stoked fans at The Grove in Anaheim, veteran charger Shane Dorian takes out the Billabong XXL Ride of the Year award for his surviving a bomb in the swell of the year at Teahupoo on November 1, 2007. After being towed into a massive slab, Dorian dropped down the face and caught a rail, putting him in a near-impossible situation. Correcting his mistake in the tube, Dorian, 35, went into a full layback and came from behind the foamball to be spat into the safety of the channel. California's Mike Parsons wins the Biggest Wave award for a 70-foot-plus ride at Cortes Bank on January 5, 2008.

NORWAY

● Rip Curl's Search crew arrives in Lofoten, Norway, in the northern Arctic Circle, to look for waves. While they wait for swell in one of the coldest places on earth, they fish for cod.

Jason and catch of the day. Photo Ted Grambeau/Rip Curl.

Shane Dorian, Billabong XXL Global Big Wave Awards. Photo Tim Jones/BillabongXXL.com.

Surftech at the Tri. Photo Duke Brouwer.

Vaca Beach cleanup. Photo Luke Thorpe.

WEEK 16
APRIL 15–21

ARIZONA

Surftech takes the sport of stand-up paddle surfing inland to the Ford ironman event in Tempe, Arizona. Surftech's team riders join with a huge turnout of amateur competitors in a special SUP leg of the triathlon. For most of the 2,500 triathletes, it is their first introduction to the sport. "It's an amazing workout," says triathlon Hall of Famer Heather Fuhr. "You're working your core the whole time."

CALIFORNIA

Snowboarder Todd Richards wins the snowboard leg of the inaugural Ultimate Boarder contest in Squaw Valley. In flawless conditions, snowboard specialists take all 10 places in the final, showing yet again that all board sports are not the same, and that crossover events are all about luck on the day. Snowboard tour veteran Richards will now wear the yellow jersey as the event moves to the surfing stage in Ventura.

INDONESIA

Bali-based photojournalist Jason Childs distributes the photo below

Snowboard podium. Photo Ruben Sanchez.

to global media, hoping to bring attention to the man-made destruction of the once-wild, surf-rich Bukit Peninsula. Home to some of the best left-hand reef waves in the world, the Bukit has become the focus for rampant development as the golden triangle of Kuta-Sanur-Nusa Dua becomes maxed out with resort hotels and shopping malls. The arid micro-climate and stark topography of the Bukit once kept developers at bay. Not any more.

Love that free stuff. Photo Phil Perez.

CALIFORNIA

Embattled Quiksilver, Inc., enjoys a rare moment of sunlight in a fairly overcast year as it emerges victorious from a long federal court battle over the Roxy trademark. Quiksilver began the action back in 2002 to prevent Kymsta Corporation from using the name Roxywear on juniors apparel.

EL SALVADOR

Billabong's Fantasy Surf Camp at Las Flores concludes with a major cleanup of nearby Vaca Beach. While Las Flores is kept in immaculate condition, neighboring Vaca was littered with plastic trash, and villagers seemed to have no concept of looking after their patch; so Billabong's Luke

Thorpe organized a "locals only" surf comp to be followed by a massive cleanup with plenty of Billabong product prizes for participants. The initiative worked wonders: Vaca had a spring clean and local kids scored big on booty.

WEEK 17
APRIL 22–28

HAWAII

Pioneer big wave surfer Woodbridge Parker "Woody" Brown dies on Maui at the age of 96. In December 1943 Brown and teenage surfer Dickie Cross drove from Honolulu to the North Shore and paddled out on their hot curl boards at Sunset Beach. The surf

Man-made erosion, Bukit Peninsula. Photo Jason Childs.

Woody Brown. Photo David L. Brown.

appeared to be about 10 feet, but the swell rose quickly and soon they were dodging massive sets. Within the hour, Sunset was closing out and as the afternoon wore on, Brown decided their best chance was to paddle three miles to Waimea Bay and get in through the deep channel. By the time they reached Waimea, 40-foot sets were closing out the bay. Paddling for shore, Cross took a huge set on the head and was never seen again. Brown also lost his board but washed ashore, where some soldiers dragged him to safety.

Woody Brown never surfed the North Shore again, and the frightening tale of Dickie Cross's loss kept surfers away for more than a decade. Born in New York, Woody went west with his young wife and became one of San Diego's first surfers before heading for Hawaii just before World War II. After the war, he built a catamaran and made his living taking tourists sailing for the next 40 years. He remained an active surfer until he was 90.

Damien Hobgood. Photo ASP Rowland © Covered Images.

FRANCE

● The French surfing community is in shock after the tragic passing of two prominent members, Reunion Island's leading longboarder Karna Goile and Arcachon's Antione Mace. The 26-year-old Mace, who was to be married in May, died in a work-related accident. He had been a leading competitor for more than 12 years.

AUSTRALIA

● Malfunction event promoter Sean McKeown says "agro" has forced him to move the 25-year-old longboard contest from Snapper Rocks south across the border to the NSW Tweed Coast after clashes with recreational surfers last year. McKeown was knocked back by the Gold Coast City Council when he applied for an exclusive use permit. "The surf is better at Snapper," he says, "But the Tweed is a lot less crowded."

CALIFORNIA

● New film *Between the Lines* examines the contrasting lifestyles and fortunes of two surfers whose lives are changed by the Vietnam War. Pat Farley volunteered, saw heavy combat and was discharged with a full psychiatric pension. Brant Page fled the draft and hid out in Hawaii and surfed until arrested by the FBI. Narrated by John Milius, this fascinating documentary is screening at veterans' benefits in California throughout the summer.

TAHITI

● Top pro Damien Hobgood is in doubt for the South Pacific leg of the ASP World Tour, following an accident while surfing Teahupoo last week. Hobgood went over the falls and fractured his shoulder. He remains in the draw for the Billabong Pro Tahiti but is an unlikely starter.

WEEK 18
APRIL 29—MAY 5

MEXICO

● An American surfer has been killed in a shark attack off Mexico's southern Pacific coast, officials say. The man, from San Francisco, bled to death after a gray shark bit his right thigh, leaving a 15-inch wound. The US embassy in Mexico City would not release the man's name, but he is understood to have been a 24-year-old who was surfing at Troncones Beach with a friend. The man was alive when brought to the beach, but it took so long for an ambulance to reach the remote beach, he died soon after reaching hospital.

FLORIDA

● The Florida chapter of the Surfrider Foundation wins a major battle with the passing of the Clean Ocean Act, requiring owners and operators of day-cruise gambling vessels to use waste-water pumping systems at ports rather than at sea.

HAWAII

● Beautiful Brazilian Maya Gabeira tells New Wind Press how it feels to ride 50-foot waves at Waimea Bay. To the amazement of North Shore veterans, she explains that she became addicted to riding big waves when she moved from Brazil to Hawaii in 2006,

Maya Gabeira. Photo Marcelo Maragni/ Red Bull Photofiles.

Veteran stylist Ray Gleave at home in Kingscliff. Photo www.malfunction.com.au.

Pat Farley. Photo courtesy Pat Farley.

Brant Page. Photo Robert Worthington.

arrived at the Bay as a set closed out, then paddled out on her 10-foot 4-inch board and caught four monster waves in four hours. "I think I was high for like 10 days," she recalls.

FRANCE

● Shaun Tomson's *Bustin' Down the Door* and Patrick Trefz's *Thread* share the honors at the International Surf Film Festival in St. Jean de Luz, Shaun's film securing best documentary and Patrick's best film. Jarrod Tallman's *Mundaka* wins best local film and *Hot Buttered Soul* wins best soundtrack. Shaun Tomson and *Hot Buttered* founder Terry Fitzgerald are among dignitaries at the festival.

WEEK 19
MAY 6–12

CALIFORNIA

● The Western Surfing Association announces the addition of a "challenged athletes" division to its West Coast championships at Churches, San Onofre. Eight disabled athletes will compete in the event, including renowned surfing quadriplegic Jesse Billauer.

FRANCE

● Basque country surfers gather in Guethary to pay tribute to the late Peter Viertel, who has died in Switzerland. Viertel's death follows that of his wife, the former actress Deborah Kerr, by just a month. In 1956, Viertel, a screenwriter, was working on the film of Ernest Hemingway's *The Sun Also Rises* in Biarritz and began riding his Velzy-Jacobs pig model in the waves in front of his hotel. He loaned the board to a young student named Joel de Rosnay and surfing in France began. More than half a century later, De Rosnay, still a keen surfer and a former French champion, leads the tribute.

CALIFORNIA

● Iconic trunks brand Katin announces the return of the Katin's Team Challenge in 2009. Katin's head Robert Schmidt says the return of the teams event after more than 30 years will herald the return of the Katin's brand to the mainstream surf industry. Walter and Nacy Katin were canvas sail makers in the 1950s, when they started producing canvas boardshorts after getting requests from local Seal Beach surfers, among them a grom named Corky Carroll. The pioneer brand became one of the biggest names in surfing in the 1960s, and in the '70s after Walt's death, Nancy introduced her annual teams event at Huntington Beach.

TAHITI

● The Air Tahiti Nui-Von Zipper Trials finishes as a monster swell starts to hit Teahupoo and the tow-in teams take over. Photographer Tim McKenna is on hand to capture the images on an all-time day.

NEW YORK

● Another victory for Surfrider as the Justice Court in East Hampton dismisses fines against the "Montauk 8" for surfing at Montauk Point, thereby opening up the state park to surfers.

WEEK 20
MAY 13–19

AUSTRALIA

● Ocean & Earth International announce the signing of former WCT surfer Troy Brooks. Brooks, a longtime Quiksilver team rider, quit the tour at the end of '07 to concentrate on his young family and on free surfing. One of the world's leading aerialists, Brooks will have his own model traction pad out later in the year.

TAHITI

● Reigning world champion Mick Fanning suffers his first last-place finish in two years when knocked out of the Billabong Pro Tahiti by Brazilian wildcard Bruno Santos. "Things could be better," says Fanning. "Every wave was a battle out there." In fact, the waves were a perfect four to six feet, but the champ never found his rhythm and made a shock early exit.

NEW YORK

● The world's leading waterman, Laird Hamilton, launches his own clothing line, Wonderwall. The collection, inspired by Laird's sense of style and uncompromising attitude, will be produced by New York–based Steve and Barry's, whose own uncompromising attitude to sales numbers means that no item of Wonderwall will cost more than 15 bucks.

CALIFORNIA

● Surfing champions Shaun Tomson, Brad Gerlach and Ken Bradshaw announce their participation in Operation Amped, a learn-to-surf day at Zuma Beach for combat-injured soldiers, sailors and marines. The benefit day, organized by the William Morris Agency, gives wounded vets the opportunity to experience some of the joys of the surfing lifestyle.

A Teahupoo screamer. Photo tim-mckenna.com.

The Katin setup at Huntington. Photo Jason Rodriguez.

Looking in. Photo tim-mckenna.com.

Troy Brooks. Photo Swilly.

Bruno Santos, giantkiller. Photo ASP Kirstin © Covered Images.

*Laird Hamilton. Photo Oxbow/
Darrel Wong.*

*Shaun Tomson with war vet. Photo
Ben Marcus/Operation Amped.*

Bruce Irons. Photo ASP Kirstin © Covered Images.

● Wildcoast environmental activist group applauds a decision by the International Boundary and Water Commission to cancel the Bajagua Project and to upgrade the sewage treatment plant in San Ysidro on the US-Mexico border, which currently fails to meet federal clean water standards. The beaches at the border are among the most polluted in North America. As of the end of April, Imperial Beach had been closed more than 50 days of 2008 owing to sewage discharges from Mexico.

MEXICO

● Insight wins breakthrough brand of the year at the sixth annual SIMA Image Awards, held in conjunction with the SIMA Surf Summit in Cabo San Lucas, Mexico. RVCA takes out men's apparel brand of the year and Billabong Girls the women's.

WEEK 21
MAY 20–26

CALIFORNIA

● The International Surfing Association announces that all dope testing results for finalists in the ISA World Masters were negative. The over-35 event has competitors from 17 differ-

ent countries and saw South Africa take out team honors.

● Volcom leading team rider Bruce Irons announces he will quit the ASP World Tour at the end of 2008 no matter what his final ranking is. "I'm going back to being a freesurfer," Brucey tells Surfing Magazine. "It's what I was meant to do." Long regarded as one of the most talented surfers in the world, the younger brother of three-time world champion Andy Irons has never enjoyed the same competitive success as his brother. After finishing ninth in 2005, he has slowly dropped back "in the back of the cattle truck" he tells Surfing. Volcom says it fully supports him.

FRANCE

● Quiksilver Europe hosts Sea Shepherd Conservation Society founder Captain Paul Watson at their St. Jean de Luz headquarters to announce that their Sea Shepherd clothing line, on sale in Australia since January 2007, would debut in France in October. Five dollars from the sale of each garment goes towards Sea Shepherd's global activist campaign against the slaughter of whales and dolphins.

MEXICO

● A second surfer is killed by a shark

off Mexico's Pacific Coast near Acapulco, less than a month after the death of an American surfer. The second attack takes place less than six miles from the first, claiming Osvaldo Mata Valdovinos, 21. The shark bit into his hand and leg, then dragged him underwater, according to witnesses. Following the first attack, Mexican authorities used baited hooks to catch sharks in the area, prompting complaints from environmentalists, who urged that warning signs be placed at the affected beaches.

AUSTRALIA

● After ditching plans to stage it in northwestern Australia, Rip Curl remains cagey about revealing the location of the 2008 Search Pro, running mystery advertising instead. After successfully staging the event in Reunion, Mexico and Chile, the Curl is giving nothing away about the new location, other than event manager Andy Higgins' assertion that the surfers will be

"frothing." What we do know is that "Somewhere" is a left. What we also know is that Photoshop is a wonderful thing.

Rip Curl Search Pro . . . where is it?

WEEK 22
MAY 27–JUNE 2

SOUTH AFRICA
● The best of South Africa's big wave chargers gather at Long Beach Kommetjie for a water ceremony to honor the winners of the O'Neill Raw Courage Awards. Hometown charger Andy Marr is the big winner, with R25,000 for a bomb he paddled into off Todos Santos and two seconds in the minor categories. Unlike other big wave

Andy Marr. Photo © O'Neill SA/Robyn Texeira 2008.

awards, the Raw Courage is reserved for paddle-in monsters.

CALIFORNIA
● The Save Trestles campaign receives another huge boost when California's Secretary of Commerce announces it will conduct a public hearing on the future of the 241 toll road that threatens the iconic break. This follows the California Coastal Commission's move to veto the project earlier in the year, which was subsequently appealed by the Transportation Corridor Agency. Now the public, including the Surfrider Foundation, will have another chance to put their case against the road.

● ASP World Tour rookie Dane Reynolds is at home in Ventura with a mystery virus, missing the Globe Pro in Fiji. After a solid start to the season,

Dane fell ill in Tahiti and opted to miss the vital fourth event and get his health checked.

FRANCE
● Rip Curl Europe announces the next phase of its "Project Resurrection," an environmental program to find new uses for waste neoprene from wetsuit off-cuts and old suits. The Resurrection Espadrille, a limited edition shoe made from chopped neoprene at Mauleon, in the heart of the Basque country, will be available from the end of June.

Jeremy Flores meets the minister. Photo Aquashot/Aspeurope.com.

● France's Secretary of Sport, M. Bernard Laporte, drops in on the Quiksilver ISA World Junior Championships in Hossegor, meeting and greeting officials and competitors, including France's leading light on the world tour, Jeremy Flores. The popular politician is shown behind the scenes of a world title event by Quiksilver's Pierre Agnes and ISA president Fernando Aguerre.

CALIFORNIA
● Big wave king Mike Parsons is

Dane Reynolds. Photo ASP Kirstin © Covered Images.

named surf marketing manager for Von Zipper, adding another string to the bow of one of surfing's busiest people. The unassuming "Snips," from San Clemente, California, directs ASP events for Billabong when not chasing huge mid-ocean swells with his tow partner, Brad Gerlach. A founding partner at Von Zipper, Snips says he is delighted to return to the fold.

MALDIVES
● Maldives surfing pioneer Tony Hussein Hinde dies while surfing his home break of Pasta Point. Hinde is found face down near the shore and does not respond to CPR. The drowning tragedy follows the death of his Maldivian wife, Zulfa, just four months earlier. Hinde "discovered" the surf breaks of the Maldives after a ketch he was crewing on ran aground in 1973. He eventually became a Maldivian citizen and converted to Islam to marry a local girl. After keeping the quality reef breaks of the region a secret for many years, Hinde eventually formed Atoll Adventures and opened Tari Resort in an effort to control the numbers of surfers visiting the Maldives.

WEEK 23
JUNE 3–9

FIJI
● Odds shorten on Kelly Slater taking an historic ninth world title as the phenomenon clinches his third tour victory of the season at the Globe Pro Fiji. After defeating Florida teammate CJ Hobgood in the final, Slater remains the only member of the Top 45 to have won a tour event this year, taking three out of four with a wildcard picking up the win in Tahiti.

MEXICO
● Biologists plan to tag hundreds of sharks off the Pacific Coast to help understand the cause of a rare spate of deadly attacks on humans. In the first

Mike Parsons, Billabong XXL Global Big Wave Awards. Photo Robert Brown/BillabongXXL.com.

Tony Hussein Hinde. Photo © Yep/Dara.

CJ Hobgood and Kelly Slater. Photo ASP Kirstin © Covered Images.

Bruce Irons. Photo Steve Robertson.

Happy Finisterre crew. Photo Katherine Rose.

fatal shark attacks off Mexico's Pacific Coast in more than 30 years, two surfers have been killed and one maimed in the past few weeks. The tagging with electronic devices is expected to begin within a month and the study will continue for a year.

CALIFORNIA

● Four-times world women's champion Lisa Andersen marries fiancé Tim Shannon in a private ceremony near their Newport Beach home. Lisa, who won her four titles back to back in the 1990s, also brought up her first child as a single mother during her pro career. As senior ambassador for the Roxy brand she helped create, she still travels the world to surf. Husband Tim, a keen amateur surfer, says the two plan to enjoy their honeymoon "every day all year long."

● Volcom founder Richard "Woolie" Woolcott succeeds his father, Rene, as chairman of the board. Mr. Woolcott Sr., 76, remains a member of the board, but Woolie steps up to the plate as main man on strategic direction, with former COO Jason Steris becoming president. In other Volcom news, leading team rider Bruce Irons reveals he will leave the ASP World Tour at the end of the year to go back to free surfing "regardless of how I finish."

● Meanwhile, Quiksilver reports net revenue increase of 15 percent in the second quarter, following the exclu-

sion as discontinued operations of the Rossignol Group. Much of the growth is attributable to foreign earnings against a weaker US dollar, but the brand claims satisfaction at the outlook in "tough economic times."

● Surfrider Foundation announces it will partner with surfer/musician Jack Johnson in his upcoming "All At Once" concert tour. Surfrider is one of several nonprofits chosen by Jack to be part of his unique awareness campaign, which gives environmental causes a forum. Surfrider will take the opportunity to roll out its Rise Above Plastics campaign, which seeks to educate people on the detrimental impact plastic products are having on the marine environment.

WEEK 24
JUNE 10–16

AUSTRALIA
● Former ASP Women's World Champion Chelsea Hedges gives birth to a baby girl, 5 lbs 12 oz Mieka Elizabeth. It is the first child for the Aussie powerhouse, who plans to be back on the tour next season.

CALIFORNIA
● Billabong signs California big wave charger Greg Long to its surf team. Just 25, Greg has ridden 60-foot waves, been attacked by a tiger shark and been named one of the "Fittest Fifty Ameri-

cans" by *Men's Fitness* magazine. He joins one of the strongest big wave teams in the world, headed by Mike "Snips" Parsons.

BRAZIL
● The ASP World Masters Championships, which were last held in 2003, are postponed at the last minute, causing anguish among competitors who had booked flights and accommodations. The event is rescheduled for September in Rio, but some competitors are skeptical it will go ahead. The Masters, which had its beginnings in the 1990s under an Oxbow sponsorship, then flourished with Quiksilver, features many of the pioneers of pro surfing, including more than a dozen former world champions.

● A 14-year-old surfer survives a shark attack off the coast of northeast Brazil. Juan Rodrigues Galvao de Franca was bitten on the leg while surfing at Del Cifre Beach. He managed to break free and swim ashore, where he was rescued by a passing ambulance crew. The attack occurred in an area off limits to swimmers and surfers because of the 52 shark attacks recorded there since 1992.

ENGLAND
● UK surf brand Finisterre wins the *Observer* newspaper Ethical Business Award in the fashion category for its use of recyclable fibers, beating a star-studded list of nominees. This is a major breakthrough for the four-year-old company based at St. Agnes in Cornwall. Says brand founder Tom Kay, "We don't push environmental and social issues to turn a profit. They are simply at the core of what we do."

Chelsea Hedges. Photo ASP Tostee © Covered Images.

Lisa Andersen. Photo courtesy Roxy.

Greg Long, Billabong XXL Global Big Wave Awards. Photo Al MacKinnon/BillabongXXL.com.

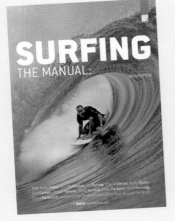

CALIFORNIA

● Surf documentary *Bustin' Down the Door* gets theatrical distribution around the US with Screen Media Films. The award-winning film, with narration by Edward Norton, will show on both coasts throughout the summer.

● Former *Surfer* editor Jim Kempton publishes *Surfing: The Manual*, a Wavefinder guidebook for advanced surfers. Kempton has tapped the surfing brains of many of the finest surfers in the world, including Kelly Slater, Andy Irons, Taj Burrow, Gerry Lopez, Laird Hamilton and Shane Dorian to provide technical information on how they make the moves they do.

WEEK 25
JUNE 17–23

CALIFORNIA

● Surf shop sales in California are down by as much as 75 percent, according to a correspondent for the UK's *Independent* newspaper. Small artisans and craftsmen are being hit the hardest, with one in five surfboard shops closing its doors or dramatically downsizing. Industry stalwarts Becker Surf, one of California's most successful surf retailers, says sales are down 75 percent in the worst summer for decades. Surf Industry Manufacturers Association director Sean Smith says 15 percent of SIMA's member companies were in "real trouble."

HAWAII

● None of the above can dissuade

Left: photo wavefinder.com. Above: Sixties Stylemasters. Photo Ben Longhurst.

Yearbook editor Phil Jarratt in the Wrecks.

master shapers Jeff Bushman and Kyle Bernhardt, who launch Country Feeling Surfboards in Hawaii, a label devoted to making environmentally friendly surfboards using soy- and sugar-based foams, plant-based resins and hemp, silk and bamboo cloth.

ENGLAND

● Saunton Sands in Devon is the site for Britain's most unusual surf contest, the 60s Stylemasters. Despite a distinct lack of swell, the style gurus strut their stuff all weekend, with James Parry beating Sam Bleakley out of the top spot.

AUSTRALIA

● Meanwhile, half a world away in Noosa, Australia, the fourth annual Wrecks and Relics Contest for the over-50s takes place in good waves at Peregian Beach and First Point, Noosa. *Pacific Longboarder* editor John Brasen takes his fourth consecutive age title in the over 55s, while Rip Curl founder Doug Warbrick is triumphant in the over 65s.

WEEK 26
JUNE 24–30

CALIFORNIA

● Record high temperatures, raging fires and a pumping south swell make for interesting times in Santa Cruz for the seventh annual Jay Moriarity Memorial Paddleboard Race. A record number of entrants, most more accustomed to cold, rough and often hazardous conditions for paddling in Santa Cruz, face sheet glass and tropical temperatures. Two-time Olympic swimmer

Chad Carvin sets a new course record for the 12 miles, finishing almost four minutes ahead of second. While prone paddlers dominate, stand-up paddler Kyle Mochizuki makes a great final run to nab second.

● Veteran surf film producer Ira Opper wins an Emmy Award for his Fuel TV series "Fins." The series takes out the award for Outstanding Achievement Magazine Program. "The award symbolizes the hard work, dedication and pure stoke that goes into crafting the series," says Opper.

INDONESIA

● The Quiksilver Foundation announces ongoing support for Children Indo Futur, a group led by Hossegor surfer and restaurateur Roland Calaudi. Having helped establish a rehabilitation center in Bali, the group is now focused on relief for Lapindo in Java, where a mine drilling accident has created an ecological disaster.

FRANCE

● The first ever Quiksilver Czech/Slovak Surfing Championships gets underway at Les Bourdaines, Hossegor, with surfers from the wave-starved Eastern European countries competing in small, fun waves. With increasing numbers of Eastern Europeans coming to France to surf each summer, Quiksilver decided to help things along by promoting the sport to them.

ENGLAND

● SAS founder and long-time environmental campaigner Chris Hines, best remembered by many as the man who chased the British environment minister around the House of Commons brandishing an inflatable turd, has received an MBE in the Queen's Birthday Honours List.

● Meanwhile in Cornwall, versatile Ben Skinner picks up a fat check from the Ford Motor Company for a day of tow-in surfing at Lusty Glaze private beach. Ben uses the tow to boost some big airs for a commercial for Ford's new S-Max car. In a busy week at Lusty Glaze, the Fat Face Night Surf has its best event yet, with thousands

Photo www.countryfeelingsurfboards.com.

Paddleboard winner Chad Carvin. Photo Duke Brouwer.

Quiksilver reps at the rehabilitation center. Photo www.indochildren-futur.com.

Ben Skinner. Photo Elliot Walker.

Lusty Glaze lights up. Photo Victoria Walker.

Ira Opper with Emmy. Photo Laura Peterson.

flocking to the beach on a balmy night to see a classic exhibition of shortboard and longboard surfing.

WEEK 27
JULY 1–7

AUSTRALIA
● After 37 years of trading, the Brothers Neilsen surf retail empire comes crashing down after liquidators deem that a deed of company arrangement agreed to by creditors 18 months ago was not capable of being completed. Brothers Neilsen began trading in 1971 in Surfers Paradise, selling a block of wax for 24 cents on its first

day. Things improved for pro surfer Paul Neilsen and his brothers Rick and Len, and at its peak the group had more than 20 major stores across Australia and in Southeast Asia. Paul Neilsen said that he was bitterly disappointed for his family and staff, but that "it's never over until the fat lady sings." Most observers felt that the chubby chick was tuning up in the wings.

Perfect day at Barber's Point for the military. Photo Mitch McEwen.

Cover of Surf-o-Rama.

● Sally Fitzgibbons, Aussie teen phenom, enters the record books by qualifying for the 2009 women's ASP World Tour before the halfway point of the women's qualifying series, a first for either men's or women's pro tours. The 17-year-old from the NSW South Coast turned her back on athletics, soccer and touch football to concentrate on her surfing, after having represented her state or country in all three. Her former athletics coach believes she could have won Olympic gold in track and field, but track and field's loss is surfing's gain.

● Australian surf historian Murray

Walding releases *Surf-o-Rama*, a new book of surf collectables and memorabilia. Walding, a former teacher whose book *Blue Heaven* presented a new take on Australian surf history, here turns his attention to his passion for beach culture, from surf movie posters to the most obscure magazine articles, beer coasters and album covers.

HAWAII
● Almost 200 military personnel and their families participate in the biggest-ever All Military Surf Classic, presented by HIC and Quiksilver. White Plains Beach, near Barber's Point and Oahu's biggest military population, offered friendly knee to shoulder-high waves for a great family day at the beach. Competitors included 97 active duty soldiers and marines.

ITALY
● Retiring veteran pro surfer Mark Occhilupo celebrates his Italian heritage with a sweep from Rome to Viareggio on Billabong's Icons Never Die tour. Making store appearances and partying with fans along the Med coast, Occy shows why the 1999 world champ is one of surfing's most popular figures.

Sally Fitzgibbons. Photo Steve Robertson.

The iconic Occy scrapbook. Photo Billabong.

Buttons Kaluhiokalani. Photo Steve McBride.

Guts Griffiths. Photo Connor Griffiths/www.gutssurfboards.com.

WEEK 29
JULY 15–21

INDONESIA
● Just days ahead of the Rip Curl Search Trials on Bali's Bukit Peninsula, an illegal 100-foot fishing vessel runs aground on the prized Padang Padang

Padang fishing vessel. Photo Jason Childs.

WEEK 28
JULY 8–14

HAWAII
● Hawaiian stylemaster and 70s innovator Buttons Kaluhiokalani makes a triumphant return to the frontline of the surf biz with his appointment to Kahuna Creations. The new sponsorship for the veteran is celebrated at an all-day picnic at Sunset Beach, where Buttons demonstrates the Kahuna Big Stick land paddle and launches the first ever land paddle race, to be held at Morro Bay, California.

ENGLAND
● More news on old dudes still in demand! Chris "Guts" Griffiths is the new hire at Team Onfire as it tackles the UK surfwear market. Guts, former Welsh and British champion and leading surfboard shaper for decades, joins a strong team that includes All Black legend Carlos Spencer.

SOUTH AFRICA
● On the eve of the Billabong Pro Jeffreys Bay, surfers protest the proposed nuclear power station at Thuyspunt, just 12 kilometers from

Cape St. Francis, made famous in the iconic 1960s surf movie *The Endless Summer*. The protest, organized by the Supertubes Surfing Association, centers on the claim that building of the nuclear plant would have a negative impact on water quality at Jeffreys Bay. Meanwhile, in an unrelated item, Super Spar Jeffreys Bay reports huge sales of condoms as the pro tour hits town. Manager Pierre Venter says, "We've had to double our order. They're definitely not just surfing when they come here."

FLORIDA
● Jaws is revisited as New Smyrna Beach, Florida, gets set to welcome thousands of summer tourists and this image pops up on the camera of local photog Ken McNair. Says McNair, "I saw something in the background and went, what was that! I backed it up just a tad and here's this spinner shark." The shark twisted on landing and disappeared, leaving swimmers and surfers none the wiser. Go figure.

NEW ZEALAND
● Kiwi longboarder Daryn McBride is revealed as a man of many talents with the release of a new series of prints and cards, which he hopes will create enough revenue to get him to ISA Surfing Games in Portugal in October. Daryn, a veteran of the not-so-lucrative longboard tour, is dad to four-year-old triplets, making his travel dreams even harder to realize.

reef. According to Rip Curl staffers on the spot, the waves are still running perfectly beside the wreck and the event will go ahead, despite fears of oil pollution from the vessel.

AUSTRALIA
● The ASP calls for expressions of interest from potential World Tour licensees for 2009, with both its men's and women's premium world tours running an event short in 2008 and further sponsor fallout expected. The governing body says it hopes to attract new event licensees for Europe, Central America, Japan and mainland USA.

SOUTH AFRICA
● While the Billabong Pro Jeffreys Bay heads towards the pointy end, surfers on hand for the event are signing a petition, started by the Supertubes Surfing Foundation, opposing the building of a nuclear power plant close to the fabled break. South Africa's former world champion Shaun Tomson is among the first to sign up, along with current world champion Mick Fanning and ratings leader Kelly Slater.

FRANCE
● Hawaii takes a long-awaited world title with Joy Monahan's victory over Australia's Chelsea Williams at the Roxy Jam women's world longboard

Believe it or leave it. Shark at New Smyrna Beach. Photo Kem McNair/Barcroft Media.

Art by Daryn McBride.

Shaun Tomson signs petition. Photo Brent Williams.   *Carissa Moore. Photo Aquashot/Aspeurope.com.*   *Jack Johnson. Photo Meike Reijerman.*

Leading shaper Luke Short. Photo Daniel Cross.

championships in Biarritz, France. In an exciting final held at Cote des Basques in the center of the picturesque old resort town, the 22-year-old from Oahu scored an excellent wave in the dying seconds to wrest the title from the favored Aussie.

AUSTRALIA

● Leading Aussie shaper Luke Short (LSD Surfboards) joins the Base Surfboards team alongside his mentor Simon Anderson and industry veterans Murray Bourton and Darren Handley. The Angourie-based shaper served his apprenticeship with Anderson, Al Merrick, Greg Webber, Maurice Cole and Rodney Dahlberg before forming Luke Short Designs (LSD) at Mona Vale in Sydney in 2000.

CALIFORNIA

● Big wave supremos Laird Hamilton and Dave Kalama co-chair a gala fundraiser for PacSun's "Pipeline to a Cure for Cystic Fibrosis" at the Hyatt Regency, Huntington Beach. The two tow-in kings joined the campaign after learning of the plight of surfer Emily Haager, a 25-year-old who has been battling the disease since she was six months old. Says Kalama: "Our duty is to help create awareness of the positive impact of surfing on CF patients. It really does help clear their sinuses and lungs."

WEEK 30
JULY 22–28

CALIFORNIA

● Just when you thought the stitched-up crew had inherited the earth, the delightfully non-PC Lost Enterprises hosts the US Open of Drinking, a three-night summer binge along Huntington Beach's notorious Main Street strip. Okay, there are more surf shops than sleazy bars in HB, and strippers, hookers and pimps . . . forget about it. But you work with what you have. The point breaks were 100 for a shot, 50 for a mixed drink and 25 for a beer, and everyone had priority.

GERMANY

● In town to play a big gig at Munich-Riem, superstar Jack Johnson does the Munich locals a favor bigger than you can imagine by sliding a few at the city's famous Eisbach river wave. Eisbach, in the middle of the beautiful old town, throws up a passable left that has been ridden as a novelty by visitors for several years. But if you're a surfer who lives in Munich, this is no novelty, this is your home break! So Jack's evening surf in boardies (despite the chill of the river) was perfectly timed as the city council had met that very day to consider banning surfing in the river for safety reasons. Jack's verdict? "Why would they want to do that? It's so cool to have a surf right in the middle of a lovely old European city."

CALIFORNIA

● Despite rumbles in the US economy, France-based Oxbow goes ahead with its long-awaited American launch, with brand guru Laird Hamilton opening Oxbow's first US retail store in Santa Monica. Laird, nearing 20 years representing the brand, paid tribute to Oxbow's commitment to surfing, particularly longboarding. Oxbow will stage the second leg of its longboard world championships at San Onofre later in the year.

● O'Neill launches "The Life," a Jamie Brisick–directed insider's look at the tough life of seven pro surfers. Says Brisick, "The reality of pro surfing is that it's not all epic waves and champagne victories. It's extremely taxing on mind, body and spirit." Yeah, but you do get to surf a lot.

● And in another neat recycling job, *Surfers: The Movie* returns to the silver screen in an updated, slicked-up revival of the epic Gotcha-sponsored 1990 flick. Producer Michael Tomson says the movie is worth another airing because the surfing shot back in the day was "so beyond." And if you look at what Pottz and crew were doing in

Jamie Mitchell. Photo Bernie Baker.

1990, he's right. Surfers kicks off with an East Coast run.

HAWAII

● Australian waterman sensation Jamie Mitchell takes out his seventh straight Quiksilver Edition Molakai to Oahu Paddleboard Race, consolidating his position as the world's leading paddleboarder. Although he finished nine minutes outside his record time in 2007, Mitchell said this was his greatest performance. "I could have just kept on paddling," he said.

WEEK 31
JULY 29–AUGUST 4

CALIFORNIA

● Pioneer surf moviemaker Bud Browne dies at San Luis Obispo, California, after a brief illness. The man who virtually invented the surf movie, creating such classics as *Locked In* and *Cat on a Hot Foam Board*, was 96. Earlier this year, he had been honored by his peers at a special film festival in

the town he had come to regard as home.

● On-line auctioneer Jim Winniman claims a world record with the sale of a wooden Tom Blake–shaped surfboard for $32,000. Winniman's auction also claims a record $19,000 for a Dora/Noll original Da Cat model, as part of a total turnover of $600,000. "People will spend more if they can stay at home," he says.

● Body Glove co-founder and Dive and Surf pioneer Bob Meistrell celebrates his 80th birthday by diving a wreck off the California coast. And in keeping with the spirit of the man who invented the wetsuit, he dives using full retro gear dating back to the 1950s. Meistrell, whose twin brother Bill passed away in 2006, is regarded as a surfing culture living treasure.

BALI

● The shipwreck on Padang Reef,

Burning boat. Photo Bernard Testemale.

Bali, is no more. Or at least, it is less than it was. In an unexplained development, the alleged pirate boat caught fire overnight and was burnt to the waterline. Go figure.

WEEK 32
AUGUST 5-11

CALIFORNIA

● The International Surfing Association announces that the 2009 World Surfing Games will take place in Playa Hermosa, Costa Rica. Some 35 countries will take part in the games between July 31 and August 9, and the entire contest will be webcast to an estimated 800 million people around the world.

EUROPE

● Over two days on the Dutch coast, 24 blind and visually impaired children learn to surf as part of the Out of

Bounds program within the O'Neill Surf Academy.

Out of Bounds is the brainchild of Santa Cruz surfer and photographer Yael Dahan, who worked with O'Neill Europe to make the Dutch clinic happen. "There were moments in the water where I looked around and could not find a single face without a smile on it," he says.

Each student was paired with an instructor as well as two volunteers—a buddy and a catcher who was there to help at the end of the wave. For 10-year-old Dion Terlingen, who is completely blind and autistic, it was not only his first time surfing but his first visit to the beach.

INDONESIA

● Dean "Dingo" Morrison, current number 18 on the ASP World Tour, pops the question to long-term girlfriend Alana Brennan during the Rip Curl Search Pro "somewhere in Indo-

Bob Meistrell on his 80th birthday. Photo Mark Kawakami.

Dean Morrison. Photo ASP Tostee © Covered Images.

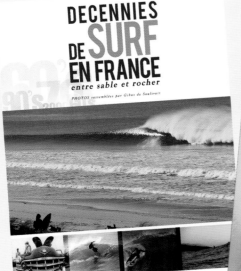

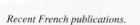

Recent French publications.

nesia," and the couple is off to the altar sometime in 2009. It was a big week for Dingo, who finished equal ninth in the Search Pro, lifting him in the ratings after a lean spell.

FRANCE

● *Decennies de surf en France (Decades of surf in France)* is published in France. The book features the work of many of the best photographers to shoot surfing in France over the past five decades, from Arnaud de Rosnay in the '60s to Gecko, Christophe Dimulle and Tim McKenna today. Some 450 photographs cover events from early days surfing at La Barre through the con-

quering of big wave spot Belharra and the arrival of what has become known as the "Flores Generation."

● Still in France, gotta love the title of France's first homegrown longboard movie. *Come On Baby* is the brainchild of Basque country local Yannick Loussouarn, and features the best of the French new wave longboarders, including Antoine Delpero and Romain Maurin.

CALIFORNIA

● The bronze bust of surfing pioneer George Freeth by sculptor Terry O'Donnell has been stolen from its

Elijah Criaco. Photo Steve Robertson.

home on Redondo Beach Pier, where it has been a feature for 31 years. Police are investigating. Freeth, who learned his surfing chops in Hawaii, is credited with popularizing surfing in southern California when he came to the Los Angeles South Bay before World War I to give surfing exhibitions promoting Henry Huntington's new coastal railroad. So he may also have been the world's first professional surfer. Wetsuit guru Bob Meistrell offers a $5,000 reward for information leading to the return of the bust.

WEEK 33
AUGUST 12–18

AUSTRALIA

● Eyewear company Arnette comes to the rescue of the former Brothers Neilsen Junior Surf Challenge on Queensland's Sunshine Coast, taking over the sponsorship from the iconic retail chain that went bust in June. The event, sponsored by Neilsens for 12 years, had appeared to be one of the first casualties of the growing world economic downturn.

HAWAII

● Presidential hopeful Senator Barack Obama returns to his youth with a body surf session

at Sandy Beach. The Democrat front-runner, who grew up in Honolulu and attended Punahou School, alma mater of such surfing greats as Gerry Lopez, Jeff Hakman and Fred Hemmings, took his daughters for a play in the rock pools at Haunama Bay before getting down and dirty with local bodyboarders at Sandy.

CALIFORNIA

● Shaping legend Bing Copeland and writer Paul Holmes launch the long-awaited book *Bing Surfboards: 50 Years of Craftsmanship and Innovation* at the Surf Heritage Foundation in San Clemente. The book, believed to be the first in a series covering the iconic surfboard brands of surf's pioneer era, covers Bing's own colorful story as well as graphically depicting the design and marketing of the most popular boards in America in the 1960s.

Obama does a Mark Cunningham move at Sandy Beach.
Photo Associated Press/Honolulu Star Bulletin.

Photo classicbingsurfboards.com.

Night rider. Photo Brian Nevins.

Surf Europe's Reader's Choice Awards winners. Photo Florence Buehr.

NEW JERSEY

● Red Bull riders light up the night sky over Atlantic City at an "extreme tow-in" event. A huge crowd fills the historic boardwalk to watch 28 of the East Coast's best surfers perform.

CHINA

● The Olympics may still take a dim view of surfing as an Olympic sport, but only one degree of separation comes between Samuel Sanchez's gold cycling medal in Beijing and surfing. Okay, Sam from Spain don't surf, but he's sponsored by Oakley, and they do! Or at least some of them do. In fact, the eyewear giant with serious surfing cred has around 500 athletes competing in Beijing.

WEEK 34
AUGUST 19–25

SOUTH CAROLINA

● A surfer who almost drowned after pushing through a heavy set in Mexico more than 20 years ago has finally come up with an invention that may save others from the frightening experience. Mark Chestnut, who had plenty of big wave

Mark Chestnut with his AIR emergency breathing device. Photo Robert Todd.

experience before his near-disaster in Cabo San Lucas in 1986, has spent years perfecting a small, portable emergency breathing device he calls AIR (Always In Reach) and now has a patent for it. AIR weighs only a couple of ounces, and according to Chestnut, represents no impediment to your surfing when worn on the upper arm. And it can make you feel a whole lot more confident as you paddle out on that killer day.

FRANCE

● World Tour front runner Jeremy Flores takes out the big one at Surf Europe's annual knees-up at the Hossegor Casino. The 20-year-old, now in his second year on the World Tour and top ten, took out the men's division as Europe's most popular surfer, while Lee-Ann Curren, the France-based daughter of legend Tom Curren, won the women's.

WEEK 35
AUGUST 26–SEPTEMBER 1

EAST COAST USA

● Montanaro Gallery unveils a major exhibition of 25 international surf artists under the banner "Surf Art Nouveau." The Newport, Rhode Island gallery's owner spent a year gathering artwork from a diverse array of creative talent, including founder of *Surfer* magazine John Severson, top young Californian longboarder Tyler "Pickle" Warren, Italy's Vincenzo Ganadu, and well-established artists like Wade Koniakowsky, Glenn Martin, Spencer Reynolds and many more. The gallery's PR blurb says, "Since the early 1880s Art Nouveau has been a leading source of inspiration to thousands of artists and designers from all over the world. Pioneers such as Alphonse Mucha, Henri de Toulouse-Lautrec and Gustav Klimt helped spread this movement to all corners of the earth." But did those old dudes shred?

CALIFORNIA

● As airlines flail to stay in business in a tough economy and with soaring fuel costs, surfers are punished with horrendous baggage charges to fly with their boards. Rising to battle the shakedown is West Coast–based global board rental and demo company Sportsknack.com, which describes itself as a "Netflix for surfers," although Hertz or Avis might be a more accurate analogy. With boards from top labels like Firewire, Kaysen, Keahana, Channel Islands, Surf Prescriptions, Surftech and Aviso, the rental company offers a novel way for the traveling surfer to save money, eliminate the check-in hassle and still ride a top-

SportsKnack inventory. Photo Orit Benzaquen, Sports Knack, Inc/www.theendlessquiver.com.

flight board for that California dream session at Rincon, Malibu or Swamis. Reservations can be made online and boards picked up at a variety of surf shop locations.

CANADA

● A Vancouver Island college announces teaming up with Australia's Southern

Surf Story 3. Art by Wade Koniakowsky/www.koniakowsky.com.

Cross University to develop a diploma for surfers, according to Barbie Mayor, a nursing instructor and surfing mom who is coordinating the program's development. The first class of about 20 students could be heading for school and waves in September 2009.

The diploma of sport management in surfing studies is being put together by Vancouver Island's North Island College, and, once approved, classes will be held at Port Alberni and Tofino. Southern Cross students enrolled in the program complete courses in sports management, events, technology and skills, culture, and business—all with a special emphasis on surfing. Mayor said the Canadian course will be based on the Southern Cross University curriculum but with a Canadian twist, adding that in 2007 the local surfing industry accounted for about $300 million in business.

UNITED KINGDOM

● The surf-starved scions of Bournemouth, England are cheering now that the long-awaited first section of the first artificial surf reef in the northern hemisphere slowly rolls off a barge and sinks onto the Boscombe seabed. It will be at least two more months before they'll know whether the completed project will turn the spot into the south coast's equivalent of the Banzai Pipeline. But Bournemouth city councillor Beverley Dunlop was clearly stoked and optimistic, saying, "It has taken 10 years to get to this point. The surf reef will turn Bournemouth into a water sports Mecca, as it will be a free facility to be enjoyed by surfers, snorkellers, windsurfers and divers." No doubt there'll be warning signs to alert snorkellers about clean-up sets.

WEEK 36
SEPTEMBER 2–8

HAWAII

● Irrepressible artist, surfer and former media mogul John Severson is finding plenty of projects to keep himself amused in his retirement on Maui. His latest gig is designing guitars for Fender. Says Severson, "I waited 40 years for that call. I was impressed with Johnny Fain surf guitaring and al-

John Severson. Photo Jon Karcey.

ways wondered how hard it would be," he says, referring to a Fender ad that appeared in early issues of his magazine back in the day. "So I 'test drove' the Surf Fever model on some smooth glassy walls. As I took off, I swung the guitar around from my back, right into a major chord position playing my Dick Dale favorites. Duck dives and rolls resulted in some interesting horse-collar wipeouts. I chased the guitar to the rocks and luckily it was

a floater. I highly recommend it—but without the amp." As the erstwhile filmmaker and *Surfer* mag founder notes, it's just "one more thing you can do at 74!"

CALIFORNIA

● A new documentary by Ty Ponder and Scott Bass titled *Between the Lines* has its Hollywood premiere and raises money for veterans charities in a gala event at the Beverly Hills Fine Arts Theater. Special guests who turn out for the screening include Jeff Kober and Brian Wimmer (*China Beach* TV series), Nia Peeples (*The Young and the Restless*), Simon Baker (*The Mentalist* CBS series, fall '08), Donna Spangler (*Blades of Glory, Playboy Magazine*) Joshua Feinman and Elle Travis (*Men Don't Lie*), Cherie Thibodeaux (model-comedian), Chris M. Allport (*Pirates of the Caribbean, At Worlds End*) and Brien Perry (*The Truth About Angels*).

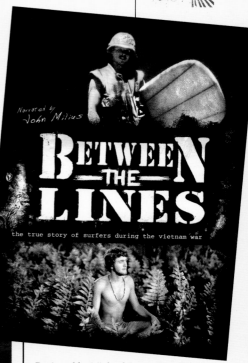

Designed by Michael Peters/Tom Luker collection and Robert Worthington.

Narrated by writer and director John Milius, who coined the immortal words "Charlie don't surf" for Lt. Col. Kilgore in *Apocalypse Now*, the film explores the Vietnam War through the prism of the surfing subculture and gives unique insight into the dramatic effect that the conflict had on young American men who rode waves—both those who served and those who dodged the draft and went underground—many of whom kept on surfing against all odds.

EAST COAST USA

● Coastal dwellers board up their windows and brace for the worst, while surfers all along the eastern shore wax up their boards and get ready with gleeful anticipation. A series

First reef section at Boscombe. Photo Bournemouth Tourism/www.thesurfreef.co.uk.

ALMANAC SEPTEMBER

of three tropical storms, all potential hurricanes, are lined up like a string of pearls across the Atlantic, promising days, even weeks, of great swell. It's been only a few days since Gustav crashed into the coast of Louisiana after cutting a swath of destruction across the Caribbean and the Gulf but bringing some of the best surf in years to Texas (briefly, before all hell broke loose) and the Florida Panhandle, which was spared the brunt of the fury. Now it's time for Florida's east side, the Mid-Atlantic states and the Northeast to get their share. Meanwhile, a few naysayers are casting swine before the pearls by asking, is global warming making this "normal" for the weather? In fact, storm researchers say, 10 tropical storms is normal, but they are predicting 17 for 2008. The record-busting 2005 season, which included deadly Hurricane Katrina, had 28 storms.

AUSTRALIA

● As manager of Maddog surf shop in Byron Bay, 51-year-old John Morgan enjoys his midday surf. Imagine his surprise when his liquid lunch session between Clarks Beach and the Pass suddenly becomes a tow-in session with a shark, "There was a big swirl under the board and I knew it was a big shark underneath me and it sort of freaked me out a bit, and then it hit my leg rope and the worst thing was it got tangled in my leg rope and

started towing me out to sea really, really quickly. I was on my board lying on it, but slipping off the back because we were going so fast," says Morgan, with matter-of-fact aplomb. "I had just come off a wave when I was suddenly hauled backwards. It felt like I was riding behind a powerful jet ski." Morgan ultimately got loose by untying his leash and swimming to shore. "I'm just glad it didn't turn around and bite me," he adds in another momentous understatement.

This is the kind of shark story that gladdens the heart. No blood, no gore, nobody dies, loses a limb or goes to the hospital. It's all good!

WEEK 37
SEPTEMBER 9–15

CALIFORNIA

● San Clemente, California–based Surfing Heritage Foundation, the surfboard museum and Taj Mahal of surf culture, hosts a memorial tribute to pioneer surf movie maker Bud Browne, who passed away in July 2008. On hand for the event is a full lineup of legends, including Bruce Brown, Linda Benson, Joyce Hoffman, Mickey Muñoz, Greg Noll, L. J. Richards, Paul Strauch, Ron Sizemore, and many other special guests. Browne was an all-time great water photographer and the first to take a movie cam-

Hurricane shoes make an appearance. Photo Suzanne Stoll.

era out at Pipeline, all of which earned him the nickname "Barracuda." He finally hung up his water housings in 1977, following a stint working on the John Milius/Warner Bros cult classic *Big Wednesday.*

HAWAII

● Alec Cooke, aka Ace Cool, the accomplished big wave rider who made his reputation after being dropped in from a helicopter to surf Kaena Point and Outside Log Cabins on the North Shore during huge swells in the mid-'80s, is on his ninth day swimming around the entire island of Oahu. "I am

exhausted and got some stings, but I am in good shape, a few blisters and I am sore," says Cooke. "It's been a great experience." Cooke's latest extreme waterman adventure is designed to raise public awareness about in-shore pollution, the plight of Hawaii's coral reefs and, as he puts it so succinctly, "to remind people to keep their trash out of the ocean."

FLORIDA

● For the ultra chic trendsetters of Miami's South Beach, the daily decisions of what to wear are always made in the eye of fashion's storm. But with the 2008 hurricane season peaking this month, fretting over footwear could really be a life or death deal. For supermodels dreading a deluge at the disco, here's the answer: Hurricane Shoes, out just in time for the action sports trade show circuit. Featuring a sexy stiletto heel and fabulous frog feet in a rainbow array of colors, these shoes are way more cool than wearing an inflatable rubber ring—ready for an elegant exit from any storm surge. No branding rights have yet been granted, but when fashion combines function like these shoes do, that's nothing to sneeze at, Jimmy Choo.

WEEK 38
SEPTEMBER 16–22

BANGLADESH

● It's a truism that surf is where you find it, and here's more proof. While most men Jafar Alam's age in Bangladesh are obsessed with cricket, this 25-year-old is more likely to be found surfing the waves on one of the world's longest beaches—a 125-kilometer (78-mile) stretch of coast. You can find it by going to India and turning right.

Alam started the Cox's Bazar Surf Club in 2002, based out of the two-room house he shares with five family members. He now has 48 students, including 12 girls, and is about to hold

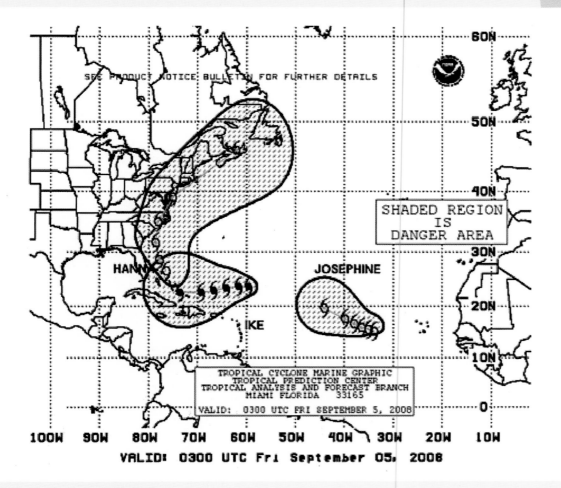

The perfect storms. Chart courtesy NOAA.

Bangladesh Surf Club. Photos Surfing the Nations.

Your local lineup to be? Photo Ted Grambeau.

the nation's fourth annual surf contest.

A decade ago Alam bought a surfboard from a visiting Australian tourist for 20 bucks, and for five years tried to teach himself. Finally he was spotted by Tom Bauer, founder of the Honolulu-based nonprofit organization Surfing the Nations, which promotes surfing in impoverished countries. "He gave me a proper leash and polished my board with wax," Alam says, which we have to assume made things a bit easier. Bauer will return to Cox's Bazar for this month's competition, and he likens the surfing conditions in southern Bangladesh to those at California's Huntington Beach. But less crowded, no doubt.

CALIFORNIA

● Despite a $5,000 reward, there's still no sign of the bronze bust of George Freeth, the first surfer in southern California (1907), which was stolen last month from its perch on the Redondo Beach pier. So now, Bob Meistrell, the local wetsuit pioneer (Dive 'n' Surf/ Body Glove) who put up the reward

money, has another idea—to replace it. Luckily, the original mold has been kept in the city's historical museum for the 31 years since the tribute was first installed. While the bust's creator, Terry O'Donnell, died in January 2008, his daughter is donating some of her father's stash of bronze to the cause. It's thought that the bust was stolen for its value as scrap metal.

THE WORLD

● Just when you were getting adjusted to the concept of global warming, the world is set for a 'big chill,' possibly a mini-ice age, according to the venerable and whimsical *Old Farmer's Almanac*, first published in 1792 and the United States' oldest continuously published periodical.

The 2009 edition, which came out earlier this month, predicts that the earth already has entered a sustained period of global cooling. True to form, the almanac also includes tips on such items as how to

stay warm all winter with just one log on your fire.

The almanac is predicting a period of global cooling partly due to the lack of sunspots, which some scientists believe causes cooling on the sun and, subsequently, the earth. But just think, all the money you'll save on air conditioning and iced mocha frappacinos will enable you to buy a better wetsuit. Original source: Michael Hirtzer at Reuters.

● Big braddah is watching your board. Well, not really, but all surfboards, SUPS, and other such surf and snow gear purchased with the SBT system and registered on the Surfboard Tracker website can now be covered by a global tracking system

similar to such services as LoJack for cars. According to SBT, the system contributes to the reduction and risk of board theft and comes with insurance underwritten by Lloyds of London. But hey, that also means your secret spot is vulnerable to curious staffers at the system, since they'll know where you're surfing all the time!

WEEK 39
SEPTEMBER 23–29

MEXICO

● The infamous Puerto Escondido is renowned for its board-snapping beachbreak bombs and barrels and might be considered a highly unlikely location for an SUP surf contest. But Maui's Noah Shimabukuro (currently a resident of Oceanside, California) walks away $4,000 richer after besting an elite field of competitors from Hawaii, California, Puerto Rico and Mexico in a four-day event that delivers everything from clean overhead tubes to small mushier paddle-pushers. Like it oar not, (it's a pun, not a typo) the SUP thing is catching fire everywhere.

Noah Shimabukuru. Photo Jaime Torres/Velauno.

The exhibit room. Photo LionelMLN.

Mundaka. Photo ASP Karen © Covered Images.

FRANCE

● The exhibition "Surfing Art by Shapers" rolls out in the cultural center at Bourdaines à Seignosse, just north of Biarritz, with a second annual event sponsored by Jacky Rott, the pioneer French surfboard maker who partnered Barland-Rott surfboards. At least 20 shaper-artists take part in the show, which features highly art-inspired boards, paintings, prints, sculptures, videos and more, in addition to more than 100 pieces of surfboard art designs submitted by regular Jeans and Jeanettes with that *je ne sais quoi* French penchant for *des artes*. Sylvain Thiery conceived and curated the show and the event also featured a live music soirée headlined by electro-rock ensemble the Golden Tatas. No photos of Tatas. Sorry, *desolé, vraiment.*

Princess Kaiulani.
Photo Janeresture.com.

UNITED KINGDOM

● British surfing may be older than once thought. According to Kristin Zambucka, who has written three books on the Hawaiian royal family, Princess Kaiulani loved surfing and introduced the sport to Europe when she was studying in England in the early 1890s. Malika Dudley Kaiulani, who was born in 1875, surfed in English Channel waters at Brighton, Zambucka says. According to documents at the British Surfing Museum there, "The tall foreign dignitary stood erect on a thin board with her hair blowing in the wind and rode the chilly waters." After learning of the princess surfing, some of the nobility of Europe were soon giving it a go, Zambucka says, adding that when the princess returned home in 1897, she surfed regularly at Waikiki and her 7' 6" board is preserved in Honolulu's Bishop Museum. But wait, how does a Hawaiian princess end up with a middle name like Dudley? And why is the Union Jack still part of the Hawaiian flag? That's the problem with surfing history: one factoid leads to more questions, like how come there are never any action pictures to back up such stories?

WEEK 40
SEPTEMBER 30–
OCTOBER 6

SPAIN

● Save The Waves Coalition, based in Davenport, California, announces the release of its first Surfonomics study

measuring the value of the waves at Mundaka. This is a place whose economy relies heavily on surf tourism, and in 2005 the surf there was temporarily lost due to river dredging for a large ship-building project.

"A beautiful surfing wave like Mundaka is truly a world treasure," says executive director Dean LaTourrette. "This study provides evidence of not just the environmental value

Kelly Slater's ninth. Photo ASP Cestari © Covered Images.

of a Mundaka, but of the economic value as well, reinforcing the notion that it and other spots like it need to be protected." A summary of key findings: an estimated positive economic impact of up to $4.5 million per year to the local economy in a town of approximately 1,900 people, adding up to $1.5 million in annual personal income to the local population and supporting up to 95 jobs. A majority of survey respondents claim they would no longer visit if the waves were significantly degraded. Local businesses estimate that up to 40 percent of their customers are surfers or surf spectators, and that the loss of business due to the degradation of the surf and the cancellation of the ASP pro contest could be as high as 50 percent. There was no comment, apparently, from the innkeeper's daughter.

FLORIDA

● Cocoa Beach's Kelly Slater, 36, wins a record ninth ASP World Title after advancing out of Round 3 of the Billabong Pro Mundaka—the 9th event of 11 on the 2008 ASP World Tour. "It's going to take a little while to sink in," Slater says when mobbed at the water's edge. "I'm probably going to have to call home and talk to family for it to really hit me."

Slater's 2008 crowning comes 16 years after securing his first ASP World Title at age 20. He is now both the oldest and youngest surfer in ASP history to win a world title. Slater joined the tour in 1991 and won his first ASP World Title in 1992. When asked if he had ever dreamed about achieving such a feat when he came onto the scene 17 years ago, Slater was close to speechless, "I never even thought about it," Slater said. "It never even popped into my head. It's crazy.

Dominating five of the season's first eight contests, Slater accrued enough points to clinch the 2008 crown with two scheduled ASP World Tour contests yet to be surfed. The unprecedented title means that the ubertalent freak of nature surf-dog formerly referred to as SL8ER, will now be known as K-NINE.

WESTERN AUSTRALIA

● Fergal Smith, 21, is surfing off the coast of Perth, Western Australia, when a shark comes within a few feet of him. The visiting surfer, from County Mayo, Ireland, only discovers his close shave after a local photographer, Phil Gallagher, shows him the picture. Fergal Smith says he

Fegral Smith takes aim at a great white in WA. Photo www.philgallagher.com.

Giant Mavericks. Photo Curt Myers/Towsurfer.com.

"couldn't help but laugh" when he saw the photograph, adding that his mother, Brid, 51, "freaked out big time." He adds, "I saw a gray shape in the wave, but I thought it was the reflection of a slab of rock. How wrong was I?" Shutterbugger Gallagher adds, "Great whites are common out here, but I have never seen one that near to a surfer before."

Since 1876 great white sharks have been responsible for 65 deaths and 242 recorded non-fatal attacks worldwide. Australia has had the most fatal great white attacks in the world with 27 deaths, the most recent in 2005. There are no records of great white attacks on Irish persons. Shark deterrent? Perhaps it's the Guinness and the Bushmills. Or just the luck of the Irish?

WEEK 41
OCTOBER 7–14

UNITED KINGDOM

● Here's a novel way to while away some time on a flat day and a must-pack item for a surf trip: a surfer's deck of playing cards from the folks at Low Pressure/Stormrider Guides—54 of the world's best waves displayed in full color with wave descriptions, latitude/longitude and other fascinating factoids. The corners display normal playing card suits, numbers and jokers. No more wooden-faced kings or queens, just killer photos of the planet's primo surf spots. How about making Hawaii trumps, waves over 20 feet penalty cards or all rivermouths wildcards? What about getting up a high-stakes game where the winner takes the pot and cashes out on a surfari to all the breaks in the winning hand?

Layne Beachley. ASP Morris © Covered Images.

Courtesy www.lowpressure.co.uk/

CALIFORNIA

● Early October and sleeping giant Mavericks wakes up for the first big winter swell of the season. Hawaiian tow-in team Garrett McNamara and Eric Akiskalian happen to be in California on business, so after seeing the forecast, they head up the coast to Half Moon Bay. By early afternoon the swell is on the rise and they luck into a few nuggets and with no one around. Before long the waves are cracking solid 15 to 18 feet, with even a few bigger waves managing to get away. A short while later the first paddler goes out, so they switch to their own traditional boards and re-join the line-up along with local surfers Grant Washburn, Ben Andrews, John Bowling, Mark Sponsler, Randy Cone, Lance Harriman, Mark Alfaro, Jeff Clever, Jeff Harrison, August Hidalgo, "Big Wave Dave" Barnett, Christy Davis, John Raymond, Alex Martins, Colin Brown, Haley Fiske and a few others. "Last year's season opener consisted of surfers from all over the world and this year it was mostly all locals," comments McNamara. "The Northern Hemisphere is lighting up and I can't wait to see what Mother Nature delivers next!"

Ricky Carroll. Photo courtesy Ice Nine Foamwork.

AUSTRALIA

● Layne Beachley, 36, the record-breaking seven-time ASP Women's World Champion, officially announces her retirement from full-time competition, effective at the end of the year. Beachley's announcement comes as a surprise, given that she's so close to yet another world crown, in the No. 3 spot on the ratings. "Even though I am in my career best form," Beachley says, "I have to be honest with myself—I'm not committing 100 percent time and energy and effort and focus into winning world titles. Even though I love what I do, I'm beginning to love what I'm doing out of the water more. My passion for competitive surfing has been diluted. So now I've had to make a decision and I'm convinced I'm doing the right thing." The Sydney-sider is the most accomplished female surfer in the history of the sport, winning six world titles in a row from 1998–2004, and coming back to take another one in 2006. Along the ways she's racked up 29 world tour event victories.

WEEK 42
OCTOBER 14–20

CALIFORNIA

● The second annual Sacred Craft Consumer Surfboard Expo goes off in Del Mar, just north of San Diego with more than 70 surfboard companies showing their wares (and selling some of them) to a wide-eyed set of several thousand stoked civilians who can't get in to see such things at the usual industry-insiders-only trade shows. As part of many events, demonstrations, seminars and what-not there's a "Tribute to the Masters Shape-off," pitting a half-dozen top shapers against each other in a 90-minute challenge to replicate a Bill Caster four-channel, wing-pintail, single-fin Chris O'Rourke model board from the 1970s. Florida's Ricky Carroll wins the contest for the second year running, with Chris Christenson, Ned Mahon, Ward Coffey, Timmy Patterson and Matt Calvani all putting up some stiff competition.

HAWAII

● The announcement of the upcoming North Shore surf contest season focuses on big waves and big money. This year's Vans Triple Crown of Surfing, now in its 26th season, offers $815,000 in prize money, but its value to the local economy goes much deeper as it attracts contestants, media, judges, officials and spectators to the world's seven-mile miracle of surfing. The last independent economic impact study, conducted in the winter of 2006, showed that the Vans Triple Crown of Surfing directly attracted a total number of 7,000 participants and spectators to the North Shore. Those participants and visitors generated $14.6 million in spending, including $8.9 million in direct spending. Studies for the Hawaii Tourism Authority also show that 51 percent of overnight visitors to Oahu venture out to the North Shore. "There's not much in life that's free these days," says Triple Crown director Randy Rarick. "But the waves and world class surfing events still don't cost a dime here. Even the

parking's free, and that makes events like ours even more attractive at times like these."

Meanwhile, "Members of the surf industry, pro surfers and visitors will be paying up to $30,000 a month to rent beach-side homes on the North Shore this winter," according to the announcement. What it doesn't say is that split 30 ways, six people per room, that adds up to only $1,000 per head but raises questions like, "Hey, who stole my beer outta da fridge?"

UNITED KINGDOM

● It was Britain's best-kept surfing secret. Some claim the spot rivals some of the best waves in Australia and Hawaii and its precise location has been known to only a few—until now. Apparently the wave, Broad Bench, comes ashore at Kimmeridge beach on Dorset's "Jurassic Coast." Local surfers decided to reveal the big wave's existence because the Ministry of Defense is restricting access on grounds that it is adjacent to the army's Bovington and Lulworth training camps. Increased use of nearby shooting ranges has prompted the military to close the beach to the public for most of the year. The MoD's move has Dorset surfers so irate they decided to reveal the location in an online campaign calling itself the Access Broad Bench Association (ABBA) to allow them to ride "surfing's holy grail" freely again. One surfer describes the MoD's actions as like "telling a climber they can't go up Mount Everest"—which is kind of right, except that if you die on Everest it's not likely because you've been shot. Jurassic Coast? ABBA? Surfing's holy grail? How can we be sure this isn't a Monty Python skit? Where are the photos?

PORTUGAL

● Australia wins its third consecutive International Surfing Association's World Surfing Games team championship gold medal in Costa de Caparica, Portugal, with USA taking silver, Brazil claiming bronze and France holding copper. Newly crowned ISA world champions include Sally Fitzgibbons (AUS) in Open Women; CJ Hobgood (USA) Open Men; Marcus Lima (BRA) Bodyboard Men; Natasha Sagardia (PRI) Bodyboard Women; Mat-

The World Tour gets even better. Photo ASP Karen © Covered Images.

thew Moir (ZAF) Longboard. Even with the ending of the World Surfing Games, the ISA is still busy with the 1st Asian Beach Games currently being held in Bali, Indonesia. This is the first time in history that teams representing their national Olympic Committees include surfers competing in an IOC-recognized event. Should surfing be an Olympic sport, according to ISA's objectives?—Discuss. No prizes or medals for the winning essays.

WEEK 43
OCTOBER 21–27

FRANCE

● An artist with "multiple facets," Benoît Alcouffe, aka Malagit, puts on a riveting exhibition of metal surfboards at the Oxbow store in Anglet, Biarritz. Dubbed "Full Metal Surfing," the show features three monumental surfboards between 1.80m and 3m tall,

in copper, zinc and brass. Fer enough? (Not a typo—bilingual pun.)

AUSTRALIA

● According to world governing body, the Association of Surfing Professionals, "Following one of the most historic board meetings to date, the ASP has introduced the option for a new competition format to be implemented in ASP World Tour events in 2009. "While the traditional 48-man format will still be available, events can elect to implement an altered 48-man format consisting of two opening elimination man-on-man rounds. Round 1 will consist of 32 surfers, those rated 17–27 on the ASP World Tour, three Tour/Injury wildcards, the Top 15–rated surfers on the ASP WQS and three event wildcards. "The seeding formula will remain the same as the traditional format, with the No. 17 seed up against the No. 32 seed in Heat 8, the No. 18 seed against the No. 31 seed in Heat 9, etc. After Round

Team Australia, world champions. Photo ISA.

Full Metal Surfing. Photo Oxbow.

1, all remaining competitors will be re-seeded for Round 2. "The Top 16 on the ASP World Tour are seeded directly in Round 2, where they will meet the 16 victors from Round 1 in the re-seeded draw. The Top 10 from the previous year's World Tour will be guaranteed a Round 2 seed all year long, while the next 6 seeds have to maintain their seeded position and can be replaced by better-performing back 32 surfers after the third ASP "Dream Tour" event of the year." Say what? Dream Tour or nightmare? Remember when pro contests were understandable—man-on-man heats based on a world championship seeding order; winner goes to the next round; loser goes to the pub; last man standing wins?

WEEK 44
OCTOBER 28–NOVEMBER 3

UNITED KINGDOM
● My, how time flies. Remember when the Boscombe artificial reef project was going to be complete by the end of October? Well, that was counting on the cooperation of the British weather and, as usual, it didn't. With shorter days and colder water setting in, work by New Zealand-based construction firm ASR Ltd. has been suspended until April 2009. Bournemouth Borough Council now hopes to open the £2.68m reef some four or five months later. That's little consolation for more than 100 competitors who'd been hoping to use the reef in November for the annual South Coast Surfing Championship. Instead, heats will run at the Boscombe Pier.

FLORIDA
● Bruce Reynolds, a 53-year-old self-taught mixed-media artist and surfer from Cocoa Beach, has never met Barrack Obama but was so inspired his message that he created a one-of-a-kind assemblage featuring the presidential candidate. Reynolds says his inspiration derives from Obama's calm approach to dealing with difficult, stressful situations. "When I was growing up, all the surfers I looked up to were intuitive on how to act with grace and style," says the artist. Reynolds' artwork features Obama "pulling ahead of a breaking wave on a single-fin, throwing a Hawaiian shaka sign with his left hand and the word "HOPE" written vertically along the top right-hand corner." Any surfer who's been in this situation will be able to relate: airborne with the lip about the axe the back of your neck, you need all the hope (and luck) you can get. Which is maybe how Obama feels about the election going in, but he wins it handily just a day or two later. Phew!

ITALY
● A strong storm passes through Eu-rope, bringing the coldest and snowiest October day to many places and also causing huge waves on the coast of Portugal (OK fine, they have the Atlantic there) and on the coast of Italy from the Mediterranean Sea. SkyNews reports that a ferry nearly capsizes in the port of Genoa amid 70 mph winds. No reports on epic surf sessions after the storm, but did you know Italy hosts the most surfing contests of any country in Europe, with over 150 contests annually?

WEEK 45
NOVEMBER 4–10

CALIFORNIA
● Will Barack Obama save Trestles? The environmental group Wildcoast chimes in on the indirect role the newly elected next president might play in preventing the highly controversial construction of a toll road through a portion of San Onofre State Beach. "Surfers everywhere are thrilled that a man who grew up in the global surfing centers of Indonesia

Trestles. Photo ASP Tostee © Covered Images.

and Oahu is to be our next president," Serge Dedina, executive director of Wildcoast, says in a news release. "This victory will have a critical impact on efforts to stop the TCA from placing a private toll road through San Onofre State Beach Park and efforts to preserve the coast worldwide." Nice idea, of course, but President Obama may have other items on his mind: like global economic meltdown, war in Iraq and Afghanistan, India and Pakistan on the brink of mutual nuclear annhilation, one or two things like that.

ICELAND
● Cold water adventurer Josh Mulcoy hits ice-cold gold in Iceland along with Timmy Turner and Sam Hammer thanks largely to the 6mm high tech neoprene that's essential to survive and thrive in potentially deadly cold water temperatures. On this trip the crew goes totally feral, camping in sub-polar tents and sleeping bags on Iceland's rugged coastal slopes, weathering

Josh Mulcoy. Photo Chris Burkard.

snow, strong winds and freezing night-time temperatures. Oh, apparently they did have thick jackets and camp fires, so that's cozy. They surf heavy slabs, walk on glaciers to rivermouths fed by glacial waters, score quality reef breaks and relax in hot geothermal baths. The Icelandic coast, blessed with a wide-open swell window, produces waves ranging from shoulder high to a couple feet overhead. Look for it on a map—middle of nowhere, deep North Atlantic Ocean. Other than the geothermal baths, this sounds like the surf trip from Viking hell. And nothing to eat but cold dried fish, alluvial gravel and crunchy volcanic pumice, no doubt. Brrrrr! Fuggedaboudit!

ALABAMA, USA
● This item is titled "Shark Industry News"—which can only mean that sharks mean business, and based on the number of Surfer's Village shark-related postings, that's surely true. But other folks have bigger ideas perhaps, like sharkskin golf balls and wetsuits. OK, here's the deal: "Shortfin mako sharks can shoot through the ocean at up to 50 miles (80 km) per hour. Now a trick that helps them to reach such speeds has been discovered—the sharks can raise their scales to create tiny wells across the surface of their skin, reducing drag like the dimples on a golf ball. "The minute scales—just 200 micrometers long—are made from tough enamel, such as that found on teeth, giving the skin a rough texture like sandpaper. Amy Lang from the University of Alabama in Tuscaloosa decided to investigate whether this could help sharks travel at high speeds. Her team created artificial shark skin with a 16 x 24 array of synthetic scales, each 2 centimeters in length and angled at 90° to the surface. They then placed the arrangement in a stream of water traveling at a steady 20 centimeters per second. The water contained silver-coated nanospheres, which a laser illuminated to reveal the nature of the flow around the scales. "The experiments revealed that tiny vortices or whirlpools formed within the cavities between the scales. These vortices form a kind of 'buffer layer' between the skin's surface and the fast-moving fluid, preventing a turbulent wake from forming behind the shark. Eliminating this wake decreases the overall drag on the shark, allowing it to travel faster." See? It's the golf ball effect. Get a dimpled wetsuit to escape the bastards.

WEEK 46
NOVEMBER 11–17

HAWAII
● The Triple Crown gets underway with the Reef Hawaiian Pro—the first event of the $815,000 three-event season. "From seasoned veterans the likes of Mark Occhilupo, 42, (Australia) . . . to young local rookies like Lahaina, Maui's Dusty Payne, 19, Haleiwa served up the best conditions possible for the opening day," according to the press release. But wait a sec, Mark Occhilupo is 42? "It was a nostalgic moment when retired former world champion Mark Occhilupo took to the waves. Over the past 20 years he has provided some of the most memorable moments of the Vans Triple Crown and without a doubt was the biggest drawcard of the day. He emerged from round one with one of the top 10 heat

Occy. Photo ASP Rowland © Covered Images.

Ghost Tree. Photo Mike Jones/Azhiaziam.com.

scores of the day—15.33 out of 20 points—then backed it up in round two with another 15.0 victory. 'I need a bit of a wave like that to get me going and I thoroughly enjoyed it,' said Occhilupo. 'I always want to do the Triple Crown and I'll do it as long as I can. It's great to see everyone having a go at Haleiwa, Sunset and Pipe.' Occhilupo has been granted a wildcard into all three of the Vans Triple Crown events. Incredibly, over all these years, he has only ever won one event here: the 1985 Pipeline Masters." On the other hand, he has a new book just out, *The Rise and Fall and Rise of Mark Occhilupo.* At 42 he's much older than Kelly Slater. And that young feller has two books already. Look out for Occy's sequel.

WEEK 47
NOVEMBER 18–24

AUSTRALIA
● "An obscure, alien-looking 6' 7" duel-finned surfboard is discovered washed up on a Tweed Heads backbeach after heavy storms.

"Horrified residents of the area have bolted doors and windows for fear of more attacks. Meanwhile the first sighter of the alien object, Mr. Baron Von Weirdo, comments: 'I was

down at my local beach just checking the conditions when this unusual object caught my eye. I approached with caution, but upon closer inspection, found it to be quite harmless.'

"Plasticologists around the globe do not share the Baron's optimism. Local expert, Mr. Larkin, said he would not be surprised at what the object was capable of and advised extreme caution."

What does this mean? Who ever heard of a lord going by the handle of Mr. Baron? Does a monarch call herself Mrs. Queen? Who's this plastics expert Mr. Larrikin and if he's a "local" how come he speaks for the "global" pundits of polymers? Ecch, don't believe a word of it!

CALIFORNIA
● The Office of National Marine Sanctuaries releases its regulatory changes for California's protected shoreline. Among the changes is a re-definition of personal watercraft, which effectively eliminates tow-in surfing within the Monterey Bay National Marine Sanctuary—an area that includes the notorious Ghost Tree big-wave spot adjacent to renowned Pebble Beach golf course. Monterey paddle-in surfer Peter Davi died there last year after attempting a monstrous wave.

Tow-in surfers are not happy with

the decision, which takes effect in February or March 2009. "It definitely narrows the possibilities of big-wave surfing," says Don Curry, 49, the Carmel surfer credited with pioneering tow-in surfing at Ghost Tree. "It's nice to be close to home and have a world-class big wave in my backyard."

A seasonal exemption will be granted for Mavericks near Half Moon Bay, allowing surfers to tow in there from December to February.

UNITED KINGDOM
● Check it out: huge fish poop caught on film!

Biologists were so excited they even scooped the poop out of the water so they could keep it! But it's not as grim as it sounds—by testing it they can find out loads more about the giant creatures.

Despite being the world's biggest fish, very little's known about whale sharks. They are related to great whites, but they're far less scary. To eat, they swim about with their huge mouths open so they can scoop up whatever

tasty treats are floating in their path.

Dr. Mark Meekan says the shark's poo sample has helped them learn much more about their feeding habits. "One way to work out what is going in one end is to look at what is coming out of the other. But it is pretty rare—they are usually doing their business down in much deeper water."

The whale shark is the largest living fish, up to 65 feet long. It feeds on a variety of microscopic and larger free-swimming prey, such as small crustaceans, schooling fish, tuna and squid, and a variety of microscopic and larger plants. It is generally considered harmless to humans. But you wouldn't want one to poop on you.

WEEK 48
NOVEMBER 25–DECEMBER 1

CALIFORNIA
● Mavericks produces an epic feast for many of the world's top big-wave riders during two of the most perfect

Baron Von Weirdo. Photo www.vonweirdos.com.

Nathan Fletcher (left) with Alex Martins in the pit, Billabong XXL Global Big Wave Awards. Photo Frank Quirarte/BillabongXXL.com.

Sunday action. Photo Richard Hallman/FreelanceImaging.com.

days ever seen at the legendary Northern California surf break.

An extremely long-period swell hits Mavericks at an ideal angle, magnifying the face heights of the bigger sets to the 30- to 45-foot range. Rogue sets break unexpectedly along reefs and breakwaters throughout the region, capsizing a 26-foot power boat less than a mile from Mavericks, which sits just outside Princeton Harbor in Half Moon Bay, a half-hour south of San Francisco. Two fishermen die in the accident.

The surf sessions are not without their own degree of peril. California big wave star Greg Long catches one of the biggest waves to roll in, but straightens out as he's overrun by a mass of whitewater. Long is thrust so deep underwater he suffers a broken eardrum, eventually surfacing with a total loss of equilibrium.

Thanks to a strong leash and a quick rescue by Mavericks pioneer Jeff Clark on a personal water craft, Long is brought to safety before being swept through the notorious rocks inside of the main break.

A group of globetrotting big wave chasers jets into Half Moon Bay ahead of the swell. South African Grant "Twiggy" Baker proves that his victory at the Mavericks Surf Contest two years ago was no fluke, consistently taking off the deepest and making it again and again. Mark Healey and Dave Wassel are in from Hawaii and make the most of the two days of intense surfing. Rusty Long and Nathan Fletcher stand out as two of the most passionate wave hunters from southern California. But the local crew—Grant Washburn, Skindog Collins, Nic Lamb, Shawn Rhodes and Lance Harriman—all take off on bombs. Among the largest waves of the swell is the vast green

wall caught by San Francisco's Alex Martins.

OREGON, USA
● Adam Replogle and Alistair Craft wins the Lincoln City–based 2008 Nelscott Reef Tow In Classic for the second year in a row on a beautiful day in perfect surf conditions. Keallii Mamala goes home with the win for the first ever paddle-in contest at Nelscott Reef.

After a day of thick fog, the field of 16 tow teams and nine paddle-in contestants wake up to sunny skies and big surf for the contest. Waves are in the 20- to 30-foot range, wind is calm, skies clear, and the temperature hits 64 degrees F.

Almost all the tow-in teams in the finals, including the winners Adam Replogle and Alistair Craft, are from Santa Cruz, but the surprise of the event is the team for Australia, Jeff and Josiah Schmucker, a father and son team who had never before competed in a big wave competition. Their second place finish among some of the best teams in the world is impressive. Russell and Tyler Smith takes third place and the Wormhoudt brothers, Jake and Zach, are fourth.

"We could not be more excited about the outcome of the event," says John Forse, event organizer. "We like to think of Nelscott as a family event, and this year the finals had a father-son team and two brother teams." Operating in a three-month holding period, John Forse has proven his

local knowledge of the reef he pioneered, with four years of calling the contest on the best day of the year.

CALIFORNIA
● Surfing America, the national governing body for surfing in the United States, announces that the National Scholastic Surfing Association (NSSA) has rejoined as a Member Organization.

"This is a tremendous and historic day for Surfing America and the sport of surfing," said Mike Gerard, Surfing America's executive director. "NSSA is an extremely important piece to the American surfing landscape. And,

Stephanie Gilmore. Photo ASP Kirstin © Covered Images.

as Surfing America operates under a philosophy of inclusion, to have such a large and prestigious organization outside of the system was troubling."

NSSA executive director, Janice Aragon, mirrored the sentiment. "I believe we are making a very positive statement to the sport," she stated. "The NSSA is committed to promoting Surfing America and its mission in a highly visible way—and we're more determined than ever to help and encourage the USA Surf Team to achieve gold!" NSSA surfers will now be eligible to take part in ISA World Surfing Games and other international events. As a result of NSSA's reengagement, which ends an almost year-long political standoff, dozens of qualified NSSA athletes will be invited to participate in the 2009 SIMA Surfing America USA Championships scheduled for August 25-30, 2009, at the Huntington Beach Pier. Other member organizations include the Eastern Surfing Association (ESA), the Western Surfing

Association (WSA), the Texas Gulf Surfing Association (TGSA), and the Hawaii Surfing Association (HSA).

WEEK 49
DECEMBER 2–8

HAWAII
● Stephanie "Happy" Gilmore has more to be happy about. Only 12 months after making history as the only rookie—male or female—to claim an ASP World Title, the 20-year-old Australian backs it up with her second World Title by winning the Roxy Pro at Sunset Beach, Oahu.

With one contest remaining in the 2008 season, Gilmore has already

Islamic surfboard art. Photo Lynne Roberts-Goodwin © 2008.

netted four event wins. Coming into Sunset, she held a slight ratings leads over former World Champions Sofia Mulanovich (PER) and Layne Beachley (AUS). "I had no idea this was going to happen today when I woke up this morning," Gilmore says. "Sofia went down and then Layne went down and I found myself in the Final with a chance to clinch it. It feels unbelievable. The second World Title definitely feels better than the first one."

AUSTRALIA

● Artist Phillip George releases a range of surfboards featuring Islamic art motifs in an attempt to create a greater understanding between East and West. George was inspired by his trips to the Middle East and by riots in 2005 when Lebanese Australians were targeted on a beach in Sydney.

He calls the range the Inshallah—or God Willing—surfboards and has them on exhibition in Sydney. There are 30 surfboards in all and the artist hopes they'll help bridge cultural and religious misunderstandings within Australia.

"What I've done to bring the joy and the interest of our Islamic art to an Australian audience," he says, "I have actually transposed a lot of my photographic images—tiles and shots of the mosque—onto a surfboard so that they become a lot more acceptable or easy to digest for an Australian audience."

Yakutat, Alaska. Photo Tony Harrington/Wheresharro.com.

WEEK 50
DECEMBER 9–15

ALASKA

● Snow is falling in Anchorage. In Nome it is minus 20. In southeast Alaska, however, the sun is shining, a rainbow arcs the sky, the air temperature hovers around the freezing mark, and the water ain't much warmer. Meanwhile, some surfers are towing into 20-foot waves off Yakutat, watched by a crowd of locals warming themselves by a bonfire. What makes people like Hawaii's Jamie Sterling, Brazilian Maya Gabiera, Tahitian Raimana Van Bostaloer and others forsake the tropics and head toward the Arctic to freeze

their coconuts off? Well, their sponsors make 'em do it, and it beats having a real job, eh?

MAUI

● Starved for surf at Honolua Bay while waiting to finalize the Billabong Pro Maui, Layne Beachley and Silvana Lima don mask, snorkel and fins and find themselves swimming alongside a playful pod of hundreds of spinner dolphins. "It was one of those amazing moments in life for me," says Beachley. "They were alongside of us, under us, all around us. It was serene and surreal to be with wild dolphins in their own environment."

The last women's pro contest of the year does eventually run, but not until organizers move the whole shebang to Hookipa on the other side of the island as they run out of time to wait for waves at Honolua.

CALIFORNIA

● The Surf Industry Manufacturers Association (SIMA) weighs in on the airline board surcharge issue, encouraging surfers to add their signatures to the Surfboard Baggage Fee Petition website (www.ipetitions.com/petition/StopUnfairSurfboardFees) and singling out Delta Airlines in particular for some harsh words. SIMA quotes Delta's website: "One item of surfing equipment is accepted as baggage for $175 (for travel within the United States, U.S. Virgin Islands, and Puerto Rico) and $300 (for travel outside the United States, U.S. Virgin Islands, and Puerto Rico)."

Simply put, says SIMA, traveling with two boards to a surf destination could cost you $1,200 round trip, likely far in excess of the price of a seat on the very same plane. "We are also keenly aware that on the very same web page, it is clear that golf bags, skis and snowboards travel free,

clearly indicating that Delta is acting in a discriminatory manner towards surfers."

"We will use our collective voice through this petition and every other means necessary to let Delta and other airlines know that we will NOT fly Delta for ANY reason, business or pleasure, unless and until these discriminatory fees are changed."

HAWAII

● This year's Vans Triple Crown of Surfing Title goes to Australia's Joel Parkinson, who finishes fifth in the first two contests held at Haleiwa and Sunset Beach and ninth at the Billabong Pipeline Masters. Triple Crown runners-up are Dusty Payne (HI), Tom Whitaker (AUS), CJ Hobgood (FL) and Chris Ward (CA).

"I've come runner-up to the Triple Crown a couple of times," says Parkinson. "Andy (Irons) nabbed it from me both times, so no hard feelings to Wardo, but I really didn't want that to happen again. It feels amazing to actually take it home this time."

The victory is doubly sweet for Parko, who made headlines earlier in the week by earning the first ever perfect 20 out of 20 heat score total at Pipeline—one of only two perfect heat scores in ASP history under the two-wave judging format.

CALIFORNIA

● Members of the Santa Cruz surfing community are in talks with the city to take over the operation of the Santa Cruz Surfing Museum. Facing a financial crisis, like many cities across the nation, Santa Cruz elected officials are cutting funds for museums, parks and recreation, and other services. Members of the newly incorporated Santa Cruz Surfing Club Museum Preservation Society are stepping up to find solutions to keep the facility open either by leasing it or through an outright purchase after the January 31, 2009, closing date set by the city.

WEEK 51
DECEMBER 16–22

EUROPE

● With the conclusion of the pro contest year, the Association of Surfing Professionals (ASP) officially announces its new Top 45 surfers in the starting lineup on its World Tour for the world title in 2009. Among them are a record breaking seven surfers from Europe: Jeremy Flores (FRA), Miky Picon (FRA), Tiago Pires (PRT), Marlon Lipke (DEU), Tim Boal (FRA), Michel Bourez (PYF) and Aritz Aranburu (EUK). What many

Jeremy Flores. Photo ASP Rowland © Covered Images.

Joel Parkinson. Photo ASP Kirstin © Covered Images.

Kelly Slater & Hives. Photo Fuel TV.

"I want to be an example for all the kids in my neighborhood, El Libano. Let them see that you can really come forward. I can succeed in studying. I grew up in contact with the sea and that is why I like to surf. When I surf, it's emotional and I feel happy."

FLORIDA

● Researchers report that sharks have wimpy bites for their size and can crunch through their prey only because they have very sharp teeth and because they can grow to be so big. "Pound for pound, sharks don't bite all that hard," says Daniel Huber of the University of Tampa in Florida, who led the study. Huber and colleagues had trouble collecting data for their study, "due to the experimental intractability of these animals," they note dryly in their report published in *Physiological and Biochemical Zoology*. Their studies of shark jaws show that lions or tigers win hands down when it comes to jaw strength, but sharks prevail in the water because of their wide jaw size. "Our analyses show that large sharks do not bite hard for their body size, but they generally have larger heads."

A 20-foot (6-meter) great white shark can "bite through anything that you come across," he adds. Many must use a sawing motion to break apart their prey, says Huber, whose team studied 10 different species of shark. Mammals have evolved much more efficient jaw muscles, he notes.

Apparently no scientists were actually bitten during the tests, although several complained of having received nasty sucks.

CALIFORNIA

● Every New Year's Day a massive parade takes place through the streets of Pasadena, California, with marching bands, high-stepping equestrians and scores of mobile floats with fanciful artwork made from flowers, petals, nuts and seeds. As its press release informs: " In honor of its 100th Anniversary of Incorporation, the City of Huntington Beach (also known as Surf City USA®), presents its first-ever float in the 120th Rose Parade®. The float captures 'the essence of living in Surf City USA®).' Measuring 55-feet long and 30-feet high, the float features waves, surfboards, local ocean life such as fish, pelicans, seagulls and dolphins, and a Surfing Family having a barbecue on a giant surfboard with their faithful dog in attendance. Although built with the help of a professional float company, hundreds of volunteers assisted in the decoration of the float, which features thousands of flowers including the Centennial Geranium™—a flower propagated in honor of Huntington Beach's Centennial."

In 2009, HB will move to trademark, copyright and register the word *pier*.

people thought was historic in 2008 when four EU men qualified, is clearly only the beginning of an era that could possibly see a European surfer become an ASP World Champion.

CALIFORNIA

● Speaking of world champions, niner Kelly Slater appears on Fuel TV's *The Daily Habit* to talk about his record breaking (again) title, and his new book (again), *For the Love*. Musical guests on the show are Swedish rockers The Hives, who are described as a "garage band," although it's clear from the way they dress that they're no grease monkeys. A stylist for the show apparently told K-nine he should wear black-and-white gear so that the on-air presentation would have a consistent look. Although he was only too willing to try to fit in, his oh-so-surfie plaid shirt didn't quite do the trick. Still, those blokes would look a bit out of place on the beach, don't you think?

WASHINGTON, DC

● Trestles saved? The U.S. Department of Commerce announces that it will uphold the California Coastal Commission's ruling that found a proposed extension of the 241 Toll Road inconsistent with the California Coastal Act. In a release issued from the Department of Commerce, they "determined that there is at least one reasonable alternative to the project [and] that the project is not necessary in the interest of national security." Says Surfrider Foundation's Assistant Environmental Director Mark Rauscher, "This decision is a significant milestone in our efforts to protect San Onofre State Beach Park and the surrounding environment, and underscores the effectiveness of grassroots activism." Don't start polishing the car

with those Save Trestles and Stop the Toll Road tee shirts just yet, though. Within days, the agency promoting the toll road takes out a full-page ad in the *Los Angeles Times* saying they intend to keep pushing the project.

WEEK 52
DECEMBER 23–31

COLOMBIA

● It's always nice to find a feel-good story for the holiday season and the end of the year. And 11-year-old Howard Gómez gets a cool yule present when he becomes the youngest recipient ever of the International Surfing Association (ISA) Individual Scholarship.

Howard was born in Cartagena de Indias and started surfing because of his father, who was the 2004 Colombian National Champ. Howard has been competing since he was six. In 2007 he was the National Under-12 champ at 10 years of age. He comes from a poor family and doesn't have enough money to buy appropriate boards for his size, so he surfs with bigger boards and it is amazing the way he rides them. In his application for the scholarship, one of the requirements was to write an essay, Why I deserve an ISA Scholarship. This is part of what he wrote:

"I would buy a house for my mother, pay for my studies, travel to tournaments outside Colombia. I would buy a bed, refrigerator, kitchen, I would buy everything for my house and clothing for my sister. With my family, I would like to leave behind poverty and my neighborhood because I don't want to see it anymore, like drugs and gang fights.

*Howard Gomez.
Photo ISA.*

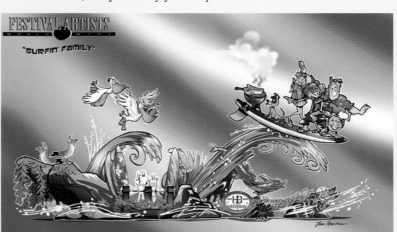

Courtesy of Festival Artists and the City of Huntington Beach.

Kelly Slater:

The Greatest Athlete Ever?

By Mark Richards

Twenty years before Kelly Slater started rewriting surfing's record books, Mark Richards was the winningest surfer in history. In this tribute, the four-time world champ from Australia argues that Slater's dominance of the sport has placed him on a pedestal no other athlete has reached.

I can't remember exactly when I first met Kelly Slater, but he tells a story about a trade show in Florida back in the early '80s. He remembers it; I don't.

Anyway, I'm sure I became aware of him pretty soon after that, because he started popping up in the magazines, and it doesn't matter where they come from, even if it's Cocoa Beach, Florida, you take notice of who's coming up. Word went out on the grapevine. It didn't happen then the way it does now with video on the internet, but it happened, and people were talking about this kid from Florida as a future world champion.

Strangely, though, it wasn't until the release of *Kelly Slater in Black & White* (1992), which I regard as one of the greatest marketing campaigns in surfing, that I became fully aware of his ability. My first thought when I saw that video was that Kelly was doing things that most of the guys on tour wouldn't even begin to understand. I knew then that he'd be famous whether he pulled on the colored singlet or not. This kid was going to change surfing. I knew that instinctively.

I think the first time I saw him surf in the flesh was when I surfed with him in an expression session at the Newcastle Surf Fest, and that was long after he'd started winning world titles. But by that time I'd made a complete video study of him, and the more I saw him surf, the more I felt sorry for the other guys.

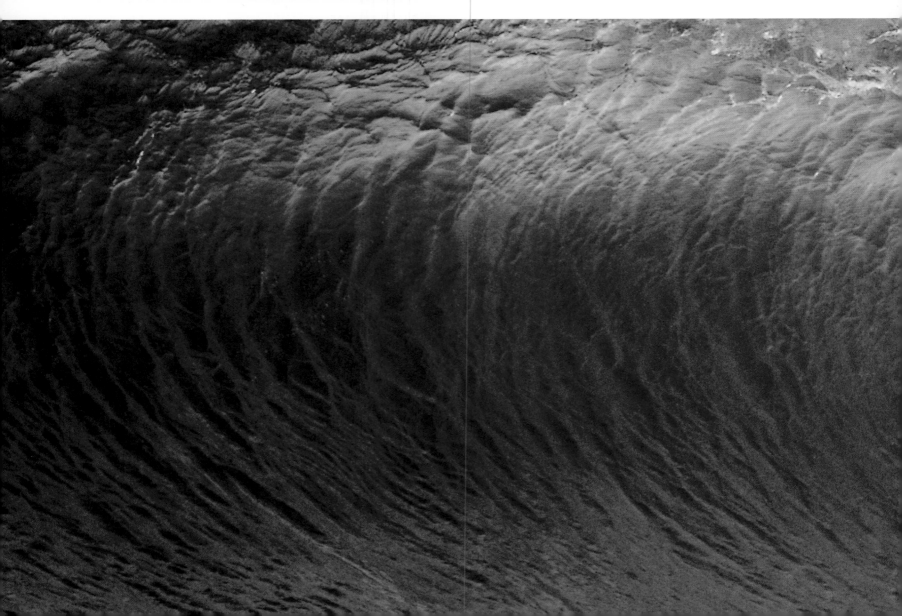

If you're a professional athlete, part of your motivation is to destroy other people's careers. That might sound harsh, but it's just the way it is. You destroy theirs or they destroy yours. I'm sure that over the years Kelly and Andy Irons have felt really good about beating each other. There might be a few guys on tour that you don't feel so strongly about, but when it comes to your major rivals, you have to have that focus.

The dominant surfer of any era has a huge impact on his rivals, and we've seen that in 2008 so clearly as Kelly has simply decimated his opponents and left them emotionally and psychologically crippled. They just don't have an answer for him. I know I've always been aware of the profound effect I had on Cheyne Horan's life back in the early 1980s. From a personal and competitive perspective, I was someone who just got in the way of what he wanted to achieve in his life. He could have been world champion four times and I was responsible for three of those failures. At the time I was probably gloating because we had a fierce rivalry, no doubt about that. But as you get older you analyze the things you've done and you put yourself in the other guy's place. I've often wondered how he coped with it, because I've wondered how I would have coped if it had been me. I know it's only a sporting contest, but it's who we are, it's what we do. I lost a lot of times, but when it really mattered I was the one who was fortunate enough to win.

With Kelly, I think it was very revealing the time he just missed out on winning the title (2003) and there was that video of him crying in the shower. I think it was his brother who pointed out that this was the first time Kelly hadn't won what he set out to win, the first time he'd lost something that really meant something to him. I laughed when I saw one of the magazines use that incident to pull the curtain on the Kelly era. I thought they'd totally screwed that up because they'd antagonized the greatest competitive surfer in history, possibly the most competitive person in any sport! They'd waved a red flag at him, so now he had no option but to come out and ruin a few more lives! It might have all come from that moment crying in the shower. His thinking may have been, I'm never going to let this happen again. This sucks and I'm going to make some one else cry in the shower. That might sound vindictive, but winning is vindictive.

I rate Kelly Slater as one of—if not the—greatest athletes ever. You can throw your Alis and Schumachers and Tigers and Armstrongs and whoever you like at me, but my premise for this belief is that surfing is one of the most difficult sports to excel at. Most people can hit each other or play tennis or drive a car. Maybe not very well, but most people can handle the basics. You put them on a surfboard in waves and they drown in the shorebreak. Think about how far Kelly has taken the act of surfing, the things he can do on a board on a wave. People are in awe of what Olympic gymnasts do. Kelly does what they do while standing on a six-foot piece of foam on waves that would drown most people, a few inches over a razor-sharp reef that's going to kill you if you fall off. The couch potato sports fans don't get that, and probably never will.

What separates some world champion surfers from others is the fact that they have actually advanced the sport through the way they've ridden waves or the way they've changed performance through equipment advances. Kelly's done both. When I came along on a twin fin, my attitude was, I'm going to show these guys where you can go on a wave, and I did. Kelly did the same thing with his approach, and he has never sat back and said, well, that's as far as I can go. He always wants to go farther, and that's his greatness. Most surfers can recall the days when you used to sit in school doodling these stick men carving impossible turns, or getting barreled backwards. Kelly Slater has taken those doodle dreams and turned them into reality.

I'm impressed by most aspects of Kelly's personality, particularly the way he's handled his fame. I don't know how he does it, to be honest. When he goes to a contest there are 47 guys who want him to bomb out in the first round, then there are 10,000 people outside the rope fence who all want to touch him or get him to write his name on their breasts! He just handles all that and goes out and wins.

I don't know where Kelly Slater's career goes from here. I'm sure he's capable of winning #10 and even beyond, if that's what he wants to do. And I'm equally sure that it's hard for him to plan an exit strategy because life on tour is so much fun, if you're a competitive animal. I just hope that he senses the moment when the motivation is no longer there, and goes out on top. I couldn't bear to see Kelly Slater finish his remarkable career at #17 in the world.

And, of course, there IS life after the pro tour. When you're 50, it's hard to cuddle up to your nine world title trophies. My life so far has been in two parts, and they've both been good journeys. I don't get as much satisfaction out of work as I did out of competing, but the satisfaction you get from family is more enduring than any of it. I hope Kelly's second journey will be just as fulfilling.

Parts of this interview with Mark Richards are published in Kelly Slater: For the Love, *by Kelly Slater and Phil Jarratt (Chronicle Books, 2008). Photos are from the same book, courtesy Chronicle and Quiksilver, Inc.*

ASP Report
A Word from the President

There was much anticipation going into th '08 season launch. Gold Coast duo Mick Fanning and Stephanie Gilmore had just been crowned ASP World Champions and were now about to open their defense on home turf, Snapper Rocks. The Quiksilver Pro and Roxy Pro may not have reached epic proportions surfwise, but the chemistry was heady stuff. The contenders included an awesome lineup of talent. Still with us were veterans such as Taylor Knox and eight-time World Champion Kelly Slater; there was the established Big Five of Mick Fanning, Andy Irons, Taj Burrow, Joel Parkinson and recent arrival Bede Durbidge; and then there were the much heralded tour debutantes Jordy Smith and Dane Reynolds.

The stellar lineup overshadowed all other World Tour elements. This was always going to be a year of great challenges and big questions. Could Fanning repeat? Was his emphatic title victory in '07 motivation for Parko and Taj? Where were Kelly and Andy's heads at? And the biggest if, were Jordy and Dane going to blow past everyone? On the women's front, was there any force that could stop Stephanie Gilmore establishing a dynastic reign as World Champion?

The opening exchanges were portents of the shape of things to come. The highlight was during the Kelly/Mick final. Nobody knows the lay of the land behind the rock better then Mick Fanning, but somehow Kelly schooled the new champ, getting under his guard, and under his skin, to jag the advantage and win the event.

What happened next was destiny. Kelly returned to Santa Barbara, unsure of his commitment to the tour year. With only days to go before the Rip Curl Bells, I was informed by Tour Manager Renato Hickel that Kelly had not confirmed either way. I said to put a rocket under him by giving him until 2:00 PM that day to confirm or he would be replaced. That got his attention; he rang back and inquired about the forecast. There was some promise of a swell and Renato told him it would be 10 feet and the swell had his name written all over it. He ummed and ahhed and I extended the deadline to 5:00 PM but that was final. At 4:55 PM he rang and confirmed, mumbling under his breath. Of course he went on to defeat Bede Durbidge in the final with the famous "Hail Mary" ride from Rincon.

The Women's title race also hotted up. After a shocker at her home break, Stephanie Gilmore rode to victory at Bells and clearly set up a rivalry with former World Champion Sofia Mulanovich, with seven-time World Champion Layne Beachley lurking ominously in the shadows. Kelly had opened with a perfect Aussie season, and although he went down early at

the Billabong Pro Teahupoo, he roared back and won the next two, the Globe Pro Fiji and Billabong Pro J Bay. Even in his loss, to event wildcard Bruno Santos, the cards fell his way. None of the other contenders made up ground, wildcards Bruno and Manoa Drollet neutralizing the points, and after five events, Kelly, with one throwaway, was still averaging perfection with four wins.

In his testimonial year, Bruce Irons, who had declared his tour innings, triumphed in the Rip Curl Search Indo, again

Rabbit still ripping in 2008. Photo Jake White.

blocking Kelly's nearest rivals from the major points, and the writing was well and truly on the wall. An irrepressible Slater lit up Trestles for an emphatic Boost Mobile Pro victory and the only talk was if he would clinch at Hossegor or Mundaka.

Meanwhile, the women's race was getting serious. Fourteen-year-old Tyler Wright dealt Gilmore a massive blow by knocking her in the early rounds of the Beachley Classic, Mulanovich zooming out front courtesy of a second in the points-rich event, and with the next event in her home country, the Peruvian looked rather daunting. Gilmore, however, had other intentions, dominating the latter part of the season, including a clean sweep of the major titles in Hawaii, to nail a second straight World Crown.

There is an amazing array of talent coming through the women's ranks. Leading the challengers are Hawaii's Carissa Moore and Aussie Sally Fitzgibbon. These two will surely develop a great rivalry, Fitzgibbon qualifying for the World Tour in record time, and there are a bunch of hotties about to bust down the door and take on the likes of Stephanie Gilmore and Sylvana Lima.

Two thousand eight also marked the end of full-time touring for seven-time World Champion Layne Beachley. After an illustrious career, the queen of world surfing announced her retirement at the Beachley Classic, but far from going quietly, the star challenged all the way, only succumbing to the might of Gilmore in a Billabong Pro Maui semifinal that was all class. A win would have seen Beachley depart with a third Vans Triple Crown title, and she took it

to Gilmore all the way, going down by the narrowest of margins. Layne's legacy of excellence hovers over the next generation of rippers.

The inevitable Slater coronation did go down in Europe; after five wins everyone else ran out of time, and speculation began immediately as to whether Kelly would commit to contending for a tenth title. There was also some interesting speculation as to Slater's place in the pantheon of sporting greats, comparisons being made in the mainstream media to Tiger Woods, Roger Federer, Lance Armstrong, Michael Schumacher, Michael Jordan and Wayne Gretzky. I think Kelly has a solid case, he has achieved domination over two decades, and importantly, raised his game big time to take on and eventually overcome three-time World Champion Andy Irons.

On the longboard front, it was a story of the return of a king as Hawaii's champion Bonga Perkins took out the ASP Men's Longboard Championship, winning out over a two-event Oxbow Longboard World Tour. Bonga had to win the final at San Onofre, California, to claim his second World Title. Harley Ingleby of Australia had convincingly won the opening tour event in France and was right in calculations at San Onofre, but it was Frenchman Antoine Delpero that threw down the gauntlet, making both finals and challenging Perkins all the way.

Another champion was crowned at the iconic Cote des Basques in Biarritz when Joy Monaghan took out the Roxy Women's World Longboard Championship. The Women's discipline is really gaining momentum throughout the world, and Roxy have established several qualifying events to cater for the deepening talent pool developing globally.

In a somewhat challenging year, confronted by economic meltdowns and tough times in the surf industry, it was great to see out a successful conclusion on all fronts. ASP has some exciting and innovative measures that will provide extra stimulus to the media, the sponsors and the global fan base, and we are already deep into the planning and activation of a great set of World Tours and Championships in 2009.

All the very best for an awesome '09.

— Wayne "Rabbit" Bartholomew
ASP President

QUIKSILVER PRO GOLD COAST
ASP Men's World Tour Event #1 | Coolangatta, Australia | February 23–March 5, 2008

He's Back! Slater Starts Season Back on Top

After a lackluster finish to the 2007 season to finish third, eight-time world champion Kelly Slater, now 36, showed he'd lost none of the fire when he defeated reigning world champion Mick Fanning at his home break to claim first blood for the '08 season.

Slater took the final at the Snapper Rocks "Superbank" 17.94 to 15.23 to claim his second Quiksilver Pro Gold Coast title and to regain the ratings lead for the first time since 2006. "It's really satisfying," Slater said of the win. "I didn't feel like I really got into motion last year. This is the best result I've had in six months and it feels great."

Slater and Fanning have now met in ASP competition nine times, with Slater in the lead 5–4, but previous to this win, he had not beaten Fanning since 2003. The two champions have won the last four Quiksilver Pro Gold Coast events, Fanning in 2005 and 2007, Slater in 2006 and 2008.

Slater complimented Fanning as "the best competitor in the world right now," but did he feel badly about beating him in front of his home crowd? "Not in the least. He'd won it twice and I had to catch up."

Slater's victory did not come easily on the final day. He had to beat former World Champion and nemesis Andy Irons to reach the semis, where he met 2007 rookie of the year and Slater protégé Jeremy Flores of France. It was a rare encounter this late in an event for top seeds Slater and Irons, their first man-on-man heat in more than two years. But despite showing early form, Irons could not find a high-scoring second wave. Quiksilver Young Gun Flores had his mentor "combo-ed" halfway through the semi, needing two high scores to take the lead. Slater appeared tired but still managed to pull out the scores before the hooter,

Kelly Slater, back on the podium and loving it. Photo ASP Kirstin © Covered Images.

winning by the most slender of margins.

Fanning, who took the number one spot in the ratings at this event in 2007 and had not relinquished it until the Quik Pro final, also had a hard road to the final, having to take out fellow locals Dean Morrison and the in-form Bede Durbidge. The latter's semifinal was a repeat of the previous year's final, with both surfers performing unbelievable stunts on the mechanical waves, but Fanning just getting the better of the exchange.

Once again the Quiksilver Pro Gold Coast enjoyed excellent waves, great weather and huge crowds, frequently causing traffic jams in the normally sleepy resort town of Coolangatta.

Kelly Slater. Photo ASP Robertson © Covered Images.

Jeremy Flores. Photo ASP Robertson © Covered Images.

FINAL

Kelly Slater (USA) 17.94		DEF	Mick Fanning (AUS) 15.23

SEMI FINALS

Mick Fanning (AUS) 17.23	Bede Durbidge (AUS) 16.70	Kelly Slater (USA) 15.47	Jeremy Flores (FRA) 15.17

QUARTER FINALS

	Bede Durbidge (AUS) 16.66		Jeremy Flores (FRA) 15.94
DEF	Joel Parkinson (AUS) 15.34	DEF	Adrian Buchan (AUS) 11.16
	Mick Fanning (AUS) 14.34		Kelly Slater (USA) 17.00
DEF	Dean Morrison (AUS) 13.06	DEF	Andy Irons (HAW) 10.94

TOUR RATINGS AFTER EVENT #1

1. Kelly Slater (USA) 1200
2. Mick Fanning (AUS) 1032
3. Jeremy Flores (FRA) 876
4. Bede Dubridge (AUS) 876

RIP CURL PRO
ASP Men's World Tour Event #2 | Bells Beach, Australia | March 18–29, 2008

Slater Steals the Show

Finding something from nothing in the dying seconds of a windswept final, Kelly Slater again asserted his dominance of world surfing by winning his third Rip Curl Pro bell trophy.

Trailing Australia's Bede Durbidge for 27 minutes of the final, Slater had all but given up when he made a last-ditch paddle across to Rincon, the point break at Bells Beach, which had shown little inclination to break all day. Miraculously, while Durbidge, who held priority, left it to him, the eight-time world champion launched into a lumpy wave and managed to boost a daring double-grab aerial ahead of a series of snap turns down the line. He was awarded 8.83 and took the final with a minute to spare, while Durbidge just shook his head in disbelief.

Slater's audacious victory gives him two for two in the 2008 world title race, replicating the position from which he began his 2006 title hunt. Is number 9 on the cards? As ever, Slater refused to be drawn, saying he would take each event as it comes. "It'd be silly to say it's not on the radar somewhere," he said, "but my whole approach [to the tour] at this point is just to have fun."

Durbidge, who moved to world number two with his result, was disappointed but accepted that when you surf against Slater "freakish things happen." Australia's Taj Burrow, defeated by Slater in the semifinals, said that he believed he was still a 2008 contender. "A third is a keeper for sure," he said. "It's frustrating to be beaten like that, when you can't get a wave in the chop, but Kelly found them while I couldn't. He's going well but we've got a lot of surfing to go this year and I'm right in there and hungry."

The Bells Beach event enjoyed good conditions in earlier rounds, particularly at neighboring break Winki Pop, but with the swell expected to decline, organizers elected to press on to the finish despite unfavorable onshore winds. Slater showed yet again that poor conditions are just something you factor in on your way to victory.

Slater winning air. Photo ASP Robertson © Covered Images.

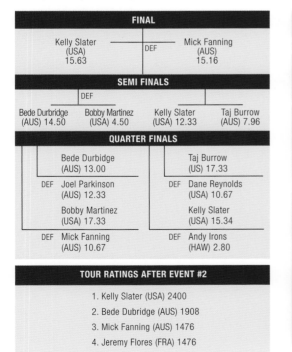

FINAL		
Kelly Slater (USA) 15.63	DEF	Mick Fanning (AUS) 15.16

SEMI FINALS			
	DEF		
Bede Durbidge (AUS) 14.50	Bobby Martinez (USA) 4.50	Kelly Slater (USA) 12.33	Taj Burrow (AUS) 7.96

QUARTER FINALS			
	Bede Durbidge (AUS) 13.00		Taj Burrow (US) 17.33
DEF	Joel Parkinson (AUS) 12.33	DEF	Dane Reynolds (USA) 10.67
	Bobby Martinez (USA) 17.33		Kelly Slater (USA) 15.34
DEF	Mick Fanning (AUS) 10.67	DEF	Andy Irons (HAW) 2.80

TOUR RATINGS AFTER EVENT #2

1. Kelly Slater (USA) 2400
2. Bede Dubridge (AUS) 1908
3. Mick Fanning (AUS) 1476
4. Jeremy Flores (FRA) 1476

Bede Durbidge and Kelly Slater on the podium. Photo ASP Robertson © Covered Images.

BILLABONG PRO TAHITI / Presented by Air Tahiti Nui
ASP Men's World Tour Event #3 | Teahupoo, Tahiti | May 8–18, 2008

Wildcard Crashes Through at Teahupoo

Wildcard Bruno Santos became the first Brazilian to win a WCT event in five years when he defeated Tahitian wildcard Manoa Drollet to win the Billabong Pro Tahiti in uncharacteristically small waves at Teahupoo. But the all-wildcard final means that Kelly Slater's position at the top of the ratings is unchallenged.

Drollet, long recognized as one of the best chargers in the Teahupoo lineup, scored two perfect 10s on his way to the final and knocked Slater out in round three, but a home victory eluded him as the supercharged Santos pulled out all stops to become the first Brazilian WCT winner since Neco Padaratz won the Quiksilver Pro France in 2003. "The waves are not great but this is the best day of my life," he said, after winning the low-scoring final on a borrowed board in lackluster waves.

Santos defeated CJ Hobgood (USA) in the semifinals with a solid performance, but it was Drollet who appeared to be on a roll, knocking out Joel Parkinson (AUS) with one of his two perfect scores and a heat score of 18.33. But in the deteriorating conditions and dropping swell, the final was very much left to chance. Santos managed to pick up two waves that barreled, and then the waves stopped coming, much to the frustration of both surfers, but particularly Drollet, who simply didn't have a backup wave.

FINAL		
Bruno Santos (BRA) 9.16	DEF	Manoa Drollet (PYF) 6.83

SEMI FINALS			
	DEF		
Manoa Drollet (PYF) 18.33	Joel Parkinson (AUS) 10.27	Bruno Santos (BRA) 14.34	CJ Hobgood (USA) 8.67

QUARTER FINALS			
	Joel Parkinson (AUS) 16.33		Bruno Santos (BRA) 9.83
DEF	Andy Irons (HAW) 6.14	DEF	Adriano De Souza (BRA) 9.07
	Manoa Drollet (PYF) 17.84		CJ Hobgood (USA) 15.00
DEF	Adrian Buchan (AUS) 9.83	DEF	Bruce Irons (HAW) 10.16

TOUR RATINGS AFTER EVENT #3

1. Kelly Slater (USA) 2810
2. Joel Parkinson (AUS) 2340
3. Bede Dubridge (AUS) 1908
4. Andy Irons (HAW) 21964
5. Mick Fanning (AUS) 1989

Bruno victorious. Photo ASP Kirstin © Covered Images.

Manoa Drollet. Photo ASP Rowland © Covered Images.

Bruno Santos. Photo ASP Kirstin © Covered Images.

FIJI GLOBE PRO
ASP Men's World Tour Event #4 | Tavarua, Fiji | May 25–June 6, 2008

Slater Takes Number 3 in Fiji

Kelly pops a few fins on the way to #3. Photo ASP Rowland © Covered Images.

CJ Hobgood. Photo Rowland ASP © Covered Images

Eight-time world champion and 2008 tour leader Kelly Slater increased his stranglehold on the ASP by making it three out of four at the Globe Pro Fiji, concluded in excellent two-meter waves at Cloudbreak.

Slater took the final from Florida beach-mate and 2001 world champion CJ Hobgood, 16.67 points to 13.27 in a tense but moderate-scoring heat. "There were some 10s out there, but we just couldn't find them," said an elated Slater, who nevertheless extended his numerical and psychological advantage, and looked to be on track, even at this early stage, for an unprecedented ninth title.

The major factor in Slater's favor, other than his extraordinary form, was the fact that no other ASP surfer had won an event this season, the previous in Tahiti having been won by a wildcard.

Hobgood's second took him to sixth position on the tour ratings, closing the gap on the Aussies and Brazil's Adriano de Souza, whose equal 3rd took the tour youngster a notch ahead of Australia's Taj Burrow. Burrow, beaten convincingly by Slater in the semifinals, watched another rung in the world championship ladder slip him by, after brilliant performances earlier in the event.

For Slater it was another banner event at his other Pacific home, Tavarua Island. The champion knows the waves of Cloudbreak and Restaurants inside out, and clearly feels relaxed and at home there.

Adriano de Souza. Photo ASP Rowland © Covered Images.

FINAL		
Kelly Slater (USA) 16.67	DEF	CJ Hobgood (USA) 13.27

SEMI FINALS			
	DEF		DEF
Kelly Slater (USA) 18.70	Taj Burrow (AUS) 12.84	CJ Hobgood (USA) 17.64	Adriano de Souza (BRA) 13.87

QUARTER FINALS			
	Taj Burrow (AUS) 14.60		CJ Hobgood (USA) 17.50
DEF	Bede Durbidge (AUS) 12.73	DEF	Mick Fanning (AUS) 6.84
	Kelly Slater (USA) 14.27		Adriano de Souza (BRA) 13.00
DEF	Bobby Martinez (USA) 13.67	DEF	Joel Parkinson (AUS) 12.66

TOUR RATINGS AFTER EVENT #4
1. Kelly Slater (USA) 4010
2. Joel Parkinson (AUS) 3072
3. Bede Durbidge (AUS) 3050
4. Adriano de Souza (BRA) 2808
5. Taj Burrow (AUS) 2762

BILLABONG PRO JEFFREYS BAY
ASP Men's World Tour Event #5 | Jeffreys Bay, South Africa | July 9–20, 2008

Stop us if you've heard this before... Slater Does It Again at J-Bay!

Taj Burrow. Photo ASP Cestari © Covered Images.

Kelly Slater. Photo ASP Kirstin © Covered Images.

He's done it again! That was pretty much all the world surf media and his 44 fellow competitors on surfing's World Tour could say when Kelly Slater chalked up his fourth victory from five starts in the '08 ASP World Tour, putting him in a commanding position to claim an unprecedented ninth world title.

Slater grabbed his 38th tour victory by defeating 2007 world champion Mick Fanning (AUS) 16.73 to 9.40 in challenging, onshore conditions where Fanning simply could not find a backup score. Said

Slater, "You have to really change your frame of mind because [earlier] we were looking at 30- to 45-second rides and doing six to eight maneuvers. In the final it was three maneuvers is a good wave. I didn't catch on until towards the end of the heat, but then I realized that a three-move wave would probably seal it."

Fanning was more blunt: "I surfed like an idiot," he said. "I don't know what happened, I just had a shocker." Fanning's disappointment was palpable. He also lost to Slater in the year's first final at his home beach, Snapper Rocks. But all was not lost. His second

placing, beating fellow Australian Taj Burrow in the semis, took him to fourth place on the ratings. Slater took out Joel Parkinson (AUS) in the other semi.

After enjoying epic conditions for much of the event, Billabong Pro organizers opted to run out the final heats in rapidly deteriorating conditions with the swell predicted to die overnight and the contest window almost gone. The quality of World Tour surfing was demonstrated again when spectators were treated to an amazing display despite the adverse surface conditions, with an onshore wind howling up the point.

Kelly victorious. Photo ASP Kirstin © Covered Images.

FINAL		
Kelly Slater (USA) 16.73	DEF	Mick Fanning (AUS) 9.40

SEMI FINALS			
	DEF		DEF
Kelly Slater (USA) 15.00	Joel Parkinson (AUS) 14.17	Mick Fanning (ASU) 16.84	Taj Burrow (AUS) 11.83

QUARTER FINALS			
	Joel Parkinson (AUS) 17.74		Mick Fanning (AUS) 14.27
DEF	Bede Durbidge (AUS) 14.00	DEF	CJ Hobgood (USA) 9.60
	Kelly Slater (USA) 15.17		Taj Burrow (AUS) 13.57
DEF	Adriano de Souza (BRA) 9.84	DEF	Andy Irons (HAW) 8.47

TOUR RATINGS AFTER EVENT #5

1. Kelly Slater (USA) 5210
2. Joel Parkinson (AUS) 3948
3. Bede Durbidge (AUS) 3782
4. Mick Fanning (AUS) 3753
5. Taj Burrow (AUS) 3638

RIP CURL PRO SEARCH
ASP Men's World Tour Event #6 | Somewhere in Indonisia | July 30–August 10, 2008

Irons on Fire

An all-Hawaiian final completed the Rip Curl Pro Search in rifling left-handers at a "mysto" reef break known only to anyone who's been anywhere in the past 30 years, with Bruce Irons defeating Fred Patacchia in a barrel shoot-out.

Despite the hype surrounding Rip Curl's presentation of a Search event in one of surfing's best-known wave playgrounds—Bali's Bukit Peninsula—the quality of the waves and the hospitality of the locals won the day, and the cameras captured some epic moments, none more so than the last ten minutes of the final, when Irons came from behind with a succession of deep barrels and dry reef re-entries to claim his first World Tour victory. Ironically, it may also be his last, since the volatile younger brother of former World Champion Andy Irons announced before the event that he was leaving the tour at the end of the season.

Long recognized by his peers as one of the most explosive and talented free surfers on the planet, "Brucey" has never really put it together at the highest level, except for those magical days when he does. Fred Patacchia, calmly threading his way through long barrels with a much-needed victory in sight, never knew what hit him. He said, "Bruce and I are friends but we were super competitive out there, hassling and trash-talking and everything!"

On his way to the crown, Irons took out Aussie rookie Ben Dunn and California's Chris Ward, while Patacchia ended a dream run for Portugal's Tiago Pires, who, earlier in the event, had claimed the scalp of ratings leader Kelly Slater. Slater, whose only previous loss this season was to a wildcard, still owns the top of the ratings board with most serious rivals for the 2008 title out before the quarters.

Bruce Irons. Photo ASP Kirstin © Covered Images.

Kai Otton. Photo ASP Kirstin © Covered Images.

FINAL

Bruce Irons (HAW) 17.66	DEF	Fred Patacchia (HAW) 11.16

SEMI FINALS

	DEF			DEF	
Fred Patacchia (HAW) 10.16	Tiago Pires (PRT) 8.50		Bruce Irons (HAW) 13.70	Chris Ward (USA) 13.50	

QUARTER FINALS

	Fred Patacchia (HAW) 16.50		Bruce Irons (HAW) 19.40
DEF	Kai Otton (AUS) 14.17	DEF	Ben Dunn (AUS) 9.67
	Tiago Pires (PRT) 12.00		Chris Ward (USA) 16.34
DEF	Kieren Perrow (AUS) 11.34	DEF	Taj Burrow (AUS) 13.90

TOUR RATINGS AFTER EVENT #6

1. Kelly Slater (USA) 5620
2. Joel Parkinson (AUS) 4548
3. Bede Durbidge (AUS) 4382
4. Taj Burrow (AUS) 4370
5. Mick Fanning (AUS) 4353

Fred and Brucey. Photo ASP Kirstin © Covered Images.

BOOST MOBILE PRO OF SURF / Presented by Hurley
ASP Men's World Tour Event #7 | Trestles, San Clemente, California | September 7–13, 2008

Close, but Kelly Again

Kelly Slater. Photo ASP Rowland © Covered Images.

Taj Burrow. Photo ASP Rowland © Covered Images.

Kelly celebrating another win. Photo ASP Rowland © Covered Images.

Europe's Jeremy Flores. Photo ASP Covered Images.

FINAL		
Kelly Slater (USA) 18.97	DEF	Taj Burrow (AUS) 18.63

SEMI FINALS			
	DEF		DEF
Kelly Slater (USA) 15.67	Bede Durbridge (AUS) 15.10	Taj Burrow (AUS) 17.33	Jeremy Flores (FRA) 16.50

QUARTER FINALS			
	Bede Durbridge (AUS) 16.90		Jeremy Flores (FRA) 17.57
DEF	Dane Reynolds (USA) 14.10	DEF	Mick Fanning (AUS) 15.67
	Kelly Slater (USA) 17.16		Taj Burrow (AUS) 18.50
DEF	Bobby Martinez (USA) 15.16	DEF	Heitor Alves (BRA) 6.34

TOUR RATINGS AFTER EVENT #7
1. Kelly Slater (USA) 6820
2. Taj Burrow (AUS) 5402
3. Bede Durbridge (AUS) 5258
4. Joel Parkinson (AUS) 5148
5. Mick Fanning (AUS) 5085

It would be downright boring . . . if it wasn't so damned exciting! In yet another display of skill and determination under duress, Kelly Slater surged from behind to beat Taj Burrow in the final of the Boost at Trestles, claiming his third Boost title and stepping still closer to an historic ninth world title.

Given Slater's dominance of the 2008 tour, this could have been a ho-hum, predictable result, but Western Australian powerhouse Taj Burrow is always formidable at Trestles, and appeared to have this one in the bag before the halfway point in the final, with Slater "combo-ed"—needing a combination of two waves to get back in the race. Burrow's first wave was a 9.00, which he quickly backed up with a near-perfect 9.63

Said Slater, "I was out there just trying to save face. Taj was on fire and I thought he had me." But the eight-time world champion caught a smaller wave on the inside part of the reef, seeing its potential to peel down the line, and it was his uncanny wave sense that paid off with a score of 9.70. With the clock ticking, Slater still needed a substantial 8.93 for victory, and at the two-minute mark, holding priority, Burrow allowed Slater a very ordinary wave that appeared to have little potential, and the champion milked it to the beach to win the event.

A disappointed Burrow said, "I felt like I had won. I didn't think that wave had scoring potential. I picked the best waves and surfed them well, so it's frustrating."

Slater now has a chance to claim his ninth world title at the next event, should he win it and Burrow finish worse than third.

QUIKSILVER PRO FRANCE
ASP Men's World Tour Event #8 | South West France | September 19–28, 2008

Ace in the Hole

Adrian Buchan. Photo ASP Cestari © Covered Images.

It was the anti-climax of the season, and it took a tour rookie to make it happen. A huge contingent of French fans—not to mention the millions watching the webcast—held their collective breath as an out-of-sorts Kelly Slater took on the relatively unknown rookie from Australia, Adrian "Ace" Buchan, in a small-wave final at Les Bourdaines. At stake, not just the Quiksilver Pro France winner's check, but Slater's ninth world title.

Having watched his nearest rivals tumble earlier in the event, it seemed a foregone conclusion that Slater would pull something out of the shorebreak—as he had done several times already this season—to claim his historic ninth crown. Ace Buchan, in his first World Tour final, had other ideas.

Slater's major sponsor, Quiksilver, had yearned for the opportunity to have him clinch a world title at this event, having missed out narrowly on two previous successful title campaigns. Quiksilver Europe president Pierre Agnes, who hosts Slater at his Capbreton home during the European season and is his biggest fan, had chilled the champagne and booked the venue for the celebration, but again it was not to be.

Having dispatched Brazil's Adriano De Souza in a tight semifinal, Slater seemed tired going into the final and lacked his usual pyrotechnics. An amped-up Buchan took the lead early and held it, with Slater needing a 7.51 going down to the wire. Needing maybe an air and two tail slides for his crown, Slater

took with three seconds to spare and pumped hard along the face. But for once the surf gods didn't smile on him. "I would have been bummed if they gave me the score," he said after the final. "Ace was the one in sync."

"I can't believe it, I'm speechless," Buchan said, and proved to be so.

And now it goes on to Mundaka, with Slater needing just a ninth to take the title, and a gazillion Euro fans heading south to watch him do it.

Aces high. Photo ASP Kirstin © Covered Images.

FINAL		
Adrian Buchan (AUS) 15.74	DEF	Kelly Slater (USA) 15.16

SEMI FINALS			
	DEF		DEF
Kelly Slater (USA) 14.90	Adriano De Souza (BRA) 13.97	Adrian Buchan (AUS) 15.17	Damien Hobgood (USA) 8.83

QUARTER FINALS		
Adriano De Souza (BRA) 114.93		Adrian Buchan (AUS) 17.00
DEF Bobby Martinez (USA) 12.40		DEF Dane Reynolds (USA) 13.34
Kelly Slater (USA) 17.50		Damien Hobgood (USA) 13.34
DEF Mick Campbell (AUS) 12.33		DEF Michel Bourez (PYF) 13.00

TOUR RATINGS AFTER EVENT #8

1. Kelly Slater (USA) 7852
2. Taj Burrow (AUS) 6002
3. Bede Durbidge (AUS) 5668
4. Adriano De Souza (BRA) 5426
5. Joel Parkinson (AUS) 5373

BILLABONG PRO MUNDAKA
ASP Men's World Tour Event #9 | Mundaka, Euskadi / Spain | September 30–October 12, 2008

CJ Takes Mundaka, Kelly Takes 9

The Bilabong Pro Mundaka, the most fickle event of the tour and sometimes the most wonderful, seemed to be suffering from Slater fatigue as it kicked off on the beach breaks at distant Zarautz. Resigned to another Slater world title, some of the pros had begged off, citing injuries or personal issues. It was all a bit, here we go again.

But a solid Mundaka swell, with superb clean lines wrapping into the picturesque bay beyond the church, made all the difference. Even perpetual World Tour bridesmaid Joel Parkinson, who had freely admitted that he had lost interest in the title race, began to pay attention as he found himself heading towards the pointy end.

With the Slater title out of the way and the new champ out in round four to Aussie Tom Whitaker, attention was focused on Parkinson, always a stellar performer when Mundaka fires, winner in France Ace Buchan who seemed to have hit a purple patch, and veteran campaigner and former World Champ CJ Hobgood. When CJ eliminated Aussie Luke Stedman and Parko took out in-form Buchan, the final became a showdown between the front-side and back-side approach of the masters.

Parkinson appeared to have it covered after he recovered from the shock of Hobgood's near-perfect 9.93 opening barrel, got two good ones and led by 5.90 with 15 seconds to go. Holding priority, the Aussie took the first wave of the set, hoping to extend his lead, but Hobgood scratched onto the next wave on the hooter; it opened up and he blasted his way to victory. More salt in the wounds for Parkinson, who has looked good but come up short all season.

CJ Hobgood. Photo ASP Kirstin © Covered Images.

Joel Parkinson. Photo ASP Kirstin © Covered Images.

CJ takes the plunge. Photo ASP Cestari © Covered Images.

FINAL		
CJ Hobgood (USA) 18.50	DEF	Joel Parkinson (AUS) 15.83

SEMI FINALS			
	DEF		DEF
Joel Parkinson (AUS) 17.80	Adrian Buchan (AUS) 14.50	CJ Hobgood (USA) 14.66	Luke Stedman (AUS) 6.70

QUARTER FINALS		
Joel Pakinson (AUS) 14.34		CJ Hobgood (USA) 15.34
DEF Adriano De Souza (BRA) 6.14		DEF Taj Burrow (AUS) 8.10
Jeremy Flores (FRA) 17.57		Mick Fanning (AUS) 15.67
DEF Taj Burrow (AUS) 18.50		DEF Heitor Alves (BRA) 6.34

TOUR RATINGS AFTER EVENT #9
1. Kelly Slater (USA) 8042
2. Taj Burrow (AUS) 6324
3. Joel Parkinson (AUS) 6180
4. Bede Durbidge (AUS) 5990
5. Adriano De Souza (BRA) 5748

HANG LOOSE SANTA CATARINA PRO
ASP Men's World Team Event #10 | Imbituba, Santa Catarina, Brazil | October 28–November 5, 2008

Durbridge Back at Number 2

Bede Durbidge. Photo ASP Kirstin © Covered Images.

Australia's Bede Durbidge claimed his third ASP World Tour victory in Imbituba, Brazil, pushing him back to number two in the rankings behind Kelly Slater, with just one tour event to come.

With Slater's historic ninth world title already sealed, there was a high level of absenteeism at the Hang Loose Pro, giving local wildcards a chance to show their skills. But by the quarterfinals, the three remaining Brazilians had bowed out.

Durbidge took out France's Jeremy Flores in a one-sided final, 17.76 to 9.86. Flores seemed to be out of position for the sets, while Durbidge was totally in rhythm, securing the two best waves of the heat early on and then maintaining his lead throughout. It was a World Tour final debut for Flores, 20, who is now ranked number 10 despite carrying an ankle injury for the last three events.

On his way to the final Flores claimed the scalp of countryman and mentor Miky Picon, but since the third placing secured his place in the 2009 top 44, it was a happy ending for both Frenchmen. Next year they will be joined on tour by qualifier Tim Boal, giving France its largest representation ever.

Hawaii's Fred Patacchia equalled his best result in Brazil with an equal third, taking him to number 11 in the ratings. He surfed well throughout the event but could not get past a rampaging Durbidge.

Bede Durbidge. Photo ASP Kirstin © Covered Images.

FINAL		
Bede Durbidge (AUS) 17.76	DEF	Jeremy Flores (FRA) 9.86

SEMI FINALS			
	DEF		DEF
Jeremy Flores (FRA) 14.00	Mikael Picon (FRA) 13.73	Bede Durbidge (AUS) 12.33	Fred Patacchia (HAW) 8.50

QUARTER FINALS			
Jeremy Flores (FRA) 18.06		Bede Durbidge (AUS) 17.17	
DEF Leonardo Neves (BRA) 14.03		DEF Bernardo Miranda (BRA) 12.30	
Mikael Picon (FRA) 12.23		Fred Patacchia (HAW) 11.83	
DEF Daniel Ross (AUS) 11.83		DEF Heitor Alves (BRA) 9.40	

TOUR RATINGS AFTER EVENT #10
1 Kelly Slater (USA) 8042
2 Bede Durbidge (AUS) 6780
3 Taj Burrow (AUS) 6324
4 Joel Parkinson (AUS) 6180
5 CJ Hobgood (USA) 5860

Jeremy Flores. Photo ASP Kirstin © Covered Images.

BILLABONG PIPELINE MASTERS
ASP Men's World Tour Event #11 | Banzai Pipeline, Oahu, Hawaii | December 8-20, 2008

Slater Caps a Perfect Year

Kelly Slater. Photo ASP Kirstin © Covered Images. Inset: Finalists Ward and Slater with Pipe legend Gerry Lopez. Photo ASP Kirstin © Covered Images.

Can life get any better for Kelly Slater? The champ arrived at Pipeline moments before his heat, having just flown in from an exotic surf locale, blitzed it and barely raised a sweat in winning his sixth Masters crown and his sixth tour event of the season. So the Slater machine finished the year just as he started it—in total domination.

The nine-time World Champion surfed four times on finals day in solid but unpredictable conditions, eventually beating Chris Ward (USA) in the final.

He faltered only once, being "combo-ed" by Timmy Reyes (USA) in the semifinal until the final five minutes, when the champion scored a 9.0 and a perfect 10 in quick succession.

Australia's Joel Parkinson finished 9th after being knocked out by Tim Reyes, but it was enough for him to claim the Triple Crown after sensationally scoring a perfect heat 20 earlier in the Masters, only the second time the feat had been achieved at Pipeline.

FINAL		
Kelly Slater (USA) 14.00	DEF	Chris Ward (USA) 7.23

SEMI FINALS			
	DEF		DEF
Kelly Slater (USA) 19.00	Tim Reyes (USA) 15.60	Chris Ward (USA) 16.46	Adrian Buchan (AUS) 10.16

QUARTER FINALS			
	Tim Reyes (USA) 16.17		Adrian Buchan (AUS) 14.33
DEF	Luke Stedman (AUS) 6.67	DEF	Kamalei Alexander (HAW) 2.67
	Kelly Slater (USA) 18.63		Chris Ward (USA) 8.06
DEF	Jamie O'Brien (HAW) 11.84	DEF	Andy Irons (HAW) 7.43

TOUR RATINGS AFTER EVENT #11
1 Kelly Slater (USA) 8832
2 Bede Durbidge (AUS) 6780
3 Taj Burrow (AUS) 6324
4 Joel Parkinson (AUS) 6180
5 CJ Hobgood (USA) 5860

Chris Ward. Photo ASP Rowland © Covered Images.

Adrian Buchan. Photo ASP Rowland © Covered Images.

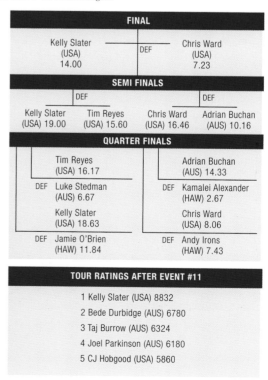

ROXY PRO GOLD COAST
ASP World Tour Women's Event #1 | Coolangatta, Australia | February 23–March 5, 2008

Former Champ Devastating in Season Opener

The 2004 Women's World Champion and 2007 runner-up Sofia Mulanovich of Peru was in sensational form as the 2008 Women's Tour got underway at the Snapper Rocks Suerbank. Mulanovich never faltered in the clean one-meter waves and pressed home her psychological advantage to take out Australia's Sam Cornish in a one-sided final.

Cornish had to surf four times on the final day and appeared too weary to hunt down the performance waves. Gracious in defeat, 2007's World number four said she simply hadn't found the waves that linked up, whereas Mulanovich had. "But congrats to Sofia anyway. She was ripping and deserved to win."

Earlier, reigning World Champion Steph Gilmore (Australia) was taken out at her home break by Hawaiian teen phenom Carissa Moore, who thrilled the big crowd with new-school tail slides. Runner-up in this event last year, Moore looked set for another final until Cornish got the better of her in the semis.

Mulanovich. Photo ASP Robertson © Covered Images.

Sam Cornish and Sofia Mulanovich. Photo ASP Kirstin © Covered Images.

FINAL

Sofia Mulanovich (PER) 17.34	DEF	Samantha Cornish (AUS) 7.83

SEMI FINALS

	DEF		DEF
Samantha Cornish (AUS) 16.90	Carissa Moore (HAW) 15.53	Sofia Mulanovich (PER) 13.50	Amee Donohoe (AUS) 10.33

QUARTER FINALS

	Samantha Cornish (AUS) 15.60	Sofia Mulanovich (PER) 13.16
DEF	Layne Beachley (AUS) 12.00	DEF Rebecca Woods (AUS) 7.10
	Carissa Moore (HAW) 17.57	Amee Donohoe (AUS) 10.73
DEF	Melanie Bartels (HAW) 9.07	DEF Julia De La Rosa (PER) 10.33

TOUR RATINGS AFTER EVENT #1

1. Sofia Mulanovich (PER) 1200
2. Samantha Cornish (AUS) 972
3. Amee Donohoe (AUS) 756
4. Layne Beachley (AUS) 552

Cornish. Photo ASP Robertson © Covered Images.

RIP CURL WOMENS PRO / Presented by Ford Fiesta
ASP World Tour Women's Event #2 | Bells Beach, Australia | March 18-29, 2008

Mulanovich Storming, But Steph Too Strong

Hot on the heels of her first blood for the season at the Roxy Pro Gold Coast, Sofia Mulanovich looked to be heading for a perfect two at Bells Beach, but she hadn't reckoned on the resilience of reigning World Champion Stehanie Gilmore, and in a repeat of the 2007 final, the two squared off in the Bells bowl, with Steph emerging victorious to claim her second consecutive Bell.

"That is probably the best performance I've put on in my career," Gilmore said after having trailed for most of the final before stroking into a solid wave with five minutes remaining and stylishly weaving through a series of floaters and top turns to score the highest wave of the day—a 9.33. On her way to the final, Gilmore took out seven-time World Champion Layne Beachley after the Sydney veteran made an uncharacteristic priority mistake and gifted the younger surfer a high-scoring ride. Beachley, who normally thrives under pressure, then choked on the wave that could have made the difference and fell off. Beachley said, "Equal third is a good result but to come so close to a victory when it's been a while . . . well, it's really frustrating. One of these days I'm going to get these groms back!"

Stephanie Gilmore, on the waves and in victory. Photos ASP Kirstin © Covered Images.

Mulanovich. Photo ASP Robertson © Covered Images.

FINAL		
Sofia Mulanovich (PER) 17.34	DEF	Samantha Cornish (AUS) 7.83

SEMI FINALS			
	DEF		DEF
Stephanie Gilmore (AUS) 14.50	Layne Beachley (AUS) 10.17	Sofia Mulanovich (PER) 13.67	Amee Donohoe (AUS) 7.34

QUARTER FINALS

	Layne Beachley (AUS) 16.33		Sofia Mulanovich (PER) 16.17
DEF	Samantha Cornish (AUS) 11.00	DEF	Jessi Miley-Dyer (AUS) 12.16
	Stephanie Gilmore (AUS) 11.83		Amee Donohoe (AUS) 10.50
DEF	Megan Abubo (HAW) 8.83	DEF	Claire Bevilacqua (PER) 10.33

TOUR RATINGS AFTER EVENT #2

1. Sofia Mulanovich (PER) 2172
2. Stephanie Gilmore (AUS) 1560
3. Samantha Cornish (AUS) 1524
4. Amee Donohoe (AUS) 1512
5. Layne Beachley (AUS) 1308

RIP CURL PRO MADEMOISELLE
ASP World Tour Women's Event #3 | Hossegor / Seignosse, France | August 28–September 1, 2008

Champ Back on Top in France

Gilmore cutback. Photo ASP Cestari © Covered Images.

Reigning World Champion Stephanie Gilmore stepped back into the limelight in an all-Aussie final at the Rip Curl Pro Medemoiselle in Southwest France, defeating seven-time World Champion Layne Beachley in clean, small waves at Les Bourdaines in the Les Landes.

Having been defeated in the season opener at her home beach, Snapper Rocks in Australia, by former World Champ Sofia Mulanovich, Gilmore battled hard and turned the tables in the final of tour stop #2 at Bells, but it is not proving to be an easy season for the 20-year-old tyro, with veteran Beachley taking her to the wire.

Beachley, ever the diplomat, said after the final, "I'm really proud of Steph. She's been the form surfer all season and really deserved the win."

Lee-Ann Curren, 19, French-born daughter of surfing legend Tom Curren, continued her meteoric rise through the women's ranks with a 3rd placing, having surfed brilliantly before Beachley took her down.

Layne Beachley and Steph Gilmore. Photo ASP Cestari © Covered Images.

FINAL

Stephanie Gilmore (AUS) 16.66	DEF	Layne Beachley (AUS) 11.00

SEMI FINALS

	DEF			DEF	
Layne Beachley (AUS) 14.33		Lee-Ann Curren (FRA) 5.84	Stephanie Gilmore (AUS) 13.33		Silvana Lima (BRA) 2.20

QUARTER FINALS

	Layne Beachley (AUS) 15.50			Stephanie Gilmore (AUS) 18.40
DEF	Amee Donohoe (AUS) 11.87		DEF	Jacqueline Silva (BRA) 5.33
	Lee-Ann Curren (FRA) 13.50			Silvana Lima (BRA) 14.20
DEF	Jessi Miley-Dyer (AUS) 8.00		DEF	Samantha Cornish (AUS) 13.17

TOUR RATINGS AFTER EVENT #3

1. Stephanie Gilmore (AUS) 2760
2. Sofia Mulanovich (PER) 2532
3. Layne Beachley (AUS) 2280
4. Samantha Cornish (AUS) 2076
5. Silvana Lima (BRA) 1272

BILLABONG RIO
ASP World Tour Women's Event #4 | Barra de Tijuca, Rio de Janero, Brazil | September 8–18, 2008

Bartels' Comeback Marks Billabong Rio

Melanie Bartels. Photo ASP Morris © Covered Images.

Hawaii's Melanie Bartels rocketed from 14th place to 6th in the rankings after an exciting win over former World Champion Sofia Mulanovich in rifling barrels at Barra da Tijuca in Rio. While the event had to wade through some rather ordinary conditions early on, it concluded in excellent quality 4-foot waves.

Bartels, 26, claimed her second tour victory after missing an event early in the season, and clearly enjoyed competing in classic conditions. The waves started to deteriorate during the final, but Bartels had already done enough to win. It was her win against reigning World Champion Stephanie Gilmore in the semis, however, that had the crowd to its feet, with both surfers trading barrels as the surf peaked. Said Bartels, "That's the most fun I've had in a heat for a very long time. It pumped out there!"

Gilmore, who had been in devastating form throughout, scored a perfect 10 during the encounter, but it was not enough to stop the raging Bartels.

Melanie Bartels. Photo ASP Mariana © Covered Images.

FINAL		
Melanie Bartels (HAW) 14.34	DEF	Sofia Mulanovich (PER) 10.60

SEMI FINALS			
	DEF		DEF
Melanie Bartels (HAW) 19.00	Stephanie Gilmore (AUS) 18.50	Sofia Mulanovich (PER) 11.67	Layne Beachley (AUS) 9.46

QUARTER FINALS			
	Melanie Bartels (HAW) 8.84		Sofia Mulanovich (PER) 11.74
DEF	Samantha Cornish (AUS) 5.23	DEF	Jessi Miley-Dyer (AUS) 8.60
	Stephanie Gilmore (AUS) 16.47		Layne Beachley (AUS) 14.83
DEF	Jacqueline Silva (BRA) 8.50	DEF	Silvana Lima (BRA) 10.33

TOUR RATINGS AFTER EVENT #4
1. Stephanie Gilmore (AUS) 3516
2. Sofia Mulanovich (PER) 3504
3. Layne Beachley (AUS) 3036
4. Samantha Cornish (AUS) 2628
5. Amee Donohoe (AUS) 2424

Sofia Mulanovich. Photo ASP Morris © Covered Images.

BEACHLEY CLASSIC
ASP World Tour Women's Event #5 | Manly Beach, Australia | October 9–14, 2008

Tyler Wright Makes History at Beachley Classic

Tyler Wright. Photo ASP Robertson © Covered Images.

Tyler Wright. Photo ASP Robertson © Covered Images.

Australia's Tyler Wright rewrote the record books for a World Tour event when she enjoyed a dream run all the way from the trials to the winner's podium.

Wright won her entry into the main event with an impressive win in the Oakley Trials the week before, and once on the main stage she never looked back, ultimately defeating Brazil's Silvana Lima in an exciting final in consistent 3-foot waves at Sydney's famous Manly Beach. With bigger prize money and more ratings points on offer at the Beachley than other tour events, Wright faced tough opposition and highly competitive tactics as the girls high on the tour ratings came up against her, but she held to her game plan to "just surf" and took out Brazil's Jacqueline Silva and Australia's Amee Donohoe on her way to the final.

The event was marked by the emotional retirement announcement of seven-time World Champion Layne Beachley, 36, who used her own event to call it a day on a stellar career.

Tyler Wright with Layne Beachley. Photo ASP Robertson © Covered Images.

FINAL

Tyler Wright (AUS) 13.64	DEF	Silvana Lima (BRA) 12.84

SEMI FINALS

	DEF			DEF	
Tyler Wright (AUS) 14.17	Amee Donohoe (AUS) 10.00		Silvana Lima (BRA) 15.10	Sofia Mulanovich (PER) 14.00	

QUARTER FINALS

	Amee Donohoe (AUS) 10.83		Sofia Mulanovich (PER) 9.00	
DEF	Julia de la Rosa Toro (PER) 9.60	DEF	Rebecca Woods (AUS) 2.00	
	Tyler Wright (AUS) 14.17		Silvana Lima (BRA) 13.93	
DEF	Jacqueline Silva (BRA) 12.83	DEF	Layne Beachley (AUS) 12.07	

TOUR RATINGS AFTER EVENT #5

1. Sofia Mulanovich (PER) 4411
2. Stephanie Gilmore (AUS) 3948
3. Layne Beachley (AUS) 3698
4. Amee Donohoe (AUS) 3331
5. Silvana Lima (BRA) 3194

MOVISTAR CLASSIC, presented by Rip Curl
ASP Womens WCT Event #6 | Marcora, Peru | November 3–8, 2008

Back to Back Peru Classics for the Champ

Stephanie Gilmore. Photo ASP Cestari © Covered Images.

Silvana Lima. Photo ASP Cestari © Covered Images.

Reigning women's World Champion Stephanie Gilmore returned to the top of the ratings with a convincing win against Brazil's Silvana Lima in challenging left-handers at the Movistar Classic. The win represented a successful defense of her 2007 Movistar title.

After posting an equal 9th in the previous event, the Beachley Classic in Sydney, and losing her ratings lead, Gilmore is now back on track to secure her second World crown with just two events remaining.

Movistar Classic organizers shifted the event 90 minutes south to Piscina to take advantage of a solid 4-foot swell and long left-handers. It proved a good call, with excellent conditions to complete the event.

Australia's Rebecca Woods delivered the shock of the day when she eliminated hometown favorite and former World Champion Sofia Mulanovich, leaving Brazilian Silvana Lima to carry South America's hopes into the semifinals. The in-form Lima ended Woods' run and a rampaging Gilmore stopped seven-time World Champion Layne Beachley.

Lima's second final in two events opened with a 7.7, but it was not enough to stop Gilmore, who seemed to gain strength with each encounter through the final rounds. But a second was good enough to put Lima into 4th on the ratings, and looking forward to Hawaii.

Stephanie Gilmore. Photo ASP Cestari © Covered Images.

FINAL		
Stephanie Gilmore (AUS) 16.10	DEF	Silvana Lima (BRA) 14.70

SEMI FINALS			
	DEF		DEF
Silvana Lima (BRA) 13.73	Rebecca Woods (AUS) 13.16	Stephanie Gilmore (AUS) 15.60	Layne Beachley (AUS) 15.23

QUARTER FINALS	
Silvana Lima (BRA) 13.83	Stephanie Gilmore (AUS) 15.00
DEF Karina Petroni (USA) 8.83	DEF Jacqueline Silva (BRA) 11.87
Rebecca Woods (AUS) 11.50	Layne Beachley (AUS) 12.94
DEF Sofia Mulanovich (PER) 9.83	DEF Samantha Cornish (AUS) 10.17

TOUR RATINGS AFTER EVENT #6
1. Stephanie Gilmore (AUS) 5148
2. Sofia Mulanovich (PER) 4963
3. Layne Beachley (AUS) 4454
4. Silvana Lima (BRA) 4166
5. Amee Donohoe (AUS) 3691

ROXY PRO SUNSET

ASP Women's World Tour Event #7 | Sunset Beach, Oahu, Hawaii | November 24–December 6, 2008

Gilmore Claims Roxy Pro & 2nd World Title

Steph Gilmore. Photo ASP Cestari © Covered Images.

Silvana Lima. Photo ASP Kirstin © Covered Images.

Australia's Stephanie Gilmore scored an emphatic victory in 3- to 5-foot waves at Sunset Beach to take the Roxy Pro title and her second consecutive ASP Women's World crown.

A stoked Gilmore said she had no idea she would clinch the World title when she arrived at the beach with a big job ahead of her, but she held on while main rivals Sofia Mulanovich (PER) and Layne Beachley (AUS) were eliminated, leaving only Silvana Lima (BRA) to get past. Lima beat the champion in their semifinal, but both advanced and in the final Gilmore found a wave late, to wrest the lead from the consistent Brazilian.

For Lima, the form surfer of the event, it was a third consecutive 2nd place. "I don't know what I have to do to win," said the disappointed surfer.

Young Aussie contenders Jessi Miley-Dyer and Nicola Atherton finished 3rd and 4th respectively.

Steph Gilmore triumphant again. Photo ASP Cestari © Covered Images.

FINAL		
Stephanie Gilmore (AUS) 15.83	DEF	Silvana Lima (PER) 14.16

SEMI FINALS			
	DEF		DEF
Silvana Lima (BRA) 16.17	Stephanie Gilmore (AUS) 12.40	Nicola Atherton (AUS) 13.17	Jessi Miley-Dyer (AUS) 12.03

QUARTER FINALS		
Silvana Lima (BRA) 10.80		Nicola Atherton (AUS) 13.43
DEF Serena Brooke (AUS) 10.67		DEF Jessi Miley-Dyer (AUS) 12.40
Stephanie Gilmore (AUS) 14.33		Layne Beachley (AUS) 15.57
DEF Megan Abubo (HAW) 10.94		DEF Lee-Ann Curren (FRA) 11.43

TOUR RATINGS AFTER EVENT #7
1. Stephanie Gilmore (AUS) 6348
2. Sofia Mulanovich (PER) 5233
3. Silvana Lima (BRA) 5138
4. Layne Beachley (AUS) 5006
5. Samantha Cornish (AUS) 3882

BILLABONG PRO MAUI
ASP Women's World Tour Event #8 | Maui, Hawaii | December 18–20, 2008

Gilmore Wins Maui, Claims Triple Crown

Steph Gilmore. Photo ASP Cestari © Covered Images.

Steph Gilmore. Photo ASP Kirstin © Covered Images.

Stephanie Gilmore (AUS), 20, newly crowned two-time ASP Women's World Champion, defeated Melanie Bartels (HAW), 26, to claim the her second consecutive Billabong Pro Maui in clean 2- to 3-foot (1-meter) waves on offer at Ho'okipa Beach Park, earning the young Australian her first Vans Triple Crown of Surfing title.

The final event of the 2008 ASP Women's World Tour opted for a relocation from Honolua Bay to Ho'okipa Beach Park (the first relocation in the event's 10-year history) in order take advantage of the swell on offer, and the action didn't disappoint.

Gilmore opened the final strongly, posting a solid 7.33 out of a possible 10, but Bartels fought back with two solid scores of her own. Then, in an exciting exchange that saw the Hawaiian pull ahead on the first wave, Gilmore answered back with the highest score of the day, a 9.57, to retake the lead, immediately following it up with an 8.03 for a massive forehand turn combination. Bartels was unable to answer.

"It feels incredible to win the Vans Triple Crown Title," Gilmore said. "We had really fun waves at Haleiwa and then solid surf at Sunset Beach and we had a beautiful opening day of competition at Honolua Bay before finishing today at Ho'okipa. It's a real honor to be considered a good surfer in Hawaii and in such a variety of conditions."

Gilmore will now head home to Australia to rest and recharge for the 2009 ASP Women's World Tour, and with two ASP Women's World Titles, a Vans triple Crown Title and 11 elite tour victories under her belt (five in 2008 alone), the makings of a legend appear in place.

With a bevy of young guns joining the ASP

Last wave on tour, Layne Beachley. Photo ASP Cestari © Covered Images.

Women's World Tour in 2009, Bartels, who rocketed into seventh ranking after her Maui performance, will look to continue her momentum in the off-season in preparation for an ASP Women's World Title campaign next season.

Layne Beachley (AUS), 36, former seven-time ASP Women's World Champion, has announced that 2008 will be her final season as a full-time ASP World Tour competitor. Despite a solid quarter-final win over Rosanne Hodge (ZAF), 21, Beachley was unable to overcome eventual winner Gilmore in their hard-fought semifinal bout, going down 15.07 to Gilmore's 16.80.

"I think it was a great way to go out," Beachley said. "We all have to lose sometime and to go down to Steph [Gilmore], who I consider my protégé and the one I am passing the torch to, is probably the most fitting way."

Silvana Lima (BRA), 24, went down in the semifinals to Bartels, but her solid equal 3rd-place finish at the Billabong Pro Maui saw the young Brazilian finish a career-best number two on the ASP Women's World Tour.

Returning surfers to the 2009 ASP Women's World Tour will be reigning and two-time ASP Women's World Champion Stephanie Gilmore (AUS), 20, Silvana Lima (BRA), 24, Sofia Mulanovich (PER), 25, Amee Donohoe (AUS), 28, Samantha Cornish (AUS), 28, Melanie Bartels (HAW), 26, Rebecca Woods (AUS), 24, Jessi Miley-Dyer (AUS), 22, Jacqueline Silva (BRA), 29, and Rosanne Hodge (ZAF), 21 (via the ASP World Qualifying Series). New faces to next year's ASP Women's World Tour will be Sally Fitzgibbons (AUS), 18, Bruna Schmitz (BRA), 18, Paige Hareb (NZL), 18, Alana Blanchard (HAW), 18, and Coco Ho (HAW), 17.

FINAL		
Stephanie Gilmore (AUS) 17.60	DEF	Melanie Bartels (HAW) 14.80

SEMI FINALS			
	DEF		DEF
Stephanie Gilmore (AUS) 16.80	Layne Beachley (AUS) 15.07	Melanie Bartels (HAW) 13.07	Silvana Lima (BRA) 11.07

QUARTER FINALS		
Layne Beachley (AUS) 11.07		Melanie Bartels (HAW) 14.66
DEF Rosanne Hodge (ZAF) 9.67		DEF Carissa Moore (HAW) 11.33
Stephanie Gilmore (AUS) 15.33		Silvana Lima (BRA) 13.13
DEF Rebecca Woods (AUS) 11.87		DEF Megan Abubo (HAW) 10.23

2008 ASP WOMEN'S WORLD TOUR FINAL RATINGS

1. Stephanie Gilmore (AUS) 7188	10. Jacqueline Silva (BRA) 3398
2. Silvana Lima (BRA) 5534	11. Megan Abubo (HAW) 2988
3. Sofia Mulanovich (PER) 5323	12. Rosanne Hodge (ZAF) 2784
4. Layne Beachley (AUS) 5210	13. Nicola Atherton (AUS) 2670
5. Amee Donohoe (AUS) 4051	14. Julia De La Rosa Toro (PER) 2654
6. Samantha Cornish (AUS) 3972	15. Karina Petroni (USA) 2604
7. Melanie Bartels (HAW) 3876	16. Melanie Redman-Carr (AUS) 2232
8. Rebecca Woods (AUS) 3602	17. Serena Brooke (AUS) 2094
9. Jessi Miley-Dyer (AUS) 3564	

OXBOW WORLD MENS LONGBOARD TOUR Longtime supporters of the pro longboard tour, France-based Oxbow, this year coincided its

OXBOW WLT
ASP World Longboard Tour Event #1 | Anglet, France | May 6–11, 2008

First Blood to the Aussies

Australia's hottest longboarding prospect for the past couple of years, Coffs Harbour's Harley Ingleby took the first leg of the Oxbow World Tour with a powerful display of precision surfing in good three-foot waves at Les Cavalieres, Anglet. The Aussie's win was all the more pleasing because he beat the hometown favorite, France's new kid on the block, Antoine Delpero in front of a very partisan French crowd.

Ingleby had to first beat off a strong challenge from reigning World Champion Phil Rajzman (BRA) in the semifinals. Just a year earlier it had been Rajzman who had taken him out in the one-event World title at the same beach, with Ingleby finishing fifth. Now, he stands poised to take the World title if he can back it up in California in November.

Winner Ingleby. Photo Aquashot/Aspeurope.com.

Harley Ingleby. Photo Aquashot/Aspeurope.com.

Antoine Delpero. Photo ASP Morris © Covered Images.

FINAL

Harley Ingleby (AUS) 16.65	DEF	Antoine Delpero (FRA) 14.50

SEMI FINALS

	DEF		DEF
Harley Ingleby (AUS) 15.00	Phil Rajzman (BRA) 13.50	Antoine Delpero (FRA) 18.25	Bonga Perkins (HAW) 17.05

QUARTER FINALS

	Harley Ingleby (AUS) 13.65		Antoine Delpero (FRA) 16.75
DEF	Carlos Bahia (BRA) 11.25	DEF	Amaro Matos (BRA) 10.85
	Phil Rajzman (BRA) 14.85		Bonga Perkins (HAW) 16.25
DEF	Matthew Moir (ZAF) 14.85	DEF	Colin McPhillips (USA) 13.90

launch on the American market with a two-event world championship, starting at Anglet, France, and concluding at San Onofre, California.

OXBOW WLT
ASP World Longboard Tour Event #2 | San Onofre, California, USA | November 5–9, 2008

But Hawaii Takes the Title

Twelve years after his first longboard world title, the great Hawaiian waterman Bonga Perkins was speechless when he claimed his second title at the age of 36. And the event, held at California's capital of longboarding, San Onofre, went right down to the wire, with both Perkins and France's Antoine Delpero going into the final with the title up for grabs.

This was longboarding at its absolute best, with two surfers representing different styles of the art, from opposite sides of the world, one a veteran, the other a rookie. And while Delpero's two 2nds in the World Tour this year, his youthful exuberance and his beautiful style have endeared him to many, no one was sorry to see Perkins, who had surfed superbly throughout the event, take the crown again, perhaps capping a stellar career in which stand-up paddle surfing seemed to have gained the upper hand in recent years. But this was the Bonga of old, powering down the line at the kelpy reef.

Much can be expected of Antoine Delpero in the future, and his second placing on the tour was just 12 points off winning. Two other surfers are worthy of special mention. Brazil's Alex Salazar finished 10th, at 41 the oldest competitor. And Australia's Bryce Young, at 17 the youngest competitor, finished 15th.

Bonga Perkins. Photo ASP Rowland © Covered Images.

FINAL		
Bonga Perkins (HAW) 16.95	DEF	Antoine Delpero (FRA) 13.90

SEMI FINALS			
DEF		DEF	
Bonga Perkins (HAW) 16.20	Ned Snow (HAW) 14.00	Antoine Delpro (FRA) 17.65	Alex Salazar (BRA) 14.25

QUARTER FINALS			
	Bonga Perkins (HAW) 16.75		Antoine Delpero (FRA) 16.85
DEF	Timothee Creignout (FRA) 13.00	DEF	Josh Baxter (USA) 14.25
	Ned Snow (HAW) 16.35		Alex Salazar (BRA) 15.65
DEF	Eduardo Bage (BRA) 13.00	DEF	Matthew Moir (ZAF) 14.00

2008 World Pro Longboard Champ Bonga Perkins. Photo ASP Morris © Covered Images.

ROXY JAM BIARRITZ
ASP Women's Longboard Championships | Cote des Basques, France | July 11–16, 2008

Hawaii's Monahan Claims World Title

Joy Monahan. Photo Aquashot/Aspeurope.com.

Hawaii's Joy Monahan completed an impressive three-year campaign with her victory at the Roxy Jam Biarritz securing her a first World Longboard title. Ninth in 2006 and fifth in 2007, Monahan took out defending champion Jen Smith (USA) in the semifinals, then defeated Australia's Chelsea Williams in a tense and exciting final.

Conditions at Cotes des Basques, France's longboarding capital in the old resort town of Biarritz, were small but contestable, making the final a battle of strategy for the two girls, one a stylist (Monahan), the other (Williams) a power surfer. In the end, it was Monahan's style that prevailed over the highly fancied Williams, whose form in the event had been superb. In the end it got down to wave choice, finding the right one that peeled to the beach and created a performance platform. Despite the fact that France's last chance, Justine Dupont, bowed out in the quarterfinals, the big crowd along the strand and on the receding beach gave both finalists huge support.

Joy Monahan claims it! Photo ASP Rowland © Covered Images.

FINAL		
Joy Monahan (HAW) 14.10	DEF	Chelsea Williams (AUS) 13.50

SEMI FINALS			
	DEF		DEF
Joy Monahan (HAW) 13.50	Jennifer Smith (USA) 12.20	Chelsea Williams (AUS) 15.00	Leah Dawson (USA) 7.35

QUARTER FINALS			
	Joy Monahan (HAW) 16.25		Leah Dawson (USA) 11.65
DEF	Rachel Barry (USA) 8.85	DEF	Justine Dupont (FRA) 10.75
	Jennifer Smith (USA) 14.40		Chelsea Williams (AUS) 12.65
DEF	Kassia Meador (USA) 9.75	DEF	Julie Cox (USA) 8.20

BILLABONG WORLD JUNIOR CHAMPIONSHIP
ASP World Junior Championship | North Narrabeen, Australia | January 3–10, 2009

Barger & Ado Crowned ASP Junior Champions

Kai the victor. Photo ASP Steve Robertson © Covered Images.

Kai Barger in the final. Photo ASP Steve Robertson © Covered Images.

Victorious Pauline Ado. Photo ASP Steve Robertson © Covered Images.

Kai Barger (HAW), 19, won the Billabong ASP World Junior Championships, defeating Jadson Andre (BRA), 20, to claim the ASP World Junior Title.

"I'm as high as Saturn's kite baby!" Barger said. "Out of all the incredible surfers in this event, like Dusty (Payne) and Granger (Larsen) and Julian (Wilson), I probably had the least amount of confidence, but I guess this goes to show that every dog has his day and today's mine!"

While Andre opened up the final with two strong scores, Barger quickly rallied, grabbing a 6.67 before usurping the Brazilian with an explosive 8.67 for a series of forehand blasts on the Narrabeen left-handers. The Hawaiian's 15.34 out of a possible 20 would prove too much for Andre to overtake and would see Barger crowned the new ASP World Junior Champion.

Barger now joins one of the most prestigious clubs in professional surfing. Past champions include World Tour stalwarts such as Joel Parkinson (AUS), 27, Jordy Smith (ZAF), 20, Adriano de Souza (BRA), 21, and fellow Hawaiian's Kekoa Bacalso (HAW), 23, and three-time ASP World Champion Andy Irons (HAW), 30.

Pauline Ado. Photo ASP Steve Robertson © Covered Images.

Gutsy Bethany Hamilton. Photo ASP Steve Robertson © Covered Images.

Earlier Pauline Ado (FRA), 17, made ASP history as the first non-Australian female to claim the ASP Junior World Title, defeating Bethany Hamilton (HAW), 18, in a hard-fought final.

Clean 3- to 4-foot (1-meter) waves were on offer at Sydney's legendary North Narrabeen beach, and after completing round 3 of the Men's division, the dramatic women's action commenced with the quarterfinals before culminating with the crowning of Ado as ASP World Junior Champion.

"I'm speechless," Ado said. "This is a dream come true. I can't believe that I won. When I woke up this morning, I never imagined that this would happen."

While her opponent Hamilton exhibited patience throughout the day, Ado wasted no time in busying herself on both the lefts and rights in the final, and although the lead flipped back-and-forth, it was the young Frenchwoman who sealed the deal with a solid 13.43 out of a possible 20.

MEN'S JUNIOR FINAL

Kai Barger (HAW) 15.34	DEF	Jadson Andre (BRA) 13.67	

SEMI FINALS

	DEF		DEF
Jadson Andre (BRA) 18.00	Tanner Gudauskas (USA) 14.34	Kai Barger (HAW) 16.73	Marc Lacomare (FRA) 8.84

QUARTER FINALS

	Tanner Gudauskas (USA) 17.23		Marc Lacomare (FRA) 14.00
DEF	Tamaroa McComb (PYF) 14.50	DEF	Maxime Huscenot (REU) 13.77
	Jadson Andre (BRA) 18.30		Kai Barger (HAW) 17.60
DEF	Kiron Jabour (HAW) 12.60	DEF	Matt Wilkinson (AUS) 13.16

WOMEN'S JUNIOR FINAL

Pauline Ado (FRA) 13.43	DEF	Bethany Hamilton (HAW) 12.47	

SEMI FINALS

	DEF		DEF
Pauline Ado (FRA) 12.17	Courtney Conlogue (USA) 10.00	Bethany Hamilton (HAW) 11.50	Leila Hurst (HAW) 10.07

QUARTER FINALS

	Pauline Ado (FRA) 16.33		Leila Hurst (HAW) 11.17
DEF	Airini Mason (NZL) 11.87	DEF	Diana Cristina (BRA) 9.23
	Courtney Conlogue (USA) 18.23		Bethany Hamilton (HAW) 14.83
DEF	Paige Hareb (NZL) 10.33	DEF	Laura Enever (AUS) 12.77

DREAMTOUR

ASP WORLD CHAMPIONS : KELLY SLATER STEPH GILMORE

08

ASPWORLDTOUR.COM

Sands of the World ceremony,
2008 Quiksilver ISA WJSC

Nataly Bernold, Costa Rica

CJ Hobgood, 2008
ISA World Surfing
Games Gold
Medalist

Team South Africa, Silver Medalists
of 2008 WSG Aloha Cup

Tamaroa McComb, Tahiti
2008 Junior U16 Gold Medalist

Morocco and Israel
flags fly side by side

Jonathan Hicks, New Zealand

Alejo Muniz, 2008
ISA U18 Junior
Gold Medalist

Portuguese pow-wow

Australia, 2008 Quiksilver ISA World
Junior Team Champions

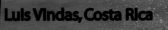

Luis Vindas, Costa Rica

ISA's Sand of the World ceremony, an important symbol. Photo courtesy ISA.

Japan's Ocean Dome, heading in the right direction. Photo JS Callahan/tropicalpix.

towards the long road that will take surfing to the Olympic Games.

WAVE PARKS

One of the ISA goals is for surfing to be available to all people, not just those who live near the oceans. For this reason, the ISA has started to interact with wave technology development companies in order to materialize man-made great waves suitable for surfing competition. Working together with the main manufacturers and specialists in wave parks, we are going to develop the ideal wave, something of fundamental importance for surfing to become part of the Olympic Games. Since the Olympic movement will not always come to the waves, we are prepared to take the waves to where the Games will be held.

This goal is part of the ISA's vision for a more democratic sport, with easier access to a wider segment of the population. We firmly believe that in the same way that the public sector in each country builds soccer and basketball stadiums, as well as arenas for many other sports, under the ISA leadership, they should start building wave parks, as soon as proper and cost efficient technology is available. We expect this to happen within the next 12 to 24 months.

ISA SURFING DEVELOPMENT PROGRAMS ON THE MOVE

Several ISA Programs such as Judging and Officiating, Coaching and Instructing, Surf School Register, Adapted Surfing, Individual Scholarship and Surfing Library have shown an incredible growth during 2008.

The ISA Scholarship Program had a humble beginning in 2007 with five grants. In 2008 it grew 400% with 20 grants. For 2009, the program will expand to 40 recipients. These scholarships provide much needed financial support to under-18 year-old surfers who have proven their case for funds to support their surfing and academic lives, while being inspirational for their communities. The grants may only be used for supporting their studying or surfing. With this program the ISA helps them achieve their dreams.

The first ISA film, "For a Better Surfing Future", was launched in May 2008 featuring the stories of the first five scholarship winners in five short films produced by local filmmakers from their native countries. This DVD was distributed free of charge all over the world.

The ISA Judging, Coaching and surfing instruction programs, expanded around the world. About 100 of these were administered by ISA licensed specialists in Oceania, Asia, the Americas, Europe and Africa. These ISA standardized programs have proven to be key building blocks for a better surfing future around the world, not only in the traditionally surfing nations but also in those where the sport is taking its first steps.

In addition, in 2008 the ISA created the Surfing School Registration Program, where ISA lists recognized surfing schools that are committed to ISA education standards.

Finally, the Director of the ISA Adapted Surfing Program, Alcino Neto, aka "Pirata", started working on the ISA-created, and Quiksilver Foundation-funded second DVD for challenged surfers. It includes instructions and a video introduction to the different techniques for teaching surfing to the disabled and challenged surfers of the world. This film will be a fundamental tool for all those that are including this program in their work scheme.

ISA AND THE SURFING INDUSTRY LEADING BRANDS ALLIANCE

The two leading surfing brands of the world, Quiksilver and Billabong, support the top two ISA events, the World Junior Surfing Championship and the World Surfing Games, respectively, through multi-year title sponsorship agreements. Their involvement has provided stability to the ISA World Championships and the national championships that select the national teams around the world.

Our ISA/Quiksilver partnership is in its sixth year, with the latest event held in May 2008 in France. Billabong begins its partnership with the ISA in the August 2009, with the Billabong ISA World Surfing Games to be held in Jacó Beach, Costa Rica.

At the same time, the Quiksilver Foundation, Billabong, Global Surf Industries and Reef Redemption announced the renewal of their donations to the ISA Individual Scholarship Program for 2009. Thus, they show that while they are market competitors, when a better future in surfing is at stake, they all join forces to work together as members of the same family.

On the environmental side, and as testimony to the ISA's commitment to the preservation of our waves, an alliance with the NGO "Save the Waves" was announced in December 2008. This organization fights for the preservation of our most important resources. The agreement partners the ISA and Save the Waves in the creation of a World Wave Reserves directory, involving private and public sectors in the preservation of the surfing areas.

FINAL WORDS

The ISA's job is not limited to the above-mentioned matters, but continues in other areas and projects that would require a whole book to describe. This work is carried out by the ISA and the more than 50 member federations, the management staff, volunteers and surfers around the world. Our job is carried out by all those who strive on a daily basis for a better surfing future.

For 2009 we will continue to lead and assist in the development of surfing around the world, with a special focus on the expansion of surfing to more countries, with Africa, Asia, and Latin America areas in the forefront.

With the help of thousands of volunteers, the public and private sectors, and especially the surfing industry, I plan to continue to lead the ISA and the surfing world in our passionate path towards a better surfing future.

Muchas gracias y un fuerte abrazo,

Fernando Aguerre
President
International Surfing Association

ISA WORLD SURFING GAMES

Australia Wins Three in a Row

By Pablo Zannochi

World Surfing Games. Sagardia led her heat from the beginning until the end. A combined score of 13.96 gave her the win.

She was carried in the arms of her teammates and cried all the way up the beach. "I can't stop crying! I'm super excited. I don't know if this is real! This is a dream come true. I've been working so hard to be here, I can't even believe it."

SALLY FITZGIBBONS MAKES HISTORY TOO

At 17, Sally Fitzgibbons (AUS) also made the record books by winning a Gold Medal in both the ISA World Junior Surfing Championship and the ISA World Surfing Games in the same year. She won in Portugal, after already winning the ASP WQS women's tour as well. No one has ever achieved this before, not even close.

Sally started slowly in her final heat against Marie Dejean (FRA), Camila Cassia (BRA) and Laureen Sweeney (USA). She waited 12 minutes

Hobgood, Fitzgibbons, Lima, and Moir are the new ISA World Champions. Photo courtesy ISA.

The mighty Aussies. Photo courtesy ISA.

The best 233 surfers from 29 different countries gathered together from October 11-19 in Costa de Caparica, Portugal for the 22nd World Games.

The Games had exciting moments in almost every heat of the five different divisions - Open Men, Open Women, Bodyboard Men, Bodyboard Women and Longboard, with conditions varying from solid five feet to well-shaped two foot waves.

AUSTRALIAN TEAM SUPREMACY

Australian patriotism and high energy surfing sidelined their rivals yet again, giving the Aussies their third consecutive ISA World Surfing Games Gold Medal in the Team Standings, the fourth out of the past six. In addition, Australia has also won three straight titles at the Quiksilver ISA World Junior Surfing Championships.

Australia got the gold medal in Open Women thanks to Sally Fitzgibbons, the silver, bronze and copper medals in Open Men thanks to Heath Joske, Dayyan Neve and Kai Otton, respectively. They also won silver in Longboard through the talented Harley Ingleby and the copper medal in Bodyboard Women thanks to Lilly Pollard. The Australians managed to have 60 percent of their team on the podium. They won the Golden Team medal with a resounding 3,000

points difference from United States.

Once Mark Lane, Surfing Australia CEO, knew his country would win one more time, he said: "I think the key to this team is that we have fun all the time, and that's one of our goals, to laugh the most we can. And an important aspect of Australian culture, we never give up, we keep going".

BRAZILIAN MARCUS LIMA SHINES IN BODYBOARD

In a tough final in which the favorites were the locals Manuel Centeno and Hugo Pinheiro (gold and silver medal winners in the 2006 Games) surfing on their home turf, Brazilian Marcus Lima stole the show.

He put some early scores under his belt, then started to work his strategy on Centeno, who was second. This caused a hassle that resulted in an interference call: Centeno on Lima. Pinheiro and Lee also had interference calls. With the other bodyboarders, Pinheiro and David Lee (ZAF) not catching many waves, the Brazilian was announced as the new ISA World Champion when the horn sounded.

PUERTO RICANS WIN THEIR FIRST EVER WSG GOLD MEDAL

Natasha Sagardia entered surfing history, becoming the first Puerto Rican to win a Gold Medal in the ISA

for a good wave. When it came, she scored an 8.90 then an 8.20 soon afterwards to take the lead and become the ISA World Champion.

MOIR WINS BACK TO BACK GOLD

Matthew Moir (ZAF) won for the second time in a row the Gold Medal in the Longboard division of the Games. He not only won the final of both events, he actually won every heat he entered at Huntington Beach 2006 and at Costa de Caparica in 2008. He's now looking forward to match Marcelo Freitas (BRA) record as a three-time consecutive Longboard winner.

Moir posted an almost perfect 18.12 combined score (9.22 and 8.90) to leave Harley Ingleby (AUS) in a close second, Taylor Jensen (USA) in third and Phil Rajzman (BRA) in fourth.

HOBGOOD WINS AGAINST THREE AUSSIES

Team USA surfer and ASP World Tour World Champion in 2001, CJ Hobgood had a great final day. It started with him forced to come back through the repechage final, but it ended amazingly with a Gold medal around his neck.

The Open Men's final included three World Tour surfers but started with Aussie Heath Joske posting a solid 8.40 and taking the lead for the first 10 minutes. But the US surfer maintained calm and, midway

through the heat, he took the lead after riding a nice right and scoring an 8.60 that was backed up with a 7.20.

With three minutes to go and Joske needing a 7.41, CJ started using tactics and didn't let the Aussie catch a wave. When the horn sounded, he was all smiles, winning his first ISA World Championship

CLOSING CEREMONY

An emotional Closing Ceremony took place on the beach in front of a great crowd of locals and the Games' participants from 29 nations. ISA President Fernando Aguerre thanked the Authorities of the hosting city, Almada; the organizer, Natural Factor; the ISA Contest Officials and the teams that travelled from all over the world to be part of the competition.

"This is a show of surfing but it is, most importantly, a show of brotherhood between the nations of the world. In the last heat of today we saw one US surfer and three Australians. Their surfing in that heat symbolized the World Surfing Games and the ISA spirit. In any other contest, it would've been very difficult for one athlete to beat all three surfers of the same nation, but in that final, good sportsmanship and fair play prevailed. They all surfed together in that spirit. What a great way to finish the World Surfing Games," Aguerre said.

WORLD CHAMPIONS

Gold: Australia – 17.238 pts.
Silver: USA – 14.284 pts.
Bronze: Brazil – 12.610 pts.
Copper: France – 11.819 pts.

MEN OPEN

Gold: CJ Hobgood (USA)
Silver: Heath Joske (AUS)
Bronze: Dayyan Neve (AUS)
Copper: Kai Otton (AUS)

WOMEN OPEN

Gold: Sally Fitzgibbons (AUS)
Silver: Marie Dejean (FRA)
Bronze: Camila Cassia (BRA)
Copper: Lauren Sweeney (USA)

MEN BODYBOARD

Gold: Marcus Lima (BRA)
Silver: Manuel Centeno (POR)
Bronze: Hugo Pinheiro (POR)
Copper: David Lee (ZAF)

WOMEN BODYBOARD

Gold: Natasha Sagardia (PRI)
Silver: Heloise Bourroux (FRA)
Bronze: Rita Pires (POR)
Copper: Lilly Pollard (AUS)

MEN LONGBOARD

Gold: Matthew Moir (ZAF)
Silver: Harley Ingleby (AUS)
Bronze: Taylor Jensen (USA)
Copper: Phil Rajzman (BRA)

ALOHA CUP

Gold: France
Silver: Portugal
Bronze: Costa Rica
Copper: South Africa

New World Champion, CJ Hobgood. Photo courtesy ISA.

Bronze medallist in longboard, Taylor Jensen. Photo courtesy ISA.

Going for it in the bodyboard. Photo courtesy ISA.

Supporters club. Photo courtesy ISA.

The ISA World Juniors

By Pablo Zannochi

Aussie gold! Photo courtesy ISA.

The world's best Under 18 surfers gathered from May 24 to June 1 at La Plage du Penon in Seignosse, France, for the biggest junior tournament on the planet: the 2008 Quiksilver ISA World Junior Surfing Championships.

Almost 300 surfers from 27 different countries participated in the event for a whole week in three divisions: Boys Under 18 and Under 16 and Girls Under 18. Once again, friendship was in the air. It was clear that surfing encourages living in peace and unity among different races, religions and colours. On the beautiful French Atlantic coast, young Muslims, Catholics, Jews, white people, black people, yellow people—each with their different traditions, languages and cultures—mingled with each other in an experience they probably will never forget.

Competitors enjoyed a week of near-perfect waves, especially good on the last day (Saturday, May 31), with long glassy 4- to 5-foot rights, as a perfect finale to the festival.

The most promising surfers in the world competed in the three finals, with the first celebration coming with Brazilian Alejo Muniz in the Boys Under 18. Tahitian Tamaroa McComb followed him in the Boys Under 16, and the event concluded with Australia's Laura Enever winning the Girls Under 18.

Australia pulled off an amazing third consecutive Quiksilver ISA World Junior Surfing Championship title, the fourth gold medal Australia has won out of the six editions of the event. It is quite clear that Aussies are not only dominant in the Pro scene now but look very solid for the future too.

At the awards ceremony, winners' national anthems were sung and the president of the International Surfing Association, Fernando Aguerre, closed the event and welcomed everyone back for Ecuador 2009.

Said Fernando, "What a wonderful week! It was raining cats and dogs an hour before the opening ceremony, but a moment before it began the sun was shining. ISA's karma is very good."

He added, "Surfing is alive and full of energy. One day after tomorrow the Olympic Committee will meet in Athens, and I will be there again fighting for surfing to become an Olympic sport. It's just a matter of time."

Boys 16 winner, Tamaroa McComb. Photo courtesy ISA.

ABOVE: Boys 18 winner Alejo Muniz. Photo courtesy ISA.
BELOW: Girls winner Laura Enever overcome with emotion. Photo courtesy ISA.

Opening ceremony. Photo courtesy ISA.

JUNIOR WORLD CHAMPIONS

Gold: Australia
Silver: Brazil
Bronze: Hawaii
Copper: United States

BOYS UNDER 18

Gold: Alejo Muniz (BRA)
Silver: Owen Wright (AUS)
Bronze: Tyler Newton (HAW)
Copper: Marc Lacomare (FRA)

GIRLS UNDER 18

Gold: Laura Enever (AUS)
Silver: Tyler Wright (AUS)
Bronze: Courtney Conlogue (USA)
Copper: Airini Mason (NZ)

BOYS UNDER 16

Gold: Tamaroa McComb (TAH)
Silver: Peterson Crisanto (BRA)
Bronze: Matty Costa (HAW)
Copper: Ian Fontaine (FRA)

ALOHA CUP

Aloha Cup
1. New Zealand
2. Australia
3. France
4. South Africa

The ISA Masters

By Pablo Zannochi

Women's finalists. Photo courtesy ISA.

*"You don't stop surfing because you grow old;
you grow old because you stop surfing."*

A real surfing celebration took place from March 30 through April 6, in the classic waves of Punta Rocas, for the second edition of the annual ISA World Masters Surfing Championship. With the ASP professional masters tournament on hold since 2003, this is the only world tournament for surfers older than 35 years of age.

More than 100 of the best veteran surfers from 18 different nations came to enjoy the six days of surfing action with waves that were never smaller than six feet.

South Africa walked away again with the World Team Gold Medal, having scored victories in the following divisions: Ladies Masters with Heather Clark, Grand Kahunas with an excellent victory by Chris Knutsen, and Marc Wright prevailing over his fellow countryman Nick Pike in the final thrust.

Juan Ashton of Puerto Rico obtained his second consecutive victory in the Masters division, with Ricardo Toledo of Brazil coming in second, Rob Page of Australia in third place, and Jay Sharpe also from Australia in fourth position.

The championship's grand finale was performed by the Grandmasters. An interesting exchange of good waves deployed by 1988 Pipe Master Robbie Page and defending champion Magoo de la Rosa, who was playing the local card, was breathtaking to all spectators. Seconds before the horn blew, de la Rosa took off on a set wave, but it closed out and that was the end. Robbie Page was watching from the sand and the emotion reduced him to tears. His Peruvian friend congratulated him. Later they celebrated, joined by Jojó de Olivença from Brazil and South Africa's Andre Malherbe, who placed third and fourth respectively.

Apart from the competition, it is important to mention the great camaraderie that reigned among all surfers during the entire event. All participants returned home as winners. What could be better to a surfer than having ten days of perfect waves breaking endlessly and shared with friends from all over the world?

It also became clear how long in life someone can keep up an excellent surfing level. It was really impressive to watch people over 50 surfing like teenagers. What ISA President Fernando Aguerre expressed in his opening and closing statements was fully confirmed: "You don't stop surfing because you get old, but you get old because you stop surfing."

The best over-35-year-old surfers from the world will come together again next year. The location has not been yet established.

Opening ceremony. Photo courtesy ISA.

FINAL TEAM CLASSIFICATION

1. South Africa
2. Australia
3. Brazil
4. Peru

MEDALISTS
MASTERS (OVER 35)

Gold: Juan Ashton (PRC)

Silver: Ricardo Toledo (BRA)

Bronze: Rob Page (AUS)

Copper: Jay Sharpe (AUS)

GRANDMASTERS (OVER 40)

Gold: Rob Page (AUS)

Silver: Magoo de la Rosa (PER)

Bronze: Jojó de Olivença (BRA)

Copper: Andre Malherbe (ZAF)

KAHUNAS (OVER 45)

Gold: Marc Wright (ZAF)

Silver: Nick Pike (ZAF)

Bronze: Jorge Posso (PER)

Copper: Rod Baldwin (AUS)

GRAND KAHUNAS (OVER 50)

Gold: Chris Knutsen (ZAF)

Silver: Paco del Castillo (PER)

Bronze: Frank Hayter (AUS)

Copper: René González (PRC)

LADIES MASTERS (OVER 35)

Gold: Heather Clark (ZAF)

Silver: Rocío Larrañaga (PER)

Bronze: Sandra English (AUS)

Copper: Briggite Mayer (BRA)

ABOVE: Robbie Page. BELOW: Tortura demonstration, opening ceremony. Photos courtesy ISA.

ISA Regional Roundup
By Pablo Zannochi

‹ISA›

Africa

On the African continent, ISA saw major progress every single day of 2008. Senegal joined the NGBs group, after its debut participation in the World Junior Surfing Championship with two excellent surfers.

South Africa, the continent's major surfing power, had an excellent year in international competition, winning the ISA World Masters Surfing Championship for the second year in a row, and seventh place at the Quiksilver ISA World Junior Surfing Championship and the ISA World Surfing Games.

At the same time, South Africa placed four athletes on the ASP World Tour: from youngest to oldest, Jordy Smith, Ricky Basnett, Royden Bryson and Travis Logie.

ISA has its eye on where it wants to attain more National Governing Bodies in Africa. To date, members are Cape Verde Islands, Ivory Coast, Morocco, Namibia, Senegal and South Africa.

Australasia

Australasia's highlight of the year—and one of the most important for the surfing world—was the inclusion of Surfing in the First Asian Beach Games that took place in Bali, Indonesia, in October.

Japan, Maldives, Indonesia, Vietnam and Philippines made their first surfing appearances within the Olympic Movement. The home team won the medal tally.

On the other hand, one must also highlight the almost perfect performance of Australia in the International Surfing Association events this year. The Aussies won the Quiksilver ISA World Junior Surfing Championship and the ISA World Surfing Games and placed second at the ISA World Masters Surfing Championship.

Europe

The evolution of European surfing could be plainly seen during 2008 in the number of surfers joining the ASP World Tour, like Tiago Pires (POR), Mikael Picon (FRA) and Aritz Aramburu (SPA), but also we noted their ability and interest in organizing ISA championships.

Two of the three main 2008 ISA events were carried out in Europe: the Quiksilver ISA World Junior Surfing Championship, in Seignosse, France, and the ISA World Surfing Games in Costa de Caparica, Portugal.

These events, together with the excellent performance of their outstanding surfers, prove that Europe has become a new world-level surfing power.

South America

South America also showed enormous growth during 2008. Peru, with its great surfing tradition, managed to be present at all ISA events with a complete team, and was the best representative of the region at all events. It was positioned fourth in the Masters, ninth in the Juniors and eleventh at the World Surfing Games.

The ISA World Masters Surfing Championship was held on the Peruvian coasts in a week of big and perfect waves at the legendary Punta Rocas, that saw the best over-35 surfers competing for the greatest honor that a veteran surfer can attain.

The administration carried out by the Argentinean Surfing Federation is also worth mentioning, since after several years of incomplete teams, the country managed to participate in all the year's events with a full team.

One must also underline the work carried out by the Ecuadorian Surfing Federation that won the application process to be host of the Quiksilver ISA World Junior Surfing Championship. Thus, South America will hold once again a world event in its region.

Beginning a long walk towards having surfing at the Olympic Games, Uruguay, a country with a long sport tradition, will seed the First South American Beach Games (ODESUR). Surfing will be one of the ten official sports in the event that will take place on the beaches of Montevideo and Punta del Este in early December 2009.

Furthermore, Brazil followed the path it has trod over the last several years, obtaining second place in the Junior World Championship, third in the Masters as well as the World Surfing Games.

BELOW and LEFT: The joy of representing your country. Photos courtesy ISA.

Central America and the Caribbean

A country in Central America and the Caribbean zone that set people talking in 2008 was surely Costa Rica. Their athletes managed to write their names in the books of world surfing history by obtaining a historic fifth place in the overall team ranking in the World Surfing Games, and were left without the copper medal by a mere point in more than 11,000.

The Costa Rican feat was built on a basis of consistency, teamwork and a surfing level that has grown exponentially in the last ten years. Of the six best Open category surfers, two were Costa Rican:

Jason Torres (5th) and Luis Vindas (6th); while on the ladies side, Nataly Bernold achieved a 6th position.

A fifth place in the general team's position was an outstanding result and the best-ever performance of a Central American and Caribbean country.

We must also draw attention to the effort by the Costa Rican Surf Federation, which won the application process to host the Billabong World Surfing Games 2009. Central America will consequently host their first world championship ever.

Finally, we must also highlight the performance of Puerto Rico in 2008, obtaining two gold medals in ISA events. Legendary Juan Ashton won his

second World Masters consecutive title in Peru, while Natasha Sagardia obtained her first medal for her country in a World Surfing Games after winning the gold medal in Ladies Bodyboard.

North America / United States

After Surfing America was created and subsequently recognized by ISA as the National Governing Body of U.S. surfing, Team USA managed a considerable success in the rankings of each one of the main ISA events carried out in 2008.

The U.S. team came from nineteenth place in the 2004 WSG held in Ecuador, to a third place in Huntington 2006, consolidating a second place in Portugal 2008, including the gold medal in the Open category, courtesy of CJ Hobgood. This team also boasted World Tour surfer Ben Bourgeois, and won the teams Gold Medal.

In the Juniors, Surfing America made a similar effort and placed its major stars in the Quiksilver ISA World Junior Surfing Championship, thus obtaining, since 2004, a place among the first five.

It's clear that the United States is back and shows its best weapons during all ISA events, based in good management and fundraising.

Mexico

The Mexican Surfing Federation has had a new board of directors since mid-2008. They were in charge of organizing the first professional surfing circuit ever carried out in Mexican history, as well as completing a national circuit that classified the best athletes to the World Surfing Games with a complete team.

Two greats of the ISA—president Fernando Aguerre and founder Eduardo Arena. Photo courtesy ISA.

Alizée Arnaud. Photo courtesy ISA.

Features

No Shortage of Surfers:
Why Are Shapers Crying the Blues?

By Paul Holmes

Painting by Vincenzo Ganadu

Unless you're a lonely soul surfer out on an isolated frontier like Iceland or Kodiak Island, Alaska, you've probably noticed that surfing continues to grow in popularity and local lineups are more crowded than ever.

With more and more surfers taking to the waves, why are surfboard shapers from Newquay to Noosa crying into their Friday-night beer because business is so bad? And just how bad is it?

In California, still a bellwether market, surfboard builders' sales are down 20 to 30 percent this year alone. A random survey of established makers, both large and small, around the world confirms that surfboard sales lately have been flat at best to dismally in decline. The reason? "It's the economy, stupid." But while board builders agree that tough times are a factor, almost all offer another major impact: cheap imports from China. Globalization bites back—even in the surfboard business.

"Sales are off about 60 percent from their 2004 peak," says Bill Bahne, chairman of the Board Builders Committee at the U.S.–based Surf Industry Manufacturers Association. "Companies are feeling the pinch of large retail inventories, mainly foreign-made products, clogging up the shops. There's no rack space for local manufacturers. Boards aren't selling through quickly, so those importer guys are dropping their prices even more so they can clear out their inventories. Our guys can't afford to do that. Our materials costs are going up and there's not that much profit; we're operating on bare bones margins, basically just working for wages. Sure, people are getting cheaper boards, but it's hurting the American manufacturer." It's the same story all over the world, Bahne says, and it's likely to be another bad year to come.

In the U.S., the rot began to set in with Clark Foam's sudden exit from the surfboard blank business in December 2005. Clark had so dominated polyurethane foam production in America that it was a virtual monopoly. When Clark quit, surfboard shapers from labels large and small were left scrambling for their essential raw material. True, the global marketplace responded relatively quickly with imported foam blanks shipped into the U.S. from Europe, South Africa and Australia. And foam makers raced to start up new blank factories both in California and just over the border in Mexico, where environmental controls were more lenient and labor costs lower. But that all took time—in ordering, production and shipping blanks from overseas and in establishing the infrastructure of new facilities with molds, permits, chemical suppliers, production methods and more.

Traditional handcraft surfboard makers ground to a halt or embarked on the steep learning curve of adapting to the "new" construction methods using polystyrene foam and epoxy-based glassing. Meanwhile, established manufacturers of "sandwich" construction polystyrene and epoxy boards like SurfTech and Global Surf Industries (GSI) stepped in fast to fill the void. They were soon followed by opportunistic entrepreneurs making traditional style polyurethane/polyester boards that were machine milled and hand finished in China—under the instruction and tutelage of Australian and American surfboard industry experts quick to make a buck as partners or consultants. Unlike the name shaper-designed sandwich boards made under license in Thailand, such boards didn't have the cachet of a master shaper or a well-known logo, but they had two impossible to ignore advantages: they were well made (computer-driven cutting tools don't have off-form days and the techniques of glassing and finishing can be taught to keen workers anywhere) and they offered retailers a low-cost board with a bigger profit margin.

Even big companies like SurfTech are feeling the pressure. "Our boards are available pretty much everywhere there's surf," says founder, Randy French. "The domestic U.S. is our most difficult market right now, but sales are up in Hawaii, so that's a bright spot for us." Even so, he says, the downturn is "affecting everyone." The economy, and a barrage of negative news, he says, leads people to freeze up and just stop buying anything that's nonessential. But, he adds, what's affecting the surfboard business is a combination of factors: "The ease of duplication and the fact that China has gotten really good at it, that's some of it. Also, the biggest true negative ramification of Clark's closing, and all the publicity that received, attracted investors and business people to become board makers—people who don't surf making non-shaper boards under made-up brands with very aggressive pricing. They brought in container loads and when their warehouses were overstocked, they just started dumping to liquidate inventory."

Surfboard buyers, meanwhile, could be excused for feeling confused. In the post-Clark era, they were faced with all kinds of unfamiliar options: EPS and epoxy? Brands they'd never heard of? Untested foam companies? In 2006 and 2007 many potential buyers decided to wait and see, fix up a few dings, swap out their fin setups, even try one of those "molded" jobs from Thailand, even if their local shaper had been decrying them as "pop-outs"—pretty much anything to avoid ordering a new board until they felt more confident about their choice. And then the global economy began circling the drain. When it came to surfboards, price apparently became the biggest issue for those in the market.

So what does this mean for the custom-built, handcrafted surfboard and the surfers who ride them? Are we witnessing the beginning of the end? Will skilled and experienced surfboard shapers go the way of wheelwrights and tinsmiths? Will computer numeric cutting (CNC) machines take the place of artists and artisans? Will software determine the next wave of design, rather than the face-to-face dialog between shapers and surfers?

Probably not, or at least not entirely, although the handcrafted board business faces some serious challenges according to most experienced industry insiders. From production, to marketing, to remaining competitive in an era of outsourced everything and tough times economically, surfboard builders everywhere are having to rethink how they've been doing things. There's already been fallout in the U.S. as a result. Faced with declining production, glassing shops have been closing up or merging, and laying off workers as contracts from high-volume producers have been curtailed.

"Shaping machines are a great tool," says Rusty Priesendorfer, whose San Diego–based R-dot logo has been seen on the boards of many top pros during the past 20-plus years. "On the one hand, machines make it possible for me not to have to spend every day in the shaping room, turning out the same 6' 2" thruster over and over again, and instead focus on the special needs of a team rider or the next little refinement in design. On the other hand, machines and computer scanning has made it very easy for anyone to copy a design that I, or others like me, have spent years developing. Any businessman who wants to make a buck out of surfing can walk into a surf shop, buy a

Bing Surfboards designed for YOU!

BING SURFBOARDS

Come in or write for mail order information NO DEALERS PLEASE
1820 Pacific Coast Highway / Hermosa Beach, California / Call FRontier 2-1248

Early Bing advertisement. Photo courtesy Think Bing by Paul Holmes.

board, have it scanned and set up a factory in China churning them out under some made-up label."

Priesendorfer, of course, knows of what he speaks. His company, along with Al Merrick's Channel Islands, Matt Biolas's . . . Lost and Australian John Stevenson's JS label have been among the world's most successful surfboard companies in recent years. At their premium level, all these shapers do custom orders for top team riders and clients willing to spend good money for face time with a master designer-shaper. Machine-milled shapes offer retailers a way to stock exact replicas of their work for customers walking in off the street. These stock boards are handcrafted in every way except one: if the master shaper laid hands on the board at all it was only to give it a blessing of quality control.

"I think that the years of surfboard companies having production runs of 5,000 or 10,000 boards may be over with the exception of one or two players," says Priesendorfer. "I understand that retailers want better margins because they are struggling too. But mostly what I want is to keep doing the custom work." Somewhere there's a solution, he says. "The main thing is that all of us do this because we love it, it's a lifestyle. In 10 or 15 years perhaps macro-economics will level the playing field, get the non-surfing businessmen out of the game as China's economy grows, their labor costs go up and there are more controls over their pollution issues, just like we have here in California. I know it goes against the current free market ideology, but perhaps even tariffs and protectionism will get more play in the economy." And, he adds, "Retailers are asking me why we can't make our stock boards in China, so that the shops can still make their margins at prices their customers are willing to pay. It's something I really have to consider, and we're already doing it for some boards going to Japan."

Meanwhile, over in England, Nigel Semmens is wrestling with the same problems. His Ocean Magic surfboard sales are off by 50 percent this year and 65 percent down from a 2006 peak. And he attributes most of that decline to "cheap boards from China." Says Semmens, "I think we need to all look after our local markets and stick together as surfboard manufacturers rather than fighting each other with silly little politics. This way we may still be here in 10 years time to shape boards for our surfers and not have boards made in China by people who have never surfed or even seen the sea. This is just not what surfing is all about."

From Newcastle, Australia, four-time world champion Mark Richards offers another perspective on the downturn. With groceries and fuel prices "out of control," he says the economy is a major factor, and in hard times most customers view a new surfboard as a luxury item. But, he adds, "The surfboard industry shot itself in the foot a few years back by trying to convince surfers that they all needed 18" wide, 2" thick, concave-bottom thrusters just like top pros were riding. A lot of recreational surfers got stitched up with boards they just couldn't ride. We're only now coming out of that with retro-twins, fishes and other hybrids. Shapers are finally giving recreational surfers something they can have fun on. But that bad experience made many people hesitant about shelling out $700 or $800 for their next board, because it's recreational surfers who pay full price for their boards, not the team riders and pros. Once you add to that a bad summer and a really cold winter, like we had in Australia, surfboard sales are down."

Allan Byrne of Burning Spears also in Australia has already made the adjustment. Although he has had the opportunity and reputation to be a big brand in the global marketplace, and once was, he decided to take his surfboard business back to its roots. "I decided it just wasn't worth it," he says." I've gone back more or less to the way I started, making 10

Are Surfboards Too Expensive?

A comparison of custom surfboard prices from 1965 and 2008 shows some remarkable similarities—and some stark differences. Just for the exercise, we took 1965 price lists from Bing Surfboards, Hobie Surfboards and Dewey Weber Surfboards and adjusted them to current dollar values. The result? The price of a board today is almost 20 percent less. "There was never any money in it," said pioneer and veteran Hobie Alter recently. "People only did it to support their surfing lifestyle." The more things change, the more they stay the same, it seems: handcrafted surfboard makers today are operating on much smaller profits and margins than they were more than four decades ago.

In 1965, the era of makers selling stock boards at wholesale to retail surf shops was in its infancy. Most board makers ran factories that had a showroom out front and production in back—everything from shaping to polishing was done in-house. Most boards sold were showroom stock or custom orders fetching full retail price. Wholesale boards sold to dealers at lower margins were just icing on the production cake, keeping the mill churning. A custom order, by contrast, meant a surfer could talk to the shaper, describe his or her unique needs and desires, select a stringer configuration for the glue-up, stipulate color for the glass and gloss job, even tell the laminator where they'd like the logo placed.

Fast forward 40 years and the scene is very different. First up, few surfboard companies have a showroom and custom orders are no longer the mainstay of the business, so full-price retail sales are but a small part of most labels' income stream. Wholesale prices, set to meet buyer demands based on comparisons to the price tags on China-based boards, have led to razor-thin profit margins for manufacturers and retailers alike. Oh, and did we mention that in the freewheeling days of the '60s there were few legal requirements on minimum wages, worker health hazards, waste disposal, and other costly and time-consuming issues of compliance for modern board builders? Or that oil back then was the equivalent of $20 per barrel and so materials like resin and fiberglass—petro-based and needing lots of energy to produce—were comparatively far less expensive than they are today?

But also consider this: in 1965, boards were much heavier, but also commensurately stronger. Surfers back then very rarely broke boards except in extreme big-wave conditions. Today, it's commonplace. Even if not broken, modern lightweight shortboards made in the traditional way have a lifespan of a few months, or a year at most, of regular surfing. Such boards are constructed at the lowest limits of the strength-weight ratio of their materials. Boards from the mid-sixties, by contrast, are still around, bought and sold among collectors, and there'd be even more of them had not so many of them been stripped of glass and re-shaped by shortboard revolutionaries at the decade's end.

Surfboards makers say that surfboards prices today are artificially low, that they've suppressed inflationary increases in part because they know that today's lightweight boards have a limited life and they counted on more frequent repeat business to keep them in business. Chinese-made boards have thrown a monkey wrench in that works. In Southern California, for example, such a board can be bought on the Internet for as little as $280 to $375. And that wouldn't even cover the raw costs of making an similar board locally.

Seen in this light, a locally made board is a bigger bargain now than ever before.

BING SURFBOARDS
1820 Pacific Coast Highway
Hermosa Beach, California
FRontier 2-1248

PRICE LIST

Up to 9'	$120.00
9'1" to 9'6"	125.00
9'7" to 10'	130.00
10'1" to 11'	140.00
11'1" to 12'	150.00

KATAMACAVE SHAPE .... $10.00 EXTRA

ABOVE PRICES INCLUDE YOUR CHOICE OF:

"T" Band - Reverse "T" Band - Foam "T" Band
or ¾" Redwood .... Center Strip
Laminated Black Walnut or Cured Foam .... Tail Block
Laminated White Glass, Black Glass, or Black Walnut
with ½" Glass Bead .... Fin
All Bing Surfboards are built of Clark isophthalic polyester foam, and two layers of 10 oz. fiberglass cloth impregnated with light stabilized isophthalic resin.

EXTRAS

Balsa Strips, (per inch)	$ 3.00
Additional Redwood Strips, (each)	6.00
One Color Design	10.00
Each Additional Color	3.00

MAIL ORDERS

Free shipping to any location in California; $10.00 shipping charge to all other states of the United States.
A minimum of $25.00 deposit* is required on all mail orders.

ACCESSORIES

Decals	10¢, 15¢ and 30¢
Sew-On Patches	60¢
"T" Shirts	$2.25
Wet-Suits - All Sizes	$25.00

* DEPOSITS CAN NOT BE REFUNDED

Dexter Color California, Inc., 3460 Wilshire Blvd., Los Angeles, Calif. 90005
585-C

Courtesy Think Bing by Paul Holmes.

boards a week with one other guy, doing all the work ourselves. I can make a better living doing what I love making custom boards. I don't have the stress and I have more time to surf."

Byrne is not the only one around the world who is retrenching. On both sides of the Pacific surfboard makers who'd once striven for growth via increased production volumes using shaping machines and outsourced glassing are having to readjust to the new market realities. Says veteran shaper Gary Linden, "I see labels, myself included, going back to smaller runs, having fewer workers and doing all the work ourselves. With margins being so slim you make the same amount of money by doing five or 10 boards a week as you did trying to make 50 boards. People do this for the lifestyle, not the money, and that won't ever change."

So is there any silver lining to the dark clouds hanging over the surfboard building business? Despite the challenges, perhaps surprisingly, the answer is yes. Firstly, in the spurt of creativity that followed Clark Foam's demise, the international surfboard blank business has become much more diversified, leading to greater competition and, by extension, proactive and ongoing development of improved foam. Secondly, the post-Clark aftermath has opened minds to new technologies in surfboard construction, especially in the realm of EPS/epoxy boards and handmade "compsand" (composite sandwich) boards. Thirdly, the rapid rise of interest in stand up paddle (SUP) surfing and racing has been a boon for many board builders.

For the makers of high-end sandwich boards in Thailand once derided as "pop-outs" there's been a shift in perception among many surfers and even die-hard traditionalist board makers, who are now perhaps reluctantly recognizing that "they" are not the problem since their boards tend to be priced in the high end of the retail range. SurfTech's French, for one, is gratified. "We always resented being lumped in as an offshore manufacturer," says French. "We have always supported shapers and paid them well for every board sold of models that carry their name. As a business practice we've always resisted dumping and discounts, except when we've had to be creative about some models we just had too many of."

Finally, for anyone (like this writer) who attended the 2008 Sacred Craft Consumer Surfboard Expo in Del Mar, California, last October it was hard not to be impressed with the resilience and creativity of the 70-plus board builders who were showing their wares to a general public that is usually shut out of industry insider trade shows. With two shaping bays offering demonstrations of the craft and contests among some of the most skilled foam mowers in the business, it offered a fascinating, real-time insight to regular Joes and Josettes as to what really goes into creating that work of functional art we refer to all too glibly as a "stick."

Also much in evidence was the work of solo artisans making beautiful and functional boards out of wood—complex constructions with an aesthetic that was reassuring to those who thought the era of skillfully crafted boards was coming to a close. Hobbyists? Perhaps. But don't forget that it was in backyard board building during the 1970s—another troubled time of recession—where many of today's design gurus honed their chops.

It was glassing expertise, though, that impressed most informed viewers at Sacred Craft. Superbly executed, cut-lap resin tints, colorful abstract art laminations, even design-your-own lightweight fabric prints that can be incorporated into any surfer's custom board, all added up to an overall impression that surfboard makers are responding to hard times with a renewed level of creative energy. The message to their customers is clear: you may pay a little more, maybe even twice as much as some bargain basement Chinese import, but we'll make you a better board that will get you stoked—and those in the know will recognize that your ride is the surfboard equivalent of a Lamborghini or Ferrari, not a Hyundai or Kia.

With so much going on in new materials and all that passion and creativity at work in handmade surfboards, there can still be a bright future for the industry. Now the question is, will surfers see its value?

The impact of the economic meltdown wasn't just the biggest surf industry story of the year: it was the *only* story.

Of course, this is not the first time that economic events beyond their direct control had adversely affected the big surfwear brands and their retailers—in recent history think 9/11, the diabolical rockabilly summer of '91, when no-brand white tees ruled and pollution closed beaches, and the Wall Street crash of '87—and when the big guys sneeze, the entire industry catches cold. But, even when the equities markets staged a comeback in late 2007 and it seemed for a minute like the sub-prime crisis was a storm in a teacup—even back in those innocent days of just a year ago there were significant differences

company president Bernard Mariette. Mariette, formerly a sales executive with L'Oreal and Timberland, was headhunted by Quiksilver in the mid-'90s to oversee the growth of its recently acquired European licensee. The sometimes charismatic, always ebullient Frenchman was, rightly or wrongly, given much of the credit for Quiksilver's dramatic growth in Europe through the late '90s, and in the wake of the post-9/11 downturn in the U.S., was promoted to global president. By 2004 he had consolidated his authority enough to unveil a grand plan to double Quiksilver's revenue almost overnight through the acquisition of Rossignol. Quiksilver's board lapped it up.

But Rossignol was deeply in debt and had not turned a profit in a decade.

Annus Horribilis

By Phil Jarratt

It was the best of times, the worst of times . . . all in 12 frickin' months!

between this calamity and those that have preceded it.

For one thing, Gordon Gecko and '80s junk bonds are like child's play compared with the shitstorm we are now suffering as a result of a generation of corporate greed and stupidity. For another thing, the surf industry can no longer throw its hands up and say, hey, we're just surf dudes so let's just surf until the storm blows through and the market glasses off. The surf sector might still be but a blip on the radar of big business, but our big brands are as culpable in this mess as the next multi-national corporate sausage machine, paying the honchos and buddies too much and investing in the future too little. And while America's two biggest surf retailers, Pacific Sunwear and Zumiez, took a lot of heat for their seriously diminishing returns in 2008, the biggest hurt was reserved for surf's biggest manufacturer.

Long-time industry leader Quiksilver, Inc., announced in November the finalization of the sale of its Rossignol snow brand to Chartreuse & Mont Blanc (a company majority-owned by Australia's troubled investment bank Macquarie Group) for $37 million cash. But the severing of a poisoned limb was no cause for celebration. Quiksilver bought the iconic but ailing French ski brand in 2005 for $560 million and subsequently invested a fortune in servicing its debt, streamlining its outmoded hardware production and in global infrastructure to establish it as Quiksilver's entrée card to the much bigger market segment known as "outdoors." But for surf's biggest brand, the great outdoors proved to be a little chillier than expected.

The problems of integration of the brand into the Quiksilver family were immediately apparent, but the Quiksilver board persevered with the strategy, hemorrhaging money all the while, largely because of its faith in the strategy's architect,

Quiksilver had to turn it around while implementing a major cultural shift—away from surf—within its core company. The monumental task proved beyond them. By the beginning of 2008, Quiksilver's debt had ballooned fivefold to more than $1 billion from less than $200 million in 2004. Mariette departed in February and Rossignol followed in November, but at such a paltry cash price that credit rater Moody's gave Quiksilver a junk bond rating as its shares slid below a dollar and short-term debt became due for refinancing.

The unthinkable had happened. Bullet-proof Quiksilver was on its knees, and if it could happen at the top, it could happen anywhere. That was the salutary lesson of 2008. And why had it happened? The deepening of the global financial crisis and the credit squeeze of the second half of 2008 were certainly factors, but the life-threatening malaise was the giant leap from boardriding into the unknown universe of outdoors. Despite the company's claims that it had saturated existing markets so much that it had no choice, the fact is that Quiksilver has not conquered snow and only the 2004 acquisition of DC Shoes has given it real cred in skate. Quiksilver had other growth options, but it chose to take the scary leap and suffered the consequences.

Conversely, the big corporations who bought into surf, notably Nike and VF Corporation, fared relatively well in 2008. Nike's lead brand, Hurley, acquired in 2004, recorded its best ever results in the first quarter of 2008, with revenues increasing 33 percent, according to its parent company. This seems like a lot in a tough economy, but in fact even the strugglers (like Quiksilver) were helped enormously by the dive in the US dollar increasing the value of their export sales in Europe and Asia.

VF Corporation, the thriving brand stable that is home to Reef and Vans,

keeps its internal sales numbers cleverly disguised, but the company overall defied the downturn and seemed certain to post excellent numbers in its surf and skate division. And, as SIMA chairman emeritus Dick Baker told a seminar in October, "Everybody freaked out when VF entered [the surf industry] but they're solid citizens and they're doing the right things with their brands."

Of the other major brands, Billabong probably enjoyed the best 2008, due to its sound management strategies of vertical growth through the acquisition of manageable and culturally fitting companies to fill in gaps in their product offering or increase their retail reach—Da Kine in August was the fifth acquisition in 12 months, but they did take a few hits, like everyone else. In the U.S. they backed out of opening a high-cost retail store in Chicago and in Australia went to court to try to recover $600,000 from failed retailer Brothers Neilsen. Still, there are some brands that would be quite happy to have problems of that ilk this year. The brand reported a 5.5 percent lift in full-year net profit to June 30, to $A176.4 million off revenue of $A1.3 billion. Said CEO Derek O'Neill: "It is a pleasing result, but [with 80 percent of revenue offshore] we would have liked to have a lower Australian dollar." O'Neill got his wish. The Aussie had dropped 30 percent against the greenback by December.

Rip Curl, meanwhile, continued in its quiet way to add value for its private shareholders, issuing a special dividend of $A34 million. A prominent member of the brand's business-savvy board, National Australia Bank CEO Ahmed Fahour, increased his investment in the company by $A1.8 million. At the shopfront, the Curl kept up its solid and respected product offering, while marketing received a huge boost from having dual Aussie world champions Mick Fanning and Steph Gilmore as a double act, and the Search World Tour event in Bali demonstrated

Rip Curl's commitment to support of its strategic neighbors.

In the U.S. Volcom had a tough year, with a flagging share price and internal problems most out of character for the happy, hippie troupe that Richard Woolcott had led for years, with Wooly vacating the president's chair in July. The brand also had serious inventory problems by year's end, with retail business on both U.S. coasts and in Europe decidedly down. And while U.S. retailer Pacific Sunwear had its own share of problems, it also seemed to be the answer to Volcom's, with sales to PacSun increasing by an enormous 80 percent.

In Europe, Headworx went bust, while Oxbow made its long-anticipated run on the American market at precisely the worst possible time, although this didn't stop the French brand from capitalizing on its World Longboard Title finale in San Clemente.

In Australia, leading retail chain Brothers Neilsen, held together by a rescue mission 18 months before, finally collapsed after more than 35 years. Devastated founder Paul Neilsen toughed it out as he had always done as a pro surfing champion in the 1970s, blaming no one but himself. Nevertheless, the shock waves and fallout filled the blogs for months, with the Australian surfing public divided as to whether the creditors—in large part, the "big three" of Quiksilver, Billabong and Rip Curl—should be hostile or sympathetic. In Billabong's case, as noted earlier, it was the former. Meanwhile struggling Globe pulled out of its World Tour event in Fiji – perhaps not the last $2-million event to fade away from the World Tour— while angry shareholders began to ask questions about the management style of the founding Hill brothers.

Also apparently on the ropes, with its advertizing and real estate disappearing in tandem, was Cult Industries, the brainchild of former Billabong heavy Doug Spong. Cult headquarters in Burleigh Heads, a cathedral-like edifice designed to dwarf its neighbors, Billabong and Rip Curl, was the first to be put on the market. Cult's high-profile Main Street, Huntington Beach retail store soon followed. The pony-tailed entrepreneur was tight-lipped about the future of the brand.

Despite, or perhaps because of, the prevailing doom and gloom, new and young brands continued to surface, and yesterday's new brands, like RVCA, continued to thrive. Insight, an Aussie-based board brand re-invented as edgy apparel in the U.S. by former surf journalist Jesse Faen, won best advertising campaign and breakthrough brand at the SIMA Summit, but the brand's strengths went beyond smoke and mirrors. Faen and his team managed to create a new and exciting twist on the art/music/ surf axis, much as Volcom had done a decade earlier and Gotcha had done a decade before that, and to back it with quality product. While Insight continued to fight for shelf space in an ever-introspective market, their support base grew stronger where it counts.

Like Oxbow, Australia's Rhythm could have chosen a better time for its run on the American market, but it still managed to make inroads on the trade show circuit and achieve placement with core retailers. Currently the "it" brand in Australia, Rhythm is looking to achieve similar status in global markets through its fun approach to the surf lifestyle. It has a long way to go, but watch this space.

In an interesting twist on the conventional wisdom, in May Hurley founder Bob Hurley used his keynote address to the annual Surf Industry Manufacturers Association Summit in Los Cabos, Mexico, to turn the "grow the pond" thesis on its head. Grow the Pond, a catch-cry launched by Quiksilver's Bob McKnight at the Summit several years earlier, was a call to the industry to circle the wagons and help each other's growth to prevent the invading hordes of non-surf corporations from taking over.

Hurley, who now works for Nike, put forth the astounding success of Hollister Co. as evidence that surf cred meant very little to the consumer. Bring it on, was his central message, and let the customers sort out who is worthy of support.

Hollister Co., meanwhile, went from strength to strength in the malls of America, ambushing much of PacSun's market while climbing to revenues of $1.6 billion at the end of 2007. Not bad for a brand invented by Abercrombie & Fitch CEO Michael Jeffries in 2000, in response to his company's difficulties capturing the affluent, young, coastal market. Where the existing brands, such as O'Neill, Rip Curl and Quiksilver, had genuine and colorful histories dating back half a century, Jeffries simply borrowed the name of a private surf break and made his history up—something about a "Pacific merchant" named JM Hollister who founded the company in 1922, not that it mattered much to the consumers who fell in love with the slick, club-like retail template.

As *Transworld Business* magazine noted in an in-depth coverage of Hollister mid-year, the genuine surf industry can scream hoax as much as they like, but the truth is that Hollister is successful because they have very deep pockets ($10 million investment in flat screens in 2007 so that their 450 stores can display Huntington Beach surf conditions all over the country) and they are simply better at retailing than traditional surf retailers.

No one in the surf industry seems to have an answer to the Hollister steamroller, but one thing seems certain: the company's profits are not going to be ploughed back into surfing anytime soon. And as the tough times drag on, we seem likely to see the World Tour turn into a nightmare for the ASP (although the Big Three have promised ongoing support) and massive spending cutbacks affect industry support of the sport and culture of surfing across the board.

In fact, it's already happening, and ironically the brand that led the way with big money sponsorships and daring event strategies for more than two decades is leading the way again. Late in the year Quiksilver announced its withdrawal from most of its Australian event sponsorships, although the cost-heavy Quiksilver Pro Gold Coast was spared for 2009.

The author is a former Quiksilver executive and a shareholder in Quiksilver, Volcom and Billabong.

Bernard Mariette (left) and Bob McKnight outside Quiksilver's Huntington Beach HQ, 2003. Photo Maurice Rebeix.

Who Are We?
The Surfersvillage Global Consumer Survey

In 2008 Surfervillage, the world's leading surfing news website, gave its regular visitors around the world the opportunity to participate in the first truly global consumer survey of surfers. While many found answering the 50 detailed questions a hard task in the era of SMS speak and sound bites, several thousand respondents answered some of the questions and almost 600 completed the full questionnaire. A full analysis of the results is in progress, but we cherry-picked the responses to present a fascinating snapshot of the 2008 surfer.

What makes you happy? Surfing, of course. A bit of a no-brainer to start with, but we were pleasantly surprised to find that today's surfers are almost as happy amongst friends and family. While surfing accounted for 41%, family/friends was a close second with 34%. Finding love came in equal third with achievement at 12%, while 10% said they were happiest when having fun (whatever that might entail) and 9.7% said the natural environment made them joyful.

WHAT MAKES YOU HAPPY?	
Surfing	41%
Family/Friends	34%
Love	12%
Achievement	12%

WHERE DO YOU LIVE?	
With parents	15.5%
Rent	47.8%
Own	36.7%

HOW MUCH DO YOU EARN?	
Less than $US 50,000	57%
$US 50-100,000	28%
More than $US 100,000	15%

While a high number of student responses skewed our overall figures for income and home ownership, it is quite clear that a significant percentage of today's surfers have considerable discretionary income. More than 40% claimed that they spent more than $US 100 a month on surfing products and 17% claimed they spent more than $US 500. Average number of surfboards owned was an astounding 5.3, with many claiming double-digit quivers.

The evidence was that these boards actually got used,

FAVORITE SURFER?	
Kelly Slater	63%
Tom Curren	6%
Mick Fanning	5%
Layne Beachley	3.5%
Mark Occhilupo	2.2%

FAVORITE SURFING DESTINATION?	
Indonesia/Bali	26%
Hawaii	20%
Australia	10%
Mexico	6%
France	6%
Maldives	6%

too, with 62% of respondents claiming they surfed at least once a week. No prizes for guessing who their favorite surfer was: Kelly Slater topped the poll with an amazing 63%, with California icon Tom Curren a distant second at 6%. Australia's Layne Beachley was the highest polling woman with 3.5%. Duke Kahanamoku, dead for more than 40 years, still pulled 1.4%, while Irish/Hawaiian surfer George Freeth, dead for nearly a century, score a couple of votes.

FAVORITE SURF BRAND?	
Quiksilver	18%
Rip Curl	16%
Billabong	14%
Volcom	10%
O'Neill	8%

Overall brand preference pretty much went with global market share, although Rip Curl punched way above its weight, and there was significant support for emerging brands like RVCA (6%) and Australia's Rhythm (2%).

BOARDSHORTS?	
Quiksilver/Roxy	28%
Billabong	22%
O'Neill	8%
Hurley/Rip Curl	4%

No clearcut winners here in a diverse field that includes many regional favorites. Only four fairly predictable shoe brands made double digit shares.

FOOTWEAR?	
Nike	10%
Globe	10%
Reef	10%
Vans	10%

EYEWEAR?	
Oakley	16%
Smith	10%
Electric	8%
Von Zipper	6%
Spy	6%
Ray Ban	6%

Perhaps not surprisingly for an on-line survey, all respondents were web-savvy, with a significant number seriously addicted. More than 28% said they spent more than four hours a day on-line, while 34% clocked between two and four hours. What are they doing on-line? Visiting surf sites, of course, for the latest news, for surf conditions and, more and more, to watch live webcasts of surfing events around the world.

HOURS A DAY ON-LINE?	
More than 4	28%
2-4	34%
Less than 2	38%

FAVORITE SURFING WEBSITES?	
Surfersvillage	34%
Surfline	22%
MagicSeaweed	16%
ASP World Tour	8%

HOW OFTEN DO YOU CHECK SURFCAMS AND FORECASTS?	
At least once daily	65.8%
Occasionally	24.0%
Rarely	10.2%

HOW OFTEN DO YOU WATCH SURFING EVENT WEBCASTS?	
Never	14.3%
Occasionally	43.9%
Often	25.0%
Never miss one	16.8%

While event webcasts, accessed either through ASP or sponsor sites are clearly gaining in popularity, there is considerable blue sky to pursue. Forecast sites, both regional and global, appear to have almost saturation market share already, despite heated opposition to them around the blogosphere.

Despite a fairly dire prognosis, old-world media continues to survive, if not thrive, although there are indications that the nexus between websites and print alternatives—like Coastalwatch and Surfing World, Surfers Path and Wetsand—might actually help grow the print market over coming years. The future for the surf vid does not look so rosy.

HOW OFTEN DO YOU BUY A SURFING MAGAZINE?	
Never	8.1%
Rarely	32.0%
Frequently	59.9%

HOW OFTEN DO YOU BUY A SURF DVD?	
Never	21.2%
Rarely	60.8%
Frequently	18.0%

PREFERRED CELLULAR PHONE?	
Nokia	34%
Motorola	12%
Sony Erickson	8%
Samsung	8%

PREFERRED CAR?	
Toyota	24%
VW	12%
Subaru	6%
Mitsubishi	4%

Beyond their brand preferences, we also wanted to find out a little about the hopes and fears of today's surfers, and how they were responding to the challenging times. By and large we discovered their hearts were in the right places, although desire for change hadn't necessarily translated into action . . . yet. Often, too, a key word was used to create several different causal associations, making interpretation difficult.

GREATEST FEAR?	
Environmental disaster	23%
Ignorance	15%
War	10%
Global warming	8%
Old age/infirmity	7%

ARE YOU A MEMBER OF AN ENVIRONMENTAL GROUP?	
No	60%
Yes	40%
(Surfrider Foundation	14%)

Attitudes to drugs and alcohol seem to have firmed in the negative, perhaps the result of role models like Kelly Slater, or perhaps the result of watching reverse role model Baby Boomer parents grow old and very confused. While alcohol was considered far more socially acceptable than cigarettes or drugs, most who said they used it qualified the admission with "in moderation." Cigarette smoking seems to be almost universally condemned in the surfing world now, with many respondents finding it "disgusting" or worse. Recreational drugs such as marijuana still have cells of support, but, again, often with qualifications like "only occasionally." Hard drugs and performance-enhancing drugs have no place in the surfing

lifestyle, our respondents voted overwhelmingly.

DO YOU APPROVE OF ALCOHOL?	
No	14%
Yes, but in moderation	50%
Yes	30%

DO YOU APPROVE OF SMOKING?	
No, it's disgusting	40%
No	48%
Yes	12%

DO YOU APPROVE OF RECREATIONAL DRUGS?	
No	64%
Medical grounds only	2%
Yes	24%

DO YOU APPROVE OF HARD DRUGS?	
No	88.9%
Yes	2.4%

DO YOU APPROVE OF PERFORMANCE-ENHANCING DRUGS?	
No	92%
Yes	6%

Bringing Waves to the World

The World Wide Web has changed the face of surfing forever. Many are the locals' calls out against webcams drawing the attention of the masses to their home breaks, the intrusive apertures murdering the once time-honored tradition of the dawn surf check. But for all the controversy it has raised, this visual technology has given back infinitely more than it has taken.

Over a decade ago, in 1997, Portuguese telephony company Telepac trailed over six kilometers of data cable across Praia Grande Beach to bring the world the first-ever webcast of a surf event. Live images, audio commentary and results were beamed across the planet in what would become the birth of an entirely new technology.

Fast-forward to 2008 and almost every contest, from the highest-rated ASP competition all the way down to local junior events, is being streamed across the web. The most popular World Tour stage, at Pipeline in Hawaii, holds the attention of some 61,000 viewers every second, around one million viewers throughout the event, from as far afield as Siberia and Alaska, as well as the more conventional locations of America, Europe and Australia.

Quite simply, webcast technology has brought surfing to the world, expanding sponsorship viability, raising the sport's profile and generating awareness in a way impossible were it not for the digital ether encompassing the planet.

As the ASP's Al Hunt states concisely, "For the viewers, the general 'wannabe' surfers, it brought surfing to their attention, brought it to their table."

This increase in popularity has been lifeblood for the surfing industry, injecting millions of dollars in revenue into it, giving back to the consumer through increased and continually improved media coverage.

We now have the ability to share with the uppermost echelons of our global surfing community their moments of glory at the precise moment they occur, often thousands of miles from where we sit; the elation on Bobby Martinez' face as he is flung from Mundaka's quayside after winning the 2006 Billabong Pro, Kelly Slater's barrel-enveloped, beer chugging antics at Teahupoo after his extraordinary, perfect, 20-point final heat.

But the glory of webcasts isn't confined to the surf action alone. The ability to have roving cameras throughout contests allows for on-the-spot interviews, surfers still dripping from their last heat, and behind-the-scenes footage that gives the viewer the experience of actually being at the event.

Take Mick Fanning's jubilant victory procession up the beach at Snapper Rocks. The world had watched as young Mick, on home turf, duelled it out with Bede Durbidge in perfect Snapper barrels. But post-surf, we got to share in the jubilant celebrations, wherever we were watching from. We could practically feel the saline spray on our faces, hear the roar of the crowd ringing through our ears, taste the Fosters on our lips—all thanks to the miracle of the webcast.

And in November of 2005, although there was

ASP webcast team. Photo ASP Robertson © Covered Images.

a wealth of action occurring in the Brazilian waves of the Nova Schin Pro, courtesy of Andy Irons and Nathan Hedge, where was the attention focussed? Not on the surfing but squarely upon Kelly Slater's tension-contorted face as he awaited the fate of his closest rival, Irons, and so his own potential World Tour victory.

Webcasts have given us the ability to never miss a beat of the hundreds of surf contests that take place around the globe every year, but they have also assisted in expanding our little subculture exponentially.

Whatever the outcome, webcams have given multifold for those minimal aspects they may have taken, making armchair surfers of us all and allowing us front-row seats at every exotic location, through every blow of every event, everywhere in the world.

The New Waterman

Ride 'em all, as one of the brands suggests. It's also the mantra of a new kind of surfer who takes his inspiration from an old kind of surfer. **Nick Carroll** *reports*

Recently I had one of those odd side-slippy moments—the cultural equivalent of losing a fin in a cutback, when all you thought was normal suddenly takes on a whole new feel.

This happened during a visit to a friend of mine, a former top-ranked professional surfer, a guy with considerable style both in and out of the water, who's always prided himself on staying tuned to high-performance surfing, and equipment too. So what was he into now? Longboard? Retro Fish? Cop-out. No way.

As soon as I walked in the door, he insisted we go stand up paddleboarding. A 14-foot C4 Vortic —a colossal, kayak-like craft—sat on his deck, next to an 11-footer that almost seemed wider than it was long. "Come on!" he insisted. "You can use the big one!"

Within 10 minutes we were in the nearest body of water, SUPing away and discussing the collapse of Western financial systems, when my mate suddenly blurted out, "Guess what? The canoe's gonna be here in a month!"

What the . . . ? Turns out he has purchased a four-man

The New Waterman ethic isn't all macho, but big cojones help. Kerby Brown, Western Australia. Photo Shorty.

Hawaiian-style outrigger canoe. Just like the ones Brian Keaulana and Mel Pu'u steer through the wilds of the Makaha shore dump. It's on its way to Australia in a container, sharing space with a couple of similar craft—one for some of the boys down at Bells, the other for Queensland's surfer-ocean-racer duo Mick Dibetta and Jamie Mitchell.

"Just think," he went on, "when that thing gets here, we can get a crew . . . ride waves . . . learn this the Hawaiian way." About then I had my side-slippy moment and in the midst of it I realized: holy crap, this bloke is no longer just a *surfer*! He's a . . . WATERMAN!

H₂O

Waterman! What a term! What an idea! Redolent of pure machismo, yet oddly innocent, it harks back to a fascinating time in surfing history: the post-war hell-man era, the late 1950s and early 1960s, when wild boys from California and Australia got together with some like-minded locals on Oahu's North and West Shores, and began the seriously unhinged business of kicking Makaha's, Waimea's and Sunset Beach's, and eventually Pipeline's, collective ass.

This was the time of Greg Noll, Buzzy Trent, Jose Angel, Pat Curren and Bob Pike—a time and place when surfing was less refined skill and more just pure invincibility in the face of crazy, overwhelming aquatic challenge. These were the original Watermen—re-forgers of a life not lived since pre-missionary Hawaii. The wild boys built on layers of myth and legend set down by the likes of Tom Blake, Tommy Zahn, the lifeguard movement in California and the Beach Boy act in Hawaii, and the elite skills of Australia's top surfer/lifesavers. They dived for coral and for their dinners, rode the biggest surf they could find, swam for miles through whitewater piles, raced each other on paddleboards, and were generally about as primitively, magnificently Watermale as you could possibly fathom.

Then crowds, shorter boards, and surfing skill arrived, and Watermanliness got the boot. Between 1970 and 1990, the sport of surfing was inhabited almost solely by loose young men between 15 and 30 years of age, pretty much all chasing a singular goal: to be the Best Surfer in the Water. Nobody aspired to much else, and thus for a long time, the surf culture was dominated by the Pro Tour—best of the best, champions in search of a champion. Trying to bung on the Waterman approach in those grommet-infested days . . . well, you'd just look out of date, silly.

But in the past 20 years, as the surfing demographic has broken wide open, the market for identity in surfing has done the same. Today's surf culture is like a closet full of different outfits. The Best Surfer is still a classic cut, but it's constantly being shoved to the back of the rack by newer arrivals. Faux Soul-rider? Mermaid? Air-trick Rebel without a Cause? Zen Eco-Master? Psycho Charger? Venerable Kahuna? What works for you? Pick what you like! Mix and match!

Thus the New Waterman — that old suit, re-cut, refurbished, and dusted off to fit an entirely different day.

Once you're tipped to this trend, you'll find signs of the New Waterman everywhere. In the *Surfer's Journal* garage quiver photos of amazing guys like Dave Kalama, with the ocean racing paddleboard, Hawaiian sling spear, swim fins, seagoing kayak, jet-ski, longboards, shortboards, canoes, SUPs. In the stealthy emergence of labels like C4 Waterman, Honolua, QuiksilverEdition, Kaenon sunglasses, even fringe-dwellers like Patagonia, slowly clustering around the New Waterman image. In the calendar of racing events on California's recently spawned website, paddleboard.com, and in surf mag articles about sea-kayak trips down the northern Cali coast.

You can see it in intriguing, unexpected shifts in surfboard design. Who'd have thought, for instance, that in 2008, one of the biggest underground buzzes would be generated by a re-worked version of a finless wooden surfboard—the alaia—that had lain dormant for over a century? Or that in the same year, there'd actually be an increase in demand for top-of-the-line, custom-ordered, hand-crafted surfboards?

Yet both have occurred, with Noosa-based Californian Tom Wegener even being voted *Surfing* magazine's 2009 Shaper of the Year on the basis of his pawlonia-wood alaia revivals, and uber New Waterman Dave Rastovich riding the boards exclusively for an upcoming Thomas Campbell movie.

On the handcrafted front, veteran shaper/artist Mitchell Rae is just one example; Mitchell's Australia-based Outer Island label has been slammed with dozens of orders for handmade balsa guns—at $3000-plus a pop. "They're not collectors," Rae says of his customers, "they're buying the boards to surf 'em . . . I think they really just want to have a board they can feel really was made just for them."

H₂O

As Mitchell's words imply, New Waterman is essentially about setting yourself apart from the pack. Which doesn't rule out getting together in packs, or even competing, as long as it's suitably select.

The invite-only Quiksilver in Memory of Eddie Aikau is a signal New Waterman event. Indeed, the "Eddie," named as it is in honor of the ultimate Waterman, may have been the first indication of the trend. Yet charging hard on the biggest goddam waves you can find, as balls-out as it is, is not really New Waterman stuff. A New Waterman only rides 30-foot triple sucking slabs as a side-project; his true mission is to wrestle with the forces of the Ocean, to become one with it, in as many ways as are humanly possible.

The undoubted peak of New Watermanliness, the unassailable Everest, then, is Molokai: the QuiksilverEdition Molokai to Oahu Paddleboard Race.

This race, held in late July each year since 1997 and run by indefatigable Sunset Beach surfer-paddler Mike Takahashi, has swiftly become surrounded by its own mythic aura—perhaps best expressed by its own incredible superhero, Australia's Jamie Mitchell, who's won the race a staggering seven times running. "It's not about winning," Jamie tells everyone each year during the pre-race luau, and amazingly, he means it. "It's a journey. Just doing the crossing is enough."

Molokai has given rise to its own semi-secret organization: the 20-30 Club, open only to surfers who've paddled 30 miles or more, straight, under their own steam (i.e., Molokai), and caught a 20-foot wave or bigger, also under their own steam. Takahashi figures the club has had around 50 members, worldwide . . . ever.

Members of this club include surfers who might not be ultra famous but whose names are held in high regard in the world of Watermen: the likes of Brian Keaulana, Buzzy Kerbox, Guy Pere, Clark Abbey, Charlie Walker, Chris Owens, and Dennis Pang, who's been paddleboarding and charging Waimea Bay for two decades or more.

What's the common thread? "It's desire," Dennis reckons. "Not everyone wants to surf big Waimea, and not everyone can imagine paddling across that channel. People are in awe of that effort, because they can see nobody's really doing it for a big reward—guys just want to see if they can do it, make it across without giving up. Same with getting a big wave at the Bay.

"It's a long range thing, both of them, there's a lot of preparation, physically, mentally, spiritually."

H₂O

Which brings us to the biggest difficulty the New Waterman movement faces—being an actual

Waterman is really fricking difficult.

I mean . . . who seriously has the time or the willingness to train up for something like Molokai? Or paddle-in at maxed-out Phantom Reef? Or free-dive 120 feet for your 100-pound tuna supper?

No, if you're gonna be a New Waterman, the task has to be within your grasp. Perhaps this goes some way to explaining the sudden global expansion of SUP—Stand Up Paddleboarding. Put simply, SUP has given the New Waterman movement wings. It's also where—for now at least—the divide between New Waterman and plain ol' surfer is most apparent.

Much is made in the Stand Up world of its apparent roots in Waikiki beachboy surf culture; it's practiced by Dave Kalama, Tom Carroll, Dave Parmenter, Bonga Perkins, Todd Bradley, Brian Keaulana, and Laird Hamilton. In other words, it's got Waterman cred. At the same time,

Master waterman Laird Hamilton sticks it to a Teahupoo barrel. Photo Oxbow/Darrel Wong.

there *is* something almost indefinably dorky about the SUP craze— something that runs astonishingly counter to the bad-boy surf star glamour groove so beloved of surf culture. As a sale sign in a Sydney, Australia, surfboard store recently blared, "Dad needs to get off the couch and lose some weight? Get him a STAND UP PADDLEBOARD."

Among other things, Mark Kelly of Global Surf Industries is an acute spotter of trends. He says SUP distribution has been rapid— unexpectedly so. "Stand-ups are part of what's kept the global surfboard business growing," says Kelly, whose company has shipped thousands of the craft worldwide in 2008.

But many hard-core surfers— unreconstructed Best Surfers by nature—find the SUP irritating almost beyond comprehension. "There's a growing resentment, for sure," says *Surfing* magazine's editor Evan Slater of the generic vibe in perhaps the

world's most trend-driven surf zone, Southern California. "But you can't deny the popularity of it. They're everywhere. Recently at San O they had a big get-together, and there were hundreds of entries."

Evan hasn't taken to the SUP— yet. But, he says, "A lot of guys, friends of mine, are secretly into it— they do it but they don't talk about it. Then there's the guys like Al Merrick, who swear it's changed their lives.

"If you tried to do it at Lowers [Trestles] you'd get heckled out of the water. Those competitive spots with a tradition of high-performance surfing, they can't make inroads there."

He's been somewhat cast as the Anti-SUP surf mag editor after *Surfing* published a rant from a trend-despising contributor. *USA Today* and *CBS News* have been on his case, wanting an explanation of why anybody in surfing would oppose the views of, say, SUP super-pioneer Laird Hamilton.

Evan doesn't see himself that way—indeed, as a qualified Mavericks charger and distance swimmer, he's a bit of a New Waterman in his own right—but he does wonder if SUP might have jumped the shark: "There's something about it that's almost mocking a Hawaiian tradition . . . they're trying to follow it but doing it soooo wrongly. Maybe it's wrong place, wrong time."

H₂O

A simple analysis might end up laying responsibility for this spectacular trend at the feet of Laird Hamilton. After all, Laird is kinda the Kelly Slater of Watermanship. Paddler, SUPer, conqueror of sporting goddesses and 60-foot surf, he's the guy nobody can beat at his own game.

But that's to ignore something bigger even than Laird: long-term

demographic shift.

It's no accident that most of the leaders and followers of the New Waterman trend are males over 35, often heading into their 50s. Many such surfers, unable or unwilling anymore to pursue grommetish levels of high performance, are facing an interesting choice: do more exercise, change the tempo, or give up surfing altogether.

New Waterman gives such surfers a clear identity to pursue—somehow resonating with that old-school Alpha Male Hell-man thing, with its unshakable macho credibility . . . and its convenient focus on things other than raw surfing prowess.

As my Vortice-owning, canoe-importing buddy says, "I can go out for 45 minutes, paddle, keep my fitness up with nothing around me but peace and quiet, and it's on the water. How could anything be wrong with that?"

Who's Bluffing?

H$_2$O

Just about every noted waterman, it seems, has discovered Shipstern's Bluff, Tasmania, Australia, an isolated slab at the bottom of a vast continent. It has become the vague du jour for the hairy-chested crew, with some absolutely epic rides recorded in 2008. None more so than this sequence of Aussie hellman Ryan Hipwood, who survives an airy moment with grace on the face.

H$_2$O

Ryan Hipwood. Photos Rod Owen.

The Emancipation
Surf Culture Comes of Age

You know something's afoot when you can read about an Australian surfer's new novel in the *Times Literary Supplement*, or watch one of the world's greatest classical violinists performing to surfing footage at a series of coastal concerts, or watch politicians hovering for photo opportunities with surf stars at the declaration of the latest "National Surfing Reserve."

I know it's been coming for years, but there can no longer be any doubt—surfing is respectable, dammit! And 2008 might well be seen as the historical "tipping point," when any notions of wave riding as a form of social rebellion have become downright laughable.

But more than respectable, surfing

seems to have become . . . well . . . dare I say it . . . cultural. I cannot count the number of PhD students I've come across lately tackling all sorts of weighty academic studies about surfing's cultural significance to this and that. Or the arty surf films focusing on whimsical characters riding alternative surfcraft, making gentle folk music or producing avant-garde artwork.

Now, all this might drive some of you slightly mad—as if we really need another fish-riding folk muso strolling thoughtfully along an empty beach, or gazing into a campfire, to remind us how special the surfing lifestyle really is.

But, beyond the nouveau soul fashion fads, there does seem to be some sort of

surf cultural renaissance afoot, perhaps as a critical mass of surfers reach a certain age, maturity and level of proficiency in their chosen fields. The music of violinist Richard Tognetti, the writing of Tim Winton, the traditional timber alaia boards of Tom Wegener, the films of Andrew Kidman, Thomas Campbell and others, the mercurial rise of Jack Johnson—can these things all be seen as part of some broader movement, a blossoming of surf culture?

"The great thing at the moment is that there's a kind of eclecticism that wasn't visible 20 years ago, not just in what craft surfers are riding, but in the ways that surfers express themselves," says Tim Winton, perhaps Australia's greatest living

of the Surfs

By Tim Baker Photos by Sean Davey

novelist, whose latest novel, *Breath*, tells the story of two young surfers in south-west Australia tackling increasingly huge and outrageous surf. "The fact that surfing has outgrown its youth-cult boundaries is important. It seems that there's finally room for more articulate voices and that's encouraging."

I have to confess to a certain, biased enthusiasm for this phenomenon. As a relative veteran now of 20-odd years in the surf media, perhaps jaded and world-wearied by too many pro contests, strained interviews with reluctant surf stars, and thrash/punk throwaway surf videos, I get excited to see artful presentations of the surfing lifestyle in all its forms.

And if you're looking for starting points of this cultural blossoming I can suggest a couple. Andrew Kidman, Jon Frank and Mark Sutherland's 1996 surf movie release *Litmus* arrived as a potent counterpoint to Taylor Steele's highly touted new school shredfest flicks of the same era. Featuring an eclectic cast of fringe-dwellers and shadowy legends, like Joel Fitzgerald, Occy before his comeback and Wayne Lynch, with a free-form music sound track recorded live in a day, *Litmus* evoked echoes of *Morning of the Earth*, a yearning for simpler, more innocent times, celebrating an intimacy with nature, the joys of travel and exploration over surf celebrity or pro tour glory. *Litmus* inspired a string of imitators, particularly the celebrated

Derek Hynd floats free on a fish in the Southern Ocean.

surf films from Chris Malloy and Jack Johnson's stable, Woodshed Films—*Thicker Than Water*, *Shelter* and *Brokedown Melody*.

At the same time, and as featured in *Litmus*, the alternative surfboard design tastes of one Derek Hynd broadened design parameters and turned a new generation on to the delights of forgotten relics from the '60s and '70s. One of Hynd's most eager students was world champ in exile Tom Curren, who set the surfing world alight with footage of him riding a tiny, Tommy Peterson–shaped Fireball Fish in huge Indo barrels.

Curren and Hynd's surfing/music tours through the US, the balladeering of surf minstrels like Pico (featured on *The Search* series of movies from Rip Curl), and the shift of pro tour events to exotic quality locations like Grajagan, Cloudbreak, and Teahupoo all came as a blast of fresh air to a surfing public wearied by four-to-the-beach, slop gymnastics at big-city pro events.

In the new millennium, when a surfer as talented as Dave Rastovich walked away from the competitive scene to pursue an uncertain path as a sponsored free surfer, exploring music, spiritualism and environmental activism along the way, it seemed pro surfing's career parameters had been blown wide open. That Billabong has continued to support Rasta is to their credit, and their ultimate benefit, as new eco-friendly boardshorts made from recycled plastic bottles—promoted primarily by Rasta—become one of their biggest sellers.

The Noosa Festival of Surfing is another example of this blossoming—a genuine cultural happening, pulling together high-performance surfing athletes, surfboard craftsmen, artists, musicians, collectors, writers, salty legends and obsessive old fanatics alike. What was once a longboard contest is now a celebration of lifestyle, combining art, music, literature, history and athleticism, as well as the sort of frantic socializing we have come to expect from any serious surf gathering.

Southern California's Cosmic Creek Challenge is another flowering of alternative surf consciousness—as big-name pros ride weird and whacky craft from the past, then groove to soulful tunes from Donavan Frankenreiter and friends into the evening, all while raising money for worthy causes. Serious surf culture gatherings, film festivals, museums and exhibitions from San Diego to Sao Paulo are furthering surfing's standing as a culture worthy of serious study.

Perhaps the most intriguing example is the classical music/alternative surf craft experiment undertaken by Derek Hynd and Richard Tognetti and documented in a fascinating film, *Musica Surfica*, made by Mick Sowry. Riding finless surfboards—ancient alaias, and weird modern/retro hybrids—while exploring surfing's synergy with classical music, the *Musica Surfica* crew took their various instruments to remote King Island, in southern Australia, and let their collective creative juices loose. "This idea of *Musica Surfica* is getting the two forces, the so-called fine art and high art and seeing how they collide with surfing," says Richard Tognetti, director of the Australian Chamber Orchestra. "We wanted to open up the field musically and in surfing and see what we came up with." The result is some truly wild surfing, 50-year-old Hynd spinning down the line like a top, that seems to suit Tognetti's equally wild violin playing perfectly. There's a nice synergy, too, in Tognetti playing a rare 200-year-old violin, valued at around $10 million, as accompaniment to surfers riding replicas of ancient Hawaiian boards that date back perhaps 1,000 years.

All this, of course, has changed the way the rest of the world sees surfing—challenging old Jeff Spicoli typecasting and awakening a widespread envy for the beauty surfing offers, in a world that sorely needs more beauty.

There was a moment at Angourie a couple of years ago when it was ordained as a National Surfing Reserve, as the politicians hovered about Luke Egan and Mark Occhilupo after the ceremony, like bees to a honey pot, that I found myself thinking, "Wow, we've won."

Not in a self-congratulatory kind of way, but in genuine amazement. The once reviled and despised "surfies" were now seen as politically advantageous props for a bit of government PR, and our prized surf spots were being enshrined in law as places of special social, recreational and environmental significance, protected from insensitive development. How far we've come. That night, as a few of us jammed, shared a few beers and even the odd combustible relaxant, to celebrate the historic occasion, it seemed to me surfing had scored some kind of moral victory. Much has been written and spoken about surfing's drift into the mainstream, but perhaps the mainstream has moved towards surfing more than we realize. The people involved in the campaign to have Angourie

Great way to start the day. Martha's, King Island.

Surfer/musician Richard Tognetti entertains a lucky few on King Island.

recognized as a surfing reserve are not well-known pro surfers or industry moguls—they are regular, recreational surfers working regular jobs, who were able to negotiate their way through the maze of government departments to have their surf spot protected. Step outside the pro surfing and industry bubbles, and most surfers are still doing what they've always done, chasing waves and good times ahead of profiteering and career building, and the outside world, it seems, has started to come around to our way of thinking. As stock markets crash, once mighty banking institutions topple, as the spectre of climate change throws the relentless march of industrialization and so-called "progress" into ever sharper question, perhaps the simple, live-for-today, pleasure-seeking lifestyle of the dedicated surfer, tuned into the cycles of nature, has more currency than ever before.

As more surfers reach middle, and even old, age, I sense a growing awareness too that surfing has added something meaningful and important to

our lives, far beyond mere recreation. Perhaps as we advance in age and look about our peer groups we can see the physical evidence in bodies, eye shine, posture, simple "joy of life," that surfing represents a valid, lifelong guide to life.

As Winton observed in my own book *High Surf*, in a large part inspired by this cultural shift: "Surfers need to broaden, I think, to see the bigger picture, and there's more hope for this now that we're not forced to pretend we're all fifteen. Much of what comes from the surfing media is deadly embarrassing, but I think men and women who are passionate about surfing can bring something grown-up to the wider culture. I'm talking human wisdom here, not market share."

For those of us who might sometimes feel like we've wasted a large chunk of our lives chasing and riding waves, embracing the idea of surfing as art might provide some consolation. As Richard Tognetti says in *Musica Surfica*, "It is art that makes grand our own stupid lives."

Tognetti waits for a set.

Jardim Do Mar, Madeira, Portugal. The "last jewel" of the Atlantic. Save The Waves continues the struggle to avoid such losses in the future through public awareness campaigning. Photo Save The Waves.

The Fan Effect

By Drew Kampion

La Constitucion, Chile. The fight continues here for the introduction of chlorine-free paper to reduce pulp mill pollution. Photo Save The Waves.

It was 2008 and the situation was hopeless. The poles were melting and the seas were on the rise. A vast continent of plastic was gyring in the center of the North Pacific. As Western assents drained towards the world's oil-exporting nations, pressure was mounting to increase offshore drilling around the world and to open vast tracks of the last wild places to the heavy artillery of resource extraction. It was the same game that's been playing out for the last hundred or five hundred years, except for now—in the words of that maniac Rev. Jeremiah Wright, the chickens were coming home to roost. The shit had hit the fan, and it was on everyone.

To make matters worse, surfers were big contributors to the problem, sucking on the same petro-teat as the rest of industrialized mankind: surfboards, wax, wetsuits, leashes, rashguards, boardshorts (almost all of it petrochemicals) and the multimodal transportation network necessary to deliver enthusiasts to their pleasure zones. A dawning awareness of these facts and the quickening global climate crisis have no doubt been catalysts for surfing's accelerating green shift.

The roots of surfing environmentalism are fairly deep; they draw from a wellspring of pantheism (God = Nature) as promulgated by Tom Blake. Surf-related environmental activism began with John Kelly and Save Our Surf in Hawaii in the early '60s, evolved into editorializing in *Surfer* magazine in the later '60s, was spurred to action by the Santa Barbara oil spill of 1969 and the OPEC oil embargo of 1973-4, and has found broad expression throughout surf media in the post-millennium as even people with terrible vision can now read the writing on the wall.

So it was that 2008 also saw an unprecedented riptide of countercurrent, pushing back against the looming and apocalyptic swells of population growth and unsustainable consumption. A building wave of green consciousness was pushing to transform the surfing world into a global model for alternative culture and technology . . . in some cases, with success. Here's a brief (and hopefully representative) look at some of the year's environmental action.

Founded in 1984, the Surfrider Foundation's campaign to "Save Trestles" from encroachment by a new toll road harkened back to John Kelly's seed organization, Save Our Surf, which prevented the destruction of dozens of surf spots in Hawaii in the 1960s. Surfrider chapters around the world took on aggressive roles in preventing surf-spot destruction (i.e., new break-walls at Bastion Point in Victoria, Australia, and the dredge-and-fill of the reefs at Lake Worth, Florida), protesting ocean pollution (like the proposed offshore discharge of nuclear waste from a reprocessing plant at Rokkasho, Japan and the continuing plume of sewage at Newport, Oregon), advocating for surfers access to the coast (i.e., the successful campaign to drop charges against the Montauk 8 and lobbying for marine parks), and continuing to fight for ocean water quality improvement everywhere, but especially in France and elsewhere in the EU, where several beaches are under threat of health closures. Tidbit: Surfrider's US membership has more than doubled in the past six years, despite an influx of competing environmental and humanitarian nonprofits. www.surfrider.org

Save The Waves Coalition found itself with a full plate in 2008, as surf spots came under attack worldwide, and these guys mobilized local, national, and international support to combat threats at a series of locations, from Salsa Brava on the Gulf coast of Costa Rica, to New Zealand's Whangamata harbor mouth. They organized protests of the pollution from CELCO pulp mills at Pichilemu and elsewhere in Chile, and they met with surfers and government officials in the Canary Islands to save surf spots there by demonstrating the value of surf tourism to the local economy. As STW fought to save Sweden's best point break (Molle) and other threatened surf spots, it also chronicled the loss of the effort to prevent the armoring of the coast at Jardim do Mar, the celebrated big-wave right-hander off the island of Madeira, and this year released the documentary DVD of that struggle, *Lost Jewel of the Atlantic.* www.savethewaves.org

In June, Wildcoast, the bi-national nonprofit that has fought to prevent the loss of multiple Baja point waves to harbors, partnered with Mex's TV-Azteca to promote Mexico's first-ever national coastal cleanup (the United Nations reports that plastic is killing over a million seabirds and 100,000 mammals and sea turtles each year; check out riseaboveplastics.blogspot.com). Elsewhere, the org lobbied far and wide in Baja to forestall new megaports at Punta Colonet, to prevent the harvest of turtle eggs (and the rising popularity of consumption of the threatened creature and its eggs), as well as campaigned against offshore drilling. Nothing easy about the work these people are doing, and 2008 was the most challenging year yet.

Across the Atlantic, the prototype surf-environmental organization in the British Isles, Surfers Against Sewage, has typically used innovative and outrageous guerrilla tactics to bring attention to its causes. These guys are inspired troublemakers (this year, a giant inflatable turd called attention to their namesake issue) that challenge the industrial status quo. SAS had a banner year in 2008, organizing cleanups of spills from overboard shipping containers (not as uncommon as you might think!), giving away reusable shopping bags to small donors, beach cleanups around the UK (including Scotland and Wales), advocating successfully for regulation of dangerous ship-to-ship oil transfers, and continuing to advocate vocally and with unorthodox methodologies against sewage discharges.

In Japan, Australian surfer Dave Rastovich and a small crew of guerrilla activists interrupted and publicized the annual dolphin slaughter at Taiji Bay on behalf of Surfers For Cetaceans, an organization Rasta founded. Rastovich is one of a growing number of surfers who support the radical environmentalism of Paul Watson's Sea Shepherd Conservation Society. Meanwhile, the Surf Industry Manufacturers Association's annual Waterman's Ball raised hundreds of thousands of dollars for an array of nonprofits that benefit from its environmental fund. (SIMA now also puts on the annual Liquid Nation Ball, which raises hundreds of thousands of dollars for surf-related humanitarian organizations worldwide.)

Elsewhere around the world, 2008 saw surfers mobilized on all fronts—around hundreds of localized environmental causes (like opposition to the Superferry in Hawaii, which was allowed to operate by the governor despite the lack of an environmental-impact study!), taking water samples, fighting for access, preventing shoreline armoring. Meanwhile, there's been a veritable deluge of new and greener surf products—organic clothing, shoes made from recycled materials, biodegradable wax, sunscreens that won't kill reefs, green suppliers for do-it-yourself surfboard construction, and companies specializing in recycling old surfboards. There are even surf shops with sustainable missions, like Loose Fit in the UK and Wetsand in the US, and more to come . . . very soon!

Add to all this a host of green websites with scads of great ideas and strategies, like phoresia.org, greensurfing.blogspot.com, cleanoceanproject.blogspot.com, and so on. Then there are the carbon-free and carbon neutral schemes . . . and the 1% for the Planet campaign, created by Patagonia, which has increasingly become a surf company over the years . . . and wetsuits made from limestone instead of oil (forget for now that it takes more oil to transform the mineral into the rubber; at least it's a push in an alternative direction) . . . and don't forget surf media! *The Surfer's Path* went "green" in 2004 (100 percent post-consumer recycled paper, no chlorine bleach, soy inks), and in 2008 both *Surfer* and *Surfing* published "green editions" of their mags, as *Surfer*

moved to recycled paper, and *Surfing* announced it was a "carbon neutral" publication.

Consider, too, the shift to electronic media and . . . you get the picture. Surfers are doing a lot! And we should. It will take millions of surfers making individual efforts to reverse the entropic slide into oblivion—surfers packing out beach trash and recycling it, surfers cutting back on travel and buddying up for rides to the beach, surfers making the right buying decisions, surfers alerting the powers that be as to what's ending up downstream of a world out of balance.

Which leads me to ask: If surfers don't represent the best hope for the planet, who does? Surfers are like canaries in the mine shafts. As "ordinary" folk spend less and less time in what's left of the natural or wild world, it's up to surfers to alert the rest of the populace to the problems civilization is creating in our oceans. Because all of life on Earth ultimately depends on the quality of life in the oceans.

As glaciers and polar caps melt and a tide of awareness begins to sweep the world, much of the immediate impact of global warming will be felt on the coasts, in the zone of waves and beaches, which has been the sacred ecotopia of surf culture everywhere. It's on the coast that the brunt of rising waters and punishing hurricanes and soaring pollution will be concentrated. The biggest environmental issue facing surfers in 2008 is, increasingly, survival. Surfers should realize that without an environment to surf in, there will be no surfing.

Ocean Minded organizes China's first-ever beach cleanup. Photo Ocean Minded.

Surfers paddle around NYC to raise awareness. Photo Andrew Brusso/www.seasurfer.org.

Save the Waves Coalition

Save the Waves is an environmental coalition dedicated to preserving the world's surf spots and their surrounding environments. Our goal is to preserve and protect surfing locations around the planet and to educate the public about their value. Save the Waves works in partnership with local communities, foreign and national governments, as well as other conservation groups to prevent coastal development from entering the surf zone.

Some of the world's best surfing waves have vanished forever, buried by large coastal developments. Killer Dana, Petacalco, La Barre—all were among the world's best, and yet they were buried without much of a fight. As the world population of surfers grows, overcrowding in the line-up has become a pervasive problem. Most surfers will concur that what this world needs is

more places to surf, not less of them.

The culprit in most of these cases has been the construction of marinas (Dana Point) or jetties (La Barre, Petacalco), which either bury a spot or vastly alter the natural sand flow patterns. If these developments had been given the proper coastal impact studies, these waves might still exist. Today, there are many other waves in the world that are facing a similar fate.

There are also numerous places in the world where the water is too polluted to surf, yet another of the ocean's most pervasive environmental threats. Save the Waves works to protect surfers from whatever might keep them out of the water.

Save the Waves uses many tactics to promote the argument that surf spots have a very high social and economic value. Every threat to a surf spot is different, depending on the country where

it is occurring, local laws and culture, and the enforcement of environmental law. Each campaign is approached in a careful and unique manner, taking all of these factors into account. Our objective is to achieve the goal of complete surf spot protection. To do so, we often create alliances with local or international environmental organizations, and join forces to create a campaign that will most effectively ensure the protection of surfing resources.

Save the Waves Coalition is the only nonprofit that protects the rights of surfers on an international scale, no matter where the problem might be. We are close partners with many other organizations that do work similar to our own, such as the Surfrider Foundation, and differ only in our intense focus on protecting the surf zone, and the international scope of our campaigns.

Reckon the big surf companies are all a bunch of filthy capitalists, raping our sport's spiritual health while stashing away vast fortunes?

Well, you nasty cynic, you might have to think again. Because an odd thing has been happening amid the upper echelons of the surfing industry, not to mention capitalism itself. People and corporations that have spent a great deal of time and energy accumulating money are . . . giving the stuff away! Billionaires like investment guru Warren Buffett and Microsoft founder Bill Gates might be setting the pace, donating large chunks of their gargantuan wealth to worthy causes, like AIDS prevention in Africa. But it seems many in the surf industry have contracted the philanthropic bug.

The Surf Industry Manufacturers Association (SIMA) in the US began its environmental fund in 1989, and in that time has awarded some $4 million worth of grants to various environmental groups—including the Surfrider Foundation, the Save The Waves Coalition, and the North Shore Community Land Trust. More recently, SIMA added a Humanitarian Fund to its philanthropic activities, inspired largely by Reef cofounder Santiago Aguerre's support for SurfAid International, an Indonesian-based aid agency. Now, SIMA's Liquid National Ball is an annual highlight of the California social/surfing calendar, as well as a fund-raising windfall for numerous humanitarian causes. The latest LNB in 2008 raised US$230,000—awarded as grants to over a dozen charities, including SurfAid, the Life Rolls On Foundation and Surfers Healing.

As well, SurfAid founder Dr. Dave Jenkins was honored as SIMA's inaugural Humanitarian of the Year. Surfwear giants Billabong and Quiksilver have become major supporters of SurfAid, to the tune of several hundred thousand dollars each annually, as well as personal contributions from senior management and staff. Quiksilver has its own Quiksilver Foundation to coordinate its philanthropic activities—donating funds to everything from Reef Check programs to breast cancer research—and their nine-time world champ Kelly Slater even has his own charitable foundation. Seven-time Women's World Champ Layne Beachley has her Aim for the Stars Foundation, to help women from all walks of life achieve their dreams through financial grants and mentoring.

Then you have surf musician Jack Johnson, who has turned his concert tours into a global vehicle for fund and awareness raising for environmental groups wherever he goes. Johnson's tours even come with an "environmental rider." Instead of demanding crates of imported beer and club sandwiches, Johnson's touring party insists venues meet a strict list of environmental measures, from energy-saving light bulbs to waste recycling. Local environmental groups are given free stall space at his concerts and fans can fill a special "green" passport by visiting each stall and then receive preferential seating at his gigs. Johnson even offered to match any donations to the Surfrider Foundation in Australia for a month recently.

In Australia, surf forecasting website Coastalwatch has become a major supporter of SurfAid and the Surfrider Foundation, providing SurfAid's Australian office space free of charge, and regularly donating large sums to both causes.

But the pacesetter for corporate responsibility for many years has been Patagonia, the Santa Barbara-based outdoor/adventure wear company. Patagonia, which has been making increasing inroads into the surf market in recent years, was advocating best practice in environmental and social responsibility on multiple levels, long before it became fashionable. Patagonia's founder and owner Yvon Chouinard outlines his radical philosophies in his biography, *Let My People Go Surfing: The Education of a Reluctant Businessman.*

"Patagonia exists to challenge conventional wisdom and present a new style of responsible business," he writes in his introduction. Chouinard co-founded 1% for the Planet, a coalition of businesses that donate 1 percent of annual revenues to environmental organizations. To date, Patagonia has given away $31 million to over 1,000 organizations. Patagonia's mission statement is simple but bold: "Build the best product, cause no unnecessary harm, and use business to inspire and implement solutions to the environmental crisis."

The beginnings of the mainstream surf industry's humanitarian awakening might be traced back to a meeting of the Surf Industry Manufacturer's Association at their annual conference in Cabo San Lucas, Mexico, in 2003. Amid the usual few days of networking, surf sessions, and cocktails, Dr. Dave Jenkins was granted 16 minutes to present his vision of a surfing-led aid agency in the Mentawai Islands, Indonesia.

Dr. Jenkins' fledgling organization SurfAid had come to the attention of Reef cofounder Santiago Aguerre through an article in *Surfer* magazine, "The Jungle Is Looking Back." In it, writer Steve Barilotti described the early efforts of SurfAid volunteers to help reduce rampant malaria in the Mentawai Islands with the aid of insecticide-treated mosquito nets.

Santiago remembers reading the article and experiencing a kind of epiphany, after learning that up to 50 percent of Mentawai children die before the age of five from easily preventable diseases. "I'd just come back from the islands, and I read that in the worst areas the chances of a kid making it to five is the toss of the coin," recalls Santiago. "My two kids at the time walked by and I thought, okay, which one of the two is going to make it. Sometimes you get grabbed by the throat."

The article made such an impact on Aguerre, he wrote an impassioned open letter to the surf industry to get behind SurfAid's efforts. "SurfAid is the work of a dreamer with a lot of courage and a big humanitarian heart, and a band of crazy people that feel passionate enough to drop their jobs to help and sensible enough not to look the other way," Santiago wrote. "Today, Dave and his Team are looking at us—surfers, industry people, boat operators, pros, yes, all of us—to see if we can help further their dream of making this effort an ongoing humanitarian crusade. I will help. Will you?"

Santiago flew Dr. Dave to Cabo for the SIMA conference, and badgered organizers to give him a

Giving Back
Surfing gets all philanthropic on us

By Tim Baker

Young Balinese surfers paddle for peace, just days before the executions of the Bali bombers. Photo Wayan.

slot in the schedule. Dave remembers his speech to SIMA as a defining moment for SurfAid.

"We'd had some success at that stage. We'd just done our parasite rates and we had a 75 percent reduction (in malaria), so I stood up at Cabo to the industry and said, this is what we've done and we'd like you to be a part of it," Dave recalls. "I was in another zone during that speech. I could hardly remember it, as if some other force entered me and helped me express how important it was. This came across powerfully and made grown men cry. The next day we were talking to Billabong and Quiksilver."

"Today you would not even think of buying a product from a company that does not care to look if its practices are harming the environment while its products are sold, made or even transported. This is a key issue affecting the buying decision of today's young consumer," he says. "In another 10 years, the general consumer will feel the same about humanitarian issues before he buys its products."

And there is a growing list of surfing enterprises which take it as a given that their activities should include a philanthropic component.

a stunning willingness to dive in and simply do what needed to be done to reach survivors and alleviate suffering. Surf charter skippers who knew the remote Indonesian islands better than anyone simply filled their boats with emergency relief supplies and headed out into the worst affected areas, in many cases days before the established aid agencies could get there. Boat owners made their vessels available for extended periods free of charge, and bearing considerable costs themselves. Major surf companies kicked in the funds to make the whole thing happen. SurfAid provided a central

Santiago concurs: "These are tough guys, and they had tears in their eyes. We hit a chord here. This is going to change the surf industry, the chemistry's there."

Santiago says SurfAid is a great example of what the surf industry can do when it unites for a cause. "Competitors in the marketplace that were at each other's throats on every other issue left their differences behind, dropped their weapons and each took on a piece of SurfAid," he says. "They didn't try and compete for this association. They said, basically, this is right. This tells you what kind of industry we are . . . It was like the lions and the tigers having dinner together."

Santiago says there has been a profound shift in both the industry and the marketplace in recent times, requiring a radical rethink of the concept of corporate responsibility.

The Noosa Festival of Surfing raised more than $100,000 in 2008 for local charities, as part of its weeklong celebration of surf culture. Holidays With Purpose is a surf charter company based in Sumatra, which offers the classic Indo surf trip, along with the opportunity to participate in community projects with remote island communities.

Breast cancer research has become a favorite cause for many of the top professional female surfers, inspiring a range of fund-raising activities through organizations like Keep Abreast and Boarding For Breast Cancer.

But perhaps the surfing industry's philanthropic instincts reached their fullest expression during the coordinated response to the devastating Boxing Day Tsunami in 2004, which caused so much death and destruction in Indonesia. From local surf charter operators to major surfwear companies., there was

coordinating role from Padang, and surfers from all over the world simply made their way to the disaster zones by whatever means they could to do whatever they could to help. "The synchronicity that happened between us and the boat captains and the surf industry, that was fantastic," says Dr. Dave, who reckons their surfing experience made them uniquely qualified to function in such a demanding environment. "It meant our productivity was way beyond what anyone could have expected—including the UN, who made comments, and AusAID and NZAID: "Who's this SurfAid? Why are they the only people getting into these remote isolated villages that no one else has got to?'"

Who would have thought all that time in the impact zone would make us so well-qualified for aid work? Hopefully it's an ability more and more surfers will choose to exercise in the years ahead.

SurfAid International

A Year of Learning, Implementation and Progress

Nowhere has the impact of the surfing community working together for humanitarian causes been better demonstrated than in SurfAid's work in Indonesia. **Kirk Willcox** reports

Tucked inside a West Sumatran barrel. Photo Simon Williams.

The Disneyland of surfing, the islands off West Sumatra, got off to a shaky start in 2008 when a 6.2 Richter scale earthquake hit Nias on January 23, claiming one life and seriously injuring three people.

A series of strong earthquakes followed in February that hit the Mentawai Islands to the south, leading to the Bupati (Regent) declaring a state of emergency for three weeks. While the earthquakes weren't of the magnitude of the previous September—when an 8.4 (the largest in the world in 2007) and a 7.9 hit the Mentawai—the February earthquakes still killed two people and damaged hundreds of homes, making the island communities extremely nervous about their future. The people of Berimanua, near the well-known break of Telescopes, were so rattled by the further destruction in their village that they actually abandoned it and moved to safer areas.

Many of these earthquakes receive scant news headlines. The region is radically unstable and experts predict that it is only a matter of time before another giant earthquake hits the Mentawai, with the strong possibility of a tsunami, as pressure builds between the Indo-Australian and Eurasian tectonic plates as they push against each other near the island chain.

One of the foremost experts in this field is Professor Kerry Sieh, formerly a professor at the Californian Institute of Technology and now the founding director of the Earth Observatory of Singapore. "West Sumatra appears to be a crucible in which humankind is destined to test its ability and resolve to take a new approach to how it addresses natural hazards," Sieh says.

But it's not only earthquakes and tsunamis that the islanders have to worry about. The infant mortality rate (children under five) in the Mentawai Islands is 93 per 1,000 live births, nearly one in 10, and in Nias the rate is 66 deaths per 1,000. In industrialized countries, on average there are six deaths for every 1,000 live births. The island children are dying from preventable diseases like malnutrition, chest infections, malaria and diarrhea.

It is in this unstable and challenging environment, sometimes referred to as the Forgotten Islands, that SurfAid International has chosen to work, rolling out its emergency preparedness, health, and water and sanitation programs. In partnership with the island communities and government, SurfAid strives to prevent disease, suffering and death through educational programs. The main goal is to empower communities to make sustainable, healthy lifestyle changes that improve their resilience to disease.

SurfAid, whose programs are supported by the Australian and New Zealand governments, the surfing industry—particularly Billabong—and generous individuals and foundations, has now worked in the region for nine years.

Today the non-profit humanitarian organization has 130 staff—85 per cent of whom are Indonesian nationals living and working with the communities in the villages. In many cases, they are Mentawai and Nias locals who speak the dialect and are working with their own people.

The 2008 year marked a series of milestones for SurfAid:

In Emergency Preparedness, SurfAid completed two-thirds of a three-year program sponsored by AusAID, the Australian government's overseas aid program. The E-Prep program is designed to improve both village and district disaster management systems so the local communities are better prepared for natural disasters. As part of the program, community-elected village disaster management

committees were established in all 56 SurfAid villages in the Mentawai and Nias.

These village committees are based on the Indonesian Government model of SATLINMAS (Community Protection Units) and include a number of important sub-units such as early warning, first aid, search and rescue, evacuation and community kitchen. Between June and September 2008, E-Prep staff trained more than 2,500 disaster preparedness team members and held community disaster response simulations: being better prepared means saving lives.

The Malaria Free Mentawai (MFM) program has been a long-term SurfAid program, dating back to the organization's beginnings in 2000. SurfAid was on track to deliver specially treated mosquito nets and malaria education to nearly 90 percent of the 70,000 Mentawai population by December 2008.

The specially trained SurfAid staff can only access many villages by local dugout canoe and long jungle walks but had still managed to reach 53,000 Mentawai people in some of the most outlying areas of three islands—Siberut, and North and South Pagai—by March 2008.

As well as delivering 22,000 insecticide-treated nets to 15,000 households, SurfAid ran an education program, which included a play about

SurfAid undertook a joint Watsan (water and sanitation) program with UNICEF and NZAID.

The 99 facilities, in 26 villages in Sirombu and Teluk Dalam, include new water tanks, tapped spring water systems, new and reconditioned wells, rainwater harvesting systems and two separate types of latrines. All have been constructed with community participation.

Following the success of this first Watsan program, SurfAid initiated a second phase for Nias, starting with an assessment of eight villages in Afulu and Alasa. SurfAid will also extend the Watsan program to the Mentawai Islands and is currently raising money to fund these projects.

SurfAid also runs a Community Based Health Program in the Mentawai and Nias, aiming to reduce the high infant mortality rate of children under five. SurfAid teaches groups of volunteer women, called Care Groups, to deliver health behavior messages on nutrition, hygiene and sanitation to their neighboring households. They also identify at-risk households—those with the sickest children who need immediate attention.

By December 2008, between the Mentawai and Nias, it was anticipated there would be:

- Almost 1,200 Care Group meetings
- 6,600 times volunteers will attend Care Group meetings
- 23,000 home visits by Care Group volunteers
- 900 visits to households classified as high-risk
- Almost 900 health messages delivered in church, mosque or other religious meetings.

The Quiksilver SurfAid Community Health Training Centre at Katiet, on Sipora Island, continues to evolve as a model for best practice and training in nutrition, basic hygiene, malaria prevention and sustainable living that can be replicated far beyond Katiet and the Mentawai. An earthquake-resistant house was completed at the site in May 2008, and vitamin gardens have been established.

SurfAid also continued to roll out its schools program, supported by Billabong, which gives students the opportunity to learn about the geography, economy, culture, health and living conditions of the Mentawai people. The program is using the activities of SurfAid as a case study to learn about global citizenship, which is about having an awareness of the world as a global community and recognizing and respecting the rights and responsibilities of citizens within it. The program is running in Australia and New Zealand and will be piloted in California and other American states in 2009.

Dave Jenkins, who co-founded the organization in 2000, said SurfAid continued to trial new, innovative strategies that demonstrate a continued organizational determination to seek the most cost-effective strategies to create lasting change.

"As these programs roll out, we track their impacts, refine the processes and build replicable tools that will enable future, efficient expansion to assist more people," he said. "Giving donors the best return for their donation is a primary objective and I would like to thank all our donors for their ongoing support that allows us to help create increasingly healthy communities in the Mentawai and Nias who are self-reliant and prepared for future emergencies."

You can donate to SurfAid via their website at surfaidinternational.org and the SurfAid schools website for free, online educational resources is schools. surfaidinternational.org

Dr. Dave Jenkins with poor Mentawai family. Photo Bob Barker / RovingEye.com.

mosquitoes and malaria, and tested 11,000 children under the age of nine for the malaria parasite.

In September 2008, SurfAid started to roll out the MFM program on Sipora Island, the final leg to complete the Mentawai chain, and the team was scheduled to reach 10,000 villagers with nets and education before the end of December.

SurfAid CEO and founder Dr. Dave Jenkins said the Malaria Free Mentawai campaign is a major step towards fulfilling SurfAid's aim to get the majority of children and adults in the Mentawai sleeping under the long-lasting nets that will save many lives and prevent extreme human suffering.

SurfAid reached another major milestone during 2008 with the completion of nearly 100 water projects on Nias, which was devastated by the March 2005 earthquake measuring 8.7 on the Richter scale.

The earthquake badly affected the water supply as it lifted coral reefs on the west and south coasts by one to three meters, raising the level of many community wells above the water table. Wells were also destroyed or badly damaged, so

SurfAid with Care Group mothers in the Mentawai. Photo Bob Barker / RovingEye.com.

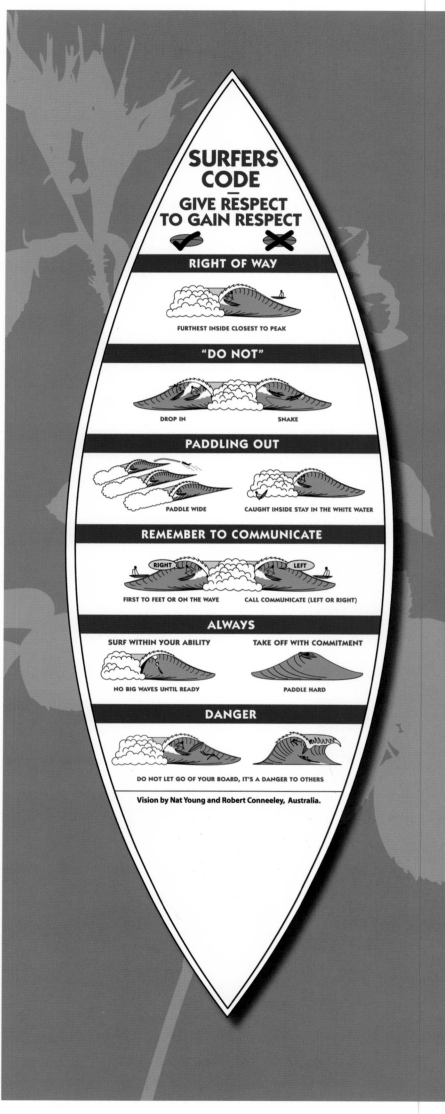

SURFERS CODE — GIVE RESPECT TO GAIN RESPECT
✓ ✗

RIGHT OF WAY
FURTHEST INSIDE CLOSEST TO PEAK

"DO NOT"
DROP IN   SNAKE

PADDLING OUT
PADDLE WIDE   CAUGHT INSIDE STAY IN THE WHITE WATER

REMEMBER TO COMMUNICATE
RIGHT   LEFT
FIRST TO FEET OR ON THE WAVE   CALL COMMUNICATE (LEFT OR RIGHT)

ALWAYS
SURF WITHIN YOUR ABILITY   TAKE OFF WITH COMMITMENT
NO BIG WAVES UNTIL READY   PADDLE HARD

DANGER
DO NOT LET GO OF YOUR BOARD, IT'S A DANGER TO OTHERS

Vision by Nat Young and Robert Conneeley, Australia.

This Original

Surfriders' Code of Ethics" sign was erected at Margaret River in Western Australia by Rosco Kermode and Robert Conneely in 1986.

Since then six surfers' code plaques exactly the same have been erected. The first two were in Byron Bay in 2004. A further two were put up on the Sunshine Coast, north of Brisbane. Two signs are now standing in California, one in C Street, Ventura, and the other at the perfect point break of Rincon.

The first French plaque went up in Anglet, north of Biarritz, in May 2008.

— NAT YOUNG

There Will Always Be Another Wave.

Surfing is more popular than ever, and the waves are getting crowded. One of surfing's most prominent figures, 1966 world champion Nat Young, got his face pounded black and blue by another surfer not too long ago while surfing his home break of Angourie, Australia. The incident prompted him to publish a book called *Surf Rage*, and a number of socially minded surfers contributed to the volume. One of them, Glen Hening, co-founded the Surfrider Foundation and later helped create the Groundswell Society, a grassroots organization that promotes social and educational issues related to ocean activities. I spoke at their annual conference in Ventura, and that address inspired my own book, *Surfers Code*.

Glen asked me to tell a group of young people what I have learned from the ocean. I decided to pass on the most important lessons of my career. I sat down and wrote them out very quickly off the top of my head, printed them on a card and handed them out that day. This is one of them.

It is true that really crowded surf breaks can be a catalyst for physical aggression, but it is certainly not inevitable. Sometimes we simply need to adjust our frame of mind. Imagine this scenario: a surfer is sitting on his board in a crowded line-up. A wave rolls in, and he is in a position to catch it. Suddenly he turns to the man or woman sitting alongside him and says, "You take this one."

What has he done? With four words he has immediately created a less competitive atmosphere in the surf, and most likely the surfer who enjoyed the wave will return the favor down the line, and pass a wave along to someone else. It is tough out in the water today. We all get frustrated at crowded surf spots, but it is easy enough to help create some unexpected goodwill in the water.

One thing I know – another wave will always come through.

— SHAUN TOMSON

Adapted from Surfer's Code *by Shaun Tomson with Patrick Moser, published by Gibbs Smith.*

A SURFER'S CODE

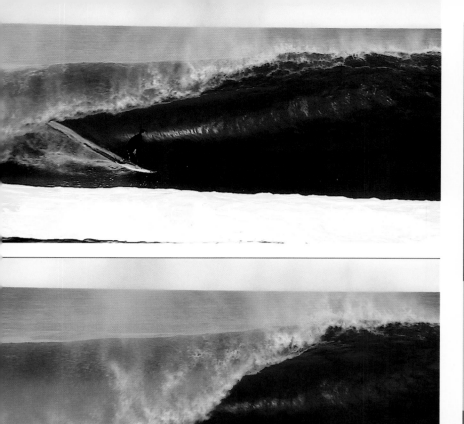

Old School Road Trip

*One day can sometimes offer so much . . .
if you make the effort to be in the right
place at the right time.*

Words and photos by Tim Bonython

Thursday, November 20, offered a good northeasterly swell. Swell forecaster Ben McCartney and I studied the maps and drove down the night before, booking into a motel in Ulladulla. We knew it was going to be an early start.

But at 5:00 a.m. we were seriously disappointed with what we saw. We decided to hang out and wait with the boys: Hippo, Dean Bowen, Karl Atkins, Damien Wills and Clint Kimmins. Waiting turned out to be a

good call. At 10.30 a.m. the wave, the wind and tide all turned in our favor, and it pumped. All day.

Then, almost exactly the way it started, it ended. It had begun with a bang as soon as the winds switched from the northeast to a warm and gusty northwest, the barrels lined up and firing. Then at around six in the evening a southerly came crashing through. No warning, not forecast and not even suspected by locals.

It was like God just decided to hit the off switch.

I was frantically trying to put my big TV camera into my bag while the salt spray was gusting up onto the reef—it was pretty hectic.

Meanwhile all the surfers headed off as quickly as they could, wanting to get their jet skis back to the beach a couple of kilometers down the coast.

So I walked across the rocks with camera and tripod to check another spot, which works in south winds, and I couldn't believe it. Perfect and no one out. Three-to-six-foot perfect right-hand barrels—like Kirra but easier.

I set up my camera, fretting over what I was missing, but I bagged a couple line-up shots. Within 10 minutes there were about four locals who lapped it up like there was no tomorrow.

What a way to end an epic day.

The Regions

Africa Report

By Paul Botha

While Morocco has long-standing claims as the "Mexico of Europe" and there are pockets of surfing in most of the coastal countries in Africa, it is South Africa's 3,000 kilometers of swell-rich coastline, highly developed surf industry and administration that have made it the most populous surfing destination on the African continent.

And 2008 was another banner year for surfing, as both the sport and lifestyle aspects grew. Surf schools and tour operators offered easy access to the waves, surf brands promoted the healthy, exciting, trendy and fashion-conscious image that surfing embraces, and South African surfers earned international accolades and challenged some of the biggest waves ever recorded in the region.

Extreme weather and wave events battered the southern tip of Africa from May to September, and Cape Town's reputation as a premier big-wave playground was confirmed when the 10th edition of Red Bull Big Wave Africa produced one of the most spectacular paddle-in surfing contests of all time.

Durban's Grant "Twiggy" Baker charged to victory in the maxing 20-to-25-foot swell at Dungeons, with Californian Greg Long scoring one of the biggest barrels ever documented. And two weeks later, Long towed Baker into arguably Africa's biggest recorded wave at Tafelberg Reef, two kilometers outside Dungeons. At the end of August swells peaked at 17.8 meters (58 feet), the largest ever measured, causing extensive damage to coastal property as big-wave chargers abandoned Cape Town to ride some of the biggest waves ever seen at Jeffreys Bay.

In May the country's big-wave brigade was deservedly acknowledged in the inaugural O'Neill Raw Courage Awards that saw ever-cheerful legend Andrew Marr take top prize for paddling into a monster at Todos Santos. Marr also finished second to Mike Schlebach in the Ultimate Ride of the Year, with both rides coming at Dungeons. Twiggy Baker won the Biggest Wave award for his tow-in ride at Cortes Bank in February, just a week before grabbing second place at the Mavericks event, and Cape Town standouts Mickey Duffus and James Taylor scooped the Balls to the Wall award for their commitment during countless life-threatening sessions.

International honors came at the ISA World Masters Surfing Championships in Peru, where Team South Africa was the top nation for the second successive year. Heather Clark dominated the Women's Masters event, Chris Knutsen added the Grand Kahunas (over 50) title to the Kahunas (over 45) crown he won the year before in Puerto Rico, and Marc Wright clinched the Kahunas gold medal ahead of teammate Nick Pike.

Matthew Moir captured his second consecutive Longboard title at the ISA World Surfing Games in Portugal in October. Dale Staples beat the world's best 16-year-olds to win the Rip Curl Gromsearch International final at Bells Beach at Easter and Shaun Joubert, 17, and Nick Godfrey, 16, enhanced their international reputations by third and fifth respectively in the Oakley Pro Junior Global Challenge, the world's richest junior event, in Bali in September.

Two thousand eight was another banner year for surfing as surf schools and tour operators offered easy access to the waves, and South African surfers earned international accolades and challenged some of the biggest waves ever recorded in the region.

Matthew Moir takes a second World Longboard title. Photo ISA.

Superfreak Jordy Smith was crowned SA's Surfer of the Year for the second straight time at a glittering awards ceremony where Frenchy Fredericks and legendary surfboard shaper Spider Murphy were inducted into the Hall of Fame, Rosanne Hodge was honored as SA's top International Women's Surfer and Rudy Palmboom Jr took the Junior award.

Jordy was the only one of the four SA surfers on the 2008 ASP World Tour to re-qualify for 2009, as his more experienced compatriots Travis Logie, Royden Bryson and Ricky Basnett dropped back onto the WQS. David Weare and Greg Emslie earned their second and ninth seasons at surfing's top table thanks to stellar performances on the WQS.

Meanwhile, Rosanne Hodge continued to fly the SA flag on the Women's World Tour for a second year, racking up heat wins over the world champion and others. But consistent 9th-place finishes saw the East Londoner having to use her excellent 2008 WQS results to qualify for the 2009 World Tour.

Events in South Africa saw Kelly Slater defeat 2007 World Champ Mick Fanning to win the Billabong Pro at Jeffreys Bay for a record fourth time. Weare beat all-comers at the 6-Star Prime Quiksilver Pro Durban in his

home town, Emslie won the Lizzard and Chris Davidson (AUS) triumphed in the 6-star Mr. Price Pro. Shane Thorne pocketed R75,000 for taking out the Quiksilver Goodwave specialty event in epic barrels at his home break of North Beach, while Shaun Payne clinched the Men's title at the SA Championships and Heather Clark won her umpteenth Women's SA crown.

Junior contests proliferated and groms from 10 to 20 years old racked up thousands of air miles as they chased cash, points and glory from one end of the coastline to the other. Klee Strachan was the standout Pro Junior performer, topping the rankings in both the ASP Africa and SSA Pro Surf Tour standings, while Tarryn Chudleigh and rising stars Bianca Buitendag and Sarah Baum dominated the Girls' standings.

The core surfing media was boosted when John McCarthy and Iain Evans created theBOMBsurf. com which utilizes new media platforms to provide an authentic take on the local beach lifestyle. Atoll Media's Zigzag grew to 10 issues per annum, but the core boardsports offering *Blunt Magazine*, was withdrawn when holding company Touchline rationalized its youth culture operations.

African Surfrider mag flourished, as did the annual Wavescapes Surf Film Festival, where SA surfing legend Shaun Tomson premiered his seminal *Breaking Down the Door* surf movie in July. And '60s surfing icon Donald Paarman published *Lunatic Surfer or Destiny*, a fascinating autobiography of his life and times.

Awareness increased about climate change, and surfers and others protested stridently when Eskom, the national electricity provider,

proposed that the country's second nuclear power station be built about 20 kilometers from the SA surfing Mecca of Jeffreys Bay. The Supertubes Foundation's praiseworthy efforts maintained and enhanced the Jeffreys Bay coastline for future generations, while pressure continued over plans to develop Durban's entry-level surf break of Vetch's Pier as a small boat harbor.

As 2008 drew to an end, surf industry entrepreneurs began anticipating increased interest in the lifestyle as the eyes of the world become focused on the southern tip of Africa during the lead-up to and after the 2010 FIFA World Cup, while tens of thousands of surfers were simply stoked to be riding pristine waves and hoping that the surf keeps on pumping.

ABOVE: Twiggy Baker, Tafelberg Reef. Photo Craig Kolesky.  *BELOW: Heather Clark. Photo Jake White.*

Future stars. Photo KZN Surfing.

LOTTO FUTURE STARS CHALLENGE
LONG BEACH, KOMMETJIE, SOUTH AFRICA
January 20

Kommetjie twins Lisa and Daniel Mace posted almost identical scores to win the Under 18 Girls and Boys titles, held in contestable small surf. Western Province dominated the event, winning both Tag Team and Overall Teams titles.

UNDER 18 BOYS
1. Daniel Mace
2. Tommie Kruger
3. Grant Arendse
4. Nicholas Grondman

UNDER 18 GIRLS
1. Lisa Mace
2. Chantelle Rautenbach
3. Tanika Hoffman
4. Holly Armstrong

UNDER 16 BOYS
1. Max Armstrong
2. James Lowe
3. Jarred Veldhuis
4. Daniel Wilson

TEAMS
1. Western Province
2. Boland
3. Future Stars
4. Mavericks

BILLABONG "GIRLS GET OUT THERE" SUMMER SERIES #3
TABLEVIEW, CAPE TOWN
February 2–3

Tarryn Chudleigh, 17, confirmed her emergence as one of SA's top female surf stars by winning both the Open and Pro Junior titles at the third (and first for 2008) of four Billabong "Get Out There" events for the summer. Rain curtailed some of the beach celebrations, but the girls were all business in the onshore but contestable waves. Surfing back-to-back finals, Chudleigh romped through the Junior but had to fight hard to take the Open in a lead-changing, nail-biting heat.

OPEN WOMEN
1. Tarryn Chudleigh
2. Bianca Buitendag
3. Tammy-Lee Smith
4. Kirsty Delport

PRO JUNIOR (UNDER 20 GIRLS)
1. Tarryn Chudleigh
2. Chantelle Rautenbach
3. Bianca Buitendag
4. Sarah Baum

UNDER 15 GIRLS
1. Cara McDonald
2. Holly Armstrong
3. Tanika Hoffman
4. Anoush Zakarian

NOVICES
1. Ruth Armstrong
2. Inge McLaren
3. Chloe Meacham
4. Grace Steel

BILLABONG "GIRLS GET OUT THERE" SUMMER SERIES #4
SCOTTSBURGH, KZN COAST
February 16–17

Cloudless skies, glassy one-meter waves and a packed crowd loving the whole scene made the final Girls Get Out There a fitting finale to a great summer. In a weekend of great surfing, top touring pro Heather Clark claimed the Open series title by the narrowest of margins, while Tarryn Chudleigh held on just long enough to claim a fourth in the Pro Junior final and win the series title.

OPEN WOMEN
1. Tammy-Lee Smith
2. Stacey Guy
3. Heather Clark
4. Sarah Baum

PRO JUNIOR
1. Heidi Palmboom
2. Bianca Buitendag
3. Alice McGregor
4. Tarryn Chudleigh

UNDER 15 GIRLS
1. Holly Armstrong
2. Cara McDonald
3. Chantelle Botha
4. Tanika Hoffman

NOVICES
1. Inge McLaren
2. Jordyn Vanhoutte
3. Demi Mason
4. Janelle Rademeyer

SERIES WINNERS
OPEN
Heather Clark
PRO JUNIOR
Tarryn Chudleigh
UNDER 15
Holly Armstrong

BILLABONG JUNIOR SERIES
ST. MICHAELS-ON-SEA, KZN
February 21–24

Durban's Kyle Beach claimed his first Pro Junior title, scoring a narrow victory over Klee Strachan (Winkelspruit) in excellent overhead waves at St. Mike's. Strachan, a two-time South African team captain, was left needing a 9.5 in the dying minutes. He threw caution to the wind and produced a strong series of maneuvers on his final wave but fell short at 9.25. Beach now holds a ratings lead in the series.

PRO JUNIOR (UNDER 20 BOYS)
1. Kyle Beach
2. Klee Strachan
3. Rudy Palmboom Jr
3. Casey Grant
5. Beyrick de Vries
5. Kyle Lane
5. Brendon Gibbens
5. Chad du Toit

UNDER 16 BOYS
1. Beyrick de Vries
2. Davey Brand
3. Dane Staples
4. David van Zyl

UNDER 14 BOYS
1. Diran Zakarian
2. Steven Sawyer
3. Slade Prestwich
4. Jarred Veldhuis

UNDER 12 BOYS
1. Benji Brand

2. Max Armstrong
3. Simo Mkhize
4. Jordy Maree

VON ZIPPER AIR SHOW
Shaun Joubert

KZNSA SENIOR CHAMPIONSHIPS
NEW PIER, DURBAN
March 1–2

After atrocious onshore conditions on the first day, the Chemspec Seniors were concluded in clean 2-to-3-foot waves, with ISA champion Chris Knutsen surprising no one in taking out the Grand Masters.

GRANDMASTERS
Chris Knutsen
SENIORS
John McCarthy
VETERANS
Warren Waring
OPEN MEN
Rudy Palmboom Jr
OPEN WOMEN
Heidi Palmboom

ROXY INVITATIONAL MOZAMBIQUE, PRESENTED BY SALT WATER GIRL
PONTO DO ORO, MOZAMBIQUE
March 4–11

Veteran Heather Clark outfoxed a trio of young hotties to take out the Roxy invitational event in perfect waves at Ponto Do Oro in southern Mozambique. Organizers ran the preliminaries in fair surf, but then took advantage of the eight-day waiting period to hold out for perfection at the right-hand point break. Ironically, all four finalists were goofy-footers who raised the bar for backhand performance. With an unlimited wave count, jet ski assist and 45 minutes for the final, the girls were exhausted after riding more than 10 waves each, many of them more than 200 meters long.

Heidi Palmboom. Photo MoonRocket.

FINAL
1. Heather Clark
2. Sarah Baum
3. Chantelle Rautenbach
4. Bianca Buitendag

QUIKSILVER KING OF THE GROMS, PRESENTED BY VIRGIN MOBILE
KOMMETJIE, CAPE TOWN
March 8–9

Powerful surfing was the order of the day when the Quiksilver Groms enjoyed excellent conditions for the second and final day, with waves barreling over the sandbar. Nick Godfrey pulled one out of the hat in the last moments of the U/20 final, while in the U/16 Devin Lane held on to his lead in a low-scoring match-up.

UNDER 20 MEN
1. Nick Godfrey
2. Brendon Gibbens
3. Dale Staples
3. Casey Grant

UNDER 16 BOYS
1. Devin Lane
2. Mikey February
3. Beyrick de Vries
3. Dane Staples

OAKLEY PRO JUNIOR
NEW PIER, DURBAN
March 21–23

Oakley team rider Shaun Joubert (Mossel Bay) overcame a strong challenge by Nic Godfrey (Cape St. Francis) to snatch victory in clean one-meter offshore waves. The inaugural Oakley Juniors event was a highlight of the Vodacom Easter Adrenaline Festival on the Durban beachfront. As a result of their placings, both Joubert and Godfrey qualify for the Oakley Pro Junior Global Challenge in Bali later in the year.

FINAL
1. Shaun Joubert
2. Nic Godfrey

SEMIFINAL 1
1. Shaun Joubert
2. Klee Strachan
SEMIFINAL 2
1. Nic Godfrey
2. Hayden McNicol

17TH REEF WETSUITS SA GROMMET SURFING GAMES
THE PIPE, POLLOCK BEACH, PORT ELIZABETH
March 23

Almost 150 girls and boys enjoyed

great surf and fine weather for this event, presented by Nelson Mandela Bay Tourism. The accent of the games is on participation throughout provincial areas of South Africa, and organizers were delighted by the turnout from rural villages as far afield as Southern KZN and Eastern and Western Cape.

UNDER 16 BOYS
1. Donavan Jacobs
2. Chad Coullie
3. Roger Vuanza
4. Levi Fraser
UNDER 16 GIRLS
1. Gina Smith
2. Nikita Kekana
3. Jessica Barnard
4. Kerri Lee Viljoen
UNDER 14 BOYS
1. Brandon Benjamin
2. Sebastian Barrett
3. Marco Loubser
4. Talente Mkhize
UNDER 14 GIRLS
1. Jordyn Vanhoutte
2. Roxy Giles
3. Azraa Moodaley
4. Camden Ravenscroft
UNDER 12 BOYS
1. Jonah Paarman
2. Matthew McGillivray
3. Jonny Hollis
4. Dylan Wichman
UNDER 12 GIRLS
1. Courtenay Ellish
2. Inga McLaren
3. Kim Van Greunen
4. Tosca Wynand
5. Amy Perrins
TEAM RESULTS
1. Western Province
2. Eastern Province
3. Boland
4. Southern KZN
5. Border
6. Southern Cape
7. Kwazulu Natal

O'NEILL SCOTTBURGH PRO
SCOTTBURGH BEACH, KZN
March 29–30

Former WCT pro Dave Weare was the standout surfer of the event, blazing his way back to form after an injury, to clinch the Open Men division from Antonio Bortoletto in an all-Durban final. Chantelle Rautenbach (Melkbos) took out the Women's and Casey Grant (Durban) the Pro Junior.

PRO JUNIOR FINAL
4. Matthew Bromley
3. Justin Gray
2. Casey Grant
1. Kyle Lane
SEMIFINAL 1
4. Brendon Gibbens
3. Beyrick De Vries
2. Shawn Dennis
1. Matthew Bromley
SEMIFINAL 2
4. Klee Strachan
3. Justin Gray
2. Kyle Lane
1. Casey Grant
WOMEN FINAL
1. Chantelle Rautenbach

2. Tasha Mentasti
3. Michelle Imeson
4. Nicole Annells
SEMIFINAL 1
1. Tasha Mentasti
2. Michelle Imeson
3. Sarah Maritz
4. Tara Hassack
SEMIFINAL 2
1. Chantelle Rautenbach

Benji Brand. Photo MoonRocket.

2. Nicole Annells
3. Tam De Maraussem
4. Kirsty Delport
OPEN MEN FINAL
1. David Weare
2. Antonio Bortoletto
3. Devyn Mattheys
4. Klee Strachan
SEMIFINAL 1
1. David Weare
2. Devyn Mattheys
3. Gary Van Wierengen
4. Manfred Adrio
SEMIFINAL 2
1. Klee Strachan
2. Antonio Bortoletto
3. Simon Nicholson
4. Kelvin Zehmke

WESTERN PROVINCE OPEN OF SURFING
LONG BEACH, KOMMETJIE
April 5

Brandon Roberts of Sun Valley won the 2008 Western Province Open and a R2000 winner's check in excellent four-foot surf at Long Beach. Unbeaten on his way to the final, Roberts saved his best for last, with a 9.83 ride to secure the title, his first since 2005.

FINAL
1. Brandon Roberts
2. Mathew Kruger
3. Mathew Bromley
4. Wesley Grey
SEMIFINAL 1
1. Brandon Roberts
2. Matthew Kruger
3. Shaun Payne
4. Jarred Veldhuis
SEMIFINAL 2
1. Mathew Bromley
2. Wesley Grey
3. Gary Van Wieringen
4. Adam Hansen

QUARTERFINAL 1
1. Shaun Payne
2. Jarred Veldhuis
3. Dagan Gold
4. Ryan Payne
QUARTERFINAL 2
1. Brandon Roberts
2. Mathew Kruger
3. Philip Nel
4. Michael February

Brandon Roberts. Photo Mark Hoffman.

QUARTERFINAL 3
1. Mathew Bromley
2. Gary Van Wieringen
3. Ruebin Pearce
4. Avro Johnson
QUARTERFINAL 4
1. Wesley Grey
2. Adam Hansen
3. Keegan Nel
4. Mikhial Thompson

KOMMUNITY PROJECT FUTURE STARS
NEW PIER, DURBAN
April 10

In the lead-up to the Quiksilver Pro Junior, the top eight juniors who had progressed through Surfing South Africa's Transformation and Development Program did battle for a slot into the second round of the main event. Uhmlanga's Bo Shabalala pulled out the stops in the dying

seconds of the final and secured a six-pointer to just scrape home.

FINAL
1. Bo Shabalaba
2. Lungani Memani
3. Bertjie Stuurman
4. David Solomons
SEMIFINAL 1
1. Bertjie Stuurman
2. Lungani Memani
3. Grant Arendse
4. Roger Vuanza
SEMIFINAL 2
1. Bo Shabalaba
2. David Solomons
3. James Maddocks
4. Dominic Abersailie

QUIKSILVER PRO DURBAN • MEN'S 6-STAR WQS PRIME
NEW PIER, DURBAN
April 13–20

An inspired performance in excellent surf at alternative venue Ansteys, on the Bluff near Durban, gave Durban's Davey Weare victory over the USA's Austin Ware. Although only one letter separates their names, there was a world of difference between the surfers in a one-sided final, with Weare peaking in front of a huge hometown crowd.

FINAL
1. David Weare
2. Austin Ware
SEMIFINAL 1
1. Austin Ware
2. Jihad Khodr
SEMIFINAL 2
1. David Weare
2. Tiago Pires
QUARTERFINAL 1
1. Austin Ware
2. Josh Kerr
QUARTERFINAL 2
1. Jihad Khodr
2. Heitor Alves
QUARTERFINAL 3
1. David Weare
2. Justin Barca

QUARTERFINAL 4
1. Tiago Pires
2. Leigh Sedley

QUIKSILVER GOODWAVE
NEW PIER, DURBAN
April 13

Durban local Shane Thorne was R75,000 richer after an incredible day's surfing in six foot plus sets at New Pier for the Quiksilver Goodwave. Rudy Palmboom Jr set the bar for the day with a perfect 10 point ride in which he emerged from a seemingly impossible barrel. In grinding waves for the final, Thorne pulled off he win with a long one on the hooter for 8.75.

FINAL
1. Shane Thorne
2. Dan Redman
3. Sean Holmes
4. Paul Canning
SEMIFINAL 1
1. Paul Canning
2. Dan Redman
3. Frankie Oberholzer
4. Dane Logie
SEMIFINAL 2
1. Sean Holmes
2. Shane Thorne
3. Simon Nicholson
4. Rudy Palmboom

BILLABONG JUNIOR SERIES AFRICA #2
BAY OF PLENTY
April 25–27

Klee Strachan continued a phenomenal run of form that has seen him reach the top five in the last four Pro Juniors when he won the second stop of the Billabong Pro Junior Series in Durban. Strachan used superior wave strategy in the long right-handers at Bay of Plenty.

PRO JUNIOR (UNDER 20 MEN)
1. Klee Strachan
2. Mark Shepperson
3. Shawn Dennis
4. Chad du Toit
UNDER 16 BOYS
1. Michael February
2. Jacob Mellish
3. Davey Brand
4. Beyrick de Vries
UNDER 14 BOYS
1. Slade Prestwich
2. Jarred Veldhuis
3. Dylan Lightfoot
4. Brandon Benjamin
UNDER 12 BOYS
1. Benji Brand
2. Max Armstrong
3. Jordy Maree
4. Jonah Paarman

JEEP SOUTH AFRICAN LONGBOARD 2008 CHAMPS
NOORDHOEK/LONG BEACH, KOMMETJIE
April 26–May 2

South Africa's top longboarder Mat-

Beyrick de Vries. Photo gregewingphoto.com.

thew Moir again showed his mettle in winning the Jeep SA Titles over a week of competition in varying conditions.

FINAL
1. Matthew Moir
2. Thomas King
3. Justin Bing
4. Johnno Rosslind

BILLABONG JUNIOR SERIES AFRICA #3
BIG BAY, CAPE TOWN
May 9–11

Chad du Toit put on a brilliant display to win the premier U/20 division in cross-shore conditions at Big Bay in Cape Town. Du Toit combo'ed his opponent, Rudy Palmboom, in the man-on-man final after a 9-point ride.

PRO JUNIOR (UNDER 20 MEN)
1. Chad du Toit
2. Rudy Palmboom
3. Kyle Beach
4. Dale Staples
UNDER 16 BOYS
1. Beyrick de Vries
2. Davey Brand
3. Devin Lane
4. Dane Staples
UNDER 14 BOYS
1. Steven Sawyer
2. Slade Prestwich
3. Diran Zakarian
4. Dylan Lightfoot
UNDER 12 BOYS
1. Benji Brand
2. Max Armstrong
3. Jason Harris
4. Jordan Maree

LIZZARD NANDO'S SURF PRO • MEN'S 1-STAR WQS EVENT #14 / GRADE 1 ASP JUNIOR MEN'S EVENT / SSA WOMEN'S 2A PRO DIVISION
NORTH BEACH, DURBAN
May 15–18

Casey Grant (Scottburgh) won the international Pro Junior event at the Lizzard Nando's, overcoming a strong challenge from Klee Strachan (Winkelspruit). Greg Emslie overcame tricky conditions to take

out the Men's Pro, while Nikita Robb beat veteran Heather Clark in the Women.

FINAL
1. Casey Grant
2. Klee Strachan
3. Kyle Lane
4. Nic Godfrey
MEN OPEN
1. Greg Emslie
2. Dan Redman
WOMEN OPEN
1. Nikita Robb
2. Heather Clark

LIZZARD TAG SERIES #1
STRAND BEACH, WESTERN CAPE
May 31

Chilly weather greeted contestants at Strand Beach, but by lunchtime the sun was out and the waves were firing, as 50 girls and boys competed in tag teams for the title.

FINAL
1. Whipping Wave Warriors
    Jacob Mellish
    Dumile Sukati
    Marco Laubscher
    Tyler Terblanche
    Bradley Roberts
2. Rebel Reverts
    Rigard Smit
    Charl de Waal
    Tosca Wynand
    Benjamin De Castro
    Ryan Hayes
3. Gecko's
    Elroy Thomas
    Leon Du Preez
    Stephen Jamieson
    Tammy Wynand
    Brett Roberts
4. Young Guns 5
    Chandre Bodenstein
    Papi Makhanyani
    Ethan Fletcher
    David Burrows
    Matthew Marais

QUIKSILVER KING OF THE GROMS
INNER POOL, MOSSEL BAY
June 14–15

Form surfer Davey Brand took out his first crown in waves varying from good to excellent at Mossel Bay.

UNDER 20 MEN
1. Shaun Joubert
2. Klee Strachan
3. Davey Brand
4. Nick Godfrey
UNDER 16 GROMS
1. Davey Brand
2. Mikey February
3. Benji Brand
4. Steve Sawyer

REEF WETSUITS SOUTH AFRICAN MASTERS CHAMPS
NAHOON REEF, EAST LONDON
June 12–15

Host province Border won the team title at the Reef Wetsuits Masters held in excellent four-foot waves at Nahoon Reef.

SENIORS (OVER 30)
1. Ryan Ribbink
2. Gary Van Wieringen
3. Graeme Field
4. Tristan Johnson
MASTERS (OVER 35)
1. Wayne Monk
2. Andrew Carter
3. Rob Pollock
4. Carl Roux
GRANDMASTERS (OVER 40)
1. Dave Malherbe
2. Andre Malherbe
3. Gareth Sepp
4. Steve Adshade
KAHUNAS (OVER 45)
1. Steven Hair
2. Nick Pike
3. Colin Buitendag
4. David Stubbs
GRANDKAHUNAS (OVER 50)
1. Chris Knutsen
2. Brian Heathcote
3. Jeremy Zinn
4. Tortie Cloete
VETERANS (OVER 55)
1. Dave Fish
2. Mush Hide
3. Rob Head
4. Mike Godfrey
PROVINCIAL TEAMS
1. Border
2. Eastern Province
3. Kwazulunatal
4. Western Province
5. Boland
6. Southern Cape
7. Southern Kzn

RIP CURL GROMSEARCH DURBAN, PRESENTED BY ISLAND TRIBE
DAIRY BEACH, DURBAN
June 21–22

Beyrick de Vries defeated national junior team-mate Davey Brand to take out the Under 16 Boys division of the first GromSearch for 2008. The lead see-sawed in a tight final before 15-year-old de Vries scored a 7.75 to take the title. De Vries dedicated his win to plucky junior surfer Mik le Roux who competed despite losing his mother and sister in a horrific car accident the night before.

UNDER 16 BOYS
1. Beyrick de Vries
2. Davey Brand
UNDER 16 GIRLS
1. Bianca Buitendag
2. Sarah Baum
UNDER 14 BOYS
1. Benji Brand
2. Josh Smit
UNDER 14 GIRLS
1. Sarah Baum
2. Chanelle Botha
UNDER 12 BOYS
1. Benji Brand
2. Jason Harris

INSIGHT SURFING OPEN
STRAND BEACH
June 21

Thirty-two surfers of all ages took part in the inaugural Insight Open, held in contestable 2-to-4-foot surf.

FINAL
1. Joske de Beer
2. Frank Solomons
3. Philip Visagie
4. Jurie van Staden

Chris Davidson. Photo Debiky/Mr. Price.

BILLABONG SASSU CHAMPIONSHIPS
CAPE ST FRANCIS
June 23-25

Josh Salie and Telana Flanagan took the individual titles, while the University of Cape Town took Men's team honors and Nelson Mandela Metropolitan the Women's in windswept half-meter waves at the fabled point.

MEN OPEN
1. Josh Sailie
2. Chris Bond
3. Kyle Jacobs
4. Greg Hayseldon
WOMEN OPEN
1. Telana Flanagan
2. Kerri-Leigh Anderson
3. Angelique Laurie
4. Lara Humby

MR. PRICE PRO JUNIOR
NORTH BEACH, DURBAN
June 26–29

Southern Cape surfers Shaun Joubert and Bianca Buitendag outshone

Silvana Lima. Photo ASP Cestari © Covered Images.

the competition in clean half-meter waves to take their respective divisions of the Mr. Price Pro Junior, curtain-raiser for the Mr. Price Pro WQS event. A stoked Joubert won a wildcard into the main event.

JUNIOR MEN
1. Shaun Joubert
2. Kyle Lane
3. Rudy Palmboom
4. Casey Grant
JUNIOR GIRLS
1. Bianca Buitendag
2. Chantel Rautenbag
3. Tarryn Chudleigh
4. Faye Zoetmulder

MR. PRICE PRO • ASP 6-STAR WQS MEN'S EVENT 19 / ASP 5-STAR WQS WOMEN'S EVENT 7
NORTH BEACH, DURBAN
June 29–July 6

Australia's Chris Davidson crushed Travis Logie's hopes of becoming only the second South African to win the Mr. Price before a patriotic crowd at New Pier. The crumbly small surf appeared to favor the Aussie, whose powerful frontside attack saw him score 16.10, to win comfortably from the local and move to seventh on the ratings. The former WCT competitor who is on the comeback trail finished with a brilliant 9.43 to put Logie out of the running.

MEN FINAL
1. Chris Davidson
2. Travis Logie
SEMIFINAL 1
1. Travis Logie
2. Patrick Gudauskas
SEMIFINAL 2
1. Chris Davidson
2. Neco Padaratz
QUARTERFINAL 1
1. Patrick Gudauskas
2. Jeremy Flores
QUARTERFINAL 2
1. Travis Logie
2. Jordy Smith
QUARTERFINAL 3
1. Neco Padaratz
2. Nathan Yeomans
QUARTERFINAL 4
1. Chris Davidson
2. Drew Courtney

Former Women's World number three Silvana Lima from Brazil scored a perfect 10 in a stellar performance to become the second-ever Brazilian Women's champion at the Mr. Price. The experienced and often radical Lima had all the answers for French schoolgirl Pauline Ado.

WOMEN FINAL
1. Silvana Lima
2. Pauline Ado
SEMIFINAL 1
1. Silvana Lima
2. Bruna Schmitz
SEMIFINAL 2
1. Pauline Ado
2. Lee Ann Curren
QUARTERFINAL 1
1. Bruna Schmitz
2. Heather Clark

QUARTERFINAL 2
1. Silvana Lima
2. Sally Fitzgibbons
QUARTERFINAL 3
1. Pauline Ado
2. Rosanne Hodge
QUARTERFINAL 4
1. Lee-Ann Curren
2. Laurina McGrath

RED BULL BIG WAVE AFRICA
DUNGEONS
July 24–August 31

South African hellman Grant Twiggy Baker caught two heart-stopping waves in raging 15-to-20-foot at Dungeons Reef to take out the international final at the Red Bull Big Wave Africa. Finals day produced some of the best waves ever ridden at Dungeons, as well as some of the most dangerous. Durban surfer Jason Ribbink suffered a concussion and had to withdraw after going over the falls backwards in a massive wipeout. Former champion Greg Long set up a huge bowl section barrel for a perfect 10, but it was to be Baker's day.

Grant (Twiggy) Baker on a bomb. Photo Alan van Gysen.

Nick Godfrey. Photo MoonRocket.

1. Grant Baker
2. Carlos Burle
3. Greg Long
4. James Taylor
5. Anthony Tashnick
6. Mark Healey

LIZZARD TAG SERIES #2
POLLOCK BEACH, PORT ELIZABETH
July 27

Team Men In Black fought their way through the repecharge heats to finally take out the second Lizzard tag event of the season in clean waves. Each team includes boys, girls and rookies.

1. Men In Black
   Ismaeel Abrahams
   Dave Kelly
   Kerri Viljoen
   Dylan Lightfoot
   Jonathan Naude
2. The Nutters
   Grant Beck
   Gay Thomas
   Tahra Uren

   Carl Barnard
   Nafees Salie
3. Sand Lizzards
   Remi Petersen
   Jordan Zeelie
   Kyla Naude
   Andre Scheepers
   Keane Hansen
4. Amphibious Dudes
   Merrick Fairall
   Jason Wells
   Tess Saunders
   Tobias Schroeder
   Matthew McGillivray

REEF WETSUITS SOUTH AFRICAN CHAMPIONSHIPS
VICTORIA BAY
July 24–27

The Eastern Province surfing team made history on the final day of the Reef Championships when they won the President's Cup for the first time. Thanks to brilliant performances by newly crowned SA men's champion Shaun Payne and Under 20 Boys champion Nick Godfrey, the EP team nudged out

Mikey February. Photo Greg Ewing/Quiksilver.

Border in a thrilling finish in 4-to-6-foot clean surf.

OPEN MEN
1. Shaun Payne
2. Simon Fish
3. Llewellyn Whittaker
4. Matt Kruger
OPEN WOMEN
1. Heather Clark
2. Stacey Guy
3. Kirsty Delport
4. Roxy Towill
UNDER 20 MEN
1. Nick Godfrey
2. Shaun Joubert
3. Michael February
4. Clinton Gravett
UNDER 20 WOMEN
1. Bianca Buitendag
2. Faye Zoetmuller
3. Alice McGregor
4. Chantelle Rautenbach

BILLABONG JUNIOR SERIES AFRICA #4
VICTORIA BAY
August 7–10

Nick Godfrey revelled in near-

perfect overhead conditions to defeat top seed Klee Strachan in the premier Boys division. Beyrick de Vries took his third U/16 title of the year in a convincing display of power surfing.

UNDER 20 MEN
1. Nick Godfrey
2. Klee Strachan
UNDER 16 BOYS
1. Beyrick de Vries
2. Michael February
3. David van Zyl
4. Dane Staples

QUIKSILVER KING OF THE GROMS MOSSEL BAY
SCOTTBURGH, KZN
August 16–17

Kommetjie's Mikey February is the new South African King of the Groms. Despite being eliminated in the quarterfinals, he had accumulated enough points to earn him the crown and a trip to France to compete in the International King of the Groms.

PREMIER GROMS
1. Dane Staples
2. Jacob Mellish
3. Remi Petersen
3. David van Zyl
UNDER 20S
1. Casey Grant
2. Klee Strachan
3. Chad Du Toit
3. Chris Leppan

O'NEILL COLDWATER CLASSIC
MOBILE ON THE CAPE
August 21–24

Josh Redman employed his pat-

Josh Redman. Photo Craig Kolesky.

ented power approach in double overhead surf at the Crayfish Factory big-wave spot near Cape Town to take the O'Neill Coldwater Classic. But it wasn't an easy win for the strongly built 20-year-old from Durban. He won on a count-back after tying with local Ian Armstrong. The Women's title went to Kirsty Delport from Durban.

OPEN MEN
1. Josh Redman
2. Ian Armstrong
3. Clinton Gravett
4. Matthew Bromley

OPEN WOMEN
1. Kirsty Delport
2. Tarryn Chudleigh
3. Chantelle Rautenbach
4. Tasha Mentasti

OPEN BOYS
1. Casey Grant
2. Davey Brand
3. Chris Leppan
4. Michael February

RIP CURL GROMSEARCH #2
MOSSEL BAY, SOUTHERN CAPE
September 6–7

The Kommetjie-based duo of Davey Brand and Tanika Hoffman clinched the premier divisions at the second of four stops on the Rip Curl GromSearch at Inner Pool, Mossel Bay. With the waves ruffled slightly from an onshore breeze, but still offering plenty of scoring opportunities, Brand took the lead from Jacob Mellish eight minutes into the final and then used his priority to good effect. In the Girls, Hoffman was on fire all day, never losing a heat.

UNDER 16 BOYS
1. Davey Brand
2. Jacob Mellish
3. JC Susan
4. Dane Staples

UNDER 16 GIRLS
1. Tanika Hoffman
2. Anna Notten
3. Sabrina Scott
4. Holly Armstrong

UNDER 14 BOYS
1. Steven Sawyer
2. Dylan Lightfoot
3. Benji Brand
4. Daniel Buitendag

UNDER 14 GIRLS
1. Emma Smith
2. Gina Smith
3. Amy Bosworth
4. Tahra Uren

UNDER 12 BOYS
1. Max Armstrong
2. Benji Brand
3. Jordy Maree
4. Donovan Wichman

LIZZARD TAG SERIES #3
ST. MICHAELS ON SEA, KZN
September 13

The strongest northeast wind seen all year on the KwazaZulu coast hammered the Lizzard Tag teams and turned the St. Mikes surf into a washing machine, making it extremely hazardous for the juniors. Nine-year-old Wesley Goodwin had to use all of his nipper lifesaving skills to avoid being smashed onto the rocks at one point.

1. Bombers
2. Sharks
3. Potatoes
4. Hobos

BILLABONG JUNIOR SERIES FINAL EVENT
JEFFREYS BAY
September 18–21

Dale Staples took out the final event of the Billabong Junior Series, but it was consistent Klee Strachan who

Dale Staples. Photo MoonRocket.

clinched the prestigious series title, despite finishing equal fifth at Jeffreys. Klee secured a trip to Australia for the World Series in January.

UNDER 12 BOYS
1. Max Armstrong
2. Benji Brand
3. Jonah Paarman
4. Donovan Wichman

PRO JUNIOR BOYS SERIES
1. Klee Strachan

UNDER 16 BOYS
1. Beyrick de Vries

UNDER 14 BOYS
1. Slade Prestwich

UNDER 12 BOYS
1. Benji Brand

JEFFREYS BAY EVENT (#5)

PRO JUNIOR BOYS
1. Dale Staples
2. Rudy Palmboom
3. Shaun Joubert
4. Chris Leppan

PRO JUNIOR GIRLS
1. Sarah Baum
2. Bianca Buitendag
3. Nikita Robb
4. Tarryn Chudleigh

UNDER 16 BOYS
1. Jacob Mellish
2. Davey Brand
3. Beyrick de Vries
4. David van Zyl

RIP CURL GROMSEARCH
KOMMETJIE, CAPE TOWN
September 27–28

Davey Brand and Sarah Baum took out the premier divisions in the third round of the Rip Curl GromSearch in tiny waves at Long Beach. The two 14-year-old goofy-footers dominated in the difficult conditions.

UNDER 16 BOYS
1. Davey Brand
2. JC Susan
3. Bradley van Zyl
4. Jacob Mellish

UNDER 16 GIRLS
1. Sarah Baum
2. Tanika Hoffman
3. Anna Notten
4. Sabrina Scott

UNDER 14 BOYS
1. Benji Brand
2. Jarred Veldhuis
3. Max Armstrong
4. Slade Prestwich

UNDER 14 GIRLS
1. Sarah Baum
2. Anoush Zakarian
3. Amy Bosworth
4. Camden Ravenscroft

REEF WETSUITS SA NATIONAL JUNIORS
ST MIKES, KZN
October 1–5

KwaZulu-Natal claimed provincial honors and the Freedom Cup at the Reef Juniors after five days of mixed conditions.

UNDER18 BOYS
1. Matthew Bromley
2. Chad Du Toit
3. Brendan Gibbens
4. Shawn Dennis

UNDER 18 GIRLS
1. Chantelle Rautenbach
2. Kirsty Delport
3. Alice McGregor
4. Faye Zoetmuller

UNDER 16 BOYS
1. Davey Brand
2. Michael February
3. Jacob Mellish
4. Devin Lane

UNDER 16 GIRLS
1. Bianca Buitendag
2. Heidi Palmboom
3. Tanika Hoffman
4 Holly Armstrong

FREEDOM CUP
1. KZN
2. Western Province
3. Eastern Province
4. Boland

REEF WETSUITS SA SCHOOLS CHAMPIONSHIPS
CAPE PENINSULA
October 25–26

Perfect weather and three-foot waves produced ideal conditions for this schools teams event.

Primary school champs Sun Valley. Photo Ali Forder.

HIGH SCHOOLS
1. Durban High
2. Fellowship College, Melkbosstrand
3. Northwood High, Durban
4. Silvermine Academy

PRIMARY SCHOOLS
1. Sun Valley
2. Kommetjie
3. Fish Hoek
4. Lantana

RIP CURL GROMSEARCH GRAND FINAL
SOUTHBROOM, KZN
November 1–2

Beyrick de Vries and Sarah Baum won tickets to Australia and invitations into the Rip Curl International GromSearch when they won the premier divisions in solid surf at Southbroom Point.

UNDER 16 BOYS
1. Beyrick de Vries
2. Davey Brand
3. Michael February
4. JC Susan

UNDER 16 GIRLS
1. Sarah Baum
2. Tanika Hoffman
3. Holly Armstrong
4. Bianca Buitendag

UNDER 14 BOYS
1. Benji Brand
2. Jarred Veldhuis
3. Max Armstrong
4. Dylan Lightfoot

UNDER 14 GIRLS
1. Sarah Baum
2. Caryn McNicol
3. Emma Smith
4. Chantelle Botha

UNDER 12 BOYS
1. Max Armstrong
2. Benji Brand
3. Jason Harris
4. Dylan Wichman

SOUTH COAST SURF CARNIVAL
SCOTTBURG MAIN BEACH
November 1–2

The 2008 edition of the South Coast Surf Carnival, presented by Jeep Apparel and the Independent on Saturday, was blessed with perfect conditions over both days, with Durban's Jason Ribbink taking full advantage to snatch the SALSA (South African Longboard Surfing Association) sanctioned Premier open division.

In the race to capture the first-ever Stand Up Paddleboard (SUP) title in South Africa, Dylan

Beyrick de Vries. Photo Craig Kolesky.

Tarryn Chudleigh. Photo B. Tuck.

McCleod (Eastern Cape) was clearly the most consistent performer and rightly claimed the prestigious title and the main prize of a BILT SUP valued at R12 500.

In addition to the Longboard and SUP divisions, the crowd at Scottburgh's main beach witnessed some radical maneuvers in the longest-running kitesurfing event in the country, thanks in part to the strong southwesterly wind that blew all Sunday.

Here, Craig Chrystal (Durban) and Lyle Bottcher (Durban North) took 1st and 2nd place respectively in the Men's Open event, while Nicole Annells (Warner Beach) triumphed in the Women's division, defeating pre-event favorite Kathryn Clarke-Mcleod (Amanzimtoti). Bryce Rawlins (Umhlanga) cemented his position as one of the country's leading up-and-coming kitesurfers when he successfully defended his Junior title.

In the longboarding event, a Women's division, as well as a Grandmasters (age 35+) and Over 50 division were contested. Competition was strong due to the large field, but it was Zanie Cawood (Durban) who clinched victory in the Women's event.

OPEN LONGBOARD
Jason Ribbink
STAND UP PADDLE
Dylan McCleod
KITESURFING (MEN)
Craig Chrystal
WOMEN
Nicole Annells

VOLCOM ELEPHANTFISH VQS
PORT ALFRED, SOUTH AFRICA
November 8–9

Excellent surf running down the Port Alfred sandbanks greeted the Totally Crustaceous Tour competitors gathered for the Volcom Elephantfish event. Surfers who were blowing up from their first round heats were the likes of Shaun Payne from St. Francis, Brandon Jackson from Durban, East Londoner Devyn Matthys and Warwick "Wok" Wright

from Durban. The girl surfers who were ripping in the predominant right-handers were Capetonian Tarryn Chudleigh, who finished first in the Ladies division ahead of Faye Zoetmulder, Karen McDonald and Alice MacGregor.

Groms were also finding the Port Alfred waves to their liking, and it was Dylan Lightfoot who set the pace in the final, winning ahead of Steve Sawyer, Matthew MacGilroy and Benji Brand.

The junior surfers were cutting loose, and showing the other surfers and spectators alike where the next South African surfing push is going to be coming from. It was Davey Brand's turn for victory, placing ahead of Grant Beck, Jean Du Plessis and Phillip Britz.

It was the Open division that saw the big hitters racking up some top scores, with Shaun Payne doing some of the massive hits for those high scores. The final was all about Payne, as he was the only surfer to find an elusive barrel-ride for the highest score of the heat that saw him clinch victory.

GIRLS
Tarryn Chudleigh
BOYS
Davey Brand
OPEN
Shaun Payne

VOLCOM STONE BABOONFISH VQS
CAPE TOWN, SOUTH AFRICA
November 15–16

A weekend that delivered excellent surf and fine weather in Cape Town saw local surfer Craig Johnson claim victory in the third event of the Volcom Totally Crustaceous Tour. The earlier rounds saw fun and highly contestable surf at Misty Cliffs, and Durban surfers Josh Redman and Chris Leppan were tearing through the early heats.

The Grom division saw an on-form Jarred Veldhuis show fellow Kommetjie surfer Max Armstrong how it's done by scooping 1st place, with Armstrong in 2nd. Leon Du Preez was in 3rd place, while Diran

Jason Ribbink. Photo Paul Godwin/Nerve Events/South Africa.

Zacharian was 4th.

Tarryn Chudleigh kept the Cape flag flying high by winning the Women's division, outpointing Melkbosstrand surfer Stacey Guy. Holly Armstrong from Kommetjie was in 3rd and Bluff surfer Heidi Palmboom came in 4th.

Always a hotbed of up-and-coming talent, the Junior division saw some of the hottest surfing of the day, with these surfers competing intensely for the title. Local ripper Brendon Gibbens fought a fierce battle against Nicky Godfrey from St. Francis in the final, with Gibbens getting the nod against Godfrey. Kommetjie surfer Mikey February came in 3rd place, with JC Susan trailing in at 4th.

Craig Johnson blasted all the way to the final of the Open division, showing just how much local knowledge counts in these tightly fought events, beating fellow local Brendon Gibbens.

GROMS
1. Jarred Veldhuis
2. Max Armstrong
3. Leon Du Preez
4. Diran Zacharian
JUNIORS
1. Brendon Gibbens
2. Nicky Godfrey
3. Mikey February
4. JC Susan
WOMEN
1. Tarryn Chudleigh

2. Stacey Guy
3. Holly Armstrong
4. Heidi Palmboom
OPEN MEN
1. Craig Johnson
2. Brendon Gibbens
3. Mikhael Thompson
4. Andrew Lange

ROXY WAHINE CUP, PRESENTED BY VIRGIN MOBILE
SUNCOAST BEACH, DURBAN
December 6–7

There wasn't much room to move at the 10th Edition of the Roxy Wahine Cup, as thousands of spectators arrived to watch the best female surfers in the country battle it out for top honors. In small but fun surf, the girls took to the water, all vying for a place in the finals and a share of the prize money.

The first final to hit the water was the Novice division final, with a one-year Roxy sponsorship as first prize. New face Mia Hordyk from Durban surfed impressively to score 17.25 (out of a possible 20) in the fun waves, winning the Novice Division and securing her Roxy Sponsorship. An amazing fact is that Mia first learned to surf by participating in the Roxy Learn to Surf Tour.

In the Under 14 division, Durban ripper Sarah Baum showed her local knowledge and completely

outshone her opponents, winning the final with a massive margin from 2nd placed Chanelle Botha. Courtnay Ellish and Emma Smith came in 3rd and 4th spots.

The Under 16 division final was another clear-cut victory, with the honors going to Tanika Hoffman from Kommetjie, who completely out pointed her fellow competitors.

International experience shone through when Nikita Robb from East London surfed through to a comfortable win in the U/20 division. Nikita has been competing hard on the WQS this year and just returned from a season in Hawaii to surf this event.

The Open division was a tight affair, with some interference calls and some seriously competitive surfing going down. Nikita Robb was surfing well and looking like she might win this division as well, but she was penalized in the final with an interference call and ended up placing 4th. In the end, it was an ecstatic Tarryn Chudleigh who emerged victorious, beating Chantelle Rautenbach into 2nd, with Tammy Lee Smith coming 3rd. Tarryn, a stylish goofy-footer from Kommetjie, surfed exceptionally well throughout the event and was a deserving winner.

NOVICES
1. Mia Hordyk
2. Jodie Kennedy
3. Bianca Potgieter
4. Paige Orbe
UNDER 14
1. Sarah Baum
2. Chanelle Botha
3. Courtnay Ellish
4. Emma Smith
UNDER 16
1. Tanika Hoffman
2. Nikita Kekana
3. Heather Klug
4. Sabrina Scott
UNDER 20
1. Nikita Robb
2. Chantelle Rautenbach
3. Alice McGregor
4. Heidi Palmboom
OPEN WOMEN
1. Tarryn Chudleigh
2. Chantell Rautenbach
3. Tammy-Lee Smith
4. Nikita Robb

OCEAN BE

A N D

earth

Pic: Morris

Pic: Morris

Pic: Morris

Australia

Mick Fanning, 27, and Steph Gilmore, 19, returned to Australia to unanimous applause after claiming the nation's first world pro title sweep since 1999. The thrill didn't last long: Steph was eliminated in round three of the first event of the year, the Roxy Pro at her home break of Snapper Rocks, by 15-year-old phenom Carissa Moore, while Mick broke his wrist snowboarding in Japan. Fanning came back to record second and fifth at Snapper and Bells Beach respectively. Kelly Slater, 36, won both events to take a quick lead in the championship race.

Warning signs of a plateau in the local surf industry's growth curve continued to flash, with flat surf shop retail sales and a broad mood of uncertainty in the core hard goods arena. Firewire Surfboards, based in Burleigh Heads, moved most of its production offshore to a factory in Thailand to reduce costs. Later in the year, increasing economic gloom caused iconic surf company Quiksilver to abandon sponsorship of regional Sate junior championships throughout the nation for 2009, and of the Roxy World Qualifying Series event at Phillip Island, Victoria.

Alex "Alfy" Cater won the Biggest Wave award of the Oakley Surfing Life Big Wave Awards, for a 45-footer ridden off West Australia's Cow Bombie reef. Alfy got A$20,000 and a jetski for the win. Other winners included Marti Paradisis (Best Overall) and Jamie Scott (Shooter Award).

Koby Abberton, star of the *Bra Boys* documentary, was quoted in one of the nation's Sunday newspapers as saying that Mark Wahlberg had signed to play him in a movie version of the story; Wahlberg's agents denied the claim. Koby also struck a deal with prosecutors in Hawaii, who had charged him over an alleged assault on a Honolulu nightclub bouncer. In November he was sentenced to three days' jail.

Darren Longbottom, 35, a skilled surfer and surf shop owner from Kiama, went over the falls on a five-foot wave at Thunders in the Mentawais, struck his board with the top of his head, and was rendered quadriplegic; an impromptu evacuation by helicopter followed. It was Darren's first trip to the area. In a farcical postscript, the helicopter pilot, New Zealand doctor Derek Allan, had his aircraft impounded by Indonesian authorities for not filing a flight plan. An assistance fund for future evacs is being raised. Contributions can be made to www.troppodoc.com.

Semi-pro "adventure" surf missions continued to explore the southern facing coasts of the continent, with a number of astonishing reef breaks being uncovered and ridden via the PWC. The moviemaking team of Ross Clarke-Jones and Justin McMillan spent several months working on a showcase piece for the USA's Discovery Channel; in late June, accompanied by Tom Carroll, Ian Walsh and several support crew, they rode the "Dangerous Bank" off Trial Harbour in Tasmania, in sleet and 30-knot onshores, and followed it up with an expedition to Eddystone Rock off southern Tasmania. The results were aired on the TV current affairs show "60 Minutes".

Australasia Report
By Nick Carroll

Seven-time champ Layne Beachley battled to find co-sponsorship for her eponymous event at Manly Beach, finally securing a bank; later, in a tearful press conference, Layne announced her forthcoming retirement from the ASP world tour. The event was won by 14-year-old Tyler Wright, from Culburra on the NSW south coast . . .

Australia's first double world champions since 1999 enjoy the moment. Photo ASP Kirstin © Covered Images.

Layne Beachley announces her retirement. Photo Nick Carroll.   *Peter Troy, mid-1960s. Photo Barrie Sutherland.*

Retro cool continued almost unabated; in September a "Morning Of The Earth" concert was held in Sydney, featuring the original bands playing the soundtrack while the movie itself flickered onscreen behind. It was greeted with rapture by an audience that included several of the old movie's surf stars. In fascinating contrast, Peter Drouyn, 58, a former Australian champion and creator of the original pro man-on-man system at the 1977 Stubbies Classic, announced his intention to undergo gender reassignment surgery, telling tabloid TV news show "Today Tonight" that his new name is "Westerly Windina" and that he hoped to develop a career on the stage.

In environmental news, the Tweed River sand bypass pumping system responsible for the so-called "Superbank" eased its load from around 800,000 cubic metres of sand per year to around 500,000; over time, it is expected the easing may result

in some recovery for the currently sand-choked Kirra Point. Several surf spots, including Maroubra, Cronulla, Crescent Head, Lennox Head and Angourie, were given honorary status as National Surfing Reserves; while this status has no particular force in law, it is seen as a first step toward ongoing legal protection of the nation's finest surfing zones. Numerous other surf spots, including Bastion Point in eastern Victoria and "The Farm" just south of Sydney, remain under threat from development.

Layne Beachley, 36, seven-time World Women's Pro Champ, released a biography, written by Michael Gordon. She battled to find co-sponsorship for her eponymous event at Manly Beach, finally securing a bank; later, in a tearful press conference, Layne announced her forthcoming retirement from the ASP world tour. The event was won by 14-year-old Tyler Wright, from Culburra on the NSW south coast; Tyler became the youngest ever

winner of a WCT.

Team Australia won its third successive overall ISA World Surfing Games title, winning the Women's via Sally Fitzgibbons and dominating the Men's final with three of the four finalists. But Heath Joske, Dayyan Neve and Kai Otton couldn't quite get the better of the USA's CJ Hobgood in the final.

Several Australian surfers died in the waves, including Maldives pioneer Tony Hussein Hinde, and a holidaying honeymooner at Gnaraloo, Western Australia. Peter Troy, legendary surf traveller and raconteur, died from a blood clot in his lung.

Asia

Bali's expatriate population continued to swell, with numerous pros, ex-pros, media and surf industry people from California, Hawaii and Australia setting up home on the enchanted isle. Permanent or near-permanent residents now include Taylor Steele, Rob Machado, Mikala Jones, Jake Paterson, Christian Fletcher, photographer Dustin Humphrey, journalist Nathan Myers; constant visitors include just about anyone who wants to be in one of Taylor's movies. The Rip Curl Search event ran at Uluwatu and Padang Padang while battling to maintain the fictional secrecy of its "Somewhere in Indo" location; the event was won by Bruce Irons, who'd previously announced his intention of

quitting the ASP World Tour, very likely in order to go surfing more often in Bali. At the same time, the island was haunted by the specter of coastal overdevelopment and its associated problems of pollution and degrading local services; the issue was highlighted by a dramatic hotel development overlooking Dreamland at the base of the Bukit peninsula, where local warung vendors were evicted by the developers.

Thailand, Taiwan and China continued to play an essential role in filling the world's surfboard supply; despite a slight downturn in overall numbers, the eastern Asian surfboard complex pushed out an estimated 350,000 boards of various kinds through 2008, or around a third of the global market.

New Zealand

After a 15-year battle over its possible effects on the legendary Whangamata rivermouth sandbar, a $20 million marina development project finally got underway inside the rivermouth. Surfers fear the project will result in constant dredging, which could lead to the destruction of the break. Whangamata is the nation's second best known break after Raglan.

It was a year for women in New Zealand surfing, where the world's only remaining chicks-only hardcore surf mag - "Curl" - is published. Susie Smith, 62, received a letter of apology after going to court over an alleged assault in the surf by a 58-year-old man (who can't be named). Some local surfers at Te Awanga, where the alleged assault occurred, said Smith and her husband were being too greedy for waves. At the other end of the scale, 17-year-old Paige Hareb finished seventh on the ASP's women's WQS rankings for 2008, almost certainly sealing NZ's first ever women's WCT place. Paige will be NZ's only elite ASP WCT rep for 2009.

Lonely left, appreciative kangaroos. Photo MickeySmith.com.

HYUNDAI PRO LONGBOARD TOUR

MOUNT MAUNGANUI, NEW ZEALAND
January 5–6

Winner Rique Smith. Photo Terry Kavanaugh.

Lee-Ann Curren. Photo Steve Robertson.

Fun conditions greeted the finalists for New Zealand's premiere surfing event. Last year's victor, Daniel Kereopa, proved indomitable in what was to be a back-to-back win for the Raglan local. A crisp, 3-foot swell gave ample opportunities for all to display their finest work, with Kereopa being the definitive winner and local favorite Daryn McBride following up with a fine performance. Daisy Thomas brought her shortboard savvy to the event, outperforming her peers with a collection of progressive maneuvers.

OPEN MEN
FINAL
1. Daniel Kereopa
2. Daryn McBride
3. Dylan Barnfield
4. Ant McColl
SEMIFINAL 1
1. Daniel Kereopa
2. Dylan Barnfield
3. Thomas Kibblewhite
4. Michael Burling
SEMIFINAL 2
1. Ant McColl
2. Daryn McBride
3. Kelly Ryan
4. Sam Guthrie
QUARTERFINAL 1
1. Michael Burling
2. Thomas Kibblewhite
3. Daniel Proctor
4. Matt Hands
QUARTERFINAL 2
1. Daniel Kereopa
2. Dylan Barnfield
3. Matt Cockayne
4. Paul Culpan
QUARTERFINAL 3
1. Sam Guthrie
2. Ant McColl
3. Lynden Jennings
4. Sam Johnson
QUARTERFINAL 4
1. Kelly Ryan
2. Daryn McBride
3. Kirk Beyer
4. Steve Tyro
OVER 40 MEN
FINAL
1. Lynden Jennings
2. Michael Fitzharris
3. Mike Thomson
4. Mal Brady
SEMIFINAL 1
1. Mike Thomson
2. Mal Brady
3. David Storck
SEMIFINAL 2
1. Lynden Jennings
2. Michael Fitzharris
3. Grant Cochrane
OVER 50 MEN
FINAL
1. Viv Treacy
2. David Storck
3. Mike Thomson
4. Grant Cochrane
SEMIFINAL 1
1. Viv Treacy
2. Grant Cochrane
3. Ian Parker
SEMIFINAL 2
1. Mike Thomson
2. David Storck
3. Warwick Gray
UNDER 18 MEN
1. Sam Guthrie
2. Rick Williamson
3. Shaun Goddard
4. Hone Douglas
OPEN WOMEN
FINAL
1. Daisy Thomas
2. Shelly Jones
3. Claire Norman
4. Belinda Galley
SEMIFINAL 1
1. Claire Norman
2. Belinda Galley
3. Kirstie Thomsen
SEMIFINAL 2
1. Daisy Thomas
2. Shelly Jones
3. Michelle Langdon

HONOLUA BURLEIGH BOARDRIDERS SINGLE FIN CLASSIC

BURLEIGH HEADS QLD
January 5

Not the most perfect ocean for the finals of the Single Fin Classic, a stormy week flooding the lineup and beaches with all manner of flotsam and jetsam, including a dead cow. The four finalists, nevertheless, produced an admirable display of surfing on their pre-1985 equipment. Smith's father, the legendary, late Col Smith, shaped the Egan shooter on which his son won the event way back yesteryear. But Rique's prowess belied the antiquity of his equipment, with nothing short of a high performance display taking him to first place. Another Col Smith, this a channelled Free Flight pin tail, was ridden into third place by Neil Nicholas, with Alby Ross and pro-longboarder Jackson Close riding a G&S and a Richard Harvey respectively.

OPEN MEN
1. Rique Smith
2. Alby Ross
3. Neil Nicholas
4. Jackson Close

KUSTOM JETTY SURF PRO JUNIOR

BELLS BEACH, VICTORIA
January 8–14

Bells Beach unleashed its exceptional form for the Under 18 event, where 6-foot waves proved challenging for some and others revelled in the glassy conditions. Stuart Kennedy stormed the final of the contest, claiming the win a clear three points ahead of his rival Nick Vasicek in the man-on-man heat. The girls had to make the most of a lesser swell with onshore winds, but still managed to produce some exceptional surfing. Lee-Ann Curren, daughter of the great Tom Curren, stood out as the only non-Australian in the semifinals, going on to take the biggest win of her career thus far in the event's final.

BOYS
FINAL
1. Stuart Kennedy
2. Nick Vasicek
SEMIFINAL 1
1. Nick Vasicek
2. Nick Riley
SEMIFINAL 2
1. Stuart Kennedy
2. Klee Strachan
QUARTERFINAL 1
1. Nick Riley
2. Chris Friend
QUARTERFINAL 2
1. Nick Vasicek
2. Ellis Ericson
QUARTERFINAL 3
1. Klee Strachan
2. Granger Larson
QUARTERFINAL 4
1. Stuart Kennedy
2. Maxime Huscenot
GIRLS
FINAL
1. Lee-Ann Curren
2. Lori Kelly
SEMIFINAL 1
1. Angela Keighran
2. Lori Kelly
SEMIFINAL 2
1. Lee-Ann Curren
2. Sally Fitzgibbons

OZMOSIS / NOVA PRO JUNIOR • ASP AUSTRALASIA GRADE 3 JUNIOR MEN'S EVENT / ASP AUSTRALASIA GRADE 1 JUNIOR WOMEN'S EVENT

GUNNAMATTA, VICTORIA
January 16–20

Excellent waves and stellar performances greeted spectators for the two finals days of the Ozmosis/Nova Pro Junior. The Girls final came on the penultimate day, with Sally Fitzgibbons reinforcing her reputation as an exceptional force and a world champ in the making stepping up under pressure in the final ten minutes. The following day saw Newcastle's Craig Anderson take a nail biter, barely defeating Julian Wilson in the final minute of contest. The biggest win of his career, Anderson was elated at the win.

BOYS
FINAL
1. Craig Anderson
2. Julian Wilson
SEMIFINAL 1
1. Julian Wilson
2. Davey Cathels
SEMIFINAL 2
1. Craig Anderson
2. Richard Christie
QUARTERFINAL 1
1. Davey Cathels
2. Stuart Kennedy
QUARTERFINAL 2
1. Julian Wilson
2. Lincoln Taylor
QUARTERFINAL 3
1. Richard Christie
2. Perth Standlick
QUARTERFINAL 4
1. Craig Anderson
2. Chris Salisbury
GIRLS
FINAL
1. Sally Fitzgibbons
2. Kirby Wright

HYUNDAI NATIONAL SURFING CHAMPIONSHIPS, PRESENTED BY QUIKSILVER

GISBORNE, NEW ZEALAND
January 12–19

Jay Quinn swept the board at the Hyundai Nationals, taking the crowns for both the Open Men and Longboard divisions. Kaiaua Bay, on New Zealand's east coast, provided substantial waves for the final day of competition, with competitors challenged by, but reveling in, the 4- to 6-foot conditions. A shaky start saw the Gisborne local threatened by eventual runner-up Matt Scorringe, but Quinn stepped up to take the first place. Angie Koops of Kaikoura excelled in the ladies' division, combo'ing her fellow competitors to claim the convincing win.

OPEN MEN
1. Jay Quinn
2. Matt Scorringe
3. Bobby Hansen
4. Zennor Wernham
UNDER 18 BOYS
1. Sean Peggs
2. Johnny Hicks
3. Alex Dive
4. Buck Woods
MEN LONGBOARD
1. Jay Quinn
2. Thomas Kibblewhite
3. Dylan Barnfield
4. Trent Dickey
OVER 28 MEN
1. Damon Gunness
2. Motu Mataa
3. Mark Dovey
4. Larry Fisher
OVER 35 MEN
1. Matt Groube
2. Clint Daly
3. Shawn Collier
4. Doug Te Ranga
OVER 40 MEN
1. Michael Fitzharris
2. Eddie Daly
3. Glenn Shuker
4. Clinton Ashill
OVER 45 MEN
1. John Gisby
2. Glenn Shuker

Jay Quinn. Photo NZ Surfing Magazine.

3. Barry McCulloch
4. Rod Welch
OVER 50 MEN
1. John Gisby
2. Barry MacCulloch
3. Rod Welch
4. Gary Stevenson
OPEN WOMEN
1. Angie Koops
2. Daisy Thomas
3. Mischa Davis
4. Rosa Thompson
OVER 30 WOMEN
1. Michelle McCarthy
2. Janine Williams
3. Sherene McCormick
4. Cherie Wallis

2. Brendan Hay
3. Will Morrison
4. Navarone Davis
UNDER 16 GIRLS
1. Ellie-Jean Coffey
2. Paige Haggerston
3. Freya Prumm
4. Ali Kelly
UNDER 14 GIRLS
1. Ellie-Jean Coffey
2. Gemma Saunders
3. Sarah Kokkin
4. Emily Clapaudis
UNDER 12 GIRLS
1. Kirsten Ogden
2. Brooke Peachy
3. Remy Randall
4. Cali McDonagh

RIP CURL GROMSEARCH
CRONULLA,
NEW SOUTH WALES
January 19–22

South Cronulla turned on for the finals of the Rip Curl Gromsearch, a 4- to 5-foot swell giving ample opportunity for all competitors to show their talents. Davey Cathels proved to be too much for his fellow peers, posting a near-flawless 9.27 in the event's final. This was Cathels' first hurdle to claiming back-to-back wins in the national final event at Bells. Crescent Heads' Ellie-Jean Coffey showed expert competition form in the Girls final of the U/16 Rip Curl Gromsearch, trailing for much of the heat before coming back strongly to claim the title. Paige Haggerston (Coal Point) looked to be the shoe-in for the victory, but Coffey's mature attitude and critical wave selection won out. The win secured her a position in the Easter grand finals, held at Bells Beach. It was to be a double win for the young Central Coaster, who also went on to take out the U/14 division.

UNDER 16 BOYS
1. Davey Cathels
2. Oscar Scaners
3. Sam Patterson
4. Kurt Kiggins
UNDER 14 BOYS
1. Jake Scott
2. Saxon Lumsden
3. Tylah Hutchinson
4. Josh Hay
UNDER 12 BOYS
1. Jordan Olsson

BILLABONG ALLEY CLASSIC, PRESENTED BY PRINTPOINT
CURRUMBIN ALLEY,
QUEENSLAND
January 19–20

Local knowledge, alongside significant talents, gave Coolangatta's Luke Dorrington the upper edge in the final of the Billabong Alley Classic. Competing in the 3- to 4-foot right-handers of the Alley, the natural-footer showed strength and consummate competitive savvy to lead the final from the outset. A final score of 17.60 (out of a potential 20) proved to fellow competitors and spectators alike that Dorrington was the event's deserved winner.

FINAL
1. Luke Dorrington
2. Shaun Gossmann
3. Luke Hitchings
4. John Cummings

TAJ'S SMALL FRIES
YALLINGUP,
WESTERN AUSTRALIA
January 18–20

With junior surfers converging on WA's Shallows Beach, just north of Yallingup, from across the country, competition was always sure to be fierce. Relative newcomer Regan Fredricks (Cabarita) held a commanding position from the start of the four-man final, going on to take the win over Matt Banting (NSW),

Jack Freestone (QLD) and WA local Nathan Kikiros. Banting didn't walk away from the event empty-handed, though, claiming number one in the U/14 division. Sisters Laura and Bronte Macauley (Gracetown, WA) dominated the girls' competition, gaining first and second respectively, in the U/16, over local favorite, Felicity Palmateer (Hillarys) and Victorian India Payne. Bronte also went on to take out the U/14.

UNDER 16 BOYS
1. Regan Fredricks
2. Matt Banting
3. Jack Freestone
4. Nathan Kikiros
UNDER 14 BOYS
1. Matt Banting
2. Soli Bailey
3. Jesse Horner
4. Mitch Parkinson
UNDER 12 BOYS
1. Jack Robinson
2. Jacob Wilcox
3. James Flemming
4. James Young
UNDER 16 GIRLS
1. Laura Macauley
2. Bronte Macauley
3. Felicity Palmateer
4. India Payne
UNDER 14 GIRLS
1. Bronte Macauley
2. India Payne
3. Carly Lynch
4. Eliza Greene

ROXY SURF FESTIVAL • ASP WOMEN 3-STAR WWLT EVENT/ ASP WOMEN 6-STAR WQS EVENT / ASP WOMEN 6-STAR PRO JUNIOR EVENT
PHILLIP ISLAND, VICTORIA
January 21–28

Sally Fitzgibbons reinforced her reputation as one of Australia's "next big thing's" with a confident win in the Roxy Surf Festival 6-star WQS contest. Defeating ASP surfer Jessi Miley-Dyer in the semis, the 17-year-old giant slayer went on to post a nine-point ride in the final. But her adversary, Brazilian Bruna Schmitz, matched her score to put the final in the balance. Fitzgibbons refused to bow down, though, following her score up with an immaculate ride just .25 points shy of perfect, to claim the title.

6-STAR WQS
FINAL
1. Sally Fitzgibbons
2. Bruna Schmitz
SEMIFINAL 1
1. Sally Fitzgibbons
2. Jessi Miley- Dyer
SEMIFINAL 2
1. Bruna Schmitz
2. Bethany Hamilton
ASP WOMEN 3-STAR WWLT
FINAL
1. Jennifer Smith
2. Cassia Meador
3. Chelsea Williams
4. Emma Wilson

HURLEY BURLEIGH PRO JUNIOR • ASP GRADE 2 MEN PRO JUNIOR
BURLEIGH HEADS,
QUEENSLAND
January 22–28

Burleigh Heads hosted a wealth of talent for the Hurley-sponsored Pro Junior event, where Tamaroa McComb proved once more that he is a powerful force on the junior circuit. The Tahitian Gold Coast transplant defeated Stuart Kennedy (Coolum, QLD) in the 35-minute final, in front of a formidable local crowd. After a slow start, the 17-year-old came into his own, posting a pair of substantial wave scores to come out on top. The win also gave him a boost in the overall Pro Junior rankings, giving him a clear lead over Pro Junior number two, Nick Riley.

FINAL
1. Tamaroa McComb
2. Stuart Kennedy
SEMIFINAL 1
1. Stuart Kennedy
2. Billy Kean
SEMIFINAL 2
1. Tamaroa McComb
2. Heath Joske

BILLABONG PRO CORONA CROWN SERIES EVENT 3
WHANGAMATA,
NEW ZEALAND
January 26–28

Conditions at Whangamata were fun for the man-on-man final of the Billabong Pro, Maz Quinn doing well to take the win over Raglan's Zennor Wernham. Wernham had completed a solid run through the heats to reach the final but was stopped in his tracks by Quinn, who held his own in the 4- to 5-foot waves. Aukland's Mischa Davis stood out from the start of the four-way women's final, an early high score giving her the lead that remained undisputed throughout the heat.

OPEN MEN
FINAL
1. Maz Quinn
2. Zennor Wernham
SEMIFINAL 1
1. Maz Quinn
2. Jeremy Evans
SEMIFINAL 2
1. Zennor Wernham
2. Bobby Hansen
QUARTERFINAL 1
1. Jeremy Evans
2. Leon Santorik
QUARTERFINAL 2
1. Maz Quinn
2. Dru Adler
QUARTERFINAL 3
1. Bobby Hansen
2. Blair Stewart
QUARTERFINAL 4
1. Zennor Wernham
2. Jay Quinn

UNDER 18 MEN
FINAL
1. Keone Campbell
2. Johnny Hicks
3. Michael Mallalieu
4. Sean Peggs
SEMIFINAL 1
1. Sean Peggs
2. Michael Mallalieu
3. Braedon Williams
4. Adam Cranston
SEMIFINAL 2
1. Keone Campbell
2. Johnny Hicks
3. Buck Woods
4. Matt Hewitt
OPEN WOMEN
FINAL
1. Mischa Davis
2. Jessica Santorik
3. Daisy Thomas
4. Laura Rishworth
SEMIFINAL 1
1. Mischa Davis
2. Jessica Santorik
3. Rosa Thompson
4. Alexis Poulter
SEMIFINAL 2
1. Daisy Thomas
2. Laura Rishworth
3. Angie Koops
4. Kara Stephenson
QUARTERFINAL 1
1. Rosa Thompson
2. Kara Stephenson
3. Bronte Mannix
4. Nicola Colson-Koster
QUARTERFINAL 2
1. Daisy Thomas
2. Mischa Davis
3. Grace Spiers
4. Michelle Langdon
QUARTERFINAL 3
1. Jessica Santorik
2. Angie Koops
3. Thandi Durham
4. Anna Hadfield
QUARTERFINAL 4
1. Laura Rishworth
2. Alexis Poulter
3. Ella Williams
4. Pipi Sopp

MACCA'S OCEAN & EARTH TEENAGE RAMPAGE
SOUTH BROULEE,
NEW SOUTH WALES
February 2–3

Backed by pro surfer Phil MacDonald, the Teenage Rampage gives young surfers the opportunity to compete without elimination, giving them vital competition experience. Currarong's Jordi Watson dominated the event to take his second Teenage Rampage victory in a row, raising his profile on the national junior circuit. The Under 16 Girls title was taken out by Hayley Murray (Culburra Beach), who maintained a solid lead from the outset.

UNDER 16 BOYS
1. Jordi Watson
2. Justin Arnold
3. Kieran Quinn
4. Doug Chandler
UNDER 16 GIRLS
1. Hayley Murray

Clint Kimmins. Photo Jake White.

2. Erin Dark
3. Rachael Folder
4. Eve Davis-Boermans

UNDER 13 BOYS
1. Michael Wright
2. Matt King
3. Darcy Piper
4. Russel Bierke

UNDER 13 GIRLS
1. Tess Mawson
2. Christie Arthur
3. Chiara Arthur
4. Jasmin Boscheinen

RIP CURL MP CLASSIC, PRESENTED BY TRACKS MAGAZINE
GOLD COAST, QUEENSLAND
February 2–3

Clint Kimmins proved himself the new King of Kirra with a significant win in the Rip Curl MP Classic, presided over by not only the man himself, Michael Peterson, but also former world champion and Gold Coast local Mick Fanning. A perfect 10-point ride saw Kimmins gain an early lead and then remained undisputed for the duration of the heat. Kirra Point regained some of its former, pre-Superbank glory, turning on some reeling right-handers for the event and giving the regular-footed winner ample opportunity to back up his early score and take the $2,000 first prize, as well as a replica of an original MP surfboard.

FINAL
1. Clint Kimmins
2. Blake Wilson
3. Josh Dowthwaite
4. Corey Ziems

2008 HYUNDAI PRO LONGBOARD TOUR
SANDY BAY, NEW ZEALAND
February 2–3

Backing up his second place of the previous Hyundai Pro contest, Daryn McBride went one better with a first place in the Open Men event. Conditions were far from favorable, but competitors still managed some exceptional displays of high-performance longboarding. It was no walk-in-the-park final for McBride, the Mt. Maunganui local having to pull out all the stops against fellow finalists Sam Johnson and Daniel Proctor. But it was McBride's per-

sistence that won out, a 9.33 in the latter stages giving him the edge he would maintain to the conclusion.

OPEN MEN
FINAL
1. Daryn McBride
2. Mike Burling
3. Sam Johnson
4. Daniel Proctor
SEMIFINAL 1
1. Sam Johnson
2. Michael Burling
3. Aidan Comrie
4. Sam Guthrie
SEMIFINAL 2
1. Daryn McBride
1. Daniel Proctor
3. Daniel Kereopa
4. Alex McKenzie
OPEN WOMEN
FINAL
1. Claire Norman
2. Daisy Thomas
3. Monique Waitzer
4. Belinda Galley
SEMIFINAL 1
1. Claire Norman
2. Belinda Galley
3. Kirstie Thomson
4. Demi Poynter
SEMIFINAL 2
1. Daisy Thomas
2. Monique Waitzer
3. Rea Ansin
4. Shelly Jones
JUNIOR BOYS
FINAL
1. Sam Guthrie
2. Eli Barnfield
3. Tom Thompson
4. Hone Douglas
SEMIFINAL 1
1. Eli Barnfield
2. Tim Thompson
3. Keiran Pullman
4. Rick Williamson
SEMIFINAL 2
1. Sam Guthrie
2. Hone Douglas
3. Braedon Williams
4. Tim Gibb
OVER 40 MEN
FINAL
1. Mike Thomson
2. Viv Treacy
3. Mal Brady
4. Rupert Newbold
SEMIFINAL 1
1. Mike Thomson
2. Viv Treacy
3. Grant Cochrane
4. John Ayton
SEMIFINAL 2
1. Mal Brady

2. Rupert Newbold
3. David Storck
4. Mark Calcutt
QUARTERFINAL 1
1. Mike Thomson
2. John Ayton
3. Steve Andrews
4. Bryan Western
QUARTERFINAL 2
1. Grant Cochrane
2. Viv Treacy
3. Neil Dawber
4. Dave Burbage
QUARTERFINAL 3
1. Mal Brady
2. Mark Calcutt
3. Robert Hawkins
4. Al Ashworth
QUARTERFINAL 4
1. David Storck
2. Rupert Newbold
3. Steve Tyro
4. Dave Espiner
OVER 50 MEN
FINAL
1. Viv Treacy
2. Grant Cochrane
3. John Ayton
4. Mike Thomson
SEMIFINAL 1
1. Grant Cochrane
2. Viv Treacy
3. Ian Parker
4. Trevor Crosby
SEMIFINAL 2
1. John Ayton
2. Paul Browne
3. David Storck
4. Mike Thomson
QUARTERFINALS 1
1. Viv Treacy
2. Trevor Crosby
3. Rupert Newbold
4. John Duff
QUARTERFINAL 2
1. Grant Cochrane
2. Ian Parker
3. Dave Reed
4. Nick Matich
QUARTERFINAL 3
1. Dave Storck
2. Paul Browne
3. Alan Sykes
4. Warren Thomsen
QUARTERFINAL 4
1. Mike Thomson
2. John Ayton
3. Warrick Grey
4. Mel Eggindon

BILLABONG GROM SERIES, PRESENTED BY OCEANBRIDGE
MOUNT MAUNGANUI, NEW ZEALAND
February 2–3

Off the back of a convincing win in the National Championships, Alex Dive claimed a back-to-back victory in his own back yard. The Maunganui surfer had local knowledge on his side in the difficult-to-contest final. Fickle waves and stiff competition from adversaries Blake Myers (Whamata), Ben Poulter (Piha) and Johnny Hicks (Gis) meant Dive had to be at the top of his game, only gaining the lead mid-heat with two seven-point rides. Third place getter Poulter was upstaged by his sibling, Alexis, who took a convincing win in the Girls Under16s.

UNDER 16 BOYS
FINAL
1. Alex Dive
2. Blake Myers
3. Ben Poulter
4. Johnny Hicks
SEMIFINAL 1
1. Ben Poulter
2. Alex Dive
3. Paul Moretti
4. Fintan Cram
SEMIFINAL 2
1. Johnny Hicks
2. Blake Myers
3. Mark Parthemore
4. Todd Doyle
QUARTERFINAL 1
1. Ben Poulter
2. Fintan Cram
3. Fraser Chatham
4. Matt Brown
QUARTERFINAL 2
1. Alex Dive
2. Paul Moretti
3. Reno Marriott
4. Chad Jones
QUARTERFINAL 3
1. Johnny Hicks
2. Todd Doyle
3. Joe Moretti
4. Dune Kennings
QUARTERFINAL 4
1. Mark Parthemore
2. Blake Myers
3. Patxi Scott-Arietta
4. Peri Matenga
UNDER 14 BOYS
FINAL
1. Tane Wallis
2. Ben Poulter
3. Dune Kennings
4. Patxi Scott-Arietta
SEMIFINAL 1
1. Ben Poulter
2. Tane Wallis
3. Peri Matenga
4. Kahu Craig Te Ranga
SEMIFINAL 2
1. Patxi Scott-Arietta
2. Dune Kennings
3. Connor Pearson
4. Waretini Wano
QUARTERFINAL 1
1. Peri Matenga
2. Kahu Craig Te Ranga
3. Mackenzie Christie
4. Kurt Barker

QUARTERFINAL 2
1. Tane Wallis
2. Ben Poulter
3. Wade Kindred
4. Taylor Louie
QUARTERFINAL 3
1. Dune Kennings
2. Waretini Wano
3. Josh Taylor
4. Sam Haven
QUARTERFINAL 4
1. Patxi Scott-Arietta
2. Connor Pearson
3. Fintan Cram
4. Paul Moretti
UNDER 12 BOYS
FINAL
1. Dune Kennings
2. Elliot Paerata Reid
3. Jordan Griffin
4. Matt Hansen
SEMIFINAL 1
1. Elliot Paerata Reid
2. Jordan Griffin
3. Ben Cochrane
4. Nick Mason
SEMIFINAL 2
1. Dune Kennings
2. Matt Hansen
3. Manu Scott-Arietta
4. Quin Matenga
UNDER 16 GIRLS
FINAL
1. Alexis Poulter
2. Ella Williams
3. Rosa Thompson
4. Kristi Zarifeh
SEMIFINAL 1
1. Ella Williams
2. Kristi Zarifeh
3. Alethea Lock
SEMIFINAL 2
1. Rosa Thompson
2. Alexis Poulter
3. Jayda Fitzharris
UNDER 14 GIRLS
FINAL
1. Alethea Lock
2. Ella Williams
3. Jayda Martin-Fitzharris
4. Chloe Shutt
SEMIFINAL 1
1. Jayda Martin-Fitzharris
2. Chloe Shutt
3. Ebony Pearson
SEMIFINAL 2
1. Ella Williams

Alex Dive. Photo NZ Surfing Magazine.

Lincoln Taylor. Photo Steve Robertson.

2. Alethea Lock
3. Gabriella McCarthy-Marriott
UNDER 12 GIRLS
FINAL
1. Bianca Sansom
2. Gabriela Sansom
3. Hannah Kohn
4. Dayna Story

OAKLEY PRO JUNIOR • ASP AUSTRALASIA GRADE 4 MEN EVENT
NORTH STRADBROKE ISLAND, QUEENSLAND
February 5–10

North Stradbroke's Cylinder Beach provided the perfect setting for the inaugural Oakley Pro Junior, with 4- to 6-foot waves consistently reeling off the point for much of the event. In his first win in the Pro Junior series, local, Lincoln Taylor excelled, defeating a wealth of exceptional junior talent in his path to success. The win gave Taylor a sizeable boost to his bank balance, but more importantly, 3,500 points in the ASP Pro Junior race. Kennedy had a double win, also snatching the Best Wave category in the Stradbroke Island Beach Hotel Expression Session, whilst Hawaiian Sebastian Zeitz scored the event's Best maneuver.

FINAL
1. Lincoln Taylor
2. Julian Wilson
SEMIFINAL 1
1. Lincoln Taylor
2. Stuart Kennedy
SEMIFINAL 2
1. Julian Wilson
2. Mitch Crews

JIM BEAM SURFTAG SERIES CRONULLA
CRONULLA BEACH, NEW SOUTH WALES
February 9

Defending title holders North Steyne were denied a follow-up win by the locals in the final minutes of the Cronulla stage of the Jim Beam Surftag. Cronulla surfer Dylan Hayler swung the balance in his team's favor in the dying stages of the heat, taking them to a narrow two-point victory over the favorites, North Steyne. Waves were far from breathtaking for the event, a sloppy, 3-foot swell doing little to aid the surfers. But the breadth of talent nonetheless displayed awe-inspiring surfing, Kirk Flintoff performing exceptionally to not only assist his team in their win, but also claim the Oporto Powerwave title. With this success, Cronulla gained a place in the grand final, held at North Narrabeen the following month.

FINAL
1. Cronulla (Matt GriggS, Dylan Hannah, Kirk Flintoff, Dane Durbin, Dylan Hayler)
2. North Steyne (Beau Mitchell, Kai Otton, Dayyan Neve, Paul Evans, Andrew Froggat)
3. Queenscliff (Luke Cheadle, Sam Page, Nick Riley, Matt Toghill)
4. North Narrabeen (Nathan Webster, Christo Hall, Chris Davidson, Ben Short)
SEMIFINAL 1
1. North Narrabeen
2. Queenscliff
3. Sandon Point
4. Elouera
SEMIFINAL 2
1. North Steyne
2. Cronulla
3. Ulludulla
4. Curl Curl
QUARTERFINAL 1
1. North Narrabeen "A"
2. Queenscliff
3. Scarborough
4. Garie
QUARTERFINAL 2
1. Sandon Point
2. Elouera
3. Dee Why
4. Long Reef "A"
QUARTERFINAL 3
1. Cronulla
2. North Steyne
3. Avoca
4. Long Reef "B"
QUARTERFINAL 4
1. Curl Curl
2. Ulladulla
3. Avalon
4. North Narrabeen "B"

VOLCOM STONE'S VQS GUNNAMATTA
GUNNAMATTA, NEW SOUTH WALES
February 9

An abrupt halt was called to the proceedings of the Volcom Stone VQS when some unwelcome visitors encouraged officials to decide final placings on a countback. With the quarterfinals completed, surfers were called from the water with the sighting of two sharks—a mother of up to 30 feet and her 10-foot calf. Despite the WestPac Rescue helicopter managing to coax the sharks from the area, organizers deemed it too unsafe to continue the event, taking the overall points scored as the surfers' final rankings.

PRO-AM
1. Simon McShane
2. Finn Barry
3. Liam Jolly
4. Tex Walker
JUNIORS
1. Todd Rosewall
2. Tom Allan
3. Stuart Ferrier
4. Angus Forrest
GROMS
1. Mitch Mee
2. Harry Mann
3. Jamie Powell
4. Willis Hartigan
GIRLS
1. Nina Van Dijk
2. Georgia Fish
3. Nikki Van Dijk
4. Hannah Lethlean

BILLABONG PRO JUNIOR • ASP AUSTRALASIA GRADE 1 MEN JUNIOR EVENT / ASP AUSTRALASIA GRADE 1 WOMEN JUNIOR EVENT
COFFS HARBOUR, NEW SOUTH WALES
February 14–17

In a shock-upset, rank outsider Jesse Adam defeated the Pro Junior Series number one and number two in quality waves at Coffs Harbour. The nineteen-year-old from Merewether took down no. 2 seed, Julian Wilson (Coolum Beach) in the semis before going on to clean up current series leader, Lennox Head's Stuart Kennedy. The nail-biting semifinal could have swung either way, with only a couple of points separating Adam from Wilson. Wilson's talent and competition poise failed to deliver, though, and Adam went through. The final was a far more convincing win, a near-perfect 9.25 from the victor, leaving Kennedy on the verge of a combo situation. The position was too much for Kennedy and Adam claimed his first-ever Pro Junior victory.

FINAL
1. Jesse Adam
2. Stuart Kennedy

SEMIFINAL 1
1. Stuart Kennedy
2. Heath Joske Heat
SEMIFINAL 2
1. Jesse Adam
2. Julian Wilson

BILLABONG GROM SERIES PRESENTED BY OCEANBRIDGE
WHANGAMATA, NEW ZEALAND
February 16–17

Despite a meager swell, the clean conditions of Whangamata were put to good use in the second round of the Billabong Grom Series. Stage one's victor, Alex Dive, was denied a second win, with Gisborne's Johnny Hicks unleashing a barrage of backhand maneuvers to narrowly claim the win. The ebbing tide further diminished the minimal waves, but this didn't seem to dampen the enthusiasm of the four contenders in the final. This was also true of the quartet of girls in their Under 16s final, Rosa Thompson (Aukland) pouring copious amounts of energy and fervor into her multitude of waves. With the waves challenging all competitors, Thompson did well to gain a nine-point combined score to take the event win.

UNDER 16 BOYS
FINAL
1. Johnny Hicks
2. Alex Dive
3. Blake Myers
4. Tane Wallis
SEMIFINAL 1
1. Alex Dive
2. Blake Myers
3. James Tume
4. Joe Moretti
SEMIFINAL 2
1. Johnny Hicks
2. Tane Wallis
3. Paul Moretti
4. Darcy Bowden
QUARTERFINAL 1
1. James Tume
2. Blake Myers
3. Dune Kennings
4. Reno Marriott
QUARTERFINAL 2
1. Alex Dive
2. Joe Moretti
3. Todd Doyle

4. Ethan Burge
QUARTERFINAL 3
1. Johnny Hicks
2. Paul Moretti
3. Adam Grimson
4. Elliot Paerata - Reid
QUARTERFINAL 4
1. Tane Wallis
2. Darcy Bowden
3. Ben Poulter
4. Connor Anderson
UNDER 16 GIRLS
FINAL
1. Rosa Thompson
2. Grace Spiers
3. Jayda Martin-Fitzharris
4. Alethea Lock
SEMIFINAL 1
1. Rosa Thompson
2. Grace Spiers
3. Alexis Poulter
SEMIFINAL 2
1. Alethea Lock
2. Jayda Martin-Fitzharris
3. Ella Spiers

HYUNDAI PRO LONGBOARD TOUR, SURFING NEW ZEALAND
BRIGHTON BEACH, CHRISTCHURCH, NEW ZEALAND
February 16–17

Despite an insignificant swell, round three of the Hyundai Pro was an exciting event to the last. Daniel Kereopa was nursing an ankle injury, the limb heavily bandaged, causing him to pull out just ten minutes into round one—an unfortunate turn of events, given his run thus far in the tour. Daryn McBride was a familiar face in the final, though he couldn't match the pace of Daniel Proctor, who excelled through much of the event to become eventual winner. In the Women's Open, daisy Thomas fortified her position as series leader with another convincing win, her competent approach proving too much for her adversaries. Viv Treacy was again a powerful force in the Over 50s, proving indomitable throughout.

OPEN MEN
FINAL
1. Daniel Proctor
2. Sam Johnson
3. Daryn Mcbride
4. Dylan Barnfield

Dylan Barnfield. Photo Slide Magazine.

SEMIFINAL 1
1. Daryn Mcbride
2. Sam Johnson
3. Kirk Beyer
4. Sam Guthrie
SEMIFINAL 2
1. Daniel Proctor
2. Dylan Barnfield
3. Thomas Kibblewhite
4. Duncan Cameron
UNDER 18 BOYS
FINAL
1. Sam Guthrie
2. Sam Hawke
3. Hugh Ritchie
4. Ambrose Mc Neil
SEMIFINAL 1
1. Hugh Ritchie
2. Ambrose Mc Neil
3. Stephen Weir
SEMIFINAL 2
1. Sam Guthrie
2. Sam Hawke
3. Luke O'Neill
QUARTERFINAL 1
1. Hugh Ritchie
2. Sam Hawke
3. Nick Sarjeant
QUARTERFINAL 2
1. Sam Guthrie
2. Stephen Weir
3. Ambrose McNeill
QUARTERFINAL 3
1. Luke O'Neill
2. Ambrose Mc Neil
3. Rick Williamson
4. Nic Todd
OVER 40 MEN
FINAL
1. Dave O'Rourke
2. Mike Thomson
3. Dean Cooke
4. Mark Andrews
SEMIFINAL 1
1. Mike Thomson
2. Dave O'Rourke
3. Stephen Tyro
4. Glen Michaels
SEMIFINAL 2
1. Mark Andrews
2. Dean Cooke
3. Ian Fletcher
4. Michael Willman
OVER 50 MEN
FINAL
1. Viv Treacy
2. Paul Bennett
3. Mike Thomson
4. Grant Cochrane
SEMIFINAL 1
1. Grant Cochrane
2. Paul Bennett
3. Len Carragher
4. Warwick Gray
SEMIFINAL 2
1. Viv Treacy
2. Mike Thomson
3. David Storck
4. Tim Clemence
OPEN WOMEN
FINAL
1. Daisy Thomas
2. Claire Norman
3. Hannah Phillips
4. Eve Welch
SEMIFINAL 1
1. Hannah Phillips
2. Eve Welch
3. Kirstie Thomsen
SEMIFINAL 2
1. Daisy Thomas
2. Claire Norman
3. Kate MacDonald

RUSTY GROMFEST
KERAMAS, BALI
February 17

Bali has become recognized as not only a dream surf destination but also a breeding ground for some of the world's hottest surfers. Event victor One Anwar and his fellow finalists reinforced this recognition in the 3- to 4-foot, perfect Balinese surf. With a combination of competent barrel-riding and driving cutbacks, married with more progressive aerial maneuvers, the competitors throughout the age divisions dazzled spectators and judges alike. The close-call under-16 final was eventually claimed by Anwar, over fellow Brazillians Putu Anggara and Gazali Hamzah and Japanese visitor

Happy winner. Photo Tim Hain.

Kaohe. But it was fellow Japanese surfer Hiroto Ohara who took the day's honors, the 11-year-old convincingly taking out both the Under 12 and the Under 14 divisions, to the crowd's delight.

UNDER 16 BOYS
1. One Anwar
2. Putu Anggara
3. Gazali Hamzah
4. Kaohe
UNDER 14 BOYS
1. Hiroto Ohara
2. Edian Putra
3. Arya Wijaya
4. Yogo Kawabata
UNDER 12 BOYS
1. Hiroto Ohara
2. Koko Mitsua Antara
3. Edian Putra
4. Komang Arif

RIP CURL GROMSEARCH
PACITAN, EAST JAVA
February 20

Furthering the advancement of Indonesia's wave of young surfers, the Rip Curl GromSearch highlighted the junior talents of Javanese surfers. After a 12-hour journey from Pangandaran earlier in the week,

Augustina and Ahmad Taufik asserted their dominance, taking first and second in the Under 16 division, while Pacitan's Salina was unstoppable in the Girls event, as well as scoring the additional award for Best Wave Selection of the event.

UNDER 16 BOYS
1. Agustina
2. Ahmad Taufik
3. Hambali
4. Suprianto
UNDER 14 BOYS
1. Made Butut
2. Supri
3. Agung
4. Ivan Putra
GIRLS DIVISION
1. Salina
2. Anisa
3. Lisa
4. Wilda

EXPRESSION SESSION
BEST TRICK:
Agus Gitar
BEST WAVE SELECTION:
Salina

CORONA CROWN SERIES EVENT 4, SURFING NEW ZEALAND
MOUNT MAUNGANUI, NEW ZEALAND
February 23–24

Fresh from competing on the Pro Junior Tour in Australia, Mahia's Richard Christie put on an extraordinary display of talent to convincingly claim the win in the fourth event in the Corona Crown Series. Logging the highest heat score of the competition, Christie amassed an impressive 18.35 points, just 1.65 points away from a perfect score. Although swell was present, the messy conditions didn't lend themselves to competition particularly well, but Christie failed to let it dampen his enthusiasm. Trailing by almost seven points was Wangamata's Gauranga Ormond; locals Sam Willis and Tim O'Connor placed third and fourth respectively. Mischa Davis made it

Billy Stairmand. Photo NZ Surfing Magazine.

two in a row with another win, also clinching the series lead. The Piha surfer was unstoppable, dominating the final with a 5.25 and a late score of 9.0.

OPEN MEN
FINAL
1. Richard Christie
2. Gauranga Ormond
3. Sam Willis
4. Tim O'Connor
SEMIFINAL 1
1. Richard Christie
2. Gauranga Ormond
3. Billy Stairmand
4. Rowan Aish
SEMIFINAL 2
1. Tim O'Connor
2. Sam Willis
3. Larry Fisher
4. Braedon Williams
QUARTERFINAL 1
1. Billy Stairmand
2. Gauranga Ormond
3. Jarrod Hancox
4. Blair Stewart
QUARTERFINAL 2
1. Richard Christie
2. Rowan Aish
3. Luke Cederman
4. Sean Peggs
QUARTERFINAL 3
1. Braedon Williams
2. Larry Fisher
3. David Van Staden
4. Nathan Welch
QUARTERFINAL 4
1. Tim O'Connor
2. Sam Willis
3. Zennor Wernham
4. Ben Kennings
UNDER 18 MEN
FINAL
1. Matt Hewitt
2. Sean Peggs
3. Buck Woods
4. Tim Thompson
SEMIFINAL 1
1. Matt Hewitt
2. Buck Woods
3. Alex Dive
4. Johnny Hicks
SEMIFINAL 2
1. Sean Peggs
2. Tim Thompson
3. Keone Campbell
4. Travis McCoy
QUARTERFINAL 1
1. Matt Hewitt
2. Buck Woods
3. Michael Mallalaieu
4. Tane Wallis
QUARTERFINAL 2
1. Johnny Hicks
2. Alex Dive
3. Tyler Anderson
4. Zen Wallis
QUARTERFINAL 3
1. Sean Peggs
2. Travis McCoy
3. Blake Myers
4. Braedon Williams
QUARTERFINAL 4
1. Keone Campbell
2. Tim Thompson
3. Kieran Pullman
4. Adam Cranston
OPEN WOMEN
SEMIFINAL 1
1. Mischa Davis
2. Jessica Santorik
3. Anna Hawes
4. Nicola Colson-Koster
SEMIFINAL 2
1. Laura Rishworth
2. Rosa Thompson
3. Daisy Thomas
4. India Wray-Murane
FINAL
1. Mischa Davis
2. Laura Rishworth
3. Rosa Thompson
4. Jessica Santorik

RIP CURL PRO RAGLAN CORONA CROWN SERIES EVENT 5
MANU BAY, RAGLAN NEW ZEALAND
February 29–March 2

After a semifinal placing in the previous event of the series, Billy Stairmand went on better to take the trophy at the fifth event of the Corona Crown Series. Though a touch crumbly on occasion, the three-foot swell proved consistent throughout the competition. A 9.25 ride in the former part of the heat gave Stairmand the upper hand, but with only a brace of throwaway scores to back it up, the young local found himself chasing something significant to seal the win. An 8.0 late in the final secured that position, placing him out of reach of his rival, Leon Santorik (Rag). Always the bridesmaid, and replicating her sibling's result, Jessica Santorik (Rag) came runner-up to Taranaki's Paige Hareb. The close-run final saw the lead in the balance for much of the heat, but the experience Hareb has gained surfing in the Australasian Pro Junior Tour in Australia stood her in good stead to take the victory.

OPEN MEN

FINAL
1. Billy Stairmand
2. Leon Santorik

SEMIFINAL 1
1. Leon Santorik
2. Matt Hewitt

SEMIFINAL 2
1. Billy Stairmand
2. Jay Quinn

QUARTERFINAL 1
1. Leon Santorik
2. Ryan Hawker

QUARTERFINAL 2
1. Matt Hewitt
2. Maz Quinn

QUARTERFINAL 3
1. Billy Stairmand
2. Mike Banks

QUARTERFINAL 4
1. Jay Quinn
2. Bobby Hansen

UNDER 18 MEN

FINAL
1. Alex Dive
2. Braedon Williams

Taj Burrow. Photo Joe Murphy/Global Surftag.

3. Matt Hewitt
4. Sean Peggs

RIP CURL GROMSEARCH BOYS FINAL
1. Johnny Hicks
2. Ryan Hawker
3. Buck Woods
4. Tyler Anderson

RIP CURL GROMSEARCH GIRLS FINAL
1. Rosa Thompson
2. Alexis Poulter
3. India Wray-Murane
4. Ella Williams

OPEN WOMEN

FINAL
1. Paige Hareb
2. Jessica Santorik
3. Kara Stephenson
4. Alexis Poulter

JIM BEAM NATIONAL SURFTAG
NORTH NARRABEEN BEACH,
NEW SOUTH WALES
March 6–7

In a sensational back-to-back win, the team from North Narrabeen claimed victory in the Jim Beam National SurfTag at their home break. Mediocre conditions didn't hamper the all-star lineup, which featured a number of A-list surfers, including Phil MacDonald, Kai Otton and Taj Burrow. North Narrabeen surfed consistently throughout the event, Nathan Webster proving to be their man of the moment, leading them into the finals with solid surfing and powerful maneuvers. Despite Kai

Otton, ranking world number nine and ASP second Taj Burrow competing in opposing teams, North Narrabeen stood firm and emerged victorious. The previous day, Nathan Webster had again been on form, surfing his way to a first place in the Jim Beam Boardriders Cup, but was denied in the dying minutes by Umina's Drew Courtney, who took the win for the second time in three years.

JIM BEAM BOARDRIDERS CUP

FINAL
1. Drew Courtney
2. Nathan Webster

SEMIFINAL 1
1. Drew Courtney
2. Nick Squires

SEMIFINAL 2
1. Nathan Webster
2. Marcus Aboody

JIM BEAM NATIONAL SURFTAG

FINAL
1. North Narrabeen

2. Ulludulla
3. North Steyne
4. Yallingup

SEMIFINAL 1
1. North Steyne
2. Ulludulla
3. Cronulla
4. Elouera

SEMIFINAL 2
1. Yallingup
2. North Narrabeen
3. Seaford
4. Curl Curl

QUARTERFINAL 1
1. Cronulla
2. Elouera
3. LeBa
4. Margaret River

QUARTERFINAL 2
1. North Steyne
2. Ulludulla
3. Philip Island
4. Scarborough

QUARTERFINAL 3
1. North Narrabeen
2. Yallingup
3. Kirra
4. Sandon Point

QUARTERFINAL 4
1. Seaford
2. Curl Curl
3. Snapper Rocks
4. Queenscliff

O'NEILL

SURFER OF THE SERIES AWARD
Taj Burrow (Wave average of 27.54)

OPORTO POWERWAVE COMPETITION
Taj Burrow (highest wave score of 9.0)

**VMOTO AWARD FOR HIGHEST WAVE
SCORE IN THE FINAL**
Kai Otton (28.9)

BILLABONG PRO JUNIOR TARANAKI • ASP JUNIOR GRADE 1 MEN'S EVENT / ASP JUNIOR GRADE 1 WOMEN'S EVENT
TARANAKI, NEW ZEALAND
March 6–8

Josh Constable. Photo Steve Robertson.

Owen Wright (Culburra) and Laura Enever (Narrabeen) made the short trip across the Tasman Sea from Australia to take wins in this stage of the Billabong Pro Juniors. Finals day saw a welcomed increase in swell, the 3- to 4-foot waves providing long, clean faces to maximise potential for the competitors. Wright's first-ever Pro Junior win was only narrowly accomplished, the series leader at the time of competition, Stuart Kennedy (Lennox Head), nearly denying Wright the title. A mere 0.25 points separated the pair when the final horn sounded. Laura Enever had a gratifying win over ex-local, Airini Mason, now of the Gold Coast. Enever's victory gave her some much-needed catch-up points over current ratings leader Sally Fitzgibbons, who didn't attend the New Zealand event.

OPEN MEN

FINAL
1. Owen Wright
2. Stuart Kennedy

SEMIFINAL 1
1. Stuart Kennedy
2. Madison Williams

SEMIFINAL 2
1. Owen Wright
2. Richard Christie

QUARTERFINAL 1
1. Stuart Kennedy
2. Dean Iezzi

QUARTERFINAL 2
1. Madison Williams
2. Jayke Sharp

QUARTERFINAL 3
1. Richard Christie
2. Chris Salisbury

QUARTERFINAL 4
1. Owen Wright
2. Tamaroa McComb

OPEN WOMEN

FINAL
1. Laura Enever
2. Airini Mason

SEMIFINAL 1
1. Airni Mason
2. Kirsti Jones

SEMIFINAL 2
1. Laura Enever
2. Paige Hareb

QUARTERFINAL 1
1. Airini Mason
2. Kirstie Jones
3. Dimitry Stoyle
4. Kirby Wright

QUARTERFINAL 2
1. Laura Enever
2. Paige Hareb

3. Nikita Robb
4. Wini Paul

GLOBAL SURF INDUSTRIES NOOSA FESTIVAL OF SURFING • ASP LQS 2-STAR MEN'S EVENT / BANANA BOAT WOMEN'S PRO
NOOSA, QUEENSLAND
March 3–9

After a week of grovelling surf conditions, the Noosa Festival of Surfing was blessed with a swell pulse that set Noosa's First Point alight for finals day. Defending event champion Josh Constable did well against an all-Australian lineup to land the two-in-a-row victory, also managing to make the finals of the SUP event. U.S. world champion Jennifer Smith, was the undisputed Banana Boat Women's Pro victor, having been on form for the entire event and not relenting in the slightest for the multinational finale. Spectacular surfing was seen throughout the final day of competition, Christian Wach being one of the finest standouts. The young Californian, riding a hollow-carbon-fiber board, was victorious in the Noserider division, clocking up a staggering amount of tip time and finishing well ahead of his still impressive adversaries.

TELSTRA MEN PRO
1. Josh Constable
2. Seb Wilson
3. Grant Thomas
4. Jackson Close

GSI ONE DESIGN
1. Alan Atkins
2. Ben Wallace
3. Bonga Perkins
4. Grant Price
5. Steve Waldon
6. Jamie Willems.

SUP C4
1. Bonga Perkins
2. Brian Keaulana
3. Luke Egan
4. James Watson
5. Josh Constable
6. Matt Lumley

OLD MALIBU
1. Isaac Fields
2. Rahn Goddard
3. Justin Healy
4. Jacob Stuth
5. Sage Joske
6. Louis English

NOSERIDER
1. Christian Wach
2. Ezra Norris
3. Matt Cuddihy
4. Jai Lee

AMATEUR OPEN MEN
1. Ben Haworth
2. Jordie Brown

UNDER 18 BOYS
1. Bryce Young
2. Fraser Biden
3. Max Weston
4. Dan McComb
5. Josh Cooper
6. Jackson Winter.

UNDER 15 BOYS
1. Dylan Hunt
2. George Cunningham
3. Ezra Norris
4. Ed Cunningham
5. Nic Jones
6. Zye Norris
3. Mitch Fraser
4. Josh Cooper
5. Rahn Goddard
6. Matt Cuddihy.

OVER 35 MEN
1. Damian Coulter
2. Mark McNamarra
3. Chris Prewitt
4. Chris McHutchinson
5. Steve Montell
6. Reid Johnson

OVER 50 MEN
1. Michael Thompson
2. Phil Baggs
3. Peter Barley
4. Patrick Sweeney
5. Peter White
6. David Smith

OVER 55 MEN
1. Bruce Channon
2. Steve O'Donnell
3. Paul Smith
4. Steve Cleveland
5. Randy Rarick
6. Ken McCulloch

OVER 60 MEN
1. Geoff Channon
2. Neville Smith
3. Otis Sistrunk
4. Bob Smith
5. David O'Donnell
6. Ian Walding

UNDER 18 GIRLS
1. Rachel Pinsak
2. Kelly Winter
3. Samantha Walker
4. Georgia Roach
5. Monique Keane
6. Jess Kelly

BANANA BOAT WOMEN PRO
1. Jennifer Smith
2. Janna Irons
3. Justine Dupont
4. Selby Riddle

AMATEUR OPEN WOMEN
1. Monique Keane
2. Sharon Jackson
3. Jess Kelly

4. Kirsty Quirk
5. Bianca Anstiss
6. Kara Nobbs
TANDEM
1. Rico and Sarah
2. Kalani and Ala
3. Brian and Kathy
4. Chuck and Tiffany
OVER 35 WOMEN
1. Sharon Jackson
2. Sue McComb
3. Michelle Finucane
4. Roslyn Coombes
5. Kristen Ross-Munro
6. Katharine Brown
WSHF INVITE

OPEN MEN
FINAL
1. Leigh Sedley
2. Shaun Gossmann
SEMIFINAL 1
1. Shaun Gossmann
2. Gavin Gillette
SEMIFINAL 2
1. Leigh Sedley
2. Toby Martin
QUARTERFINAL 1
1. Gavin Gillette
2. Khy Vaughan
QUARTERFINAL 2
1. Shaun Gossmann
2. Michael Campbell

Classic, with glassy conditions and pristine weather welcoming competitors. Taking a more fun-oriented format, the competition allowed everyone two surfs each, their accumulative total being their overall score. Open winners Blair O'Keefe and Josh Rees, placing first and second respectively, showed form throughout the day, marrying traditional single-fin surfing with modernday performance maneuvers. Dan Warren couldn't retain his Seniors title of the previous year, coming a close second to the consistent performance of Tony Shaefer, while Johnny Fenton relived his youth in style to take the Masters division.

OPEN MEN
1. Blair O'Keefe
2. Josh Rees
3. Tom Entwistle
4. Manu Schafer
5. Kane Marshall
6. Dee Maynard
SENIORS
1. Tony Schafer
2. Dan Warren
3. Ken Beaumont
4. Aaron Beaumont
5. Paul Weaffer
MASTERS
1 Johnny Fenton
2. Mike William
3. Andrew Pickering

dominating much of the event and retaining her first place on the Corona Crown Series. The U/18 and U/16 divisions provided much excitement, with Rosa Thompson (Aukland) and Alexis Poulter (Raglan) in a feisty battle for first. Fortunately, both surfers surfed in both events, Thompson taking the U/18 title, while Poulter redeemed herself in the U/16 division. Thompson also did well to make third place in the open finals against her more mature peers. Poulter, meanwhile, showed her versatility, taking second place in the longboard event.

OPEN WOMEN
FINAL
1. Jessica Santorik
2. Daisy Thomas
3. Rosa Thompson
4. Mischa Davis
SEMIFINAL 1
1. Jessica Santorik
2. Rosa Thompson
3. Laura Rishworth
4. Thandi Durham
SEMIFINAL 2
1. Daisy Thomas
2. Mischa Davis
3. Alexis Poulter
4. Marie Boyer
UNDER 18 GIRLS
FINAL
1. Rosa Thompson

UNDER 12 GIRLS
1. Gabriela Sansom
2. Bianca Sansom
3. Hannah Kohn
4. Demi Hewitt
OPEN WOMEN LONGBOARD
FINAL
1. Daisy Thomas
2. Alexis Poulter
3. Rea Ansin
4. Shelly Jones
SEMIFINAL 1
1. Alexis Poulter
2. Rea Ansin
3. Ella Williams
4. Anna Jolly
SEMIFINAL 2
1. Daisy Thomas
2. Shelly Jones
3. Cheryl Lowe
4. Chloe Shutt
OVER 30 WOMEN
FINAL
1. Renee Jacobsen
2. Gina Samson
3. Gina Kennings
4. Cheryl Lowe
SEMIFINAL 1
1. Gina Samson
2. Cheryl Lowe
3. Sherene McCormick
SEMIFINAL 2
1. Renee Jacobsen
2. Gina Kennings
3. Anna Jolly

Sally Fitzgibbons. Photo Steve Robertson.

Dave Wilson (Best Wave)
Doug Warbrick (Noseride)
Barry McGuigan (Best move)
Ron Adler (Sportsmanship)
CEO CHALLENGE
1. Quiksilver Europe
2. Quiksilver
3. Billabong

ARRIVE ALIVE CENTRAL COAST PRO MEN'S 4-STAR WQS EVENT / WOMEN'S 4-STAR WQS EVENT
SOLDIERS BEACH, NORAH HEAD
March 11–16

Sunshine Coast surfer Leigh Sedley took a momentous victory in the Arrive Alive Central Coast Pro. Though not epic conditions, the glassy, two-foot waves were more than contestable, making for a visually spectacular final, the closely vied battle eventually being won by Sedley over Shaun Gossman (Gold Coast). Sedley's maiden WQS victory saw him elevated to 19th position on the overall table. Sally Fitzgibbons (Gerroa) was up against event favorite, local girl Amee Donohue (McMasters Beach) in the semis, but refused to bow to the crowd's preferences, taking the heat confidently before going on to claim the crown over 16-year-old Laura Enever. Enever surfed beyond her years, but Fitzgibbons affirmed why she is a secure tip for a 2008 WQS win.

QUARTERFINAL 3
1. Leigh Sedley
2. Rhys Bombaci
QUARTERFINAL 4
1. Toby Martin
2. Matt Jones
OPEN WOMEN
FINAL
1. Sally Fitzgibbons
2. Laura Enever
SEMIFINAL 1
1. Sally Fitzgibbons
2. Amee Donohoe
SEMIFINAL 2
1. Laura Enever
2. Julie De La Rosa Toro
QUARTERFINAL 1
1. Sally Fitzgibbons
2. Pauline Ado
QUARTERFINAL 2
1. Amee Donohoe
2. Mizuki Hagiwara
QUARTERFINAL 3
1. Laura Enever
2. Laurina McGrath
QUARTERFINAL 4
1. Jul De La Rosa Toro
2. Airini Mason

CENTRAL SURF SINGLE FIN SURFING CLASSIC, POINT SURF TEAM BOARDRIDERS
CHRISTCHURCH, NEW ZEALAND
March 8

Hickory Bay was the venue for the 2008 Central Surf Single Fin

Dale Staples. Photo Steve Robertson.

4. Paul Robb
5. Stu Mckinnon
OPEN WOMEN
1.Sophia Moore
2 Kristi Zafrieh
3. Leilani Morgan
4. Nicola Sidon

RIP CURL CLEAN & CLEAR WOMEN'S PRO
TAY STREET, MOUNT MAUN-GANUI, NEW ZEALAND
March 15–16

Clean and clear was the phrase of the day at Mount Maunganui, perfect waves, offshore winds and clear skies blessing the event. Jessica Santorik (Aukland) was the one to watch from start to finish,

2. Alexis Poulter
3. Jayda Martin-Fitzharris
4. Chloe Shutt
SEMIFINAL 1
1. Alexis Poulter
2. Chloe Shutt
3. Abigail Daunton
SEMIFINAL 2
1. Rosa Thompson
2. Jayda Martin-Fitzharris
3. Nicola Colson-Koster
UNDER 16 GIRLS
1. Alexis Poulter
2. Rosa Thompson
3. Grace Spiers
4. Gabriella McCarthy-Marriott
UNDER 14 GIRLS
1. Ella Spiers
2. Gabriella McCarthy-Marriott
3. Ella Williams
4. Chloe Shutt

BILLABONG CREEK TO CREEK CLASSIC, PRESENTED BY PRINTPOINT • BILLABONG QLD CHAMP CIRUIT EVENT #2
GOLD COAST, QUEENSLAND
March 15–16

The second event of the Billabong Queensland Championship Circuit (QCC) was a close-fought affair, the final comprising a former QCC champion in Reardon-Smith, Mann, a winner of the event in previous years, and ex-World Tour competitor Wehner. But it was Corey Ziems who took the day's honors, leading for much of the heat after an early seven-point ride left his opponents chasing substantial rides that remained illusive. The win provided Ziems with a much-needed boost in the QCC ratings, reigniting his hopes and chances of a series win.

FINAL
1. Corey Ziems
2. Dave Reardon-Smith
3. Samba Mann
4. Shane Wehner

RNR SOUTH ISLAND INTERNATIONAL LONGBOARD PRO-AM, HYUNDAI PRO LONG-BOARD TOUR EVENT # 5
KAIKOURA, NEW ZEALAND
March 14–16

Stage Five of the Hyundai Pro saw some critical surfing in trying conditions. Daniel Kereopa won his semifinal heat despite his still-injured ankle remaining heavily strapped, but his form couldn't remain through the tempestuous conditions and he could only muster a third place. Australian visitor Jackson Close nearly denied the locals a win, but Michael Burling (Gisborne) managed to stave off his attacks, resulting in a convincing win over the rest of the field. Sophia Moore eclipsed her competition, easily winning her heat, whilst the noserider division went down to the wire, Jackson Close being the trans-Tasman victor despite an altercation with the littoral rocks.

OPEN MEN
FINAL
1. Michael Burling
2. Jackson Close
3. Daniel Kereopa
4. Kirk Beyer
SEMI-FINAL 1
1. Daniel Kereopa
2. Kirk Beyer
3. Mathew Cockayne
4. Dylan Barnfield
SEMIFINAL 2
1. Michael Burling
2. Jackson Close
3. Shayne Baxter
4. Daniel Proctor
UNDER 18 MEN
1. Le Roy Rust
2. Eli Barnfield

Under 12 finalists. Photo Tim Hain.

3. Sam Hawke
4. Hone Douglas
OVER 40 MEN
1. Glen Shuker
2. Mike Thomson
3. Mike Pimm
4. Michael Willman
OVER 50 MEN
1. Mike Pimm
2. David Storck
3. Viv Treacy
4. Mike Thomson
OVER 55 MEN
1. Ross Tyson
2. Ron Carter
3. Peter Stevens
4. Kevin Merdock
NOSERIDER
1. Jackson Close
2. Darren McBride
3. Matt Cockayne
4. Dylan Barnfield
OLD MAL
1. Daryn McBride
2. Paul Culpan
3. Troy Scott
4. Jason Lawn
OPEN WOMEN
1. Sophia Moore

2. Anau Burling
3. Claire Norman
4. Josephine Moore

RUSTY GROMFEST
CANGGU BEACH, BALI
March 16

The youth of Bali had the chance to prove themselves to the world again with Rusty's Bali stage of the Gromfest. The Keramas stage winner, One Anwar, couldn't double up, only managing a fourth place, conceding victory to Putra Hermawan, despite an exceptionally close-fought final. The surfers, not least the Under 12s, refused to be deterred by the four-foot swell, unleashing a barrage of progressive moves comparable to, if not exceeding, those of their international peers.

UNDER 12
1. Nyoman Satria 'Blacky'
2. Edian Putra
3. Koming
4. Mansyur
UNDER 14
1. Ediana Putra
2. Surya Atmaja Putra
3. Koko Mitsua Antara
4. Arya Wijaya 'Blerong'
UNDER 16
1. Putra Hermawan

RIP CURL GROMSEARCH INTERNATIONAL FINALS, PRESENTED BY SNICKERS
BELLS BEACH, VICTORIA
April 22

An international contingent converged on Bells Beach for the world finals of Rip Curl's Gromsearch, each having won passage to the event in their own regions. Australian surfers were denied in both the Boys and Girls divisions, South Africans and a Hawaiian proving to be strong competition in the under 16 event. Dale Staples (St. Francis Bay, ZAF) managed to secure a pair of substantial scores through his patience and expert wave selection, with Sydney's Davey Cathels unable to find a significant backup

for an early eight-point ride. James Woods, formerly of South Africa and now living on the Gold Coast, was held back in third place, with local Todd Rosewall relegated to fourth place. Meanwhile, Hawaii's Malia Manuel won with a pair of rides, her closest adversary, Phillipa Anderson (Newcastle), mirroring Cathels' performance, failing to find a partner for her early eight-point wave.

BOYS FINAL
1. Dale Staples
2. Davey Cathels
3. James Woods
4. Todd Rosewall
GIRLS FINAL
1. Malia Manuel
2. Phillipa Anderson
3. Sarah Baum
4. Laura Enever

RIP CURL GROMSEARCH #2, INDONESIAN PRO SURFING TOUR
SEGER BEACH, KUTA, LOMBOK
March 23

Seger Beach produced a clean but

Owen Wright. Photo Kirstin Scholtz.

fickle swell for the second leg of the Rip Curl Gromsearch Indonesia, the right-hand reef break never quite living up to expectations, rarely barrelling and eventually refusing to break at all. But this didn't dampen the spirits of the 38 young locals who had journeyed from near and far to take part in the ISC-sanctioned event. Senggigi's Mulyadi had the misfortune of losing his board in the final, a fact that may possibly have cost him the title, given his enthusiasm and fervor in the heat's latter stages. But it was Taka Arwada of Gerupuk whose backside attack won favor with the judges and earned him the victory.

UNDER 16 BOYS
1. Taka Arwada
2. Mahatta
3. Mulyadi
4. Semang
UNDER 14 BOYS
1. M. Rifai
2. Sayid Hamjah

3. Dani Abdullah
4. Fahmi
EXPRESSION SESSION
Best Wave: Mul – Kuta
Best Trick: Ketok Ovan

SURFEST MOTOROLA JUNIOR • ASP AUSTRALASIA GRADE 1 MEN'S JUNIOR EVENT / ASP AUSTRALASIA GRADE 1 WOMEN'S JUNIOR EVENT
MEREWETHER BEACH, NEW SSOUTH WALES
March 27–30

Following convincing wins in the previous ASP Juniors, Laura Enever and Owen Wright gave everyone a touch of déjà vu, both winning their respective divisions. Oozing confidence from his previous win, Wright showed form from the opening, producing a 19.5-point combined score in the event's early stages. The girls' event was a far closer-run race, going down to the wire, Enever managing to secure a high-scoring wave in the dying minutes to take a win over perpetual rival Sally Fitzgibbons.

BOYS FINAL
1. Owen Wright
2. Dean Bowen
GIRLS
FINAL
1. Laura Enever
2. Sally Fitzgibbons
SEMIFINAL 1
1. Sally Fitzgibbons
2. Tyler Wright
SEMIFINAL 2
1. Laura Enever
2. Kirby Wright

CORONA CROWN SERIES FINAL EVENT, SURFING NEW ZEALAND
PIHA BEACH, AUCKLAND
March 29–30

Despite an injured foot, Gisborne surfer Maz Quinn defined himself as possibly New Zealand's finest surfer, winning not only this final stage

but also the entire Corona Crown Series. In a close call, Quinn had to battle Luke Cederman throughout the event, Cederman receiving a 9.0-point ride midway through the final. But Quinn's consistency couldn't be beaten and he remained in front, claiming the double win. Mischa Davis followed suit, winning both the event and the series, Jessica Santorik unable to stop Davis in her tracks. The North vs. South tag team challenge had the expected result: North Island surfers making the most of the average conditions to convincingly defeat their southern counterparts.

OPEN MEN
FINAL
1. Maz Quinn
2. Luke Cederman
3. Bobby Hansen
4. Zennor Wernham
SEMIFINAL 1
1. Luke Cederman
2. Maz Quinn
3. Billy Stairmand
4. Keone Campbell
SEMIFINAL 2
1. Bobby Hansen
2. Zennor Wernham
3. Leon Santorik
4. Jay Quinn
OPEN WOMEN
FINAL
1. Mischa Davis
2. Jessica Santorik
ROUND ROBIN 1
1. Laura Rishworth
2. Daisy Thomas
3. Jessica Santorik
4. Mischa Davis
ROUND ROBIN 2
1. Mischa Davis
2. Jessica Santorik
3. Daisy Thomas
4. Laura Rishworth
INTERCLUB CHAMPIONSHIP
1. Point Boardriders
2. Bay Boardriders
3. Whanga Boardriders
4. Lion Rock Boardriders
NORTH VS SOUTH CHALLENGE
1. North Island
2. South Island

MARK RICHARDS PRO / MIDORI PRO • MEN'S 4-STAR WQS EVENT #7 / WOMEN'S 6-STAR WQS EVENT #4
MEREWETHER, NEWCASTLE, NSW
March 26–April 6

Conditions for the final of the Mark Richards Pro left much to be desired, with meager swell and onshore winds making things difficult for all surfers. Brazilian Adriano de Souza stood tall in conditions similar to those he frequently experiences at his home breaks, Frenchman, Jeremy Flores, doing his best to hold off the Brazilian's threats, but unable to come close, falling almost nine points off the mark. Stephanie Gilmore, 2007 WCT World Champion, won convincingly. But it was the once-again impressive surfing of 17-year-old Sally Fitzgibbons that impressed most as she overcame

Adriano de Souza. Photo ASP Kirstin © Covered Images.

several current and ex-World Tour surfers on her path to the final. The second place in the six-star event almost guaranteed Fitzgibbons a position in the top echelon of surfing, the ASP.

MEN 4 STAR
FINAL
1. Adriano de Souza
2. Jeremy Flores
SEMIFINAL 1
1. Jeremy Flores
2. Jarrad Sullivan
SEMIFINAL 2
1. Adriano de Souza
2. Shaun Gossmann
QUARTERFINAL 1
1. Jeremy Flores
2. Willian Cardoso
QUARTERFINAL 2
1. Jarrad Sullivan
2. Rhys Bombaci
QUARTERFINAL 3
1. Shaun Gossmann
2. Kirk Flintoff
QUARTERFINAL 4
1. Adriano de Souza
2. Adam Melling
WOMEN 6 STAR
FINAL
1. Stephanie Gilmore
2. Sally Fitzgibbons
SEMIFINAL 1
1. Stephanie Gilmore
2. Rosanne Hodge
SEMIFINAL 2
1. Sally Fitzgibbons
2. Alana Blanchard
QUARTERFINAL 1
1. Stephanie Gilmore
2. Rebecca Woods
QUARTERFINAL 2
1. Rosanne Hodge
2. Megan Abubo
QUARTERFINAL 3
1. Alana Blanchard
2. Bruna Schmitz
QUARTERFINAL 4
1. Sally Fitzgibbons
2. Jessi Miley-Dyer

HYUNDAI PRO LONGBOARD TOUR EVENT # 7, SURFING NEW ZEALAND
TITAHI BAY, WELLINGTON, NEW ZEALAND
April 4–5

With just one event remaining in the Hyundai Pro Longboard Tour,

Daryn McBride swept into the lead, overcoming some of the world's best longboarders, including Australians Jackson Close and Harley Ingleby and ex-World Champion, Bonga Perkins (HAW). Although the waves were far from cooperating, the wealth of talent provided an exciting spectacle for the crowds, New Zealand's finest doing battle to save face on home turf. The locals succeeded in taking one, two and three in the Open Men finals, but the ladies couldn't follow suit, Claire Norman, over from Sydney, denying the Kiwis their prize. Viv Treacy was a familiar face on the podium, the Over 50s competitor again topping the list.

OPEN MEN
FINAL
1. Daryn Mcbride
2. Daniel Kereopa
3. Michael Burling
4. Bonga Perkins
SEMIFINAL 1
1. Daniel Kereopa
2. Daryn Mcbride
3. Thomas Kibblewhite
4. Sam Johnson
SEMIFINAL 2
1. Michael Burling
2. Bonga Perkins
3. Jackson Close
4. Harley Ingleby
UNDER 18 BOYS
FINAL
1. Luke O'Neill
2. Shaun Goddard
3. Hone Douglas
4. Hugh Ritchie
SEMIFINAL 1
1. Shaun Goddard
2. Hugh Ritchie
3. Sam Guthrie
SEMIFINAL 2
1. Hone Douglas
2. Luke O'Neill
3. Sam Hawke
OVER 40 MEN
1. Mike Thomson
2. Viv Tracey
3. Mal Brady
4. David Storck
5. Stephen Tyro
6. Dave Burbage
OVER 50 MEN
1. Viv Treacy
2. Ian Gall
3. Mike Thomson
4. Warwick Grey
5. John Goddard
6. David Storck

OPEN WOMEN
FINAL
1. Claire Norman
2. Daisy Thomas
3. Shelly Jones
4. Hannah Phillips
SEMIFINAL 1
1. Daisy Thomas
2. Shelly Jones
3. Shereen Lobb
4. Belinda Galley
SEMIFINAL 2
1. Hannah Phillips
2. Claire Norman
3. Kirstie Thomsen
4. Melody Spaul

NEW ZEALAND BILLABONG GROM SERIES, PRESENTED BY OCEANBRIDGE, SURFING NEW ZEALAND
PIHA BEACH, AUCKLAND, NEW ZEALAND
April 5–6

Ever an imposing threat on the New Zealand circuit, sibling duo Ben and Alexis Poulter dominated the Aukland stage of the New Zealand Billabong Grom Series in challenging four-foot surf. Winning his semifinal heat, Ben also did well in the Under 14 division but, with so many heats under his belt, faltered in the final, allowing Tane Wallis a dramatic win in the dying seconds. Wallis had also joined Poulter in the Under 16 final, placing fourth. The Poulter siblings extended their dominance with younger brother Sam performing well in the Under 12s but conceding victory to Elliot Paerata Reid (Piha) and Whangamata's Dune Kennings.

UNDER 16 BOYS
FINAL
1. Ben Poulter
2. Alex Dive
3. Johnny Hicks
4. Tane Wallis
SEMIFINAL 1
1. Alex Dive
2. Ben Poulter
3. Peri Matenga
4. Todd Doyle
SEMIFINAL 2
1. Johnny Hicks
2. Tane Wallis
3. Joe Moretti
4. Blake Myers
QUARTERFINAL 1
1. Todd Doyle
2. Ben Poulter
3. Dune Kennings
4. Kahu Craig-Ranga
QUARTERFINAL 2
1. Alex Dive
2. Peri Matenga
3. Nat Hughes
4. Reno Marriott
QUARTERFINAL 3
1. Tane Wallis
2. Johnny Hicks
3. Aaron Reid
4. Fraser Chatham
QUARTERFINAL 4
1. Blake Myers
2. Joe Moretti
3. Jacob Kohn
4. James Tume

UNDER 14 BOYS
FINAL
1. Tane Wallis
2. Waretini Wano
3. Ben Poulter
4. Kahu Craig Te Ranga
SEMIFINAL 1
1. Tane Wallis
2. Waretini Wano
3. Fintan Cram
4. Paul Moretti
SEMIFINAL 2
1. Ben Poulter
2. Kahu Craig Te Ranga
3. Kurt Geiseler
4. Jules Craft
QUARTERFINAL 1
1. Waretini Wano
2. Paul Moretti
3. Peri Matenga
4. Mackenzie Christie
QUARTERFINAL 2
1. Tane Wallis
2. Fintan Cram
3. Ian Luscombe Jnr
4. Connor Pearson
QUARTERFINAL 3
1. Ben Poulter
2. Kurt Geiseler
3. Adam Grimson
4. Josh Taylor
QUARTERFINAL 4
1. Kahu Craig Te Ranga
2. Jules Craft
3. Patxi Scott-Arrieta
4. Dune Kennings
UNDER 12 BOYS
FINAL
1. Elliot Paerata Reid
2. Dune Kennings
3. Sam Poulter
4. Quin Matenga
SEMIFINAL 1
1. Dune Kennings
2. Quin Matenga
3. Jordan Griffin
n/s. Morgan Munroe
SEMIFINAL 2
1. Elliot Paerata Reid
2. Sam Poulter
3. Matt Hanson
4. Leo Copley
UNDER 16 GIRLS
1. Alexis Poulter
2. Georgia Cooper
3. Rosa Thompson
4. Ella Williams
UNDER 14 GIRLS
1. Gabriella McCarthy-Marriott
2. Chloe Shutt
3. Ella Williams
4. Alethea Lock
UNDER 12 GIRLS
FINAL
1. Milly Crewe
2. Bianca Sansom

3. Gabriella McDonnell
4. Gabriela Sansom
SEMIFINAL 1
1. Milly Crewe
2. Gabriella McDonnell
3. Britt Kindred
SEMIFINAL 2
1. Gabriela Sansom
2. Bianca Sansom
3. Demi Hewitt

VOLCOM STONE'S VQS GRAND CHAMPS MANLY
MANLY BEACH, NEW SOUTH WALES
April 4–5

With two tickets to America for the $100,000 VQS Grand Finals, the Australian Grand Championships were always going to be a hotly contested event. Glassy waves failed to swell to any great size, but that didn't stop all competitors unleashing their finest moves. The majority of finals could have swung either way, both surfers in each division equally matched and in with a strong chance of a win. Almost all were decided in the final minutes, except for the Pro-Am. Luke Cheadle went into the final as the favorite, but Tom Salverson wasn't going to let it be an easy victory, hounding Cheadle into a double interference call. But two solid waves in the heat's latter half gave Cheadle the win and the chance to compete in the VQS Grand Finals.

PRO-AM MEN FINAL
1. Luke Cheadle
2. Tom Salverson
UNDER 16 BOYS
1. James Woods
2. Mitch Crews
UNDER 14 BOYS
1. Oscar Scanes
2. Cooper Chapman
GIRLS FINAL
1. Tyler Wright
2. Dimity Stoyle

BILLABONG PARKO GROM STOMP
SUNSHINE COAST, QUEENSLAND
April 7–11

Junior sensation Tamaroa McComb once again dominated over his fellow competitors, this time in the Billabong Parko Grom Stomp. The

Tom Whitaker. Photo Steve Robertson.

Tahitian-born surfer who now lives on the Gold Coast has been an outstanding force in Under 16s events since his migration to Australia. There was rarely a doubt that McComb would come out on top, although runner-up Tim McDonald did well to remain within a point of McComb. Matt Banting was a stand-out in the Under 14 division, but it was a fortuitous circumstance that landed him in first place. Creed McTaggart posed a very real threat to the eventual winner, but an interference call relegated McTaggart into third place. WA surfer, Felicity Palmateer narrowly missed out on a win, Phillipa Anderson (Merewether) just pipped her by a mere 0.17 points.

UNDER 16 BOYS
1. Tamaroa McComb
2. Tim McDonald
3. Jack Freestone
4. Thomas Woods
UNDER 14 BOYS
1. Matt Banting
2. Tyla Hutchinson
3. Creed McTaggart
4. Tommy Boucout
UNDER 12 BOYS
1. Joshua Szele
2. Jack Germain
3. Jackson Baker
4. Harry Bryant
UNDER 16 GIRLS
1. Phillipa Anderson
2. Felicity Palmateer
3. Naomi Stevic
4. Georgia Fish
UNDER 14 GIRLS
1. Sarah Mason
2. Eden Putland
3. Ellie Jean Coffey
4. Amaia Doyle

DRUG AWARE PRO MARGARET RIVER, PRESENTED BY O'NEILL • MEN'S 6-STAR PRIME WQS EVENT #8 / WOMEN'S 6-STAR PRIME WQS EVENT #5
SURFERS PT, MARGARET RIVER, WESTERN AUSTRALIA
April 7–13

Tom Whitaker and Paige Hareb both sealed maiden victories at Margaret River, in a pair of all-international finals. For Hareb (NZ) it was a very close race, the 17-year-old overcoming South Africa's Rosanne Hodge in the latter half of her heat. For Whitaker, the path to success was considerably easier. Surfing against Californian, Chris Ward, a fellow ex-World Tour surfer, Whitaker (Bronte, NSW) had the heat on his side, easily defeating his rival to take the US$15,000 first prize.

OPEN MEN
FINAL
1. Tom Whitaker
2. Chris Ward
SEMIFINAL 1
1. Chris Ward
2. Daniel Ross
SEMIFINAL 2
1. Tom Whitaker

2. Chris Davidson
OPEN WOMEN
FINAL
1. Paige Hareb
2. Rosanne Hodge
SEMIFINAL 1
1. Paige Hareb
2. Rebecca Woods
SEMIFINAL 2
1. Rosanne Hodge
2. Clair Bevilacqua

Todd Rosewall. Photo Steve Robertson.

HYUNDAI PRO LONGBOARD TOUR, SURFING NEW ZEALAND
SUNSET BEACH, PORT WAIKATO
April 12–13

Despite only finishing in seventh place, Daryn McBride managed to secure enough points in the final stage of the Hyundai Pro Longboard Tour to claim overall series victory. Australians dominated the Men's Open, Jackson Close barely edging out Harley Ingleby to take the stage win. Hawaiian visitor Bonga Perkins couldn't make it out of the quarterfinals, McBride and Close simply being too good on the day. Australia again overshadowed the locals in the Women's Open, Sydney's Claire Norman claiming her second series victory in a row over Daisy Thomas. Notwithstanding, Thomas's Tour record stood her in good stead, the Christchurch surfer securing first place on the overall points tally.

OPEN MEN
FINAL
1. Jackson Close
2. Harley Ingleby
3. Dylan Barnfield
4. Daniel Proctor
SEMIFINAL 1
1. Dylan Barnfield
2. Jackson Close
3. Kirk Beyer
4. Daryn Mcbride
SEMIFINAL 2
1. Daniel Proctor
2. Harley Ingleby
3. Michael Burling
4. Sam Johnson
QUARTERFINAL 1
1. Dylan Barnfield
2. Kirk Beyer
3. Dave Elley

n/s. Jay Reeve
QUARTERFINAL 2
1. Daryn Mcbride
2. Jackson Close
3. Bonga Perkins
4. Thomas Kibblewhite
QUARTERFINAL 3
1. Harley Ingleby
2. Sam Johnson
3. Rob Norman
4. Paul Culpan

QUARTERFINAL 4
1. Daniel Proctor
2. Michael Burling
3. Ant McColl
4. Matt Gillespie
UNDER 18 BOYS
1. Rick Williamson
2. Sam Guthrie
3. Hone Douglas
4. Eli Barnfield
OVER 40 MEN
FINAL
1. Mike Thomson
2. David Storck
3. Rupert Newbold
4. Mal Brady
SEMIFINAL 1
1. Mal Brady
2. David Storck
3. Bryan Western
4. Simon Bennett
SEMIFINAL 2
1. Rupert Newbold
2. Mike Thomson
3. Stephen Tyro
4. Richard Benson Cooper
OVER 50 MEN
FINAL
1. Mike Thomson
2. Viv Treacy
3. Paul Browne
4. Ruepert Newbold
SEMIFINAL 1
1. Mike Thomson
2. Viv Treacy
3. David Storck
SEMIFINAL 2
1. Paul Browne
2. Ruepert Newbold
3. Warrick Gray
OPEN WOMEN
FINAL
1. Claire Norman
2. Daisy Thomas
3. Shelly Jones
4. Kirstie Thomsen
SEMIFINAL 1
1. Kirstie Thomsen
2. Shelly Jones
3. Rea Ansin
SEMIFINAL 2
1. Daisy Thomas

2. Claire Norman
3. Shereen Lobb

QUIKSILVER STATE JUNIOR TITLES, EVENT 2 OF 3
PHILLIP ISLAND, VICTORIA
April 11–13

The second round of the Quiksilver State Junior Titles was surfed in clean waves, overhead for many of the young competitors. Todd Rosewall was a powerful force throughout the event, not dropping a heat from the outset and going on to remain strong through the final for the win. Jess Laing did well in the challenging waves, defeating Georgia Fish of Flinders and fellow Phillip Islanders Sophie Collins and Emma Demos. Closeouts, chops and rips made the going difficult, but Torquay's Harry Mann surfed with tenacity and skill to emerge victorious in the Under 16s.

UNDER 18 BOYS
1. Todd Rosewall
2. Mitch Baker
3. Elliot Mann
4. Johnno Spitteri
UNDER 16 BOYS
1. Harry Mann
2. Marcus Wright
3. Jamie Powell
4. Tom Cole
UNDER 18 GIRLS
1. Jess Laing
2. Georgia Fish
3. Sophie Collins
4. Ella Demos
UNDER 16 GIRLS
1. Nikki Van Dijk
2. India Payne

RUSTY GROMFEST SERIES
HALFWAY BEACH, BALI
April 15

A glorious day welcomed the competitors for Rusty's third and final Indonesian Gromfest. Four-foot glassy waves and blue skies made for a perfect day of competition. Australia's Alex Swading was prevalent in the Under 16 division, having the upper hand for the majority of the heat. In the Under 14s, Ediana Putra was surf-

ing for the series win. Unable to match the consistency of eventual winner, Ornot, Putra nonetheless came second, the points gained enough to place him at the top of the overall ladder. Koko Mitsua Antara took the double win in the under 12 event, coming out on top for the day, so by cementing his place as the 2008 Gromfest victor.

Owen Wright. Photo Steve Robertson.

UNDER 16 BOYS
1. Alex Swading
2. Agus Frimanto
3. Gazali Hamzah
4. Darmaputra Tonjo
UNDER 14 BOYS
1. Ornot
2. Ediana Putra
3. Arya Wijaya
4. Abi Azwar Anas
UNDER 12 BOYS
1. Koko Mitsua Antara
2. Luke Hynd
3. Komang Arip
4. Kadek Yoga

BOOST MOBILE SURF SHO, PRESENTED BY NOKIA • ASP 2008 SPECIALTY EVENT
SURFERS PARADISE, QUEENSLAND
April 18–20

Overcoming a field of world-class surfers, Owen Wright boosted his way to victory in the Boost Mobile Surf Sho. The wildcard to the event was indomitable in the perfect three-foot waves, defeating Mick Fanning, Bede Durbidge and 2007 Boost Mobile Surf Sho winner Taj Burrow. Wright, known for his propensity toward aerial maneuvers, soared high in a series of lofty airs to claim the $25,000 prize. The unique format required surfers to perform tricks based on the spin of a wheel, evening the playing field somewhat and giving everyone the opportunity to perform at their utmost.

OPEN MEN
1. Owen Wright
2. Luke Stickley
Equ. 3. Dru Alder
Equ. 3. Julian Wilson
Equ. 3. Asher Pacey

QUIKSILVER / ROXY OPEN, KERAMAS, PRESENTED BY JIM BEAM • 6-STAR ISC MEN'S EVENT
KERAMAS, BALI, INDONESIA
April 17–27

The Quiksilver Open commenced in classic Indonesian surf: three-foot and glassy, with a gentle offshore grooming the faces. Dede Suryana was the man to watch, a hunger to better last year's second place driving the local hard. Last year's victor, Lee Wilson, barely missed out

Billy Stairmand. Photo www.andrewchristie.com.

on advancing from the quarters, Dede nearly following suit in his heat against Rizal Tanjung. Tanjung's talents were proven when he pulled into a tight barrel for a good score, but Suryana wouldn't roll over, matching Tanjung's barrel and bettering his score to the tune of nine points. A tight final saw Suryana pocket another nine-point ride, Pepen Hendrik unable to answer. A see-sawing final had Suryana again having to work hard, this time against Raditya Rondi. Suryana's work was made even tougher by the fact that he had surfed his way up through the trials, the now exhausted surfer having to draw on all his motivation and reserves to out-surf his rival. Third place getter Pepen Hendrik had a consolation prize: his wife, Yesco, convincingly claiming first place in the Roxy Open.

ISC MEN PRO DIVISION
1. Dede Suryana
2. Raditya Rondi
3. Pepen Hendrik / Tipi Jabrik

ISC MEN MASTERS DIVISION
1. Made Artha
2. Wayan Pica
3. Wayan Widiartha
4. Sachang

ROXY OPEN FINAL
1. Yesco
2. Mikiko
3. Yasnyar Gea aka Bonnie
4. Ayako

VOLCOM VQS CHAMPS NZ
RAGLAN, NEW ZEALAND
April 19

The VQS Champs were blessed, Raglan's Manu Bay turning on some epic six-foot surf for the event and the Over 18s all the way through to the grommets reveling in the first-class conditions. Locals Billy Stairmand and Zennor Wenham showed their knowledge of the break, placing first and second, Stairmand taking the grand prize of tickets and entry to the World VQS Finals in California. The 15-17-year-old division saw Matt Hewitt take his second .win in as many years, whilst in the grommets' final, wildcard Fraser Chatham overthrew Tane Wallis in the upset of the day, the heat so close many were left guessing until the presentations were made. Also a surprise to the podium was Mischa Davis, the Piha surfer, along with Mt.Maunganui's Laura Rishworth, reaching the final after the defeats of favorites Jess Santorik and Kara Stephenson.

PRO-AM 18+
1. Billy Stairmand
2. Zennor Wenham
3. Luke Cederman
3. Jarrod Hancox
4. Chris O'Leary
4. Jarrod Toomey
5. Owen Barnes
5. Damon Gunness
5. Leon Santorik
6. Jesse Lewis
6. Chris Malone
6. Jeremy Granger
7. Reuben Knoble
7. Morehu Roberts
7. Conrad Doyle
7. Hamish Mathieson
7. Tim O'Connor
7. Rangi Ormond
8. Larry Fisher
8. Conan James
8. Isaac Patersen
8. Dean Hishon
8. Nick Moses
8. Matt Scorringe

JUNIORS
1. Matt Hewitt

2. Blake Myers
3. Brandon Williams
3. Storm Carrol
4. Tyler Anderson
4. Mike Mallaleu
5. Peter Ralph
5. Mark Pathmore
6. Alex Dive
6. Zen Wallis
6. Paul Moretti
6. John Courian
7. Adam Cranston
7. Tom Smith
7. Rob Courian
7. James Tume

GROMS
1. Fraser Chatham
2. Tane Wallis
3. Subarm Linklater
3. Joe Moretti
4. Stefan Gross
4. Todd Doyle
5. Conner Anderson
5. Ethan Burge
6. Chad Joes
6. Mac Christie
6. Fintan Cram
6. Paul Moretti
7. Ryan Sutton
7. James Tume
7. Josh Kettle

GIRL'S OPEN
1. Mischa Davis

Chelsea Williams. Photo www.malfunction.com.au.

2. Laura Rishworth
3. Jess Santorik
3. Thandi Durham
4. Kara Stephenson
4. Wini Paul
5. Gabby Sansom
5. Jayda Fitz
6. Biance Sansom

HYUNDAI MALFUNCTION SURF FESTIVAL • ASP WORLD LONGBOARD QUALIFYING SERIES
NEW TWEED COAST, QUEENSLAND
April 22–27

In its new home of Kingscliff on the New South Wales – Queensland border, the Hyundai Malfunction was a huge success, locals and visitors alike enjoying the event's relocation. Dane Pioli made it a back-to-back victory, having also won last year's contest, this year being a more prestigious award, being the event's 25th anniversary. Defeating Harley Ingleby, Josh Constable and Ray Lawrence in the tricky conditions of the Surftech Men's Professional WLQS final, Pioli did well to achieve a score of 14 from a possible 20. Ingleby had a reprieve, taking out the retro division with ease. Chelsea Williams was again a force to be reckoned with, winning the equivalent ladies' competition, but her score, a meager 9.33, reflected the ordinary conditions.

SURFTECH MEN PROFESSIONAL WLQS FINAL
1. Dane Pioli
2. Harley Ingleby
3. Josh Constable
4. Ray Lawrence

9FT AMATEUR MEN FINAL
1. Ben Williams
2. Justin Healy
3. Nick Farago
4. Mitch Surman
5. Ben Johnson
6. Blair McDonald

SURFTECH WOMEN PROFESSIONAL WLQS FINAL
1. Chelsea Williams
2. Rosie Locke
3. Selby Riddle
4. Tessa Davidson

9FT .AMATEUR WOMEN FINAL
1. Bianca Anstiss
2. Monique Keane
3. Kathryn Hughes
4. Emma Claxton
5. Sally Paxton
6. Jade Foster

ABOOD CRANE TRUCKS UNDER 18 BOYS FINAL
1. Mitch Surman
2. Jackson Winter
3. Tim Cloxton
4. Clinton Guest
5. Nick Jorgensen
6. Damien Farago

SEA MASTER FISHING CHARTER AUSSIE COUCH UNDER 18 GIRLS FINAL
1. Georgie Roach
2. Bianca Anstiss
3. Kelly Winter
4. Grace Bullen
5. Beth Palmer
6. Kathryn Hughes

GOLDEN BREED RETRO OPEN FINAL
1. Harley Ingleby
2. Kyle Neilsen
3. Tai Graham
3. Cameron Gleave

GOLDEN BREED UNDER 18 BOYS FINAL
1. Mitchell James
2. Tim Claxton
3. Dominque Wall
4. N/A -

GOLDEN BREED OLD MAL FINAL
1. Justin Healy
2. Ray Gleave
3. Isaac Fields
4. Grant Davies
5. Nick Jorgenson
6. Tony Abood

HONOLUA MEN STAND UP PADDLE BOARDS FINAL
1. Kerien Taylor
2. Woody Jack
3. Guy Walker
4. Ray Gleave

ANZ KINGSCLIFF OVER 40 MEN FINAL
1. Ray Gleave
2. Grant Davies
3. Mick Riddle
4. Ian Pearson
5. Steve Jackson
6. Robin Yates

DUKES LONGBOARDS OVER 50 MEN FINAL
1. Peter Becker
2. Mike Pimm
3. Tony Abood
4. David Storck
5. Jeff Arnold
6. Peter Dunn

ROBERT AUGUST LONGBOARDS OVER 60 MEN FINAL
1. Neville Smith
2. Dennis Lowe
3. Malcom Brough
4. Bob Smith

RIP CURL GROMSEARCH TARANAKI
TARANAKI'S BACK BEACH, NEW ZEALAND
April 26–27

The Poulters were at it again, flexing their competition muscle to take two firsts and a third in the Rip Curl Gromsearch. Ben Poulter couldn't manage to get out of the semis of the Boys Under 16 division, but managed to seal a victory in the U/14. Little brother Sam secured a second in the Under 12s, whilst their female counterpart, sister Alexis, scored first in the Under 16 Girls final. Gisborne's Johnny Hicks asked his granddad, who had passed away the previous week, for good waves and the old guy must have been listening, Hicks scoring the majority of good waves in the four-way final heat and taking the win with ease.

UNDER 16 BOYS FINAL
1. Johnny Hicks
2. Mark Pathemore
3. Blake Myers
4. Tane Wallis

SEMIFINAL 1
1. Tane Wallis
2. Blake Myers
3. Alex Dive
4. James Tume

SEMIFINAL 2
1. Johnny Hicks
2. Mark Pathemore
3. Ben Poulter
4. Cody McCusker

UNDER 14 BOYS FINAL
1. Ben Poulter

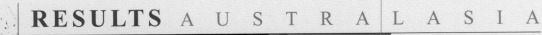

2. Tane Wallis
3. Patxi Scott – Arrieta
4. Paul Moretti
SEMIFINAL 1
1. Tane Wallis
2. Paul Moretti
3. Fintan Cram
4. Jules Craft
SEMIFINAL 2
1. Ben Poulter
2. Patxi Scott – Arrieta
3. Dune Kennings
4. Kahu Craig Te Ranga
QUARTERFINAL 1
1. Paul Moretti
2. Fintan Cram
3. Peri Matenga
4. Taylor Louie
QUARTERFINAL 2
1. Tane Wallis
2. Jules Craft
3. Waretini Wano

Julian Wilson. Photo Jake White.

4. Levi Stewart
QUARTERFINAL 3
1. Ben Poulter
2. Dune Kennings
3. Josh Kettle
4. Adam Grimson
QUARTERFINAL 4
1. Kahu Craig Te Ranga
2. Patxi Scott – Arrieta
3. Brad Pitcher
4. Mackenzie Chritie
UNDER 12 BOYS
FINAL
1. Dune Kennings
2. Sam Poulter
3. Manu Scot – Arrieta
4. Korbin Hutchings
SEMIFINAL 1
1. Manu Scot – Arrieta
2. Sam Poulter
3. Quin Matenga
SEMIFINAL 2
1. Dune Kennings
2. Korbin Hutchings
3. Jordan Griffin
UNDER 16 GIRLS
FINAL
1. Alexis Poulter
2. Rosa Thompson
3. Jayda Martin – Fitzharris
4. Ella Williams
SEMIFINAL 1
1. Rosa Thompson
2. Jayda Martin – Fitzharris
3. Alethea Lock
4. Chloe Shutt
SEMIFINAL 2
1. Alexis Poulter

2. Ella Williams
3. Hayley Baxter
4. Gabreilla McCarthy – Marriott
UNDER 14 GIRLS
FINALS
1. Jayda Martin-Fitzharris
2. Ella Williams
3. Alethea Lock
4. Gabriella McCarthy-Marriott
SEMIFINAL 1
1. Alethea Lock
2. Gabriella McCarthy-Marriott
3. Eloise Stevens
4. Emma Croton
SEMIFINAL 2
1. Jayda Martin-Fitzharris
2. Ella Williams
3. Alexandra Potter
4. Chloe Shutt
UNDER 12 GIRLS
FINAL
1. Gabriela Sansom

2. Bianca Sansom
3. Milly Crewe
4. Hannah Kohn

BROTHERS NEILSEN PRO JUNIOR • GRADE 3 ASP MEN'S PRO JUNIOR / GRADE 1 ASP WOMEN'S PRO JUNIOR
BURLEIGH HEADS, QUEENSLAND
April 28–May 4

Julian Wilson claimed his first Brothers Neilsen Pro Junior crown with a narrow win over Coffs Harbour surfer Jayke Sharp. Taking advantage of better swell conditions, the event was moved south to Duranbah. The tight final heat saw the lead swapping frequently throughout the 30 minutes, Wilson snatching the pole position in the final seconds of the competition. Contrasting his finals performance, Wilson was the distinct standout in his semi against Heath Joske. Likewise, Sharp dominated over Dean Iezzi to make his final berth. Sally Fitzgibbons extended her series lead with a victory over perpetual bridesmaid Laura Enever, who was simply unable to find the waves she needed to develop any significant score. Fitzgibbons was indefatigable throughout the

event, showing her consummate professionalism throughout her heats.

OPEN MEN
FINAL
1. Julian Wilson
2. Jayke Sharp
SEMIFINAL 1
1. Jayke Sharp
2. Dean Iezzi
SEMIFINAL 2
1. Julian Wilson
2. Heath Joske
OPEN WOMEN
FINAL
1. Sally Fitzgibbons
2. Laura Enever
SEMIFINAL 1

Sally Fitzgibbons. Photo Jake White.

1. Sally Fitzgibbons
2. Tyler Wright
SEMIFINAL 2
1. Laura Enever
2. Kirstie Jones

SMOKEFREE NATIONAL SCHOLASTIC SURF CHAMPIONSHIPS, SURFING NEW ZEALAND
OPUNAKE, TARANAKI, NEW ZEALAND
April 29–May 3

The Waikato scholastic surfing team proved far too talented for their rivals in the waves of Taranaki for the Smokefree National Scholastic Surf contest. Aided by the ever-proficient Poulter duo, Ben and Alexis, and Under 18 winner Buck Woods, the team defied all challenges, winning the Under 18 and 14 Boys divisions and the Girls Under 16s. Surfers were tested to their limits by messy conditions, finding a peak and making the most of the crumbling faces often denying the contestants of any significant scores. Alex Dive, always an assertive force in Kiwi events, masterfully surfed into the lead in the Under 16 division and, with the assistance of Mitch Tomelson's win in the Under 18 bodyboard competition, managed to secure second place overall for his Bay of Plenty team.

TEAM PLACINGS
1. Waikato
2. Bay Of Plenty
3. Coromandel
4. Auckland
5. Gisborne
6. Taranaki
7. Northland
8. Canterbury
9. Otago
10. Hawkes Bay
11. Wellington
12. West Coast
UNDER 18 BOYS
FINAL
1. Buck Woods
2. Paco Divers
3. Sean Parker
4. Braedon Williams
SEMIFINAL 1
1. Buck Woods
2. Braedon Williams
3. Charlie Denniston
SEMIFINAL 2
1. Sean Parker
2. Paco Divers
3. Tim Thompson
UNDER 16 BOYS
FINAL
1. Alex Dive
2. Ben Bennett
3. James Tume
4. Blake Myers
SEMIFINAL 1
1. Alex Dive
2. James Tume
3. Fraser Chatham
4. Todd Doyle
SEMIFINAL 2
1. Blake Myers
2. Ben Bennett
3. Mark Parthemore

4. Johnny Hicks
UNDER 14 BOYS
1. Ben Poulter
2. Taylor Louie
3. Brad Pitcher
4. Patxi Scott-Arrieta
UNDER 18 GIRLS
FINAL
1. India Wray - Murane
2. Nicola Colson - Koster
3. Anna Hawes
4. Lucy Brankin
SEMIFINAL 1
1. Lucy Brankin
2. Anna Hawes
3. Grace Spiers
4. Demi Poynter
SEMIFINAL 2
1. India Wray - Murane)
2. Nicola Colson - Koster
3. Sharnae Van Der Helder
4. Grace Mora
UNDER 16 GIRLS
1. Alexis Poulter
2. Rosa Thompson
3. Georgia Cooper
4. Kristi Zarifeh
UNDER 14 GIRLS
1. Ella Williams
2. Jayda Martin-Fitzharris
3. Alethea Lock
4. Gabriella McCarthy-Marriott
UNDER 18 BOYS LONGBOARD
1. Leroy Rust
2. Sam Guthrie
3. Charlie Brown
4. Dylan Mayor
UNDER 18 BOYS BODYBOARD
1. Mitch Tomelson
2. Luke Elliot
3. Aran Naismith
4. Kurt Randell

LIZZY SURF SERIES ROUND 1, SURFING QUEENSLAND
SURFERS PARADISE, QUEENSLAND
May 9–11

Central Coast surfer Ellie-Jean Coffey overcame a wealth of talent, including Dimity Stoyle and Naomi Stevic, to claim the title in stage one of the inaugural Lizzy Surf Series. The three-stop tour kicked off in Surfers Paradise in average waves but with much enthusiasm from all competitors. Seven divisions, from the Under 14 grommets right up to the "more experienced" Over 35s, more than 70 entrants in total, surfed it out in the small, wind-swept conditions. Coffey needed to be at the very top of her game, barely managing to scrape a lead from Stoyle, taking the win by a mere 0.11 points. Sarah Mason (Tugun) excelled, following in her big sister Airini's footsteps to win both the Under 16 and Under 14 contests.

WOOPEN MEN
1. Ellie-Jean Coffey
2. Dimity Stoyle
3. Naomi Stevic
4. Linda Fisher
UNDER 21 WINNER
Brittani Nicholl
UNDER 18 WINNER
Dimity Stoyle
UNDER 16 WINNER
Sarah Mason
UNDER 14 WINNER
Sarah Mason
OVER 28 WINNER
Bel Hardwick
OVER 35 WINNER
Sharon Jackson

SALTWATER WINE SURF CLASSIC, HURLEY NSW CHAMPION CIRCUIT
OLD BAR, NEW SOUTH WALES
May 10–11

Rhys Bombaci took his first win of the year at Old Bar for the Salt Water Wine Classic, despite an exceptional WQS ratings position. In a contest that saw a phenomenal level of surfing talent, Bombaci overcame Drew Courtney (Umina, NSW), defending champion Darren O'Rafferty (Bonny Hills, NSW) and local standout Joel Reading (Wallabi Point, NSW) to take the gratifying win. Ty Watson did well to finish equal fifth in the open division, but excelled in the Under 18s to take the win. A tight heat for the Under 16s saw the finalists separated by less than two points, local lad Oscar Scanes delighting the home crowd in emerging victorious.

OPEN MEN
1. Rhys Bombaci
2. Drew Courtney
3. Darren O'Rafferty
4. Joel Reading

UNDER 18 BOYS
1. Ty Watson
2. Sam Schuman
3. Matt Dunlop
4. Mitchell Sykes

UNDER 16 BOYS
1. Oscar Scanes
2. Jordi Watson
3. Matt Banning
4. Jake Sylvester

QUIKSILVER STATE JUNIOR TITLES VICTORIA, SURFING VICTORIA

JAN JUC, VICTORIA
May 10–11

Good conditions blessed competitors at Jan Juc for the Quiksilver state titles. But despite swell and wind direction working for the event, high-scoring waves proved elusive. Todd Rosewall used his local knowledge to find the pick of the banks, enabling a collection of waves that gave him the edge over his fellow competitors. Jess Laing defined herself as a highly talented surfer, finishing almost seven points clear of her closest rival, Georgia Fish. Nikki Van Dijk continued her indomitable form, taking out the Under 16 Girls division, her third victory in as many events of the Victoria Junior series.

UNDER 18 BOYS
1. Todd Rosewall
2. Mitch Baker
3. Shyama Buttonshaw
4. Adam Rawson

UNDER 18 GIRLS
1. Jess Laing
2. Georgia Fish
3. Molly Kenwood
4. Sophie Collins

UNDER 16 BOYS
1. Harry Mann
2. Jamie Powell
3. Tom Cole
4. Sam Chalmers

UNDER 16 GIRLS
1. Nikki Van Dijk
2. India Payne

UNDER 13 BOYS
1. Joe Van Dijk
2. Darcy Day
3. Francis Meade
4. Matthew Lawrie

UNDER 13 GIRLS
1. Ginger Brown
2. Zoe Clarke
3. Julia Mann
4. Kelly Laity

RUSTY RUMBLE IN DA JUNGLE • 6-STAR ISC EVENT

BANGSAL BEACH, SANUR
May 2–14

With four-foot hollow waves reeling across the reef at Sanur, the final of the Rusty Rumble in Da Jungle was set to be spectacular. Made Awan made the final his, pulling in deep before carving hard on the open faces and throwing up the occasional aerial maneuver to defeat his rivals. Despite his easy entry into the semifinals, his round four and quarterfinal adversaries failing to show up, so giving him free passage, there was no denying Awan's superior talent. Getting the first wave of the final, Awan gained the early upper hand. But Wayan "Betet" Merta wasn't going to allow Awan an easy vistory. Betet was in fine form, holding out for the set waves and greater barrel potential. But his patience would be his undoing, the waves failing to provide the points he needed and, Awan's voracious thirst for waves bettering his rival's calmer approach.

PRO RESULTS
1. Made Awan
2. Wayan "Betet" Merta
3. Devis Ratif / Tipi Jabrik

MASTERS RESULTS
1. Gacang
2. Made Artha
3. Wayan Gantiyasa

MACBETH BEST BARREL AWARD
Tipi Jabrik

BILLABONG COOLUM CLASSIC, PRESENTED BY PRINT-POINT, BILLABONG QUEENSLAND CHAMPIONSHIP CIRCUIT

SUNSHINE COAST, QUEENSLAND
May 17–18

Blake Wilson proved himself the unlikely winner of the latest stage of the Queensland Championship Circuit, overcoming a WQS contender and an ex-World Tour surfer on his path to the final. Wilson, who only entered the event on the encouragement of a friend, made the most of insignificant conditions. Trailing Matt Jones, Wilson was playing

Inside barrel for Made Awan. Photo Tim Hain.

catch-up for much of the final. But a couple of expertly selected waves gave him the opportunity to step up and take the lead in the dying minutes of the heat.

FINAL
1. Blake Wilson
2. Matt Jones
3. Dave Reardon-Smith
4. Jamie Thomson

SUNSMART PRO JUNIOR • GRADE 4 MEN'S ASP PRO JUNIOR / GRADE 3 WOMEN'S ASP PRO JUNIOR

TRIGG POINT, WESTERN AUSTRALIA
May 15–18

Stuart Kennedy and Tyler Wright were outstanding in the ASP Pro Junior event, held in three-foot waves at Trigg Point. With only three stages remaining after this, the pressure was on for all contestants. Sunday was the scheduled final day of contest, but a dying swell urged the contest organizers to push on while the waves remained. Kennedy's win extended his overall series lead, Jayke Sharp's second place assisting in advancing on his third ranking. Tyler Wright proved herself as a huge force on the world stage and a future star, the 14-year-old proving that age doesn't matter in her win over defending Australasian Pro Junior Series champion Airini Mason.

MEN PRO JUNIOR
1. Stuart Kennedy
2. Jayke Sharp

WOMEN PRO JUNIOR
1. Tyler Wright
2. Airini Mason

DRIPPING WET PRO, HURLEY NSW CHAMPIONSHIP CIRCUIT

FRESHWATER BEACH, NEW SOUTH WALES
May 24–25

The second stage of the Hurley NSW Championship Circuit proved as spectacular as the first, with North Narrabeen's Chris Davidson defeating ex-World Tour surfer Nathan Hedge, Under 20s champion Ty Watson, and victor Rhys Bombaci in an electric final. Watson's performance was, at times, quite literally faultless, a perfect 10 in the semis, proving that the surfer was in fine form and a favorite for the final. His skills didn't abate for the final, a 9.33 proving to his fellow finalists that he was on a mission to win. Ty Watson showed a wealth of potential, the third-place getter winning the Under 20 division the previous day, before advancing to the final of the main event.

FINAL
1. Chris Davidson
2. Nathan Hedge

3. Ty Watson
4. Rhys Bombaci

TRIPLE BULL PRO, HURLEY NSW CHAMPIONSHIP CIRCUIT

WANDA BEACH, CRONULLA, NEW SOUTH WALES
May 31–June 1

Umina's Drew Courtney illuminated the lineup in the third stop on the Hurley NSW Championship Circuit. Despite challenging conditions, Courtney amassed a two-wave score of 17.93 to overcome adversaries Joe Sear (Cronulla), Luke Cheadle (Culburra) and Nick Riley (Harbord). Courtney was a significant presence throughout the event but was given a run for his money in the final, local surfer Sear challenging his more experienced peers throughout the final. Locals again fell short of a win in the Cadets, with Connor O'Leary (Cronulla) being edged out by Currarong's Jordy Watson. Current Hurley NSW Championship Circuit ratings leader Oscar Scanes (Old Bar) and Justin Arnold (Gerringong) came in third and fourth respectively.

OPEN MEN
1. Drew Courtney
2. Joe Sear
3. Luke Cheadle
4. Nick Riley

CADET BOYS
1. Jordy Watson
2. Connor O'Leary
3. Oscar Scanes
4. Justin Arnold

AUAHI KORE MĀORI TRI SERIES, SURFING NEW ZEALAND

GISBORNE, NEW ZEALAND
May 31

A perfect swell greeted competitors in the first event of the Auahi Kore Maori Tri Series, three-foot peelers making the chilled New Zealand morning that bit more acceptable. The Chrises—Daly and Malone—showed indefatigable form, surfing excellently throughout their heats, the Over 35 and Open respectively. Both surfers took an early lead, Malone securing a 9.5 and 7.5 after only ten min-

utes, to make himself undefeatable by his rivals. Daniel Proctor sewed up the Open Longboard division, a performance of consummate professionalism proving too much for the other finalists. And wahine Jayda Martin-Fitzharris had local knowledge on her side, surfing the Kiwi Pipe with flair and style for a division win.

Martyn Matenga. Photo Cory/NZ Surfing Magazine.

TEAM
1. Tauranga Moana
2. Turanganui a Kiwa

OPEN MEN
1. Chris Malone
2. Tim O'Connor
3. James Fowell
4. Khan Butler

MEN LONGBOARD
1. Daniel Proctor
2. James Atutahi
3. Martin Matenga
4. Reagen Fairle

JUNIOR
1. Jay Paddock
2. Reno Marriot
3. Dylan Mayor
4. Ryan Elliot

OVER 35 MEN
1. Clint Daly
2. Khan Butler
3. Ronnie Mayor
4. Grant Marriot

WAHINE
1. Jayda Martin Fitzharris
2. Gabe McCarthy-Marriott
3. Maiha Morten

FCS MANUFACTURERS CUP

DURANBAH, GOLD COAST
May 30

Proving that they know more than just how to make surfboards, teams from some of Queensland's best surfboard manufacturers came together for the Sunshine State leg of the FCS Manufacturers' Cup. Tackling a feisty ocean, competitors representing their brands did battle. Ben Webb, Matt Hurworth and Paul Ward of Shaping Co gained the upper hand over the other teams to advance to the October final of the series.

RESULTS
1. Shaping Co
2. Venom
3. JS 1
4. Empire 1

QUIKSILVER QUEENSLAND JUNIOR SERIES
GOLD COAST AUSTRALIA
June 7–9

James Woods, 2006 State Champion, brought his wealth of talent to the stormy seas of Duranbah to take out the first stage of this year's Quiksilver Queensland Junior Series. The young former South African brought his much-hyped talents to the event, showing that, at just 16 years old, he has a very bright future in surfing. An early 8.7 score was backed up with a near-perfect 9.8, proving Woods' undeniable prevalence in the event and in Australia's ranks of high-class junior surfers. Bridey McNeven of Tugun did well to overcome Naomi Stevic (Sunrise Beach) and Dimity Stoyle (Buderim) to take out the Under 18 Girls final, Stevic and Stoyle both hot contenders for a win in every event they enter. Noa Deane, son of Gold Coast surfing legend Wayne Deane, showed that surfing is genetic, his approach defying his younger years and netting him a first place in the Boys Under 16.

UNDER 18 BOYS
1. James Woods
2. Tim MacDonald
3. Jack Freestone
4. Thomas Freestone

UNDER 18 GIRLS
1. Bridey McNeven
2. Naomi Stevic
3. Dimity Stoyle
4. Amy Hubbard

UNDER 16 BOYS
1. Noa Deane
2. Sol Pereira Ryan
3. Thomas Cervi
4. Harry Wheeler

UNDER 16 GIRLS
1. Brodie Doyle

SRI LANKAN AIRLINES PRO, PRESENTED BY THE MALDIVES • ASP 6-STAR WQS EVENT #16
PASTA POINT, MALDIVES
June 9–15

Firsts abound in the Sri Lankan Airlines Pro at Pasta Point, with an all-Hawaiian final producing a first-ever win for WQS top ten surfer Kekoa Bacalso. Joined by fellow islander Dustin Barca, a fellow front-runner on the series, Bacalso had his work cut out for him, trailing at multiple stages of the heat. Barca had his own first in a finals berth, and for the early part of the heat looked like going on to double up his firsts with a win. But patience won out for Bacalso, an excellent wave presenting itself and the Hawaiian taking full advantage to the tune of nine points. Barca still had opportunity to recover but an 8.7 from his opponent sealed his fate.

FINAL
1. Kekoa Bacalso
2. Dustin Barca

SEMIFINAL 1
1. Kekoa Bacalso
2. Joel Centeio

SEMIFINAL 2
1. Dustin Barca
2. Leonardo Neves

BRADNAM'S WINDOWS & DOORS QLD LONGBOARD TITLES, SURFING QUEENSLAND
GOLD COAST, QUEENSLAND
June 14–15

Superb waves highlighted superb surfing at the renowned Gold Coast right-hander of Currumbin. Josh Constable (Peregian Beach) once again proved his dominance in the Australian longboarding world, overcoming local favorite Jackson Close (Currumbin) in a breathtaking final that saw the pair neck and neck for the majority of the 25-minute final. It was a near-perfect score of 9.75 inside the last ten minutes that drove the nail in Close's coffin, thrusting Constable from fourth place—behind Close and fellow finalists Oliver Shaw (Coolangatta) and Mitch Surman (Maroochydore)—into first. Constable didn't relinquish the lead in the dying minutes and emerged victorious. Selby Riddle (Coolangatta) used her intimate knowledge of the break to overthrow Kelly Winter (Sunshine Beach), Rosie Locke (Sunnybank Hills) and Georgie Roach (Maroochydore). Riddle's powerful style suited the gutsy four-foot waves perfectly, the local surfer adding yet another victory to her already vastly impressive tally.

OPEN MEN
1. Josh Constable
2. Jackson Close
3. Oliver Shaw
4. Mitch Surman

UNDER 18 BOYS
Clint Guest

UNDER 18 GIRLS
Georgie Roach

OVER 35 MEN
Damien Coulter

OVER 35 WOMEN
Sharon Jackson

OVER 40 MEN
Brad Sultmann

OVER 45 MEN
Michael Corcoran

OVER 50 MEN
Paul Newman

OVER 60 MEN
Neville Smith

OPEN WOMEN
1. Selby Riddle
2. Kelly Winter
3. Rosie Locke
4. Georgie Roach

AUAHI KORE MAORI TRI SERIES #2, SURFING NEW ZEALAND
MATAKANA ISLAND, TAURANGA MOANA, NEW ZEALAND
June 14–15

The second stage of the Auahi Kore Maori Tri Series began with a mass migration from the original contest site, which resembled a millpond, to the swell magnet of Matakana Island. Khan Butler immediately went to work on the two-foot peaks, really milking the waves for all they were worth. His tenacity paid off, landing him a win in the Open Men division. Runner-up Thomas Hardwick had a consolation prize, taking out the junior division with confidence. Duncan Cameron and Hone Douglas (both Whakatohea) were spectacular in the Hyundai Longboard event, and, despite Cameron's well-deserved win, Douglas stunned the crowd, the 13-year-old holding his own against his peers and proving that the future of longboarding is alive and well on Kiwi shores.

BILLABONG OPEN MEN
1. Khan Butler
2. Thomas Hardwick
3. Brooke Elliot
4. Reece Horne

BILLABONG JUNIOR MEN
1. Thomas Hardwick
2. Peri Matenga
3. Dylan Elliot
4. Hone Douglas

QUIKSILVER UNDER 12 BOYS
1. Quinn Matenga
2. Kaya Horne
3. Max Yeager
4. Tama Yeager

HYUNDAI MEN LONGBOARD
1. Duncan Cameron
2. Hone Douglas
3. Pete Smith
4. Doug Te Ranga

SENIOR MEN
1. Lance Yeager
2. Ronnie Mayor
3. Jake Barbarich
4. Doug Te Ranga

BILLABONG PRO JR SERIES INDONESIA EVENT #1, INDONESIAN SURFING CHAMPIONSHIP
KERAMAS BEACH, BALI
June 18–22

Keramas Beach produced flawless five-foot barrels for the inaugural event of the Indonesian Pro Junior Series. Heath Joske took the conditions in his stride, pulling in to numerous close-out barrels before finally breaking through for a mid-range score. This was enough to give Joske the edge over fellow finalist Nick Vasicek, who, try as he might, couldn't gather a solid pair of scores. Joske found a backup score of a mid-seven to put him out of reach of his opponent. The earlier heats saw the higher tide opening up the barrels somewhat, allowing for some exceptional tuberiding. Joske clocked a near-perfect 9.77 to give him passage into the final. On the other side of the draw, Vasicek matched Joske's form, a 9.5, putting an end to Sam Wrench's finals aspirations.

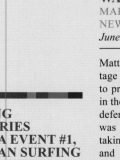
Heath Joske. Photo Tim Hain.

FINAL
1. Heath Joske
2. Nick Vasicek

SEMIFINAL 1
1. Heath Joske
2. Brendon Leckie

SEMIFINAL 2
1. Nick Vasicek
2. Sam Wrench

QUARTERFINAL 1
1. Heath Joske
2. Billy Keane

QUARTERFINAL 2
1. Brendon Leckie
2. Madison Williams

QUARTERFINAL 3
1. Nick Vasicek
2. Dean Iezzi

QUARTERFINAL 4
1. Sam Wrench
2. NA

NSW OPEN, PRESENTED BY WALSH'S PHARMACY
MAROUBRA BEACH, NEW SOUTH WALES
June 22

Matt Bembrose took full advantage of Maroubra's two-foot swell to produce a winning performance in the New South Wales Open. The defending Australian champion was indomitable form the outset, taking all challengers on with style and skill to take the gold medal. Bembrose's path to victory was made a tough journey by the likes of runner-up Luke Cheadle, but the victor's form didn't flounder for an instant, giving him an undisputed win.

FINAL
1. Matt Bembrose
2. Luke Cheadle
3. Joel Reading
4. Rodney Morgan

LIZZY SURF SERIES
SUNSHINE COAST, QUEENSLAND
June 21–22

Dimity Stoyle, 16-year-old Sunshine Coast sensation, landed a convincing win in the second of Lizzard's surf contest for girls, the Lizzy Surf Series. Stoyle launched into the four-way final with a superb 9.07 ride inside the first minute, following it up with a near-faultless 9.87 to project herself into an indisputable first place over Naomi Stevic (Sunrise Beach), Tara Christie (Coolum) and Jess Grimwood (Batemans Bay). As if this wasn't enough, Stoyle also picked up the first place in the Under 21 division. Another double winner was fellow Sunshine Coaster Sharon Jackson. Always a contender in the more senior divisions, Jackson claimed both the Over 28 and the Over 35 titles.

OPEN WOMEN
1. Dimity Stoyle
2. Naomi Stevic
3. Tara Christie
4. Jess Grimwood

UNDER 14 GIRLS
Renee Heazlewood

UNDER 16 GIRLS
Eden Putland

UNDER 18 GIRLS
Naomi Stevic

UNDER 21 GIRLS
Dimity Stoyle

MASTERS (OVER 35)
Sharon Jackson

SENIORS (OVER 28)
Sharon Jackson

AUAHI KORE MAORI TRI SERIES #3, SURFING NEW ZEALAND
RUAPUKE BEACH, WHAINGAROA, NEW ZEALAND
June 21

Blessed with another day of excellent surf, the third of the Auahi Kore Maori Tri Series was again an awesome display of native New Zealand surfing. Chris Malone stepped up to the plate to take the crown, but it was Jess Santorik who got tongues wagging. The reason for the attention was the young girl's inclusion

Douglas Te Ranga. Photo Cory/NZ Surfing Magazine.

in the Open Men division, in which she advanced throughout the heats to the final, securing a third place against her male counterparts. Martin Matenga barely edged out his competition in the longboard final to take a low-scoring win, whilst the fourth-place holder, Reece Horne, made the trip to the podium twice after also landing a third in the Over 35 division

BILLABONG OPEN MEN
1. Chris Malone
2. Brook Elliot
3. Jess Santorik
4. Wayne Cooper
BILLABONG JUNIOR MEN
1. Haami Martin
2. James Tume
3. Ryan Elliot
4. Wiremu Campbell
HYUNDAI MEN LONGBOARD
1. Martin Matenga
2. Doug Te Ranga
3. Isaac Johnston
4. Reece Horne
QUIKSILVER UNDER 12 BOYS
1. Max Yeager
2. Tangaroa Rawiri
3. Kaya Horne
4. Monique Redman
5. Tama Yeager
OVER 35 MEN
1. Doug Te Ranaga
2. Ronnie Mayor
3. Reece Horn
4. Lance Yeager

QUIKSILVER QUEENSLAND STATE JUNIOR SERIES, SURFING QUEENSLAND
NORTH STRADBROKE ISLAND, QUEENSLAND
July 1–3

James Woods took another great step towards becoming the 2008 Queensland State Junior Champion, winning his second state title in as many months. Woods was unstoppable in the final, decimating the competition in a display of high-performance surfing. Trying conditions tested the finalists to their limits, all

needing to search hard for a reasonable wave amongst the wind-blown, minimal swell. Woods, formerly of South Africa, has emerged as a major talent in Australia's junior surfing and is certain to do well, both on home turf and overseas. Dimity Stoyle bettered her third place of the last series event, placing first over the same three finalists she had met previously. Thomas Cervi had a fortunate win in the Under 16s, the Noosa surfer stealing the victory from third place in the heat's final minute.

UNDER 18 BOYS
1. James Woods
2. Tim MacDonald
3. Matt Johnson
4. Jack Miliken
UNDER 18 GIRLS
1. Dimity Stoyle
2. Naomi Stevic
3. Bridey McNeven
4. Amy Hubbard
UNDER 16 BOYS
1. Thomas Cervi
2. Nick Edgerton
3. Noa Deane
4. Hayden Welch

QUIKSILVER OPEN LAKEYS, PRESENTED BY COCA-COLA ISC TOUR EVENT
LAKEY PEAK, SUMBAWA
July 1–4

After a very shaky start, Made "Garu" Widiarta pulled his form together to take his first ISC victory in two years. The Kuta surfer reveled in the four-foot lefts of Lakey Peak, which, although not perfectly glassy, were substantial enough to give the surfers a host of opportunities. Wayan "Gobleg" Suyadnya

(Uluwatu) took an early lead in the final, sitting on the inside to take the lesser quality, though more frequent, waves. Widiarta waited patiently and was rewarded when a three-foot set wave came through, affording him an 8.5 ride. A high six swiftly followed, Suyadnya unable to gain the nearly perfect score required to regain the lead.

PRO DIVISION
1. Made "Garut" Widiarta
2. Wayan "Gobleg" Suyadnya
3. Lee Wilson
4. Devis Ratif
MASTERS DIVISION
1. Ketut Menda
2. Wayan "Gachang" Wisma
3. Moh Ali
4. Jimmy Hamsah
WOMEN DIVISION
1. Yasnyiar "Bonnne" Yea
2. Nyoman Satri
3. Fesi Klink
4. Desy Try Wilujeng

NSW SURFMASTERS, SURFING NSW
PORT MACQUARIE, NEW SOUTH WALES
July 5–6

New South Wales' best seniors had their moment in the sun with the state's surfmasters event being held in three-foot waves at Bonny Hills. Already defending Australian champion, Wayne Hudson (Mid North Coast) netted his second NSW Surfmasters victory, overcoming Joel Gribble (Central Coast), Jeremy Cohen (Central Coast) and Dan Frodsham (Newcastle) to do so. Hudson's role made him the one to beat in the four-man final, his backhand finesse proving too much for his fellow finalists. Wayne Morrison, achieved victory on home turf, taking out the Over 35 division, his adversaries unable to match his assault. Melissa Sherringham (Central Coast) dominated the Open Women event, a standout through the earlier heats and just as confident in the final.

OVER 28 MEN
1. Wayne Hudson
2. Joel Gribble
3. Jeremy Cohen
4. Dan Frodsham
OVER 35 MEN
1. Wayne Morrison

2. Brett Bannister
3. Jay Sharp
4. Scott Myers
OVER 40 MEN
1. David Sparenberg
2. Rod Baldwin
3. Mark Cameron
4. Matt Hucker
OVER 45 MEN WINNER
Max Perrot
OVER 50 MEN WINNER
Matt Phelan
OPEN WOMEN
1. Melissa Sherringham
2. Lara Reading
3. Yvonne Byron
4. Jenny Boggis
OVER 35 WOMEN WINNER
Sandra English
OPEN KNEEBOARD WINNER
Glen Bitton

BILLABONG OCCY'S GROM COMP
DURANBAH, GOLD COAST
July 5–9

Billabong's Grom Comp again created astonishment at the level of Australia's youth, the under 16-year-old surfers throughout the divisions. Small, friendly waves at Duranbah didn't abate for the finals, all surfers finding adequate opportunity to perform. Tyler Wright (Culburra) continued her phenomenal roll, claiming the win over Naomi Stevic (Sunrise Beach), who has herself been performing excellently throughout the year. On the men's side of the contest, Jack Freestone (Coolangatta) won out over Avoca's Wade Carmichael, Banora Point's Sam Clift and Jordi Watson (Currarong). Freestone's final tally was edging on perfection, dropping less than two points over his two-wave result, his closest rival, Camichael, almost five points off the pace.

UNDER 16 BOYS
1. Jack Freestone
2. Wade Carmichael
3. Sam Clift
4. Jordi Watson
UNDER 14 BOYS
1. Matt Banting
2. Noa Deane
3. Harrison Mann
4. Mitchell Parkinson
UNDER 12 BOYS
1. Michael Wright
2. Jack Germain
3. Jackson Baker

4. William Prickett
UNDER 16 GIRLS
1. Tyler Wright
2. Naomi Stevic
3. Laura Macaulay
4. Cody Klein
UNDER 14 GIRLS
1. Sarah Mason
2. Amiya Doyle
3. Ellie-Jean Coffey
4. Bronte Macaulay

BILLABONG PRO JR SERIES INDONESIA EVENT #2, INDONESIAN SURFING CHAMPIONSHIP
KUTA REEF, BALI
July 9–13

Kuta Reef was the setting for stage two of the Indonesian Billabong Pro Junior Series and would also develop into somewhat of a battleground for the highly talented entrants. A slightly shell-shocked Caleb Boquist mounted the second-place podium for the presentations, the highest spot being taken by Ketut Mega Yoga Semadhi, who had defied predictions to claim the prize of US$2,000. In the shadow of Boquist's 9.5 wave, Semadhi had all the work to do, some on the beach already discounting him from contention. But the ocean provided what Semadhi needed, a nice three-foot wave coming through to give the eventual victor ample occasion to unleash his bag of tricks. A collection of critical turns and carving cutbacks were punctuated with an air, to give him the edge he maintained to the finish.

FINAL
1. Ketut Mega Yoga Semadhi
2. Caleb Boquist

BILLABONG WINTER CLASSIC, PRESENTED BY PRINTPOINT, QUEENSLAND CHAMPIONSHIP CIRCUIT
GOLD COAST, QUEENSLAND
July 12–13

Shaun Gossmann succeeded in emerging victorious in the fourth stage of the Queensland Championship Circuit, held on the Gold Coast.

David Sparenberg . Photo Michael Tyrpenou/Surfing NSW.

Ketut "Mega" Semadhi. Photo Tim Hain.

Complete results are available at www.SurfingYearBook.com/Results2008 | **153**

The South African transplant hadn't won an event for three years, the Winter Classic victory giving him much-needed points on the QCC. Coming third, Corey Ziems still gained enough points to secure his position at the top of the series, but with two competitions remaining, no season win could be claimed. Fellow finalist Blake Wilson had been lined up nicely for the win, posting two significant scores, to require a near-perfect wave of Gossmann. Unfortunately for Wilson, Gossmann happened to have that near-perfection in him, posting a 9.5 inside the remaining four minutes to secure the gold.

OPEN MEN
1. Shaun Gossmann
2. Blake Wilson
3. Corey Ziems
4. Ryan Campbell

RUSTY GROMFEST
LENNOX HEAD,
NEW SOUTH WALES
July 11–15

Jack Freestone made it a double with his win at the Rusty Gromfest following hot on the heels of his victory at the Billabong Occy's Grom Comp. The young surfer from Coolangatta made his mark on Under 16s surfing in Australia with a last-minute defeat of his rivals, Mitchell Baker (Cowes), Guillermo Satt (Chile) and Jake Sylvester (Bar Beach). Freestone looked in trouble as, with just four minutes remaining, he was yet to catch a single wave. But the young Gold Coaster came good, scoring enough points in that time for a convincing win. Tyler Wright (Culburra) continued her domination of the Girls divisions, cleaning up the Under 14 final over an on-form Sarah Mason. Phillipa Anderson bettered her second place of last year by making it to the top. Anderson looked to be surfing with a vendetta, her performance full of gusto with underlying professionalism.

UNDER 16 BOYS
1. Jack Freestone
2. Mitchell Baker
3. Guillermo Satt
4. Jake Sylvester
UNDER 16 GIRLS
1. Phillipa Anderson
2. Georgia Fish
3. Lyla Wright
4. Naomi Stevic
UNDER 14 BOYS
Matt Banting
UNDER 14 GIRLS
1. Tyler Wright
2. Sarah Mason
3. Manuel Hereiti
4. Eden Putland
UNDER 12 BOYS
1. Benji Brand
2. Michael Wright
3. Nic Doran
4. Jack Robinson
UNDER 12 GIRLS
1. Karelle Poppke
2. Zoe Clarke
3. Laura Poncini
4. Olivia Wheeler

WHALEBONE CLASSIC • ASP AUSTRALASIA LQS 1-STAR EVENT
COTTESLOE, PERTH,
WESTERN AUSTRALIA
July 12–13

Wollongong's Dane Pioli denied locals a win in the LQS 1-Star Whalebone Classic, held in meager, yet clean, surf on the West Coast. Cottesloe Beach drew the best in Australian longboarding for the renowned event, including 2006 World Champion Josh Constable, and the series leader at the time, Harley Ingleby. Pioli surfed to strong heat, produc-

Shaun Gossmann. Photo Jake White.

ing two waves in the seven-point range to give him the edge over his adversaries. The win boosted Pioli's overall ranking, drawing him closer to Ingleby and the prospect of an LQS victory. Claire Finnucane produced a familiarly solid performance to claim the trophy in the Open Women division.

9FT PRO MEN
FINAL
1. Dane Pioli
2. Rahn Goddard
3. Jock Bahen
4. Jared Neal
SEMIFINAL 1
1. Dane Pioli
2. Rahn Goddard
3. Paul Scholten
4. Ben Proudfoot
SEMIFINAL 2
1. Jock Bahen
2. Jared Neal
3. Tim Fitzpatrick
4. Harley Ingleby
JUNIOR MEN
1. Lindsay Small
2. Tod Quartermaine
3. Lachlan Shaw
4. Dan Refeld
5. Mitch Corbett
6. Lachlan Bahen
UNDER 40 MEN
1. Michael McCormick
2. Daniel Corbett
3. Michael Corbett
4. Ryan Clarke
5. Kent Turkish
6. Damien Lipscombe
OVER 40 MEN
1. Kevin Anderson
2. Ray Barker
3. Steve Del Rosso
4. Brad Belcher
5. Brett Merrifield

6. Ron Dobich
OVER 50 MEN
1. Michael Cottier
2. Martin Richardson
3. Tony Wiggersmith
4. Peter Dunn
5. Gary McCormick
6. Gary Tucker
OVER 55 MEN
1. Bob Monkman
2. Norm Bateman
3. John Geyer
4. John Laming
5. Brian Hood
6. Mick Marlin
OLD MAL
1. Jock Bahen
2. Rahn Goddard
3. Ryan Clarke

4. Kevin Anderson
5. Joe Warwick
6. Kent Turkish
OPEN WOMEN
1. Claire Finnucane
2. Jennypher Sorbier
3. Zanny Wilson
4. Lucy Burrows
5. Kym Davey
6. Michelle Finnucane

FANTASTIC CUP PRO JR, PRESENTED BY NIPPY'S • ASP GRADE 2 MEN'S PRO JUNIOR / ASP GRADE 1 WOMEN'S PRO JUNIOR
VICTOR HARBOUR,
SOUTH AUSTRALIA
July 17–20

South Australia provided a bounty of waves for the inaugural Fantastic Cup Pro Junior, with Owen Wright and Paige Hareb demolishing all contenders to claim the titles. Wright excelled in the three-foot waves of his final heat against Lennox Head's Stuart Kennedy. Kennedy had performed exceptionally throughout the event, but Wright had the upper hand, in faultless form for the finale. Hareb met 2007 World Junior Champion Laura Enever in her final, but the grandiose title failed to intimidate the Kiwi, Hareb taking the win with confidence.

MEN PRO JUNIOR FINAL
1. Owen Wright
2. Stuart Kennedy
SEMIFINAL 1
1. Stuart Kennedy

2. Tom Salveson
SEMIFINAL 2
1. Owen Wright
2. Lincoln Taylor
GIRLS PRO JUNIOR FINAL
1. Paige Hareb
2. Laura Enever

RIP CURL GROMSEARCH #2
GISBORNE, NEW ZEALAND
July 19–20

The Poulter siblings have once again dominated New Zealand's junior surfing circuit, brothers Ben and Sam reaching the Under 16 and Under 12 semis respectively, Ben winning the Under 14s and sister, Alexis representing the family with a win in the Under 16 Girls division. Curiously, the winners' lineup matched precisely the results of ten weeks previous, in the first stage of the Rip Curl Gromsearch. Johnny Hicks again took the first in the Under 16 Boys final, but Tane Wallis impressed equally, placing second in the U/16 and U/14 divisions, the 13-year-old displaying boundless energy and talent beyond his years.

UNDER 16 BOYS
FINAL
1. Johnny Hicks
2. Tane Wallis
3. Mark Parthemore
4. Haami Martin
SEMIFINAL 1
1. Johnny Hicks
2. Tane Wallis
3. Ben Poulter
4. Reno Marriott
SEMIFINAL 2
1. Mark Parthemore
2. Haami Martin
3. Joe Moretti
4. Todd Doyle
QUARTERFINAL 1
1. Ben Poulter
2. Tane Wallis
3. Nat Hughes
4. Stefan Gross
QUARTERFINAL 2
1. Johnny Hicks
2. Reno Marriott
3. Matt Brown
4. Paul Moreiti
QUARTERFINAL 3
1. Mark Parthemore
2. Haami Martin
3. Patxi Scott-Arietta
4. Jules Craft
QUARTERFINAL 4
1. Joe Moretti
2. Todd Doyle
3. Ethan Burge
4. Blake Myers
UNDER 14 BOYS
FINAL
1. Ben Poulter
2. Tane Wallis
3. Adam Grimson
4. Dune Kennings
SEMIFINAL 1
1. Adam Grimson
2. Tane Wallis
3. Patxi Scott-Arrieta
4. Fintan Cram
SEMIFINAL 2
1. Ben Poulter
2. Dune Kennings
3. Elliot Paerata - Reid

4. Peri Matenga
QUARTERFINAL 1
1. Patxi Scott-Arrieta
2. Fintan Cram
3. Paul Moretti
4. Chris Ludgate
QUARTERFINAL 2
1. Tane Wallis
2. Adam Grimson
3. Brad Pitcher
4. Mitchell Davis
QUARTERFINAL 3
1. Ben Poulter
2. Peri Matenga
3. Waretini Wano
4. Mackenzie Christie
QUARTERFINAL 4
1. Elliot Paerata - Reid
2. Dune Kennings
3. Taylor Louie
4. Kurt Geiseler
UNDER 12 BOYS
FINAL
1. Dune Kennings
2. Elliot Paerata Reid
3. Jordan Griffin
4. Korbin Hutchings
SEMIFINAL 1
1. Dune Kennings
2. Jordan Griffin
3. Sam Poulter
SEMIFINAL 2
1. Elliot Paerata Reid
2. Korbin Hutchings
3. Manu Scott-Arietta
QUARTERFINAL 1
1. Dune Kennings
2. Manu Scott-Arietta
3. Jack Virtue
QUARTERFINAL 2
1. Korbin Hutchings
2. Sam Poulter
3. Quin Matenga
4. Ben McCulloch
QUARTERFINAL 3
1. Elliot Paerata Reid
2. Jordan Griffin
3. Nick Mason
UNDER 16 GIRLS
FINAL
1. Alexis Poulter
2. Rosa Thompson
3. Jayda Martin-Fitzharris
4. Ella Williams
SEMIFINAL 1
1. Rosa Thompson
2. Jayda Martin-Fitzharris
3. Chloe Shutt
SEMIFINAL 2
1. Alexis Poulter
2. Ella Williams
3. Hayley Baxter
UNDER 14 GIRLS
1. Jayda Martin-Fitzharris
2. Ella Williams
3. Chloe Shutt
4. Madison Atkins
UNDER 12 GIRLS
1. Gabriela Sansom
2. Bianca Sansom
3. Hannah Kohn

QUIKSILVER QUEENSLAND STATE JUNIOR TITLES, SURFING QUEENSLAND
SUNSHINE COAST,
QUEENSLAND
July 19–20

Jack Freestone made it a hat trick, with a third win in as many weeks in the Queensland State Junior Titles. The Coolangatta surfer surfed an incredible heat to defeat Thomas Woods (Coolangatta), Ice Ryan (Coolangatta) and Eli Criaco (Coolum) at Coolum on the Sunshine Coast. But despite Freestone's win in triplicate, it was James Woods who claimed the series title. Woods' pair of wins earlier in the season, coupled with further high rankings and a semifinal placing in this final event gained the South African enough ratings points to hold the lead overall. Noa Deane (Coolangatta) mustered a third place against Nick Edgerton (Wurtulla) and Sol Ryan (Coolangatta), enough to give him the series title in the Under 16 division. Dimity Stoyle (Buderim) finally resolved the three-way tussle in the U/18 Girls, defeating Naomi Stevic (Sunrise Beach) and Bridey McNeven (Tugun), the series results reflecting the championship's final heat.

UBDER 18 BOYS
1. Jack Freestone
2. Thomas Woods
3. Ice Ryan
4. Eli Criaco

UNDER 16 BOYS
1. Nick Edgerton
2. Sol Ryan
3. Noa Deane
4. Trini Tonga

UNDER 18 GIRLS
1. Dimity Stoyle
2. Naomi Stevic
3. Bridey McNeven

UNDER 16 GIRLS
1. Eden Putland
2. Amiya Doyle
3. Brodie Doyle
4. Ashley Goodall

RIP CURL CUP AT ULUWATU, ISC TOUR
ULUWATU, BALI
July 26

Landing himself 20 million rupiah, 3,500 ISC Championship points, and Rip Curl's exclusive "Ticket to Somewhere," a wild card entry into the Rip Curl Pro Search '08 World Championship Tour event, Komang "Gogo" Sujaya defeated a gamut of talent in Indonesia's most prestigious ISC event. Gogo had to fight hard, the goofy-footer contesting on his backhand, renowned Indonesian surfer Dede Suryana pushing to the very last before finally conceding victory to Gogo in the final minutes of the final. Last year's ISC champion, Lee Wilson, tied third place with local Made Lapur.

PRO DIVISION RESULTS
1. Komang "Gogo" Sujaya
2. Dede Suryana
3. Made Lapur
3. Lee Wilson
COCA-COLA
ISC BEST MANEUVER AWARD
Made Lana

QUIKSILVER NEW SOUTH WALES STATE JUNIOR TITLES, SURFING NEW SOUTH WALES
MAROUBRA BEACH, NEW SOUTH WALES
July 30–August 3

Glassy four-foot waves graced the contest site for the final of the Quiksilver New South Wales State Junior Titles, Dean Bowen (Gerroa) and Matt Banting (Port Macquarie) emerging victorious from the two divisions. Under 18 champion Bowen proved his abilities earlier in the competition, a perfect ten-point wave showing onlookers and opponents alike that he was motivated for the series win. Ryan Callinan (Merewether), Max Ayshford (Maroubra) and Jordi Watson (Currarong) fought hard in the four-man final but simply couldn't match the tenacity or ability in larger surf of Bowen. Matt Banting continued his run of exceptional results, adding the Under 16 title to his fast-swelling resume, opponents Cooper Chapman (North Narrabeen), Jackson O'Donnell (Crescent Head) and Leroy Davies (Wombarra) trying hard to hold the winner down, but to no avail.

UNDER 18 BOYS
1. Dean Bowen
2. Ryan Callinan
3. Max Ayshford
4. Jordi Watson
UNDER 16 BOYS
1. Matt Banting
2. Cooper Chapman
3. Jackson O'Donnell
4. Leroy Davies

YUMEYA BILLABONG PRO TAHARA • MEN'S 6-STAR WQS
AKABANE BEACH, TAHARA, JAPAN
July 27–August 3

In an all-international final, Hawaii's Dustin Cuizon defeated Pedro Henrique (Brazil) to take the win at the six-star Yumeya Billabong Pro Tahara. In groveling one-foot waves, Cuizon and Henrique had to resort to surfing above the lip, performing aerial maneuvers to gain higher scores. Cuizon dispensed with former World Tour surfer Greg Emslie (ZAF) in the semifinals, Henrique ending fellow Brazilian Jadson Andre's finals aspirations. The WQS points scored from the event advanced Cuizon to 21st position on the WQS ladder. Henrique, meanwhile, looked set for a 2009 World Tour berth, holding fourth place on the 'QS.

Dimity Stoyle. Photo Jake White.

Uluwatu winners. Photo Tim Hain.

FINAL RESULTS
1. Dustin Cuizon
2. Pedro Henrique
3. Greg Emslie
3. Jadson Andre
5. Nathaniel Curran
5. Andre Silva
5. Shaun Gossmann
5. Marlon Lipke

QUIKSILVER NSW STATE JUNIOR TITLES, SURFING NEW SOUTH WALES
MAROUBRA BEACH, NEW SOUTH WALES
July 30–August 3

Kirby Wright (Culburra) overcame a field of talent in the Quiksilver NSW State Junior Titles to claim the title and opportunity of representing her state in the December finals of the series, to be held at Margaret River. Leaving Phillipa Anderson (Merewether), Paige Haggerston (Coal Point) and Rachel Pinsak (Terrigal) in her wake, Wright dominated the finals, increasing the reputation of her family name. Perfect, 2- to 3-foot waves graced the finals day, offering up crisp, clean faces for the state's best juniors. Wright's Siblings, Tyler and Michael, succeeded in placing second in the Under 16 Girls and Under 14 Boys divisions respectively, whilst Crescent Heads' Ellie Jean Coffey's proficient skills afforded her the win over defending champion Wright, in the U/16 Girls.

UNDER 18 GIRLS
1. Kirby Wright
2. Phillipa Anderson
3. Paige Haggerston
4. Rachel Pinsak
UNDER 16 GIRLS
1. Ellie Jean Coffey
2. Tyler Wright
3. Emily Clapoudis
4. Rachel Campbell
UNDER 14 GIRLS
1. Indianna Greene
2. Coco Beeby
3. Stephanie Single
4. Veronica Charles
UNDER 14 BOYS
1. Soli Bailey
2. Michael Wright
3. Tommy Boucaut
4. Jackson Baker

OAKLEY PRO JUNIOR JAPAN • ASP JAPAN GRADE 1 MEN'S JUNIOR EVENT
SHIDA-SHITA POINT, CHIBA, JAPAN
August 9

Locals swept the board in the final of the Japanese Oakley Pro Junior. The ASP Grade 1 event was postponed from its early start due to a low-lying fog making for difficult judging. When the finalists did eventually enter the water, it was to a meager swell, but one that was utilized to its fullest by the eight finalists across the two divisions. Pro Junior victor Nobuyuki Osawa was tested to his fullest in the final, onshore winds corrupting the already fickle surf and his finals counterparts, including an ASP World Pro Junior Champion and Team Japan member in Shota Nakamura and Kento Takahashi. Winner of the cadet division, Arashi Kato added this win to his collection, which includes the title of 2007 Cadet Grand Champion.

PRO JUNIOR (20 & UNDER)
1. Nobuyuki Osawa
2. Shota Nakamura
3. Keito Matsuoka
4. Kento Takahashi
CADET (15 & UNDER)
1. Arashi Kato
2. Sho Kobayashi
3. Mao Terashima
4. Hiroto Ohara

BILLABONG PRO JUNIOR SERIES CANGGU, BALI, INDONESIAN SURFING CHAMPIONSHIP
CANGGU, BALIM, INDONESIA
August 13-17

Powerful waves abound for the final day of the Balinese leg of the Billabong Pro Junior Series. Hawaiian Keanu Asing unleashed a barrage of aerial maneuvers to overcome a formidable lineup, including Nic Vasicek, the current ratings leader, event favorite Tamaroa McComb and defending event champion Heath Joske. Locals had solid representation, with Raditya Rondi and Wayan Susiana placing joint-third and joint-fifth respectively overall. Tamaroa McComb had the consolation of taking the crown in the Billabong Occy's Grom Comp, whilst Creed McTaggart had to work hard to secure the Under 14 title, the young West Australian landing an 8.5 ride in the final minutes of his heat to defeat his adversaries. Despite only making the semifinals, Nic Vasicek amassed enough points throughout the three-stage series to be awarded a Nixon watch as Indonesian Pro Junior victor.

PRO JUNIOR BOYS
1. Keanu Asing
2. Ice Periera
BILLABONG OCCY'S GROM COMP WINNER
Tamaroa McComb
UNDER 14 BOYS WINNER
Creed McTaggart

RED BULL JUNIOR SURF MASTERS, SURFING NEW SOUTH WALES
MEREWETHER BEACH, NEWCASTLE
August 16–17

Surfing beyond his years, local surfer Wes Bainbridge unleashed an array of tricks and carves to take a victory of fellow Merewether surfer Jesse Adam, Dane Atcheson (Avoca) and Sam Lendrum (Newcastle). All four finalists qualifies for the series final, to be held

Keanu Asing. Photo Steve Robertson.

in at Queenscliff at the end of the month. Bainbridge's display was exceptional throughout the event, taking on all challengers with the mature poise of a seasoned professional.

RED BULL JUNIOR SURF MASTERS
1. Wes Bainbridge
2. Jesse Adam
3. Dane Atcheson
4. Sam Lendrum

FIREWIRE LITTLE THUNDER SHONAN SUPER KIDS PRO JUNIOR • ASP GRADE 1 MEN'S JUNIOR EVENT
KANAGAWA, SHONAN, JAPAN
August 15–17

Sloppy waves and a gentle onshore could not dampen the enthusiasm of surfers in the Firewire Little Thunder Shonan Super Kids Pro Junior. Shota Nakamura was the strongest surfer on the final day, gaining the upper hand over some of Japan's hottest talent, including current ratings leader Nobuyuki Osawa. Defending event champion Keito Matsuoka fell in the quarterfinals, whilst Nakamura and Osawa competed head to head in a final for the second time in as many weeks, having met also in the previous week's Oakley Pro Junior event.

1. Shota Nakamura
2. Nobuyuki Osawa

VOLCOM STONE TOTALLY CRUSTACEOUS SURF TOUR, VQS SUNSHINE COAST
CALOUNDRA, QUEENSLAND
August 16

A pulsing three-foot swell broke at Caloundra's Ann Street for the Sunshine Coast stop of the VQS. The familiar finals faces of Naomi Stevic and Dimity Stoyle graced the podium when the final bell rang, Stevic just edging out her rival. Both girls, along with third- and fourth-place getters Tahita Replard and Maddy

Dede Suryana. Photo Tim Hain.

Dunn, in making the finals qualified for the VQS Series final held in April of 2009. Trini Tonga made a sterling impression, stepping up against Tom Cervi, Jake Fissendon and Kai Hing. The young gun managed to somehow find a barrel in the two-foot swell, adding to it some carving cutbacks to make secure his winning position. Shannon Neil lost by the skin of his teeth to take the win in the Pro-Am division, an impressive wave in the dying minutes, edging out Luke Jory.

GROMS
1. Trini Tonga
2. Tom Cervi
3. Jake Fissendon
4. Kai Hing

JUNIORS
1. Nick McDonald
2. Paul McGregor
3. Tim Ollier
4. Matt Johnson

PRO-AM
1. Shannon Neil
2. Luke Jory
3. Andy Johnson
4. Kalan Schloss

GIRL'S OPEN
1. Naomi Stevic
2. Dimity Stoyle
3. Tahita Replard
4. Maddy Dunn

SURF FOR BALI KIDS CHARITY COMPETITION, ISC
PADMA BEACH, BALI
August 20

With 3,000 ISC Championship points on offer, the Surf for Bali Kids Charity Comp gave entrants an ulterior motive for entering. Dede Suryana took the gold medal over Lee Wilson, both finalists donating 20 percent of their combined Rp 15 million (AU$1,850) prize purse to charity. The win, in an uneven three-foot swell, launched Suryana into second place overall on the ISC tally, within striking distance of the series victory. Pepen Hendrik shared third place with Made Awan, and, as with the Quiksilver / Roxy Open back in April, Hendrik's third was made more acceptable by his wife, Yesco's, first place in the Women's Pro division.

ISC MEN PRO
1. Dede Suryana
2. Lee Wilson
3. Pepen Hendrik – Made Awan

ISC WOMEN PRO
1. Yesco
2. Bone
3. Sena
4. Jasmine

OXBOW AUSTRALIAN LONGBOARD TITLES, COUNTRY ENERGY AUSTRALIAN SURF FESTIVAL
PORT MACQUARIE, NEW SOUTH WALES
August 16–30

Peregian Beach's Josh Constable reinforced why he was 2006 World Longboard champion and already three-time winner of the Oxbow Australian Longboard Titles, with a convincing fourth win in the Open Men division. Dropping just 1.25 points from his combined two-wave score, Constable held off Harley Ingelby, Sam Dunton and Paul Scholton for the win. Sizeable, wind-blown swell made the contest difficult, but Chelsea Williams took the event in her stride, decimating her competition for yet another unquestionable victory. David "Sput" Keevers led the charge in the Over 45s, the Byron Bay surfer always a serious threat to any challenger.

OPEN MEN
1. Josh Constable
2. Harley Ingelby
3. Sam Dunton
4. Paul Scholton

JUNIOR MEN
1. Beau Nixon
2. Adam Lynch
3. Tas Dunton
4. Clint Guest

OVER 35 MEN
1. Matt Rawson
2. Dean Cook
3. Nigel Canterbury
4. Jason Weeks

OVER 40 MEN
1. Richard Smith
2. Hayden Swan
3. Scott Downing
4. Mark McNamara

OVER 45 MEN
1. David Keevers
2. Paul O'Grady
3. John Fraser
4. John Lane

OVER 50 MEN
1. Ric Chalmers
2. Paul Guthrie
3. Phil Roxburgh
4. John Ayton

OVER 55 MEN
1. Phil Baggs
2. Bruce Channon
3. Peter Hudson
4. Garry Taylor

OVER 60 MEN
1. David Pimm
2. Daniel Bond
3. Bob Smith
4. Roy Forbes

OPEN WOMEN
1. Chelsea Williams
2. Kelly Winter
3. Rosie Locke
4. Rachell Pinsak

JUNIOR WOMEN
1. Georgie Roach
2. Jess Kelly
3. Rachel Pinsak
4. Samantha White

OVER 35 WOMEN
1. Lisa Nicholson
2. Sharon Jackson
3. Heather Peck
4. Gayle Rezenbrink

NA PAPA AUSTRALIAN SURFMASTERS TITLES, SURFING NSW
PORT MACQUARIE, NEW SOUTH WALES
August 24–30

Amidst a gamut of stellar performances in the Na Papa Australian Surfmasters Titles, Jenny Boggis emerged as the stand-out competitor of this year's event. Winning both the Open and Over 28 divisions, Boggis blazed through her heats with panache from the outset. A win in either category would have been admirable, the double victory exceptional. Former World Tour surfer Toby Martin proved that he has lost none of his world class form to take out the Men Over 28, while 2007 Open winner Matt Bemrose missed out on a back-to-back victory, coming in second to a thrilled Dane Atcheson. Also of note was Max Perrott's victory, the Over 45 competitor dropping just half a point to claim the win.

OPEN MEN
1. Dane Atcheson
2. Matt Bemrose
3. Stephen Walsh
4. Trevor Tripcony

OVER 28 MEN
1. Toby Martin
2. Gurt Du Preez
3. Wayne Hudson
4. Joel Spillane

OVER 35 MEN
1. Brett Bannister
2. Jay Sharpe
3. Wayne Morrison
4. Scott Myers

OVER 40 MEN
1. David Sparenburg
2. Vic Levett
3. Rod Baldwin
4. Matt Hucker

OVER 45 MEN
1. Max Perrot
2. Rod Baldwin
3. Brent Moss
4. Vic Levett

OVER 50 MEN
1. Brent Moss
2. Mark Phelan
3. Peter Eales
4. Gordon Barnes

OPEN KNEEBOARD
Glenn Bitton
1. Darren Cooper
2. Anthony Cridland
3. Peter Whitehouse
4. Shane Whitehouse

OPEN WOMEN
1. Jenny Boggis
2. Melissa Sherringham
3. Lara Reading
4. Leah Wright

OVER 28 WOMEN
1. Jenny Boggis
2. Michelle Richens
3. Ladine Smith
4. Roslyn Franklin

OVER 35 WOMEN
1. Sandra English
2. Kellie O'Brien
3. Heather Peck
4. Roslyn Franklin

RED BULL JUNIOR SURF MASTERS, PRESENTED BY MICK FANNING
CRONULLA, NEW SOUTH WALES
September 2

Tricky conditions made the going tough for competitors in the final stage of the Red Bull Junior Surf Masters fought a close battle against junior sensation, Owen Wright, who held the advantage for the first half

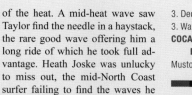

of the heat. A mid-heat wave saw Taylor find the needle in a haystack, the rare good wave offering him a long ride of which he took full advantage. Heath Joske was unlucky to miss out, the mid-North Coast surfer failing to find the waves he needed to advance.

FINAL
1. Lincoln Taylor
2. Owen Wright
3. Heath Joske and Chris Salisbury

SCAR REEF PRO, PRESENTED BY RIP CURL • 6-STAR PRIME COCA-COLA ISC TOUR EVENT
WEST SUMBAWA, INDONESIA
August 28–September 5

Glassy barrels and long rides blessed the participants of the Coca-Cola-ISC Men Pro, a solid five-foot swell hitting Sumbawa's Scar Reef to form beautifully contestable, though sometimes fickle, waves. Bali's Rahtu Suargita succeeded in defeating fellow Balinese surfer Garut Widiarta, a fantastic ride cementing his victory. Pulling in to one hollow barrel, Suargita emerged only to be enveloped again. Exiting the second barrel of the wave, Suargita was given a confident lead, with a 9.25 score, that he refused to relinquish for the heat's duration. Dede Suryana, surfing on his backhand, secured the event's only perfect ride, completing three barrels on the one wave, a justified ten points, advancing him to the semifinals. The waves became tricky on the falling tide, but Mustofa Jeksen made use of the altered conditions, boosting a clean air-reverse to claim the Best Maneuver award and its Rp one million prize.

COCA-COLA-ISC MEN PRO RESULTS
1. Rahtu Suargita
2. Garut Widiarta

Rahtu Suargita. Photo Tim Hain.

3. Dede Suryana
3. Wayan Wirtama
COCA-COLA ISC
    BEST MANEUVER AWARD
Mustofa Jeksen

BILLABONG PRO JUNIOR • ASP PRO JUNIOR BOYS / ASP PRO JUNIOR GIRLS
PORT STEPHENS, NEW SOUTH WALES
September 4–7

Tahitian import Tamaroa McComb proved himself once more with a record-breaking win at the Billabong Pro Junior event at Port Stephens. The 16-year-old defeated Lincoln Taylor in fantastic form, an 8.5-point ride sealing the win with style and conviction. Local Jesse Adam nearly put an end to McComb's progression, a particularly close semifinal looking like going either way. McComb just edged out the Merewether surfer and took his motivation through to the final. Paige Hareb staved off the threats of Tyler Wright. Both surfers had had an exceptional year, but Hareb gained the upper hand midway through the final with a nine-point wave, Wright unable to answer. Nonetheless, 14-year-old Wright's second has placed her in a good position to be able to steal the runner-up prize on the Billabong Pro Junior Series from Laura Enever.

ASP PRO JUNIOR BOYS
FINAL
1. Tamaroa McComb
2. Lincoln Taylor
SEMIFINAL 1
1. Tamaroa McComb
2. Jesse Adam
SEMIFINAL 2
1. Lincoln Taylor
2. David Vlug
ASP PRO JUNIOR GIRLS
1. Paige Hareb
2. Tyler Wright

MURASAKI PRO KITAIZUMI • ASP MEN'S 2-STAR WQS EVENT #28 / ASP LQS 2-STAR SUN'S PRO LONGBOARD / ASP PRO JUNIOR
FUKUSHIMA, JAPAN
September 2–7

Inclement weather hampered competition in the early stages of the Murasaki Pro Kitaizumi, but despite a bleak forecast, it soon improved, making way for a day of superb surfing. Four events were being played out over the six days of action; the ASP Men and Women WQS events, the ASP Pro Junior and the ASP LQS Sun's Pro Longboard division. Shota Nakamura was in fine form, victorious in the Pro Junior division and second in the Open. The young Japanese surfer has a bright future. The smaller waves were a little more conducive to the Longboarding division, a blend of styles making for interesting viewing. Kevin Connelly threw in a traditional element, while Bonga Perkins and Kekoa Uemura added a more powerful aspect to the proceedings, with Keegan Edwards injecting some smaller wave performance surfing to make the semis an all-round affair. Despite being more at home in the big stuff, it was Bonga Perkins who managed to amass the greatest point tally from the modest surf.

ASP MEN 2-STAR WQS EVENT #28
SEMIFINAL 1
FINAL
1. Hideyoshi Tanaka
2. Shota Nakamura
SEMIFINAL
1. Shota Nakamura

2. Naohisa Ogawa
SEMIFINAL 2
1. Hideyoshi Tanaka
2. Takayuki Wakita
PRO JUNIOR BOYS
1. Shota Nakamura
2. Shu Hagiwara
3. Arashi Kato
4. Koki Nakamura
ASP LQS 2-STAR SUN'S PRO LONGBOARD
FINAL
1. Bonga Perkins
2. Keegan Edwards
SEMIFINAL 1
1. Bonga Perkins
2. Kevin Connelly
SEMIFINAL 2
1. Keegan Edwards
2. Kekoa Uemura
OPEN WOMEN
1. Sayuri Hashimoto
2. Nao Omura
3. Asako Mizuno
4. Nagisa Tahiro

WILD SURF CO. MATTARA, HURLEY NSWCC
NEWCASTLE, NEW SOUTH WALES
September 13–14

The 46th Wild Surf Co. Mattara commenced with blue skies and good surf, a collection of superbly talented surfers eager to make the most of the two feet of swell. Leaving a host of experienced surfers in his wake, including former World Tour competitor Toby Martin, Joel Reading climbed the podium, ecstatic at his second win in the contest, the first being way back in 2002. It was an exceedingly tight race in the four-way final, each competitor more than capable of taking the title. But Reading's form on the day was the one that counted, the Wallabi Point surfer making the most of every wave he caught.

FINAL
1. Joel Reading
2. Toby Martin
3. Mitch Noonan
4. Chris Enever

BILLABONG NORTH SHORE CLASSIC, PRESENTED BY PRINTPOINT, BILLABONG QUEENSLAND CHAMPIONSHIP CIRCUIT
MAROOCHYDORE'S NORTH SHORE, QUEENSLAND
September 13–14

A scattered swell was breaking for the penultimate QCC stage, sizeable but onshore, challenging the competitors every step of the way. Chris Friend gave local representation, alongside fellow Sunshine Coaster Luke Jory, Friend winning out to the delight of the spectators. A $2,000 check was awarded to Friend, along with 1,000 valuable QCC points, giving him a much-welcomed boost for the final event. The four-man final heat was a struggle in every

sense of the word, both in terms of wave consistency and competition. Conditions made finding a scoring ride exceedingly tricky for all finalists, Friend lucky to take the win, holding just 0.3 points over closest rival Jory.

FINAL
1. Chris Friend
2. Luke Jory
3. Matt Jones
4. Jamie Thomson

SUNSMART SURFMASTERS • ASP WQS MEN'S 1-STAR EVENT
FLAT ROCKS, GERALDTON, WESTERN AUSTRALIA
September 11–14

Defending title holder Ben Godwin denied locals a victory at Geraldton's Sunsmart Surfmasters, scoring a back-to-back win in the ASP 1-star event. The double victor dominated, his semifinal opponent Ben McDonald struggling hard to catch up inside the first ten minutes of the heat but unable to find the scoring wave in the four-foot stormy swell. Facing West Coaster Kit Rayner in the final, Godwin once again stepped up. Challenged by Rayner in the heat's earlier stages, Godwin soon found his rhythm, proving exactly why he was defending champion and validating his brace of wins.

FINAL
1. Ben Godwin
2. Kit Rayner
SEMIFINAL 1
1. Kit Rayner
2. Danny Williams
SEMIFINAL 2
1. Ben Godwin
2. Ben McDonald

MAMBO PRO JUNIOR, PRESENTED BY DAKINE • ASP AUSTRALASIA PRO JUNIOR / SKULL CANDY CADET CUP, SURFING NSW
MANLY BEACH, NEW SOUTH WALES
September 18–21

Owen Wright (Culburra) again validated the hype surrounding him as a "Next Big Thing" with a win over former Tahitian Gold Coast surfer Tamaroa McComb in the Mambo Pro Junior, Manly Beach. "That was probably the hardest final I've ever surfed," confessed Wright of his heat, surfed in immaculate two-foot waves. The two surfers both had to perform at their utmost in the final, both of exceptional talent and fully aware of each other's potential. But it was Wright who would impress the judges most when all was said and done. The Skull Candy Cadet Cup ran in conjunction with the Mambo Pro Junior, allowing the under 16s their turn in competition singlets. Wade Carmichael of

Joel Reading. Photo Michael Tyrpenou/Surfing NSW.

Avoca snatched victory from under the nose of Old Bar's Oscar Scanes, paddling into the winning wave with just 40 seconds remaining on the clock.

MAMBO PRO JUNIOR FINAL
1. Owen Wright
2. Tamaroa McComb

SKULL CANDY CADET CUP FINAL
1. Wade Carmichael
2. Oscar Scanes

RIP CURL GROMSEARCH, PRESENTED BY SNICKERS, SURFING AUSTRALIA
JAN JUC, VICTORIA
September 23–26

Victoria's under 16s were tested to their limits in the Rip Curl Gromsearch, a wealth of talent flocking from other states, including New South Wales and Tasmania, to contest the title of 2008 champion. Thomas Woods had made the long haul from the Gold Coast to attend the event and didn't let the journey go to waste, confidently claiming first his semifinal heat and then the final over Ryan Callinan. Wade Carmichael couldn't continue his form in the previous week's Skull Candy Cadet Cup, having to settle for fourth. Local surfer Nikki Van Dijk surfed two divisions, the sensational 14-year-old surfer coming second to Ellie Jean Coffey in the U/14s but taking the win in the U/16 division.

UNDER 16 BOYS
1. Thomas Woods
2. Ryan Callinan
3. Wade Carmichael
4. Jack Scollard

UNDER 16 GIRLS
1. Nikki Van Dijk
2. Jessica Laing
3. Lauren McAleer
4. Kate Raines

UNDER 14 BOYS
1. Harrison Mann
2. Tyler Hutchinson
3. Jake Scott
4. Joshua Hay

UNDER 14 GIRLS
1. Ellie Jean Coffey
2. Nikki Van Dijk
3. Zoe Clarke
4. Lauren McAleer

UNDER 12 BOYS
1. Jackson Bake
2. Brendan Hay
3. Joe Van Dijk
4. Tristan Evans

UNDER 12 GIRLS
1. Zoe Clarke
2. Iona Renwick
3. Kelly Laity

BILLABONG CLOUD 9 INVITATIONAL, SURFING AUSTRALIA
CLOUD 9, SIARGAO ISLAND, PHILIPINES
September 23–30

Philippines surfer Edito "Peso" Alcala defeated Queensland's Wade

Ben Godwin. Photo Nick Woolacott.

Goodall in an awesome display of tube-riding at the Philipine break of Cloud 9. The local held a strong position in the final, perfectly in control in the four-foot barreling waves. Goodall, always a solid adversary in any event, led for a significant portion of the event, but it was an expertly negotiated barrel in the latter stages that gave Alcala a 0.39 point advantage over the previous year's champion. Goodall couldn't regain the points and had to settle for second, to the elation of a jubilant and US$7,500 richer Alcala.

FINAL
1. Edito 'Peso' Alcala
2. Wade Goodall

SEMIFINAL 1
1. Edito 'Peso' Alcala
2. Granger Larsen

SEMIFINAL 2
1. Wade Goodall
2. Lee Wilson

ARNETTE JUNIOR SURF CHALLENGE, SURFING AUSTRALIA
SUNSHINE COAST
September 29–October 3

Five days of competition saw some of the Sunshine Coast's finest young surfers go head to head for the Arnette Junior Surf Challenge. Jaiden Egley (Palm Beach) managed to sneak past Maroochydore's Ben Milgate, the Gold Coast surfer managing to take a late wave and gain himself nine points to take the victory. Local surfer Charlie Roach dominated the girls' side of contest, convincingly winning both the Under 16 and the Under 14 divisions, whilst outstanding young gun Eli Steele was exceptional. The Moffat Beach surfer illuminated the two-foot waves to come out on top, landing the event's only perfect 10 ride.

UNDER 18 BOYS
1. Jaiden Elgey
2. Ben Milgate
3. James Cervi
4. One Anwar

UNDER 16 BOYS
1. Damo Norman
2. Nick Edgerton
3. Adam Parnell

4. Sol Ryan

UNDER 14 BOYS
1. Eli Steele
2. Hayden Cervi
3. Harry Bryant
4. Tommy Boucout

UNDER 16 GIRLS
1. Charlie Roach
2. Tahlija Redgard
3. Keely Andrew
4. Ashley Goodall

BILLABONG PRO JUNIOR • ASP GRADE 3 MEN'S PRO JUNIOR EVENT / ASP GRADE 1 WOMEN'S PRO JUNIOR EVENT
BELLS BEACH
VICTORIA AUSTRALIA
September 30–October 4

In an outstanding performance of talented surfing, Heath Joske dominated at Bells Beach for the Billabong Pro Junior contest. Sometimes under duress from his exceptional opponents, Joske held his calm, taking on all comers to claim a win in triplicate. The three-way win came first with the event victory. This then gave Joske the Pro Junior series win for 2008 and landed him a position in the ASP World Junior Championships in January of 2009. Bells, not up to its finest standard yet healthily contestable, was also good to barely-teen sensation Tyler Wright. A convincing win over Kiwi import Airini Mason gave Wright a berth in the World Juniors, upstaging series adversary Laura Enever, who failed to progress beyond the semis. Enever will now be fighting hard for the remainder of the year in an attempt to secure her own spot at the Worlds.

MEN PRO JUNIOR FINAL
1. Heath Joske
2. Jayke Sharpe

SEMIFINAL 1
1. Heath Joske
2. Nic Vasicek

SEMIFINAL 2
1. Jayke Sharpe
2. Madison Williams

WOMEN PRO JUNIOR FINAL
1. Tyler Wright
2. Airini Mason

RIP CURL GROMSEARCH EVENT 3, SURFING NEW ZEALAND
ST. CLAIR BEACH, DUNEDIN, NEW ZEALAND
October 4–5

Tricky conditions tested competitors, but the finals were no less electric, all surfers pushing hard to impress the judges. Alex Dive proved that previous wins have been no mere strokes of luck, another victory under his belt in the third installment of the Rip Curl Gromsearch. Dive relegated eternal runner-up Ben Poulter into second place, the young surfer tackling both the U/16 and the U/14 and doing well to make the finals of both. More fortunate sister Alexis made the grade again, another win in the Girls Under 16 to add to her collection of already impressive victories for the year.

UNDER 16 BOYS
1. Alex Dive

Thomas Woods. Photo Steve Robertson.

2. Ben Poulter
3. Johnny Hicks
4. Tane Wallis

UNDER 16 GIRLS
1. Alexis Poulter
2. Jayda Martin-Fitzharris
3. Rosa Thompson
4. Chloe Shutt

UNDER 14 BOYS
1. Tane Wallis
2. Peri Matenga
3. Elliot Paerata-Reid
4. Ben Poulter

UNDER 14 GIRLS
1. Jayda Martin-Fitzharris
2. Gabriella McCarthy-Marriott
3. Alethea Lock
4. Chloe Shutt

UNDER 12 BOYS
1. Elliot Paerata Reid
2. Jordan Griffin
3. Korbin Hutchings
4. Matt Hanson
5. Quin Matenga

RIP CURL GROMSEARCH, PRESENTED BY SNICKERS SURFING, NEW SOUTH WALES
COFFS HARBOUR, NEW SOUTH WALES
October 3–6

The second event of the Rip Curl Gromsearch series was no less spectacular than the first. Despite a

fog layer permeating the lineup, the waves were cooperating, a clean, two-foot swell running through the lineup. Avalon's Billy Bain secured himself a place in the national finals, the Northern Beaches surfer showing talent and maturity to take the crown in the Boys Under 16 division. Ellie-Jean Coffey had her work cut out, surfing in both the Under 16 and Under 14 Girls divisions. But the Crescent Head surfer didn't stretch herself too far, with enough energy left to come out third in the older division and securing a win in the U/14. Merewether's Jackson Baker left a lasting impression, surfing beyond his years to score not only the highest wave but also the highest heat score of the entire event.

UNDER 16 BOYS
1. Billy Bain
2. Thomas Woods
3. Nikolas Hoskin
4. Max Weston

UNDER 16 GIRLS
1. Rachel Campbell
2. Skye Burgess

3. Ellie-Jean Coffey
4. Pheobe Miley-Dyer

UNDER 14 BOYS WINNER
Soli Bailey

UNDER 14 GIRLS WINNER
Ellie-Jean Coffey

UNDER 12 BOYS WINNER
Jackson Baker

UNDER 12 GIRLS WINNER
Holly Wawn

ZINK SURF SOUTH COAST OPEN, HURLEY NSW CHAMPIONSHIP CIRCUIT
WERRI BEACH, NEW SOUTH WALES
October 11–12

The penultimate stage of the Hurley NSW Championship Circuit crowned a surprise champion in Ashley King of Ulladulla. King, who hadn't been exceptionally prominent throughout the 2008 season, surfed with flair and confidence, defeating his opponents with ease to take the win. The three-foot waves of Werri Beach forced King onto his backhand, but this seemed to suit him better as he unleashed a succession of cutbacks and vertical maneuvers. Sam Wrench (Mollymook), Nick Riley (Manly) and Ben Godwin (Forster) came second, third and fourth respectively, Godwin's placing taking him to fourth place overall coming into the final stage of the circuit.

FINAL
1. Ashley King
2. Sam Wrench
3. Nick Riley
4. Ben Godwin

VOLCOM STONE'S HELIFISH SURF SERIES VQS

CIMAJA,
SUNSET BEACH, WEST JAVA,
October 11

A day of uncharacteristic small swell, punctuated by rain, did little to dampen the enthusiasm of the contestants in Volcom's Helifish series. As the event progressed, sunshine soon bathed the arena, Ujang Jitli standing out on his way to the final. Runner-up Cakrayudha struggled to overcome the eventual winner, but fell just one point short when the final bell sounded. As consolation, the second-place getter came top in the Under 17 division, proving that he has a very bright future in the Javanese surfing world.

MEN PRO AM FINAL
1. Ujang Jitli
2. Cakrayudha
3. Saprudin
4. Parman

UNDER 17 BOYS
1. Cakrayudha
2. Monot
3. Dwinuka
4. Sandi Slamet

UNDER 14 BOYS
1. Andre Julian
2. Ryan Hidayat
3. Aripin
4. Jimi

CAMBO'S OCEAN AND EARTH TEENAGE RAMPAGE

PORT MACQUARIE,
NEW SOUTH WALES
September 18–19

ASP World Tour surfer Mick Campbell did his part for promoting and supporting Australia's youth with the Ocean and Earth Teenage Rampage. Presiding over the event, Campbell witnessed some of New South Wales' finest 16 and unders do battle for the opportunity to compete in the national final later in the year. Matt Banting stood tall against all comers, leading the way through heat after heat and continuing his fine form into the finals. Oscar Scanes could not bring his best to the final; Banting dominated from the opening, an early 9.57 immediately putting his adversaries on the back foot. The girls' final was the polar opposite, Kelly Delang snatching the win by a mere tenth of a point. The heat remained in the balance until the final second had fallen, runner-up Fiona Casey coming up short by the narrowest of margins.

UNDER 16 BOYS
1. Matt Banting
2. Oscar Scanes
3. Todd Bourke

4. Will Coy

UNDER 16 GIRLS
1. Kelly Delang
2. Fiona Casey
3. Emily Clapoudis
4. Ashley Simms

UNDER 16 BOYS WINNER
Jack Germain

UNDER 16 GIRLS WINNER
Kirstin Ogden

OCEAN AND EARTH TEENAGE RAMPAGE, SURFING NEW SOUTH WALES

NEWCASTLE,
NEW SOUTH WALES
October 25–26

A mirror image of the inaugural event, the second stage of the Ocean and Earth Teenage Rampage saw a nail-biting Boys final and a heavily one-sided girls' final take place in

Hamish Renwick. Photo Steve Robertson.

pristine, three-foot surf. Shane Holmes held firm against Jake Sylvester, Joshua Hay and Tylah Hutchinson to take the Boys event, continually under pressure from his opponents and taking a narrow lead in the latter stages of the four-way heat. Philippa Anderson was indomitable on the girls' side of the event, a standout in each heat, taking the finals with ease over Annable Barratt (Dee Why), Sarah Kokkin (Merewether) and Cromer's Gemma Saunders.

UNDER 16 BOYS
1. Shane Holmes
2. Jake Sylvester
3. Joshua Hay
4. Tylah Hutchinson

UNDER 16 GIRLS
1. Philippa Anderson
2. Annable Barratt
3. Sarah Kokkin
4. Gemma Saunders

UNDER 16 BOYS WINNER
Jake Thompson

UNDER 16 GIRLS WINNER
Indianna Green

RIP CURL GROMSEARCH, PRESENTED BY SNICKERS, SURFING AUSTRALIA

CLIFTON BEACH, TASMANIA
October 25–26

The midway event of the Rip Curl Gromsearch took place in tricky two-foot conditions on Tasmania's

Roaring Beach. Reinforcing their leads and reputations, Thomas Woods and Nikki Van Dijk were impressive in the Under 16 finals, while local Hamish Renwick was outstanding in the Under 14s, securing a 9.5-point ride in the semifinals and driving hard to also dominate the final. Woods' form has been impeccable all year, this being his second win of four events, a second also in his tally. Likewise, Van Dijk's season has been rife with success, a pair of wins standing her in good stead for the remaining three events of the series. Renwick's inspiring performance in the Under 14 semis not only allowed him passage into the finals, where he would go on to win, but also netted him the Snickers Wave of the Day.

UNDER 16 BOYS
1. Thomas Woods
2. Jake Fawcett

3. Doug Chandler
4. George Allan

UNDER 14 BOYS
1. Hamish Renwick
2. Jamie Powell
3. Jake Cumberland
4. Grant Williams

UNDER 12 BOYS WINNER
Jake Morrison

UNDER 16 GIRLS
1. Nikki Van Dijk
2. Georgia Fish
3. Bronte MacCauley
4. Sophie Bourke

UNDER 14 GIRLS WINNER
Matilda McLellan

UNDER 12 GIRLS WINNER
Iona Renwick

RIP CURL SURF AND MUSIC FEST, COCA-COLA INDONESIAN CHAMPIONSHIP EVENT

KUTA BEACH,
BALI, INDONESIA
October 26

Japanese surfer Yesco continued her dominance of women's surfing in Bali, another title secured with a convincing win in the Rip Curl Surf and Music Fest. Wife of prominent Indonesian surfer Pepen Hendrik, Yesco, who now calls Bali home, has claimed victory in almost every event she has entered throughout the year. Defeating Yasniar Gea (Bonne), Nyoman Satria and Diah Rahayu Dewi in the testing onshore conditions, Yesco was the standout from the outset, a win almost guaranteed with over half the heat remaining. The series title was in the balance in the Men's Pro division, both Lee Wilson and Dede Suryana in the running for the championship crown. From the early heats, there was no doubt of Suryana's intentions, carving and boosting his way through to the final. Wilson, on the other hand, wasn't favored by lady luck; the 2007 champion was relegated to second series place, knocked out of the event by Made Awan in round four. Awan's proficient performance was too much for Wilson, a crisp air 360 grab netting him the heat win as well as the Coca-Cola Best Maneuver award.

MEN PRO DIVISION
1. Dede Suryana
2. Dedy Santoso
3. Mustofa Jekson / Raditya Rondi

WOMEN DIVISION
1. Yesco (JPN)
2. Yasniar Gea
3. Nyoman Satria
4. Diah Rahayu Dewi

MASTERS DIVISION
1. Wayan Widiartha
2. Made Artha

3. Gus Rai
4. Ketut Menda

AUAHI KORE MAORI SURFING TITLES, SURFING NEW ZEALAND

ROCKY LEFTS, TARANAKI,
NEW ZEALAND
October 25–26

One and a half decades after his first victory in the Auahi Kore Maori Surfing Titles, Jason Lellman returned to reclaim the title. Proving that the 15 years have done nothing to hinder his abilities or dampen his enthusiasm, Lellman surfed proficiently throughout the event to make the finals. An early high score in the heat immediately placed his opponents, Morehu Roberts, Buck Woods and Danny Carse, on the defensive. An excellent 9.5-point wave from 16-year-old Buck Woods stole the lead from Lellman, who was then forced into a catch-up situation. An 8.5 returned the lead to Lellman, but it was Morehu Roberts who left the lasting impression, a perfect 10-point score elevating him to second place. Jayda Martin-Fitzharris impressed in the Roxy Open. At just 13 years of age, the Gisborne surfer showed maturity and talent to defeat Jessica Terrill, Thandi Durham and Lana Yearbury, patiently waiting until the very last minute to register her winning score.

BILLABONG OPEN MEN
1. Jason Lellman
2. Morehu Roberts
3. Buck Woods
4. Danny Carse

RIP CURL UNDER 18 MEN
1. Haami Martin
2. Buck Woods
3. Johnny Hicks
4. Reno Marriott

RAPU UNDER 16 BOYS
1. Johnny Hicks
2. Haami Martin
3. Reno Marriott
4. James Tumes

QUIKSILVER UNDER 12 BOYS
1. Elliot Paerata-Reid
2. Mahorahora Mcleod

Made Awan. Photo Tim Hain.

Dimity Stoyle. Photo Steve Robertson.

3. Te Rapai Barbarich-Love
4. Indika Ratima

ROXY OPEN WOMEN
1. Jayda Martin-Fitzharris
2. Jessica Terrill
3. Thandi Durham
4. Lana Yearbury

HYUNDAI MEN LONGBOARD
1. Jason Matthews
2. Jamie Andrews
3. Daniel Proctor
4. Kirk Beyer

MOTZSTAR OVER 30 MEN
1. James Fowell
2. Motu Mataa
3. Wayne Cooper
4. Jamie Andrews

AOTEAROA

BORN AND BREED OVER 35 MEN
1. Jason Lellman
2. Phil Willoughby
3. Shaun Coffey
4. Stacey Lamb

SEED OVER 40 MEN
1. Doug Te Ranga
2. Pipi Ngaia
3. Peter Schafer
4. Jason Matthews

SLIMES SURF CLASSIC, HURLEY NSW CHAMPIONSHIP CIRCUIT
AVOCA, NEW SOUTH WALES
November 1–2

Drew Courtney, 2009 ASP World Tour qualifier, posted wins multifold in the final leg of the Hurley NSW Championship Circuit, earning four separate titles at the Slimes Surf Classic. The definitive event win also afforded Courtney the series victory, the Umina surfer having stood out in each of the six series stages. Fierce competition from fellow finalists, Blake Thornton, Rhys Bombaci and Joel Reading necessitated in Courtney focus and competence, more than adequately displayed with the event's highest wave and highest heat scores. Thornton, Bombaci and Reading preformed admirably, continually keeping Courtney on his toes to defend his lead, but when the final seconds ticked over, there was no doubt that Courtney would emerge victorious. A powerful end to the year for the new World Tour initiate. Jordi Watson also secured a double victory in the Cadet division. Enter-

ing the finals, Watson was already assured of the series win, closest rival, Oscar Scanes (Old Bar) being eliminated in the semis and out of the running for the overall win. But Watson wasn't content, refusing to back down, an 8.5 ride in the heat's early stages proffering the lead that was never relinquished

OPEN MEN
1. Drew Courtney
2. Blake Thornton
3. Rhys Bombaci
4. Joel Reading

CADETS – 16 & UNDER
1. Jordi Watson
2. Wade Carmichael
3. Beau Foster
4. Rory Jenkins

ROXY PRO TRIALS FOR TRIALS
GOLD COAST, QUEENSLAND
November 2

Sunshine Coast wunderkind, Dimity Stoyle, earned herself the opportunity to compete against some of the finest non-Pro Tour surfers in the world at the 2009 Gold Coast Roxy Pro Trials with a dominating win in the Roxy Pro Trials for Trials. Duranbah Beach provided the setting for Stoyle's conquest, the opening five minutes being all she needed to secure 15.6 points and the lead she would maintain for the duration of the heat. Taking on Talina Christensen (Currumundi), Brittany Nicholl (Cabarita) and Wini Paul (Tugun), there was little doubt from the outset that Stoyle would come out on top, her powerful and diverse style a valediction to her adversaries.

FINAL
1. Dimity Stoyle
2. Talina Christensen
3. Brittany Nicholl
4. Wini Paul

O'NEILL SEQUENCE SURF SHOP PRO, SURFING NEW ZEALAND
GISBORNE, NEW ZEALAND
November 1–3

In the first event of the new season, Bobby Hansen snatched a win from

under the nose of fellow Gisborne surfer Maz Quinn. Tested to their limits in the very unimpressive conditions, surfers had to struggle hard to make the most of every wave that came their way. Hansen was under threat of losing the final, gaining the upper hand late in the final, both of his scoring waves only coming in the dying minutes. Favorite Quinn had to settle for second, a harder pill to swallow coming so late in the heat when he surely must have been entertaining thoughts of his own victory. Despite only taking the bronze medal, Jayda Martin-Fitzharris again impressed, her age belying her talent, the 13-year-old surfing strongly against some highly skilled, more experienced peers, including heat winner Jessica Santorik. Santorik was the undisputed winner, an eight-point wave sealing her victory and placing all three of her adversaries in a combination situation, an excellent result for the 21-year-old at the start of the 2009 season.

OPEN MEN
FINAL
1. Bobby Hansen
2. Maz Quinn
3. Luke Cederman
4. James Fowell
SEMIFINAL 1
1. Maz Quinn
2. Luke Cederman
3. Tim O'Connor
4. Damon Gunness
SEMIFINAL 2
1. Bobby Hansen
2. James Fowell
3. Keone Campbell
4. Ryan Hawker
QUARTERFINAL 1
1. Luke Cederman
2. Damon Gunness
3. Jeremy Evans
4. Gauranga Ormond
QUARTERFINAL 2
1. Maz Quinn
2. Tim O'Connor
3. Blair Stewart
4. Buck Woods
QUARTERFINAL 3
1. James Fowell
2. Keone Campbell
3. Chris Malone
4. Sol Paans
QUARTERFINAL 4
1. Bobby Hansen
2. Ryan Hawker
3. Clint Daly
4. Paco Divers
JUNIOR MEN
FINALS
1. Sean Peggs
2. Alex Dive
3. Paco Divers
4. Johnny Hicks
SEMIFINAL 1
1. Sean Peggs
2. Paco Divers
3. Ryan Hawker
4. Zen Wallis
SEMIFINAL 2
1. Alex Dive

2. Johnny Hicks
3. Braedon Williams
4. Tane Wallis
OPEN WOMEN
FINAL
1. Jessica Santorik
2. India Wray-Murane
3. Jayda Martin-Fitzharris
4. Ella Williams
SEMIFINAL 1
1. Ella Williams
2. India Wray-Murane
3. Anna Hawes
SEMIFINAL 2
1. Jessica Santorik
2. Jayda Martin-Fitzharris
3. Alexis Poulter

PRINTPOINT QUEENSLAND MASTERS, SURFING QUEENSLAND MASTERS SURFING CIRCUIT
NORTH STADBROKE ISLAND, QUEENSLAND
November 8–9

North Stradbroke Island weaved its magic for the Printpoint Queensland Masters, three-foot peaks littering the beaches and a gentle breeze grooming the waves. Mark Richardson snatched a close victory over Peter Boyd in the Over 28s, the defeat being reversed in the Over 35 division. With the win in the 28 and the second placing

Chris Brooks. Photo Jake White.

in the 35, Richardson claimed both state titles for the series. Fellow Currumbinite Chris Brooks barreled his way to a state title, denying Nick Ryan (Mermaid Beach), Terry Landsberg (Currumundi) and David Masters (Mooloolaba) in his path to victory.

OVER 28 MEN
1. Mark Richardson
2. Peter Boyd
3. Simon Massey
4. Michael Betts
OVER 35 MEN
1. Peter Boyd
2. Mark Richardson

OVER 40 MEN
1. Chris Brooks
2. Nick Ryan
3. Terry Landsberg
4. David Masters
OVER 45 MEN
1. Mark Traucnieks
2. Andrew Harris
3. Paul Fisher
4. Craig Frampton
OVER 50 MEN WINNER
Neville Williams
OVER 55 MEN WINNER
Paul Neilsen

MACCA'S OCEAN AND EARTH TEENAGE RAMPAGE, SURFING NEW SOUTH WALES
CRONULLA BEACH, NEW SOUTH WALES
November 8–9

The final event of the Ocean and Earth Teenage Rampage was an awesome punctuation to a blistering series. Jarrod Campbell surfed phenomenally from start to finish, overcoming all opponents in his division heats, the local surfer using his familiarity of the break to monopolize on his bag of tricks. Skye Burgess was equally as impressive in the 16 and Under Girls division, surfing proficiently throughout the event but stepping her performance up a level to leave her challengers, Rachel Campbell (Stanwell Park), April Charles (Woolooware) and Renee Savas (Caringbah), in a combination situation. Both victors earned themselves places in the international finals at Curl Curl Beach in December.

UNDER 16 BOYS
1. Jarrod Campbell
2. Max Ayshford
3. Kurt Kiggins
4. Jesse Horner
UNDER 16 GIRLS
1. Skye Burgess
2. Rachel Campbell
3. April Charles
4. Renee Savas

UNDER 13 BOYS WINNER
Chris Robertson
UNDER GIRLS WINNER
Tayla Ayshford

JIM BEAM WOMEN'S SURFTAG, SURFING NEW SOUTH WALES
CURL CURL
NEW SOUTH WALES
November 15

The North Narrabeen Surftag team of Ellie Northey, Katie Allan, Belinda Hardwick, Tess de Josselin and Shelley Carrier dominated the Women division of the 2008 series. Belinda Hardwick led the charge, posting a nine-point ride to add to the highest heat score of 25 points (out of a possible 40), to assist her team to the win. Trying conditions challenged all contestants, but the Narrbeen wahines stepped up to that challenge admirably, banding together to bring their team to victory and the $3,000 prize purse.

FINAL
1. North Narrabeen
2. Manly
3. Bondi 2
4. Trimmin Women (Newcastle and Central Coast regions)

LIZZY SURF SERIES EVENT #3, SURFING QUEENSLAND
GOLD COAST QUEENSLAND
November 15–16

A multitude of divisions, from Under 14s to Over 35s, fought it out in choppy 2- to 3-foot waves on Gold Coast's Main Beach in the final stage of the Lizzy Surf Series. Ashleigh Smith brought her local knowledge to the Open Women division, going hard against series top-rankers Ellie-Jean Coffey and Dimity Stoyle to take the series win. But it was Stoyle who claimed the biggest prize. Despite placing third in the day's event, Stoyle's previous series results gave her adequate accumulative points to emerge champion of the Lizzy Surf Series. Coffey pipped Stoyle to second place but the higher place wasn't a significant enough deficit to make up the 250 points needed to claim the series victory.

FINAL
1. Ashleigh Smith
2. Ellie-Jean Coffey
3. Dimity Stoyle
4. Courtney Bell

VOLCOM STONE STALEFISH VQS
WERRI BEACH, GERRINGONG, NEW SOUTH WALES
November 15

Ty Watson had a battle on his hands from the outset of the second Volcom Stone Stalefish event, Tom

Salvesen, Byron Bartlett and Ash King fighting hard to deny him a victory. But their challenges fell short, Watson's talents too complete to be held back. In the juniors, Dean Bowen continued his exceptional roll, illuminating the lineup with his comprehensive skills and taking the title with confidence. Katherin Turk refused to let her opponents get the better of her, Skye Burgess, Freya Prum and Jessica Relf failing to hold down the young surfer, the Volcom win firmly in her grasp when the heat's remaining seconds died.

MEN PRO-AM DIVISION
1. Ty Watson
2. Tom Salvesen
3. Byron Bartlett
4. Ash King
JUNIOR DIVISION
1. Dean Bowen
2. Matt Gale
3. Kurt Kiggins
4. Max Ashford
GROMS DIVISION
1. Jack Scott
2. Zac Scott
3. Michael Wright
4. Nick Clifford
GIRLS DIVISION
1. Katherin Turk
2. Skye Burgess
3. Freya Prum
4. Jessica Relf

JIM BEAM INDUSTRY CHALLENGE, GLOBAL SURFTAG
DEE WHY, NEW SOUTH WALES
November 21

Matt Hoy and former two-time ASP World Champion Tom Carroll led the Quiksilver industry team to a convincing victory in the Global Surftag Jim Beam Industry Challenge. Fun surf at Sydney's Dee Why beach may not have given big-wave contender Carroll his usual choice of swells, but he and Hoy brought

their high-class, professional talent to the minimal conditions. Team Ocean and Earth stayed in close touch with the team of the Mountain and Wave, but couldn't draw them in close enough to strike, falling almost five points short of their conquerors. Queens-cliff proved to be worthy of the win in the team Paddle Race, bettering Dee Why , North Narrabeen , Curl Curl and Long Reef, who were second to fifth respectively.

FINAL STANDINGS
1. Quiksilver
2. Ocean & Earth
3. RVCA and Chilli Surfboards
4. Aloha Surfboards
JIM BEAM PADDLE RACE
1. Queenscliff
2. Dee Why
3. North Narrabeen
4. Curl Curl
5. Long Reef

VOLCOM STONE'S STALEFISH VQS
AVALON BEACH, NEW SOUTH WALES
November 22

Fighting for the chance to compete in the Australian Grand Championships at Manly Beach in April of 2009, competitors poured passion into their performances in the 3- to 4-foot waves of Avalon Beach. Tim Taplin took the bull by the horns, reveling in the pristine conditions and defeating Isaac Buckley, Sam Rhodes and Dylan Cram with confidence if not ease. Ali Kelly did likewise in the Girls division, Heidi Hammester drawing close to the eventual winner, but unable to come through when the final gong sounded.

MEN PRO-AM
1. Tim Taplin
2. Isaac Buckley
3. Sam Rhodes
4. Dylan Cram

JUNIORS
1. Tom Myers
2. Billy Bain
3. Max Tag
4. Parker Graham
GROMS
1. Matt Crowe
2. Cooper Chapman
3. Ryan Hunt
4. Bodi Smith
GIRLS
1. Ali Kelly
2. Heidi Hammester
3. Skye Burgess
4. Lauren McAleer

AUSTRALIAN JUNIOR SURFING TITLES, SURFING AUSTRALIA
MARGARET RIVER, WEST AUSTRALIA
December 1–7

Proving once more that he is an exceptional talent destined for a huge future, Dean Bowen dominated the Australian Junior Surfing Titles, winning convincingly and adding yet another trophy to his burgeoning collection. Second to fourth places were a closer-fought battle, places exchanging continually between Tim McDonald, Jordi Watson and Khai Adams. Bowen's lead was undisputed, a mid-eight-point ride soon backed up with a higher eight. In the latter half of the heat, Bowen went one better, landing a near-perfect 9.5 to seal the victory. The ladies had a little tougher competition on their hands, Paige Haggerston toughing it out against Kirby Wright, with Philipa Anderson and Felicity Palmateer snapping at their heals. At the sound of the final horn, Haggerston and Wright were tied, both holding a combined score of 14.10. A count-back revealed Haggerston's best wave to be just one tenth of a point higher than that of Wright, giving her the win by the narrowest of margins.

UNDER 18 BOYS
1. Dean Bowen
2. Tim McDonald
3. Jordi Watson
4. Khai Adams
UNDER 18 GIRLS
1. Paige Haggerston
2. Kirby Wright
3. Philipa Anderson
4. Felicity Palmeteer
UNDER 16 BOYS
1. Cooper Chapman
2. Dylan Cummings
3. Hamish Renwick
4. Harrison Mann
UNDER 16 GIRLS
1. Tyler Wright
2. M. Greene
3. B. Doyle
4. Nicola Van Dijk

RIP CURL GROM-SEARCH, SURFING NEW ZEALAND
PIHA BEACH, AUCKLAND, NEW ZEALAND
December 6–7

The finale of the Rip Curl Grom-Search gifted two of New Zealand's most prominent surfers with early Christmas presents, Gisborne's Johnny Hicks and Alexis Poulter of Raglan achieving wins in the Under 16 Boys and Under 16 Girls divisions respectively. An outstanding 9.75 wave midway through the final secured Hicks' victory, though there was still a very real threat from runner-up Alex Dive. Dive had an exceptional 2008 season and matched Hicks' performance closely, falling frustratingly short of the victor. Almost three points ahead of her rivals, Alexis Poulter posted a far more convincing win. The Raglan local, unlike the previous three GromSearches, all of which she won, focused her energy on the under 16 division, making it four for four in her winning streak.

UNDER 16 BOYS
FINAL
1. Johnny Hicks
2. Alex Dive
3. Tane Wallis
4. Mark Parthemore
SEMIFINAL 1
1. Johnny Hicks
2. Tane Wallis
3. Joe Moretti
4. Adam Grimson
SEMIFINAL 2
1. Alex Dive
2. Mark Parthemore
3. Ben Poulter
4. Subarn Linklater
UNDER 14 BOYS
FINAL
1. Tane Wallis
2. Peri Matenga
3. Ben Poulter
4. Dune Kennings
SEMIFINAL 1
1. Tane Wallis
2. Peri Matenga
3. Paul Moretti
4. Adam Grimson
SEMIFINAL 1
1. Dune Kennings
2. Ben Poulter

North Narrabeen team. Photo Michael Tyrpenou/Global Surftag.

Johnny Hicks. Photo NZ Surfing Magazine.

3. Fintan Cram
4. Patxi Scott-Arrieta

UNDER 12 BOYS
FINAL
1. Elliot Paerata Reid
2. Dune Kennings
3. Manu Scott-Arietta
4. Jordan Griffin

SEMIFINAL 1
1. Jordan Griffin
2. Elliot Paerata Reid
3. Sam Poulter
4. Blake Haven

SEMIFINAL 2
1. Dune Kennings
2. Manu Scott-Arietta
3. Korbin Hutchings
4. Quin Matenga

UNDER 16 GIRLS
FINAL
1. Alexis Poulter
2. Rosa Thompson
3. Jayda Martin-Fitzharris
4. Ella Williams

SEMIFINAL 1
1. Alexis Poulter
2. Ella Williams
3. Gabriella McCarthy-Marriott
N/S Madison Atkins

SEMIFINAL 2
1. Rosa Thompson
2. Jayda Martin-Fitzharris
3. Maiya Thompson
4. Ruby Meade

UNDER 14 GIRLS
FINAL
1. Ella Williams
2. Jayda Martin-Fitzharris
3. Gabriella McCarthy-Marriott
4. Maiya Thompson

SEMIFINAL 1
1. Gabriella McCarthy-Marriott
2. Maiya Thompson
3. Madison Atkins

SEMIFINAL 2
1. Jayda Martin-Fitzharris
2. Ella Williams
3. Hannah Kohn
4. Gabriella McCarthy-Marriott

UNDER 12 GIRLS
FINAL
1. Gabriela Sansom
2. Bianca Sansom
3. Demi Hewitt
4. Britt Kindred

SEMIFINAL 1
1. Demi Hewitt

2. Britt Kindred
3. Claudia Fraser

SEMIFINAL 2
1. Bianca Sansom
2. Gabriela Sansom
3. Hannah Kohn

WAHU SUPER GROM COMP
MAIN BEACH, GOLD COAST, QUEENSLAND
December 14

A distinct lack of swell did little to hamper the finalists of the Wahu Super Grom Comp, competitors defying the unfriendly conditions to put on a display that rivaled any in it's class. Matt Banting finished the year with flair, convincingly dominating the U/15 Boys event. Banting was the only surfer to break the ten-point mark in the final, almost doubling the figures of closest rival Kurtis Herman. The Sunshine Coast's Sophie Callister also had a significant victory, far out-surfing her peers in the Girls Under 15 division.

UNDER 15 BOYS
1. Matt Banting
2. Kurtis Herman
3. Eli Steele
4. Will Morrison

UNDER 15 GIRLS
1. Sophie Callister
2. Eden Putland
3. Naomi McCarthy
4. Skye Fagan

UNDER 13 BOYS
1. Joshua Szele
2. Luke Hynd
3. Kai Hing
4. Blaine Johnson

UNDER 13 GIRLS
1. Renee Heazlewood
2. Jade Wheatley
3. Laura Poncini
4. Iluka Enright

UNDER 11 BOYS
1. Jarrod Szele
2. Zac Wrightman
3. Reef Heazlewood
4. Leonard Rawlings

UNDER 9 BOYS & GIRLS
1. Dextar Muskens

2. Sandon Whitaker
3. Kyuss King
4. Tiger Rawlings

BILLABONG GROM COMPETITION
SUMMER BEACH, CHRISTCHURCH, NEW ZEALAND
December 13–14

The final Billabong Grom Comp series victory was laid squarely in the hands of Ben Bennett, the Dunedin surfer narrowly overcoming Christchurch's Cody McCusker. Small conditions and brisk winds prevailed in the series final, surfers having to make the most of a one-foot swell. But despite the conservative conditions, surfers across the divisions performed spectacularly. With a fifth and a second placing already under his belt in the series, the event's victory also gave Bennett the inaugural Billabong Grom Comp Series title, Taylor McNeill (Christchurch) netting second place for the series. Christchurch's Kristi Zarifeh went into the final of the Under 16 Girls, holding a second place in the series. Her work was cut out, with fellow Christchurch surfer and series leader Alethea Lock meeting her in the final. But pure grit and determination saw Zarifeh take the event victory and in doing so claiming the series win also.

UNDER 16 BOYS
FINAL
1. Ben Bennett
2. Cody McCusker
3. Sam Courtney
4. Michael Dalrymple

SEMIFINAL 1
1. Sam Courtney
2. Michael Dalrymple
3. Geordi Dearn

SEMIFINAL 2
1. Cody McCusker
2. Ben Bennett
3. Taylor McNeill

QUARTERFINAL 1
1. Sam Courtney
2. Cody McCusker

3. Hugh Ritchie
4. Jack Hawke

QUARTERFINAL 2
1. Ben Bennett
2. Michael Dalrymple
3. Billy Harmon
4. Luke O'Neill

QUARTERFINAL 3
1. Taylor McNeill
2. Geordi Dearn
3. Sam Blackman
4. Quinn Harmon

UNDER 14 BOYS
ROUND 1, HEAT 1
1. Luke O'Neill
2. Niwa Ututaonga
3. Cam Malcolm
4. Ryan Robertson

ROUND 1, HEAT 2
1. Billy Harmon
2. Jack Hawke
3. Ashlee Sullivan
4. Max Cooke

ROUND 2, HEAT 1
1. Luke O'Neill
2. Ashlee Sullivan
3. Cam Malcolm
4. Max Cooke

ROUND 2, HEAT 2
1. Billy Harmon
2. Niwa Ututaonga
3. Jack Hawke
4. Ryan Robertson

UNDER 14 BOYS
HEAT TOTALS
1. Billy Harmon
2. Luke O'Neill
3. Ashlee Sullivan
4. Jack Hawke

UNDER 12 BOYS
ROUND 1, HEAT 1
1. Lachie Malcolm
2. Jack Wilson
3. Matt Robin

ROUND 1, HEAT 2
1. Max Marshall
2. Harrison Whiteside
3. Samuel Sands

ROUND 2, HEAT 1
1. Max Marshall
2. Samuel Sands
3. Harrison Whiteside

ROUND 2, HEAT 2
1. Lachie Malcolm
2. Matt Robin
3. Jack Wilson

UNDER 12 BOYS
HEAT TOTALS
1. Lachie Malcolm
2. Max Marshall
3. Harrison Whiteside
4. Samuel Sands

UNDER 16 GIRLS
ROUND 1, HEAT 1
1. Kristi Zarifeh
2. Alethea Lock
3. Grace Nicolson
4. Emily Nicolson

ROUND 1, HEAT 2
1. Alethea Lock
2. Kristi Zarifeh
3. Emily Nicolson
4. Grace Nicolson

ROUND 1, HEAT 3
1. Kristi Zarifeh
2. Alethea Lock
3. Emily Nicolson
4. Grace Nicolson

UNDER 16 GIRLS
HEAT TOTALS
1. Kristi Zarifeh
2. Alethea Lock
3. Emily Nicolson
4. Grace Nicolson

UNDER 14 GIRLS
HEAT 1
1. Alethea Lock
2. Alessa Whitfield

HEAT 2
1. Alethea Lock
2. Alessa Whitfield

UNDER 12 GIRLS
ROUND 1, HEAT 1
1. Katie Nicolson
2. Brittany Andrews
3. Lilly Molloy-Wolt

ROUND 1, HEAT 2
1. Lilly Molloy-Wolt
2. Katie Nicolson
3. Brittany Andrews

UNDER 12 GIRLS
HEAT TOTALS
1. Katie Nicolson
2. Lilly Molloy-Wolt
3. Brittany Andrews

VOLCOM STONE'S FISH FINGERS VQS,
MT. MAUNGANUI, NEW ZEALAND
December 13–14

The final stop of the Volcom Crustaceous Tour saw the usual suspects on New Zealand's circuit fighting it out in the meager conditions plaguing the South Island throughout early December. Billy Stairmand, Alex Dive, Jess Santorik and Tane Wallis made up the event's winners list, all evidently proficient at finding needles in haystacks, or the high-scoring sections in very mediocre surf, as the case may be. Stairmand did well to link up maneuvers in his final, managing to maximize his use of the cleaner portions of the small, crumbling conditions to defeat Ricardo Christie by a whisker.

MEN PRO-AM OPEN
1. Billy Stairmand
2. Ricardo Christie
3. Luke Ashman
4. Mark Dovey

JUNIORS 15-17
1. Alex Dive
2. Matt Hewitt
3. Zen Wallis
4. Ryan Heath

GROMS 14 & UNDER
1. Tane Wallis
2. Dune Kennings
3. Peri Matunga
4. Chad Kleiman

GIRLS
1. Jess Santorik
2. Laura Rickworth
3. Hester Stacey
4. Jazmin West

RIP CURL GROMSEARCH, SURFING AUSTRALIA
DURANBAH BEACH, QUEENSLAND
December 15–19

The penultimate qualification event of the 2008 Rip Curl GromSearch took place in clean, balmy, but slightly undersized conditions at the Gold Coast's Seaway Spit. Taking the victories, two overseas surfers who now call the Gold Coast home dominated their heats to gain entry into the grand finale in April of 2009. One Anwar, who had recently emigrated from Indonesia to Palm Beach, claimed the Under 16 Boys division, while Sarah Mason, the former New Zealander, surfed superbly throughout the event to emerge victorious in both the Under 16 and Under 14 Girls division. Anwar was threatened by Kingscliff surfer James Mitchell, who posted a solid eight-point ride, but the Indonesian's solid style gave him a pair of scores that Mitchell failed to equal. Mason was indomitable, with high eight- and nine-point rides peppering both of her finals heats.

UNDER 16 BOYS
FINAL
1. Oney Anwar Hanzah
2. James Mitchell
3. Nicholas Hoskin
4. Wade Carmichael
SEMIFINAL 1
1. Nicholas Hoskin
2. James Mitchell
3. Jackson O'Donnell
SEMIFINAL 2
1. Oney Anwar Hanzah
2. Wade Carmichael
3. Connor O'Leary
UNDER 16 GIRLS
FINAL
1. Sarah Mason
2. Ellie Jean Coffey
3. Amiya Doyle
4. Brodie Doyle
SEMIFINAL 1
1. Sarah Mason
2. Brodie Doyle
3. Codie Klein
4. Nao Oomura
SEMIFINAL 2
1. Ellie Jean Coffey
2. Amiya Doyle
3. Emily Clapoudis
4. Namomi Stevic

O'NEILL GROMTAG
AVALON BEACH, NEW SOUTH WALES
December 20–21

Chris Enever and Davey Cathels led their North Narrabeen team to victory in O'Neill's Gromtag event, Avalon providing a solid swell for the occasion. Three-foot waves curled into the beach, giving the defending champions of Narrabeen the perfect stage on which to mount their victory. Convincingly defeating the local team from Avalon, Narrabeen were never in doubt, in their minds or those of the spectators, of having a podium finish, the final placing justified, with all team members performing exceptionally.

FINAL
1. North Narrabeen
2. Avalon
3. Ulladulla
4. Cronulla
5. Avoca
6. Elouera
7. Werri
8. Newport
9. North Shelley
10. North Narrabeen "B"
11. Dee Why
12. Freshwater
SEMIFINAL 1
1. Ulladulla
2. North Narrabeen
3. Avoca
SEMIFINAL 2
1. Cronulla
2. Avalon
3. Elouera

BILLABONG QUEENSLAND CHAMPIONSHIP CIRCUIT EVENT, PRESENTED BY PRINTPOINT, SURFING QUEENSLAND
BURLEIGH POINT, QUEENSLAND
December 21

South African emigrant Shaun Gossmann sealed the series crown for this year's Queensland Championship Circuit, despite only placing fourth in the final event of the series. Gossmann surfed well throughout the event, but in the end had to concede the day's victory, still gaining sufficient points to stave off closest Circuit rival Corey Ziems. The battle may have been significantly more poignant, had Ziems been competing in the final event, the Currumbin surfer landlocked having sustained damage to his spine. Though perhaps not has gratifying as a series win, Brent Dorrington held aloft the trophy for the stage victory, surfing strongly in Burleigh's clean, two-foot conditions. Blake Wilson and Nick Vasicek made up the numbers in the final, placing second and third respectively.

QCC EVENT FINAL
1. Brent Dorrington
2. Blake Wilson
3. Nick Vasicek
4. Shaun Gossmann
QUEENSLAND CHAMPIONSHIP CIRCUIT FINAL SERIES RESULTS
1. Shaun Gossmann
2. Corey Ziems
4. Matt Jones

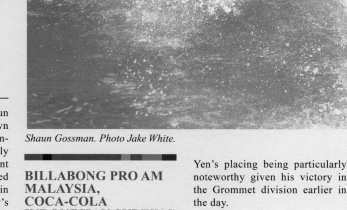

Shaun Gossman. Photo Jake White.

BILLABONG PRO AM MALAYSIA, COCA-COLA INDONESIAN SURFING CHAMPIONSHIPS
CHERATING POINT, PAHANG, MALAYSIA
December 19–21

What began as a contest in fun surf turned into a struggle to find scoring waves for the Coca-Cola Indonesian Surfing Championships. Early rounds saw 2- to 3-foot peelers curling into the contest arena at Cherating Point, Malaysia, but come finals day, the surfers were forced to fight over scraps in a desperate effort to achieve any ride of note. Local surfer Mamat gave his all and, as one of the larger surfers in the final, was the surprise victor, by his own admittance. His knowledge of the break allowed him to find the right peaks, maximizing his chances of gaining a significant score. Yen, Khairil and Mohd Fairoz made up the numbers in the final, gaining second, third and fourth places respectively, Yen's placing being particularly noteworthy given his victory in the Grommet division earlier in the day.

MENS OPEN
1. Mamat
2. Yen
3. Khairil
4. Mohd Fairoz
MASTERS FINAL
1. Paul Anderson
2. Michael Robert
3. Art
4. Tim Brent
GROMMETS FINAL
1. Yen
2. Didaqt
3. Sammy
4. Shahir
MEN BODYBOARD
1. Jarul Aliff Zulkifli
2. Hatta Abu Bakar
3. Omar Emad
4. Aman Ishak
WOMEN FINAL
1. Noriko Kanno
2. Mariam Abbas
3. Angela Wisco
4. Wani Norizan

OCEAN AND EARTH INTERNATIONAL TEENAGE RAMPAGE, SURFING AUSTRALIA
CURL CURL BEACH, NEW SOUTH WALES
December 27–30

Julian Wilson (Coolum) added yet another trophy to an already overloaded cabinet on the penultimate day of 2008 at Curl Curl Beach for Ocean & Earth's Teenage Rampage. Wilson was a potent force in the event, surpassing Nambucca Heads' Heath Joske to take the win. A hiatus on the competitive scene seemed not to have affected Wilson, a 9 and a 7.5 ride proving that he maintained his talents despite the time off due to injury. Matt Banting (Port Macquarie) reinforced his reputation as one of Australia's foremost young talents with a substantial win in the Under 16 division, whilst Merewether's Phillipa Anderson claimed trophies in both the Under 16 and Under 20 divisions.

UNDER 20 MEN
1. Julian Wilson
2. Heathe Joske
3. Magno Pacheco
4. Matt Wilkinson
UNDER 16 BOYS
1. Matt Banting
2. Jack Freestone
3. Ryan Callinan
4. Max Ayshford
UNDER 13 BOYS
1. Eli Steele
2. O'Neil Massin
3. Matt King
4. Chris Robertson
UNDER 20 WOMEN
Phillipa Anderson
UNDER 16 GIRLS
1. Phillipa Anderson
2. Nao Oura
3. Brodie Doyle
4. Skye Burgess
UNDER 13 GIRLS
1. Kirsten Ogden
2. Stephanie Single
3. Sophie Bernard
4. Cali McDonagh

Julian Wilson. Photo Kirstin Scholtz.

ABOVE: Keramas rail grab. BELOW: Ghost ship at Padang.

Bali Is Back!
Words and photos by Jason Childs

Balinese people love to smile, and with the return of tourists and surfers here for the season, the place is rocking and everyone is smiling. Flights full, hotels packed, bars overflowing and bikinis everywhere—Bali is back and bigger and better than ever. The surf season has been consistent, but what happened to the big swells lighting up Padang Padang and Outside corner at Uluwatu?

Even without those true standout days, Bali is where the future of high-performance surfing is happening. Early in the season, performance levels were at an all-time high as top surfers fought for their part in the latest Taylor Steele production; then later in the year the Rip Curl Search event brought everyman and his dog to town. These are just some of the visitors we've had this year: Andy Irons, Joel Parkinson, Kai Otton, Dusty Payne, Julian Wilson, Jordy Smith, Bruce Irons, CJ Hobgood, Luke Stedman, Taj Burrow, Kalani Robb, Rob Machado, Pat O'Connell, and Kelly Slater. Phew!

Bali was thumped by a big south swell on Sunday, April 13, and that opened the real surf season. The surf was pretty epic at Keramas. Damien Wills (Aussie Hurley team rider) scored the biggest barrel we have seen at Keramas. Taj Burrow and Bruce Irons ruled, Taj pulling an epic alley-oop, freaking the crew out watching from the warungs.

Rizal Tanjung (the King of Bali) and the Bali boyz have been ruling the lineup as usual, but throwing a few set waves to pro guys.

Dreamland as we know it is gone! The once idyllic beach hangout that has been over-run the past few years with new warungs and accommodation is no longer, with the building of a massive shopping center and hotel overlooking the beach. Yes shops, just what Bali needs! All who have seen the photos or visited the beach are left feeling very sad by the new development. The area has been renamed the New Kuta. Progress?

The Balcony nightspot rocked to music by Hurley pro surfers/musicians Rob Machado, Timmy Curren and musician John Swift in front of a big crowd of tourists, expats and locals. In fact, Hurley International dominated the Bali surf season, with their surfers rotating through a team villa that boasts personal chefs, maid service and in-house massage, and accessing the world-class waves that Bali has to offer. "Bali is fast becoming the North Shore of the summertime," commented Hurley sports marketing manager Pat O'Connell. "We've been coming to Bali for years to shoot videos and photos. It was a no-brainer for us to get a team house here." Indonesian Hurley team rider Rizal Tanjung has been the surf guide to the crew.

The Taiwanese fishing boat *Ho Tsai Fa No.18*, dubbed the "ghost ship," smashed into the reef of the famous Balinese wave Padang Padang the night before the Rip Curl Cup (local contest) opening ceremony on Saturday, July 12, prompting fears of an environmental disaster and threatening to destroy one of Indonesia's finest waves. Shortly after dawn, alarmed local fishing boats had pulled up outside of the beached vessel whose hold full of oversized catch (including tuna, sharks, and mahi-mahi) had begun to be pilfered by anyone who could get out to the ship.

The *Ho Tsai Fa No. 18* had a chequered history. It was apprehended off Costa Rica in 2003 with 60,000 kilograms of illegally caught shark fin. Early this year, Greenpeace activists intercepted the ship fishing illegally in the Pacific.

Local police described the vessel as a crime scene, confirming its captain may have been murdered. It was rumored that the dozen Indonesian crew members had mutinied while fishing off Papua and thrown their Taiwanese captain overboard!

Predicted heavy swells caused fears that the boat could break up, spread wreckage and fuel along the Bukit Peninsula and possibly contaminate the waves at Uluwatu. Many attempts were made by concerned expats and local lifeguards to refloat the 35-meter fishing vessel.

Local environmental group the ROLE Foundation attempted to coordinate salvage efforts to move the ship. Rising waves and tides finally pushed it farther onto the rocks, taking it off Padang Padang's famous surf break but complicating salvage attempts. ROLE staff then moved in to contain oil slicks before the ship broke up. But in the end the ship mysteriously caught fire and burned to the ground.

The Rip Curl WCT Search and the Oakley Pro Junior Global Challenge put Bali back on the contest map with some of the year's best contest waves, and then the ocean went to sleep for nearly two months in one of the worst wave droughts in memory.

But the drought broke in October when up-and-coming surfing hotshot Dusty Payne barreled his way to victory in the Oakley Pro Junior Global Challenge to claim the world's biggest ever payday for a Pro Junior event. Keramas, an ultra-perfect right-hand reef break, lived up to its hype, serving out epic barreling waves for the final day of the inaugural competition.

And to round out the year, Indonesia's #1 surfer for 2008 (newly crowned ISC champ) Dede Suryana completely dominated the Aerial competition at the inaugural Asian Beach Games at Kuta Beach, Bali. Dede was the second Indonesian to win a surfing gold medal at the games, held in October. The Beach Games brought together 17 sports, people competing for Olympic medals around the Bali locations of Sanur, Nusa Dua, Serangan Island and Kuta Beach.

Above: Rizal, the king on his throne.
Below: Keramas air.

Below: Kelly hanging high and loose.

The Island of the Gods has had a rough few years, with fear of new terrorism outbreaks reducing tourism to a trickle, but in '08 the elements all aligned and Bali was not only cool again—it was positively hot!

Your Magic

SHAPED BY Peter Daniels

Pukas

www.pukassurf.com

Europe Report

By Gibus de Soultrait

For Europeans the stoke started with France's Jeremy Flores, 20, finishing his '07 WCT season as the "rookie of the year" and being reinforced in the Euro team for 2008 with the arrival of three European beach buddies, Miky Picon (Fr), 29, Tiago Pires (Prt), 28, and Aritz Arumburu (Sp), 23. No longer an illusion, the Euroforce became a reality. Among the highlights: a 3rd place for Jeremy at tour stop #1 at Snapper, and Tiago at Uluwatu tour stop #6 becoming the first ASP competitor to stop Slater's succession of victories. Bad luck for Aritz, who was badly injured and didn't find his top level. For the Euroforce, perhaps the ultimate moment was Miky and Jeremy battling a semi in Brazil.

Winter 07/08 turned to a search of Atlantic thrills for European tow-in riders. Going back and forth between Ireland and Spain, the French warrior Benjamin Sanchis, with two Spanish big-swell-addicted surfers Ibon Amatrian and Asier Munian, opened the wild scale of two new European dramatic slabs.

On January 2, the Gascogne Gulf was on fire with the right wind on the coast. Belharra's pioneers jumped at the opportunity. The huge reef had not been surfed since 2003. During this session Vincent Lartizien rushed down the longest ocean slope of his life—no time to look back to the avalanche behind him—and a drop that put him in the Billabong XXXL finals. Tahitian Manoa Drollet was second in the XXL with a majestic ride on a Teahupoo bomb. Manoa continued at his home spot, where, as a wildcard, he twice defeated King Kelly to finish 2nd in the Billabong Pro. Waiting for his glory at Teahupoo but already seriously riding the famous spot, Tamaroa MacComb also held up the Tahitian flag during the Quiksilver World Junior Championship (ISA) at Seignosse, winning the first place in the Under 16s.

Also in the spring, the O'Neill Mission went running for the right waves between Brittany and the Basque Coast. Ten pro riders with an army of photographers, filmmakers and big buses did a lot of miles during a week of weak swell but an interesting attempt in unexpected spots that finally gave victory to Aussie Julian Wilson. Less air and more fluidity with no road stress was the Oxbow Longboard Championships '08 first contest, held at Anglet. There was a real French flavor for the local

Tim Boal, 2008 ASP Europe Champion. Photo Alex Laurel.

supporters watching the local stylist Antoine Delpero, who finished second in a dancing final against Aussie opponent Harley Engleby.

With Nat Young backstage signing the new version of his *History of Surfing* book, the Oxbow Worlds spread a cultural atmosphere, creating an appetite for the following Surf Film Festival in St. Jean de Luz. Onstage there, Nat again, fellow Aussie Terry Fitzgerald and Shaun Tomson, who had been invited with his film *Bustin' Down the Door*, in "avant-premiere." Certainly the most popular '70s pro surfer in France, as he often visited the country during his career, Shaun again touched the public with his "Free Ride" generation documentary.

Surfing history does not always belong just to the obvious countries. France could claim its own with the 50th anniversary of Barland Surfboards, where some of the legendary shapers (Cooper, Diffenderfer, Parrish, Linden) worked in the past. Not to mention that it was Michel Barland who in 1981 created the first pre-shape machine assisted by

computer, a machine still considered one of the most precise in the world. On a more minor level, *Surf Session* magazine celebrated its 250th issue with contents focused on slabs—not just the well-known ones like Shipsterns or Ours, but also new discoveries in the Atlantic and Mediterranean gnarly enough to land you in hospital.

The Rip Curl Mademoiselle event created excitement in the French camp with the performance of Lee-Ann Curren, 19, in a solid summer swell at Hossegor. A wildcard in this ASP event, she finished third and certainly made her father, Tom, proud. Another hot prospect, Marie Dejean, 16, astounded her teammates during the World Surfing Games, at Costa de Caparica, Portugal, with a 2nd place behind Australia's Sally Fitzgibbons.

A new development in Europe is the rise of the paddling sports, not only the stand-up paddleboard but also the outrigger canoe and the paddleboard, with more and more watermen ready for long-distance races, like the 63 kilometer Quiksilver Eyewear Paddleboard Race

from San Sebastian (Spain) to Capbreton (France), the longest in the world. For a third time France's Ludovic Dulou had trained hard to be ready at the start, and his main rival, Aussie Jamie Mitchell, who beat him in 2007 by 30 seconds, did not come this time. After 6 hours 41 minutes of strong paddling, Dulou broke the record, nearly 15 minutes in front of Mitchell's best time. Enough to get Jamie back in 2009?

Another battle this year was the defense of the surf spot L'Embarcadere, at La Tranche-sur-Mer. This "French Kirra" was threatened by boatmen who wanted an extension of the pier. But with the support of Surfrider Foundation, the surfing media and a petition signed by hundreds of surfers, the locals convinced the city council of the importance of the wave—a great win in an area where surfing is still a minor sport compared to sailing.

Farther south, over the Spanish border, the district of Mundaka further established its economic interest in the waves for the area. In 2005, the wave at Mundaka had been nearly destroyed by sand dredging. In 2006, the Mundaka Billabong Pro had to be cancelled and the local government ordered a study that proved the importance of the surfing income. By chance, the river mouth brought the sand back naturally, and Mundaka recovered its famous barrel. To celebrate, the swell picked up during the Mundaka Billabong Pro 08, giving Kelly Slater his ninth world title with some good barrels—not bad publicity for the area.

If Jeremy Flores, 3rd at Trestles and 2nd in Brazil, is the Euroforce leader, the group grew with the qualification of Tim Boal (Fr), 25, and Marlon Lipke (Ger), 24. The French surfer, who speaks fluent English courtesy of an Irish father, finished second at the U.S. Open (Huntington). This good result gave him the confidence to produce his elegant, snappy surfing in the following WQS contests, qualifying for the ASP before the end of the season. Marlon, a hero in Germany already, also lent his weight (along with visiting singer Jack Johnson) to the campaign to save Munich's famous Eisbach river wave from a council surfing ban. The surfers won!

French surf brand Oxbow shrugged off the economic situation and went ahead with its second World Tour Longboard event in San Onofre, California, with Hawaiian Bonga Perkins winning a second world title 12 years after the first, and France's Antoine Delpero finishing a worthy second.

UK and Ireland Report

By Sam Bleakley

North East secret spot. Photo Sharpy/surfphoto.co.uk.

Wherever the cold, turbulent Atlantic greets the United Kingdom and Ireland's rugged coastline, sometimes with a kiss, mostly with a slap, there is now a thriving surf culture. Two thousand eight started with a consistent run of long-fetch swells, as big-wave warriors faced epic Irish surf frontiers. In January, photographer Mickey Smith exposed Riley's, a death-defying left slab close to the tow-in spot Aileens, below the towering granite cliffs of Moher. Irishman Fergal Smith and Tom Lowe, from St. Ives, tackled insanely thick, glaucous green pits. Ireland's answer to Teahupoo made eye-watering copy for the UK's premier magazines *Carve* and *The Surfers Path* and was featured in Smith's film *Revolution*.

Tow partners Al Mennie (Portrush) and Andrew Cotton (North Devon) were filmed riding 30-foot-plus giants at Aileens in February. British tow team Gabe Davies (Newcastle) and Richie Fitzgerald (Bundoran) premiered *Wave Riders* at the Dublin Film Festival weeks later. This stunning documentary unravels the Emerald Isle's surfing story, from George Freeth's first foray to Aileens explosion, climaxing at Mullaghmore Head where Davies rides a 50-foot thundering left nominated for the Billabong XXL Big Wave of the Year Award.

The hollow, spinning, deep-freeze right at Thurso, Scotland, confirms this as the UK's premier contest venue. Despite hideous weather along the barren Caithness coast, clean 6- to 8-foot no-nonsense barrels blessed the Roxy 3 Degrees event in October, where Ireland's Nicole Morgan spent most of her time sheltering under the lip, to annihilate the competition. She took the overall UK Pro Surf Tour in scintillating form, losing only one event, at Portrush, to fellow Irish charger Easkey Britton. Dave Reed's thriving UK Pro Surf Tour has become a melting pot of foreign and resident surfers chasing top prize money. Newcastle's Sam Lamiroy battled bitter hail and snow to win the Quiksilver North East Open. The tall, explosive regular-foot led the UK Pro Surf Tour into the ninth and final event, the Animal Newquay Open in November. But Lamiroy's early elimination meant either Alan Stokes or Reuben Pearce could win the tour. As goofy-footer Pearce linked a series of vertical backhand turns on a head-high set in the dying minutes of the final, he did enough to snag the whole UK Pro Surf Tour. The event itself was won by Bude's lightning-fast Reubyn Ash, who finished 10th on the ASP Pro Junior Tour and was given a wild card to the Billabong Pro in Mundaka, Spain, where he surfed against Kelly Slater in his 9th ASP World Title crowning event.

At the UK Pro Surf Tour awards night, Newquay legend Russell Winter won Most Inspirational Surfer. Russell is still the only Briton to have qualified for the WCT (in 1998, 2000, and 2001), and win the nation's premier WQS contests—the Rip Curl Boardmasters at Fistral (2002), and the O'Neill Highland Pro in Thurso (2006). Russell competed in select WQS events in 2008, and dominated the national contests he was able to enter. At the October British Championships he made spaghetti of the 6-foot Fistral faces with radical torque and precise trademark hacks, to win both the Open and Seniors.

Although autumn delivered a long-overdue run of sunny days and lips clipped by stiff offshores, darkness descended on the surf economy. The "credit crunch" has led to the eclipse of numerous surf shops, and British surf clothing company Headworx collapsed. However, surf schools, sanctioned by the British Surfing Association (BSA), are booming, with an estimated 500,000 surfers in the country. The BSA itself has endured an unresolved administrative and financial rollercoaster, with numerous managerial sackings and reappointments. Board builders have faired reasonably well, and experimentation with new and sometimes green materials continues. Working in Nigel Semmens' state-of-the-art Ocean Magic board factory, Ben Skinner's freshly formed Skindog Surfboards now leads the national longboard market, pioneering carbon rail technology in 9 footers. Skinner, 2007 European Longboard Champion, dominated longboard contests, narrowly beating Sennen's Sam Bleakley to win both the UK Pro Surf Tour and the British National Longboarding Championships in sizzling 28° C July weather in Jersey. Skinner and Bleakley finished in 21st and 30th places respectively on the ASP World Longboard Tour. Britain's continued success in European longboarding shows how well suited the nation's playful beach breaks are for perfecting this art. Seeking to improve the wave quality on the less consistent south coast, construction of Europe's first artificial surf reef started at Boscombe, Bournemouth, and is set to open in September 2009.

In recognition of their enlightened environmental policy, newly formed St. Agnes outdoor surf and clothing company Finnistere won the Observer Ethical Business Award in the fashion category in June. A month later, Cornwall's Chris Hines was awarded the MBE for services to the environment. Chris was a founding member of the once-radical environmental action group Surfers Against Sewage (SAS) in 1990, and went on to pioneer the construction of a balsa-based "eco" board with Tris Cokes from Homeblown foam. Fusing surf and art, a recent auction called "Drawing Boards" raised £29,350 for *SAS*. Fourteen surfboards, made with biofoam at Laminations in St. Agnes, with artworks by luminaries such as Tracey Emin and Paul McCartney, were sold at Bonhams in London as part of the world-renowned Urban Art Auction. The UK's colorful surf heritage is beautifully documented in the recently completed book *The Surfing Tribe: A History of Surfing in Britain,* by Roger Mansfield, covering everything from Captain Cook to kook-cords and charismatic lifeguard surfers.

The age-old tension between surfers and lifeguards reared its ugly head this summer in Cornwall. Lifeguards at some beaches were having so much trouble enforcing the rules with local surfers sliding through the badly positioned swimming areas, they decided to ask for police help. In a ludicrous scheme, sensationalized by the national press, the Royal National Lifeboat Institution (RNLI), whicih runs the lifeguard service in the UK, is considering employing uniformed police officers on key beaches to arrest law breaking surfers next year!

CIRCUITO DE SURF B. SIDE ALGARVE
ALBUFEIRA, ALGARVE, PORTUGAL
January 12–13

Albufeira Algarve Portugal hosted the Circuito de Surf B. Side January 12 and 13. On the first day of competition, Leo Belime ruled the Open category, taking out main rival Miguel Mouzinho in the small but clean conditions. In the Sub 16s Goncalo Esteves nabbed the win with some stylish flair. Rain and onshore winds came up on the second day for the Sub 14 and Sub 12 divisions. Kathy Cardoso ousted Bruna Coelho to claim the Women's top spot.

OPEN MEN
1. Leo Belime
2. Melvin Lipke
3. Miguel Veterano
4. Kalu Oliveira

UNDER 16 BOYS
1. Gonçalo Esteves
2. João David
3. Tiago Silva
4. João Jóia

UNDER 14 BOYS
1. Basile Belime
2. Tiago Nunes
3. Gabriel Botelho
4. Federico Fêmea

UNDER 12 BOYS
1. Francisco Duarte
2. Tomás Alcobia
3. João Miguel
4. Manuel Kalu

OPEN WOMEN
1. Kathy Cardoso
2. Bruna Coelho
3. Francisca Coutinho
4. Inês Martins

CIRCUITO DE SURF B. SIDE ALGARVE • EVENT #2
PRAIA DE FARO, ALGARVE, PORTUGAL
February 9–10

Phase 2 of the Circuit de Surf B. Side drew 132 surfers to Praia de Faro in the Algarve. Conditions were small but clean and the groms flared. Outstanding performances also came from the Women's longboarders, who thrived in the peaks of Praia de Faro.

OPEN MEN
1. Alex Botelho
2. Nuno Corte Real
3. Manuel João
4. Paulo Almeida

MEN LONGBOARD
1. Miguel Cebola
2. Luís Esteves
3. Nuno Coelho
4. Paulo Rodrigues

UNDER 16 BOYS
1. Tiago Silva
2. João Jóia
3. Gabriel Botelho
4. Tiago Nunes

UNDER 14 BOYS
1. Frederico Fêmea
2. Tiago Nunes

3. Hugo Gonçalves
4. Miguel Costa

UNDER 12 BOYS
1. Tomás Alcobia
2. Francisco Duarte
3. José Mestre
4. Rafael Arnedo

OPEN WOMEN
1. Katy Cardoso
2. Bruna Coelho
3. Inês Martins
4. Alícia

VOLCOM LAVAFISH
PLAYA FAMARA, LANZAROTE
February 9–10

The fourth edition of the VQS Lavafish returned to Playa Famara Lanzarote. The two-day event was blessed with howling offshores and clean surf. Julian Cuello, aka "el Rey Misterio," took apart the reefbreak waves, marching over his opponents on his way to 1st place and taking out the Best Trick award for his air reverse—all of which was accomplished while donning one fierce-looking Mexican wrestling mask.

OPEN MEN
1. Julian Cuello
2. Franito
3. Manuel Lezcano
4. Damián Moro

GROMS
1. Javier Ascanio
2. Kai García
3. Luas Harman
4. Lucas Díaz

JUNIORS
1. Rubén González
2. Bentor González
3. Gary González
4. Manuel Sánchez

GIRLS
1. Davinia
2. Eider
3. Miriam
4. Carla

SOUTH TO SOUTH FROSTBITE SESSIONS
PORTREATH, CORNWALL UK
February 16

Josh Piper ruled the South to South Frostbite sessions held at Portreath by claiming the Under 18 division and nabbing 2nd place in the Un-

Josh Piper. Photo southtosouth.co.uk.

der 16 division. The frosty bite of winter Portreath air was tempered by the clean surf that attracted the area's most core surfers including 9-year-old Harry de Roth, from St. Ives.

UNDER 18 BOYS
1. Josh Piper
2. Rob Webster Blythe
3. Jack Whitefield
4. Bert Wright

UNDER 16 BOYS
1. Jack Whitefield
2. Josh Piper
3. Alex Piper
4. Seb Smart

IRISH SURFING INTERVARSITIES
LAHINCH, CO. CLARE, IRELAND
February 22–24

The NUI Galway Surf Club in association with the Irish Surfing Association (ISA) and Tubes Boardsports hosted the largest surf competition to date in Ireland. More than 250 competitors from 12 universities competed in heats run through difficult surf over two days. When all was said and done, John Burke of

Lost finalists. Photo Lucia Griggi.

Sligo IT took top honors.

OPEN MEN
1. Stephen Kilfeather
2. Eoin McCarthy Deering
3. Kevin Smith

MEN LONGBOARD
1. Aidan Byrne
2. Gareth Gargan
3. Stephen Kelleher

MEN BODYBOARD
1. Andrew Kilfeather
2. Ryan McEnroe
3. Aidan Kelly

BEGINNERS
1. John Burke
2. Brian O'Donnacha
3. Martin McAleese
4. Dan Breen
5. Elaine Tarrant
6. Stephen Keogh

OPEN WOMEN
1. Jessie Smith
2. Sophie Piggott
3. Claire Concannon

TEAM RESULTS
1. NUIG
2. SIT

NACIONAL DEEPLY SURF ESPERANÇAS
CRISMINA, CASCAIS, PORTUGAL
February 29–March 2

Blessed with good surf, the Nacional Deeply Surf Esperanças roared through three days of intense competition at Crismina Beach in Cascais. António Ribeiro and Vasco Ribeiro dominated the Boys divisions, while Margarida Guerra came up number one in the women's.

UNDER 18 BOYS
1. António Ribeiro
2. Vasco Ribeiro
3. José Ferreira
4. Pedro Pinto

UNDER 18 GIRLS
1. Margarida Guerra
2. Francisca Sousa
3. Carina Duarte
4. Ana Sarmento

UNDER 16 BOYS
1. José Ferreira
2. Francisco Alves
3. João Pereira
4. Rui Henriques

UNDER 14 BOYS
1. Vasco Ribeiro
2. Rui Henriques
3. Miguel Blanco
4. João Zenguito

UNDER 12 BOYS
1. Vasco Melo
2. Guilherme Fonseca
3. Tomás Fernandes
4. António Henriques

LOST SURF JAM TOUR
S. PEDRO DO ESTORIL, PORTUGAL
March 8–9

OPEN MEN
1. Fernando "Jó" Bento
2. Sérgio Silva
3. Miguel "Espanhol" Sanchez
4. Fernando Moreira
4. Alexandre "Xaninho" Ferreira
4. João Pelágio

UNDER 16 BOYS
1. Luís Eyre
2. Caetano Machado

GOANNA PRO TAPIA ASP WQS 1-STAR EVENT
TAPIA DE CASARIEGO ASTURIES, SPAIN
March 20–22

Marcos San Segundo, 19, clinched his first-ever ASP WQS win in testing, stormy surf at Tapia de Casariego in Spain. San Segundo, from Zarautz in the Basque Country, surfed only four waves in the thirty-minute decider but posted the highest wave score of the final with a 7.17. On his way to the win, San Segundo defeated rival and former ASP European Pro Surf Tour #2–rated Pablo Solar of Spain.

OPEN MEN
1. Marcos San Segundo
2. Simon Marchand
3. Edgar Nozes
4. Pablo Solar

NORTHCORE EAST COAST DRIFT
SCARBOROUGH'S SOUTH BAY
March 23

Snow welcomed the Northcore East Coast Drift surf competition on Easter morning as some areas of the UK East Coast received over 4 inches of the white stuff. Thirty-five competitors battled throughout the event which culminated in a backwash-marred final claimed by none other than James Kirk.

JUNIORS
James Kirk

VETERANS
Ian Kirk

GROMS
Mark Dickinson

CAMPEONATO BODY-BOARD ODECEIXE
ODECEIXE BEACH, PORTUGAL
March 21–22

OPEN MEN
1. Hugo Nunes
2. João Barciela "Jofi"
3. Francisco Pinheiro
4. João Pinheiro

OPEN WOMEN
1. Joana Schenker
2. Teresa Duarte
3. Maria Lourenço

BIARRITZ QUIKSILVER MAIDER AROSTEGUY
LA GRANDE PLAGE DE BIARRITZ, FRANCE
March 29–30

The Biarritz Maider Arosteguy drew hundreds of competitors to La Grand Plage de Biarritz. This year Vincent Duvignac bested rising star Joan Duru with some big moves and solid scoring throughout the final held in stormy surf. Supergirl Pauline Ado tromped the competition on the women's side to take 1st place, while Holy Barth took the top spot in the groms.

ROXY ONDINES CHALLENGE
1. Pauline Ado
2. Mary Dejean

Marcos San Segundo. Photo Aquashot/Aspeurope.com.

3. Justine Dupont
4. Annabelle Talouarn
OPEN MEN
1. Vincent Duvignac
2. Joan Duru
3. Abdel El Harim
4. Tristan Guilbaut
GROMS
1. Holy Barth
2. Dimitri Opens
3. Othmane Choufani
4. Antoine Servary

3RD ETAPA DO CIRCUITO DE SURF B. SIDE ALGARVE
PRAIA DE ROCHA ALGARVE, PORTUGAL
March 29–30

The third stage of the Circuito de Surf B hit Praia de Rocha with Marlon and Melvin Lipke battling it out for 1st and 2nd place in the Open division. When the spray had cleared, it was Marlon who got the nod. In the Women's, Katy Cardoso lit up the small, bumpy conditions to win, doing Clube Naval de Portimão proud in the process.

OPEN MEN
1. Marlon Lipke
2. Melvin Lipke
3. Gustavo Gouveia
4. Paulo Almeida
UNDER 16 BOYS
1. João David
2. Basile Belime
3. Tiago Silva
4. Yuri Wenting
UNDER 14 BOYS
1. Basile Belime
2. Frederico Fêmea
3. Tiago Nunes
4. Francisco Neves
UNDER 12 BOYS
1. Tomás Alcobia
2. Francisco Duarte
3. José Mestre
4. Pedro Reigoto
OPEN WOMEN
1. Katy Cardoso
2. Francisca Coutinho
3. Bruna Coelho
4. Ines Diogo – Playsurf/A.C.R.Alvor

VOLCOM RUMBLEFISH
CARCAVELOS, PORTUGAL
March 22–23

Hugo Zagalo nailed the Open division win at the Volcom Rumblefish in Carcavelos. As with most Volcom events, the real excitement came from the frothing groms competing to win prizes, in this case a free surfboard. The first kid to run to the water and swim in his clothes to the outside would receive a brand-new hand-painted surfboard from Polen surfboards. The fastest grom on the block this day was Pedro Correia.

OPEN MEN
1. Hugo Zagalo
2. Kalu Oliveira
3. Francisco Lima
4. Filipe Fernandes
5. Paulo Almeida
6. Miguel Mouzinho
JUNIORS
1. Luís Eyre
2. Francisco Sousa
3. Diogo Appleton
4. Henrique Rosa
GROMS
1. Rui Henriques
2. João Abreu
3. Guilherme Fonseca
4. António Henriques
GIRLS
1. Carolina Guerreiro
2. Maria Gonçalves
3. Mariana Figueiredo
4. Sónia Pires

THE SALTROCK OPEN
CROYDE BEACH, NORTH DEVON
April 12–13

Rough surf, strong winds and swift currents kicked off the UK Pro Surf Tour's 2008 debut event at Croyde. Last year's Saltrock Open winner Sam Lamiroy advanced confidently through the event until the semifinal, where he lost out in the tricky conditions. Another favorite, Alan Stokes looked good until he was tagged with an interference in his semifinal leaving Mark Harris and Matt Capel to battle it out in the final, where Harris triumphed.

OPEN MEN
1. Mark Harris
2. Matt Capel
3. Joss Ash
4. Johnny Fryer
PRO JUNIOR
1. Reubyn Ash
2. Tom Butler
3. Toby Donachie
4. Josh Piper
OPEN WOMEN
1. Nicole Morgan
2. Sarah Bentley
3. Jenny Horbas
4. Hanabeth Luke
UNDER 16 GIRLS
1. Zoe Sheath
2. Lucy Campbell
3. Harriet Knight
4. Jemima Knight

CREVETTES TOUR
CAPBRETON, FRANCE
April 12

Capbreton Surf Club hosted the only-14-and-under Crevettes Tour. Groms from all over Les Landes converged on the small Springtime Capbreton surf, with Théo Ribot winning the Under 10 event, Nelson Cloarec claiming the Under 12s and veteran Tom Cloarec coming out on top in the Under 14 division. Malissa Pichaud won the Girls.

UNDER 14 BOYS
1. Cloarec Tom
2. Distinguin Paul César
3. Le Barbier Léo
4. Lojou Emilien
UNDER 12 BOYS
1. Cloarec Nelson
2. Guilhemsang François
3. Trehet Victor
4. Poupinel Louis
UNDER 10 BOYS
1. Théo Ribot Soustons
2. Jonas Bachar Hossegor
3. Mattia Poirier, Capbreton
4. Louis Lambert Capbreton
GIRLS
1. Pichaud Malissa
2. Delhay Lison
3. Vaudin Maylis

THE WILKINSON SWORD WELSH INTER-CLUB CHAMPS
REST BAY, PORTHCAWL
April 12

The Welsh Coast Surf Club hosted the Wilkinson Sword Welsh Inter-club Champs in mediocre surf at Rest Bay. After a full day of heats it was Channel Coast's Club captain Mark Vaughan who stepped up to take the prized Wilkinson Sword trophy. Vaughan gave thanks to Bob and Anne Webster-Blyth, Stuart Bentley and Jamie Bateman, who'd worked hard to reinstate this popular all-Wales event.

1. Channel Coast Surf Club
2. Welsh Coast Surf Club
3. Langland Surf Division

VENDEE PRO • ASP 4-STAR MEN'S WQS
BRÉTIGNOLLES SUR MER, FRANCE
April 15–20

Romain Laulhe won his maiden WQS event in the shifty reef peaks

Romain Laulhe. Photo Aquashot/Aspeurope.com.

of La Sauzaie. This, the tenth WQS event of the year, saw surfers from all over the globe gunning for the 4-star rating points. Throughout the event Laulhe built his momentum, finally posting a solid 15.33 point heat tally to best Luke Campbell's 14.33 score in the final.

MEN FINAL
1. Romain Laulhe
2. Luke Campbell
SEMIFINAL 1
1. Luke Campbell
2. Blake Wilson
SEMIFINAL 2
1. Romain Laulhe
2. Eric Rebiere
QUARTERFINAL 1
1. Luke Campbell
2. Justin Mc Bride
QUARTERFINAL 2
1. Blake Wilson
2. Arthur Bourbon
QUARTERFINAL 3
1. Romain Laulhe
2. Hugo Savalli
QUARTERFINAL 4
1. Eric Rebiere
2. Jean Sebastien Estienne

DENNY IRISH NAT. SURFING CHAMPS
TULLAN STRAND, IRELAND
April 19

A hard-fought final between Liam Joyce and Cain Kilcullen in deteriorating conditions at Tullen Strand found Joyce dominating most of the final while his three adversaries scratched for a score worth keeping. In the dying seconds, Cain Kilcullen took off on a small wave, ripping it all the way to the beach and securing the highest score of the final and thus the win.

OPEN MEN
1. Cain Kilcullen
2. Liam Joyce
3. Fergal Smith
4. David Blount
MEN LONGBOARD
1. John Mc Curry
2. Aidan Byrne
3. Howard Robinson
4. Emmet O'Doherty
MEN BODYBOARD
1. Paul Mc Carter
2. Shane Meehan
3. Darragh Mc Carter
4. Martin Kelly
OPEN WOMEN
1. Easkey Britton
2. Nicole Morgan
3. Amy May Garvey
4. Tahlia Britton

RIP CURL PRO JÚNIOR SURF AND MUSIC FESTIVAL • ASP 3-STAR MEN'S PRO JUNIOR EVENT
BALEAL, SUPERTUBOS, PORTUGAL
April 24–27

Hossegor's Marc Iacomare took out Medi Veminardi of Reunion Island at this 3-star Men's ASP Junior event presented by Renault. Lacomare, no stranger to heaving beach-breaks, kicked off with an 8.83 point ride and posted a solid 15.00 point heat total in the final. With the win, Lacomare takes the lead in the ASP Junior Europe ratings.

MEN FINAL
1. Marc Lacomare
2. Medi Veminardi
SEMIFINAL 1
1. Marc Lacomare
2. Toyon
SEMIFINAL 2
1. Midi Veminardi
2. Maxime Huscenot

O'NEILL HIGHLAND OPEN • ASP WQS 6-STAR MEN'S EVENT
THURSO, SCOTLAND
April 22–30

Possibly the coldest event on the ASP schedule, the O'Neill Highland Open presented by Swatch drew the top WQS campaigners to the breaks of Thurso. Hawaiian Sunny Garcia signaled his World Tour bid by marching through to the quarters but came up short. In the final Aussie Adam Robertson threaded the ledgy reef tubes to take the win from Adam Melling.

MEN FINAL
1. Adam Robertson
2. Adam Melling
SEMIFINAL 1
1. Adam Robertson
2. David Weare
SEMIFINAL 2
1. Adam Melling
2. Hugo Savalli (REU)
QUARTERFINAL 1
1. Adam Robertson
2. Matt Wilkinson
QUARTERFINAL 2
1. David Weare
2. Yadin Nicol
QUARTERFINAL 3
1. Hugo Savalli (REU)
2. Michel Bourez (PYF)
QUARTERFINAL 4
1. Adam Melling
2. Sunny Garcia

Sunny Garcia. Photo Aquashot/Aspeurope.com.

HUNTER/BILLABONG BRITISH SCHOOLS SURFING CHAMPS
WOOLACOMBE, NORTH DEVON
April 27–27

The British Surfing Association's school champs lit up Devon as more than 200 competitors descended on Woolacombe to take advantage of the clean surf. At event's end, it was Tretherras who triumphed over Bruanton, thus claiming bragging rights and the cup for another year.

UNDER 18 BOYS BODYBOARD
1. Bertie Thompson
2. Nat McAbe
3. Liam Bentley
4. Ollie Arden
UNDER 16 BOYS BODYBOARD
1. Bertie Thompson
2. Jacob Sharp
3. Ollie Arden
4. Liam Bentley
GIRLS BODYBOARD
1. Tamsin Dillon
2. Sophie Good
BOY'S LONGBOARD
1. Karma Worthington
2. Zack Lawton
3. Harry Bennett
4. Zack Broad
UNDER 18 BOYS
1. Matt Burner
2. Jack Whitefield
3. Tom Bentley
4. Haydn Duck
UNDER 16 BOYS
1. George Picking
2. Max Tucker
3. Robert Merchant Greenslade
4. Jack Ellis
UNDER 14 BOYS
1. Miles Lee Hargreaves
2. Ryan Roberts
3. Paddy Daniel
4. Tassy Swallow
OPEN GIRLS
1. Holly Donnelly
2. Karma Worthington
3. Kathleen Spears
4. Tassy Swallow
OVERALL SCHOOLS WINNER 2008
1. Tretherras A team 61 points
2. Braunton 36 points

3. Bournemouth 33 points
4. Kingsbridge and Ivybridge 32 points

CIRCUITO EL DIARIO VASCO DE SURF 2008
BARINATXEN, BASQUE COUNTRY
May 1–2

More than 96 entrants signed up for the latest EHSF event in the Circuito El Diario Vasco de Surf. The contest was held in fun Spanish beachbreak, where Txaber Trojaola claimed a couple airs and the win.

OPEN B
1. Asier Ibáñez
2. Mario Azurza
3. Gorka Yarritu
4. Iñigo Idigoras
OPEN A
1. Txaber Trojaola
2. Marcos San Segundo
3. Ander Hederá
4. Jatyr Berasaluze

4TH ETAPA DO CIRCUITO DE SURF B. SIDE ALGARVE 2008
PRAIA DO AMADO, PORTUGAL
May 10–11

The fourth event of the Circuito de Surf B. Side saw Marlon Lipke take out yet another win in the Algarve surf. Marlon found time to compete in this non-ASP-rated event despite chasing a World Tour slot.

OPEN MEN
1. Marlon Lipke
2. Miguel Mouzinho
3. Luca Guichard
4. Tiago Silva
UNDER 16 BOYS
1. Basile Belime
2. Gonçalo Esteves
3. João David
4. Gabriel Botelho
UNDER 14 BOYS
1. Basile Belime
2. Tiago Nunes
3. Frederico Femia
4. Luis Vale
5. Hugo Gonçalves

Matt Burner. Photo Phil Williams.

UNDER 12 BOYS
1. Francisco Duarte
2. Martim Magalhães
3. Martim Gregório
4. Francisco Gregorio
OPEN GIRLS
1. Kathy Cardoso
2. Francisca Coutinho
3. Alicia Wiese
4. Marina

BUDE SURF CLASSIC
WIDEMOUTH BAY, NORTH CORNWALL
May 10–11

Small surf eked its way through severe tidal swings at Widemouth Bay throughout the day for this Christian Surfers UK event. After several stops and starts, the event was miraculously completed in the dying light as the last final ended at 9 pm. Rising star Joss Ash took the Men's Open.

OPEN MEN
1. Joss Ash
2. Jack Butler
3. Matt Burner
4. Simon Daly
OPEN MEN LONGBOARD
1. Dan Harris
2. Nico Keruzec
3. James Parry
4. Ben Howarth
MEN BODYBOARD
1. Phil Milson
2. Kevin Drew
3. Kris Inch
4. Matthew Budd
JUNIOR BOYS
1. Jack Butler
2. Matt Burner
3. Sam Scoble
4. Haydn Duck
OPEN WOMEN
1. Katie Block
2. Pippa Renyard
3. Jaimi Davie
4. Emily Crocker

RIP CURL GROMSEARCH PERRANPORTH
CORNWALL
May 10–11

More than 100 competitors of all ages, some as young as 8 years old, turned up to compete in small but

perfect waves at Perranporth Beach in Cornwall. Standouts included super sprite Lucy Campbell and mega mouse Will Bailey.

UNDER 16 BOYS
1. Luke Dillon
2. Seb Smart
3. Christian Jackson
4. Tom Good
UNDER 16 GIRLS
1. Megan Burns
2. Daisy Docking
3. Zoe Sheath
4. Gabi Rowe
UNDER 14 BOYS
1. Luke Dillon
2. Jack Hough
3. Harry Timson
4. Miles Lee-Hargraves
UNDER 14 GIRLS
1. Lucy Campbell
2. Masie Lawton
3. Laura Crane
4. Sophie Sainsbury
UNDER 12 BOYS
1. Will Bailey
2. Ed Smith
3. Harry De Roth
4. Dale Foster 4
UNDER 12 GIRLS
1. Flora Lawton
2. Peony Knight
3. Sophie Good
4. Tamsin Dillon 4

QUIKSILVER WELSH NATIONALS
FRESHWATER WEST, WALES
May 3–4

The Quiksilver Welsh Nationals ran off in perfect conditions over the May Day bank holiday weekend. With Swansea's Lloyd Cole taking the Open title for the second time and Pembrokeshire's Joanne Dennison successfully defending her Women's crown for a third successive time.

OPEN MEN
1. Lloyd Cole
2. Greg Owen
3. Harry Cromwell
4. Gareth Vaughan
MEN BODYBOARD
1. Mark Griffiths
2. Tom Hammett
MEN LONGBOARD
1. Elliot Dudley
2. Dan Harris

3. Chris Griffiths
4. Evan Rogers

UNDER 18 BOYS
1. Thomas Padden
2. Max Tucker
3. Tom Good
4. Tom Bentley

UNDER 18 BOYS LONGBOARD
1. Huw Bentley
2. Evan Rogers
3. Thomas Padden
4. Connor Griffiths
5. Arran Bright

UNDER 18 GIRLS
1. Hannah Griffiths
2. Mali James
3. Patsy Poutney

UNDER 16 BOYS
1. Tom Good
2. Jack Hughes

Pearce nabbed 3rd and 4th respectively.

OPEN MEN
1. Tom Butler
2. Oli Adams
3. Matt Capel
4. Reubin Pearce

MEN LONGBOARD
1 Ben Howarth
2. Ben Howey
3. James Parry
4. Ben Byfield

MEN KNEEBOARD
1. Richard Smith
2. Karl Ward
3. Richard Hewitt
4. Duncan Jones

MASTERS KNEEBOARD (OVER 35)
1. Richard Hewitt

4. Leon Mansfield

CADET BODYBOARD (UNDER 16 BOYS)
1. Luke Brabyn

YOUTH (UNDER 14 BOYS)
1. Luke Dillon
2. Liam Turner
3. Harry Timson
4. Sam Harwood

YOUTH BODYBOARD (UNDER 14 BOYS)
1. Sam Brabyn
2. Joe Logg
3. Ed Hone
4. Ed Shurlock

GROM (UNDER 12 BOYS)
1. Ed Smith
2. Dale Foster
3. Will Bailey
4. Harry DeRoth

SENIOR (OVER 28)
1. Lee Bartlett

Les Cavaliers, in Anglet, with Aussie Harley Ingleby edging out French rising star Antoine Delpero for the win. Ingleby, 24, defeated reigning ASP World Longboard Champion Phil Rajzman of Brazil in the semifinals and took the 35-minute final with a solid 16.65 point heat tally, besting Delpero's 14.50 point score. "I am the happiest kid in the world right now," said Ingleby. "I had a very testing semifinal against Phil and that win gave me a lot of confidence for the final. I found the better waves against Antoine (Delpero) and it ended up just perfectly for me in the final." Delpero beat Bonga Perkins in semifinal No. 2 with an impressive 18.25 point heat score.

FINAL
1. Harley Ingleby
2. Antoine Delpero

SEMIFINAL 1
1. Harley Ingleby
2. Phil Rajzman

SEMIFINAL 2
1. Antoine Delpero
2. Bonga Perkins

QUARTERFINAL 1
1. Harley Ingleby
2. Carlos Bahia

QUARTERFINAL 2
1. Phil Rajzman
2. Matthew Moir

QUARTERFINAL 3
1. Antoine Delpero
2. Amaro Matos

QUARTERFINAL 4
1. Bonga Perkins
2. Colin McPhillips

3. Robin Leraen
4. Yann Bole

UNDER 14 BOYS
1. Luc Herbert
2. Thomas Milochau
3. Louis Darnaud
4. Charles Macky

UNDER 12 BOYS
1. Antoine Aubry
2. Robin Roche
3. Maxime Gaborit
4. Eliot Marival

UNDER 10 BOYS
1. Augustin Amiré
2. Hugo Robin
3. Samuel Boucard
4. Roain Caiveau

GIRLS
1. Lucie Milochau
2. NolwenSugrault
3. Sophie Merceron
4. Justine Caiveau

THE O'NEILL MISSION
FRENCH COAST FROM BIARRITZ TO BRITTANY
May 17–25

When the third edition of the O'Neill Mission took to France, it was faced with a severe shortage of waves. Armed with a caravan of RVs chasing any sign of swell up and down the French coast, the event made the most of a lackluster week of surf. Julian Wilson won the event with his self-edited video of the week's highlights. Wilson's segment included many aerials, 360s, and some lively new-school rap. Julian was voted

Watergate Bay, Day 1 action. Photo Jason Feast.

3. Max Tucker
4. Rhys Alexander

UNDER 14 BOYS
1. David Williams
2. William Sharp
3. Daniel Bresnan
4. Connor Griffiths

UNDER 12 BOYS
1. William Sharp
2. Raife Gaskell
3. Arran Bright
4. Cara Gaskell

SENIORS
1. Mark Vaughan
2. Chris Griffiths
3. Craig Burrows
4. Andrew James

MASTERS
1. Simon Tucker
2. Nick Bresnan
3. Chris Griffiths
4. Rob Poutney

OPEN WOMEN
1. Joanne Dennison
2. Beth Mason
3. Renee Godfrey
4. Breige Lawrence

2. Nick Barkham
3. Richard Smith
4. Jodie Winter

MEN STAND UP PADDLE SURF
1. Adam Zervas
2. Tim Mellors
3. John Hibbard
4. Lewis Timson

MEN BODYBOARD
1. Darren Halse
2. Damien Prisk
3. Jack Johns
4. P Milson

MEN DROP-KNEE BODYBOARD
1. Darren Halse
2. Brad Hut
3. Ollie Meddlam
4. Aiden Salmon

JUNIOR (UNDER 18 BOYS)
1. Lewis Clinton, Newquay
2. Lyndon Wake, N Devon, Croyde
3. Aaron Evans, Newquay
4. Matt Burner, Kingsbridge

JUNIOR LONGBOARD (UNDER 18 BOYS)
1. Zak Lawton, Croyde
2. Callum Clark
3. Ben Sowter, Newquay
4. Trev Garland, St Ives

JUNIOR BODYBOARD (UNDER 18 BOYS)
1. Luke Brabyn
2. Alex Wake
3. Joe Hone
4. Charlie Strang

UNDER 18 GIRLS
1. Kathleen Spears, Croyde
2. Lucy Campbell, Woolacombe
3. Holly Donnelly, Newquay
4. Karma Worthington, Croyde

CADET (UNDER 16 BOYS)
1. Luis Eyre, Ericeira, Portugal.
2. George Picking, Newquay.
3. Josh Piper

2. Eugene Tollemache
3. Chris Harris
4. Roger Knight

MASTERS (OVER 35)
1. Lee Bartlett
2. Chris Harris
3. Callum Mole
4. Jed Stone

VETERANS (OVER 45)
1. Jed Stone
2. Cliff Cox
3. Les Clinton
4. Phil Williams

OPEN WOMEN
1. Holly Donnelly
2. Sophie Hellyer
3. Nicola Bunt
4. Karma Worthington

WOMEN LONGBOARD
1. Candice O'Donnell
2. Sophie Skinner
3. Becky Stanhope
4. Kathryn Mepeoth

WOMEN KNEEBOARD
1. Jodie Winter (uncontested)

WOMEN BODYBOARD
1. Jemma Knight
2. Clemi Hardy
3. Harriet Knight
4. Maisie Lawton

Julian Wilson. Photo O'Neill.

MOSKITO TOUR SABLES D'OLONNE
LES SABLES D'OLONNE, FRANCE
May 17–18

Electric's ever-popular Moskito Tour stoked groms at La Tranchet. Gnarly gnat Augustin Amiré claimed the Under 10 division with his bag of tricks, while Antione Aubry took the Under 12 section. But the biggest star was Luc Herbert, who claimed the Under 14s with his smooth style and big ollies.

UNDER 16 BOYS
1. Samuel Guillet
2. Adrien Amivé

the winner by his fellow surfers, including the likes of Cory Lopez, Tim Boal, Jarrad Howse and Michel Bourez. "I'm so blown away right now," Julian said. "It's been such a good week. We have made the best out of all the conditions we faced in France."

RIP CURL GROMSEARCH, TARNOS
LA PLAGE DU "MÉTRO," TARNOS, FRANCE
June 8

For eleven and a half hours, the Rip Curl GromSearch Tarnos took full advantage of the near-solstice daylight, attracting young surfers from

HEADWORX ENGLISH NATIONALS
WATERGATE BAY, NEWQUAY UK
May 3–5

Surfers from Newquay claimed more than 10 of the 23 titles on offer at the Headworx English Nationals. Winning the prestigious Open division was 19-year-old Tom Butler, with defending champion Oli Adams taking 2nd. Headworx team riders Matt Capel and Reubin

OXBOW WLT, PRESENTED BY ORANGE • ASP WORLD LONGBOARD TOUR EVENT #1
LES CAVALIERS, ANGLET, FRANCE
May 5–11

The longboard event of the year went down in 2- to 3-foot surf at

around the Basque Coast. Ramzi Boukhiam and Joana Giansanti shined in the Under 16 divisions in the fun, waist-high surf.

UNDER 16 BOYS
1. Ramzi Boukhiam
2. Pierre Rollet
UNDER 16 GIRLS
1. Joana Giansanti
2. Marie Mitsuko Bochaton
UNDER 14 BOYS
1. Andy Crière
2. Adrian Belascain
UNDER 12 BOYS
1. Louis Fears
2. Alex Comet
UNDER 12 GIRLS
1. Delia Delanne
2. Nahia Giansanti

VOLCOM STONE'S SIDFISH
PORTHTOWAN, CORNWALL
June 7

This first event of the VQS European tour kicked off in heavy Cornish tides at Porthtowan with the Juniors division scoring the best window for waves. Lewis Clinton found the right ones and edged out Josh Pipes to take the Sidfish Junior crown, while Joss Ash made it past Shaun Skilton to claim the Open division. Oh, yes, and everyone dressed up like pirates.

OPEN MEN
1. Joss Ash
2. Shaun Skilton
3. Jack Clinton
4. Luke Patterson
GROMS
1. Harry Timson
2. Tom Good
3. Sam Hardwood
4. Max Tucker
5. Joss Brooks
6. Jack Hough
JUNIORS
1. Lewis Clinton
2. Josh Pipes
3. Zak Lanwton
4. Ben Sowter
5. Morgham Clinton
6. Veremy Bunt
GIRLS
1. Lauren Ringer
2. Emily Anderson
3. Holy Mather
4. Melissa Reid

RIP CURL GROM-SEARCH, LAHINCH
LAHINCH CO CLARE, IRELAND
June 14–15

The third leg of the UK & Ireland GromSearch series was held in small but perfect waves at Lahinch Co. Clare, Ireland, with more than 50 of the country's best Groms in attendance. This was the sixth annual GromSearch event on the Emerald Isle—the third and final qualifying event in the UK and Ireland series.

UNDER 16 BOYS
1. Cillian Ryan

2. Conor McGuire
3. James Garvey
4. Aaron Reid
UNDER 16 GIRLS
1. Niamh Kelly
2. Ayesha Garvey
UNDER 14 BOYS
1. Gearoid McDaid
2. Iaram Madden
3. Donagh Cronin
4. Gareth Morrisey
UNDER 12 BOYS
1. Aaron O Hare
2. Gearoid McDaid
3. Peter Moody
4. Mathew Crowe

'60S STYLE MASTERS
SAUNTON SANDS, DEVON
June 7–8

The contest is the only one of its kind in Britain and it has a strong following from the old-school set. And no wonder, it's a no-leash event sans seeding—all the names are thrown in a hat and then drawn out lottery style, just like in the days before electronic scoring. Shaun Marlow was the standout in the Masters division and cruised into 1st place over the evergreen Eric Davies. But the most impressive surfers of the day were James Parry and Sam Bleakley, both from Sennen and both masters of the true-grit style of longboarding.

OPEN MEN
1. James Parry
2. Sam Bleakly
3. Ben Haworth
4. Elliot Dudley
MASTERS
1. Shaun Marlow
2. Richard Emerson
3. Eric Davies
4. Minnow Green

SUPERJUNIOR 2008
LA ZURRIOLA, DONOSTIA
June 21–22

UNDER 18 BOYS:
1. Asier Makeda
2. Mitxel Lopez
3. Gorka Biggi
4. Jon Mentxaka
UNDER 16 BOYS:
1. Marcelino Botin
2. Alex Iriondo
3. Imanol Yeregi
4. Natxo Gonzalez
SUPER JUNIOR
1. Juan Merodio
2. Asier Makeda
3. Borja Agote

FAT FACE NIGHT SURF 2008 • UK PRO SURF TOUR (UK PST)
LUSTY GLAZE, NEWQUAY
June 27–29

Nick White from New Zealand claimed the Fat Face Night Surf in spectacular style, emerging from water's edge to the applause of thousands of party-minded specta-

tors at Lusty Glaze Beach. It was a truly international podium for the second stop of the UKPSA Tour, with Reuben Pearce from South Africa taking 2nd place, local lad and two time winner Alan Stokes taking 3rd and Australian-born but UK-based Matt Capel beating 150 other competitors to claim 4th place.

OPEN MEN
1. Nick White
2. Rueben Pearce
3. Alan Stokes
4. Matt Capel
MEN LONGBOARD
1. Ben Skinner
2. Sam Bleakley
3. Dan Harris
4. James Parry
OPEN WOMEN
1. Nicole Morgan
2. Natasha Bastenie
3. Jo Dennison
4. Jenny Horbas

LES BILLABONG TETARDS
COTE DE BASQUES, BIARRITZ, FRANCE
July 19–20

Held at La Côte des Basques, the Billabong Têtard comps celebrate the grommiest of groms, those rippers under the age of 14. This year's event went off in small surf, with Victor Mur claiming the top Têtard spot (ages 5–8) while Louis Fears won out in the Benjamins (ages 12–14) and Marion Bouzigues claimed the Ondines section.

TÊTARDS
Victor Mur
POUSSINS
Leo Paul Etienne
BENJAMINS
Louis Fears
MINIMES
Andy Crière
MINI-ONDINES
Délia Delanne
ONDINES
Marion Bouzigues

OXBOW KIDS WEEK SURF TOUR
ANGLET, FRANCE
July 22

More than 80 kids showed off their mad skills during the Oxbow Kids Week in Anglet, but it was uber-grom Louis Fears who shined brightest, claiming the Waterman title at Anglet's Plage de Marinella.

UNDER 16 BOYS
1. Josu Alcantra
2. Quentin Plouvier
3. Guillaumme Lozé
4. Romain Petit
UNDER 14 BOYS
1. Pierre Rollet
2. Andy Criere
3. Martin Coret
4. Leo Edmont
UNDER 12 BOYS
1. Louis Fears

2. Charly Termeau
3. Fran Previtera
4. Alex Comet
GIRLS
1. Josephine Costes
2. Marion Bouziques
3. Delia Delanne
4. Alaia Peres

VANS PRO JUNIOR • GRADE 1 MEN'S ASP JUNIOR EVENT
SAN SEBASTIAN, BASQUE COUNTRY
July 24–27

In small but consistent surf, France's rising star Marc Lacomare took the Vans Pro Junior title in a runaway final that found most of his competitors combo-ed by the time the final horn blew. This was Lacomare's second major win in a year full of promise for the young man from Hossegor. "I missed out on my qualification for the ASP World Junior Championships at Narabeen by one spot last year," Lacomare said. "With this win, I am on for the regional title and am already looking forward to the next event in Tenerife."

Côte des Basques. Photo YvesS.

FINAL
1. Marc Lacomare
2. Adrien Toyon
3. PV Laborde
4. Reubyn Ash
SEMIFINAL 1
1. Marc Lacomare
2. PV Laborde
3. Maxime Huscenot
4. Yann Martin
SEMIFINAL 2
1. Reubyn Ash
2. Adrien Toyon
3. Jatyr Berasaluce
4. Hugo Palmarini
QUARTERFINAL 1
1. Maxime Huscenot
2. Yann Martin
3. Lewis St John
4. Filipe Jervis
QUARTERFINAL 2
1. Marc Lacomare
2. PV Laborde
3. Damien Chaudoy
4. David Leboulsh
QUARTERFINAL 3
1. Hugo Palmarini
2. Jatyr Berasaluce
3. Edouard Delpero
4. Ramzi Boukiam
QUARTERFINAL 4
1. Adrien Toyon
2. Reubyn Ash
3. Kevin Bourez
4. Rudy Marechal

BRITISH NATIONAL LONGBOARDING CHAMPS, BRITISH SURFING ASSOCIATION
JERSEY, CHANNEL ISLANDS UK
July 26–27

Ben Skinner again triumphed at the British National Longboarding Championships in Jersey by claiming his fifth British title, this time on the island of Jersey. The weekend threw up a mixed bag of conditions with small onshore waves for Friday and Saturday but building to clean 3-foot waves and a stunning high of 28 degrees on Sunday.

OPEN MEN
1. Ben Skinner
2. Sam Bleakley
3. James Parry
4. Elliot Dudley
JUNIOR
1. Evan Rogers
2. Will Glenn
3. Matt Travis
4. Mike Iay

SENIORS
1. Sam Bleakley
2. Andre le Geyt
3. Ben Chapmen
4. Vic Danks
MASTERS
1. Andre Le Geyt
2. Pete Journeux
3. Eric Davies
4. Paul Gautron
VETERANS
1. Eric Davies
2. Jem Oxenden
3. Gary Rogers
4. Minnow Green

BILLABONG GIRLS CASCAIS FESTIVAL • ASP 6-STAR WQS WOMEN'S EVENT
CASCAIS, PORTUGAL
July 31–August 3

Brazilian dynamo Jacqueline Silva clinched the 6-star Billabong Girls Cascais Festival held in solid 5- to 6-foot (1.5- to 2-meter) waves at Guincho Beach in Portugal. Consistency won it for Silva, who out-pointed Women's World Tour campaigner Rebecca Woods in an epic 40-minute final. Silva posted several excellent scores throughout the two-day competition, including a 9.50 point ride and an impressive 17.00 point heat tally—respectively the best wave and second-best heat result of the event. "I had not won an event since Newquay in 2007 and I gave everything I had to get this one despite the massive conditions," said Silva.

FINAL
1. Jacqueline Silva
2. Rebecca Woods
SEMIFINAL 1
1. Jacqueline Silva
2. Airini Mason
SEMIFINAL 2
1. Rebecca Woods
2. Jessi Miley-Dyer
QUARTERFINAL 1
1. Jacqueline Silva
2. Laurina MacGrath
QUARTERFINAL 2
1. Airini Mason
2. Karina Petroni
QUARTERFINAL 3
1. Rebecca Woods
2. Rosanne Hodge

Alizée Arnaud. Photo Aquashot/Aspeurope.com.

QUARTERFINAL 4
1. Jessi Miley-Dyer
2. Alana Blanchard

EUROPEAN LONGBOARD TOUR, EVENT 1 • JLRA & ESF EUROPEAN LONGBOARD

WATERSPLASH ST. OUEN, JERSEY
July 26–27

Perfect longboarding surf reeled off in front of a huge crowd as Remy Arauzo built momentum through the 35-minute final against Antoine Delpero and company. Nearing the final horn Delpero was leading, but in the dying seconds a set approached, and a paddle battle ensued between Arauzo and Delpero. It was Delpero who fought his way onto the first set wave. However, he fell on a critical turn, and Arauzo grabbed the next wave, an 8.73 and the win.

FINAL
1. Remy Arauzo
2. Antoine Delpero
3. Timothee Creignou
4. James Parry

QUIKSILVER KING OF THE GROMS, PRESENTED BY ORANGE • EUROPEAN FINAL

SANTOCHA, CAPBRETON, FRANCE
July 30–August 3

Sometimes it all comes down to one good wave. Spanish battler Vicente Romero was crowned European King of the Groms after nabbing a solid 4-foot (1.5-meter) left, which he tore up with three giant off-the-lips and punctuated with a mini air. When added to his 13.17 heat score, it was enough for the win. "I am happy for me and for Spain," said Romero. "We won in cycling and in football. It was a wonderful final and I'm really looking forward to surfing against the top 16 in the world. I'm excited to surf alongside Kelly Slater and Mick Fanning." Romero capped off his speech with a "Merci a todos!"

FINAL
1. Vicente Romero
2. Dimitri Ouvré
3. Marc Audo
4. Toby Donachie

ISLAND STYLE PRO JUNIOR • GRADE 2 MEN'S ASP JUNIOR EVENT / GRADE 1 WOMEN'S ASP JUNIOR EVENT

SOPELANA, BASQUE COUNTRY
July 31–August 2

With major ratings points up for grabs in the regional title race, competition cranked up a notch in the quiets of the Basque Country. Medi Veminardi of Reunion Island took the men's title after defeating local Basque surfer Jatyr Berasaluce in the last minute of the final with a 7.5. The ASP Grade-1 Nikita Women's Pro Junior saw Alizee Arnaud secure her first win this season after defeating Johanne Defay, Ravi Bailleux and Fanny Brice in an all-French final. Arnaud, who was injured for

a couple of months this year, put on an exceptional performance in the final, posting an impressive 19.20 point heat tally to clinch the crown and move up in the ratings. "I had a great time in the final with the girls who are my friends," Arnaud said. "I felt good and relaxed during this event and I am stoked to get such high scores. All went my way."

MEN FINAL
1. Medi Veminardi
2. Jatyr Berasaluce
SEMIFINAL 1
1. Medi Veminardi
2. Thomas Fok Cheong
SEMIFINAL 2
1. Jatyr Berasaluce
2. Pierre Valentin Laborde
QUARTERFINAL 1
1. Medi Veminardi
2. Justin Delanne
QUARTERFINAL 2
1. Thomas Fok Choeng
2. Marc Lacomare

QUARTERFINAL 3
1. Jatyr Berasaluce
2. Jules Thomet
QUARTERFINAL 4
1. Pierre Valentin Laborde
2. Igor Muniain
GIRLS FINAL
1. Alizee Arnaud
2. Johanne Defay
3. Ravi Bailleux
4. Fanny Brice

OAKLEY PRO JUNIOR • ASP GRADE 1 MEN'S JUNIOR EVENT/ ASP GRADE 1 WOMEN'S JUNIOR EVENT

LACANAU OCEAN, FRANCE
August 7–10

In front of a massive French crowd at Lacanau, Miguel Pupo of Sao Paulo Brazil went big in the clean 3- to 4-foot (1- to 1.2-meter) surf at Lacanau to defeat Marc Lacomare, Thomas Fok Cheong and Charles Martin. Pupo, who advanced through seven heats during three days of intense action to reach the final encounter, surprised himself and won with a solid 17.16 point score tally. "The final was very hard to win and I never expected to

Wiggoly Dantas. Photo Aquashot/Aspeurope.com.

finish ahead of such good surfers," said Pupo. In the Women's Pauline Ado defeated reigning ASP European Women's Champion Lee-Ann Curren and Junior ratings leader Joahnne Defay, as well as Marie Dejean in a 100 percent French final.

MEN FINAL
1. Miguel Pupo
2. Marc Lacomare
3. Thomas Fok Cheong
4. Charles Martin
SEMIFINAL 1
1. Miguel Pupo
2. Marc Lacomare
3. Mario Azurza
4. Adrien Toyon
SEMIFINAL 2
1. Charles Martin
2. Thomas Fok Cheong
3. Dimitri Ouvre
4. Kieren Bulard
QUARTERFINAL 1
1. Marc Lacomare
2. Adrien Toyon
3. Ormand Rangi
4. Felix Delanne
QUARTERFINAL 2
1. Miguel Pupo
2. Mario Azurza
3. Maxime Huscenot
4. Tanner Gudauskas
QUARTERFINAL 3
1. Dimitri Ouvre
2. Kieren Bulard
3. Joachim Guichard
4. Jules Thomet
QUARTERFIANL 4
1. Charles Martin
2. Thomas Fok Cheong
3. Medi Veminardi
4. Vincente Romero
WOMEN FINAL
1. Pauline Ado
2. Lee-Ann Curren
3. Joahnne Defay
4. Marie Dejean
SEMIFINAL 1
1. Lee-Ann Curren
2. Pauline Ado
3. Cannelle Bulard
4. Joahnne Panzini
SEMIFINAL 2
1. Joahnne Defay
2. Marie Dejean

3. Nikita Robb
4. Alizée Arnaud
QUARTERFINAL 1
1. Lee-Ann Curren
2. Cannelle Bulard
3. Francesca de Santos
4. Alix Cranet
QUARTERFINAL 2
1. Pauline Ado
2. Joahnne Panzini
3. Merril Delanne
4. Garazi Sanchez
QUARTERFINAL 3
1. Joahnne Defay
2. Alizée Arnaud
3. Justine Dupont
4. Marjolaine Ado
QUARTERFINAL 4
1. Nikita Robb
2. Marie Dejean
3. Fransisca Sousa
4. Camille Davila

RIP CURL BOARDMASTERS • ASP WQS 5-STAR MEN'S EVENT

FISTRAL BEACH, NEWQUAY, ENGLAND
August 4–9

The boys from Brazil took over Newquay's Fistral Beach as Wiggoly Dantas of Ubatuba claimed his maiden ASP World Qualifying Series title against fellow Brazilian Pablo Paulino. Fitness made a difference for Dantas, who won by surfing four heats in a row against some of the world's best in surging 4- to 6-foot (1.2- to 2-meter) beachbreak. "We had great waves at the start [of the event] and tough ones today but it was always lots of fun," said Dantas. "So stoked to get this first title, such a big thing. It is a great confidence boost for the upcoming events." Dantas moved up the ratings from No. 122 into the Top 80.

FINAL
1. Wiggoly Dantas
2. Pablo Paulino
SEMIFINAL 1
1. Wiggoly Dantas

Alizée Arnaud. Photo Aquashot/Aspeurope.com.

2. David Weare
SEMIFINAL 2
1. Pablo Paulino
2. Pedro Henrique
QUARTERFINAL 1
1. David Weare
2. Marlon Lipke
QUARTERFINAL 2
1. Wiggoly Dantas
2. Chris Davidson
QUARTERFINAL 3
1. Pedro Henrique
2. Nathan Hedge
QUARTERFINAL 4
1. Pablo Paulino
2. Nic Muscroft

SOÖRUZ LACANAU PRO, PRESENTED BY PLAYSTATION • ASP 6-STAR WQS MEN'S EVENT
LACANAU OCEAN, FRANCE
August 7–17

Nathaniel Curran continued his hot streak in wind-blown 2-to3-foot (0.5- to 1-meter) waves at Lacanau. Curran blew up in a tit-for-tat final, defeating Dion Atkinson and closing six days of great action at the famous French beach town.

FINAL
1. Nathaniel Curran
2. Dion Atkinson
SEMIFINAL 1
1. Nathaniel Curran
2. Mike Losness
SEMIFINAL 2
1. Dion Atkinson
2. Josh Kerr
QUARTERFINAL 1
1. Nathaniel Curran
2. Tiago Pires (PRT)
QUARTERFINAL 2
1. Mike Losness
2. Joel Centeio
QUARTERFINAL 3
1. Dion Atkinson
2. Yadin Nicol
QUARTERFINAL 4
1. Josh Kerr
2. Greg Emslie

KANAMISSCUP • 2-STAR WOMEN'S ASP PRO JR EVENT
HOURTIN, FRANCE
August 15–17

Alizee Arnaud was a standout throughout the 3-day event that scored some good-quality 3-foot (1-meter) waves in KanaMiss Cup's first incarnation as solely a Pro Junior.

FINAL
1. Alizée Arnaud
2. Pauline Ado
3. Lee-Ann Curren
4. Cannelle Bulard
SEMIFINAL 1
1. Lee-Ann Curren
2. Pauline Ado
3. Idoia Meabe
4. Raine Jakson
SEMIFINAL 2
1. Alizée Arnaud
2. Cannelle Bulard
3. Marie Dejean
4. Francesca De Santos

EUSKAL SURF ZIRKUITOA 08
ZARAUTZ, BASQUE COUNTRY
August 16–17

OPEN MEN A
1. Igor Munian
2. Mario Azurza
3. Jatyr Berasaluze
4. Marcos San Segundo
OPEN MEN B
1. José María Cabrera
2. Pablo Solar
3. Mario Azurza
4. Ander Ugarte

BILLABONG MARBELLA TAG TEAM BASCS
PLAGE DE MARBELLA, BIARRITZ, FRANCE
August 14–17

Excellent surf greeted those gathered for Billabong's Marbella Tag Team contest. A tradition on the Basque Coast, the event attracts France's best, who compete in a relaxed team format. This year the hamburger enthusiasts of Team Mac Do edged out Team DC to take the win,

FINAL
1. Team Mac Do
2. Team DC
3. Team Landais
4. Team Marbella

MOSKITO TOUR
LA PISTE, CAPBRETON, FRANCE
August 16

UNDER 16 GIRLS
1. Marie Applagnat
2. Nias Desplain
3. Maitane Berzara
UNDER 14 BOYS
1. Hgo Robin
2. Andy Criere
3. Lojou Emilien
4. Descacq
UNDER 12 BOYS
1. Leonardo Fioravantil
2. Franprevitera
3. Pol Barets
4. Aldric God
UNDER 12 GIRLS
1. Josephine Coste
2. Clara Pola
3. Ariane Otxoa
4. Amsia Bllecocq
UNDER 10 BOYS
1. Thomas Debriere
2. Mattia Poirier
3. Victor Barrere
4. Antoine Mur

RIP CURL PRO HOSSEGOR/SEIGNOSSE, PRESENTED BY SPRITE • ASP 6-STAR PRIME WQS MEN'S EVENT
LES BOURDAINES, HOSSEGOR, FRANCE
August 18–24

Chris Davidson defeated an inform Jihad Khodr in the final by posting the highest heat score of the week. By clinching the crown Davo secured his second ASP World Qualifying Series win this season and confirmed his No. 2 rank on the international ratings. "I felt like it was my day because these conditions usually fit my surfing so well and there was all the potential to surf at my best," said Davidson. "I was so amped I got those two big scores straight away and just felt like I was free surfing with Jihad [Khodr]."

FINAL
1. Chris Davidson
2. Jihad Khodr
SEMIFINAL 1
1. Jihad Khodr
2. Marlon Lipke
SEMIFINAL 2
1. Chris Davidson
2. Josh Kerr
QUARTERFINAL 1
1. Marlon Lipke
2. Tim Boal
QUARTERFINAL 2
1. Jihad Khodr
2. Nathaniel Curran
QUARTERFINAL 3
1. Chris Davidson
2. Mikael Picon
QUARTERFINAL 4
1. Josh Kerr
2. Drew Courtney

BILLABONG PRO JUNIOR, PORTUGAL • ASP GRADE 2 MEN'S JUNIOR EVENT/ ASP GRADE 2 WOMEN'S JUNIOR EVENT
RIBEIRA D'ILHAS ERICEIRA, PORTUGAL
August 22–24

Alizee Arnaud won this, her third event of the summer, in a close battle with Justine Dupont and Lee-Ann Curren. Arnaud impressed the judges with her stunning rail-to-rail work and smooth style. In the Men's it was Charles Martin of Guadeloupe who took the win over Euskadi's Jatyr Berasaluce, Brazil's Wiggoly Dantas and Reubyn Ash of the UK.

MEN FINAL
1. Charles Martin
2. Jatyr Berasaluce
3. Wiggoly Dantas
4. Reubyn Ash
SEMIFINAL 1
1. Wiggoly Dantas
2. Charles Martin
3. Medi Veminardi
4. Rangi Ormond
SEMIFINAL 2
1. Jatyr Berasaluce
2. Reubyn Ash
3. PV Laborde
4. Tristan Guilbaud
WOMEN FINAL
1. Alizee Arnaud
2. Justine Dupont
3. Lee-Ann Curren
4. Canelle Bulard

RIP CURL PRO JUNIOR MADEMOISELLE • ASP GRADE 2 WOMEN'S PRO JUNIOR
LES BOURDAINES, SEIGNOSSE FRANCE
August 26–27

Hossegor threw out clean four-foot barrels for an all-French final during the Rip Curl Pro Junior Mademoiselle. Slowly building momentum throughout the event Lee-Ann Curren peaked in the final, handing in a performance that left rival Justine Dupont outpointed at the final horn. With the win Curren nabs a wildcard into the prestigious Rip Curl Pro Mademoiselle and jumps to No. 2 in the regional ratings.

FINAL
1. Lee-Ann Curren
2. Justine Dupont
3. Pauline Ado
4. Marie Dejean
SEMIFINAL 1
1. Justine Dupont
2. Lee-Ann Curren
3. Bianca Buidentag
4. Alizée Arnaud
SEMIFINAL 2
1. Marie Dejean
2. Pauline Ado
3. Bruna Schmitz
4. Nikita Robb
QUARTERFINAL 1
1. Justine Dupont
2. Bianca Buidentag
3. Marjolaine Ado
4. Cannelle Bulard
QUARTERFINAL 2
1. Lee-Ann Curren
2. Alizée Arnaud
3. Raine Jackson
4. Merril Delanne
QUARTERFINAL 3
1. Nikita Robb
2. Pauline Ado
3. Francesca De Santos
4. Alix Cranet
QUARTERFINAL 4
1. Marie Dejean
2. Bruna Schmitz
3. Laetitia Sudre
4. Leticia Canales

VOLCOM STONE'S MULLETFISH
PLAGE DE LA PALUE, CROZON, FRANCE
August 23–24

The Volcom Mulletfish roadshow left their HQ in Anglet for the 11-hour drive north to Crozon in Brittany. Eighty surfers, both novice and experienced, competed (sometimes in the same heat) throughout the day. At the final horn it was Aurélien Jacob who took the Ppen win, while Lola Boutin signaled another new wave of French talent in the Girls division.

OPEN MEN
1. Aurélien Jacob
2. Vincent Lemanceau
3. Erwan Dinnahet
4. Jean Marie Toulgoat

GROMS
1. Leo Latourte
2. Tom Croq
3. Quentin Michelet
4. Andreas Failler

JUNIOR
1. Jean Tonnerre
2. Augustin Gragnic
3. Manu Petipo
4. Mathieu Guegan

GIRLS
1. Lola Boutin
2. Lucie Milochau
3. Marie Galliou
4. Pauline Robert

BUONDI BILLABONG PRO PORTUGAL • WQS 6-STAR MEN'S EVENT
RIBEIRA D'ILHAS, ERICEIRA, PORTUGAL
August 26–31

Aussie Phillip MacDonald drew upon his tour experience to oust Patrick Gudauskas in a wave-starved final and claim the 6-Star

Ornella Pellizzari. Photo Aquashot/Aspeurope.com.

Buondi Billabong Pro in tricky 2-foot (0.5-meter) surf. With the win, Macca jumps from 31 to 14 in the WQS ratings. "I placed second many times in my career but to eventually win a big event is just amazing," MacDonald said. "It was one of the smallest contests in a long time, but a win is always a win and I am stoked I finally got the boys to hold me up in the air and get that feeling at last."

FINAL
1. Phillip MacDonald
2. Patrick Gudauskas
SEMIFINAL 1
1. Patrick Gudauskas
2. Heitor Alves
SEMIFINAL 2
1. Phillip MacDonald
2. Eneko Acero
QUARTERFINAL 1
1. Patrick Gudauskas
2. Patrick Beven
QUATERFINAL 2
1. Heitor Alves
2. Wiggoly Dantas
QUARTERFINAL 3
1. Phillip MacDonald
2. Che Stang
QUARTERFINAL 4
1. Eneko Acero
2. Tim Boal
ROUND 6 RESULTS
Heat 1: Patrick Beven Def. Pedro Henrique

Heat 2: Patrick Gudauskas Def. Marco Polo
Heat 3: Wiggoly Dantas Def. Leigh Sedley
Heat 4: Heitor Alves Def. Tonino Benson
Heat 5: Che Stang Def. Travis Logie
Heat 6: Phillip MacDonald Def. Brett Simpson
Heat 7: Eneko Acero Def. Tanner Gudauskas
Heat 8: Tim Boal Def. Rodrigo Dornelles

GUL OPEN 2008 • UK PST EVENT #4
PORTHMEOR BEACH, ST. IVES, CORNWALL
August 30–31

Reubyn Ash upped the bar for British surfing, taking to the air and nailing several air reverses to win this, the fourth event of the UKPST tour. Second place also went to one of the UK young guns, local favorite Jayce Robinson from St. Ives, who recovered from a broken leg earlier in the year. Ireland's Nicole Morgan seesawed in the final against Oz transplant Lauren Ringer (now a local at St. Ives), but it was Morgan who had the lead when the final horn blew.

MEN FINAL
1. Ruebyn Ash
2. Jayce Robinson
3. Alan Stokes
4. Johnny Fryer
SEMIFINAL 1
1. Ruebyn Ash
2. Alan Stokes
3. Tom Butler
4. Tom Pope
SEMIFINAL 2
1. Jayce Robinson
2. Johnny Fryer
3. Mike Young
4. Tim Boydell
WOMEN FINAL
1. Nicole Morgan
2. Lauren Ringer
3. Zoe Sheath
4. Sophie Hellyer

BELGISCHE KAMPIONENSCHAP GOLFSURF
HOSSEGOR, FRANCE
August 30–31

MEN SHORTBOARD
1. Lars Musschoot
2. Mathias Vanoverbeke
3. Alexander Debruycker

MEN LONGBOARD
1. Dylan Verlinde
2. Tom Soupart
3. Achile Kindt
GROMMETS
1. Erik David
2. Matt Marcantuoni
3. Sam David
GIRLS
1. Delphine Vanoverbeke
2. Anne-Laure Boucquaert
3. Mieke Mertens
3. Delphine Vanhooren

MOVISTAR O'NEILL PANTIN CLASSIC • ASP WQS 5-STAR EVENT/ ASP WOMEN'S WQS 3-STAR EVENT
PANTIN, GALICIA, SPAIN
September 2–7

Ornella Pelizzarri of Argentina clinched her maiden ASP WQS title after rocking both the massive and small surf throughout the 5-day Movistar O'Neill Pantin Classic. In the final, Pelizzarri edged out Justine Dupont, Amandine Sanchez and Marie Dejean. "I am so stoked to get this win," Pelizzarri said. "I had a disappointing year and this victory is crucial for me. I will be focusing on gaining points to make sure I start 2009 with a good seeding." Pelizzarri wasn't the only champ of the event; Justine Dupont of France became the 2008 ASP European Women's Champion. Dupont, 17, had to place third or better in the final to clinch the Euro title ahead of Pauline Ado. In the Men's WQS William Cardoso of Brazil dampened Tahitian sparkplug Michel Bourez.

MEN FINAL
1. William Cardoso
2. Michel Bourez
SEMIFINAL 1
1. William Cardoso
2. Antonio Bortoletto
SEMIFINAL 2
1. Michel Bourez
2. Nic Muscroft
QUARTERFINAL 1
1. William Cardoso
2. Patrick Gudauskas
QUARTERFINAL 2
1. Antonio Bortoletto
2. Yuri Sodre
QUARTERFINAL 3
1. Michel Bourez
2. Jarrad Sullivan
QUARTERFINAL 4:
1. Nic Muscroft
2. Hizunome Bettero
WOMEN FINAL
1. Ornella Pelizzarri
2. Justine Dupont
3. Marie Dejean
4. Amandine Sanchez
SEMIFINAL 1
1. Ornella Pelizzarri
2. Amandine Sanchez
3. Lee-Ann Curren
4. Bianca Buitendag
SEMIFINAL 2
1. Justine Dupont
2. Marie Dejean
3. Anne Cecile Le Tallec
4. Jessica Grimwood

QUARTERFINAL 1
1. Bianca Buitendag
2. Ornella Pellizzari
3. Caroline Sarran
4. Maria Gonzalez
QUARTERFINAL 2
1. Amandine Sanchez
2. Lee-Ann Curren
3. Pauline Ado
4. Filipa Prudencio
QUARTERFINAL 3
1. Marie Dejean
2. Jessica Grimwood
3. Nicole Morgan
4. Fransisca Santos
QUARTERFINAL 4
1. Justine Dupont
2. Anne-Cecile Le Tallec
3. Charlotte Hand
4. Martine Geijsels

RIP CURL PRO ZARAUTZ • ASP 5-STAR WQS MEN'S EVENT
ZARAUTZ, BASQUE COUNTRY
September 9–14

The Basque beachbreak of Zarautz tossed out clean 2- to 3-foot (0.5- to 1-meter) waves for an all-French final at the 5-Star Rip Curl Pro Zarautz. Showing consistency throughout the event, Tim Boal left Hossegor's Joan Duru almost 6 points behind by the time the final horn blew. Boal, who's been building momentum throughout the summer

Tim Boal event champion. Photo Aquashot/Aspeurope.com.

European WQS season, takes the Euro ratings lead with the win. "I am so stoked to finally get a big win" Boal said. "I was able to get the waves and surf them well, and it is great to get the feeling right. That win is the icing on the cake. I made the final in California at the U.S. Open of Surfing but failed to win it, and it was a big frustration for me . . . I just wanted to make a good final here to put that loss in California behind me."

FINAL
1. Tim Boal
2. Joan Duru
SEMIFINAL 1
1. Tim Boal
2. Michel Bourez
SEMIFINAL 2
1. Joan Duru
2. Aritz Aranburu

QUARTERFINAL 1
1. Tim Boal
2. Glenn Hall (IRE)
QUARTERFINAL 2
1. Michel Bourez
2. Blake Thornton
QUARTERFINAL 3
1. Joan Duru
2. Luke Dorrington
QUARTERFINAL 4
1. Aritz Aranburu
2. Vs Blake Wilson

JESUS SURF CLASSIC, CHRISTIAN SURFERS UK
CROYDE BAY, NORTH DEVON
September 13–14

Divine forces appeared to be at work at the 16th annual Jesus Surf Classic as great surf in a fickle, blustery corner of the world welcomed competitors. The brothers Ash split the open final, with Joss collecting the £250 check for 1st place while Reubyn had to settle for 2nd. When the comp ended and packed up on Sunday evening, the heavens opened and the rain came down for a solid 8-hour torrent. Good timing, indeed.

OPEN MEN
1. Joss Ash
2. Reubyn Ash
3. Lyndon Wake
4. Luke Hughes
YOUTH
1. Miles Lee-Hargeaves
2. Jobe Hariss
3. Harry Timson
4. Sam Harwood
JUNIOR WOMEN
1. Sophie Sainsbury
2. Tassy SwalloW
3. Gabbi Rowe
4. Karma Worthington
CADETS
1. Alex Baker
2. Toby Donachie
3. Tom Good
4. Josh Daniel

DELOITTE CHANNEL ISLANDS SURFING CHAMPS
WATERSPLASH, JERSEY
September 13–14

Good conditions were short and sweet at the Channel Island Champs. When the high tide hit the seawall during the Open final, it was Scott Eastwood who handled the mad backwash best, edging out Ben Chapman and Minky Charlton. The contest ended in traditional Jersey fashion, with sponsor Deloittes dishing out the trophies and many, many well-earned beers.

OPEN MEN
1. Scott Eastwood
2. Ben Chapman
3. Michael Charlton
4. Jon Carden

JUNIOR
1. Matt Chapman
2. Alex Vibert
3. Freddie Seymour
4. Jacob Warr

SENIOR
1. Scott Eastwood
2. Ben Chapman
3. Clayton Lidster
4. Michael Charlton

MEN LONGBOARD
1. Joe Davies
2. Will Glen
3. Cole Jouanny
4. Ben Chapman

MASTERS
1. Nigel Wray
2. Clayton Lidster
3. Mark Durbano
4. Michael Charlton

GIRLS
1. Lucy Goddard
2. Megan Jones
3. Megan Vibert

LADIES
1. Lucy Goddard
2. Arlene Maltman
3. Megan Vibert
4. Esther Lemprière

BILLABONG BRITISH JUNIOR CHAMPS, BRITISH SURFING AS-SOCIATION
FISTRAL BEACH, NEWQUAY UK
September 20–21

Fistral Beach offered up some excellent surf for competitors to test their skills against Britain's best as 180 surfers vied for various British titles. Holly Donnelly won the Under 18 Girls while Stuart Campbell took the Under 18 Boys.

UNDER 16 BOYS
1. Josh Piper
2. Toby Donachie
3. Alex Baker
4. Harry Timson
5. Angus Scotney

UNDER 14 BOYS
1. Harry Timson
2. Luke Dillon
3. Ryan Roberts
4. Patrick Daniel

UNDER 14 GIRLS
1. Tassy Swallow
2. Lucy Campbell
3. Laura Crane
4. Gabi Rowe

UNDER 12 BOYS
1. Ed Smith
2. Will Bailey
3. Ben Bates

Maxime Huscenot. Photo Eric Chauche/Quiksilver.

QUIKSILVER KING OF THE GROMS • FINAL WORLD UNDER 16S SURFING CHAMPIONSHIPS
HOSSEGOR/SEIGNOSSE, SW FRANCE
September 19–28

On the heels of a worldwide qualifying tour, 16 surfers under age 16 came together in the Landes region of southwest France to crown the King of the Groms. Reunion Island stylist Maxime Huscenot edged out California-next-big-thing Kolohe Andino in a tight back-and-forth final. The surfers swapped next-school moves until in the dying seconds Huscenot nabbed a wave that put him in front of Andino by a breath. Final tally: Andino 17.16, Huscenot 17.17 With the win Huscenot earns the privilege of competing in the trials of two ASP World Tour Quiksilver events.

1. Maxime Huscenot
2. Kolohe Andino
3. Matt Banting
4. Alex Dive

QUIKSILVER GERMAN CHAMPS
SEIGNOSSE, LANDES, FRANCE
September 27—October 4

The best German surfers from around the globe descended on Seignosse to trade blows for the Quiksilver German Surfing Champ crown. International favorite Nico von Rupp won both the Open Men and Junior titles, despite a shark scare during the Open final. "Approximately five minutes before the end of the heat I saw this big shark next me and did not know if I should tell my friends," said Von Rupp. "I thought if I tell them, they won't believe me. They'll probably just think I wanted them out of the water . . . After I got out I didn't care who won the final, I just was happy I made it thru the final."

OPEN MEN
1. Nicolaus von Rupp
2. Ricardo Lange,
3. Dieter Kuhn
4. Thomas Lange

JÚNIOR FINAL
1. Nicolaus von Rupp
2. Diogo Fragoso
3. Phillip Katzenstein
4. Severin Clasen

BRITISH BODYBOARD NATIONALS
PORTHTOWAN, CORNWALL
September 27–28

UNDER 18 BOYS
1. Dave Speller
2. Luke Brabyn
3. Stephen Hall
4. Nathan Thompson

UNDER 16 BOYS
1. Stephen Hall
2. Luke Brabyn
3. Liam Benney
4. Callum Morse

UNDER 14 BOYS
1. Sam Brabyn
2. Harry Smith
3. Lloyd Atherton
4. Ed Sherlock

MEN DROP KNEE
1. Aiden Salmon
2. Remy Geffroy
3. Alex Winkworth
4. Danny Wall

SENIORS
1. Damien Prisk

Ricardo Lange. Photo Hannibal.

2. Bjorn Storey
3. Eldred Hawke
4. Danny Catten

MASTERS
1. Eldred Hawke
2. Danny Catten
3. Colin Crowther
4. Simon Watkins
5. Alasdair Newby

INTERNATIONAL
1. Aiden Dixon
2. Ben Hughes
3. Eduardo Alfonso

OPEN WOMEN
1. Gemma Brittan
2. Clemmie Hardy
3. Olivia Smedley
4. Jasmine O'Shea

ELUSIVE WELSH PRO • STOP NO 5 OF 9 ON 2008 UK PST
REST BAY, PORTHCAWL, WALES
October 11–12

British national treasure Russell Winter utilized his global experience to take the Elusive Welsh Pro at Rest Bay. Winter squeaked past fellow Brit vet Spencer Hargraves by posting the highest scoring wave of the event, a 9.83. In the Women's division, Kathleen Spears managed to pick up the best wave of the heat in the dying seconds to score 7.0 and edge out Holly Donnelly.

OPEN MEN
1. Russel Winter
2. Reubyn Ash
3. Matt Capel
4. Spencer Hargraves

OPEN WOMEN
1. Kathleen Spears
2. Holly Donnelly
3. Raine Jackson
4. Jenny Horbas

LA SANTA SURF PRO • ASP WQS 6-STAR PRIME MEN'S EVENT
SAN JUAN, LANZAROTE, CANARY ISLANDS
October 14–19

In wind-blown 3-foot (1-meter) surf at the world-class left-hander of San Juan, Nic Muscroft defeated former ASP World Junior Champion Kekoa Bacalso. Muscroft, this year's poster child for focus and determination, hit a solid 14.43 point heat tally to best Bacalso's 14.00 in a wave-starved final. "It was gnarly, probably the gnarliest finish I have ever had," Muscroft said. "It was stressfull for me and I'm sure it was for Kekoa as well. We had fifteen minutes with no waves right after I got my last one, so I could not hope for more."

MEN FINAL
1. Nick Muscroft
2. Kekoa Bacalso

SEMIFINAL 1
1. Nic Muscroft
2. Drew Courtney

SEMIFINAL 2:
1. Kekoa Bacalso
2. Phil MacDonald

QUARTERFINAL 1
1. Nic Muscroft
2. Heitor Alves

QUARTERFINAL 2
1. Drew Courtney
2. Shaun Cansdell

QUARTERFINAL 3
1. Kekoa Bacalso
2. Nathan Yeomans

QUARTERFINAL 4
1. Phil MacDonald
2. Gabe Kling

BUCS SURF CHAMPS BRITISH SURFING, ASSOCIATION
FISTRAL BEACH, NEWQUAY UK
October 17–18

Fistral Beach hosted the British Universities & Colleges Sport (BUCS) Surfing Champs, where Falmouth claimed the Men's trophy and Swansea won the Women's division. The contest hit a record high for entries and the contest director was forced to cap contestants at 100 women and 200 men, making the BUCS event the largest British surfing competition next to the English Championships.

MEN TEAM
1. Falmouth
2. Plymouth
3. Cardiff
4. Falmouth B

Jean Da Silva. Photo Aquashot/Aspeurope.com.

WOMEN TEAM
1. Swansea
2. Plymouth B
3. Falmouth A
4. Plymouth

VOLCOM STONE CODFISH
SELE BEACH, STAVANGER, NORWAY
October 18–19

Sele Beach in Norway launched Volcom's Codfish surf series in excellent and very cold surf. While surf culture is a new import to Norway, the contest attracted—in randomness fitting for a Volcom event—a Mexican tow-in team, a Bra-boy and the younger sister of snowboarding hell-man Mads Jonsson. Camilla Pedersen shined in the Women's division, while Caspar from Denmark ruled the Juniors. In the Open it was Marcio Dias who was crowned King Codfish.

OPEN MEN
1. Marcio "Drop in" Dias
2. Aage Obrestad
3. Jaymin (Yeeeah) Rowlands
4. Kristian Haribo Engström
JUNIORS
1. Casper from Denmark
2. Chris Hartknopp
3. Baard Skeie
4. Ask Hide
GIRLS
1. Camilla Pedersen
2. Unn Haukenes
3. Hannah
4. Lene Nyberg

ESTORIL COAST PRO • ASP 6-STAR WQS MEN'S EVENT
CARCAVELOS, LISBON, PORTUGAL
October 21–26

Brazil's Jean Da Silva overcame a serious hip injury and four months of dry-dock to win the 6-Star Estoril Coast Pro. Da Silva defeated American Gabe Kling with a 9.83 total heat score after nabbing the best wave of the final. Gabe Kling was swept out of position for most of the heat, taking clean-up sets on the head and battling the strong current. Da Silva nabbed 2500 ratings points with the win and signaled his return.

MEN FINAL
1. Jean Da Silva
2. Gabe Kling
SEMIFINAL 1
1. Jean Da Silva
2. Tiago Pires
SEMIFINAL 2
1. Gabe Kling
2. Dion Atkinson
QUARTERFINAL 1
1. Tiago Pires
2. Mike Losness
QUARTERFINAL 2
1. Jean Da Silva
2. Gavin Gillette
QUARTERFINAL 3
1. Dion Atkinson
2. Marlon Lipke
QUARTERFINAL 4:
1. Gabe Kling
2. Jay Thompson

ROXY NORTH EAST WOMEN'S OPEN • STOPS NO 6–8 OF 9 ON 2008 UK PST
LONGSANDS BEACH, TYNEMOUTH
October 25–26

In tricky conditions, Caroline Perret took an early lead at Longsands, forcing the other finalists to play catch-up. Jenny Horbas came closest, earning 2nd, while 3rd went to Aussie Raine Jackson and 4th to Lauren Davies.

WOMEN FINAL
1. Caroline Perret
2. Jenny Horbas
3. Raine Jackson
4. Lauren Davies

BRITISH NATIONAL SURF CHAMPS, BRITISH SURFING ASSOCIATION
FISTRAL BEACH, NEWQUAY, CORNWALL
October 25–26

In the Open final, Oli Adams, Joss Ash, Mitch Corbett and Russell Winter traded the lead in the high-tide, potluck conditions. But with less than three minutes to go, Russell Winter paddled into a wave that opened up all the way through to the inside. He earned the high score of the final and celebrated his first British Open Champion title in over 15 years as well as the Senior's crown. In the women's Welsh wonder Jo Dennison beat out Kathleen Spears, Nicole Morgan and Rachael Taylor to take the crown.

OPEN MEN
1. Russell Winter
2. Joss Ash
3. Oli Adams
4. Mitchell Corbett
VETERANS
1. Jed Stone
2. Gary Collins
3. Phil Williams
4. Laurence Couch
MASTERS
1. Cullum Murrell
2. Chris Harris
3. Tony Good
4. Steve Winter
SENIORS
1. Russell Winter
2. Paul Kirby
3. Pete Williams
4. Chris Harris
OPEN WOMEN
1. Jo Dennison
2. Kathleen Spears
3. Nicole Morgan
4. Rachael Taylor

Portrush winners. Photo Lucia Griggi.

QUIKSILVER NORTH EAST OPEN • STOP NO 6 OF 9 ON 2008 UK PST
GILLS, POINT OF NESS, KIESS & SANDSIDE
October 25–26

The surfers and organizers drove just about as far north and about as far east as you can go in mainland UK looking for good surf. The conditions they found were harsh at best and horrific at times, with gale-force winds, snow and below-zero temperatures. In between hail and snow squalls, a few small, clean waves rolled through. Sam Lamiroy put in a lot of work and took the win, while the King of Water Sports award for the highest wave score went to Australian Jye Goffton for his 9.77.

FINAL
1. Sam Lamiroy
2. Nathan Phillips
3. Warren Tuck
4. Mike Young

QUIKSILVER / ROXY 3 DEGREES • STOP NO 7 OF 9 ON 2008 UK PST
THURSO, EAST SCOTLAND
October 29

Britain's best and a few internationals traded barrels in the final, run in firing Thurso East surf. Micah Lester kicked it off with a 9.1 and held a slim lead throughout. In the dying seconds, Reuben Pearce went big on his last wave but came up just shy of Lester's final score. Nicole Morgan claimed the Women's in solid surf. Shauna Ward won the Queen of the Waves award, scoring a 7.63 in the final.

OPEN MEN
1. Micah Lester
2. Reuben Pearce
3. Reubyn Ash
4. Spencer Hargraves
OPEN WOMEN
1. Nicole Morgan
2. Joe Dennison
3. Shauna Ward
4. Caroline Perret

RIP CURL PRO BANZAI, PRESENTED BY SMITH OPTICS
SANTA MARINELLA, ITALY
October 10—November 1

While most of Italy was under the grip of bad weather, the best surfers on the peninsula gathered for the fifth and final stage of the Italian national circuit in chest-high surf. Alessio Poli dominated the Men's division and took the win, while 2nd-place Iacopo Conti earned enough points to be crowned 2008 Italian Champ. Elena Bertolini nabbed the Women's.

OPEN MEN
1. Alessio Poli
2. Iacopo Conti
3. Nicola Bresciani
4. Francesco Palattella
OPEN WOMEN
1. Elena Bertolini
2. Alessandra Mauri
3. Greta Dalle Luche
4. Valentina D'Azzeo

ROXY PORTRUSH WOMEN'S OPEN • QUIKSILVER 3 DEGREES SERIES EVENT 3, UK PRO SURF TOUR (UK PST) EVENT 8
EAST STRAND, WHITEROCKS BEACH, PORTRUSH
November 1–2

National Irish team member Glenn Hall took home the Portrush Open title in clean 2-foot surf at White Rocks Beach in County Antrim, Northern Ireland. Glenn, who learned to surf in Australia but has returned to his Irish roots, took control of the event right from the first round. Irish surfer Easkey Britton ruled the final of the Roxy Portrush Women's Open. Easkey, who is studying in Northern Ireland, trains at the contest venues of White Rocks and the East Strand whenever she is away from her home beach of Rossnowlagh.

OPEN MEN
1. Glen Hall
2. Jayce Robinson
3. Sam Lamiroy
4. Martin Black
OPEN WOMEN
1. Easkey Britton
2. Shauna Ward
3. Sarah Bentley
4. Raine Jackson

VOLCOM LAVA FISH SURF SERIES
TENERIFE, PUNTA HIDALGO
November 1–2

The groms action heated up nicely at the Volcom Lava Fish, Tenerife. In the final, Ivan Gonzales scored a little tube and with it the win, edging out VQS veteran Kai Garcia. Eight-year-old Yael Peña earned a 3rd at his local spot, while Nico Aguirre had trouble finding a decent wave. With their placings, all finalists are now qualified for the European champs in Anglet.

OPEN MEN
1. Michel Lopez
2. Alexander Zirke
3. Nardo Lopez (senor)
4. Marc Lopez
GROMS
1. Ivan Gonzales
2. Kai Garcia
3. Yael Peña
4. Nico Aguirre
JUNIORS
1. Victo Machristi
2. Nico Kali
3. Jose Roman
4. Hanniel Bertoni
GIRLS
1. Cintia Borges
2. Monica Diaz
3. Marta de Florit
3. Marian de Tomas

Reubyn Ash and Alan Stokes. Photo Lucia Griggi.

Joss Ash. Photo Lucia Griggi.

ANIMAL SURF ACADEMY CORNISH SCHOOLS SURFCHAMPS
TOLCARNE BEACH, NEWQUAY
November 8–9

The 2008 Animal Cornish Schools Surfing Championships scored solid surf for the sixth year running as more than 160 competitors from Bude to Penzance descended on Tolcarne beach in Newquay. Stylist Leon Mansfield fired in the Under 16s, landing big scores for his top-shelf maneuvers, which were enough to roll past Tom Good, Luk Millington and Josh Damer.

UNDER 16 BOYS
1. Leon Mansfield
2. Tom Good
3. Luke Millington
4. Josh Damer
UNDER 14 BOYS
1. Jobe Harris
2. Luke Dillon
3. Ed Smith
4. Sam Harwood
MEN BODYBOARD
1. Steven Hall
2. Sam Brady
3. Lewis Annear
4. Danny Selling
GIRLS
1. Jaide Rowe
2. Kensa Munroe
3. Gabi Rowe
4. Daisy Docking
5. Tamsin Dillon

VOLCOM STONE DODO FISH
3 BASSINS, REUNION ISLAND
November 8–9

Reunion Island: perfect lefts, clear water and according to Volcom, Dodo Fish. Trois-Bassins was blessed with 4- to 6-foot surf for the more than 120 local and international competitors, including podium savant Maxime Huscenot. But it was Medi Veminardi's 3-feet-above-the-lip aerial reverse on a solid left that really stoked the crowd and earned him the Electric Volt Thrower move of the event.

OPEN MEN
1. Adrien Toyon
2. William Pasquet
3. Maxime Huscenot

4. Jeremy Attyasse
GROMS
1. Ugo Robin
2. Woody Gujon
3. Kevin Grainville
4. Pablo Goncalvez
GIRLS
1. Canelle Bullard
2. Johanne Defay
3. Johanne Panzini
4. Albanne Tatibouet
JUNIORS
1. Maxime Huscenot
2. Medi Veminardi
3. Martin Dambreville
4. YannGuyonneau

ANIMAL NEWQUAY OPEN • STOP NO 9 OF 9 ON 2008 UK PST
FISTRAL BEACH, NEWQUAY
November 15–16

Day one of the Animal Newquay Open at Fistral Beach began with some of the best conditions seen at this event in recent years, and many competitors couldn't restrain themselves from pulling double, even triple duty. Toby Donachie from St. Merryn surfed consistently well throughout three categories: Under 16s, Pro Junior and the Open division. In doing so, he progressed to both the Under 16 and Pro Junior finals. Other surfers that selected multiple duty were Tom Butler, Reubyn Ash and Jayce Robinson. All three made the final of the Pro Junior division along with Toby, but it was Reubyn Ash who won out in the Open.

OPEN MEN
1. Reubyn Ash
2. Joss Ash
3. Reuben Pearce
4. Alan Stokes
PRO JUNIOR
1. Reubyn Ash
2. Tom Butler
3. Jacye Robinson
4. Toby Donachie
UNDER 16 BOYS
1. Alex Baker
2. Toby Donachie
3. Leon Mansfield
4. Tom Good
OPEN WOMEN
1. Nicole Morgan
2. Daisy Thomas
3. Raine Jackson
4. Holly Donnelly

2008 BRITISH KNEEBOARD CHAMPIONSHIPS • UK PST
GODREVY, CORNWALL UK
November 15–16

Karl Ward's characteristic powerful surfing earned him the title of British Kneeboard Champion as he outpaced Bryn Dampney, Richard Hewitt and Marc Crawford. In the Masters division, Richard Hewitt got on top of the conditions early, narrowly beating Chris Diplock and company. Jodie Winter surfed well in the Open and made it through a Master's semifinal before a back injury stopped her. Prior to the injury she earned the Women's crown.

OPEN MEN
1. Karl Ward
2. Bryn Dampney
3. Richard Hewitt
4. Marc Crawford
MASTERS
1. Richard Hewitt
2. Chris Diplock
3. Matthew Deaves
4. Tony Bonner

TSUNAMI CUP, CHRISTIAN SURFERS UK
REST BAY, PORTHCAWL, SOUTH WALES
December 6–7

Rob Blythe was on fire for the Tsunami Cup, taking both the Open and the Longboard titles in this event organized to benefit Tsunami victims. The Women's event was won by Holly Gwazdacz, who edged ahead of Olivia Tate and Rhiannon Tate. The Junior event had a tough and close final, with Keifer Thompson securing his maiden title.

OPEN MEN
1. Rob Blythe
2. Tom Anderson
3. Greg Owen
4. Harry Cromwell
MEN LONGBOARD
1. Rob Blythe
2. Steve Horn
3. Dan Evans
JUNIOR
1. Keifer Thompson
2. Thomas Padden
3. Ezra Hanes
4. Sam Bailey
OPEN WOMEN
1. Holly Gwazdacz
2. Olivia Jones
3. Rhiannon Tate

2008 ISA EURO JUNIOR CHAMPS • FÉDÉRATION ROYALE MAROCAINE DE SURF ET BODYBOARD
IMOURANE, TAGHAZOUT, MOROCCO
December 1–7

Utilizing a mobile format at select spots in Morocco, the ISA Euro Junior Champs debuted a formidable Moroccan team that claimed a respectable 4th place, a mere 91 points behind Spain. However, as with most European events (even ones held on the African continent), France dominated nearly every single event. Marc Lacomare, Pauline Ado, Dimitri Ouvre, and Eduardo Delpero all took home 1st place trophies for France. The only event not dominated by les Bleus was the Women Bodyboard, won by Portugal's Mariana Machado.

OPEN MEN
1. Marc Lacomare
2. Charles Martin
3. Filipe J. Pereira
4. Angelo Bonomelly
MEN LONGBOARD
1. Edouard Delpero
2. Evan Rogers
3. João Veríssimo
4. Cole Jouanny
MEN BODYBOARD
1. Martin Mouradian
2. Tiago Silva
3. Ayoub Soussi
4. Kevin Rosales
UNDER 16 BOYS
1. Dimitri Ouvre
2. Maxime Huscenot
3. Frederico Morais (POR)
4. Ramzi Boukhiam (MOR)
UNDER 16 BOYS BODYBOARD
1. Yann Salaun
2. Isaac Rodriguez
3. António Lopes
4. Haddar Anas
WOMEN FINAL
1. Pauline Ado
2. Alizee Arnaud
3. Maria Abecasis
4. Garazi Sanchez
WOMEN BODYBOARD
1. Mariana Machado
2. Marine Mainguy
3. Soukaina Agouali
4. Cristina Fernandez

VOLCOM STONE TOROFISH
ANDALOUCIA, LA BARROSA, SPAIN
December 6–7

Andalousia locals Naranjito, El Bola, Emilio Oliva, Roberto and Limón put in top performances at Volcom's Torofish, while Zeus Leiba shined brightest, taking the win in the Open division. Javier Carrillo pulled into a nice bowl and won Electric's Volt Thrower award and 50€ in cash. All finalists are qualified for the European VQS final in Anglet April 25–26.

OPEN MEN
1. Zeus Leiba
2. Manu Vazquez
3. Pablo Montero
4. Jose Antonio Leiba
GROMS
1. Federico Femía
2. Ignacio Touzón
3. Javier Aragón
4. Pablo Nebreda
JUNIOR
1. David Schekahn
2. Julio Serrano
3. Carlos Capilla

4. Pedro Moreno
OPEN WOMEN
1. Raquel Nowell
2. Rita Lohmann
3. Lorena Batish
4. Sara Nowell
ELECTRIC VOLT THROWER
Javier Carrillo's tube

PUNTA GALEA BBK CHALLENGE
PUNTA GALEA, GETXO, SPAIN
December 13

Eighteen big-wave riders descended on Punta Galea for the BBK Challenge, but it was Indar Unanue who scored the biggest and deepest sets to claim the win. In waves that ranged between 3 and 4 meters, with the occasional larger bomb, Indar edged out fellow ballsy Basque Eneko Steel. Asier Legorreta earned the dubious Slap Award for the worst pounding, limping away with 700 Euros to help ease his pain.

OPEN MEN
1. Indar Unanue
2. Eneko Steel
3. David Bustamante

ETL ESTORIL EUROPEAN LONGBOARD TOUR
SAO PEDRO, ESTORIL, PORTUGAL
December 13–14

Held in beautiful, hollow right-handers at Praia Santa Amaro, the ETL Estoril saw Brit Ben Skinner claim his second consecutive title here. Skinner had been the powerful standout throughout the contest, taking advantage of the conditions with a snappy forehand approach. On his way to the winner's podium, he displaced French phenoms Antione Delperro and Rémy "Shawn" Arauzo, also knocking out fellow Brit Adam Griffiths. With Arauzo's 3rd-place finish, the Frenchman secured enough points to claim the 2008 European Longboard title.

OPEN MEN
1. Ben Skinner
2. Antoine Delpero
3. Rémy Arauzo
4. Adam Griffiths

Ben Skinner. Photo YvesS.

Hawaii Report
By Bernie Baker

It's hours short of the New Year, way beyond my deadline for this re-cap of the past 12 months of our island living, but I just wanted to make sure there was no "Eddie"-sized swell sneaking in before the clock strikes 12:00, and I think I'm safe.

Two thousand eight was rough for the world, but Hawaii's taken a particularly hard hit on the business side in the past six months, since tourism fuels this state. From the shapers to the glassers to the retailers to you-name-it, we've taken it square on the chin. It's that trickle-down effect that generates the engine, and surfing sits like a spark plug with no connected wire. Two thousand nine's going be a real test of surfing's ability to feed itself over here and weather the economic storm with everyone else.

To wrap the season in reverse, this winter's hugely successful Vans Triple Crown escaped a trap when we just finished the Billabong Pipeline Masters on a dropping swell and on the back of one of Oahu's worst-ever storm floods. Hundreds of families lost their homes or businesses when the rivers overflowed and swept through North Shore lowlands. I don't know how or why, but the weather broke open just long enough and we made it through, with the Kelly Machine devouring all who came near him at the Masters in a brilliant display of focus, knowledge and aggression. There was barely any beach left from the winter's shifting sands, so it looked like there were a million on the beach to watch it, and when you add the numbers on the internet feed, there were probably more than two million!

That day Oahu was literally buried in chocolate brown water, and still Pipe was the cleanest break along the North Shore. I don't think any of us will ever understand how that came to be, but for the next three weeks there wasn't a day over head high and the weather fell into a gray soup that's still lingering overhead.

A 2008 Triple Crown sidebar: "Uncle" Rabbit Kekai gave us a scare at Sunset Beach, where he was beach marshalling at the women's Roxy Pro final. Just after the awards presentation Rabbit blacked out in the competitors' area.

He's fine now, but I'll share a shot of humor with you: When the first lifeguard at his side held up five fingers and asked him how many he was showing, Rabbit, with the oxygen mask over his face, slowly lifted his right hand up, showing just his middle finger and muttered through the plastic, "One . . ." That tells you just how strong the 80-plus surfing legend is.

A shifting weather cycle across the Pacific haunted us at the beginning of 2008 and again at the end, loads of uber-flat periods and plenty of rain. Even the North Shore summer wind swell bumps we used to play around on in past years all but disappeared. Early morning and afternoon rinse-offs were part of the treat for living in the country, but last year when it went flat it stayed flat, not a dribble of any value till fall came around. However, the stand up paddle onslaught hasn't felt that pinch. They multiplied in numbers like termite swarms, charging even boat wake–sized stuff. The head count of SUP's in the flat water grows each month and methinks that in 2009 it will be even more popular. As a matter of fact, the one sector of Hawaii's surf business that isn't fully feeling the economic downspin is SUP board and paddle sales.

In 2008 we got a bit of everything at our doorstep. Forever local boy Gerry Lopez brought home his new book *Surf Is Where You Find It* and gave two readings to packed houses—he could have done it for another week and broken more attendance records. Dads and moms even brought their kids to the event just to hear Gerry talk. Shaun Tomson and Mark Richards shared billing for Shaun's *Bustin'*

Down the Door documentary, with premieres on Oahu and Maui and a well-received theatre run that drew a number of older guys and girls who were part of the fun side of that period out from hiding and into smiling.

The film must have carried some extra good vibes to the islands, because our summer surf wasn't that bad afterwards, and Ala Moana was center stage for one of the best pro events ever staged there. Farther up the beach, the early rumbles of changing the landscape with a series of groins in front of the Sheraton Hotel made headlines, and battle plans are now in full swing for '09—and there will be blood from this one, trust me.

There were shark sightings and attacks where we never thought of sharks hanging out. Even Hawaiian monk seals were sleeping on the beach where normally hundreds of people would be lounging. (We're still not sure if the sharks chased them in or the seals thought it was time to take back what's theirs).

We also lost a number of great people this past year from all the islands. We said aloha to surf pioneer Woody Brown, we scattered the ashes of Lee Blears (wife of Lord Tally Ho, mother to Jimmy, Laura, Clinton and Carol) at Makaha, and bade farewell to legendary surfing cinematographer Bud Browne at Ehukai Beach. Surfer Dave Skimin was a rescue jumper/diver with the Coast Guard, and when their helicopter went down this summer off of Honolulu, a fitting tribute—for a man whose life was centered around saving others 24 hours a day—was given to him and the others who perished that evening.

Finally, as a last comment on 2008, I would like to personally commend everyone associated with AccesSurf, the organization created to help share the ocean and surfing with those who simply have the desire to embrace what we all too often take for granted. They've done a great job getting people to the beach who, through physical or mental challenges, would never have had the opportunity. They do now, thanks to AccesSurf. Mahalo.

2008 was rough for the world, but Hawaii has taken a particularly hard hit; from the shapers to the glassers to the retailer to you-name-it, we've taken it square on the chin.

Farewell to Lee Blears. Photo Bernie Baker.

DA HUI BACKDOOR SHOOTOUT
PIPELINE/BACKDOOR, NORTH SHORE, OAHU
January 2–15

It was just another day in the office for Jamie O'Brien, who came from behind to win the title at Da Hui's Backdoor Shootout, taking home $50,000! Coming in second was Bruce Irons, winning $25,000. Mark Healey & Myles Padaca tied for fifth and both surfers were awarded $5000. The only thing they could not share was the beautiful Christian Riese Lassen painting that each surfer was awarded along with their winnings. So, in true local style, Mark & Myles had to face each other for one round of "jun-ken-po" (rock, paper, scissors for you non-Hawaiians). No executive decisions, no special judges meeting—just a down-home schoolyard battle—and winning the "jun-ken-po" was Da Hui's Myles Padaca!

RESULTS
1. Jamie O'Brien
2. Bruce Irons
3. Ola Eleogram
4. Marcus Hickman
5. Mark Healey and Myles Padaca

NSSA HAWAII RVCA SERIES EVENT FIVE
BANYAN TREE, KAILUA-KONA, HAWAII
January 12–13

Malia Manuel swept both the Explorer Girls and Open Women at Banyan Tree in Kailua-Kona as the fifth event of the RVCA series went down in good surf over the January 12–13 weekend. With Oahu's North Shore pushing 25 feet, the waves for the RVCA contest peaked at 8-foot faces during the Explorer Men's final, with Oahu's Billy Kemper lighting up the rights and lefts for some huge scores.

EXPLORER MEN
1. Billy Kemper

2. Chris Foster
3. Tanner Hendrickson
4. Levi Gonzales
5. Albee Layer
6. Alex Smith

EXPLORER GIRLS
1. Malia Manuel
2. Kelia Moniz
3. Nage Melamed
4. Kallee Krebs
5. Tatiana Weston Webb
6. Brianna Cope

EXPLORER WOMEN
1. Kelia Moniz
2. Alyssa Wooten
3. Nage Melamed
4. Kallee Krebs
5. Alisha Gonsalves
6. Tatiana Weston Webb

EXPLORER LONGBOARD
1. Bullet Obra
2. Dylan McNeil

OPEN MINI GROMS
1. Kalani David
2. Imaikalani DeVault
3. Kaulana Apo
4. Lucas Angulo
5. Justin Ringsby
6. Dylan Lehmann

OPEN JUNIORS
1. Keala Naihe
2. Keanu Asing
3. Tanner Hendrickson
4. Davey Brand
5. Nick Falbo
6. Nathan Carvalho

OPEN BOYS
1. Makai McNamara
2. Benji Brand
3. Lahiki Minamishin
4. Ka'oli Kahokuloa
5. Kalen Galtes
6. Kalani David

OPEN MEN
1. Kiron Jabour
2. Aaron Swanson
3. Dege O'Connell
4. Alex Smith
5. Kyle Galtes
6. Davey Brand

OPEN WOMEN
1. Malia Manuel
2. Nage Melamed
3. Gabriella Cope
4. Kallee Krebs
5. Kelia Moniz
6. Kendall Krebs

OPEN LONGBOARD
1. Bullet Obra
2. Ka'oli Kahokuloa
3. Dylan McNeil

NO FEAR/KOASTAL KAOS PRO JUNIOR, PRESENTED BY HARD ROCK • ASP GRADE 1 MEN'S PRO JUNIOR
SUNSET BEACH
January 14–25

Sunset was striking to watch as 8–12 foot sets rolled into the lineup, heaving the 20 years and under surfers into the drops of their lives! No problem for Hawaii's Kiron Jabour, who scored a 6.25 and 7.5, taking out the final and staking his claim to qualify for the World Junior Championship. Brazilian-born Jabour has lived in Hawaii since he was four years old and flies the Hawaiian flag.

RESULTS
1. Kiron Jabour
2. Tyler Newton
3. Jeronimo Vargas
4. Marco Giorgi

PADDLE CORE FITNESS PRO
SUNSET BEACH
January 20

Bonga Perkins took down a crew of international big-wave riders on 18- to 25-foot westerly peaks at Sunset Beach to claim the first-ever Paddlecorefitness.com stand up surfing event on the North Shore of Oahu. In a final that also featured Hawaiian SUP specialist Ikaika Kalama, tow and big-wave specialist Garrett McNamara and Australian paddle board champion Jamie Mitchell, Perkins' knowledge of the break and impeccable timing got him past the field of watermen.

RESULTS
1. Bonga Perkins
2. Ikaika Kalama
3. Jamie Mitchell
4. Garrett McNamara

Bonga Perkins. Photo Allen Mozo.

PUFFERFISH SURF SERIES, VOLCOM QUALIFYING SERIES
MAILE POINT, WEST SIDE, OAHU
January 26–27

The second stop of the Pufferfish Surf Series went off in clean 2- to 4-foot Maile Point.

MEN PRO-AM
1. Dustin Cuizon
2. Jason Shibata
3. Brennen Bourdeu
4. Kaupena Miranda
5. Kyle Ramey
6. Liam Mcnamara

JUNIORS
1. Billy Kemper
2. Jackson Kine
3. Dege O'Connell
4. Albee Layer
5. Ford Archbold
6. Kyle Galtez

GROMS
1. Keanu Asing
2. Isiah Moniz
3. Ezkiel Lau
4. Seth Moniz
5. Austin Vicente
6. Eala Stewart

GIRLS
1. Nage Melamed
2. Kelia Moniz
3. Alissa Wooten
4. Anna Fry
5. Cecekua Enriques
6. Dax McGill

MONSTER ENERGY PIPELINE PRO, PRESENTED BY BILLABONG • ASP 3-STAR MEN'S EVENT
PIPELINE, OAHU
January 27–February 6

Hawaii's Pancho Sullivan wiped out the opposition to claim his second Monster Energy Pipeline Pro at Backdoor Pipe in barreling waves of 6 to 8 feet. Posting a perfect 10-point tube ride as well as the highest heat score of the event—18.75 points out of 20—in the 30-minute final, Pancho left his three rivals in need of a combination of scores to turn the tables. The win earned Sullivan $7,000 and 875 WQS ratings points.

FINAL
1. Pancho Sullivan
2. Fred Patacchia
3. Roy Powers
4. Dustin Barca

SEMIFINAL 1
1. Roy Powers
2. Pancho Sullivan
3. Makuakai Rothman
4. Marcus Hickman

SEMIFINAL 2
1. Dustin Barca
2. Fred Patacchia
3. TJ Barron
4. Ian Walsh

Jamie O'Brien.
Photo Steve Robertson.

PIPELINE BODYSURFING CLASSIC, PRESENTED BY HONOLUA SURF CO.
PIPELINE, NORTH SHORE, OAHU
January 27–February 6

The Honolua Surf Company Pipeline Bodysurfing Classic wrapped up with 10-time champion Mike Stewart claiming his 11th trophy and $1000. It was a tough day for all involved as rainsqualls whipped up the 2- to 4-foot peaks that Pipeline had to offer.

The elite group of watermen charged the lineup, taking off underwater like dolphins and catapulting their bodies across big sections. It was a sight to see, as they would spin and hurl themselves up into the curl and down again, arms out, as if to say hello. " I call that move the Cunningham; he taught it to me," said champ Mike Stewart.

RESULTS
1. Mike Stewart
2. Frederic David
3. Gavin Kennelly
4. Steve Kapela
5. Mark Cunningham
6. Todd Sells

QUIKSILVEREDITION KU IKAIKA CHALLENGE, PRESENTED BY C4 WATERMAN & RED BULL
MAKAHA POINT, WEST SIDE, OAHU
January 15–February 29

The inaugural edition was a hugely successful celebration of the waterman heritage, epic surf and aloha that have been Hawaii's gifts to the world for centuries. Staged in waves that ranged throughout the day from 6 to 15 feet, the world's first big-wave stand-up paddle surfing event was more about gathering together to honor a tradition than it was about winning. The first-place winner's check of $4,000, ultimately claimed by revered Hawaiian waterman Aaron Napoleon (Pearl City, Oahu, 41), was presented on his behalf to the West Side Junior Lifeguard Foundation. Every surfer in the main event received an equal prize check of $350.

FINAL
1. Aaron Napoleon
2. Keoni Keaulana
3. Ikaika Kalama
4. Kamu Auwae

NSSA HAWAII OPEN & EXPLORER #6
PINETREES, KAUAI
February 16–17

NSSA Hawaii conference event 6 went down at Pinetrees with Tyler Newton taking the Open Men and Tanner Hendrickson claiming the Juniors division.

OPEN MEN
1. Tyler Newton
2. Granger Larsen
3. Keanu Asing
4. Aaron Swanson
5. Kai Barger
6. Tanner Hendrickson

OPEN JUNIORS
1. Tanner Hendrickson
2. Keanu Asing
3. Ian Gentil
4. Matty Costa
5. Ezekiel Lau
6. Eli Olson

OPEN BOYS
1. Makai McNamara
2. Kain Daly
3. Ian Gentil
4. Ka'oli Kahokuloa
5. Chaz Kinoshita
6. Imaikalani DeVault

OPEN MINI GROMS
1. Pierre Graham
2. Seth Moniz
3. Iamaikalani DeVault
4. Kalani David
5. Lucas Angulo
6. Dylan Lehmann

OPEN WOMEN
1. Alessa Quizon
2. Malia Manuel
3. Coco Ho
4. Nage Melamed
5. Tatiana Weston-Webb
6. Leila Hurst

OPEN LONGBOARD
1. Ka'oli Kahokuloa
2. Dylan McNeil
3. Michael Stuart

EXPLORER BOYS
1. Koa Smith
2. Ezekiel Lau
3. Matty Costa
4. Kaimana Jaquias
5. Luke Hitchcock
6. Dylan Aoki Walsh

EXPLORER MENEHUENE
1. Lahiki Minamishin
2. Ka'oli Kahokuloa
3. Makai McNamara
4. Josh Moniz
5. Koa Smith
6. Luke Hichcock

EXPLORER WOMEN
1. Coco Ho
2. Gabrielle Cope
3. Kelia Moniz
4. Alisha Gonzales

5. Monyca Byrne-Wickey
6. Nage Melamed

EXPLORER GIRLS
1. Malia Manuel
2. Nage Melamed
3. Tatiana Weston-Webb
4. Kelia Moniz
5. Leila Hurst
6. Alessa Quizon

EXPLORER LONGBOARD
1. Michael Stuart
2. Dylan McNeil

HARD ROCK CAFE SURF SERIES
MA'ILI BEACH PARK, OAHU
March 15–16

Over 20 divisions and offshore conditions, 100 plus surfers at the break, fun for all.

MENEHUNE 2A
1. Elijah Gates
2. Alex Pendleton
3. Mo Freitas
4. Kaulana Apo
5. Finn Mcgill
6. Andrew Medina

BOYS 2A
1. Sheldon Pasion
2. E.J. Mitsui
3. Dax Mcgill
4. Cole Yamamoto
5. Kaito Kino

JUNIOR MEN 2A
1. Kylen Yamakawa
2. Evyn Tyndzik
3. Christian Pendleton
4. Keoni Jones
5. Barak Maor
6. Kainoa Haas

MEN 2A
1. Davin Jaime
2. Pancho Peterson
3. Fumi Hirano
4. Bruno Silva

OPEN MEN
1. Brice Yamashita
2. Davin Jaime
3. Scott Shimoda
4. Pancho Peterson

MASTERS
1. Scott Shimoda
2. Darren Mahoe
3. Brice Yamashita
4. Alessandro Costa
5. Satoshi Ito

SENIOR MEN
1. Greg Hunter
2. Stephen Obrien
3. Matt Kenny
4. Adam Traubman
5. Robert Howard
6. Michael Estencion

GRANDMASTERS
1. Tommy Reyes
2. Raymond Shito
3. John Limahai
4. Kimo Miranda
5. Kal Faurot
6. Gilbert Perez

GIRLS
1. Dax Mcgill
2. Maili Enos Branigan
3. Missy Valdez
4. Hana Harrison
5. Megan Steele

WOMEN
1. Dana Tortuga
2. Glennel Warren
3. Izumi Baldwin
4. Susan Nishida

Aaron Napolean. Photo Bernie Baker.

NSSA/RVCA HAWAII REGIONAL CHAMPS
KEWALO BASIN, OAHU
March 15–20

OPEN MEN
1. Granger Larsen
2. Billy Kemper
3. Albee Layer
4. Kai Barger

OPEN WOMEN
1. Alessa Quizon
2. Nage Melamed
3. Monyca Byrne-Wickey
4. Malia Manuel

OPEN JUNIORS
1. Tanner Hendrickson
2. Ezekiel Lau
3. John John Florence
4. Keanu Asing
5. Matty Costa
6. Makana Eleogram

OPEN BOYS
1. Koa Smith
2. Ian Gentil
3. Luke Hitchcock
4. Kain Daly
5. Makai McNamara
6. Seth Moniz

OPEN MINI GROMS
1. Imaikalani DeVault
2. Kalani David
3. Kaulana Apo
4. Seth Moniz
5. Pierre Graham
6. Kona Olivira

OPEN LONGBOARD
1. Ka'oli Kahokuloa
2. Bullet Obra
3. D.K. Walsh
4. Michael Sturat
5. Kazuma Saita
6. Shaun Walsh

EXPLORER MEN
1. Kai Barger
2. John John Florence
3. Dylan Goodale
4. Granger Larsen
5. Albee Layer
6. Alex Smith

EXPLORER JUNIORS
1. John John Florence
2. Levi Gonzales
3. Granger Larsen
4. Tyler Newton
5. Albee Layer
6. Alex Smith

EXPLORER BOYS

1. Kaimana Jaquias
2. Keanu Asing
3. Ezekiel Lau
4. Luke Hitchcock
5. Makai McNamara
6. Matty Costa

EXPLORER MENEHUENES
1. Seth Moniz
2. Luke Hitchcock
3. Makai McNamara
4. Koa Smith
5. Joshua Moniz
6. Ian Gentil

EXPLORER WOMEN
1. Coco Ho
2. Leila Hurst
3. Alessa Quizon
4. Nage Melamed
5. Monyca Bryne-Wickey
6. Alisha Gonsalves

EXPLORER GIRLS
1. Leila Hurst
2. Alessa Quizon
3. Nage Melamed
4. Alisha Gonsalves
5. Kelia Moniz
6. Malia Manuel

EXPLORER LONGBOARD
1. Bullet Obra
2. Kazuma Saita
3. D.K. Walsh
4. Shaun Walsh
5. Michael Sturat

EXPLORER MASTERS
1. Christian Budroe
2. Scott Shimoda
3. Dale Sabate

EXPLORER SENIORS
1. Dale Sabate
2. Eric Olson
3. Christian Budroe
4. Bryan Suratt
5. Raymond Shito

EXPLORER SUPER SENIORS
1. Raymond Shito

STEINLAGER SHAKA LONGBOARD SERIES
SUNSET BEACH
April 5–6

The Steinlager Shaka Longboard Series was completed in some wild and windblown surf at Sunset Beach with wave heights reaching 12-foot faces at times. Over 90 surfers from around the state showed up to brave

the cool north winds and shifty peaks, and while some survived, a half dozen not so lucky ones went home with two-piece souvenirs as the power of Sunset took wrath on those competitors.

LONGBOARD
1. Ikaika Kalama
2. Kamu Auwae
3. Kai Sallas
4. Koa Enriquez

STAND UP PADDLEBOARD
1. Kamu Auwae
2. Dave Parmenter
3. Leleo Kinimaka
4. Nolan Martin

HARD ROCK CAFE SERIES, PRESENTED BY QUIKSILVER
KEWALO BASIN, OAHU
May 10

The Hard Rock Cafe Surfing Series completed its last event for the season as the Quiksilver Kewalo event drew 120 competitors. Two- to three-foot faces on the south shore reef break raised the bar once again for the top-level amateurs.

MENEHUNE 2A
1. Kaulana Apo
2. Kalani David
3. Alex Pendleton
4. Joshua Moniz
5. Ivan Florence
6. Mo Freitas

BOYS 2A
1. Kaito Kino
2. Nathan Florence
3. Matty Costa
4. John Quizon
5. Sheldon Paishon
6. Ha'a Aikau

JUNIOR MEN 2A
1. John Florence
2. Hizon Linkee
3. Derek Wong
4. Kaiea Bosgra
5. Eli Olson
6. Kylen Yamakawa

MEN 2A
1. Davin Jaime
2. Fumi Hirano
3. Bruno Silva
4. Mo Siscon

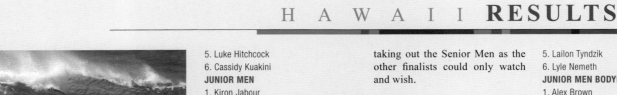

Kamu Auwae. Photo Bernie Baker.

MASTERS
1. Darren Mahoe
2. Scott Shimoda
3. Derrick Chang
4. Alessandro Costa
5. Brice Yamashita
6. Ryota Seki

SENIOR MEN
1. Robert Howard
2. Todd Murashige
3. Richard Tom
4. Adam Traubman
5. Stephen O'Brien
6. Greg Hunter

OPEN MEN
1. Hizon Linkee
2. Ronson Silva
3. Evyn Tyndzik
4. Kaiea Bosgra
5. Richard Tom
6. Keoni Jones

GIRLS
1. Missy Valdez
2. Hana Harrison
3. Alyssa Wooten
4. Maili Enos Branigan

WOMEN
1. Izumi Baldwin
2. Dana Tortuga
3. Sheila Finnegan
4. Gennel Warren
5. Susan Nishida

3. Flynn Novak
4. Love Hodel

SEMIFINAL 1
1. Love Hodel
2. TJ Barron
3. Jason Shibata
4. Hank Gaskell

SEMIFINAL 2
1. Joel Centeio
2. Flynn Novak
3. Shane Beschen
4. Chris Foster

QUARTERFINAL 1
1. Jason Shibata
2. TJ Barron
3. Kiron Jabour
4. Isaac Stant

QUARTERFINAL 2
1. Hank Gaskell
2. Love Hodel
3. Makuakai Rothman
4. Evan Valiere

QUARTERFINAL 3
1. Joel Centeio
2. Chris Foster
3. Nathan Carroll
4. Dylan Melamed

QUARTERFINAL 4
1. Shane Beschen
2. Flynn Novak
3. Daniel Jones
4. Rainos Hayes

MACY'S E-SERIES EVENT #1
MAILI POINT, OAHU
May 15–18

A mix of building southwest and declining northwest swells was the perfect concoction of contestable conditions for TJ Barron to win the Macy's E-Series Event #1. Barron's victory in the 1-star World Qualifying Series (WQS) event held at Maili Point in fun, two-foot surf, earned him $2,500 dollars and 250 WQS points.

Second place went to Joel Centeio (Makakilo, $1,000, 219 points), third was Flynn Novak (North Shore, $800, 188 points), and fourth was Love Hodel (North Shore, $700, 178 points).

Although Maili is predominantly a left-breaking wave, Barron won the 30-minute final by going right. The 25-year-old regular-foot used his front side attack brilliantly, linking up a tail slide, snap, and two roundhouse cutbacks over barely submerged reef.

FINAL
1. TJ Barron
2. Joel Centeio

LOCAL MOTION SURF INTO SUMMER, PRESENTED BY BILLABONG
ALA MOANA BOWLS, OAHU
May 24–29

The Local Motion Surf Into Summer presented by Billabong finished off the three-day holiday weekend at the Ala Moana Bowl with head-high surf, tons of prizes and burgers on the beach for all the contestants, wrapping up the biggest amateur contest in Hawaii. Leading the charge was Brennan Boudreau from Makakilo, taking top honors in the Open Men with the North Shore's Kiron Jabour winning the Junior division.

MENEHUNE
1. Joshua Moniz
2. Seth Moniz
3. Kalani David
4. Ivan Florence
5. Landon McNamara
6. Kaulanu Apo

BOYS
1. Ha'a Aikau
2. Makai McNamara
3. Ezekiel Lau
4. Isaiah Moniz

5. Luke Hitchcock
6. Cassidy Kuakini

JUNIOR MEN
1. Kiron Jabour
2. John John Florence
3. Kainoa Haas
4. Hizson Lin Kee Jr.
5. Jedediah Pacheco
6. Kapu Ping

MEN
1. Brennan Boudreau
2. Jared Clapper
3. Gregg Nakamura
4. Makana Ciotti
5. Scott Saito
6. Derek Wong

MASTERS
1. Scott Shimoda
2. Michael Chun
3. Kris Grimm
4. Gabriel Lietz
5. Jorge Chong
6. Kevin Whitton

SENIOR MEN
1. Todd Murashige
2. Edrick Baldwin
3. Mike Akima
4. Richard Tom
5. Robert Howard
6. Brad Chang

GIRLS
1. Kelia Moniz
2. Alyssha Gonsalves
3. Kaili Rodman
4. Dax McGill
5. Kendall Krebb
6. Alyssa Wooten

WOMEN
1. Missy Valdez
2. Lane Davey
3. Izumi Baldwin
4. Michelle Watkins
5. Cecilia Enriquez
6. Jenny Kono

LONGBOARD MEN
1. Nelson Ahina
2. Geoff Wong
3. Nainoa Ciotti
4. DeKrammer Hatae
5. Shane Stedman
6. Kupe Rosser

LONGBOARD MASTERS
1. Gavin Hasegawa
2. Lucas Won
3. Ash Marzouki
4. Gino Bell
5. Daniel Stein
6. Rober Fernandez

LONGBOARD WOMEN
1. Ashley Ahina
2. Ashley Quintal
3. Chie Matsuoka
4. Stacia Ahina
5. Leah Cantrell
6. Rachel Spear

BURGER KING HASA CHAMPS
ALA MOANA BOWL, OAHU
June 4–6

Whopper-sized waves treated finalists to some heavy action at the Ala Moana Bowl as double-overhead surf took competitors by surprise for the final day of competition. Ala Moana local Kal Farot used local knowledge in capturing the Grandmasters title as he took positioning on the best sets of his heat. Not to be outdone, Todd Murashige from Honolulu found a couple of nice hollow pits in

taking out the Senior Men as the other finalists could only watch and wish.

MENEHEUNE
1. Chaz Kinoshita
2. Ian Gentil
3. Elijah Gates
4. Imai Devault
5. Tatiana Weston Webb
6. Uluboy Napeahi

BOYS
1. Ha'a Aikau
2. Keanu Asing
3. Kaoli Kahokuloa
4. Sheldon Pashion

JUNIOR MEN
1. Kylen Yamakawa
2. Dege O'Connell
3. Kapu Ping
4. Levi Gonsalez

MEN
1. Dain Jaime
2. Theodore Landt
3. Nakoa Decoite
4. Shawn Pila
5. Josh Rex

OPEN MEN
1. Christian Enns
2. Keanu Asing
3. Forrest Troxell
4. Tanner Hendrickson
5. Dege O'Connell
6. Scott Shimoda

MASTERS
1. Scott Shimoda
2. Chrstian Enns
3. Darren Mahoe
4. Brice Yamashita
5. Alessandro Costa
6. Derrick Chang

SENIOR MEN
1. Todd Murashige
2. Miguel Graham
3. Adam Escobar
4. Robert Howard
5. Greg Hunter
6. Stephen O'Brien

GRANDMASTERS
1. Kal Farot
2. Mark Shima
3. Les Tabuchi
4. Eddie Pieper
5. Raymond Shito
6. Tommy Reyes

BOYS BODYBOARD
1. Matthew Holzman
2. Kainoa French
3. Cody Lucas
4. Storm Magsaday

5. Lailon Tyndzik
6. Lyle Nemeth

JUNIOR MEN BODYBOARD
1. Alex Brown
2. Travis Smith
3. Kaena La'a
4. Oliver Seitz
5. Rusty Akeo
6. Corin Foster

MEN BODYBOARD
1. James Clancy
2. Bradda La'a
3. Dayne Kim
4. Mark Gervacio

GIRLS
1. Nage Melamed
2. Missy Valdez
3. Lani Doherty
4. Erika Steiner

WOMEN
1. Mia Melamed
2. Dana Tortuga
3. Kalindi Jacoby
4. Virginia Fajardo
5. Nina Dodge
6. Takako Yago

STEINLAGER SHAKA LONGBOARD SERIES EVENT #2
QUEEN'S KUHIO BEACH, OAHU
May 31–June 1

Contestants scored some fun 3- to 4-foot faces at the Queen's surf break at Kuhio Beach amongst the thousands of tourists surrounding the shores of Waikiki. Leading the charge in the longboard competition was Waianae's Kamu Auwae, as he took down a field of 32 professional surfers to claim first and take the series lead along with $1,200 in prize money. Second place went to another Waianae local, Duane DeSoto.

PRO DIVISION
1. Kamu Auwae
2. Duane DeSoto
3. Kekoa Auwae
4. Keegan Edwards

OPEN STAND UP PADDLE
1. Ikaika Kalama
2. Kamu Auwae
3. Duane DeSoto
4. Kekoa Auwae

MENEHUNE
1. Jackson Hollingsworth

Junior Men's winner Kiron Jabour. Photo Bernie Baker.

2. Maika DeSoto
3. Trevor Collins
4. Vanina Walsh

JUNIOR MEN
1. Nelson Ahina
2. Kody Gedge
3. Cody Harada
4. Marc Logan

MEN
1. Dane McCallum
2. Keoni Duey
3. Daniel Johnson
4. Daniel Teijiro

MASTERS
1. Shane Hamamoto
2. Lucas Won
3. Paul McDonnell
4. Jared Katakura

SENIOR MEN
1. Daniel Stein
2. Alika Willis
3. Gino Bello
4. Kevin Pascua

GRANDMASTERS
1. Stephan Katayama
2. Lance Ohata
3. Bob Kim
4. Jim Gartland

LEGENDS
1. Soyu Kawamoto
2. Arnold Lum
3. George Matsuda

JUNIOR WAHINE
1. Megan Godinez
2. Tracy Pruse
3. Vanina Walsh
4. Jodie Clark

WAHINE
1. Leah Dawson
2. Akoi Pada
3. Chie Matsuoka
4. Kim Miyashiro

HIC ALL MILITARY SURF CLASSIC, PRESENTED BY QUIKSILVER & MWR
LADIES BARBER'S POINT, OAHU
June 21

The annual All Military Surf Classic, presented by HIC, Quiksilver and MWR once again brought active U.S. military personnel, retirees, dependants and their families together for a day of surf, sun, competition and camaraderie on the sands of White Plains Beach.

MILITARY S.B. 17–29 YEARS OLD
1. Shawn Clamlee
2. Fredrick Aquias
3. James Maxcey
4. Craig Replogle
5. Salvador Fiesta
6. Mike Fazio

MILITARY S.B. 30 & OVER
1. Rod Behrend
2. Edwin Nakazato
3. Fabian Enanoria
4. Jason Tangalin
5. Randy Ferriman
6. Darwin Thomas

MILITARY L.B. 17–29 YEARS OLD
1. Shawn Clamlee
2. Duke Yim
3. Matt Okerson
4. Robert Villanueva
5. Mathew Toole
6. Craig Replogle

MILITARY L.B. 30 & OVER
1. Fabian Enanoria
2. Johnny Dodge

3. Rod Behrend
4. Tim Ige
5. Darwin Thomas
6. Edwin Nakazato

MILITARY WOMEN L.B.
1. Dee Marques
2. Carmel Tomlins
3. Terrish Bilbrey
4. Michelle Parlette
5. Nadia Aquias

OPEN S.B. 12 & UNDER
1. Elijah Gates
2. Tiare Blanco
3. Nicole Brueggemann
4. Chris Bluthardt
5. Nathan Chester
6. Devon Brueggemann

RIP CURL GROMSEARCH, HAWAII PRESENTED BY BOOST MOBILE
LAHAINA HARBOR, MAUI
July 12

With fun, rippable surf gracing the line-up, the Rip Curl GromSearch, presented by BOOST Mobile showcased top talents in all divisions.

UNDER 16 BOYS
1. Tanner Hendrickson
2. Alfred Layer
3. Dylan Goodale
4. Makana Eleogram

Finn McGill. Photo Mike Latronic/Freesurfingmagazine.com.

UNDER 16 GIRLS
1. Lani Doherty
2. Hanna Harrison
3. Alyssa Wooten
4. Kulia Doherty

UNDER 14 BOYS
1. Kain Daly
2. Dylan Walsh
3. Luke Hitchcock
4. Cole Walter

UNDER 12 BOYS
1. Imaikalani Devault
2. Kain Daly
3. Nathan Schlea
4. Luke Hitchcock
5. Cole Walter
6. Justice Patao

MACY'S E SERIES • ASP 1-STAR MEN'S WQS
BOWLS SOUTH SHORE, OAHU
July 16

The E Series 1-star WQS ended on an all-time high, claimed as the greatest day of pro surfing ever seen on the South Shore. Saving the best for last in the nine-day waiting period, Bowls pumped out waves with machine-like consistency with 6- to 8-foot barrels.

FINAL
1. Flynn Novak
2. David Gonsalves
3. Jason Shibata
4. Kaipo Jaquias

QUIKSILVER SURF SHOP CHALLENGE
ALA MOANA, OAHU
July 19

The sinking sailboat in the channel wasn't the only thing going down at Ala Moana as seven teams took to the lineup for the regional qualifier for the Quiksilver Surf Shop Challenge, presented by *Surfer Magazine*. The building south swell, light winds and blazing sun made for ideal conditions, and Town & Country, last year's national runners-up, picked up where they left off, grabbing the highest score of the first round. T & C will now join other regional winners on September 8 at the nationals at Huntington Beach, California.

1. Town & Country
2. Nukumoi
3. Pacific Vibrations
4. HIC

11TH ANNUAL T & C SURF GROM CONTEST
QUEENS, WAIKIKI, OAHU
July 12–13

After a week of flat conditions, Queens surged to life when nearly

Kyle Galtes. Photo Tony Heff/Freesurfingmagazine.com.

200 groms hit the water for the T & C Groms. With plenty of fun and not much pressure, champions were crowned in Longboard, Shortboard and Bodyboard divisions. The groms ranged in age from 3 to 14.

BODYBOARD 9 YEARS AND UNDER
Honolua Blomfield
BODYBOARD 10–14
Titus Lafradez
SHORTBOARD 7 YEARS AND UNDER
Keola Auwae
SHORTBOARD 8–11
Dane Rust
SHORTBOARD 12–14
Cole Yamakawa
SHORTBOARD GIRLS 9 AND UNDER
Moana Jones
SHORTBOARD GIRLS 10–14
Cayla Moore

LONGBOARD 9 AND UNDER
Finn McGill
LONGBOARD 10–14
Eala Stewart

HENNESSEY'S INTERNATIONAL PADDLEBOARD CHAMPIONSHIPS
TURTLE BAY TO WAIMEA BAY
July 20

World paddleboard champion Jamie Mitchell of Australia posted his fourth win of an undefeated season, winning the $15,000 Hennessey by a conclusive margin. With inconsistent trade winds along the seven-mile route, there were no records broken, but Mitchell still set a blistering flat water pace. It was a great lead-in to the upcoming Quiksilver Edition Molokai to Oahu race for defending champion Mitchell.

MEN
1. Jamie Mitchell
2. Jackson English
3. Nathan Henderson

WOMEN
1. Kanesa Duncan
2. Shakira Westdorp
3. Sarah Herrington

STAND UP PADDLEBOARD
1. Guy Pere
2. Brendan Shea

3. Aaron Napoleon

NSSA HAWAII EVENT #1
PK'S, KAUAI
July 26–27

The NSSA season opened with a lip-smackin' 2- to 4-foot surf at PK's on the Kauai south shore. The new NSSA format, which allows only resident island surfers to compete, was a big positive, with many new faces appearing. Newcomer James Thesken took an impressive double in winning the Open Boys and Explorer Meneheunes, while Kyle Galtes blew up to win the Open Men and Explorer Juniors. As if that wasn't enough, celebrity Jada Pinkett-Smith showed up to cheer on the Kinemaka sisters.

Flynn Novak. Photo Bernie Baker.

OPEN MEN
1. Kyle Galtes
2. Dylan Goodale
3. Kaimana Jaquias
4. Chatson Barrett
5. Nathan Carvalho
6. Gavin Klein

OPEN JUNIORS
1. Kaimana Jaquias
2 Kalen Galtes
3. Kaikea Elias
4. Jesse Gugliemana
5. Troy Weston-Webb
6. Ry Cowan

OPEN BOYS
1. James Thesken
2. Lucas Angulo
3. Dorian Blanchard
4. Kai Haugland
5. Pierre Graham
6. Tabin Shamblin

OPEN MINI GROMS
1. Mainei Kinemaka

OPEN WOMEN
1. Leila Hurst
2. Nage Melamed
3. Tatiana Weston-Webb
4. Maluhia Kinemaka
5. Brianna Cope
6. Lianna Patey

Joy Monahan, on the platform and in the water. Photos Bernie Baker.

VOLCOM PUFFERFISH SURF SERIES
LAHAINA, MAUI
August 9–10

The new Pufferfish series kicked off with a bang in Lahaina Harbor when some tidy lines showed up, even though no surf was predicted. A cool vibe presided over the event, with Gavin Beschen in charge of the barbie and hanging with the 100-plus groms all day.

MEN PRO AM
1. Jason Shibata
2. Matt Meola
3. Wesley Larson
4. Buzzy Statner
5. Charlie Carroll
6. Kea Espiritu

JUNIORS
1. Tanner Hendrickson
2. Makana Eleogram
3. Kyle Galtes
4. Dylan Goodale
5. Albee Layer
6. Baker Grant

GROMS
1. Ian Gentil
2. Kaoli Kahokua
3. Ezekiel Lau
4. Imaikalani Devault
5. Dylan Walsh
6. Sheldon Paishon

GIRLS
1. Lani Dougherty
2. Monyca Byrne-Wickey
3. Helena Suehiro
4. Kayla Eubank
5. Kulia Dougherty
6. Alicia Yamada

SEA HAWAII GIRLS WHO SURF PRO AM
KEWALO BASIN PARK, OAHU
August 16–17

Two perfect days of surf at Kewalo Basin for the girls who surf!

It ranged in the 2- to 5-foot area throughout with sunny skies, big moves and broad smiles all round.

STAND UP PADDLEBOARD
1. Candice Appleby
2. Jennifer Koki
3. Kalii Rodman
4. Kawehi Whitford
5. Heather Jeppesen

LONGBOARD
1. Carissa Moore
2. Leah Dawson
3. Crystal Dzigas
4. Miku Uemura

SHORTBOARD
1. Carissa Moore
2. Aleesa Quizon
3. Hana Harrison
4. Nage Melamed

MACY'S E SERIES
KUHIO BEACH, OAHU
August 18

Maui's Kai Barger scored the first major pro junior victory of his career, taking out big names Clay Marzo, Casey Brown and Ha'a Aikau along the way. Surf for the event was contestable most of the day, but the finalists struggled with the high-tide blues, with only 13 waves ridden in the final.

RESULT
1. Kai Barger
2. Sebastien Zietz
3. Keanu Asing
4. Albee Layer

RVCA NSSA SERIES
LAHAINA HARBOR, MAUI
August 16

Another great contest at Lahaina Harbor. The first day of the event saw some very contestable conditions. Typical morning glass and waist- to chest-high sets with the occasional head-high bomb. This being a highly rated 5-star event, most of the top Hawaii amateurs

showed at Lahaina for the event. A 10-point ride was the highlight on the first day for Maui's Tanner Hendrickson, as well as scooping up wins in the Open Men, Explorer Juniors and Explorer Men. Coming off her U.S. Open win, Kauai's Malia Manuel took both the Open and Explorer Women. Another Kauai contender, Maluhia Kinimaka, showed the harbor crowd where the future of the girls is by winning the Explorer division.

OPEN MEN
1. Tanner Hendrickson
2. Ezekiel Lau
3. Makana Eleogram
4. Derek Wong
5. Lahiki Minamishin
6. Kyle Galtes

OPEN WOMEN
1. Malia Manuel
2. Leila Hurst
3. Lani Doherty
4. Kelia Moniz
5. Lianna Patey
6. Alisha Gonsalves

OPEN JUNIORS
1. Kolohe Andino
2. Ezekiel Lau
3. Tosh Peila
4. Matty Costa
5. Luke Hitchcock
6. Ian Gentil

OPEN BOYS
1. Ian Gentil
2. Imaikalani DeVault
3. Seth Moniz
4. Cole Walter
5. Kalani David
6. Kaulana Apo

OPEN MINI GROMS
1. Noa Mizuno
2. Dylan Lehmann
3. Kala Willard
4. Kaulana Apo
5. Dax McGill
6. Monte Grant

OPEN LONGBOARD
1. DK Walsh
2. Shaun Walsh
3. Kai Lenny
4. Justin Ringsby
5. Pierce Watumull

ROXY JAM HONOLULU, PRESENTED BY SCHICK QUATTRO FOR WOMEN • ASP WLT 3-STAR WOMEN'S EVENT
QUEEN'S OAHU HAWAII
August 20–23

Newly crowned women's world longboarding champion Joy Monahan (Honolulu) capped off the summer of her life by winning the Roxy Jam Honolulu, presented by Schick. The event was held at Waikiki Beach as part of the Duke's OceanFest. Monahan, 22, surfed to a convincing win over a stellar local lineup in the final and earned $2,000 for her result. Runner-up for the second consecutive year was 15-year-old Roxy team-rider Kelia Moniz (Honolulu). While Moniz demonstrated the most impressive nose-riding of the event—clocking up weightless "cheetah fives" and "hang tens," her wave selection left her short on the critical points in the final. "It has been an amazing summer, one of my favorites for sure," said Monahan, who heads back to college in Utah next week.

FINAL
1. Joy Monahan
2. Kelia Moniz
3. Geodee Clark
4. Malia Kaleopaa

SEMIFINAL 1
1. Geodee Clark
2. Joy Monahan
3. Kaitlyn Maguire

4. Crystal Dzigas

SEMIFINAL 2
1. Kelia Moniz
2. Malia Kaleopaa
3. Jennifer Koki
4. Ashley Quintal

C4 WATERMAN/HONOLUA SURF CO SUP
QUEEN'S WAIKIKI OAHU HAWAII
August 17–24

In another first for the sport of stand-up paddle (SUP) surfing, the major honors for the C4 Waterman/Honolua Surf Co. competition, presented by Blue Planet, went to a woman. Waikiki's Candice Appleby out-performed a field of world-class SUP surfers to win both the Pro division and the Women's category. Among Appleby's casualties in the pro ranks were Brian Keaulana (Makaha), Noland Martin (Makaha), and Noah

Candice Appleby. Photo Bernie Baker.

Shimabukuro (Kula, Maui). It was also a day of double victories for 13-year-old Maui stand-up paddler Slater Trout. Trout won the highest-scoring heat of all the finals—the men's amateur division against surfers more than twice his age—as well as the 12-mile C4 Waterman/Honolua Surf Co. paddleboard race from Hawaii Kai to Duke's Restaurant, Waikiki, held earlier in the day.

PRO DIVISION
1. Candice Appleby
2. Noland Martin
3. Noah Shimabukuro
4. Brian Keaulana

WOMEN
1. Candice Appleby
2. Pinoi Makalena
3. Jennifer Koki
4. Geodee Clark
5. Tiare Lawrence
6. Heather Jeppesen

JUNIORS
1. Kai Lenny
2. Brendan Bradley
3. Kawika Kinimaka
4. Micah Liana
5. Connor Baxter
6. Noah Yap

AMATEURS
1. Slater Trout
2. Chris Martin
3. Stuart Murray
4. Dennis Matos
5. Mike Mendez
6. Bill Ward

HARD ROCK CAFE SURF SERIES, HAWAII SURFING ASSOCIATION (HSA)
KEWALO'S, HONOLULU
September 6–7

At 15 years of age, Keanu Asing (Ewa Beach, Hawaii) represents the new face of surfing superstars who have a laser focus on the future. On the fast track to becoming one of Hawaii's leading international surf stars, his latest victory came in the second of 10 events that comprise the Hard Rock Cafe Surf Series, presented by the Hawaii Surfing Association (HSA), at Kewalo's, Honolulu. Asing's summer of celebrations began in May with his 15th birthday. Over the next three months he racked up wins in the NSSA Nationals in California, the Billabong Junior Pro in Bali, and

took U.S. Championship titles in both the 16 and 18 year divisions in California; two third placings in the Occy Grom contest in Bali and the Macy's Junior Pro at Waikiki; as well as a reputable showing in the ISA World Juniors in France. His goal now in the Hard Rock Cafe Surf Series at home is to qualify again for the ISA World Juniors and this time take it all the way to the winner's dais. Beyond that, his plan is to embark upon the World Pro Surfing Tour when he turns 18. Already boasting half a lifetime of competitive experience, Asing leads a crop of highly polished and extremely talented young surfers out of Hawaii who are set on taking their careers farther than that of their predecessors. The Hard Rock Cafe HSA series offers a division for every surfer, from the beginner menehune (ages 11 and under), to all ages of men, women, longboarders, bodyboarders and stand-up paddle surfers. But the most hotly contested division, without a doubt, is Asing's Junior Men division for surfers aged 15 to 17.

SHORTBOARD
JUNIOR MEN FINAL (AGE 15-17):
1. Keanu Asing
2. Kylen Yamakawa
3. Matty Costa
4. Ezekiel Lau

BOYS FINAL (AGE 12-14)
1. Eala Stewart
2. Makai McNamara
3. Isaiah Moniz
4. Cole Yamakawa

MEN FINAL (18-24)
1. Soleil Farnsworth
2. Jared Clapper
3. Kapu Ping
4. Davin Jaime

OPEN MEN FINAL
1. Matty Costa
2. Davin Jaime
3. Keanu Asing
4. Igor Lumuertz

RVCA NSSA SERIES
LAHAINA HARBOR, MAUI
September 6

The waves fired up as the Maui-competitors-only NSSA Hawaii RVCA series contest saw the best waves of summer blast through the Lahaina Harbor surf break. Four- to eight-foot faces came through for some heavy right-handers on the south shore

Pancho Sullivan. Photo ASP Towner © Covered Images.

break as the fierce competition brought out some bar level raising action. Maui veteran surfer and shaper Matt Kinoshita said, "The waves are as good as it gets."

OPEN MEN
1. Tanner Hendrickson
2. Tyle Grant
3. Nick Falbo
4. Makana Eleogram
5. Theo Niarchos
6. Michael Stuart

OPEN JUNIORS
1. Kain Daly
2. Tyler Grant
3. Dylan Aoki-Walsh
4. Ian Gentil
5. Zane Schweitzer
6. Alfred Rice

OPEN BOYS
1. Ian Gentil
2. Chaz Kinoshita
3. Imaikalani DeVault
4. Andrew Nieman
5. Cole Walter
6. Kala Willard

OPEN MINI GROMS
1. Kala Willard
2. Dylan Lehmann
3. Monte Grant
4. Hojo Pou
5. Elijah Hanneman
6. Kelson Lau

OPEN WOMEN
1. Lani Doherty
2. Alexis Aquera
3. Shelby Schweitzer
4. Cathrine Heenan
5. KatiKai Minami

OPEN LONGBOARD
1. DK Walsh
2. Kawika Kinimaka
3. Dylan McNeil
4. Shaun Walsh
5. Justin Ringsby
6. Kai Lenny

XCEL PRO, PRESENTED BY HONOLUA • ASP 4-STAR MEN'S WQS EVENT
SUNSET BEACH, OAHU HAWAII
October 26–November 10

In an all-Hawaiian, high-scoring 30-minute final, ASP World Tour surfer Pancho Sullivan took home his fourth Xcel Pro title, having previously won the event in 1998, 2000, and 2003. Sullivan dominated from the start, hitting a contest-high 9.77 that put him firmly in the driver's seat over fellow finalists Kamalei Alexander (2nd), Danny Fuller (3rd), and Makua Rothman (4th). "Epic," "pristine," and "all-time" were just a few ways used to describe the glassy morning conditions, as a new northwest swell came in overnight and brought clean, corduroy lines to Sunset Beach. The long-period swell stayed clean through the finals, challenging riders to stay in position off Sunset Point for optimal set wave selection.

1. Pancho Sullivan
2. Kamalei Alexander
3. Danny Fuller
4. Makua Rothman

#4 OF HARD ROCK CAFE SURF SERIES PRESENTED BY THE HAWAII SURFING ASSOCIATION
RENNICKS OAHU
November 15–16

Ezekiel Lau, 14, of Honolulu, has won stop #4 of the Hard Rock Cafe Surf Series, presented by the Hawaii Surfing Association, to finally break out of a victory drought that spanned "forever" and qualify for the State Championships. Lau boosted tail-free turns and airs without hesitation in the final. He opened up the heat with an 8-point ride out of a possible 10. The Kamehameha School freshman also surfed without a leash in the final, allowing him to surf faster in the small waves. "I usually don't surf out here with a leash anyways and it's tiny," Lau said. "You go faster because there's less drag."

JUNIOR MEN SHORTBOARD
1. Ezekiel Lau
2. Kylen Yamakawa
3. Matty Costa
4. Buddy Wiggins

MEN SHORTBOARD
1. Davin Jaime
2. Scott Saito

MENEHUNE 1-A SHORTBOARD
1. Finn McGill
2. Michael Ikalani
3. Christopher Bluhardt
4. Klaus Eyre

MENEHUNE 2-A SHORTBOARD
1. Seth Moniz
2. Kaulana Apo
3. Elijah Gates
4. Kalani David

BOYS SHORTBOARD
1. Isiah Moniz

2. Coley Yamakawa
3. Kaito Kino
4. Josh Moniz

MASTER SHORTBOARD
1. Brice Yamashita
2. Thomas Spear
3. Alessandro Costa
4. Bruce Foley

SENIOR MEN SHORTBOARD
1. Shannon Silva
2. Sheldon Poirier
3. Stephen O'Brien
4. Hank Hundhausen

GRANDMASTER SHORTBOARD
1. Kal Faurot
2. Raymond Shito
3. Gilbert Perea
4. Beau Hodges

OPEN MEN SHORTBOARD
1. Matty Costa
2. Davin Jaime
3. Matthew Oshiro
4. Thomas Spear

GIRLS SHORTBOARD
1. Kallee Krebs
2. Dax McGill
3. Maile Enos Branigan
4. Nicole Brueffemann

WOMEN SHORTBOARD
1. Bonnie Campanella
2. Izumi Baldwin
3. Mari Sullivan
4. Susan Nishida

BOYS BODYBOARD
1. Micah Liana

MEN BODYBOARD
1. James Clancy
2. Mark Gervacaio

MEN DROP KNEE
1. James Clancy
2. Mark Gervacio

MENEHUNE LONGBOARD
1. Micah Liana
2. Jordan Brueggemann
3. Klans Eyre
4. Vincent Starn

JUNIOR LONGBOARD
1. Nelson Ahina

MEN LONGBOARD
1. Justin Mitsui
2. Mau Ah Hee
3. Daniel Teijeiro

SENIOR MEN LONGBOARD
1. Alika Willis
2. Gino Bell
3. Frederico Algono
4. Gavin Hasegawa

GIRLS LONGBOARD
1. Tracy Pruse
2. Kelly Graf
3. Keisha Eyre
4. Bailey Nagy

Keanu Asing. Photo Bernie Baker.

Carissa Moore. Photo APS Rowland © Covered Images.

Michel Bourez. Photo ASP Rowland © Covered Images.

NIXON WTA
PIPELINE, OAHU
December 8–20

Nixon announced Joel Parkinson as the winner of the fourth and final stop of the 2008 Nixon WTA, after winning the Vans Triple Crown.

Parkinson made a solid showing in this year's three events, kicking off with a fifth place finish at both the Reef Hawaiian Pro as well as at the O'Neill World Cup of Surfing. He rounded out his performance with a 9th place finish at the Billabong Pipe Masters. Hailing from Australia's Gold Coast, Parkinson has been a key player on tour all year, with perhaps one of the most memorable achievements when he scored the first-ever 20 out of 20 at Pipeline.

Parkinson will be rewarded for his win with a custom Nixon 51-30 tide watch with nearly two carats of white baguette diamonds on the bezel crowned with a black onyx countdown timer marker.

WOMEN LONGBOARD
1. Izumi Baldwin
2. Dana Tortuga

LEGENDS LONGBOARD
1. Layton Sun
2. Lance Ohata
3. George Matsuda
4. Wink Arnott

OPEN LONGBOARD
1. Nelson Ahina
2. Mau Ah Hee
3. Daniel Teijeiro
4. Gino Bell

STAND UP PADDLEBOARD
1. Nelson Ahina
2. Chris Martin
3. Alika Willis
4. Micah Liana

REEF HAWAIIAN PRO • ASP 6-STAR WQS MEN'S AND WOMEN'S
HALEIWA, OAHU
November 12–23

The 2008 Reef Hawaiian Pro was always going to be about the new guard of women's surfing from the opening heat of competition, and in the end Haleiwa crowned its youngest-ever Vans Triple Crown of Surfing event champion in 16-year-old Carissa Moore (Honolulu). Moore won her way through every round of the competition from the preliminary trials heat that awarded one wildcard spot into the event. Three teenagers and a 36-year-old, seven-time World Champion featured in the 30-minute final. Moore won, multiple World Champ Layne Beachley (Manly, Australia) was second, 17-year-old Laura Enever (Narrabeen, Australia) was third, and North Shore local Coco Ho, 17, was fourth. Haleiwa's Ali'i Beach Park offered up clean and highly contestable 4- to 5-foot surf for the women's final day of action, with left-handers the order of the day. In the final, 17-year-old Coco Ho was at the center of a drama. A win here would have guaranteed Ho a start on the 2009 elite World Tour, but after finding herself in fourth for most of the heat, her focus shifted to securing the win for Moore. With less than a minute remaining, Beachley was in need of little more than six points to steal the win. Ho took off, dropping in on Beachley,

popping an air above her head and effectively shutting down Layne's scoring potential in a classic case of schoolgirl tactics. While it will never be known if Layne would have earned the score she needed to win, it's indisputable that Moore earned the victory on the merits of her surfing alone.

FINAL
1. Carisssa Moore
2. Layne Beachley
3. Laura Enever
4. Coco Ho

SEMIFINAL 1
1. Coco Ho
2. Laura Enever
3. Melanie Bartels
4. Claire Bevilacqua

SEMIFINAL 2
1. Carissa Moore
2. Layne Beachley
3. Rosanne Hodge
4. Rebecca Woods

QUARTERFINAL 1
1. Claire Bevilacqua
2. Melanie Bartels
3. Bruna Schmitz
4. Stephanie Gilmore

QUARTERFINAL 2
1. Coco Ho
2. Laura Enever
3. Courtney Conlogue
4. Samantha Cornish

QUARTERFINAL 3
1. Layne Beachley
2. Rebecca Woods
3. Sally Fitzgibbons
4. Kyla Langen

QUARTERFINAL 4
1. Carissa Moore
2. Rosanne Hodge
3. Silvana Lima
4. Alana Blanchard

Tahitian Michel Bourez, 22, scored a career-best win, taking first place and $15,000 in the $135,000 Reef Hawaiian Pro and an early lead on the prestigious Vans Triple Crown of Surfing Series ratings. Prior to this, Bourez's best result was a minor event win in the Canary Islands in 2005. Runner-up was Brazil's Jihad Khodr, 24 ($7,500); third was Hawaii's Kekoa Bacalso (Mililani, $4,500); and fourth was Maui's Dusty Payne, the youngest of the finalists at 19 and the only surfer to come all the way through from

the very first round, surfing eight times to earn $4,400.

FINAL
1. Michel Bourez
2. Jihad Khodr
3. Kekoa Bacalso
4. Dusty Payne

SEMIFINAL 1
1. Michel Bourez
2. Kekoa Bacalso
3. Nic Muscroft
4. Brett Simpson

SEMIFINAL 2
1. Jihad Khodr
2. Dusty Payne
3. Joel Parkinson
4. Bede Durbidge

QUARTERFINAL 1
1. Kekoa Bacalso
2. Michel Bourez
3. Evan Valiere
4. Greg Emslie

QUARTERFINAL 2
1. Nic Muscroft
2. Brett Simpson
3. Sunny Garcia
4. Kieren Perrow

QUARTERFINAL 3
1. Bede Durbidge
2. Dusty Payne
3. Chris Ward
4. Dayyan Neve

QUARTERFINAL 4
1. Jihad Khodr
2. Joel Parkinson
3. Dustin Barca
4. Tim Reyes

O'NEILL WORLD CUP OF SURFING • ASP WQS 6-STAR MEN'S
SUNSET BEACH, OAHU
November 25–December 6

Florida's C.J. Hobgood, 29, won the O'Neill World Cup of Surfing in clean 20- to 30-foot wave face heights, making Hobgood the first goofy-footer in 11 years to win at Sunset Beach. Australia's Michael Romelse was the last goofy-foot to win at Sunset, in 1997; he also won the Vans Triple Crown of Surfing title the same year. On his backhand, Hobgood, who was the 2001 ASP World Champ, charged his way to victory, nabbing the biggest wave of the 35-minute final.

FINAL
1. CJ Hobgood

2. Tom Whitaker
3. Marcus Hickman
4. Jordy Smith

SEMIFINAL 1
1. CJ Hobgood
2. Marcus Hickman
3. Dusty Payne
4. Mick Fanning

CJ Hobgood. Photo ASP Cestari © Covered Images.

SEMIFINAL 2
1. Jordy Smith
2. Tom Whitaker
3. Joel Parkinson
4. Ian Walsh

QUARTERFINAL 1
1. CJ Hobgood
2. Dusty Payne
3. Yadin Nicol
4. Rhys Bombaci

QUARTERFINAL 2
1. Mick Fanning
2. Marcus Hickman
3. David Weare
4. Torrey Meister

QUARTERFINAL 3
1. Jordy Smith
2. Joel Parkinson
3. Kamalei Alexander
4. Bede Durbidge

QUARTERFINAL 4
1. Tom Whitaker
2. Ian Walsh
3. Greg Emslie
4. Dion Atkinson

The one-of-a-kind watch also features three crowns to commemorate the event for which the watch was commissioned: a triple gasket screw crown, an easy adjust button to set the tide subdial, and a final crown, which houses a compact screwdriver to make band adjustments. This timepiece also features a custom-engraved case back along with the names of the three locations of the Vans Triple Crown events etched into the side of the case wall.

This year's WTA has showcased unique talent with Ryan Hipwood (AUS), Taylor Knox (USA) and Royden Bryson (ZAF) claiming victory for the previous three Nixon WTA titles. Their respective wins were for heaviest wave in Teahupoo this past May, highest heat score at J-Bay in July and longest tube ride in Mundaka in late September. Competition for the Nixon WTA will resume in May 2009 at the Billabong Pro in Tahiti.

North Shore Magic

This fairly well-known break looks almost empty. Photo Bernie Baker.

Marcus Hickman Sunset drop. Photo ASP Rowland © Covered Images.

Pancho Sullivan, grace on the face at Sunset. Photo Bernie Baker.

Once known as the "ghetto du surf," Oahu's North Shore is these days millionaires row, with the threat of un-wanted development a constant thorn in the side of long-term residents. For the surfers who flock there each winter from around the world, it can be a crazy, heartless place where sensible wave selection is a necessity for continued good health. But the North Shore still has its magic moments. Here are a few of them from a better-than-average '08 season.

Dusty Payne inside Sunset.
Photo Bernie Baker.

Sunset contest village. Photo ASP
Rowland © Covered Images.

...lost

MASON HO
'Waterman'

...on his 5'5" X 19 1/4" 'paddlefish'

Tupat

The O'Neill SI Pro launched the 2008 ASP WQS season at Sebastian Inlet, Florida, in January with an all-American final and Pat Gudauskas taking a five star win over fellow San Clemente local Mike Losness. Pro surfer Chris Ward was arrested and charged with assault in Mammoth Lakes while on a snowboarding vacation.

Greg Long took out the Mavericks Surf Contest with a perfect 10, edging out Grant "Twiggy" Baker. The other finalists were Evan Slater, Grant Washburn, Jamie Sterling and Tyler Smith. Long insisted the finalists split the $75,000 prize money evenly.

Super Brand Surfboards was launched by a group of the US's hottest young surfers: Clay Marzo, Kolohe Andino and pro Skater Tosh Townend, along with Aussies Dion Agius and Ry Craike. Volcom purchased Electric for $25.3 million in cash plus future earnings incentives. Electric, founded in 2000, produces sunglasses and goggles and had 2007 sales of $23.5 million.

Shaun Tomson's docudrama *Bustin' Down the Door* premiered at the Santa Barbara Film Festival and sold out the 2,000-plus-seat Arlington theatre. The six stars, Wayne "Rabbit" Bartholomew, Mark Richards, Peter "PT" Townend, Ian Cairns, Michael Tomson and Shaun himself were on hand, along with master of ceremonies actor Gregory Harrison and a who's who of the California surf industry.

Bernard Mariette resigned the Quiksliver presidency with CEO Bob McKnight taking over his duties. The announcement came in the wake of news that Quiksilver had hired J.P. Morgan to pursue a sale of the Rossignol Group, which they had acquired under Mariette's leadership.

The Toll Road hearing at the Del Mar Fairgrounds was attended by thousands and was debated in front of the California Coastal Commission. After over 15 hours of debate, the commission ruled against the tollway that would go through San Onofre State Beach, saying it would violate environmental laws that regulate development along 1,100 miles of California coastline.

North Carolina's Tony Silvagni won the 44th Ron Jon's Easter Surf Festival Pro Longboarding event in Cocoa Beach to open the U.S. longboarding season.

Bra Boys premiered in the U.S in Los Angeles and then opened in select U.S. theatres in coastal communities. The Abberton brothers flew to LA for the Hollywood premiere hosted by action sports TV host Sal Masekela, whose company Berkela Films distributed the film in the U.S.

The first Ultimate Boarder compe-

North America Report

By Peter Townend

tition combining surfing, skateboarding and snowboarding was held in Squaw Valley and Ventura, with Aaron Astorga walking away with $30,000. Runner-up was Kristian Phillip, followed by Chad Shetler, Shayne Popisil, Tosh Townend, John Warren, Nathan Fletcher, Kurt Wastell and Clint Allen.

Steve Long, a 34-year veteran of the State Parks in Orange County and father of surfers Greg and Rusty Long, retired. He had overseen the Trestles location for 30 of those years and helped establish the San Onofre Foundation, a park support group.

Eddie Vedder rocked San Clemente for the Kelly Slater Foundation to raise funds for Surfrider's "Save Trestles" campaign. Held at a private home overlooking Cottons, the night's 700 at-

Eddie Vedder rocked San Clemente for the Kelly Slater Foundation to raise funds for Surfrider's "Save Trestles" campaign. A highlight was a cover of Tom Petty's "I Won't Back Down," which closed with the line, "Take your [expletive] road and put it somewhere else."

Lower Trestles. Photo ASP Covered Images.   Inset: PT saves Trestles.

tendees included A-list celebrities Sean Penn, Laura Dern, Arnold's brother-in-law Bobby Shriver and Ben Harper, who got up to perform with Vedder. Highlight was the cover of Tom Petty's "I Won't Back Down," which he closed with the line, "Take your [expletive] road and put it somewhere else."

The eleventh annual Sima Surf Summit in Cabo San Lucas was highlighted by Bob Hurley's opening address. The big winners in the Sima Image Awards were Billabong, with three of the ten awards, RVCA, which got the granddaddy Men's Apparel Brand of the Year, and Aussie brand Insight, which won Breakthrough Brand of the Year. Other category winners included Xcel for wetsuits, Sanuk for footwear and L-Space for women's swim.

USA Surf Team finished fourth at the Quiksilver ISA Junior Championships in France. The top U.S. performer was Courtney Conlogue who took a bronze medal in the Women's division. Sage Erickson, Dillion Perillo and Nat Young made the top ten in their respective divisions.

Surfwise, a documentary on the life of Dorian "Doc" Paskowitz and his nine children with wife Juliette, told the story of the their upbringing in an alternative surfing lifestyle in a 24-foot camper van. It opened in Orange County to strong reviews.

Sports TV network ESPN dropped surfing from the X Games, claiming that they've been unable to draw the ASP's top tour surfers to match up with the world's best in the other disciplines like skateboarding, motocross and BMX.

Quiksilver announced that following its successful launch of the Hawk skateboarding apparel exclusively in mid-tier mass retailer Kohl's, it will work with the retailer again to bring back iconic surf brand Hang Ten in the summer of 2009.

Billabong International continued its acquisition strategy by acquiring San Diego–based skateboarding company Sector 9. Volcom acquired Laguna Beach retailer Laguna Surf & Sports, one of the longest standing specialty retailers. This announcement came hot on the heels of Billabong acquiring Florida-based retailer Quiet Flight, also one of the U.S.'s early surf shops.

Nathanial Curran defeated France's Tim Boal in the man-on-man U.S. Open of Surfing final. Earlier Boal defeated local HB favorite Brett Simpson, while in the Pro Juniors Tanner Gudauskas won over Aussie Julian Wilson. In longboarding Taylor Jensen won the U.S. Open title.

Surfing Walk of Fame inducted Andy Irons as Surfing Champion, Lynn Boyer as Woman of the Year, Buzzy

Trent and Wayne Lynch as Surf Pioneers, Rich Chew as Local Hero and the NSSA Founders to the Honor Roll. Meanwhile, across the street in front of Huntington Surf & Sport, the Surfers Hall of Fame inducted Mike Parsons, Brad Gerlach, Sean Collins and Wayne "Rabbit" Bartholomew.

Mark Occhilupo, former world surfing champ, Jackson Browne, musician extraordinaire and Eduardo Arena, founder of ISA, were honored at the annual SIMA Waterman's Ball as 850 surf-industry executives and environmentalists gathered at the St. Regis Monarch Beach, Dana Point, raising over half a million dollars for environmental causes.

FIRST ANNUAL RAINBOW SANDALS
BATTLE OF THE PADDLE
WWW.RAINBOWSANDALS.COM

Jock Sutherland led his team to victory in the 15th Annual Moore's UCSD Cancer Center Legends & Luau at La Jolla Shores. U.S.–based legends of surfing again gathered to raise nearly half a million dollars for skin cancer research.

Billabong acquired Dakine, adding to its burgeoning brand portfolio.

Kelly Slater again won the Boost Mobile Pro at Trestles in an epic final, prompting San Clemente mayor Joe Anderson to present him with the keys to the city.

Aussie brand Rhythm launched in America at ASR. Peter "Tang" Grey with sons Jamahl and Ryan broke out Rhythm's quirky and colorful trunks, with California's Jye Townend their man on the ground in America.

California surfing lost one its best all-around good guys to cancer, RIP Midget Smith. Smith, a mainstay of San Clemente surfing and the surfboard industry, had been shaping surfboards for many of the world's best over the decades, including local Shane Beschen,

world champs Andy Irons and Mark Occhilupo and countless others. Smith was also one of America's most accomplished judges, having judged at the ASP level for three decades. Legendary moviemaker Bud Browne also passed. Arguably the godfather of surf moviemaking, Browne pioneered the genre and his water angles were legendary.

In Hollywood Matthew McConaghey released *Surfer, Dude*, a stoner/ surf film based on the life of a "soul surfer" who is pressured by industry bigwigs to sell out. Also starring Woody Harrelson, it has the cult classic potential to become the modern day *Fast Times at Ridgemont High*.

The battle over the toll road through Trestles continued at the Del Mar Fairgrounds, this time in a federal government hearing prompted by the Toll Road Agency's appeal of the February Coastal Commission's denial of the project. Again thousands turned out to hear passionate testimony from both sides, with a decision to come down early January whether to rescind the Coastal Commission's decision.

Can you believe it's been 30 years since the release of *Big Wednesday*, John Milius and Denny Aaberg's story of youthful friendships based on their growing up in Malibu in the sixties? Arguably Hollywood's best depiction of surfing, it has become a cult classic. A collection of the original cast and watermen assembled at Duke's restaurant in Malibu to celebrate the anniversary, including stars Gary Busey and William Katt along with co-writer Aaberg and legendary Malibu surfer Lance Carson, whose life the movie's lead character Matt Johnson was based on. Also in attendance was Ian Cairns, who was Busey's double as Leroy, and the original Gidget, Kathy Kohner Zuckerman. Highlight of the evening was the music set with Busey strapping on the Stratocaster and jamming with Denny Aaberg. Busey broke out a few Buddy Holly numbers, bringing back memories of the practice sessions during Big Wednesday's filming as he prepared for his Academy Award nomination as Buddy Holly in the movie *The Buddy Holly Story*.

The usual suspects were winners at the annual Surfer Poll, with Kelly Slater taking men's honors while Sophia Mulanovich was the women's winner. In the movie/video awards *Bustin Down the Door* won a double whammy, taking out both Movie of the Year and Best Documentary.

The second annual consumer surf-

boards show Sacred Craft was held in Del Mar, with the highlight being the shape-off where a cast of skilled craftsmen had to duplicate a Bill Caster '70s board on-site. Going back-to-back in this challenge was master shaper Ricky Carroll of Florida. All sorts of shaping luminaries were in attendance, from legends like Bing Copeland signing copies of his newly penned Paul Holmes book *Think Bing*, Skip Frye, Bobby Challenger, the *Endless Summer*'s Robert August and Mike Hynson, the Campbell "Bonzer" brothers, Aussie Alan "Byrning Spears" Byrne and modern artisans Rusty Preisendorfer and Matt Biolas.

The inaugural Gerry Lopez Battle of the Paddle was won by Dana Point's Chuck Patterson. He covered the course that combined paddling 1.5-mile laps and beach running in just over an hour to take home the $10,000 first prize. Jenny Kalmbach won the women's division.

On an October Sunday afternoon in "Surf City," Huntington Beach, the International Surfing Museum hosted a 1968 World Championships 40-year reunion, featuring the two champions, Fred Hemmings and Margo Godfrey Oberg, and a number of other competitors from the event that was held in Puerto Rico. Highlight of the afternoon was the showing of the ABC *Wide World of Sports* coverage, which hadn't been seen in 40 years.

The California Surf Museum hosted the first California Surf Film Festival, celebrating Bruce Brown's 50 years of filmmaking. The highlight was Bruce's "live" narration of his original *Endless Summer*, just like he did back in the sixties.

While many surf specialty retailers were closing locations, Jack's Surfboards opened it first inland location in Irvine. The 9,500-square-foot surf superstore features huge sections from Billabong, Quiksilver and Volcom, but most brands are well represented. In the meantime, retailers Becker Surfboards, Killer Dana and Ron Jons announced store closings in Orange County.

Quiksilver's stock price on the New York Stock exchange dropped to under a dollar. Meanwhile, the brand's biggest star, Kelly Slater, launched a national book tour in support of his *Kelly Slater: For the Love*, penned with esteemed Aussie journalist Phil Jarratt and with an introduction by his long-time surfing musician friend Jack Johnson.

CJ Hobgood continued his winning streak by winning the final WQS event of the year, the O'Neill World Cup, in macking Sunset Beach. For young Americans Brett Simpson and Pat Gudauskas it was a huge disappointment as they both fared poorly and failed to qualify for the ASP World Tour. For Gudauskas the result was bitter, as he had led the WQS rankings for much of the first half of 2008 after winning the opening WQS event, the O'Neill SI Pro, in Florida back in January.

O'NEILL SEBASTIAN INLET PRO • ASP 5-STAR WQS MEN'S EVENT
SEBASTIAN INLET, FLORIDA
January 4–11

Under sunny skies and in 1- to 3-foot surf, a pair of San Clemente standouts met in the first all-California final of the O'Neill Sebastian Inlet Pro, presented by Ron Jon. After flip-flopping the lead for the duration of the heat, Patrick Gudauskas' 8.50 proved too much for Mike Losness to overcome. With the win at the season opening event on the WQS, Gudauskas took the early ratings' lead with hopes of qualifying for the Dream Tour. Nathaniel Curran and Sterling Spencer finished equal 3rd.

FINAL
1. Patrick Gudauskas
2. Mike Losness
SEMIFINAL 1
1. Patrick Gudauskas
2. Nathaniel Curran
SEMIFINAL 2
1. Mike Losness
2. Sterling Spencer
QUARTERFINAL 1
1. Patrick Gudauskas
2. CJ Hobgood
QUARTERFINAL 2
1. Nathaniel Curran
2. Nathan Yeomans
QUARTERFINAL 3
1. Sterling Spencer
2. Cory Lopez
QUARTERFINAL 4
1. Mike Losness
2. Asher Nolan

2007/2008 MAVERICKS SURF CONTEST® BIG WAVE CONTEST
HALF MOON BAY, CALIFORNIA
January 17

Twenty-four of the world's most accomplished big-wave surfers came to one of the most infamous breaks on the planet, Mavericks and were greeted with ideal 25- to 30-foot conditions. Risking life and limb over the course of six heats, ultimately camaraderie stole the show. Facing minimal conditions in the finals, the six competitors made the decision to split the winnings evenly regardless of the outcome. With the finances handled, a set appeared on the horizon and Greg Long stroked into the wave of the heat—and arguably the history of the contest—and was rewarded with an unprecedented 10, a perfect score. "Greg's been pushing the limits," said contest director Jeff Clark. "With his natural talent it's not a surprise to see him learning the ropes quickly and becoming one of the best big-wave surfers."

OPEN MEN
1. Greg Long

Greg Long. Photo maverickssurf.com.

2. Grant "Twiggy" Baker
3. Jamie Sterling
4. Tyler Smith
5. Grant Washburn
6. Evan Slater
JAY MORIARITY AWARD
Jamie Sterling
CLIF BAR GREEN ROOM AWARD
Grant "Twiggy" Baker

2007 NELSCOTT REEF TOW-IN CLASSIC, PRESENTED BY LIQUID MILITIA
NELSCOTT REEF, LINCOLN CITY, OREGON
October 1, 2007–March 31, 2008

Facing small, windy conditions, competitors initially felt that contest organizers Behemoth LLC and John Forse had made an ill-fated call in running the event. Their opinions changed after lunchtime, when 35-foot monsters started rolling through for the only tow-in event in North America. With one set estimated at approaching the 60-foot marker, tow-in teams were provided an adequate challenge for the contest title. The Nelscott experienced duo of Adam Replogle and Alistair Craft proved to be the in-form team, winning the event with a final score of 44.75.

1ST PLACE
Adam Replogle and Alistair Craft
2ND PLACE
Yuri Soledade and Rodrigo Resende
3RD PLACE
Eraldo Gueiros and Everaldo Pato
4TH PLACE
Osh Bartlett and Tyler Fox
5TH PLACE
Homer Henard and Matt Rockhold

GATHERING OF THE TRIBES, DOHENY LONGBOARD SURFING ASSOCIATION'S 12TH ANNUAL EVENT
CHURCH BEACH, SAN ONOFRE, CALIFORNIA
January 12–13

Nearly 300 competitors descended on Church Beach to compete in the 12th annual Gathering of the Tribes surf club contest. Over the course of two days, the contest was graced with optimum conditions to decide winners in 18 divisions. No cash prizes were awarded, but winners contributed top points to the overall club standings.

UNDER 14 BOYS
1. Trevor Robbins
2. David Arganda
3. Jesse Hinkle
4. Jordon Thomas
5. Elli Gillis
6. Brody Stevens
MEN 15–19
1. Cole Robbins
2. Josh Gundulla
3. Brett Robbins
4. Travis Perkins
5. Samson Magazino
6. Chris Cravey
MEN 20–29
1. Taylor Jensen
2. Charlie Waite
3. Billy Harris
4. Cody Craig
5. Kelly Kraushaar
6. Steve Simeson
MEN 30–39
1. Mark Stewart
2. Jason MacMurray
3. Rocky McKinnon
4. Ryan Renolds
5. Sverre Strom
6. Daniel Cross
MEN 40–49
1. Guy Takayama
2. Nate Cintas
3. Dennis Bourg
4. Rob Brockman
5. Rubio Smith
6. John Welch
MEN 50–59
1. Donald McLead
2. Bobby Lombard
3. Tres Focht
4. Mark Calkins

5. Steve Cleveland
6. Bob English
UNDER 16 GIRLS
1. Kirra Kehoe
2. Torey Gilkerson
3. Halley Rohr
4. Makala Smith
5. Llailani Harrisson
6. Emily Yates
JUNIOR WOMEN 15–19
1. Kasie Perkins
2. Danica E
3. Maggie Dunn
4. Rachael Barry
5. Lauren Ngan
6. Brooke Velasquez
WOMEN 20–39
1. Anne Zelcer
2. Katlin Maguire
3. Stacey Ross
4. Wanda Snans
5. Rachael Calkins
6. Amanda Calkins
MASTERS WOMEN 40+
1. Mary Schwinn
2. Cheryl McGregor
3. Jill Nakano
4. Debbie Trauntvein
5. Mel Rogers
6. Katie Calkins
TANDEM
1. Clay & Kristen Huntington
2. Charlie & Myra
3. Brian & Illa Mcevily
4. Travis Long & Kate Anthony
5. Ryan Reynolds & Jennifer Vasques
6. Travis Perkins & Makala Smith
LEGENDS 60–69
1. Mike Dawson
2. Chris Bredeson
3. Ron Jones
4. Barry Ault
5. Tom Dolton
6. Bobby Challenger
EXTREME LEGENDS 70+
1. Mickey Munoz
2. Gary Stellern
3. George Carr
MEN SHORTBOARD 1–39
1. Jordan Gaudet
2. Steve Simeson
3. Mark Stewart
4. Cody Craig
5. Alex Calkins
6. Jay Gordan
MASTERS SHORTBOARD 40+
1. Nate Cintas
2. Donnie Wilson
3. Rob Brockman
4. Donald McLead
5. Rubio Smith
6. Tom Kunz
JUNIOR WOMEN SHORTBOARD 1–29
1. Rochelle King
2. Alexandria Souza

Mickey Munoz, George Carr & Gary Stellern. Photo Denny Michael.

3. Stacy Ross
4. Katlin Maguire
5. Cary Endich
6. Marry Mulshine
SHORTBOARD WOMEN 30+
1. Deb Trauntvein
2. Aida Welch
3. Tracey Edwards
4. Katie Taheany
5. Jill Nakano
6. Katie Calkins
PRESIDENT'S
1. Travis Long
2. Joe Baldwin
3. John Welch
4. Christian Wadman
5. Guy Takayama
6. Alec Mackenzie

NSSA SOUTHWEST EXPLORER #6
SEASIDE REEF, CARDIFF, SAN DIEGO, CALIFORNIA
January 12–13

With Seaside Reef firing with 4- to 6-foot faces, the sixth stop on the 10-event schedule was held in highly contestable conditions. Carlsbad's Brent Reilly was in top form, throwing out a number of moves from his repertoire in winning his second consecutive Juniors division. On the biggest wave ridden in the event, Senior/Masters competitor Barry Deffenbaugh recorded the only 10-point ride after throwing three huge gauges on the 10-foot face.

EXPLORER MEN
1. Chase Wilson
2. Nick Suhadolnik
3. Kyle Kennelly
4. Sean Bacon
5. Marc Everds
6. Tanner Long
EXPLORER JUNIORS
1. Brent Reilly
2. Chase Wilson
3. Kyle Kennelly
4. Christian Saenz
5. Luke Davis
6. Dane Zaun
EXPLORER BOYS
1. Jared Thorne
2. Luke Davis
3. Ian Crane
4. Jacob Halstead
5. Taylor Thorne
6. Blake Davis
EXPLORER MENEHUENE
1. Colin Moran
2. Taylor Clark
3. Johnny Elles
4. Jay Christenson
5. Addy Giddings
6. Kanoa Igarashi
EXPLORER WOMEN
1. Taylor Pitz
2. Natalie Anzivino
3. Tara Franz
4. Jena Balestar
5. Cassidy Wehsener
6. Chelsea Byland
EXPLORER GIRLS
1. Emmy Merrill
2. Charlotte Shanahan
3. Anise Guzman
4. Harley Taich
5. Melina Smith
6. Kirra Kehoe
EXPLORER MASTERS
1. Barry Deffenbaugh

2. Tom Matthews
3. Tim Senneff
4. Rick Takahashi
5. Jon Warren
6. Scott Whitmer

EXPLORER SENIORS
1. Neil Bern
2. Scott Whitmer
3. Dave Montalbano
4. Barry Deffenbaugh
5. Mike Gillard
6. Randy Cutshall

EXPLORER SUPER SENIORS
1. Andrew Halstead
2. Tim Senneff
3. Mike Gillard
4. David Winslow
5. Dale Baker
6. Rick Fignetti

EXPLORER LONGBOARD
1. Scott Brandeburg
2. Michael Lallande
3. Terry Gillard
4. Cody Ulrich
5. Mike Gillard
5. Cole Robbins

NSSA SOUTHEAST/ NORTH CONFERENCE #6
BETHUNE BEACH, FLORIDA
January 12–13

Stop No. 6 in the NSSA Southeast/ North Conference ran at Bethune Beach, with Evan Thompson finishing first in the Men's division and third in the Juniors, respectively.

OPEN MEN
1. Evan Thomson
2. Nick Rupp
3. Michael Dunphy
4. Liam Michelbrink
5. Evan Geiselman
6. Eric Templeton

Brent Reilly. Photo Giddings.

OPEN JUNIORS
1. Evan Geiselman
2. Nick Rupp
3. Evan Thompson
4. Joshua Torres
5. Ryan Croteau
6. Keto Burns

OPEN BOYS
1. Noah Schweizer
2. Cam Richards
3. Justin Croteau
4. Weston Williams
5. Knox Harris
6. Tristan Thompson

OPEN MINI GROMS
1. Evan Brownell
2. Stevie Pittman

3. Jack Umbel

OPEN WOMEN
1. Jasset Umbel
2. Kayla Durden
3. Jessie Carnes
4. Amy Nicholl
5. Chelsea Gresham
6. MJ Keglor

EXPLORER MEN
1. Liam Michelbrink
2. Nick Bland
3. Tayler Brothers
4. Eric Templeton
5. Michael Dunphy
6. Nick Rupp

EXPLORER JUNIORS
1. Nick Rupp
2. Evan Thompson
3. Liam Michelbrink
4. Tayler Brothers
5. Michael Dunphy
6. Eric Kirby

EXPLORER BOYS
1. Noah Schweizer
2. Keto Burns
3. Mason Barnes
4. Evan Geiselman
5. Julian Payne
6. Zack Bland

EXPLORER MENEHUENE
1. Weston Williams
2. Noah Schweizer
3. Cam Richards
4. Knox Harris
5. Tristan Thompson
6. Justin Croteau

EXPLORER WOMEN
1. Amy Nichol
2. Jessie Carnes
3. Kayla Durden
4. Jasset Umbel
5. Chelsea Gresham
6. MJ Keglor

EXPLORER GIRLS
1. Jasset Umbel
2. Ele Klein
3. Rossi Klein

4. Kayla Durden

EXPLORER MASTERS/SENIORS
1. Steve Moore
2. Charlie Hajak
3. Rob Parson
4. Chester Pittman
5. Chilly Willy
6. Ray Sturm

EXPLORER SUPER SENIORS
1. Rob Parson

EXPLORER LONGBOARD
1. Weston Williams
2. Morgan Leavel
3. Chelesa Grisham
4. Sam Cuminsky
5. Jimmie Cuminsky

RIP CURL WOMAN FESTIVAL FEMENINO DE SURF, PRESENTED BY SCHICK QUATTRO FOR WOMEN
YACHT CLUB DE PLAYA GRANDE, COSTA RICA
January 18–19

Rip Curl brought the festival atmosphere full of bright colors, entertainment and a "flower power" spirit to Costa Rica in an all-women contest, the only all-surfista contest in Latin America. The festival included massages, face painting, yoga, Hawaiian dance classes, and an introduction to the sport of surfing to all who were interested.

OPEN WOMEN
1. Ornella Pellizzari
2. Agostina Pellizzari
3. Sofía Borquez (Chile)
4. Lucila Gil

PRINCIPIANTES MAYORES
1. Paola Danuncio
2. Lucila Rey
3. Laura Falco
4. Martina Gainza

LONGBOARD
1. Tete Gil
2. Sofía Guatelli
3. Lucía Cosoleto
4. Natalia de la Lama

BODYBOARD
1. Ornella Pellizzari
2. Violeta Jiménez
3. Guadalupe Gallardo
4. Lucía Cosoleto
5. Carla Orfei

GIRLS
1. Lucía Cosoleto
2. Josefina Ané
3. Malena González
4. Melany González

TANDEM
1. Federico Goñi & Lucila Rey
2. Lucas Rubiño & Lucía Cosoleto
3. Agostina Pellizzari & Nahuel Amalfitano
4. Paco Garcia Rabini & Rochi Rillo

MIDGET SMITH PIER RAT CHALLENGE • WSA
SAN CLEMENTE PIER, CALIFORNIA
January 19

Clear, crisp winter conditions greeted the large crowd in atten-

dance for the Midget Smith Pier Rat Challenge in San Clemente, California. As he had done for years, Midget was on hand to observe the scene, with competitors in various divisions duking it out for bragging rights. It wasn't just competitors filling the beach but members of the surf industry as well, who were present to support Smith, who was involved with a drawn-out battle with cancer. One particularly inspiring effort came from Newport Beach's Kenny Clark. Clark took 3rd in the Men's 40+ Shortboard division, despite

Agostina Pellizzari. Photo Rip Curl.

having undergone aggressive treatment for throat cancer over the past 18 months.

MEN SHORTBOARD 40+
1. Glenn Rilly

Contest scenery. Photo Sheri Crummer.

2. Jeff Jones
3. Kenny Clark
4. Michael Skelly
5. Javier Huarcaya
6. Perry Faanes

8 & UNDER BOYS AND GIRLS
1. Sam Wickwire
2. Michael Tilly
3. Ashley Beeson
4. Tanner Deveze

GIRLS SHORTBOARD 14–17
1. Mackenzie Kessler

GIRLS LONGBOARD 17 AND UNDER
2. Hallie Rohr
3. Bryn Lutz
4. Tory Gilkerson
5. Haley Powell
6. Alexandra Adolph

WOMEN SHORTBOARD 18–25
1. Jenny Quam
2. Hether Carrick

WOMEN LONGBOARD 30+

1. Wanda Smanz
2. Sherri Crummer

BOYS LONGBOARD 17 AND UNDER
1. Dennis Whitw
2. Scott Brandenburg
3. Cody Ulrich
4. Eli Gillis
5. Casey Powell
6. Dean Hyland

MEN SHORTBOARD 26–29
1. Chris Drummy
2. Chris Cabeza
3. Micah Mullen
4. Kelly O'Connell
5. Pat Drummy
6. Brian Hill

MEN LONGBOARD 30+
1. Bryan Ballard
2. Sean Haggar
3. Kelly O'Connell
4. Skeeter DiRusso
5. Biff Cooper
6. Michael Skelly

BOYS SHORTBOARD 14–17
1. Dennis White
2. Sam Branker
3. Randy Gilkerson
4. Levi Gregory
5. Jacob Graff
6. Zach Lyons

MEN SHORTBOARD 18–25
1. Brandon Ragenovich
2. Brandt Bacha
3. Jeff Mull
4. Chase Stavron

BOYS SHORTBOARD 13 AND UNDER
1. Braden Taylor
2. Jonah Carter
3. Trevor Thornton
4. Zach Stabley
5. Ryan Graves
6. Kevin Schulz

GIRLS SHORTBOARD 13 AND UNDER
1. Bryn Lutz
2. Shelby Detmers
3. Madi Swayne
4. Anna Gillis
5. Kaerina Rozunko

MEN LONGBOARD 18 – 29
1. Tommy Lloy
2. Tommy Witt
3. Kevin Osborne
4. Tyler Warren
5. Josh Rapozo
6. Bobby Foster

RETRO SHORTBOARD OPEN
1. Brandon Ragenovich
2. Scott Finn
3. Brandt Bacha
4. Chris Cabeza
5. Tyler Warren
6. Tommy Lloy

STAND-UP PADDLE RELAY
1. Bryce Sagman and TJ Sagman

2. Eric Diamond and Chris Koerner
3. Gary Larson and Boston Titensoz
4. Sean Haggar and Tyler Warren
5. Tim Mellars and Dave Mellars

KOASTAL KAOS #5
OCEAN BEACH, SAN DIEGO, CALIFORNIA
January 26–27

Leading up to the final day of competition, conditions had been ideal for the fifth stop on the Koastal Kaos series, with glassy, rippable wave faces in the shoulder- to head-high range. However, in the wee hours of Sunday morning, the weather turned hostile and water spouts came ashore, tearing scaffolding off the ground and shredding easy-up tents. As a result, contest organizers were forced to reschedule the remaining heats. Both the Women and Masters divisions were already decided, with some familiar series faces making a case for the contest title.

OPEN WOMEN
1. BreAnne Custodio
2. Alexa Dilley
3. Winnie Riley
4. Lyndsay Hingst
MASTERS FINAL
1. Rick Takahashi
2. Tom Matthews
3. Pedro Diaz
4. Keith Dybee
5. Sean Malabanan
6. Yufu Penrose

COPA WITCH'S ROCK CIRCUITO NACIONAL DE SURF
TAMARINDO, COSTA RICA
February 2–3

With a repeat win at Circuito Nacional de Surf held at the world-renowned Witch's Rock, Puerto Viejo's Gilbert Brown further distanced himself from the pack in the overall standings of the Federacion de Surf of Costa Rica. Held in 2- to 4-foot surf near the Tamarindo Rivermouth, the other finalists couldn't keep pace with Brown. A bronze medalist at the Pan-American games, Brown managed to hold off some stiff competition, including local boy Federico Pilurzu, who's making a name for himself competing on the WQS.

OPEN MEN
1. Gilbert Brown
2. Jason Torres
3. Federico Pilurzu
4. Jairo Pérez
JUNIOR (UNDER 18)
1. Jairo Pérez
2. Ariel Agüero
3. Angelo Bonomelli
4. Anderson Tascon
OPEN WOMEN
1. Lisbeth Vindas
2. Nataly Bernold
3. Erica Valverde
4. Lupe Gallucio
MEN LONGBOARD
1. Diego Naranjo

2. Alex Gómez
3. Cedric Auffret
4. Mauricio Umaña
MASTERS (OVER 35)
1. Mauro Sergio Oliveira
2. Marcelo Matos
3. William Agüero
4. Carlos Velarde
UNDER 16 BOYS
1. Anthony Segura
2. Rudy Jiménez
3. Ángelo Bonomelli
4. Carlos Muñoz
GROMMETS
1. Noe Mar McGonagle
2. Tomas King
3. Anthony Fillingan
4. Dineth Arce
MINI GROMMETS
1. Noe Mar McGonagle
2. Manuel Mesen
3. Leonardo Calvo
4. Paco Waldschmidt
JUNIOR WOMEN (UNDER 18)
1. Nataly Bernold
2. Julie Javelle
3. Leilani McGonagle
4. Debbie Zec
MINI GROMMET WOMEN (UNDER 12)
1. Arisha Grioti
2. Leilani McGonagle
3. Avalon Esterak
4. Naomi Bernold
NOVICES
1. Yader Díaz
2. Steven Duran
3. Weine Guevara
4. Keiner Carranza
OPEN BODYBOARD
1. Joan Mojica
2. Maicel Allan Rojas
3. Jefry Gómez
4. Richard Marín
WOMEN BODYBOARD
1. Lorena Vera
2. Jimena Calvo
3. Cindy Díaz
4. Dineth Arce

NSSA SOUTHWEST EXPLORER EVENT
MISSION BEACH, SAN DIEGO, CALIFORNIA
February 2–3

Following a few days of clean surf, a storm front making its way down the California coast made for some difficult Mission Beach conditions for the final day of competition. The less than ideal conditions didn't seem to both Huntington Beach's Christian Saenz. Used to spending endless hours in the frequently windblown waves in HB, Saenz nabbed the wave of the heat, throwing several front-side turns and receiving a 9.25 out of 10 for his efforts. The Juniors division win was Saenz's first NSSA title.

EXPLORER MEN
1. Nick Suhadolnik
2. Matt Pagan
3. Dane Zaun
4. Brent Bowen
5. Tanner Long
6. Kyle Kennelly
EXPLORER JUNIORS
1. Christian Saenz
2. Thomas Clarke
3. Brent Reilly

4. Evan Kane
5. Nick Suhadolnik
6. David Suhadolnik
EXPLORER BOYS
1. Luke Davis
2. Kolohe Andino
3. Jared Thorne
4. Taylor Thorne
5. Sam Branker
6. Matt Lewis
EXPLORER MENEHUENE
1. Colin Moran
2. Jacob Davis
3. Taylor Clark
4. Addy Giddings
5. Kanoa Igarashi
6. Jake Marshall
EXPLORER WOMEN
1. Alexa Frantz
2. Erika Cook
3. Sophia Bartlow
4. Marissa Shaw
5. Taylor Pitz
6. Tara Franz
EXPLORER GIRLS
1. Melina Smith
2. Anise Guzman
3. Emmy Merrill
4. Paige Ortiz
5. Harley Taich
6. Charlotte Shanahan
EXPLORER MASTERS
1. Barry Deffenbaugh
2. Scott Whitmer
3. Rick Takahashi
4. YuFu Penrose
5. Jimmy Quintanilla
6. Steve Ling
EXPLORER SENIORS
1. Barry Deffenbaugh
2. Randy Cutshall
3. Dave Montalbano
4. Jeffrey O'Donnell
5. Rusty Phillipy
6. Scott Whitmer
EXPLORER SUPER SENIORS
1. Andrew Halstead
2. Jeffrey O'Donnell
3. Mike Gillard
4. Rick Fignetti
5. Dale Baker
6. David Winslow
EXPLORER LONGBOARD
1. Scott Brandenburg
2. Cody Ulrich
3. Cole Robbins
4. Terry Gillard
5. Michael Lallande
6. Eli Gillis

VOLCOM STONE GREAT WHITE SURF SERIES
THE LANE, SANTA CRUZ, CALIFORNIA
February 2–3

With valuable last-minute WQS qualifying points on the line, competitors pulled on the 4/3 wetsuits and booties to combat the chilly temps at Santa Cruz's best-known break, Steamer Lane. With waves in classic form, every heat from the various divisions was a worthwhile spectacle for those in attendance. In the Pro-Am final, Russell Smith mounted a late-heat comeback to knot his two-wave tally with Randy Bonds. Smith won the tie-breaker and received the winner's check.

Gilbert Brown, Costa Rica. Photo Shifisurfshots.

MEN PRO-AM
1. Russel Smith
2. Randy Bonds
3. Bud Freites
4. Anthony Ruffo
5. John John Florence
6. Josh Loya
JUNIORS
1. Nat Young
2. Miles Clanton
3. Patrick Shaugnessy
4. Collin Dyer
5. Max Karnig
6. Ashton Madeley
GROM
1. Nic Hdez
2. Noah Wegrich
3. Jake Logan
4. Micheal Joshua
5. Ethan Vanseggern
6. Seth Nowlen
GIRLS
1. Kim Mayer
2. Lexi Wilson
3. Savannah Shaugnessy
4. Sierra Partidge
5. Mackenzie Kessler
6. Isabel Bryna

JSA OPEN EVENT #1, JAMAICA SURFING ASSOCIATION
LIGHTHOUSE, PLUMB POINT, JAMAICA
February 9

Icah Wilmot established himself as the points leader on Jamaica's National Open Series after winning the first of five stops. The event was held at the famous Lighthouse beachbreak in quality 6- to 8-foot surf. In the four-man final, the title was up for grabs until late in the

heat when Wilmot stroked into a long, open-faced peak that he ripped apart all the way down the point for a score of 8.7 and the win.

OPEN MEN
1. Icah Wilmot
2. Ackeam Phillips
3. Inilek Wilmot
4. Luke Williams
5. Ishack Wilmot
6. Ivah Wilmot
7. Eneson Lightbourn
7. Shama Beckford
7. Ronley Lewis
10. Drum Drummond
10. Gabre Beckford
10. Garren Pryce
OPEN WOMEN
1. Danielle O'Hayon
2. Elim Beckford
3. Imani Wilmot
4. Esther Beckford

NSSA SOUTHWEST CONFERENCE #5
SEASIDE REEF, CARDIFF-BY-THE-SEA, CALIFORNIA
February 9–10

In a make-up event for a previously cancelled stop due to severe weather, the groms took over flawless Seaside Reef, which was firing compliments of a perfectly angled west swell. While the conditions welcomed stellar performances from any and all the talent on hand, in the fiercely competitive Men's division it was really a one-man show. Brent Reilly was again in top form. Though he only caught four waves, three of the four broke the 8-point barrier, forcing his fellow finalists

Icah Wilmot. Photo Billy Wilmot.

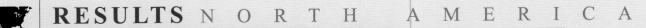
to scramble for second. Similar to Reilly's dominant performance, in the Open Women Courtney Conologue broke away from the pack early and maintained a solid cushion en route to a statement win.

OPEN MEN
1. Brent Reilly
2. Duran Barr
3. Conner Coffin
4. Andrew Bennett

OPEN JUNIORS
1. Conner Coffin
2. Taylor Thorne
3. Dale Timm
4. Kolohe Andino

OPEN BOYS
1. Taylor Clark
2. Colin Moran
3. Andrew Jacobson
4. Patrick Curren
5. Frank Curren
6. Kanoa Igarashi

OPEN MINI GROMS
1. Jacob Davis
2. Kanoa Igarashi
3. Jake Marshall
4. Decker McAllister
5. Kody Clemens
6. Blake Dresner

OPEN LONGBOARD
1. Jerry Swearingen
2. Cole Robbins
3. Scott Brandenburg
4. Andy DeLorme
5. J.R. Costello
6. Max Jessee

OPEN WOMEN
1. Courtney Conlogue
2. Kaleigh Gilchrist
3. Sara Taylor
4. Taylor Pitz

VOLCOM STONE'S GOLDFISH SURF SERIES
CAYUCOS PIER, CALIFORNIA
February 9–10

After super-sized swells started rolling through the Morro Rock lineup, the call was made to shift the contest down to Cayucos Pier, where competitors were presented more manageable 4- to 6-foot faces. In the atypical blazing heat of winter along the Central Coast, Bobby Morris finally broke his streak of second-place finishes and ended up in the winner's circle of the Pro-Am division.

PRO-AM
1. Bobby Morris

Killian. Photo Dez Cobb/Volcom.

2. Dustin Ray
3. Blake Howard
4. Nate Tyler
5. Walt Cerney
6. Rick Gannon

JUNIORS
1. Eli Cole
2. Nat Young
3. Ashton Madeley
4. Chad Underhill
5. Shaun Burns
6. Jason Hdez

GROM
1. Lucas Silveira
2. Christian Ramirez
3. Nate Gracey
4. Trent Popovich
5. Nick Taron
6. Keary Kennel

GIRLS
1. Jamie Hannula
2. Rachel Harris
3. Darlene Conolly
4. Keenan Reeser
5. Amy Covert
6. KK Cobb

VOLCOM STONE'S SEASLUG
EL PORTO, LOS ANGELES, CALIFORNIA
February 16

With the sandbars finally groomed after a series of storms, the final stop on the Volcom Sea Slug Surf Series was shaping up to be a strong finish. In the Groms final, the competitors were split in strategies. Half of the final six sat outside, while the others decided to work the inside section. Ultimately, sitting outside proved to be the better call. Conor Beatty destroyed a few of the 2- to 4-foot faces on his way to the win.

PRO-AM
1. Michel Flores
2. Marcelo Catcarth
3. Macy Mullen
4. Jamie Meistrel
5. Michael Bailey
6. Matt King

JUNIORS
1. Nick Fowler
2. David Ruderman
3. Matt Grote
4. Derek Bruinsma
5. Tim Spaulding
6. Adam Anorga

GROMS
1. Conor Beatty
2. Andrew Jacobson
3. Kanoa Igarashi
4. Andrew Andrus
5. Hunter Johnson

6. Angelo Whren

GIRLS
1. Natalie Anzivino
2. Chelsea Rauhut
3. Lisa Tuttle
4. Emily Wratschko
5. Jessica Rodgers
6. Krystal Rodriquez

KOASTAL KAOS SERIES #6
PONTO JETTY, CALIFORNIA
February 16–17

After completing make-up heats from the previous event, the sixth stop on the Koastal Kaos Series went off in 3- to 5-foot waves. The deciding heat of the day was in the Juniors final. After exchanging the lead throughout the final, Dominic

Macy Mullen. Photo tobyogden.com.

DiPietro made one last bid to take the win, but his series of hacks wasn't enough and Derrick Disney went home the victor.

MEN FINAL
1. Macy Mullen
2. Marcelo Cathcart
3. Scott Young
4. Willie Safreed

GROM FINAL
1. Kyle Timm
2. Matt Passaquindici

BOYS FINAL
1. Jacob Halstead
2. Joe Diamond
3. Matt Lewis

JUNIORS FINAL
1. Derrick Disney
2. Dominic DiPietro
3. Dale Timm

MASTERS FINAL
1. Pedro Diaz
2. Scott Quarrie
3. Ed Custodio

WOMEN FINAL
1. Lauren Nutter
2. Alexa Dilley
3. Breanne Custodio

40TH ANNUAL NEW ENGLAND MID-WINTER SURFING CHAMPS
NARRAGANSETT, RHODE ISLAND
February 16

In the true spirit of a surf contest held in late winter in New England, the wind chill was in single digits and a "Nor'Easter" was produc-

ing quality 2- to 3-foot peelers. Comeptitors were suited up in the thickest rubber they could find and frothing to take home some regional bragging rights. The major hardware winner of the day was Little Compton's Chuck Barend, who took home three titles: Senior Men, Senior Longboard and the Open division.

NSSA SOUTHEAST/NORTH #7 & COLLEGE EVENT #5
BETHUNE BEACH, FLORIDA
February 16–17

East Coast up-and-comer Evan Geiselman stole the show at the regular season finale of the NSSA Southeast region. Both Jasset Umbel and Weston Williams were double winners in their respective divisions, but Geiselman trumped all the other trophy winners by taking home three firsts and a second. Geiselman holds the Regional win record with nine. Waves were in the 2- to 3-foot range throughout the weekend of competition.

OPEN DIVISIONS

OPEN MEN
1. Michael Dunphy
2. Evan Geiselman
3. Tayler Brothers
4. Eric Templeton

OPEN JUNIORS
1. Evan Geiselman
2. Keto Burns
3. Evan Barton
4. Ryan Croteau
5. Dylan Kowalski
6. Mason Barnes

OPEN BOYS
1. Weston Williams
2. Corey Howell
3. Tristan Thompson
4. Justin Croteau

OPEN MINI GROMS
1. Evan Brownell
2. Stevie Pittman
3. Jack Umbel

OPEN WOMEN
1. Jasset Umbel
2. Amy Nicholl
3. Haley Watson
4. Pat Thompson
5. Lauren McLean
6. Chelsea Gresham

EXPLORER DIVISIONS

EXPLORER MEN
1. Michael Dunphy
2. Tanner Deprin

3. Tayler Brothers
4. Liam Michelbrink
5. Chad Carr
6. Eric Templeton

EXPLORER BOYS
1. Evan Geiselman
2. Keto Burn
3. Jonathon Hatton
4. Ryan Croteau
5. Dylan Kowalski
6. Mason Barnes

EXPLORER MENEHUENE
1. Weston Williams
2. Noah Schweizer
3. Cam Richards
4. Knox Harris
5. Tristan Thompson
6. Justin Croteau

EXPLORER WOMEN
1. Amy Nicholl
2. Lauren McLean
3. Haley Watson
4. Jasset Umbel
5. Chelsea Gresham
6. Kayla Durden

EXPLORER GIRLS
1. Jasset Umbel
2. Ele Klein
3. Kayla Durden
4. Darsha Pigford
5. Rossi Klein

EXPLORER LONGBOARD
1. Weston Williams
2. Chelsea Gresham
3. Morgan Leavel
4. Sammy Cuminsky
5. Jimmy Cuminsky

AIRSHOW
1. Evan Geiselman
2. Nick Bland

RESULTS COLLEGE EVENT #5

COLLEGE TEAM
1. DBCC
2. FCCJ
3. UCF A
4. FLAGLER A
5. FLAGLER B
6. UF A

COLLEGE MEN
1. John Lewis
2. David Holloway
3. Austin Allen
4. Chris Coyle
5. Andrew Gregory
6. Francis Molihot

COLLEGE WOMEN
1. Kayla Beckman
2. Mallory Turner
3. Lauren McLean
4. Carmen Keys
5. Abby Schweizer
6. Sarah Malone

COLLEGE LONGBOARD
1. Todd Kinsey
2. Ryan Hamby
3. Jake Radaz
4. Brent Newell
5. John Glenn
6. Austin Piazza

NSSA GOLD COAST, EVENTS 7 & 8
C STREET, VENTURA, CALIFORNIA
February 16–17

The Gold Coast doubleheader weekend at Ventura's C Street was the beneficiary of solid swell and an abundance of fabulous overhead waves pumping through both days of competition. The level of surfing in the quality conditions were evidenced in the nine perfect 10 scores through the weekend. Nat Young was one of the stars of the events, putting together three of the perfect-scoring rides on his way to a couple wins and a few solid showings.

EXPLORER MEN
1. Trevor Gordon
2. Nat Young
3. Matt Pagen
4. Adam Lambert
5. Chad Underhill
6. Chris Keet

EXPLORER JUNIORS
1. Conner Coffin
2. Kokoro Tomatsuri
3. Hans Rathje
4. Conrad Carr
5. Eli Cole
6. Colin Dwyer

EXPLORER BOYS
1. Conner Coffin
2. Andrew Jacobson
3. Duke Van Patten
4. Charlie Dentzel

Nat Young. Photo Jean-Paul Garcia, Gold Coast Groms Photography.

5. Kyle Marre
6. Parker Coffin
EXPLORER MENEHUENE
1. Nic H'dez
2. Brogie Panesi
3. Charlie Fawcett
4. Parker Coffin
5. Andrew Jacobson
6. Kanoa Igarashi
EXPLORER MASTERS
1. Chris Keet
2. Andrew Nakagawa
3. Weston Haver
EXPLORER SENIORS
1. Yari Vodraska
2. Barry Deffenbaugh
3. Tim Wyman
4. Robert Weiner
5. Mike Lamm
6. Toby Lamm
EXPLORER WOMEN
1. Demi Boelsterli
2. Sage Erickson
3. Catherine Clark
4. Chelsea Rauhut
5. Jordan DeLaVega
6. Rachel Harris
EXPLORER GIRLS
1. Catherine Clark
2. Kirra Kehoe
3. Jordan DeLaVega
4. Lakey Peterson
5. Glennie Rodgers
EXPLORER LONGBOARD
1. Cole Robbins
2. Kevin McNicol

3. JP Garcia
4. Samson Anderson Magazino
5. Gabe Biancone
6. Rory Golden
RESULTS: EVENT #8
EXPLORER MEN
1. Nat Young
2. Matt Paga
3. Adam Lambert
4. Colin Dwyer
5. Chris Keet
6. Brandon Barnes
EXPLORER JUNIORS
1. Nat Young
2. Conner Coffin
3. Gabe Boucher
4. Kokoro Tomatsuri
5. Brandon Barnes
6. David Suhadolnik
EXPLORER BOYS
1. Conner Coffin
2. Parker Coffin
3. Kyle Marre
4. Andrew Jacobson
5. Taylor Curran
6. Charlie Dentzel
EXPLORER MENEHUENE
1. Parker Coffin

2. Andrew Jacobson
3. Jake Kelley
4. Frank Curren
5. Charlie Fawcett
6. Brogie Panesi
EXPLORER MASTERS
1. Andrew Nakagawa
2. Barry Deffenbaugh
3. Weston Haver
4. Chris Keet
EXPLORER SENIORS
1. Barry Deffenbaugh
2. Yari Vodraska
3. Tim Wyman
4. Tim Burrows
5. Robert Weiner
6. Scott Whitmer
EXPLORER WOMEN
1. Sage Erickson
2. Lakey Peterson
3. Chelsea Rauhut
4. Rachel Harris
5. Catherine Clark
6. Keenan Reeser
EXPLORER GIRLS
1. Catherine Clark
2. Jordyn DeLaVega
3. Kirra Kehoe
4. Lakey Peterson
5. Glennie Rodgers
EXPLORER LONGBOARD
1. Samson Anderson Magazino
2. JP Garcia
3. Kevin McNicol
4. Gabe Biancone
5. Rory Golden

CORONA EXTRA PRO SURF CIRCUIT • APSPR EVENT #2
PLAYA DOMES, RINCÓN, PUERTO RICO
February 23–24

An infusion of youth competitors advancing into the late heats of the Corona Extra Pro event held at Playa Domes made for a entertaining and unexpected turn of events. Of the eight semifinalists, five were not even of age to drive an automobile. After battling it out for several rounds, Darren Muschett and Liza Caban each won their first professional event in their respective divisions.

CICUITO NACIONAL DE SURF TORNEO BANCO NATIONAL
PLAYA NOSARA, COSTA RICA
February 23–24

In four-foot waves, Mattias Braun overcame a tough contest lineup of competitors for his first win on the Costa Rican contest circuit after eight years of competing. The win at Nosara earned him a spot on the Costa Rica National Surf Team. On the women's side, five-time National Surf Champion Lisbeth Vindas managed her third win this season, putting herself in good position to notch a sixth title.

OPEN MEN
1. Mattías Braun
2. Carlos Muñoz
3. Gilbert Brown
4. Juan Carlos Naranjo
JUNIOR (UNDER 18)
1. Anderson Tascón
2. Jairo Pérez
3. Jordan Hernández
4. Carlos Muñoz
OPEN WOMEN
1. Lisbeth Vindas
2. Nataly Bernold
3. Debbie Zec
4. Laura Pecorano
LONGBOARD MEN
1. Cedric Auffret
2. Mauricio Umaña
3. Adolfo Gómez
4. Cristian Santamaría
MASTERS (OVER 35)
1. Mauro Sergio Oliveira
2. Cassio Carvalho
3. Marcelo Matos
4. Carlos Velarde
BOYS (UNDER 16)
1. Carlos Muñoz
2. Danny Bishko
3. Rudy Jimenez
4. José Calderón
GROMMETS (UNDER 14)
1. Manuel Mesén
2. Josué Rodríguez
3. Anthony Filligam
4. Elijah Guy
MINI GROMMETS (UNDER 12)
1. Manuel Mesén
2. Noemar McGonagle
3. Josué Rodríguez
4. Leonardo Calvo

Mattías Braun. Photo Shifisurfshots.

JUNIOR WOMEN (UNDER 18)
1. Nataly Bernold
2. Debbie Zec
3. Anatassssio Patterson
4. Julie Javelle
MINI GROMMET GIRLS (UNDER 12)
1. Martha Fillingam
2. Arishe Grioti
3. Michelle Rodríguez
4. Avalon Esterak
NOVICE
1. Vader Draz
2. David Torres
3. José Angel López
4. Andrés Gutiérrez
BODYBOARD
1. Richard Marín
2. Joan Mojice
3. Reiner Montenegro
4. Oscar Ulate
BODYBOARD WOMEN
1. Anne-Céale Lacoste
2. Jimena Calvo
3. Lorena Vera
4. Dineth Arce

NSSA SOUTHWEST EVENT #8
9TH STREET, HUNTINGTON BEACH, CALIFORNIA
February 23–24

On the final day of competition, waves started out in the waist-high range but rapidly increased in size as the finals approached. By midday some sets were approaching one-and-a-half to double overhead and forcing competitors into survival mode. With a strong current and punishing conditions, finalists in each division had difficulty picking out waves that would provide a face to perform on. Brent Reilly continued his dominant streak in the Explorer Juniors, and Luke Davis checked any fear he made of had and pulled into the highest scoring wave of his Explorer Boys final to snatch a win.

EXPLORER MEN
1. Kyle Kennelly
2. Tanner Long
3. Dane Zaun
4. Makito Shito
5. Victor Done
6. Nick Suhadolnik
EXPLORER JUNIORS
1. Brent Reilly
2. Evan Kane
3. Dane Zaun
4. Dale Timm
5. Luke Davis
6. Nick Suhadolnik
EXPLORER BOYS
1. Luke Davis

2. Josh Giddings
3. Breyden Taylor
4. Sam Branker
5. Taylor Clark
6. Zane Norman
EXPLORER MENEHUENE
1. Johnny Elles
2. Taylor Clark
3. Kanoa Igarashi
4. Jacob Davis
5. Colin Moran
6. Jake Saenz
EXPLORER WOMEN
1. Alexa Frantz
2. Chandler Parr
3. Taylor Pitz
4. Chelsea Byland
5. Marissa Shaw
6. Winnie Riley
EXPLORER GIRLS
1. Melina Smith
2. Emmy Merrill
3. Paige Ortiz
4. Shelby Detmers
5. Kirra Kehoe
6. Charlotte Shanahan
EXPLORER MASTERS
1. Jon Warren
2. Randy Cutshall
3. Rick Takahashi
4. Scott Whitmer
5. Barry Deffenbaugh
6. Jimmy Quintanilla
EXPLORER SENIORS
1. Barry Deffenbaugh
2. Scott Whitmer
3. Mike Gillard
4. Tim Senneff
5. Rusty Phillipy
6. Neil Bern
EXPLORER SUPER SENIORS
1. Tim Senneff
2. David Winslow
3. Rick Larson
4. Mike Gillard
5. Rick Fignetti
EXPLORER LONGBOARD
1. Cole Robbins
2. Mike Gillard
3. Andy DeLorme
4. Scott Brandenburg
5. Cody Ulrich
6. Eli Gillis

VOLCOM BLOWFISH SERIES
CARDIFF REEF, SAN DIEGO, CALIFORNIA
February 16–17

The third and final stop of the Blowfish series ran in stunning fashion, with sunny skies and head-high faces on hand for what would prove to be an epic day of competition. Most every final heat was stacked with top performers, which made

Connor Coffin. Photo Jean-Paul Garcia, Gold Coast Groms Photography.

picking a favorite quite difficult. In the money heat of the Pro-Am, Darrell Goodrum managed to outlast Sean Marceron in a back-and-forth exchange.

PRO-AM
1. Darrell Goodrum
2. Sean Marceron
3. Austin Ware
4. Tom Curren
5. Marcelo Catcarth
6. Nathen Carroll

JUNIORS
1. Derrick Disney
2. Austin Sheed
3. Sean Pearson
4. John Nons
5. Thomas Clark
6. Ian Garcia

GROMS
1. Cooper Jones
2. Kent Nishiya
3. Bobby Okvist
4. Kyle Marre
5. Pat Curren
6. Hunter Johnson

GIRLS
1. Lauren Sweeney
2. Darlene Conolly
3. Lauren Nutter
4. Jamie Hannula
5. Cheyenne Arnold
6. Kristi Rife

NSSA SOUTHWEST OPEN #8
SOUTH JETTY, OCEANSIDE HARBOR, CALIFORNIA
March 1–2

With a combo swell sending 4- to 6-foot wedges into the contest area, high scores and progressive maneuvers were the theme of the weekend. As he's done all season, Conner Coffin was dominating heats, winning ten heats en route to double-duty in the finals of the Open Men and Open Juniors divisions. Griffin won every heat including the finals in the Men. The only heat where he finished less than first was in the finals of the Juniors. For the ladies, Courtney Conlogue proved far too advanced for the competition, as she swiped away any doubt with ease.

OPEN MEN
1. Conner Coffin
2. Riley Metcalf
3. Christian Saenz

4. Gabe Garcia

OPEN JUNIORS
1. Ian Crane
2. Conner Coffin
3. Jared Thorne
4. Riley Metcalf

OPEN BOYS
1. Colin Moran
2. Taylor Clark
3. Nic H'dez
4. Parker Coffin
5. Kanoa Igarashi
6. Johnny Elles

OPEN MINI GROMS
1. Kanoa Igarashi
2. Jacob Davis
3. Hunter Johnson
4. Jake Marshall
5. Decker McAllister
6. Blake Dresner

OPEN WOMEN
1. Courtney Conlogue
2. Sara Taylor
3. Kaleigh Gilchrist
4. Taylor Pitz

OPEN LONGBOARD
1. Jerry Swearingen
2. Cole Robbins
3. Scott Brandenburg
4. Cody Ulrich
5. Michael Maddox
6. Max Jessee

3RD ANNUAL GOLDEN GLOVE WINTER SURF CONTEST
MANASQUAN INLET, NEW JERSEY
March 1

Close to 100 competitors turned out to battle the elements at the third edition of the annual contest. Sun, snow, wind and rain made for an interesting backdrop, but with waist-to chest-high peaks in the water, the event was able to run in contestable conditions. Rod Kelly won the 16 & Up division for the third year in a row.

15 & UNDER
1. Michael Ciaramella
2. Christian Porter
3. PJ Raia
4. Dave Terranova
5. Nick Rutkowski
6. Michael Agnew

16 & UP
1. Rob Kelly
2. Chris Eaves
3. Balaram Stack
4. Chris Manson

5. Dalton Johnson
6. Brendan Buckley

OPEN WOMEN
1. Rachel Harrell
2. Carroline Duerr
3. Kim Kepich
4. Jill Kepich
5. Beth Grant
6. Joanne Dannecker

OPEN LONGBOARD
1. Joe Gillen
2. Alex Barlow
3. Chris Makibbin
4. Michael Ciarmella
5. Bill Willem
6. Paul Aspenberg

THE SANS SOUCI PRO, PRESENTED BY SUZUKI CARIBBEAN SURF NETWORK
TOCO, TRINIDAD
February 22–24

With representatives on hand from throughout the Caribbean, the San Souci Pro presented a range of the talent found in the warm-water locales. Throughout the event, top names were falling and new ones were rising. By the end of the weekend, Barbadian Lewis St. John's stock had risen, with a pair of wins in the Juniors and Open men divisions.

JUNIORS
1. Lewis St. John
2. Bruce Mackie
3. Jesse Jarvis
4. Oneal Coa

OPEN MEN
1. Lewis St. John
2. Chris Dennis
3. Thibault Breneol
4. Mark Holder

OPEN WOMEN
1. Ametza Nicholls
2. Danielle Ohayan
3. Jade Niccolls

BILLABONG PRO JUNIOR SEBASTIAN INLET • ASP GRADE 2 MEN PRO JR. EVENT/ ASP GRADE 1 WOMEN PRO JR. EVENT
SEBASTIAN INLET, FLORIDA
March 8–9

After making the call to extend the event an extra day to accommodate improving conditions for the final day of competition at Sebastian Inlet, heats were run in adequate 2- to 3-foot wind swell. In the Men's final, Corey Arrambide didn't provide for a tense finish, as he managed to rack up the highest heat score of the event, 17.5, and comboed his fellow finalists.

MEN FINAL
1. Cory Arrambide
2. Evan Geiselman
3. Eric Geiselman
4. Evan Thompson

QUARTERFINAL 1
1. Eric Geiselman
2. Tanner Gudauskas
3. Brent Reilly
4. Eric Snortum

QUARTERFINAL 2
1. Evan Geiselman
2. Phillip Goold
3. Nat Young
4. Adam Wickwire

QUARTERFINAL 3
1. Cory Arrambide
2. Michael Dunphy
3. Jason Harris
4. Brett Barley

QUARTERFINAL 4
1. Evan Thompson
2. Blake Jones
3. Hunter Heverly
4. Travis Beckman

SEMIFINAL 1
1. Eric Geiselman
2. Evan Geiselman
3. Phillip Goold
4. Tanner Gudauskas

SEMIFINAL 2
1. Evan Thompson
2. Cory Arrambide
3. Blake Jones
4. Michael Dunphy

WOMEN FINAL
1. Christa Alves
2. Courtney Conlogue
3. Haley Watson
4. Sage Erickson

WSA/HOBIE CHAMPIONSHIP TOUR #8
HUNTINGTON BEACH PIER, CALIFORNIA
March 8–9

With a long period Northwest swell in the water, waves were in the triple-over-grom range at HB Pier. With 24 divisions contested,

2. Breyden Taylor
3. Trevor Thornton
4. Kyle Crompton
5. Brooks Bushman
6. Cameron Faris

BOYS SHORTBOARD 14 & 15
1. Tyler Packham
2. Erik Heimstaedt
3. David Slay
4. Jakeb Bradley
5. Brett Sandison
6. Ashton Malkin

BOYS SHORTBOARD 16 & 17
1. Alex Gullet
2. Erik Heimstaedt
3. Nick Hagen
4. Matthew Nickel
5. David Slay
6. Bennet Lefebvre

GIRLS LONGBOARD 13–17
1. Tory Gilkerson
2. Marissa Graham
3. Britlyn Coleman
4. Michelle Bautista Layton
5. Taylor Garrett
6. Catherine Vasquez

GIRLS SHORTBOARD 13–15
1. Shelby Detmers
2. Chelsea Byland
3. Torey Tschudin
4. Taylor Garrett
5. Madi Swayne
6. Taylor Blake

GIRLS SHORTBOARD 16 & 17
1. Heather Jordan
2. Shelby Detmers
3. Madi Swayne
4. Chelsea Byland
5. Torey Tschudin
6. Lisa Tuttle

GRANDMASTERS SHORTBOARD 50 AND OVER

Huntington Beach Pier. Photo Greg Cruse.

the weekend was packed with tense heats, upsets, standouts and memorable moments. Terry Gillard once again found himself in the finals in numerous divisions, going three for three with wins in the Open Longboard, Senior Men Longboard and Senior Men Shortboard divisions.

BOYS LONGBOARD 13 & UNDER
1. Tony Morelli
2. Tony Bartovich
3. Jesse Hinkle
4. Trevor Robbins
5. Dane Petersen
6. Zach Stabley

BOYS LONGBOARD 14–17
1. Nick Hagen
2. Eli Gillis
3. Cody Ulrich
4. Rex Pahoa
5. Trevor Robbins
6. Kris Kaliakin

BOYS SHORTBOARD 12 & 13
1. Scott Weinhardt

1. John Silver
2. Rick Fignetti
3. Patrick Schlick
4. Dave Shaughnessy
5. David Pahoa

JUNIOR WOMEN SHORTBOARD 18–29
1. Heather Carrick
2. Morgan Gore
3. Jessica Silver
4. Chrissie Canino
5. Cybil Oechsle
6. Jessica Jamison

MASTERS' SHORTBOARD 30–39
1. Roger Heath
2. Branton Slowinski
3. Brady Martin
4. Raymond Koehler
5. Ken Workman
6. Kris Wolfe

MEN SHORTBOARD 18–29
1. Zach Newsom
2. Dane Anderson
3. Gibran Garcia
4. Sean Johnson
5. Ryan Mcafee
6. Jose Velazquez Garcia

MICRO GROM BOYS/GIRLS SHORT-BOARD/LONGBOARD 8 & UNDER
1. Tyler Gunter
2. Crosby Colapinto
3. Meah Collins
4. Diego Quinonez
5. Michael Tilly
6. Griffin Foy

OPEN MEN LONGBOARD
1. Terry Gillard
2. Shawn Parkin
3. Cody Ulrich
4. Gene Rodriguez
5. Keiichiro Tomi
6. Eli Gillis

OPEN MEN SHORTBOARD
1. Alex Gullet
2. Dane Anderson
3. Gibran Garcia
4. Brady Martin
5. Zach Newsom
6. Roger Heath

OPEN WOMEN LONGBOARD
1. Blythe Bejan
2. Michelle Bautista Layton
3. Marissa Graham
4. Wanda Smans
5. Deborah Scarano
6. Lyn Burich

OPEN WOMEN SHORTBOARD
1. Madi Swayne
2. Dresden Rowlett
3. Chelsea Byland
4. Mackenzie Kessler
5. Hayley Conant
6. Mary Setterholm

SENIOR MEN SHORTBOARD 40–49
1. Terry Gillard
2. Troy Bertrand
3. Barry Bushman
4. Glen Tilly
5. Dave Hansberry
6. Witt Rowlett

SENIOR MEN LONGBOARD 30 & OLDER
1. Terry Gillard
2. Gabriel Fimbres
3. Rick Carlisle
4. Kelly O'Connell
5. Barry Bushman
6. Robert Stirrat

SUPER GROM BOYS SHORTBOARD 11 & UNDER
1. Brooks Bushman
2. Kyle Crompton
3. Chandler Stirrat
4. Ryan Harris
5. Tyler Gunter
6. Justin Harrison

SUPER GROM GIRLS LONGBOARD 12 & UNDER
1. Allyson Heinmeyer
2. Lauren Heinmeyer
3. Avalon Johnson
4. Sidney Johnson
5. Rachael Tilly

SUPER GROM GIRLS SHORTBOARD 12 & UNDER
1. Taylor Blake
2. Rachael Tilly
3. Avalon Johnson
4. Meah Collins
5. Lauren Heinmeyer
6. Malia Ward

WOMEN LONGBOARD 18 & OLDER
1. Blythe Bejan
2. Wanda Smans

WOMEN SHORTBOARD 30 & OLDER
1. Dresden Rowlett
2. Mary Setterholm
3. Heather Pine
4. Deborah Scarano
5. Lyn Burich
6. Casper Elizaga

NSSA INTER-SCHOLASTIC STATE CHAMPS, PRESENTED BY NO FEAR
CHURCH, SAN CLEMENTE, CALIFORNIA
March 7–9

Fifteen colleges, 12 high schools and 10 middle schools rolled up to Church in San Onofre State Park to compete for state supremacy. With school rivalries adding to the intensity, a number of closely contested final heats made for entertaining close to the weekend. In the college division, the team title came down to the Men's Shortboard final, with two representatives from both University of California, Santa Barbara and San Diego State University. With Matt Johnson and Charles McMahon finishing 3rd and 5th, respectively, UCSB managed to cling to its team lead. In longboarding, Troy Mothershead won his division for the sixth consecutive year, having initially won the middle division four straight years in high school and now as a freshman in college at Point Loma.

COLLEGE TEAM
1. UCSB-A
2. SDSU-A
3. Saddleback
4. CSUSM-A
5. Mira Costa –Red
6. UCSD
7. Point Loma
8. USD
9. CSUSM-B
10. UCSB-B
11. Cal Poly San Luis Obispo-A
12. Mira Costa-White
13. SDSU-B
    Cal Poly San Luis Obispo-B
15. Golden West

COLLGE MEN
1. Jason McIlwee
2. Chris Smith
3. Matt Johnson
4. Ryan Judson
5. Charles McMahon
6. Tyler Smith

COLLEGE WOMEN
1. Lauren Sweeney
2. Allie Brown
3. Ericka Cook
4. Devon Holloway
5. Michelle Reeves
6. Kristi Rife

COLLEGE LONGBOARD
1. Troy Mothershead
2. Billy Harris
3. Christian Clark
4. Chris Smith
5. Corey Hartwyk
6. Wyatt Harrison

HIGH SCHOOL TEAM
1. Huntington Beach
2. Carlsbad
3. San Dieguito
4. San Clemente
5. Edison
6. Newport Harbor
7. Carpenteria
8. Mira Costa
9. Laguna Beach
10. Santa Barbara
11. Palos Verdes
12. Marina

HIGH SCHOOL MEN
1. Doug Van Mierlo
2. Kyle McGeary
3. Dominic DiPietro
4. Kokoro Tomatsuri
5. Quinn McCrystal
6. Vance Smith

HIGH SCHOOL WOMEN
1. Kaleigh Gilchrist
2. Taylor Pitz
3. Heather Jordan
4. Alexa Dilley
5. Sara Taylor
6. Rachel Harris

HIGH SCHOOL LONGBOARD
1. Jeff Newell
2. Paul Smeltzer
3. Brent Bowen
4. Scott Brandenburg
5. Chris Cravey
6. Wade Carden

MIDDLE SCHOOL TEAM
1. Shorecliffs
2. Sowers
3. Shorecliffs
4. Dwyer
5. Marco Forster
6. Carpenteria
7. Sowers
8. Niguel Hills
9. Shorecliffs
10. Niguel Hills

MIDDLE SCHOOL BOYS
1. Ian Crane
2. Parker Coffin
3. Josh Giddings
4. Breyden Taylor
5. Trevor Thornton
6. Wyatt Brady

MIDDLE SCHOOL GIRLS
1. Melina Smith
2. Lulu Erkeneff
3. Paige Ortiz
4. Torrey Miethke
5. Emmy Lombard
6. Danielle Wyman

MIDDLE SCHOOL LONGBOARD
1. Tony Bartovich
2. Zack Stapley
3. Scott Weinhardt
4. Andy Nieblas
5. Mason Klink
6. Chandler Stirrat

WSA/HOBIE CHAMPIONSHIP TOUR #9
SALT CREEK, DANA POINT, CALIFORNIA
March 2

With epic conditions for the weekend, as a sign of respect and deference to the locals, organizers decided to run the event only on Sunday, with an extra competition area for a few hours. Waves were glassy and head-high, with sunny skies sending a shimmer across the faces. Conditions were so good that the MC opted to sign up for the Open division in order to get some time in the stunning conditions.

BOYS LONGBOARD 13 & UNDER
1. Jesse Hinkle
2. Dane Petersen
3. Tony Bartovich
4. Zach Stabley
5. Trevor Robbins

BOYS LONGBOARD 14–17
1. Cody Ulrich
2. Sam Orozco
3. Eli Gillis
4. Kevin McNicol
5. Rex Pahoa
6. Nick Hagen

BOYS SHORTBOARD 12 & 13
1. Cameron Faris
2. Trevor Thornton
3. Scott Weinhardt
4. Brooks Bushman
5. Tony Bartovich
6. Tony Morelli

BOYS SHORTBOARD 14 & 15
1. Christian Arballo
2. Shaw Kobayashi
3. Tyler Packham
4. Randy Gilkerson
5. Jonathan Koechlin
6. Cameron Faris

BOYS SHORTBOARD 16 & 17
1. Christian Arballo
2. Jason Strom
3. Nick Hagen

Salt Creek. Photos California Surfing Images.

4. Kent Nishiya
5. David Slay
6. Erik Heimstaedt

GIRLS LONGBOARD 13–17
1. Michelle Bautista Layton
2. Marissa Graham
3. Tory Gilkerson
4. Carly Martin
5. Lisa Tuttle
6. Taylor Garrett

GIRLS SHORTBOARD 13–15
1. Shelby Detmers
2. Chelsea Byland
3. Carly Martin
4. Taylor Garrett
5. Torey Tschudin
6. Madi Swayne

GIRLS SHORTBOARD 16 & 17
1. Shelby Detmers
2. Chelsea Byland
3. Mackenzie Kessler
4. Taylor Garrett
5. Lisa Tuttle
6. Jade Baer

GRANDMASTERS SHORTBOARD 50 AND OVER
1. Rick Fignetti
2. John Silver
3. Patrick Schlick
4. Dave Shaughnessy
5. John MacPherson

JUNIOR WOMEN SHORTBOARD 18–29
1. Amy Covert
2. Morgan Gore
3. Chrissie Canino
4. Jessica Silver
5. Jessica Jamison
6. Cybil Oechsle

MASTERS SHORTBOARD 30–39
1. Roger Heath
2. Ken Workman

BOYS LONGBOARD 14–17 *(continued)*
3. Brady Martin
4. Conner Erwin
5. Raymond Koehler
6. Kris Wolfe

MEN SHORTBOARD 18–29
1. Willie Watkin
2. Jose Velazquez Garcia
3. Zach Newsom
4. David Daly
5. Justin Pierson
6. Dane Anderson

MICRO GROM BOYS/GIRLS SHORT-BOARD/LONGBOARD 8 & UNDER
1. Kei Kobayashi
2. Tyler Gunter
3. Crosby Colapinto
4. Griffin Foy
5. Sam Wickwire
6. Meah Collins

OPEN MEN LONGBOARD
1. Shawn Parkin
2. Keiichiro Tomi
3. Terry Gillard
4. Eli Gillis
5. Cody Ulrich
6. Josh Rapozo

OPEN MEN SHORTBOARD
1. Marty Thomas
2. Tyler Christian
3. Dane Anderson
4. Willie Watkin
5. Jose Velazquez Garcia
6. Gibran Garcia

OPEN WOMEN LONGBOARD
1. Marissa Graham
2. Blythe Bejan
3. Michelle Bautista Layton
4. Lyn Burich
5. Wanda Smans

OPEN WOMEN SHORTBOARD
1. Heather Jordan
2. Chelsea Byland
3. Dresden Rowlett
4. Mary Setterholm
5. Morgan Gore
6. Mackenzie Kessler

SENIOR MEN SHORTBOARD 40–49
1. Witt Rowlett
2. Terry Gillard
3. Troy Bertrand
4. Jean Pierre Pereat
5. Greg Reed
6. Kevin Daniels

SENIOR MEN LONGBOARD 30 & OLDER
1. Terry Gillard
2. Kelly O'Connell
3. Barry Bushman
4. Michael Kuri
5. Gabriel Fimbres
6. Ken Workman

SUPER GROM BOYS SHORTBOARD 11 & UNDER
1. Brooks Bushman
2. Kyle Crompton
3. Tai Stratton
4. Kei Kobayashi

5. Ryan Harris
6. Griffin Colapinto

SUPER GROM GIRLS LONGBOARD 12 & UNDER
1. Allyson Heinmeyer
2. Lauren Heinmeyer
3. Avalon Johnson
4. Ashley Beeson
5. Sidney Johnson

SUPER GROM GIRLS SHORTBOARD 12 & UNDER
1. Kylie Loveland

Luis Vindas. Photo Shifisurfshots.

2. Erika Barnett
3. Lauren Heinmeyer
4. Taylor Blake
5. Sidney Johnson
6. Meah Collins

WOMEN LONGBOARD 18 & OLDER
1. Wanda Smans
2. Blythe Bejan

WOMEN SHORTBOARD 30 & OLDER
1. Dresden Rowlett
2. Lyn Burich
3. Heather Pine
4. Casper Elizaga

VOLCOM STONE CATFISH
DOMINICAN REPUBLIC
March 8–9

After consecutive years of running the event in Puerto Rico, Volcom decided to role the dice and move the event to the Dominican Republic for a change in scenery. Despite lost luggage and issues passing through customs, the event ran smoothly, with solid conditions for the hordes of competitors in attendance. The Pro-Am final was the heat of the final day. After shuffling the lead among the finalists, Dylan Graves' front-side attack proved too strong as he took home the cash prize.

PRO-AM
1. Dylan Graves
2. Brandon Sanford
3. Nate Tyler
4. Manuel Selman
5. Pedro Fernandez
6. Jason Reagen

JUNIORS
1. Taylor Brothers
2. Hector Santa-Maria
3. Daniel Aguilera
4. Yohauri Polbaco
5. Jobe Mark
6. Saul Meding

GROMS
1. Edward Santang
2. William Kirkham
3. Derek Daniel Gomez
4. Jules Guerrier
5. Jesus Alberto
6. Pablo Fourcian

GIRLS
1. Quincy Davis
2. Aubrey Faulk
3. Rachel Haslett
4. Sarah Hoffert

5. Andrea Vogel
6. Modaka Kawaguchi

CIRCUITO NACIONAL DE SURF EVENT #5
PLAYA CARMEN, COSTA RICA
March 15–16

Despite failing to win the contest Gilbert Brown had plenty of reasons to celebrate. In the difficult dumping conditions, Brown finished second behind Luis Vindas. With the points accumulated from the runner-up finish, Brown took the Circuito title in the Open division. In the Women's, defending Circuito champ Nataly Bernold notched her first win of the season. However, she trails Lisbeth Vindas, a five-time champ.

OPEN MEN
1. Luis Vindas
2. Gilbert Brown
3. Jairo Pérez
4. Juan Carlos Naranjo

JUNIORS
1. Carlos Muñoz
2. Rudy Jiménez
3. Ramon Taliani
4. Jairo Pérez

OPEN WOMEN
1. Nataly Bernold
2. Laura Pecoraro
3. Lisbeth Vindas
4. Dorothy Bugbee

LONGBOARD
1. Diego Naranjo
2. Cedric Auffret
3. Ross Packman
4. Cristian Santamaría

BOYS
1. Anthony Segura
2. Rudy Jiménez
3. Carlos Muñoz
4. Tamas King

GROMMETS
1. Tomas King

2. Josué Rodríguez
3. Elijah Guy
4. Noemar McGonagle

MINI GROMMETS
1. Noemar McGonagle
2. Manuel Mesen
3. Santana Rosales
4. Leonardo Calvo

MINI GROMMETS GIRLS
1. Leilani McGonagle
2. Naomi Bernold
3. Martha Fillingan
4. Avalon Esterak

MASTERS
1. Cassio Carvalho
2. Marcelos Matos
3. David Madigal
4. Mauro Sergio Oliveira

NOVICES
1. David Torres
2. Yader Díaz
3. Eduardo Mora
4. Alexis Chamorro

BODYBOARD
1. Joan Mojica
2. Yeric Fajardo
3. Jesús Zavala

WOMEN BODYBOARD
1. Anne Leleane Lacoste
2. Lorena Vera
3. Jimena Calvo
4. Jennifer Harder

JSA 2008 NATIONAL OPEN SURFING CHAMPS EVENT #2
MAKKA, YALLAHS, ST. THOMAS, JAMAICA
March 16

Icah Wilmot's progressive approach was too much for his fellow finalists, picking up his second win in as many contests. For the women, only two competitors showed up; Imani Wilmot won.

OPEN MEN
1. Icah Wilmot
2. Luke Williams
3. Shane Simmonds
4. Ackeam Phillips
5. Michael Panton
6. Inilek Wilmot
6. Ackeam Taylor
8. Gatey Dawkins
8. Scott Clelland
10. Dane Jefferys
10. Shama Beckford
10. Ivah Wilmot
13. Ishack Wilmot

Icah Wilmot. Photo Jamaica Surfing Association.

13. Garren Pryce
13. Jason Pusey
16. Anthony Miller
16. Ronley Lewis
16. Sean Laidley
16. Junior Hibbert
16. Alton Smith

OPEN WOMEN
1. Imani Wilmot
2. Elim Beckford

VOLCOM STONE BUTTERFISH
PIPES, VENTURA, CALIFORNIA
March 15–16

In super-gusty conditions, the final stop on the Butterfish Series ran at Pipes, with some tightly contested final heats. The Girls division final had three young ladies vying for the top spot while being judged on only a single wave. Bo Stanley pulled out the win with a late one. The majority of the day was dominated by the finalists with the patience to hold out for the better ones; solid-scoring waves were few and far between, but they were out there.

PRO-AM
1. Matt McCabe
2. Blake Howard
3. Bobby Morris
4. Tom Curren

Cory Arrambide. Photo munchphotos.com.

5. Guy Guy Quesada
6. Pierce Flynn

JUNIORS
1. Evan Watson
2. Ian Jenkins
3. Simon Murdock
4. Eli Cole
5. Antonie Allain
6. David Dittme

GROM
1. Sam Reagan
2. Kent Nishiya
3. Frank Curren
4. Skylar Lawson
5. Matt Becker
6. Jake Kelly

GIRLS
1. Bo Stanley
2. Demi Boelsterli
3. Sage Erickson
4. Lexi Vanderlieth
5. Catherine Clark
6. Keenan Reeser

CAMPEONATO CENTROAMERICANO DE SURF
PLAYA VENAO, PANAMA
March 20–24

For the third consecutive year in the three years of existence of the Central America Surf Championships, Costa Rica took home the overall team title. Tico's Jason Torres (Open Men) and Nataly Bernold (Open Women) won their respective divisions to contribute to the winning cause. The event was held over three days at Playa Venao.

TEAM RESULTS
1. Costa Rica
2. Panama
3. Nicaragua
4. El Salvador
5. Guatemala

KOASTAL KAOS EVENT #7, PRESENTED BY NO FEAR
SEASIDE REEF, SAN DIEGO
March 21–22

In an entertaining display of quality progressive surfing, a couple of the young guns lit up Seaside Reef, while a familiar face took home the $500 in the Men's division. Costa Mesa's Colin Moran and Santa Cruz's Nat Young continued their solid run of contest showings. Though the event was Young's first as part of the KK series, he's been taking down events all over Southern California. Hawaii's Macy Mullen followed up his previous contest win with another, which was solidified with a near-perfect 9.83 wave score after destroying a good one in the final.

OPEN MEN
1. Macy Mullen
2. Matt Mccabe
3. Matt Myers
4. Gabe Garcia
5. David Suhadolnik
5. Eric McHenry
BOYS
1. Taylor Clark
2. Colin Moran
3. Jacob Halstead
4. Josh Giddings
5. Nelson Kingery

Shaun Ward. Photo Vans.

6. Alec Macauley
GROMS
1. Colin Moran
2. Nelson Kingery
3. Kyle Timm
4. Kanoa Igarashi
5. Taylor Clark
6. Jay Christenson
JUNIORS
1. Nat Young
2. Derrick Disney
3. JD Lewis
4. Dale Timm
5. Britt Galland Jr
6. Sterling Weatherly
MASTERS
1. Yu Fu Penrose
2. Pedro Diaz
3. Shaun Noble
4. Rick Takahashi
5. Austin Neider
6. Tom Trier
OPEN WOMEN
1. Amy Chivers
2. Alexa Dilley
3. Danielle Dickerson
4. Alexa Thornton
5. Breanne Custodio
6. Coco Jones

VANS PIER CLASSIC, PRESENTED BY JACK'S SURFBOARDS • MEN 2-STAR WQS EVENT & EZEKIEL PRO JUNIOR, PRESENTED BY JACK'S SURFBOARDS • GRADE 2 MEN ASP JUNIOR EVENT
THE PIER, HUNTINGTON BEACH, CALIFORNIA
March 26–30

The standout all week long, Shaun Ward capped off his string of consistently strong-scoring heats by outgunning his fellow finalists en route to his first win on the ASP World Qualifying Series this season, in front of his hometown crowd. Running in conjunction with the Vans Pier Classic was the Ezekiel Junior Pro. Newly local Bruno Rodrigues, a Brazilian transplant, managed to pull out the win in one of his first contests at his new home break.

MEN FINAL
1. Shaun Ward
2. Dylan Graves
3. Brad Ettinger
4. Austin Ware
SEMIFINAL 1
1. Austin Ware
2. Brad Ettinger
3. Patrick Gudauskas
4. Kyle Ramey
SEMIFINAL 2
1. Dylan Graves
2. Shaun Ward
3. Jason Miller
4. Ian Rotgans
QUARTERFINAL 1
1. Patrick Gudauskas
2. Brad Ettinger
3. Dane Gudauskas
4. Chris Drummy
QUARTERFINAL 2
1. Kyle Ramey
2. Austin Ware
3. Matt King
4. Heath Walker
QUARTERFINAL 3
1. Dylan Graves
2. Ian Rotgans
3. Casey Brown
4. Sunny Garcia

QUARTERFINAL 4
1. Shaun Ward
2. Jason Miller
3. Jason Collins
4. Nathan Yeomans
WOMEN FINAL
1. Courtney Conlogue
2. Sage Erickson
3. Nage Malamud
4. Lauren Sweeney
SEMIFINAL 1
1. Nage Malamud
2. Lauren Sweeney
3. Anastasia Ashley
4. Christa Alves
SEMIFINAL 2
1. Courtney Conlogue
2. Sage Erickson
3. Leila Hurst
4. Bo Stanley
EZEKIEL PRO JUNIOR PRESENTED BY JACKS SURFBOARDS (ASP PRO JUNIOR GRADE-2)
JUNIORS FINAL:
1. Bruno Rodrigues
2. Travis Beckmann
3. Trevor Saunders
4. Adam Wickwire
SEMIFINAL 1
1. Trevor Saunders
2. Bruno Rodrigues
3. Austin Smith Ford
4. Jason Harris
SEMIFINAL 2
1. Adam Wickwire
2. Travis Beckman
3. Blake Jones
4. Cody Thompson
QUARTERFINAL 1
1. Jason Harris
2. Bruno Rodrigues
3. Tanner Gudauskas
4. Quinn McCrystal
QUARTERFINAL 2
1. Trevor Saunders
2. Austin Smith Ford
3. Logan Strook
4. Kekoa Cazimero
QUARTERFINAL 3
1. Blake Jones
2. Travis Beckmann
3. Eric Geiselman
4. Spencer Reagan
QUATERFINAL 4
1. Cody Thompson
2. Adam Wickwire
3. Andrew Doheny
4. Nat Young

REEF CLASSIC PANAMA 2008
PLAYA VENAO, PANAMA
March 28–30

Despite less-than-ideal conditions in the three-foot range, the championship of the Reef Classic was able to finish. Venezuelan Francisco Bellorin won his second Open Pro ALAS title in a tightly contested final of the Men's division.

OPEN MEN
1. Francisco Bellorin
2. Germain Nino Myrie
JUNIORS
1. Dylan Southworth
2. Jesus Chacón
3. Diego Silva
4. Francisco Bellorin
OPEN WOMEN
1. Agostina Pellizzari
2. Lisbeth Vindas

3. Sofia Bórquez
4. Adriana Cano

NSSA EAST COAST CHAMPS, PRESENTED BY NO FEAR
SEBASTIAN INLET, FLORIDA
March 27–30

The NSSA was blessed with fun surf and warm, sunny skies for its season-ending series on the East Coast. Sebastian Inlet presented contestable conditions courtesy of a consistent combination of ground and wind swells for waves in the waist- to shoulder-high range. Virginia Beach native Michael Dunphy was the stud of the week, putting together a trifecta in winning the Open Men, Explorer Men and Explorer Juniors. Evan Geiselman had a fine showing with four finals appearances, winning three.

OPEN MEN
1. Michael Dunphy
2. Liam Michelbrink
3. Evan Geiselman
4. Nick Rupp
JUNIORS
1. Evan Geiselman
2. Evan Thompson
3. Nick Rupp
4. Hector Santa Maria
BOYS
1. Cam Richards
2. Weston Williams
3. Corey Howell
4. Mauricio Diaz
5. Noah Schweizer
6. Sam Duggan
MINI GROMS
1. Logan Hayes
2. Stevie Pittman
3. Luke Marks
4. Evan Brownell
5. Jack Umbel
6. Izzi Gomez
OPEN WOMEN
1. Jassett Umbel
2. Ariel Engstrom
3. Alexis Engstron
4. Jennifer Morris
OPEN LONGBOARD
1. Patrick Nichols
2. Todd Kinsey
3. Michael Wood
4. Weston Williams
5. Michael Agnew
6. Chelsea Gresham
EAST COAST EXPLORER CHAMPIONSHIPS
EXPLORER MEN
1. Michael Dunphy
2. Balaram Stack
3. Tommy Orsini
4. Liam Michelbrink
5. Tayler Brothers
6. Oliver Kurtz
EXPLORER JUNIORS
1. Michael Dunphy
2. Nick Rupp
3. Oliver Kurtz
4. Balaram Stack
5. Liam Michelbrink
6. Tayler Brothers
EXPLORER BOYS
1. Evan Geiselman
2. Keto Burns
3. Christian Miller
4. Dylan Kowalski
5. Tanner Strohmenger

6. Noah Schweizer
EXPLORER MENEHUENE
1. Cam Richards
2. Mauricio Diaz
3. Tristan Thompson
4. Noah Schweizer
5. Logan Hayes
6. Weston Williams
EXPLORER WOMEN
1. Quincy Davis
2. Jassett Umbel
3. Amy Nicholl
4. Ariel Engstrom
5. Savannah Bradley
6. Alexis Engstrom
EXPLORER GIRLS
1. Jassett Umbel
2. Quincy Davis
3. Savannah Bradley
4. Nikki Viesins
5. Kayla Durden
6. Rossi Klein
EXPLORER MASTERS
1. Jason Motes
2. Lyn Meyers
3. Steve Moore
4. William Kimball
5. Chad Carr
6. Anthony Passarelli
EXPLORER SENIORS
1. Jason Motes
2. Bill McCardell
3. Chilly Gilreath
4. Charlie Hajek
5. Jim Tolliver
6. Ray Sturm
EXPLORER SUPER SENIORS
1. Charlie Hajek
2. Steve Moldenhauer
3. Rob Person
4. Jim Tolliver
5. Jim Miller
6. Bill Miller
EXPLORER LONGBOARD
1. Michael Wood
2. Steve Moldenhauer
3. Bill McCardell
4. Weston Williams
5. Wyatt Todd
6. Patrick Nichols
EAST COAST AIRSHOW CHAMPIONSHIPS
1. Evan Geiselman
2. Rob Kelly
EAST COAST COLLEGIATE CHAMPIONSHIPS
COLLEGE TEAM
1. Flagler College
2. University of Central Florida
3. Daytona Beach Community College
4. University of North Florida
5. University of Florida
6. University of North Florida
7. University of Central Florida
8. University of Central Florida
COLLEGE MEN
1. Eric Taylor
2. Ben McLeod
3. David Holloway
4. Chad Bagwell
5. John Lewis
6. Erich Hauck
COLLEGE WOMEN
1. Lauren McLean
2. Kayla Beckman
3. Ashley Francis
4. Mallory Turner
5. Sara Malone
6. Abby Schweizer
COLLEGE LONGBOARD
1. Todd Kinsey
2. Jake Radacz
3. Brent Newell
4. Erik Tanner

5. Austin Piazza
6. Travis Eubanks

TORNEO BANCO NATIONAL • CIRCUITO NACIONAL DE SURF EVENT #6
PLAYA DOMINICAL, COSTA RICA
April 5–6

Luis Vindas made it two in a row on the Circuito Nacional de Surf Series, holding off points-leader Gilbert Brown in the final. Though Brown is comfortably in the ratings lead, it may get interesting with the final event of the series coming up. Lisbeth Vindas was too much for the opposition, winning the Women's division and inching closer to a sixth national championship.

OPEN MEN
1. Luis Vindas
2. Gilbert Brown
3. Juan Carlos Naranjo
4. Jason Torres
JUNIORS
1. Carlos Muñoz
2. Jairo Pérez
3. Anderson Tascon
4. Rudy Jiménez
OPEN WOMEN
1. Lisbeth Vindas
2. Laura Pecoraro
3. Jennifer Hinds
4. Ericka Valverde
JUNIOR WOMEN
1. Nataly Bernold
2. Julie Javelle
3. Debbie Zec
4. Avalon Esterak
BOYS
1. Mykol Torres
2. Anthony Segura
3. Danny Bishkol
4. Anthony Fillingam
GROMMETS
1. Anthony Fillingam
2. Tomas King
3. Leonardo Calvo
4. Jan Gagstater
MINI GROMMETS
1. Noe Mar Mcgonagle
2. Leonardo Calvo
3. Czar Esterak
4. Kevin Montiel
MINI GROMMETS GIRLS
1. Arisha Grioti
2. Leilani McGonagle

Aston Madely. Photo Miah Klein.

3. Mar y Paz Solano
4. Marta Fillingam
LONGBOARD
1. Diego Naranjo
2. Cedric Auffret
3. Alex Gómez
4. Adolfo Gómez
MASTERS
1. Mauro Sergio Oliveira
2. Gustavo Saravia
3. Marcelo Matos
4. Mike Esterak
NOVICES
1. José Angel López
2. Rolando Zamora
3. Carlos Rivera
4. Manuele Fratini
BODYBOARD
1. Joan Mojica
2. Oscar Ulate
3. Richard Marin
4. Francisco Mendoza
BODYBOARD WOMEN
1. Jimena Calvo
2. Lorena Vera
3. Donet Arce

COPA LAS AMERICAS DE SURF CIRCUITO PROFESIONAL DE SURFING EN MEXICO
PLAYA BONFIL, MEXICO
April 3–6

Angelo Lozano took home the title on the second stop of the Mexican Professional Circuit of Surfing. Held at Playa Bonfil, waves were in the 4- to 7-foot range.

1. Angelo Lozano
2. Jose Mauel "Yuco" Trujillo
3. Dylan Southworth
4. Cristian Corso
5. Oscar Chino

RED BULL RIDERS CUP
PLEASURE POINT, SANTA CRUZ, CALIFORNIA
April 11

In competitive games throughout the week, Soquel High School was crowned the Santa Cruz regional champion of the Red Bull Riders Cup (formerly the Red Bull High School Cup). The final game between Soquel High and Harbor High brought big crowds in an action-packed game.

FINALS
SANTA CRUZ GAME #1
1. Aptos High
2. Scotts Valley High
   Most Valuable Player - Brandon Barnes, Aptos High
   Most Radical Maneuver - Aaron Godfrey, Aptos High
SANTA CRUZ GAME #2
1. Soquel High School
2. Santa Cruz High School
   Most Valuable Player - Jason Hdez, Soquel High School
   Most Radical Maneuver - Ashton Madely, Soquel High School
SANTA CRUZ GAME #3
1. Harbor High School
2. Aptos High School
   Most Valuable Player - Bjorn Temple, Harbor High School
   Most Radical Maneuver - Cheyne Pearson, Harbor High School
SANTA CRUZ GAME #4
1. Harbor High School
2. Soquel High School

VOLCOM COOTERFISH MARYLAND
OCEAN CITY, MARYLAND
April 5–6

In its last stop of the season, the Volcom Cooterfish series was run in cold, rainy weather with a nice pulse providing 3- to 4-foot surf. With water temps in the mid-40s, the groms were tweaking on Monster energy drinks enough to keep the blood pumping and provide some entertainment for the spectators. In the Pro-Am final, Noah Snyder managed to find some tubes and was able to hold off Jeff Myers and his aerial approach.

Demi Boelsterli. Photo Jean-Paul Garcia, Gold Coast Groms Photography.

PRO-AM
1. Noah Snyder
2. Jeff Meyers
3. Vince Bolanger
4. Ian Parnell
5. Billy Hume
6. Phillip Gould
JUNIORS
1. Mike Dunphy
2. Ron Harrell
3. Evan Barton
4. Sean Wooleyhan
5. Kyle Herman
6. Andrew Stweart
GROM
1. Nick Rupp
2. Austin Deppe
3. Conner Lester
4. Austin Gerachs
5. Roland Gerachs
6. Oleg Connoll
GIRLS
1. Rachel Harrell
2. Kate Faston
3. Emily Rupppert
4. Kahlyn Curren
5. Jenna Landon
6. Danielle Ariand

NSSA GOLD COAST EXPLORER #9
PISMO BEACH, CALIFORNIA
April 12

With 1- to 3-foot fun waves off the south side of Pismo Beach Pier, glassy conditions prevailing through the weekend, and daytime temperatures soaring to the low 90s, the NSSA Gold Coast contest went off in fine form.

EXPLORER MEN
1. Brandon Barnes
2. Adam Lambert
3. Kokoro Tomatsuri
4. Brandon Smith
5. Conrad Carr
6. Trevor Gordon
EXPLORER JUNIORS
1. Brandon Barnes
2. Conner Coffin
3. Kokoro Tomatsuri
4. Conrad Carr
5. Connor Walden
6. Shane Orr
EXPLORER BOYS
1. Parker Coffin
2. Conner Coffin
3. Kyle Marre
4. Kadin Panesi
5. Brogie Panesi
6. Kanoa Igarashi
EXPLORER MENEHUENE
1. Parker Coffin
2. Kanoa Igarashi
3. Kadin Panesi
4. Jake Kelley
5. Andrew Jacobson
6. Brogie Panesi
EXPLORER WOMEN
1. Demi Boelsterli
2. Sage Erickson
3. Rachel Harris
4. Catherine Clark
5. Rachel Harris
6. Lakey Peterson
EXPLORER GIRLS
1. Lakey Peterson
2. Catherine Clark
3. Kirra Kehoe
4. Jordyn De La Vega
5. Glennie Rodgers
6. Malia Faramarzi
EXPLORER MASTERS
1. John Gardner
2. Weston Haver
3. Chris Keet
EXPLORER SENIORS
1. Robert Weiner
2. Scott Whitmer
3. Yari Vodraska
4. Mike Lamm
5. Steve Dwyer
6. Matt McAllister
EXPLORER LONGBOARD
1. Rory Golden
2. Nicholas Shellhammer
3. JP Garcia
4. Kevin McNicol
5. Shayne Millhollin
6. Alec Ledbetter
2008 GOLD COAST CONFERENCE EXPLORER CHAMPIONS
Men—Kokoro Tomatsuri
Juniors—Kokoro Tomaturi
Boys—Parker Coffin
Menehuene—Parker Coffin
Women—Demi Boelsterli

Volcom Cooterfish. Photo courtesy Volcom.

Girls—Lakey Peterson
Masters—Chris Keet
Seniors—Robert Weiner
Longboard-Kevin McNicol

NORTHWEST OPEN SEASON EVENT #6
PISMO BEACH PIER
OPEN MEN
1. Shaw Kobayashi
2. Brandon Barnes
3. Conrad Carr
4. Ashton Madeley
OPEN JUNIORS
1. Shaw Kobayashi
2. John Wilson
3. Daniel Prichard
4. Theo Kirkham-Lewitt
OPEN BOYS
1. Frank Curren
2. Nic Hdez
3. Andrew Jacobson
4. Pat Curren
5. Decker McAllister
6. Brogie Panesi
OPEN MINI GROMS
1. Decker McAllister
2. Kei Kobayashi
3. John Mel
4. Noah Cooper
5. Cousteau Christopher
6. Malia Faramarzi
OPEN WOMEN
1. Demi Boelsterli
2. Rachel Harris
3. Bo Stanley
4. Sahara Ray
LONGBOARD OPEN
1. Samson Anderson Magazino
2. Kevin McNichol
3. Kai Medeiros
4. Kirra Kehoe
5. Zach Abbriscuto

2008 NORTHWEST CONFERENCE OPEN CHAMPIONS
Men—Conrad Carr
Juniors—Shaw Kobayashi
Boys—Andrew Jacobson
Mini Groms—Kei Kobayashi
Women—Demi Boelsterli
Longboard—Samson Anderson Magazino

RED BULL RIDERS CUP SOUTH FLORIDA
CARLIN PARK, JUPITER, FLORIDA
April 15–17

The Red Bull Riders Cup came to outh Florida to determine the regional champion from among four high school surf teams. Jupiter High managed to nudge past Cardinal Gibbons High for the win, and secured itself a spot in the National Championships in San Clemente, California.

SOUTH FLORIDA GAME #1 FINAL
1. Martin County High
2. Cardinal Gibbons High
  Most Valuable Player—
  Alex Walker of Cardinal Gibbons High
  Most Radical Maneuver—
  Zack Kleinfeld of Martin County High
SOUTH FLORIDA GAME #2 FINAL
1. Calvary Christian Academy
2. Jupiter High School
  Most Valuable Player—
  Ryan Weiland of Jupiter High School
  Most Radical Maneuver—
  Ryan Weiland of Jupiter High School
SOUTH FLORIDA GAME #3 FINAL
1. Cardinal Gibbons High
2. Jupiter High School

Most Valuable Player—Ryan Weiland, Jupiter High School
  Most Radical Maneuver—Taylor Hagglund, Jupiter High School

MOSKITO TOUR GUADELOUPE
BANAMIER BEACH, GUADELOUPE
May 10–11

Small waves and pleasant weather were enough to keep the 65 kids enthused in the Banamier Beach stop of the Moskito Tour. In the finals, the kids were pulling out all the maneuvers in hopes of taking home the win.

UNDER 16 BOYS
1. Oueslati Jordan
2. Merz Cyril
3. Alexi Raphael
4. Breton Louis
UNDER 16 GIRLS
1. Landres Rosana
2. Rilens Kim
3. Dubosc Oana
4. Mignot Diane
UNDER 14 BOYS
1. Dulac Alix
2. Astezano Max
3. Lahalle Corto
4. Marval Noé
UNDER 12 BOYS
1. Bierre Raphael
2. Delahaye Gatien
3. Lavole Titouan
4. Bissot Tim
UNDER 12 GIRLS
1. Cavalini Manon
2. Brendy Delannay
3. Coraline Foveau
4. Jahelia Tareau
UNDER 10 BOYS
1. Cavallini Enzo
2. Etienne Leopaul
3. Debierre Tom
4. Soret Noham
EXPRESSION SESSION
1. Hernandez Paul
2. Dulac Christopher
3. Magnin Kevin

ESA OUTER BANKS EVENT #2
ECKNER STREET, KITTY HAWK, NORTH CAROLINA
May 10

For stop No. 2 of the season for the Outer Banks District of the Eastern Surfing Association (ESA), conditions started out strong but deteriorated through the day. The winds picked up, pulling tents out of the ground. Regardless, the contest went on and competitors accrued valuable points toward qualifying for regional ESA events.

MENEHUNE
1. Beau Douglas
2. Quentin Turko
3. Daniel Brake
4. Jason Williams
3A BOYS
1. Julian Payne
2. Josh Beveridge
3. Christian VanVliet
4. Jennings Sessoms

5. Morgan-Taylor Leavel
3A JUNIORS
1. Sterling King
2. Dillon Pratt
3. Hunter Whitfield
4. Cam Fullmer
5. Devin Chambers
6. Jacob Capps
7. Michael Atkinson
3A MEN
1. Chris McDonald
2. Zach Kenny
3. Zane McKnight
4. Hunter Romeo
5. Thomas Bruce
MASTERS
1. Jason Breiholz
2. Greg Sherman
3. Lewis Molton
SENIOR MEN
1. Pat McManus
2. Joe Gillen
3. Steve Pauls
4. Brian Breiholz
5. Mark Pillsbury
6. Brad Musselman
7. Anthony French
GRANDMASTERS
1. Reese Patterson
2. Jay Hawekotte
3. John Barnes
4. Ricky Brake
5. Carmen Garcia
OPEN MEN SHORTBOARD
1. Julian Payne
2. Zach Kenny
3. Chris Hunter
4. Sterling King
5. Thomas Bruce
6. Hunter Romeo
MENEHUNE LONGBOARD
1. Julian Payne
2. Morgan-Taylor Leavel
3. Joey Gillen
JUNIOR LONGBOARD
1. Cam Fullmer
MEN LONGBOARD
1. Chris McDonald
2. Zane McKnight
3. Jason Breiholz
4. Greg Sherman
5. Hunter Romeo
6. Steve Umphlett
MASTERS LONGBOARD
1. Reese Patterson
2. Joe Gillen
3. Steve Pauls
4. Mark Pillsbury
5. Anthony French
6. Brad Musselman
7. Brian Breiholz
LEGENDS LONGBOARD
1. Carmen Garcia
2. John Barnes
3. Jay Hawekotte
MENEHUNE BODYBOARD
1. Cyrus Lewis
2. John Joyce
3. Morgan-Taylor Leavel
4. Joey Gillen
5. Christian VanVliet
OPEN MEN BODYBOARD
1. John Joyce
2. Morgan-Taylor Leavel
3. Brian Breiholz
4. Charles Shelton
5. Cyrus Lewis
6. Hunter Whitfield
7. Joey Gillen
GIRLS
1. Codie Patterson
OPEN WOMEN
1. Leanne Foster
2. Regina Foster

3. Fran Reynolds
4. Jeanne-Marie Destefano
LADIES
1. Cayce Patterson
2. Jessica Delosreyes
3. Dorothy Edwards
WOMEN LONGBOARD
1. Regina Foster
2. Leanne Foster
LADIES LONGBOARD
1. Cayce Patterson
2. Dorothy Edwards

RED BULL RIDERS CUP NEW JERSEY
3RD STREET, OCEAN CITY, NEW JERSEY
May 13–15

The local favorite, Ocean City High, lived up to its billing and held off Manasquan High. It was a tight game, but the Kelly brothers proved to be the difference in qualifying Ocean City for the national championships.

NEW JERSEY GAME #1
1. Ocean City High School
2. Southern Regional High
MOST VALUABLE PLAYER
Rob Kelly, Ocean City High School

Kolohe Andino. Photo Mike/Azhiaziam.com.

MOST RADICAL MANEUVER
Rob Kelly, Ocean City High School
NEW JERSEY GAME #2
1. Middle Township High
2. Manasquan High
MOST VALUABLE PLAYER
Brandon Buckley, Manasquan High
MOST RADICAL MANEUVER
Brandon Buckley, Manasquan High
NEW JERSEY GAME #3
1. Ocean City High School
2. Manasquan High
MOST VALUABLE PLAYER
Rob Kelly, Ocean City High School
MOST RADICAL MANEUVER
Brendon Buckley, Manasquan High

NSSA WEST COAST CHAMPS, PRESENTED BY NO FEAR
SOUTHSIDE HUNTINGTON BEACH PIER, CALIFORNIA
May 14–18

Huntington Beach Pier was firing for the 500 competitors in town for the NSSA West Coast Championships. In glassy 4- to 6-foot A-frames, high scores were fly-

ing and some tough heats went down. Kolohe Andino had a solid showing, winning the prestigious Open Men and Open Juniors. In the Open Men final, he managed to overcome a quick start by Nat Young, blowing up an HB right-hander and closing the ride with an aerial that was rewarded with a 9.17.

OPEN MEN
1. Kolohe Andino
2. Nat Young
3. Conner Coffin
4. Dillon Perillo
OPEN JUNIORS
1. Kolohe Andino
2. Conner Coffin
3. Clay Crandal
4. Jared Thorne
BOYS OPEN
1. Taylor Clark
2. Parker Coffin
3. Andrew Jacobson
4. Colin Moran
5. Kadin Panesi
6. Nic Hdez
OPEN MINI GROMS
1. Jacob Davis
2. Kanoa Igarashi
3. Jake Marshall
4. Hunter Johnson

5. Tyler Gunter
6. Kei Kobayashi
MEN LONGBOARD OPEN
1. Cole Robbins
2. Cody Ulrich
3. Samson Anderson
4. Steve Simpson
5. Andy DeLorme
6. Kevin McNicol
2008 WEST COAST EXPLORER CHAMPIONSHIPS
EXPLORER MEN
1. Kokoro Tomatsuri
2. Conrad Carr
3. Victor Done
4. Adam Lambert
5. Nick Suhadolnik
6. Dillon Perillo
EXPLORER JUNIORS
1. Conner Coffin
2. Kolohe Andino
3. Nat Young
4. Christian Saenz
5. Brent Reilly
6. Dillon Perillo
EXPLORER BOYS
1. Conner Coffin
2. Kolohe Andino
3. Taylor Thorne
4. Jared Thorne
5. Luke Davis

6. Parker Coffin

EXPLORER MENEHUENE
1. Colin Moran
2. Kanoa Igarashi
3. Parker Coffin
4. Taylor Clark
5. Nic Hdez
6. Johnny Elles

EXPLORER MASTERS
1. Randy Cutshall
2. Scott Whitmer
3. YuFu Penrose
4. Jon Warren
5. Tim Senneff
6. Taichi Maruyama

EXPLORER SENIORS
1. Chad Logan
2. Yari Vodraska
3. Rusty Phillipy
4. Randy Cutshall
5. Mike Lamm
6. Tim Senneff

EXPLORER SUPER SENIORS
1. Mike Lamm
2. Jeffrey O'Donnell
3. Mike Gillard
4. Robert Weiner
5. Rick Larson
6. Masaki Kobayashi

EXPLORER LONGBOARD
1. Cole Robbins
2. Eli Gillis
3. Mike Lallande
4. Kevin McNicol
5. Cody Ulrich
6. Michael Maddox

2008 WEST COAST AIRSHOW CHAMPIONSHIPS
1. Dane Zaun
2. Robert Curtis
3. Ian Crane
4. Kolohe Andino
5. David Suhadolnik
6. Luke Davis
6. Brock Bowden
6. Sam McGee

OPEN WOMEN
1. Courtney Conlogue
2. Sage Erickson
3. Demi Boelsterli
4. Catherine Clark

EXPLORER WOMEN
1. Sage Erickson
2. Demi Boelsterli
3. Marissa Shaw
4. Taylor Pitz
5. Natalie Anzivino
6. Lakey Peterson

EXPLORER GIRLS
1. Lakey Peterson
2. Catherine Clark
3. Charlotte Shanahan
4. Shelby Detmers
5. Emmy Merrill
6. Melina Smith

CLEAN WATER CLASSIC
WESTPORT, WASHINGTON
May 17–18

Over 150 contestants turned out for the only Pro-am contest held in the Northwest region, with contestants spanning from Oregon to British Columbia. Conditions were great, with sunny skies and a few overhead sets. Special surf guest Australian Bob McTavish was on hand, signing autographs and pulling into some of the larger waves of the weekend.

BEST WAVE
Peter Hamilton

HIGH SCORE SHORTBOARD
Peter Hamilton

HIGH SCORE LONGBOARD
Kapono Nahina

MEN PRO-AM
1. Noah Cohen
2. Kirk Tice
3. CC Unger

MASTER'S SHORTBOARD
1. Perry Abedor
2. Matt Loughran
3. Nolan West

WOMEN SHORTBOARD
1. Leah Oke
2. Annie Atkinson
3. Anne Beasley

MEN LONGBOARD
1. Kapono Nahina
2. JP Canlis
3. Andrew Cordeiro

MASTER'S LONGBOARD
1. Kevin Todd
2. Anthony Redpath
3. Ben Cockcroft

WOMEN LONGBOARD
1. Monica Todd
2. Leah Oke
3. Annie Atkinson

JUNIORS
1. Kye Peladeau
2. Ryan Gardner
3. Chad Hoh

MEN STAND-UP PADDLE
1. JP Canlis
2. Kevin Todd
3. Peter Miller

KEIKI (CHILD) WITH PARENT
1. Isabella Martinez-Ybor
2. Noah Martin
3. Scarlett Redpath
4. Nicole Simpson

RED BULL RIDERS CUP OC REGIONAL CHAMPS
HUNTINGTON BEACH PIER, CALIFORNIA
May 17–18

In a match-up between powerhouse Orange County surf schools, San Clemente High managed to out-surf Huntington Beach High in the regional championship of the Red Bull Riders Cup. Despite stormy conditions, plenty of high-performance maneuvers and tactical coaching took the stage in a close final.

HUNTINGTON BEACH GAME #1
1. San Clemente High School
2. Newport High

MOST VALUABLE PLAYER
Riley Metcalf, San Clemente High School

MOST RADICAL MANEUVER
Chase Brady, San Clemente High School

HUNTINGTON BEACH GAME #2
1. Edison High School
2. Huntington Beach High

MOST VALUABLE PLAYER
Matt Mc Mullen, Huntington Beach High School

MOST RADICAL MANEUVER
Kyle Kennelly, Huntington Beach High School

HUNTINGTON BEACH GAME #3
1. San Clemente High
2. Huntington Beach High School

MOST VALUABLE PLAYER
David Price, San Clemente High School

MOST RADICAL MANEUVER
David Price, San Clemente High School

RIP CURL GROM-SEARCH PRESENTED BY BOOST MOBILE
JOBO'S BEACH, PUERTO RICO
May 24

Dismal conditions were countered by high spirits of the hordes of young groms on hand for the event. Hector Santa Maria wont the 16/Under division, locking up the cash prize and trip to California for the Boost Mobile Pro and a spot in the Rip Curl GromSearch at Salt Creek.

UNDER 16 BOYS
1. Hector Santa Maria
2. Eric Torrez
3. Tommy Orsini
4. Ricardo Lucke

UNDER 16 GIRLS
1. Lecar Maud
2. Ocean Diamond
3. Ninotchka Acevedo
4. Nicole Luna

UNDER 14 BOYS
1. Ricardo Lucke
2. Mauricio Diaz
3. Bryan Laide
4. Christian Rivera

UNDER 12 BOYS
1. Mauricio Diaz
2. David Liceaga
3. Devan Vazquez
4. Maximilian Torres
5. Sheila Martine

9TH ANNUAL NEW ENGLAND LONG-BOARD CLASSIC, EASTERN SURFING ASSOCIATION
NANTASKET BEACH, MASSACHUSETTS
May 30

With conditions minimal, the high-scoring rides went to the most creative surfers at the 9th Annual New England Longboard Classic. Spinners, coffin rides and any other means of improvization scored well and allowed competitors to advance. Three-year-old Cade Marsden was the talk of the contest and a crowd favorite. With his father pushing him into a few small walls, Cade finished second in the Under 13 division.

UNDER 13 BOYS
1. Joe Parisi
2. Cade Marsden
3. Charlie Frodigh
4. Matt Brennan
5. Dan Parisi
6. Pat McCormack
7. Colin Merrill
8. Tim Foley

UNDER 13 GIRLS
1. Abigail Seaburg
2. Marissa Fitcher
3. Maggie Parisi
4. Cari O'Shea
5. Katie Frodigh
6. Anna McCormack

JUNIOR MEN (14–19)
1. Luke Ryan
2. John Ryan
3. James McGragham
4. Ben Fitcher
5. Chad Bruce
6. Chris Orlando
7. Adam Keally
8. Ross Lagoy
9. Tyler Brodie
10. Ryan Lagoy
11. Chris Welch

JUNIOR WOMEN (14–19)
1. Katie Zullo
2. Emily Cunningham
3. Nora Vasconcellos
4. Megan O'Shea
5. Atria Fitcher
6. Caroline McCormack
7. Rebecca Seaberg
8. Mary Scanlan

MEN (20–29)
1. Scott Habershaw
2. Tom Casserly
3. Kenny Flynn
4. Eric Greenside
5. Siawn Ou
6. Mike Jilling
7. Nick Carter
8. Tom O'Brien

WOMEN (20–29)
1. Alicia Walker
2. Jesse Miele
3. Ami Choi
4. Pilar Gutierrez

MASTERS (30–39)
1. Jim Chabot
2. Jose Gomez
3. Naoto Ohashi
4. Steve Stasiuk
5. Andy Marsden
6. Joe Daugirda
7. Todd Salmonson
8. Brian Mozinski
9. Kipp Sullivan
10. Andy Maturna

WOMEN (30–39)
1. Karen Conant
2. Angelia Daugirda
3. Chrissy Walker

SENIOR MEN (40–49)
1. Tim O'Shea
2. Scott MacGillivray
3. Ken Merrill
4. Dan Vasconcellos
5. Tim McCormack
6. John Cotter

SENIOR WOMEN (40 AND OVER)
1. Isabelle Montesi
2. Ellen Brown.

LEGENDS (50 AND OVER)
1. Peter Pan
2. Alan Bruce
3. Chris Abelli
4. Bill Devoney
5. Tim Brooks
6. John Burns
7. Tom Green
8. Branch Lane
9. Richie Simone
10. Hal Stokes

ARNETTE PRO JUNIOR, PRESENTED BY JACK'S • GRADE 2 MEN ASP PRO JUNIOR
54TH STREET, NEWPORT BEACH, CALIFORNIA
June 7–8

In 2- to 3-foot beachbreak conditions at 54th Street in Newport Beach, Cory Arrambide started out fast, leaving the competition in his wake. Arrambide stroked into three early waves, establishing a cushion and comboing most of finalists. In this, his last year of eligibility on the Juniors circuit, Arrambide leads the ratings.

MEN FINAL
1. Cory Arrambide
2. Spencer Regan
3. Matt Mohagen
4. Bruno Rodrigues

SEMI FINAL 1
1. Cory Arrambide
2. Spencer Regan
3. Andrew Doheny
4. Travis Beckmann

Carlsbad High School. Photo Klein/surfline.com.

SEMI FINAL 2
1. Bruno Rodrigues
2. Matt Mohagen
3. Chris Eneim
4. Evan Thompson

QUARTER FINAL 1
1. Cory Arrambide
2. Andrew Doheny
3. Noah Erickson
4. Nat Young

QUARTER FINAL 2
1. Travis Beckmann
2. Spencer Regan
3. Cody Thompson
4. Chase Wilson

QUARTER FINAL 4
1. Bruno Rodrigues
2. Chris Eneim
3. Jason Harris
4. Phillip Goold

QUARTER FINAL 4
1. Evan Thompson
2. Matt Mohagen
3. Austin Smith-Ford
4. Blake Jones

QUIKSILVER KING OF THE GROMS EAST COAST QUALIFIER

SEBASTIAN INLET, FLORIDA
June 7

With heaps of specialty prizes, $100 per "Skin," a trip to France and a slot in the Quiksilver King of the Groms Global Championships on the line, the groms on hand were super motivated to make the most of the 1- to 2-foot peaks. Puerto Rican Mauro Diaz ended up the top grom of the day, winning 5 skins.

1. Mauro Diaz (Puerto Rico)
2. Ryan Croteau
3. Nathan Colburn
4. Noah Schweizer
5. Jordan Heaselgrave (Barbados FWI)
6. Logan Hayes
7. Nate Behl
8. Tanner Strohmenger
9. Christopher Tucker
10. Christian Miller
11. Corey Howell
12. Justin Croteau

RED BULL RIDERS CUP NATIONAL CHAMPS

CHURCH, SAN CLEMENTE, CALIFORNIA
June 14–15

The regional champions of the Red Bull Riders Cup were greeted with perfect waves and ideal weather at Church. In a tightly contested final, showcasing some of the finest up-and-coming talents in the country, Carlsbad High managed to edge past San Clemente High for the National Championship.

ROUND ONE
GAME ONE
1. San Clemente High
2. Mira Costa High
GAME TWO
1. Ocean City High
2. Jupiter High
GAME THREE
1. Carpinteria
2. Satellite High
GAME FOUR
1. Carlsbad High
2. Soquel High (SC)
SEMI-FINALS
GAME ONE
1. San Clemente High
2. Ocean City High
GAME TWO
1. Carlsbad High
2. Carpinteria

FINALS-NATIONAL CHAMPIONSHIP
1. San Clemente High
2. Carlsbad High

RIP CURL GROMSEARCH HUNTINGTON BEACH PRESENTED BY BOOST

9TH STREET, HUNTINGTON BEACH, CALIFORNIA
June 14–15

With solid head-high waves on hand for some of the top under-16 talent around, the level of surfing for the GromSearch lived up to its billing. Luke Davis and Evan Geiselman went double-duty in the Under 16 and Under 14 and met up in both finals. Each snagged one title and both put on quite a show for spectators in attendance.

UNDER 16 BOYS
1. Luke Davis
2. Ian Crane
3. Evan Geiselman
4. Nick Rupp

UNDER 16 GIRLS
1. Nage Melamed
2. Kelia Moniz
3. Lakey Peterson
4. Brianna Cope
5. Jasset Umbel
6. Shruti Greenwood

UNDER 14 BOYS
1. Evan Geiselman
2. Luke Davis
3. Ian Gentil
4. Taylor Clark

UNDER 12 BOYS
1. Ian Gentil
2. Koa Smith
3. Colin Moran
4. Kalen Galtes

QUIET STORM DELAWARE STATE SURFING CHAMPIONSHIPS, DELMARVA DISTRICT ESA

OCEAN CITY, MARYLAND
June 14–15

The new contest directors made the right call to give the contest the go, as the incoming tide progressively grew the size of the waves on offer for the 150 contestants. Waist-high surf was more than enough to determine the placings in the various divisions.

OPEN SHORTBOARD
1. Travis Knight
2. Matt Meinhardt
3. Roy Harrell
4. Dillon Harrington
5. Jamie Crosby
6. Chris Makibbin

OPEN LONGBOARD
1. Chris Makibbin
2. Matt Meinhardt
3. Jake Buchler
4. Joe Gillan
5. Ted Smith
6. Noah Vaxmonsky

OPEN WOMEN
1. Emily Ruppert
2. Kelsey Willison
3. Rachel Harrell
4. Danielle Ariano

5. Jenna Landon
6. Kelly Powell
7. Laurel Harrington

OPEN BODYBOARD
1. Matt Landon
2. Jacob Lahr
3. Caleb Buchler
4. Josh Mitchell
5. Craig Chatterton
6. Zeus Rodriguez
7. Jake Buchler

MENEHUNE SHORTBOARD (BOYS/GIRLS 11 & UNDER)
1. Patrick Ruppert
2. Evan Conboy
3. Tyler Clazey

GIRLS SHORTBOARD (14 & UNDER)
1. Emily Ruppert

BOYS SHORTBOARD (12–14)
1. Seth Conboy
2. Brad Flora
3. John Moore
4. Avery Seig
5. Dallas Harrington
6. Richie Donofrio

JR. MEN SHORTBOARD (15–17)
1. Matt Meinhardt
2. Jamie Crosby
3. Andrew Stewart
4. Dillon Harrington
5. Caleb Buchler
6. Jake Buchler

MEN SHORTBOARD (18–24)
1. Travis Knight
2. Roy Harrell
3. Aviad Sasi
4. George Vitak
5. Dane Wooleyhan
6. Scott Tetzner
7. Andrew Mercer

WOMEN SHORTBOARD (18–29)
1. Laurel Harrington
2. Kelsey Willison
3. Sloane Doud
4. Chelsea Remines

MASTERS SHORTBOARD (25–34)
1. Ted Smith
2. Chris Makibbin
3. Gatey Dawkins
4. Jack Thomas

LADIES SHORTBOARD (30+)
1. Danielle Ariano
2. Bonnie Preziosi

SENIOR MEN SHORTBOARD (35–44)
1. Joe Gillan
2. Chris Vaxmonsky
3. Craig Garfield
4. Dave Clazey

LEGENDS SHORTBOARD (55–64)
1. Bill Helmuth
2. Brett Buchler

MENEHUNE BODYBOARD (BOYS/GIRLS 14 & UNDER)
1. Carter Michael
2. Michael Murray
3. Joey Gillan
4. Ben Vaxmonsky

MENEHUNE LONGBOARD (BOYS/GIRLS 14 & UNDER)
1. Brad Flora
2. Tyler Clazey
3. Noah Vaxmonsky
4. Joey Gillan
5. Carter Pruit
6. Ben Vaxmonsky

JUNIOR LONGBOARD (15–17)
1. Jake Buchler
2. Matt Meinhardt
3. Colton Clazey

MEN LONGBOARD (18–34)
1. Chris Makibbin
2. Aviad Sasi
3. Ted Smith

WOMEN LONGBOARD (29 & UNDER)

1. Chelsea Remines
2. Kelsey Willison

LADIES LONGBOARD (30+)
1. Bonnie Preziosi

MASTERS LONGBOARD (35-49)
1. Chris Vaxmonsky
2. Joe Gillan
3. Craig Garfield
4. Dave Clazey

LEGENDS LONGBOARD (50+)
1. Bill Helmuth
2. Bill Thompson
3. Brett Buchler

RHODE ISLAND STATE SURFING CHAMPS EASTERN SURFING ASSOCIATION

NARRAGANSETT TOWN BEACH, RHODE ISLAND
June 28–29

After having been cancelled on three previous occasions, the Rhode Island State Championships finally ran, with a 2- to 4-foot south swell wrapping workable walls into beach. Matheus de Sousa was on fire all weekend, winning the Men Shortboard and Men Longboard, and was also awarded the "Hottest Wave" award.

MENEHUNES
1. Shane Lynch
BOYS
1. Matt Bush
JUNIOR MEN
1. James McGraghan
MEN
1. Matheus de Souza
MASTERS
1. Ryan Andrews
2. Eric Greenside
3. Nick Carter

Julian Wilson. Photo Brent Hilleman.

SENIOR MEN
1. Bob Fitton
GRANDMASTERS
1. Mike Salvadore
LEGENDS
1. Peter Pan
JUNIOR WOMEN
1. Katie Zullo
WOMEN
1. Katie Ryan
SENIOR WOMEN
1. Janice Causey
OPEN
1. Peter Pan
2. Matheus de Sousa
3. James McGraghan
4. Nick Carter

5. Katie Ryan
6. Mike Salvadore
MENEHUNE LONGBOARD
1. Shane Lynch
2. Matt Bush
JUNIOR LONGBOARD
1. James McGraghan
MEN LONGBOARD
1. Matheus de Sousa
MASTERS LONGBOARD
1. Bob Fitton
2. Ryan Andrews
3. Jim Chabot
4. Nick Carter
5. Eric Greenside
LEGENDS LONGBOARD
1. Peter Pan
2. Mike Salvadore
3. Don Lynch
OPEN BODYBOARD
1. Peter Pan
2. Mike Salvadore
3. Don Lynch
4. Katie Ryan
5. Janice Causey
WOMEN LONGBOARD
1. Katie Zullo
2. Katie Ryan
SENIOR WOMEN LONGBOARD
1. Janice Causey

NIKE 6.0 PIER PRESSURE, PRESENTED BY JACK'S • GRADE 4 MEN ASP PRO JUNIOR

THE PIER, HUNTINGTON BEACH, CALIFORNIA
June 29–30

In improving 2- to 3-foot swell, Julian Wilson took home the first-place check of the Nike 6.0 Pier Pressure at Huntington Beach Pier. Surfing from round one, Wilson won every heat that he surfed. Fellow Australian Stuart Kennedy came up 2nd after having won each of his heats leading up to the final.

MEN FINAL
1. Julian Wilson
2. Stuart Kennedy
3. Chris Salisbury
4. Andrew Doheny
SEMIFINAL 1
1. Julian Wilson
2. Stuart Kennedy
3. Quinn McCrystal
4. Cory Arrambide

SEMIFINAL 2
1. Chris Salisbury
2. Andrew Doheny
3. Dillon Perillo
4. Travis Beckmann

QUARTERFINAL 1
1. Stuart Kennedy
2. Quinn McCrystal
3. Nat Young
4. Evan Thompson

QUARTERFINAL 2
1. Julian Wilson
2. Cory Arrambide
3. Brent Reiley
4. Kai Barger

QUARTERFINAL 3
1. Chris Salisbury
2. Travis Beckmann
3. Evan Geiselman
4. Cody Thompson

QUARTERFINAL 4
1. Andrew Doheny
2. Dillon Perillo
3. Blake Jones
4. Nick Rupp

DOHENY LONGBOARD MENEHUNE CHAMPS
DOHENY STATE BEACH, CALIFORNIA
June 28

Surfers ranging from first-timers to 17 years of age signed up for their respective divisions to paddle out at Boneyards as part of the annual Doheny Longboard Menehune Surfing Championships. Families made a day of the event, bringing the whole crew for fun in the sun and maybe some inter-family bragging rights.

UNDER 17 BOYS
1. Alex Calkins
2. Preston Crowell
3. Jeff Newell
4. Jason Schechter
5. Michael McGregor

UNDER 17 GIRLS
1. Rachael Barry
2. Michelle Layton
3. Amanda Baron
4. Stephanie Schechter
5. Mariah Spurlock
6. Gabriela Brugeman

UNDER 14 BOYS
1. Andy Neblis
2. Preston Crowell
3. Trevor Robbins
4. Dane Doran
5. Dean Michael

UNDER 14 GIRLS
1. Hallie Rohr
2. Makala Smith
3. Carly Mora
4. Kloee Openshaw
5. Paige Edwards
6. Kayla Garcia

UNDER 12 BOYS
1. Mason Klink
2. Kai Franz
3. Perry Rohr
4. Brock Thomson
5. Ricky Ortega
6. Jacob Orpineda
6. Tim Kam

UNDER 10 BOYS
1. Xander Morgan
2. Jacob Atwood
3. Kei Kobayashi
4. Kai Diamond
5. Myles Blazer

6. Diego Quinonez

UNDER 10 GIRLS
1. Laureen Rowe
2. Avalon Johnson
3. Ashley Beeson
4. Kailey Biggs
5. Kaeley Sterkel
6. Amber Sislin

8 & UNDER
1. Malia Faramarzi
2. Noah Atwood
3. Griffin Foy
4. Ian Diamond
5. John Garbino
6. Ava Valdez

GIRLS SHORTBOARD
1. Michelle Layton
2. Paige Edwards
3. Avalon Johnson
4. Stephanie – Schechter
5. Malia Faramarzi
6. Ashley Beeson

CHAUNCEY'S SURFABOUT EASTERN SURFING ASSOCIATION
30TH STREET, OCEAN CITY, MARYLAND
June 28

The second edition of the Chauncey's Surfabout—put on by Chauncey and Blair Rhodes of Chauncey's Surf Shop—ran in fine conditions, with the Atlantic having awoken from its early summer slumber. For the second consecutive ESA event, Matt Meinhardt took home the Juniors division in the clean, contestable conditions.

OPEN SHORTBOARD
1. Walden Remington
2. Mike Lawson
3. Dillon Harrington
4. Jamie Crosby
5. Matt Meinhardt
6. Travis Knight

MENEHUNE SHORTBOARD (BOYS/ GIRLS 11 & UNDER)
1. Shane Moore
2. Patick Ruppert
3. Tyler Clazey
4. Melissa Harrell
5. Evan Conboy
6. Jack Fager

GIRLS SHORTBOARD (14 & UNDER)
1. Tierney Loeser
2. Claire Zurkowski

BOYS SHORTBOARD (12-14)
1. Brad Flora
2. Gabe Bell
3. Avery Sieg
4. Seth Conboy
5. Dallas Harrington
6. Roland Gerachis

JUNIOR MEN SHORTBOARD (15-17)
1. Matt Meinhardt
2. Dillon Harrington
3. Jamie Crosby
4. Andrew Stewart
5. Austin Gerachis
6. Caleb Buchler

JUNIOR WOMEN SHORTBOARD (15-17)
1. Rachel Harrell
2. Kelly Powell
3. Lindsey Meeks

MEN SHORTBOARD (18-24)
1. Travis Knight
2. Waldon Remington
3. Mike Lawson
4. Roy Harrell

5. Aviad Sasi
6. George Vitak

WOMEN SHORTBOARD (18-29)
1. Laurel Harrington
2. Kaitlyn Curran
3. Kelcey Bodolus
4. Mackenzie White
5. Chelsea Remines
6. Abigail Corrin

MASTERS SHORTBOARD (25-34)
1. Ted Smith
2. Pat Merkle
3. Gatey Dawkins
4. Jack Thomas
5. Chris Makibbin
6. Andrew Snook

NSSA NATIONALS, PRESENTED BY NO FEAR
SALT CREEK & LOWERS, CALIFORNIA
June 18–28

The 30th edition of the NSSA Championships had all the fireworks and flair of the previous editions, with a few particular standout performances. Nat Young and Granger Larsen were on a crash course throughout the eight days at Salt Creek and Lowers. They met in three finals, with Larsen taking the Explorer Men and Explorer Juniors. But the crown jewel of the NSSA is the Open Men and once again, Young and Larsen had at it. After coming up short twice, Young turned to his backhand approach and destroyed Lowers rights en route to the win. Cole Robbins was the stud of the Longboard divisions, taking the Open Longboard and Explorer Longboard.

2008 NATIONAL OPEN CHAMPIONSHIPS

OPEN MEN/GOVERNOR'S CUP
1. Nat Young
2. Granger Larsen
3. Tanner Hendrickson
4. Kolohe Andino

OPEN WOMEN/GOVERNOR'S CUP
1. Courtney Conlogue
2. Sage Erickson
3. Leila Hurst
4. Malia Manuel

OPEN JUNIORS
1. Andrew Doheny
2. Evan Geiselman
3. Evan Thompson
4. Tanner Hendrickson

OPEN BOYS
1. Koa Smith
2. Luke Hitchcock
3. Makai McNamara
4. Joshua Moniz
5. Nick Hdez
6. Parker Coffin

OPEN MINI GROMS
1. Kalani David
2. Imaikalani DeVault
3. Kanoa Igarashi
4. Jacob Davis
5. Seth Moniz
6. Jake Marshall

OPEN LONGBOARD
1. Cole Robbins
2. Scott Brandenburg
3. Cody Ulrich
4. Kevin McNicol
5. Weston Williams

6. Patrick Nichols

2008 NATIONAL EXPLORER CHAMPIONSHIPS

EXPLORER MEN
1. Granger Larsen
2. Kai Barger
3. Alex Smith
4. Tyler Newton
5. Michael Dunphy
6. Nat Young

EXPLORER JUNIORS
1. Granger Larsen
2. Dillon Perillo
3. Alex Smith
4. Nat Young
5. Oliver Kurtz
6. Kolohe Andino

EXPLORER BOYS
1. Keanu Asing
2. Ezekiel Lau
3. Kolohe Andino
4. Conner Coffin
5. Luke Davis
6. Kaimana Jaquias

EXPLORER MENEHUENE
1. Koa Smith
2. Makai McNamara
3. Ian Gentil
4. Luke Hitchcock
5. Kaoli Kahokuloa
6. Seth Moniz

EXPLORER WOMEN
1. Leila Hurst
2. Monyca Byrne
3. Alesa Quizon
4. Demi Boelsterli
5. Lakey Peterson
6. Nage Melamed

EXPLORER GIRLS
1. Leila Hurst
2. Malia Manuel
3. Nage Melamed
4. Kelia Moniz
5. Alisha Gonsalves
5. Lakey Peterson

EXPLORER MASTERS
1. Tim Senneff
2. Chris Keet
3. Rick Takahashi
4. Christian Budroe
5. Steve Moore
6. Scott Whitmer

EXPLORER SENIORS
1. Chad Logan
2. Stephen Dwyer
3. Terry Gillard
4. Randy Cutshall
5. Rusty Phillipy
6. Jeff O'Donnell

EXPLORER SUPER SENIORS
1. Robert Weiner
2. Mike Gillard

Vince Boulanger. Photo Kelsey Willison.

3. Mike Lamm
4. Tim Senneff
5. Rick Fignetti
6. Jeffrey O'Donnell

EXPLORER LONGBOARD
1. Cole Robbins
2. Mike Gillard
3. Scott Brandenburg
4. Cody Ulrich
5. Eli Gillis
6. Mike Lallande

2008 NATIONAL AIRSHOW CHAMPIONSHIPS
1. Ian Crane
2. Dylan Goodale
3. Matt Meola
4. Oliver Kurtz
5. Albee Layer
6. Evan Geiselman

2008 NATIONAL INTERSCHOLASTIC CHAMPIONSHIPS

COLLEGE TEAM
1. UCSB-A
2. SDSU
3. Mira Costa–Red
4. Saddleback
5. CSUSM
6. UCSD
7. UCF
8. UCSB B
9. Cal Poly San Luis Obispo
10. U of F

COLLEGE MEN
1. Nick Olsen-Mira Costa
2. Alex Ganguli-Mira Costa
3. Keetin Devine-Mira Costa
4. Marty Weinstein-UCSD
5. Matt Johnson-UCSB
6. Andre Oziol-SDSU

COLLEGE WOMEN
1. Lauren Sweeney-UCSD
2. Lipoa Kahaleuahi-UCSB
3. Allie Brown-SDSU
4. Erika Cook-Saddleback
5. Lauren McLean-UCF
6. Lily Howard-UCSB

COLLEGE LONGBOARD
1. Christian Clark-CSUSM
2. Kevin Osborne-Saddleback
3. Chris Koerner-SDSU
4. Todd Kinsey-U of F
5. Corey Hartwyk-UCSB
6. Woody Robinson-UCSB

HIGH SCHOOL TEAM
1. Elite Element
2. Carlsbad
3. Huntington Beach
4. San Dieguito
5. Carpinteria
6. San Clemente
7. Edison
8. Laguna Beach

9. Middle Township
10. Marina
11. Manasquan
12. Keakalike

HIGH SCHOOL MEN
1. Brent Reilly-Carlsbad
2. Kiron Jabour-Elite Element
3. Tyler McGinty-Carlsbad
4. Gabe Garcia-Carlsbad
5. Quinn McCrystal-Huntington Beach
6. Conner Coffin-Carpinteria

HIGH SCHOOL WOMEN
1. Kelia Moniz-Elite Element
2. Coco Ho- Elite Element
3. Sara Taylor-Huntington Beach
4. Taylor Pitz-Laguna Beach
5. Rachel Harris-Carpenteria
6. Alexa Dilley-San Dieguito

HIGH SCHOOL LONGBOARD
1. Chris Cravey- San Dieguito
2. Cole Robbins-Carlsbad
3. Jeff Newell-Edison
4. Cody Ulrich-San Clemente
5. Mike Fisher-Huntington Beach
6. Kevin DeWald-Middle Township

MIDDLE SCHOOL TEAM
1. Shorecliffs-Red
2. Kapaa
3. Dwyer
4. Marco Forster
5. Sowers A
6. Sowers B
7. Shorecliffs White
8. Niguel Hills
9. Carpintera

MIDDLE SCHOOL BOYS
1. Kolohe Andino-Shorecliffs
2. Luke Hitchcock-Kapaa
3. Parker Coffin-Carpinteria
4. Ian Crane-Shorecliffs
5. Kalen Galtes-Kapaa
6. Jesse Guglielmana-Kapaa

MIDDLE SCHOOL GIRLS
1. Melina Smith-Shorecliffs
2. Lulu Erkeneff-Marco Forster
3. Paige Ortiz-Dwyer
4. Candi Patterson-Shorecliffs
5. Nicole Hines-Marco Forster
6. Torrey Miethke-Sowers

MIDDLE SCHOOL LONGBOARD
1. Scott Weinhardt-Marco Forster
2. Andy Nieblas-Shorecliffs
3. Tony Bartovich-Dwyer
4. Mason Klink-Shorecliffs
5. Nathan Thompson-Shorecliffs
6. Lauren Heinemeyer-Niguel Hills

REEF SWEETWATER PRO AM SURF FEST
OCEANIC STREET, WRIGHTSVILLE BEACH, NORTH CAROLINA
July 12–13

With Hurricane Bertha sitting just off the coast, the Reef Sweetwater was blessed with solid surf thoughout the weekend, sending sets in the chest-high range with the occasional head-high-plus. With the defending champ eliminated in the quarterfinals, some new blood would be taking the Pro-am crown. Jeremy Johnston managed to hang on in close final.

MEN PRO-AM
1. Jeremy Johnston
2. Nick Rosza
3. Aaron Cormican
4. Lucas Rogers

BOYS LONGBOARD OPEN
1. Tony Silvagni

2. Drake Courie
3. Ty Roach
4. Sean Simmons

OVER 15 BOYS
1. Owen Moffet
2. Jonathon Mincher
3. Cole Richards
4. Jimmy Blumenfield

UNDER 14 BOYS
1. Michael Ciaramella
2. Weston Williams
3. Cam Richards
4. Dylan Kowalski

OVER 18 GIRLS
1. Jasset Umbel
2. Haley Watson
3. Jo Pickett
4. Darsha Pigford

UNDER 17 GIRLS
1. Jasset Umble
2. Haley Watson
3. Chandler Von Cannon
4. Kate Easton

GIRLS LONGBOARD OPEN
1. Kate Easton
2. Kayleigh Winslow
3. Jo Pickett
4. Madison Huckabee

14TH ANNUAL MALIBU CLASSIC, ESA DELMARVA
8TH STREET, OCEAN CITY, MARYLAND
July 12

With bands rocking out on the surf shop steps, food grilling and some fun waves on hand, it was an all-day surf party for the 225 contestants at the 14th Annual Malibus Classic. Ian Tilghman pulled out the Open Shortboard final in the dying moments with a barrel and floater to lock up first place.

OPEN SHORTBOARD
1. Ian Tilghman
2. Ted Smith
3. Waldon Remington
4. Vince Boulanger
5. Dillon Harrington
6. Brady Dashiell

MENEHUNE SHORTBOARD (BOYS/GIRLS 11 & UNDER)
1. Sam Deeley
2. Myles Deppe
3. Jack Fager
4. Evan Conboy
5. Shane Moore
6. Patrick Ruppert
7. Simon Hetrick

GIRLS SHORTBOARD (14 & UNDER)
1. Emily Ruppert
2. Claire Zurkowski
3. Courtney Genovese

BOYS SHORTBOARD (12–14)
1. Seth Conboy
2. Brad Flora
3. Brady Dashiell
4. Avery Seig
5. Gabe Bell
6. Roland Gerachis

JUNIOR MEN SHORTBOARD (15–17)
1. Dillon Harrington
2. Austin Deppe
3. Joey Boulanger
4. Spencer Ashton
5. Austin Gerachis
6. Tommy Edmunds

JUNIOR WOMEN SHORTBOARD (15–17)
1. Kelly Powell

2. Rachel Harrell
3. Jenna Landon
4. Meegan Smith

MEN SHORTBOARD (18–24)
1. Vince Boulanger
2. Aviad Sasi
3. Mikey Lawson
4. Waldon Remington
5. Sam Svenson
6. Dan Baumgardner

WOMEN SHORTBOARD (18–29)
1. Kelsey Willison
2. Kelcey Bodolus
3. Laurel Harrington
4. Mackenzie White
5. Caitlin Whalan
6. Jen Abrams

PACSUN'S BATTLE OF THE BRANDS
THE PIER, HUNTINGTON BEACH, CALIFORNIA
July 18

With many top pros in town prior to the U.S. Open, the Battle of the Brands was choc full of top talent in its second year of existence. In 2- to 3-foot surf, Team O'Neill and Transworld Surf proved their dominance in their respective divisions.

BRANDS
1. O'Neill (Pat Gudauskas, Tanner Gudauskas, Malia Manuel, Nat Young)
2. Quiksilver (Julian Wilson, Tyler Newton, Sally Fitzgibbons, Kiron Jabour)
3. Hurley (Brett Simpson, Yadin Nicol, Daise Shayne, Evan Geiselman)
4. …Lost (Mason Ho, James Wood, Leilani Gryde, Riley Metcalf)

MEDIA
1. Transworld Surf
2. Surfing
3. Fuel TV
4. Surfline
5. Surfer

2008 CAPE COD SURFING CHAMPS RD #1
WHITECREST, SOUTH WELLFLEET, MASSACHUSETTS
July 19–20

The swell did its part, sending 4- to 5-foot A-frames into the Whitecrest beachbreak for the first stop of the Cape Cod Championships. Despite the chilly waters, classic conditions led to a high level of surfing, with a number of exciting heats from the earliest of rounds.

MENEHUNES
1. Anthony Tartaro

BOYS
1. Jonathan Tartaro

JUNIOR MEN
1. Chris Orlando
2. James McGraghan
3. Mike Viprino

MEN
1. Matheus de Souza
2. Blake Olson

MASTERS
1. Seth Sullivan
2. Justin Dalby
3. Andy Jacob

SENIOR MEN
1. Brendan McCray
2. Ron Belanger
3. Matt Richards

Pat Gudauskas. Photo A.J. Neste/SurfingAmerica.

GRAND LEGENDS
1. Kitty Pechet

OPEN MEN
1. Matheus de Souza
2. Chris Orlando
3. Siul Reis
4. Chick Frodigh
5. Ronaldo Lima

GIRLS OPEN
1. Myra Kotalac

OPEN WOMEN
1. Katie Ryan

SENIOR WOMEN
1. Sue Glidden
2. Melanie Kotalac

MENEHUNE LONGBOARD
1. Anthony Tartaro

JUNIOR LONGBOARD
1. James McGraghan
2. Chris Orlando

MEN LONGBOARD
1. Blake Olson
2. Matheus de Souza

MASTER LONGBOARD
1. Brendan McCray
2. Jeff Sullivan
3. Justin Darby

LEGENDS LONGBOARD
1. Jerry Tartaro
2. Timmy Brooks
3. Kitty Pechet

WOMEN LONGBOARD
1. Katie Ryan

SENIOR WOMEN LONGBOARD
1. Sue Glidden
2. Melanie Kotalac

VOLCOM STONE BLOWFISH
D STREET, ENCINITAS, CALIFORNIA
July 19

The first stop on the Blowfish Surf Series went off in ideal 3- to 5-foot waves at D Street in Encinitas, with kids lining up on the beach to sign up well before the first horn. Between throwing fins and launching airs, the heats in every age group were pumping up the crowd. In the Pro-Am final, Josh Buran managed to hang onto the win despite an onslaught of extreme maneuvers from his competitors.

MEN PRO-AM
1. Josh Buran
2. Sean Marceron
3. Drew Irons
4. Jeff Lukasik

5. Matt McCabe
6. Austin Sneed

JUNIORS
1. Josh Morse
2. Sterling Weatherley
3. Dale Timm
4. Nick Fowler
5. Ian Garcia
6. Nick Rowe

GROM
1. Jake Halstead
2. Tommy Mehnener
3. Kyle Marle
4. Kyle Timm
5. Ian Crene
6. Matt Passaguinni

GIRLS
1. Lauren Sweeney
2. Elise Peate
3. Cassidy Wehsner
4. Jenny Quam
5. Darlene Conolly
6. CJ Soto

10TH ANNUAL SURFSIDE SEVENTIES
ANDERSON STREET, SURFSIDE, CALIFORNIA
July 19

With the swell building throughout the day, it peaked in time for the final with some overhead sets on offer. Bobby Baker took home the win, but fun was had by all on the vast array of '70s-era boards being ridden.

RESULTS
1. Bobby Baker
2. Steve Thomas
3. Justin Hugron
4. Danny Nichols
5. Scotty Myer
6. Scotty Stopnik

BEST 10-YEAR SURFSIDE SEVENTIES VETERAN
John Kissel

BEST WIPEOUT
Shane Yoshikawa

BEST MOUSTACHE
Pat Shanahan

BEST SEVENTIES STYLE RIDE
Doug Scott

BEST CUTBACK
Bob Bellamy

BEST LIPPER
Matty Cameron

BEST DROP
Ryan Blake

BEST SOUL ARCH
Dylan Tyrnaur

Finalists. Photo Joe Nabor.

BEST BARREL
Brighton Truax
BEST UP-AND-COMERS
Joey Wangsness and Trevor Lucca

HONDA U.S. OPEN OF SURFING, PRESENTED BY O'NEILL • MEN 6-STAR WQS EVENT #22/ WOMEN 6-STAR WQS EVENT #22/ GRADE 2 MEN ASP JUNIOR EVENT
HUNTINGTON BEACH, CALIFORNIA
July 18–27

Over the course of ten days, spectators were presented more visual stimuli than most can handle. Be-

2. Gabe Kling
QUARTERFINAL 1
1. Tim Boal
2. Dusty Payne
QUARTERFINAL 2
1. Brett Simpson
2. Eric Geiselman
QUARTERFINAL 3
1. Nathaniel Curran
2. Chris Waring
QUARTERFINAL 4
1. Gabe Kling
2. Joan Duru
WOMEN FINAL
1. Malia Manuel
2. Coco Ho
SEMIFINAL 1
1. Malia Manuel
2. Sally Fitzgibbons
SEMIFINAL 2
1. Coco Ho
2. Stephanie Gilmore

Malia Manuel. Photo ASP Rowland © Covered Images.

tween the youngest Women's final in the history of the U.S. Open of Surfing, the ultra-progressive Juniors final and a fine display by the longboarders, it was almost anti-climactic once the Men's final hit the water. Nonetheless, Nathaniel Curran put on a fine display to displace Timothy Boal on his run to the title. Curran nabbed his first major win on the WQS and placed himself at the top of the ratings for the first time as well.

MEN FINAL
1. Nathaniel Curran
2. Tim Boal
SEMIFINAL 1
1. Tim Boal
2. Brett Simpson
SEMIFINAL 2
1. Nathaniel Curran

QUARTERFINAL 1
1. Malia Manuel
2. Sofia Mulanovich
QUARTERFINAL 2
1. Sally Fitzgibbons
2. Samantha Cornish
QUARTERFINAL 3
1. Coco Ho
2. Melanie Bartels
QUARTERFINAL 4
1. Stephanie Gilmore
2. Bethany Hamilton
O'NEILL U.S. OPEN PRO JUNIOR
1. Tanner Gudauskas
2. Julian Wilson
3. Chris Salisbury
4. Nat Young
O'NEILL U.S. OPEN OF LONGBOARDING
1. Taylor Jensen
2. Tony Silvagni
3. Ned Snow
4. Noah Shimabukuro

S-3 SUPERGIRL PRO JUNIOR
1. Coco Ho
2. Nikita Robb
3. Sage Erickson
4. Courtney Conlogue

CORONA STAND-UP PADDLE SURF CHALLENGE
HUNTINGTON BEACH, CALIFORNIA
July 27

The inaugural Corona Stand-up Paddle Surf Challenge took center stage on the final day of competition at the Honda U.S. Open of Surfing, with a star-studded bunch of SUPers in attendance. Longboard finalist Noah Shimabukuro put on a fine display of grace and power, navigating the powerful HB beachbreak. His long noserides and huge floaters were enough to impress the judges and give him the win.

1. Noah Shimabukuro
2. Rocky McKinnon

RIP CURL GROM-SEARCH, PRESENTED BY BOOST MOBILE
PLEASURE POINT, SANTA CRUZ, CALIFORNIA
August 2

Fighting the fog and difficult wave conditions, the final of the Under 16

Boys was also a duel between North and South. A pair of Santa Cruzians were fighting for bragging rights with a pair of SoCal groms for the cash and prize package. Ultimately, Nat Young's contest prowess proved too great for all comers, dispatching any competition and racking up yet another contest win.

UNDER 16 BOYS
1. Nat Young
2. Dale Timm
3. JD Lewis
4. Shaun Burns
UNDER 16 GIRLS
1. Asia Carpenter
2. Meah Collins
3. Cienna Norton
4. Katie Draeger
5. Brooke Giuffre
6. Brittany Rothhammer

UNDER 14 BOYS
1. Josh Giddings
2. Noah Wegrich
3. Colin Moran
4. Trevor Thornton
UNDER 12 BOYS
1. Colin Moran
2. Kadin Panesi
3. Jake Kelly
4. Garret Colfer
5. Brogie Panesi
6. Kyle Timm

RIP CURL GROM-SEARCH #6, PRESENTED BY BOOST MOBILE
NEW SMYRNA BEACH, FLORIDA
August 9–10

Following the Under 16 Girls final, gale-force winds nearly tore the contest site apart. However, only 30 minutes after it started, the weather cleared, presented light offshore winds and chest-high faces. In the Under 16 Boys final, Dustin Richardson outlasted his friends/competitors en route to the win.

UNDER 16 BOYS
1. Dustin Richardson
2. Taylor Brothers
3. Christian Miller
4. Tommy Orsini
UNDER 16 GIRLS
1. Savannah Bradley
2. Kayla Durden
3. Haley Watson

Nathaniel Curran. Photo ASP Rowland © Covered Images.

4. Chelsea Gresham
UNDER 14 BOYS
1. Ryan Croteau
2. Nathan Behl
3. Christian Miller
4. Keto Burns
UNDER 12 BOYS
1. Noah Schweizer
2. Corey Howell
3. Logan Hayes
4. Robert Merell

EAST COAST WAHINE CHAMPS, PRESENTED BY BILLABONG
WRIGHTSVILLE BEACH, NORTH CAROLINA
August 16–17

In the all-female Wahine Champi-

onships, women from various age groups competing in a range of disciplines made for an entertaining and enjoyable two-day event. Mallory Turner made the most of her first appearance at the contest, taking home two titles, three trophies and $350.

OPEN SHORTBOARD
1. Mallory Turner
2. Jessica Delosreyes
3. Terry Green
4. Liz Hauser
5. Carrie Emory
6. Erin Whittle
GROMMETTE SHORTBOARD (14 AND UNDER)
1. Madison Huckabee
2. Allison Parks
3. MT Bourque
4. Grace Muckenfuss
5. Samantha Newkirk
6. Julia McPherson
GIRLS SHORTBOARD (15-18)
1. Carly Eldred
2. Annie O'Brien
3. Katy MacFitzgerald
4. Hillary Watters
5. Christy Walker
6. Devon Klein
JUNIOR WOMEN SHORTBOARD (19-28)
1. Liz Hauser
2. Carrie Emory
3. Mallory Turner
4. Ainslee Wallace
5. LeAnn Foster
6. Brittany Golumlka
WOMEN SHORTBOARD (29-39)
1. Laura Peirano
2. Cayce Patterson
3. Liz Chirles
4. Jessica Delosreyes
5. Jennifer Butler
6. Marrie Hemmen
GODDESS SHORTBOARD (40 AND UP)
1. Terry Green
2. Mimi Munro
3. Barbara Corey
4. Becka Beitel
5. Mary Mentzer
6. Kim Watters
GIRLS LONGBOARD (15 AND UNDER)
1. Allison Parks
2. Brie Sciales
3. MT Bourque
4. Madison Huckabee
5. Rachel Nessuno
6. Savannah Jacruso
JUNIOR WOMEN LONGBOARD (16-24)
1. Mallory Turner
2. Janie McAuliffe
3. Hillary Watters
4. Sarah Walden
5. Brittany Gomulka
6. Liza Dean
WOMEN LONGBOARD (25-39)
1. Mary Schmader
2. Erin Whittle
3. Cayce Patterson
4. Kristen Kornegay
5. Carrie Emory
6. Laura Periano
GODDESS LONGBOARD (40 AND UP)
1. Mimi Munro
2. Jo Pickett
3. Lisa Muir Wakely
4. Barbara Corey
5. Kim Watters
6. Devon Plumer

CAPE COD SURFING CHAMPIONSHIPS, ESA SOUTH NEW ENGLAND
WHITECREST BEACH, SOUTH WELLFLEET, ASSACHUSETTS
August 16–17

With some of the best conditions Whitecrest Beach had seen all summer, a number of the surfers in attendance hung around after the award ceremony to get a few more. Glassy head-high waves were more than most would have asked for. With conditions being as good as they were, a number of competitors signed up for multiple divisions.

MENEHUNES
1. Jana Laurendeau
2. Ed Barend
3. Maria Barend
BOYS
1. Cob Ingalls
JUNIOR MEN
1. James McGraghan
2. Chris Orlando
SENIOR MEN
1. Chuck Barend
2. Bob Fitton
3. Ron Belanger
LEGENDS
1. Peter Pan
2. Tim Brooks
GRAND LEGENDS MALE
1. Bob Fredette
GRAND LEGENDS FEMALE
1. Kitty Pechet
OPEN
1. James McGraghan
2. Chris Orlando
3. Cob Ingalls
4. Ana Barend
5. Chuck Barend
6. Peter Pan
GIRLS
1. Mya Kotalac
SENIOR WOMEN
1. Ana Barend
2. Melanie Kotalac
MENEHUNE LONGBOARD
1. Cob Ingalls
MASTER LONGBOARD
1. Chuck Barend
2. Ron Belanger
3. Bob Fitton
LEGENDS LONGBOARD
1. Peter Pan
2. Tim Brooks
3. Bob Fredette
SENIOR WOMEN LONGBOARD
1. Ana Barend
2. Melanie Kotalac
3. Kitty Pechet
OPEN BODYBOARD
1. Pat Redmond
2. Peter Pan

QUIET STORM MARYLAND STATE SURFING CHAMPS, ESA DELMARVA OCEAN CITY, MARYLAND
August 16

After having to postpone the event on a previous date due to lack of waves, the event was given a go with the arrival of a new swell.

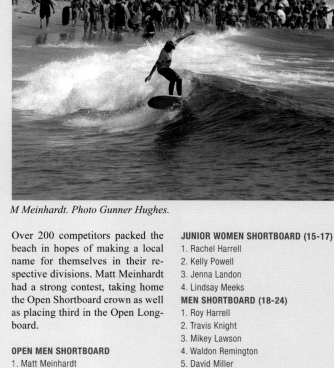

M Meinhardt. Photo Gunner Hughes.

Over 200 competitors packed the beach in hopes of making a local name for themselves in their respective divisions. Matt Meinhardt had a strong contest, taking home the Open Shortboard crown as well as placing third in the Open Longboard.

OPEN MEN SHORTBOARD
1. Matt Meinhardt
2. Dillon Harrington
3. Mike Lawson
4. Travis Knight
5. Waldon Remington
6. Jamie Crosby
OPEN WOMEN SHORTBOARD
1. Rachel Harrell
2. Daniell Ariano
3. Kelly Powell
4. Kelsey Willison
5. Jenna Landon
6. Tierney Loeser
OPEN LONGBOARD
1. Chris Makibbin
2. Chris Vaxmonsky
3. Matt Meinhardt
4. Austin Cook
5. Robert Fernandez
6. Bill Helmuth
OPEN BODYBOARD
1. Matt Landon
2. Josh Mitchell
3. Matt Meinhardt
4. Brady Faby
5. Craig Chatterton
6. Ty Webb
MENEHUNE SHORTBOARD (BOYS/GIRLS 11 & UNDER)
1. Shane Moore
2. Simon Hetrick
3. Evan Conboy
4. Jack Fager
5. Tyler Clazey
6. Melissa Harrell
GIRLS SHORTBOARD (14 & UNDER)
1. Tierney Loeser
BOYS SHORTBOARD (12–14)
1. Brad Flora
2. Seth Conboy
3. Noah Conboy
4. Dallas Harrington
5. Jimmy Edmunds
6. Ryan Thane
JUNIOR MEN SHORTBOARD (15–17)
1. Austin Deppe
2. Dillon Harrington
3. Corey Brown
4. Matt Meinhardt
5. Austin Gerachis
6. Andrew Stewart

JUNIOR WOMEN SHORTBOARD (15–17)
1. Rachel Harrell
2. Kelly Powell
3. Jenna Landon
4. Lindsay Meeks
MEN SHORTBOARD (18–24)
1. Roy Harrell
2. Travis Knight
3. Mikey Lawson
4. Waldon Remington
5. David Miller
6. Dane Woolyhan
WOMEN SHORTBOARD (18–29)
1. Chelsea Remines
2. Kelcey Bodolus
3. Kaitlyn Curren
4. Kelsey Willison
MASTERS SHORTBOARD (25–34)
1. Chris Makibbin
2. Jack Thomas
3. Matt Miller
LADIES SHORTBOARD (30+)
1. Danielle Ariano
2. Bonnie Preziosi
SENIOR MEN SHORTBOARD (35–44)
1. Keith White
2. Chris Vaxmonsky
3. Craig Garfield
GRAND MASTERS (45–54)
1. Doug Brown
2. JD Moore
LEGENDS SHORTBOARD (55–64)
1. Bill Helmuth
2. Bill Thomson
GRAND LEGENDS SHORTBOARD (65+)
1. Bryant Hungerford
MENEHUNE BODYBOARD (BOYS/GIRLS 14 & UNDER)
1. Matt Meekins
2. Brooks Gilbert
3. Brady Cooling
4. Jake Walsh
5. Carter Michael
6. Griffin McWilliams
MENEHUNE LONGBOARD (BOYS/GIRLS 14 & UNDER)
1. Robert Fernandez
2. Roland Gerachis
3. Johnny Moore
4. Shane Moore
5. Chase Schmehling
6. Carter Pruitt
JUNIOR LONGBOARD (15–17)
1. Matt Meinhardt
2. Austin Cook
MEN LONGBOARD (18–34)
1. Chris Makibbin
2. Travis Knight
WOMEN LONGBOARD (29 & UNDER)
1. Chelsea Remines
2. Rachel Harrell
3. Lindsay Meeks

LADIES LONGBOARD (30+)
1. Bonnie Preziosi
MASTERS LONGBOARD (35–49)
1. Chris Vaxmonsky
2. Doug Brown
3. Keith White
LEGENDS LONGBOARD (50+)
1. Bill Thomson
2. Bill Helmuth

VOLCOM'S STARFISH SURF SERIES
THE PIER, HUNTINGTON BEACH, CALIFORNIA
August 16–17

In 4- to 6-foot surf, the kids in attendance were amped to get into the water and make a case for their respective division titles. The Groms final was loaded with up-and-coming talent who were surfing beyond their years in the challenging conditions. East Coaster Cam Richards held off the heavily California finalists and took home the win and with it an electric guitar.

MEN PRO-AM
1. Brandon Guilmette
2. Chris Abad
3. Robert Patterson
4. Jake Kirshenbaum
5. Macy Mullen
6. Jason Harris
JUNIORS
1. Ford Archbold
2. Victor Done
3. Christian Saenz
4. Evan Kane
5. Bobby Okvist
6. Vance Smith
GROMS
1. Cam Richards
2. Parker Coffin
3. Kaikea Elias
4. Colin Moran
5. Trevor Thorton
6. Weston Williams
GIRLS
1. Demi Boelsteri
2. Jenna Balestar
3. Rachel Harris
4. Haley Watson
5. Erika Cook
6. Chelsea Rauhut

SIMA SURFING AMERICA USA CHAMPS, PRESENTED BY PACSUN
HUNTINGTON BEACH, CALIFORNIA
August 19–24

With hopes of qualifying for the USA Surf Team, a horde of top talent congregated on HB to make their case. At the close of the contest, the standout male performer was Keanu Asing, who won the Under 18 Boys and Under 16 Boys. However, since he lives in Hawaii, he is ineligible for Team USA. On the girls' end, Courtney Conlogue dethroned previous champ Sage Erickson in the Under 18 Girls division.

UNDER 18 BOYS
1. Keanu Asing
2. Conner Coffin
3. Fisher Heverly

4. Chase Wilson
UNDER 18 GIRLS
1. Courtney Conlogue
2. Taylor Pitz
3. Sage Erickson
4. Kaleigh Gilchrist
UNDER 16 BOYS
1. Keanu Asing
2. Taylor Thorne
3. Andrew Doheny
4. Nathan Carvalho
UNDER 16 GIRLS
1. Nage Melamed
2. Keenan Lineback
3. Taylor Pitz
4. Lani Doherty
UNDER 14 BOYS
1. Kolohe Andino
2. Ian Gentil
3. Parker Coffin
4. Jacob Halstead
UNDER 14 GIRLS
1. Nikki Viesins
2. Quincy Davis
3. Tatiana Weston-Webb
4. Emily Ruppert
UNDER 12 BOYS
1. Ian Gentil
2. Kanoa Igarashi
3. Daniel Glenn
4. Brogie Pansai
UNDER 12 GIRLS
1. Tatiana Weston-Webb
2. Miah Collins
3. Taylor Blake
4. Rachel Tilly

NSSA GOLD COAST EVENT #1
MANDALAY BEACH, OXNARD, CALIFORNIA
August 23

Though the waves were super-fun for most of the day, with waist- to chest-high peaks, the notorious afternoon onshores brought about windswept conditions for the finals at Mandalay Beach in Oxnard. The bumpy conditions didn't appear to bother Conrad Carr, who pulled double-duty, winning the Explorer Men and Explorer Juniors in convincing fashion.

EXPLORER MEN
1. Conrad Carr
2. Kokoro Tomatsuri
3. Shaun Burns
4. Shane Orr
5. Tanner Kehl
6. Chris Keet
EXPLORER JUNIORS
1. Conrad Carr
2. Shaun Burns
3. Chance Lawson
4. Tyler Thornsley
5. Christian Ramirez
6. Dustin Letinsky
EXPLORER BOYS
1. Kadin Panesi
2. Kyle Marre
3. Taylor Curran
4. Patrick Curren
5. Skylar Lawson
6. Charlie Fawsett
EXPLORER MENEHUENE
1. Kei Kobayashi
2. Patrick Curren
3. Decker McAllister
4. Spencer Farrar
5. Vinny Leonelli
6. Thelen McKinna

EXPLORER MASTERS
1. Tim Burrows
2. Kevin Frederick
3. Jeff Marder
4. Bryan Boyd
5. Scott Whitmer
6. Chris Keet

EXPLORER SENIORS
1. Robert Weiner
2. Mike Lamm
3. Jeff Gardner
4. Jeff Marder
5. Tim Wyman
6. Kevin Frederick

EXPLORER WOMEN
1. Keenan Reeser
2. Brittany Rothhammer
3. Frankie Harrer
4. Glennie Rodgers
5. Kirra Kehoe
6. Alexis Ross-Arroyo Grande 1.5

EXPLORER GIRLS
1. Frankie Harrer
2. Chantal Miller

EXPLORER LONGBOARD
1. Rory Golden
2. JP Garcia
3. Tim Smith
4. Alec Ledbetter
5. Zachary Svenson
6. Taylor Ross

OAKLEY PRO JUNIOR, PRESENTED BY HERITAGE SURF AND SPORT • GRADE 2 ASP PRO JUNIOR MEN EVENT
SEA ISLE CITY, NEW JERSEY
August 29–30

With only three events remaining on the ASP Pro Junior Circuit, Cory Arrambide managed to extend his ratings lead with a win in windswept 2- to 3-foot surf at Sea Isle City. In the final, Arrambide managed to overcome the local favorite, Rob Kelly, and defend his contest title. Nat Young's 3rd-place finish moved him up to third in the overall ratings.

FINAL
1. Cory Arrambide
2. Rob Kelly
3. Nat Young
4. Trevor Saunders
SEMIFINAL 1
1. Cory Arrambide
2. Trevor Saunders
3. Michael Dunphy
4. Bruno Rodrigues
SEMIFINAL 2
1. Rob Kelly
2. Nat Young
3. Travis Beckmann
4. Matt Pagan
QUARTERFINAL 1
1. Michael Dunphy
2. Trevor Saunders
3. Blake Jones
4. Marshall Alberga
QUARTERFINAL 2
1. Bruno Rodrigues
2. Cory Arrambide
3. Dillon Perillo
4. Jason Harris
QUARTERFINAL 3
1. Rob Kelly
2. Travis Beckmann
3. Spencer Regan 4. Cody Thompson

QUARTERFINAL 4
1. Nat Young
2. Matt Pagan
3. Brent Reilly
4. Kolohe Andino

FSC LEGENDS TOURNAMENT
PLAYA HERMOSA, COSTA RICA
August 29–31

In pumping 7- to 10-foot surf at Playa Hermosa, the over-35 competitors fought for a spot on the prestigious Costa Rican Masters team, which will be competing at the International Surfing Association Masters event next year in Costa de Caparica, Portugal. In the 45 to 50 category, the man who goes by "Tequila" pulled into one of the best tubes of the contest, receiving a perfect 10 score for the display and going on to win the final heat.

MEN 35–40
1. Randall Chávez
2. Tommy Bernsdorf
3. Mauro Sergio Oliveira
MEN 40–45
1. Alejandro Monge
2. Víctor Fallas
3. Christophe "Kiki" Commarieu
MEN 45–50
1. Craig "Tequila" Schieber
2. Brian Michael
3. Ian Douglas
50 AND OVER
1. Ian Douglas
2. Edward Alexander

CORONA DAIRYLAND SURF CLASSIC
SHEBOYGAN, WISCONSIN
August 30–September 1

Competitors and spectators flocked to the shores of Lake Michigan for one of the largest freshwater surf contests in the world. Considered the premiere spot on the lake, Sheboygan has been the host of the Dairyland Classic since 1988. The first year had 20 competitors and the contest has seen almost yearly growth. Competitors never count on glassy conditions, considering winds must be 20–25 mph from the S/SE or N/NE to create waves large enough to surf at the spot. Beyond the Pro Division, there was also a Women's and SUP division.

PRO MEN
1. Joe Matulis
2. Chris Matulis

Lake Michigan surf contest. Photo Mike McGinnis.

LABOR DAY SURF GAMES
NARRAGANSETT TOWN BEACH, RHODE ISLAND
August 30–31

There were waves for the 2008 ESA Labor Day Surf Games, but just barely. After holding off for a day, organizers ran the event during high tide, with plenty of rideable waves, but as the tide dropped, waves became more difficult to come by. Despite the meager conditions, competitors made the most of what was on offer and had a good time.

MENEHUNES
1. Cole Morehead
BOYS
1. Matt Nota
2. Andrew Nota
3. Mason Morehead
JUNIOR MEN
1. Alex Rastelli
MEN
1. Jarrett Parker
SENIOR MEN
1. Ron Belanger
LEGENDS
1. Peter Pan
GIRLS
1. Elizabeth Davis
WOMEN
1. Sarah Lim
SENIOR WOMEN
1. Janice Causey
MENEHUNE LONGBOARD
1. Andy Nota
2. Matt Nota
3. Mason Morehead
4. Cole Morehead
JUNIOR LONGBOARD
1. Alex Rastelli
MASTER LONGBOARD
1. Jim Chabot
2. Ron Belanger
3. Jarrett Parker
LEGENDS LONGBOARD
1. Peter Pan
WOMEN LONGBOARD
1. Sarah Lim

SENIOR WOMEN LONGBOARD
1. Janice Causey
OPEN BODYBOARD
1. Pat Redmond
2. Peter Pan
3. Elizabeth Davis
4. Janice Causey
OPEN
1. Matt Nota
2. Jarrett Parker
3. Andy Nota
4. Elizabeth Davis
5. Sarah Lim
6. Ron Belanger

MEXICO NATIONAL CHAMPIONSHIP OF SURFING
SAN JOSE, MEXICO
September 4–7

Over 200 competitors showed up to determine their standing in the echelons of Mexican surfing. Waves were 4 to 8 feet in height.

UNDER 14 BOYS SHORTBOARD
1. Diego Mignot
2. Miguel Velasco
3. Mario A. Farias
4. Aaron Hernandez
UNDER 16 BOYS SHORTBOARD
1. Martin Vazquez
2. Kai Lowe
3. Diego Mignot
4. Travis Southworth
UNDER 18 BOYS SHORTBOARD
1. Byland Southworth
2. Kai Lowe
3. Travis Southworth
4. Carlos Peralta
WOMEN SHORTBOARD
1. Nadia Buen Ostro
2. Citlaly Calleja
3. Taide Rosas
4. Andrea Gaytan
OPEN SHORTBOARD
1. Jose Manuel Trujillo
2. Heriberto Ramirez
3. Raul Medina
4. Diego Cadena
UNDER 18 BOYS BODYBOARD
1. Andres Lopez
2. Hugo Collins
3. Cesar Petroni
4. Francisco Cordoba
GIRLS BODYBOARD
1. Yoland Blanco
2. Kenia Leon
3. Paloma Aguirre
4. Alejandra Perez
OPEN BODYBOARD
1. Jose Rutherford
2. Arturo Ayala
3. Carlos Guillen
4. Juan Manuel Suazo
MEN LONGBOARD
1. Patricio Gonzalez
2. Tzahui Poo
3. Fernando Garcia
4. Alejandro Bello
SENIORS
1. Jose Zepeda
2. Jesus Velazquez
3. Alejandro Peraza
4. Tzahui Poo
MASTERS
1. Miguel Rojas
2. Alejandro Olea
3. Marco A. Islas
GRAND MASTERS
1. Sixto Mendez
2. David Santiago

3. J. Kervor
4. Adrian Valenzuela
KAHUNA
1. J. P. Kervor
2. Hector Rivero
3. Ricardo Acosta
4. Luciano Montoya
GRAND KAHUNAS
1. Hector Rivero
2. Leonel Perez
3. D. D. Paul S.
4. Ruben Villaseñor

MSA CLASSIC
FIRST POINT, MALIBU, CALIFORNIA
September 6–7

The Malibu Surfing Association emerged victorious at its home break, holding back competitors from 14 other clubs throughout California and the Virginia Longboard Federation. MSA had five division winners, but the weekend was a success for all, with 2- to 4-foot First Point Malibu for all to enjoy. An addition to this years contest was the Surfrider Foundation Celebrity Expression Session, presented by Barefoot Wines, which raised $4,000.

1. Malibu Surfing Association (MSA)
2. Santa Barbara Surf Club (SBSC)
3. Ventura Surf Club (VSC)
4. Windansea Surf Club (WnS)
5. Oceanside Longboard Surfing Club (OLSC)
6. Long Beach Surf Club (LBSC)
7. Virginia Longboard Federation (VLF)
8. Swami's Surfing Association (SSA)
9. Malibu Boardriders Club (MBC)
10. Big Stick Surfing Association (BSSA)
11. Santa Cruz Longboard Union (SCLU)
12. Colony Cool Cats (CCC)
13. Pacific Beach Surf Club (PBSC)
14. Hawaiian Longboard Federation (HLF)
15. Oxnard Waveriders (OWR)

NSSA SW CONFERENCE, EVENT 1
NINTH STREET, HUNTINGTON BEACH, CALIFORNIA
September 6–7

In the first event of the Southwest Conference Open season, a few familiar faces returned to prominence in the 2- to 4-foot surf in HB. The defending Conference, Regional and National Champion Courtney Conlogue didn't allow any early season slip-ups as she won every heat on her way to the Open Women win. Riley Metcalf also maintained his previous season form, winning the Open Men over a talented group of finalists.

OPEN MEN
1. Riley Metcalf
2. Christian Saenz
3. Dominic DiPietro
4. Derrick Disney
OPEN JUNIORS
1. Connor Coffin
2. Ian Crane
3. Tanner Rozunko
4. Jake Halstead
OPEN BOYS
1. Kanoa Igarashi
2. Nic Hdez
3. Patrick Curren

4. Jacob Davis
5. Skip McCullough
6. Addy Giddings

MINI GROM OPEN
1. Jake Marshall
2. Tyler Gunter
3. Griffin Colapinto
4. Kei Kobayashi
5. Ryland Rubens
6. Sam Wickwire

OPEN WOMEN
1. Courtney Conlogue
2. Lakey Peterson
3. Catherine Clark
4. Kaleigh Gilchrist

OPEN LONGBOARD
1. Michael Maddox
2. Scott Brandenburg
3. Matt Elias Calles
4. Shaun Thompson
5. Conor Morey
6. Tony Bartovich

NSSA SE CONFER-ENCE, EVENT #1
SEBASTIAN INLET, FLORIDA
September 6–7

After canceling two previous events, the Southeast Conference season finally got started thanks to 3- to 5-foot waves courtesy of Hurricane Ike. Tanner Strohmenger, Savannah Bradley and Luke Marks were the standouts, each winning two divisions.

OPEN MEN
1. Peter Polanski
2. Tommy Orsini
3. Alex Jackman
4. Christopher Tucker

OPEN JUNIORS
1. Tanner Stromenger
2. Sam Duggan
3. Christian Miller
4. Georgio Gomez

OPEN BOYS
1. Luke Marks
2. Matt Kaltenbach
3. Kai Walden
4. Fisher Grant

OPEN MINI GROMS
1. Luke Marks
2. Jaric Fink
3. Noah Berger
4. Noah Dovin
5. Izzi Gomez
6. Shelby Fink

OPEN WOMEN
1. Savannah Bradley
2. Emily Ruppert
3. Nikki Viesins
4. Jennifer Morris

OPEN LONGBOARD
1. Patrick Nichols
2. Frank Roper
3. Jaric Fink

EXPLORER MEN
1. Eddie Guilbeau
2. Tommy Orsini
3. Kedren Ferrero
4. Alex Jackman

EXPLORER JUNIORS
1. Kedren Ferrero
2. Tommy Orsini
3. Alex Jackman
4. Frank Roper
5. Christian Miller
6. Chad Ellingham

EXPLORER BOYS
1. Tanner Stromenger
2. Patrick Nichols
3. Georgio Gomez

4. Sam Duggan
5. Marley Puglielli
6. Jonathan Berger

EXPLORER MENEHUENE
1. Matt Kaltenbach
2. Luke Marks
3. Jaric Fink
4. Noah Berger

EXPLORER WOMEN
1. Savannah Bradley
2. Emily Ruppert
3. Nikki Viesins
4. Jennifer Morris
5. Erica Elliott

EXPLORER GIRLS
1. Emily Ruppert
2. Nikki Viesins
3. Shelby Fink
4. Izzi Gomez

EXPLORER MASTERS
1. Chad Carr
2. Dan Connover
3. Brian Corbitt
4 Andrew Bloom
5. Carlos Rodriguez
6. Gerardo Douahi

EXPLORER SENIORS
1. Jim Tolliver
2. Kevin Moon
3. Brian Corbitt
4. Andrew Bloom
5. Bill Miller

EXPLORER SUPER SENIORS
1. Steve Moldenhauer
2. Jim Tolliver
3. Sean Hayes
4. Jim Miller
5. Bill Miller

EXPLORER LONGBOARD
1. Patrick Nichols
2. Steve Moldenhauer
3. Frank Roper
4. Jordan Nichols

K-COAST/REEF OPEN EASTERN SURFING ASSOCIATION
35TH STREET, OCEAN CITY, MARYLAND
September 8

After Hurricane Hanna delivered heavy rains and wind on the eve of the contest, conditions cleared by morning, for highly contestable conditions. Head-high waves provided a perfect canvas to perform on for competitors in the four divisions. Open Shortboard winner Vince Boulanger went big from the first heats, throwing huge vertical snaps and the occasional reverse.

OPEN SHORTBOARD
1. Vince Boulanger
2. Travis Knight
3. Brad Beach
4. Roy Harrell

OPEN GIRLS
1. Rachell Harrell
2. Jassett Umble
3. Jenna Landon
4. Kaitlyn Curran

OPEN GROMS (14 AND UNDER)
1. Jassett Umble
2. Austin Deppe
3. Seth Conboy
4. Brad Flora

OPEN LONGBOARD
1. Jake Buchler
2. Dean Thompson
3. Colin Herlihy
4. Chris Shannahan

TORNEO BENEFICO DE SURF, FEDERACION DE SURF DE COSTA RICA
BOCA BARRANCA, COSTA RICA
September 13–14

In 2- to 4-foot surges at Boca Barranca, defending national champion Gilbert Brown collected yet another trophy to add to his ever-expanding collection. In the Longboard division, California's Dennis Bourg held off the Costa Rican competition to notch his first-ever win on the circuit.

OPEN MEN
1. Gilbert Brown
2. Jairo Pérez
3. Jason Torres
4. David Herrera

JUNIOR
1. Anderson Tascon
2. Anthony Flores
3. Manuel Mesén
4. Alvaro Guevara

OPEN WOMEN
1. Lisbeth Vindas
2. Macarena Ríos
3. Yanoris Godinez
4. Verónica Quiroz
5. Mar y Paz Solano

LONGBOARD MEN
1. Dennis Bourg

Nate Yeomans. Photo Brent Hilleman.

2. Luis León
3. Marco Pacheco
4. Willian Agüero

NSSA SOUTHWEST CONF. EXPLORER #1
MISSION BEACH, SAN DIEGO, CALIFORNIA
September 13–14

In small yet contestable conditions, the Southwest Conference Explorer season got its start with some high scores falling despite the dearth of swell. After taking a season off due to personal reasons, Cort Cespedes made a startling return, taking first in the Explorer Men division. San Diego locals won 7 of the 10 divisions.

EXPLORER MEN
1. Cort Cespedes
2. Colton Larson

3. Dylan Stephenson
4. Austin Rowe

EXPLORER JUNIORS
1. Shayne Nelson
2. J. D. Lewis
3. Josh Morse
4. Mason DeRieux

EXPLORER BOYS
1. Jake Halstead
2. Kanoa Igarashi
3. Taylor Clark
4. Josh Giddings

EXPLORER MENEHUENE
1. Kanoa Igarashi
2. Jake Marshall
3. Keone Betanzos
4. Skip McCullough
5. Noe McGonagle
6. Kody Clemmens

EXPLORER MASTERS
1. Rick Takahashi
2. Neil Bern
3. Tim Senneff
4. Jeff Marder
5. Chris Munsterman
6. Tom Matthews

EXPLORER SENIORS
1. Rick Takahashi
2. Rusty Phillipy
3. Jeff Marder
4. Scott Whitmer
5. Tom Matthews
6. Neil Bern

EXPLORER SUPER SENIORS
1. Rusty Phillipy
2. Mike Gillard-Coronado
3. David Winslow

4. Tim Senneff
5. Bill MacLeod
6. Randy Fox

EXPLORER WOMEN
1. Natalie Anzivino
2. Chelsea Rauhut
3. Chloe Buckley
4. Kaelin Bohl
5. Shelby Detmers
6. Harley Taich

EXPLORER GIRLS
1. Kylie Loveland
2. Shelby Detmers
3. Taylor Blake
4. Paige Ortiz
5. Lauren Heinmeyer
6. Torrey Miethke

EXPLORER LONGBOARD
1. Terry Gillard
2. Mike Gillard
3. Connor Morey
4. Lucas Dirkse
5. Brandyn Garske
6. Brian Biggins

COPAS LAS AMERICAS STOP #4
ROSARITO, BAJA CALIFORNIA
September 14

At 18 years of age, Dylan Southworth held off some stiff competition and won his second contest this season on the Copas Las Americas circuit. Though the swell was dropping, over 800 spectators turned out to take in the action.

SHORTBOARD MEN
1. Dylan Southworth
2. José Manuel Trujillo
3. Abel Estopin
4. Christian Corzo
5. Heriberto Ramirez
6. Raúl Medina
7. Diego Cadena
8. Angelo Lozano

OPEN BODYBOARD
1. Jonatan Lopéz
2. Jonatan Jimenez
3. Jorge Lopéz
4. Yolanda Blanco

OAKLEY NEWPORT BEACH PRO • ASP 2-STAR WQS MEN EVENT #34
56TH STREET, NEWPORT BEACH, CALIFORNIA
September 16–21

Nate Yeomans defended his Newport Beach Pro title, winning for the third consecutive year, and vaulted himself into the ratings lead of the Macy's Trifecta series with a single stop remaining. Waves were in the 2- to 3-foot range, providing plenty of push for the progressive approach of most of the contestants.

FINAL MEN
1. Nathan Yeomans
2. Dillon Perillo
3. Travis Mellem
4. Micah Byrne

SEMIFINAL 1
1. Dillon Perillo
2. Travis Mellem
3. Brett Barley
4. Darrell Goodrum

SEMIFINAL 2
1. Nathan Yeomans
2. Micah Byrne
3. Asher Nolan
4. Brad Ettinger

OAKLEY PRO JUNIOR • ASP GRADE 2 MEN JUNIOR EVENT
56TH STREET, NEWPORT BEACH, CALIFORNIA
September 16–21

Dillan Perillo was the in-form surfer of the weekend, winning his first Pro Junior contest, while also placing second in the Newport Beach Pro, which was running concurrently. The 18-year-old tore up the 2- to 3-foot waves with blistering backhand blasts and forehand boosts.

Dillon Perillo. Photo Brent Hilleman.

Perillo comboed the other competitors, throwing away a 7.33.

MEN FINAL
1. Dillon Perillo
2. Tanner Gudauskas
3. Michael Dunphy
4. Trevor Saunders

ROXY JAM CARDIFF, PRESENTED BY SCHICK® QUATTRO FOR WOMEN® • ASP LQS 6-STAR WOMEN EVENT
CARDIFF, SAN DIEGO, CALIFORNIA
September 19–21

Cardiff Reef-local Cori Schumacher won the Roxy Jam Cardiff in clean 2- to 4-foot surf in a stacked final heat. Schumacher took a commanding lead late in the final, requiring second-place Jen Smith (the 2007 World Champ) to net a near perfect 9.95 in order to close the gap. Schumacher's win gave her the North America Women's Longboard title and qualified her for the '09 Women's World Longboard Championships.

FINAL
1. Cori Schumacher
2. Jen Smith
3. Chelsea Williams
4. Summer Romero
SEMIFINAL 1
1. Summer Romero
2. Chelsea Williams
3. Bianca Valenti
4. Ashley Lloyd
SEMIFINAL 2
1. Cori Schumacher
2. Jen Smith
3. Kelly Nicely
4. Janna Irons
QUARTERFINAL 1
1. Bianca Valenti
2. Summer Romero
3. Crystal Dzigas
4. Kelia Moniz
QUARTERFINAL 2
1. Ashley Lloyd
2. Chelsea Williams
3. Rosie Locke
4. Jennifer Flanigan

QUARTERFINAL 3
1. Jen Smith
2. Janna Irons
3. Ashley Quintal
4. Rachel Barry
QUARTERFINAL 4
1. Cori Schumacher
2. Kelly Nicely
3. Megan Godinez
4. Kassia Meador

SURFTECH WOMEN'S SUP CHALLENGE
CARDIFF, SAN DIEGO, CALIFORNIA
September 21

The inagural Surftech Women's SUP Challenge incorporated paddling and wave-riding in a relay style event. Held in conjunction with the Roxy Jam Cardiff, the event included contest competitors and non-affiliated individuals. Though most of the teams were tight for the first half of the event, Team Love pulled away to take the win. Leah Dawson, Bianca Valenti and Geodee Clark made up the three-member Team Love.

FINAL RESULTS
1. Team Love
2. Team H.P.D.
3. Team ONE
4. Team Roxy 1
5. Team Cheddar
6. Team Santa Cruz

Jen Smith. Photo Roxy.

SQUALO LATIN PRO
IXTAPA, ZIHUATANEJO, MEXICO
September 18–21

Ernesto Nunes won the sixth stop on the ALAS Tour. Nunes and Diego Cadena traded the lead in the final heat, but Nunes locked up the win with three vertical maneuvers on a wave to provide a solid score and take the win.

MEN SHORTBOARD
1. Ernesto Nunes
2. Diego Cadena
JUNIORS
1. Francisco Bellorin
OPEN WOMEN
1. Agostina Pellizari
MEN LONGBOARD
1. Martin Perez

19TH ANNUAL DALE VELZY SURF CLASSIC AND LUAU
DOHENY STATE BEACH, CALIFORNIA
September 20

Hundreds came to the shores of Doheny to take part in the festivities of the annual Dale Velzy Surf Classic and Luau. The gathering is now a celebration of the memory of the legendary surfer/shaper Dale Velzy. The contest was a rousing success, with some hot surfing on display.

MENEHUNE BOYS
1. Andy Nieblas
2. Perry Rohr
3. Tim Kam
4. Dane Peterson
5. Cody Page
6. Noah Cordoza
7. Shane Roland
MENEHUNE GIRLS
1. Carley Mora
2. Becca Dunn
3. McKenzie Openshaw
JUNIOR MEN 15–19
1. Matt Suckle
2. Jr. Costello
3. Peter Danskin
4. Taylor Patton
5. Robert Freschaof
6. Conner Lumenzo
JUNIOR WOMEN 15–19
1. Marissa Barry
2. Lauren Ngan

3. Ashley Henderson
4. Melissa Jasnily
5. Natasha Swanson
6. Denae Thraher
WOMEN 20–44
1. Connie Hurst
2. Rachael Calkins
3. Cathy Brunmier
4. Michelle Mayo
5. Leslie Wielenga
6. Jeanette Francis
MEN 20–29
1. Maxx Dexter
2. Charlie Waite
3. Pete Casica
4. Kameron Brown
5. Zak Fritz
6. Josh Ropoza
SENIOR MEN 30–39
1. Mark Stewart
2. Jeremy Porfillo
3. Gary Siskar
4. Irwin Cabala
5. Troy Sugg
6. Robert Wielenga
PRONE PADDLE RACE
1. Mark Stewart
2. Tyler Warren
3. Bucky Barry
4. Gary Larson
5. Andy Nieblas
6. Rubio Smith
GRAND MASTERS PRONE PADDLE RACE
1. Mark Calkins
2. Cheryl MacGregor
3. Matt Albers
4. Jeff Wroe
5. Raudel Barba
6. Ed McMillen

VOLCOM STONE COOTERFISH
WRIGHTSVILLE BEACH, NORTH CAROLINA
September 20–21

Though the event was postponed three times last season, it went off on the first try in fine form this year, with 3- to 4-foot lines peeling through the impact zone. The Richards family had a strong showing in the Groms and Juniors divisions, with Cam and Cole winning their respective divisions.

MEN PRO-AM
1. Matt Gilligan
2. Shane Upchurch
3. Rob Cordova
4. Lucas Rodgers
5. Michael Powell
6. Jake Kirschenbaum
JUNIORS
1. Cole Richards
2. Evan Barton
3. Shane Burn
4. Josh Torres
5. Nick Capone
6. Chris Moore
GROMS
1. Cam Richards
2. Weston Williams
3. Dylan Kowalski
4. Tyler Faulkner
5. Conner Lester
6. Dillon Mincher
GIRLS
1. Chelsea Grisham
2. Bree Kleintop
3. Cierra Cunningham
4. Katy Mac Fitzgerald

5. Liz Hauser
6. Brittany Gomulka

VOLCOM STONE'S GREATWHITE SURF SERIES
PLEASURE POINT, SANTA CRUZ, CALIFORNIA
September 20–21

In fun 4- to 5-foot Pleasure Point surf, the Greatwhite Surf Series got off to a rousing start. The Grom and Junior divisions continued to show progress as the competitors become a little more capable, gain some size and with it, power. However, the highlight was once again the show-stopper, with a display of progressive maneuvers and classic power. Randy Bonds took a minimalist approach into the contest, holding out for the prime waves of each heat. It worked out for him as he claimed the winner's check.

PRO-AM MEN
1. Randy Bonds
2. Tyler Smith
3. Bud Freitas
4. Matt Meyers
5. Ashton Madley
6. Nick Erickson
JUNIORS
1. Shawn Burns
2. Cheyne Pearson
3. Patrick Shaughnessy
4. Noah Wegrich
5. Cody Frank
6. Aaron Godfrey
GROMS
1. Kadin Panesi
2. Seven Adams
3. Willie Eaglton
4. Jake Logan
5. Caleb Adams
6. Sachel Douphinez
GIRLS
1. Demi Boelsterli
2. Savannah Shaughnessy
3. Lexi Wilson
4. Mackenzie Kessler
5. Camila Gerard
6. Vanessa Floyd

LATIN PRO EL SALVADOR, ALAS TOUR
PUNTA ROCA, EL SALVADOR
September 26–28

In minimally contestable surf, the seventh stop on the ALAS Tour ran at Punta Roca in El Salvador. In her first contest as part of the tour, Maria Eugenia Rojas managed to advance to the finals against a seasoned group of finalists. Rojas' wave selection proved to be the difference.

OPEN MEN
1. Angelo Lozano
2. Jason Torres
OPEN WOMEN
1. Maria Eugenia Rojas
JUNIORS
1. Francisco Bellorín
LONGBOARD MEN
1. Patrick Gonzales
2. Martin Perez

CORONA EXTRA PRO, APSPR CORONA EXTRA PRO SURF CIRCUIT
MIDDLES, ISABELLA, PUERTO RICO
September 27–28

The defending champs in both the Men's Open and Women's Open returned to the shores of Puerto Rico to defend their Corona Extra Pro crowns. Both Dylan Graves and Anastasia Ashley proved successful in their intentions, winning in convincing fashion. With plenty of wind and a mixed-swell direction, challenging 5- to 7-foot faces made the champs have to work to reclaim the previous years' glory.

OPEN MEN
1. Dylan Graves
2. Carlos Cabrero
OPEN WOMEN
1. Anastasia Ashley
2. Maria Gonzales

NSSA NORTHWEST OPEN SEASON #1
LINDA MAR BEACH, PACIFICA, CALIFORNIA
September 27

Competitors from the NSSA Northwest were welcomed to the new season with rippable 2- to 3-foot beachbreak surf at Linda Mar. Prior to the event, Britt Galland had never won an NSSA contest. He'd never he made a final. But the San Diego County native's style apparently excelled in a new region as he won the Open Men division. In the Open Boys, Brogie Panesi was in stellar form throughout the event, and the 11-year-old continued the run into the finals of the Open Juniors and Open Boys. Panesi won both in impressive fashion.

OPEN MEN
1. Britt Galland
2. John Wilson
3. Kadin Panesi
4. Anthony Dunn
JUNIORS OPEN
1. Brogie Panesi
2. Kadin Panesi
3. Noe Mar McGonagle
4. Seth Nowlin
BOYS OPEN
1. Brogie Panesi
2. Noe Mar McGonagle
3. Tenzin Mendenhall
4. John Mel
MINI GROM OPEN
1. John Mel
2. Akea Tolentino
OPEN WOMEN
1. Sahara Ray
2. Asia Carpenter
3. Glennie Rodgers
LONGBOARD OPEN
1. Kevin McNicol
2. Audrey Bullwinkel
3. Liam Hession
4. Carlos Carpenter

Anastasia Ashley. Photo Osiris Torres/APSPR.

VOLCOM STONE'S BUSHFISH
CORPUS CHRISTI, TEXAS
September 27

With the issue of whether to call the event off following the wrath of Hurricane Ike, the organizers decided to give the event the go with the intention of making it the best Bushfish event to date. Extra free stuff and fun waves combined for an enjoyable event for all. In the Pro-Am, CJ Bradshaw managed to squeak out a win from the final group of six, despite solid scores for most every wave ridden.

MEN PRO-AM
1. CJ Bradshaw
2. Zach May
3. Shane Wiggins
4. Morgan Faulkner
5. Gabriel Prusmark
6. Justin Jalufka
JUNIORS
1. Adam Garrison
2. Clint Richard
3. Brandin Stevens
4. Lindsey Scroggs
5. James Berry
6. Alek Rackris
GROMS
1. Jordan Heaselgrave
2. Daniel Norton
3. Kyle Ferris
4. Daniel Daigle
5. Vincent Scroggs
6. Brandon Byas

Britt Galland. Photo tobyogden.com.

GIRLS
1. Grace Reutzel
2. Alicia Yaklin
3. Brittany Tupag
4. Kendal Baylis
5. Kristen Barden
6. Lauren Kenny

VOLCOM STONE'S COOTERFISH
KILL DEVIL HILLS, NORTH CAROLINA
September 28

In head-high, hollow conditions, the Cooterfish contest at Kill Devil Hills was one for the memory books. With 96 competitors, tons of barrels were being ridden and the high scores were dropping. The Richards brothers, Cole and Cam, continued their family dominance in the Juniors and Groms divisions. In the Pro-Am, Billy Hume found a few hollow pits and rode them to victory.

MEN PRO-AM
1. Billy Hume - $500
2. Michael Dunphy
3. Michael Powell
4. Jeff Myers
5. Slater Powell
6. Travis Ajay
JUNIORS
1. Cole Richards
2. Evan Barton
3. Nick Rupp
4. Shane Burn

5. Nathan Brake
6. Erik Kurby
GROMS
1. Cam Richards
2. Dylan Kowalski
3. Julian Payne
4. Mason Barnes
5. Weston Williams
6. Morgan Taylor Level
GIRLS
1. Jasset Umbel
2. Michelle Ketten
3. Chelsea Gresham
4. Brittany Tucker
5. Bree Kleintop
6. Kali Park

FREEDOM CALIFORNIA SURF SERIES, PRESENTED BY SURFRIDE
CALIFORNIA STREET, VENTURA
September 27

Under overcast skies, the Christian Surfing Federation event was graced with 2- to 4-foot waves at C Street in Ventura for its annual event. Chad Eastman nabbed a set in the last moments of the Open Men heat and repeated as contest champ for the Open Men.

OPEN WOMEN
1. Erica Tow
2. Erica Cook
3. Lauren Milner

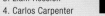
Kill Devil Hills action. Photo Volcom.

OPEN MEN
1. Chad Eastman
2. Paul Pugleisi
3. Brian Warren
GROMS
1. Charlie Fawcett
2. Charlie Taylor
3. Max Allen
SENIORS
1. Chris Williams
2. Eric Knowles
3. Patrick Schlick
LONGBOARD
1. Mike Stone
2. Ryan Cardone

TRKY TRIPLE CROWN, EVENT 1
THALIA STREET, LAGUNA BEACH, CALIFORNIA
October 5

In solid 4- to 6-foot peaks at Thalia Street, the first event of the TRKY Triple Crown went off with some solid performances from the under-20 crowd competing. The "Best TRKY Toob of the Day" went to 12-year-old Timmy Gamboa, who pulled into a clean 3-foot stand-up pit on a left off the reef.

UNDER 18 BOYS
1. Porter Hogan
2. Daschel Pierson
3. Christian St. Clair
4. Andrew Palmer
UNDER 15 BOYS
1. Andrew Redding-Kaufman
2. Dane Zarinelli
3. Hunter Smith
4. Adam Mejia
UNDER 12 BOYS
1. Teague Hamilton
2. Timmy Gamboa
3. Derek Strombotne
4. Shane Chapman
GIRLS
1. Brenda Joseph
2. Kennedi Gherardini

NSSA SOUTHWEST CONFERENCE EXPLORER EVENT #3
9TH STREET, HUNTINGTON BEACH, CALIFORNIA
October 11–12

In varying weather conditions, a peaking NW wind swell joined with strong side-shore winds to produce steep, feathering head-high peaks with overhead sets for the young shredders in attendance on day one. But with a dwindling swell, the surfers were left with challenging conditions by the time the finals rolled around. Despite the raucous conditions, Austin Rowe found enough room to work and win his first Explorer Men event of the season.

EXPLORER MEN
1. Austin Rowe
2. Britt Galland
3. Colton Larson
4. Brent Bowen
EXPLORER JUNIORS
1. Cooper Jones
2. Dale Timm
3. Porter Hogan
4. Mason DeRieux
EXPLORER BOYS
1. Trevor Thornton
2. Matt Lewis
3. Scott Weinhardt
4. Ian Simmons

EXPLORER MENEHUENE
1. Kanoa Igarashi
2. Jake Marshall
3. Skip McCullough
4. Keone Betanzos
5. Jay Christenson
6. Kody Clemmons

EXPLORER MASTERS
1. Rick Takahashi
2. Jeff Marder
3. Scott Whitmer
4. Neil Bern
5. Tim Senneff
6. Tom Matthews

EXPLORER SENIORS
1. Rick Takahashi
2. Neil Bern
3. Rusty Phillip
4. Mike Gillard
5. Tim Senneff
6. Tom Matthews

EXPLORER SUPER SENIORS
1. Rusty Phillip
2. Mike Gillard
3. Rick Fignetti
4. Randy Fox
5. Tim Senneff
6. Toby Lamm

EXPLORER WOMEN
1. Chloe Buckley
2. Shelby Detmers
3. Chelsea Rauhut
4. Natalie Anzivino
5. Harley Taich
6. Kaelin Bohl

EXPLORER GIRLS
1. Harley Taich
2. Melina Smith
3. Shelby Detmers
4. Paige Ortiz
5. Taylor Blake
6. Kylie Loveland

EXPLORER LONGBOARD
1. Mike Gillard
2. Terry Gillard
3. Lucas Dirkse
4. Brandyn Garske
5. Conner Morey
6. Brian Biggins

PACSUN WSA PRIME, EVENT #2, WESTERN SURFING ASSOCIATION
CHURCH, SAN ONOFRE, CALIFORNIA
October 11

The expected surge in swell from Hurricane Norbert never materialized for the invite-only competitors at the second-ever PacSun WSA Prime event. Courtney Conlogue won a hard-fought Under 18 Girls final over Lakey Peterson, her second in as many events. In the U/16 Boys final, Taylor Thorne held off Kolohe Andino to take the win. Taylor's brother, Jared, took third.

UNDER 18 BOYS
1. Dane Zaun
2. Christian Arballo
3. Chase Wilson
4. Victor Done

UNDER 16 BOYS
1. Taylor Thorne
2. Kolohe Andino
3. Jared Thorne
4. Ian Crane

UNDER 16 GIRLS
1. Courtney Conlogue
2. Lakey Peterson

3. Taylor Pitz
4. Cassidy Wehsener

UNDER 14 BOYS
1. Kanoa Igarashi
2. Colin Moran
3. Jacob Davis
4. Jake Marshall

UNDER 14 GIRLS
1. Melina Smith
2. Anise Guzman
3. Emmy Merrill
4. Catherine Clark

VOLCOM STONE'S GOLDFISH SURF SERIES
MORRO BAY, CALIFORNIA
September 20–21

The first Goldfish event of the year kicked off in true Central Cal fashion with some big, stormy surf and gale-force winds. In the Pro-Am division, Nate Tyler found a bit of retribution after having lost to Walt Cerney in the event last year. Tyler was simply too much with his wide range of maneuvers, which garnered the $500 check.

MEN PRO-AM
1. Nate Tyler
2. Walt Cerney
3. Dustin Ray
4. Jimmy Herrick
5. Eric Soderquist
6. Chad Jackson

JUNIORS
1. Simon Murdock
2. Jackson Newel
3. Cody Lewis
4. Christian Ramirez
5. Josh Printup
6. Frankie Soares

GROMS
1. Trent Popovich
2. Johnny McElgunn
3. Keary Kennedy
4. Rocky Allen
5. Joel Wilkie
6. Austin Thidodeaux

GIRLS
1. Rachel Harris
2. Amy Covert
3. Alex White
4. Katie Draeger
5. Marissa Kuiken

BILLABONG/WILD-COAST DEMPSEY HOLDER OCEAN FESTIVAL AND SURF CONTEST
IMPERIAL BEACH PIER PLAZA, SAN DIEGO, CALIFORNIA
October 19

A record number of competitors turned up for the annual Dempsey Holder Surf Contest. With 165 individuals signed up to compete in the 2- to 3-foot surf near Imperial Beach Pier, the action was nonstop from sunup to sundown. Though the contest lended to bragging rights, the contest sheds light on the important environmental work being done by the folks at Wildcoast.

MENEHUNE BOYS
1. Daniel Dedina
2. Joshua Johnson
3. Vincent Claunch

MENEHUNE GIRLS
1. Hannah Erbe-Smith
2. Grace Jackson
3. Kayla Rojas

UNDER 15 BOYS
1. Andre Arana
2. Sven Karlsson
3. Jack Alldredge

UNDER 18 BOYS
1. Tyler Smith
2. Jason Voorhies
3. Kyle Johnson

UNDER 18 GIRLS
1. Natalia Palmatier
2. Michelle McDonald
3. Michaela Branscomb

LONGBOARD MEN
1. Mike Gillard
2. Doug Smith
3. Richard Cacanindin

RETRO
1. Kelly Kraus
2. Dane Cosby
3. John Holder

STAND UP PADDLEBOARD
1. Mike Galliard
2. Kelly Kraus
3. John Ashley

OPEN MEN
1. Mike Galliard
2. Kevin Ferris
3. Balthazar Macias

OPEN WOMEN
1. Landy Spencer
2. Nicole Pratt
3. Antonette Guitierrez

OPEN MASTERS
1. Gary Trieschman
2. Mark Wraight
3. Billy Huddleston

BODYBOARD MEN
1. Anthony Zabrano
2. Peter Cosgrove
3. Paloma Aguirre

NSSA NORTHEAST HIGH SCHOOL CHAMPS, PRESENTED BY NO FEAR
OCEAN CITY, NEW JERSEY
October 19

Overhead surf, with north winds gusting to 30 mph were the order of the day as competitors faced brutal conditions for the NSSA Northeast Championships. The challenging conditions didn't appear to faze Chris Kelly, who posted two perfect 10s. One of those scores for Kelly came in the final, where he locked up the High School Men title.

HIGH SCHOOL TEAM RESULTS
1. Ocean City A
2. Southern Regional A
3. Ocean City B
4. Manasquan A
5. Middle Township A
6. Ocean City C
7. Atlantic City A
8. Point Pleasant Boro A
9. Manasquan B
10. Ocean City D
11. Ocean City E
12. Southern Regional B
13. Monsignor Donovan A
14. Middle Township B
15. St Augustine's A
16. Point Pleasant Beach A
17. Holy Spirit A

HIGH SCHOOL MEN
1. Chris Kelly
2. Ian Bloch
3. Jordan Beverly
4. Mike Ciaramella
5. Chris Eaves
6. Sean Santiago

HIGH SCHOOL WOMEN
1. Meridith Miedama
2. Jenna Scahmbach
3. Molly Guldin
4. Morgan Becker
5. Lacy Nichol
6. Grace Becker

HIGH SCHOOL LONGBOARD
1. Kevin DeWald
2. Mark Miedama Jr
3. Alex Branch
4. Sean Molyneaux
5. Jordan Baker
6. Ted Lyons

NSSA SOUTHEAST CONFERENCE #3
SEBASTIAN INLET, FLORIDA
October 18

Sebastian Inlet turned on for the third stop on the NSSA Southwest contest calendar, providing glassy

offshore peaks for the over-amped groms to tear apart. Both Jasset Umbel and Luke Marks were successful in their double-duty bids. Umbel won the Open and Explorer Women, while Marks took the Open Mini Groms and Open Boys.

OPEN MEN
1. Peter Polanski
2. Tanner Strohmenger
3. Shande Holmes
4. Alex Jackman
5. Chris Tucker
6. Gavin Greenwood

OPEN JUNIORS
1. Tanner Stromenger
2. Giorgio Gomez
3. Sam Duggan
4. Parker Greenwood

OPEN BOYS
1. Luke Marks
2. Logan Hayes
3. Matt Kaltenbach
4. Fisher Grant
5. Marley Puglielli

OPEN MINI GROMS
1. Luke Marks
2. Noah Dovin
3. Izzy Gomez
4. Jaric Fink
5. Zachary Goberville
6. Shelby Fink

OPEN WOMEN
1. Jasset Umbel
2. Savannah Bradley
3. Nikki Viesins
4. Jennifer Morris
5. Emily Ruppert

OPEN LONGBOARD MEN
1. Michael Wood
2. Tommy Evans
3. Patrick Nichols
4. Frank Roper

EXPLORER DIVISIONS

EXPLORER MEN
1. Chris Tucker
2. Tommy Orsini
3. Stephen Kaltenbach
4. Alex Jackman
5. Kedren Ferrero
6. Chad Carr

EXPLORER JUNIORS
1. Chris Miller
2. Chad Ellingham
3. Kedren Ferrero
4. Tommy Orsini
5. Shane Holmes
6. Alex Jackman

EXPLORER BOYS
1. Tanner Strohmenger
2. Giorgio Gomez
3. Marley Puglielli
4. Patrick Nichols
5. Logan Hayes
6. Sam Duggan

EXPLORER MENEHUENE
1. Logan Hayes
2. Luke Marks
3. Fisher Grant
4. Matt Kaltenbach
5. Jaric Fink

EXPLORER WOMEN
1. Jasset Umbel
2. Savannah Bradley
3. Nikki Viesins
4. Haley Dawson
5. Jennifer Morris

EXPLORER GIRLS
1. Nikki Viesins
2. Emily Ruppert
3. Shelby Fink
4. Izzy Gomez

Dane Zaun. Photo Jack McDaniel/WSA Prime.

Mason Ho. Photo Divel.

EXPLORER MASTERS
1. Dan Conover
2. Chad Carr
3. Bill Kimball
4. Brian Corbitt
5. Carlos Rodriguez
6. Gerardo Douaihi

EXPLORER SENIORS
1. Bill Kimball
2. Brian Corbitt
3. Jim Tolliver
4. Kevin Moon
5. Dave Walker
6. Bill Miller

EXPLORER SUPER SENIORS
1. Sean Hayes
2. Jim Tolliver
3. Jim Miller
4. Bill Miller

EXPLORER LONGBOARD
1. Michael Wood
2. Nick Gregory
3. Patrick Nichols
4. Frank Roper

FREAK AIRSHOW
Kedren Ferrero

NSSA WEST COAST COLLEGE TEAMS SEASON, EVENT #1
BLACKS BEACH,
SAN DIEGO, CALIFORNIA
October 18–19

Unfortunately for the college crowd, Blacks wasn't working quite the way it's been known to. Despite meager 1- to 3-foot faces, there were still some fine displays of quality surfing. In Marty Weinstein's third-round heat, he tallied a perfect 10 after a few huge lip bashes and turns, topped off with a 360 air-reverse re-entry. In the Longboard division, Troy Mothershead continued his NSSA contest prowess, taking yet another title.

COLLEGE TEAM POINTS
1. SDSU A
2. Pt. Loma A
3. Mira Costa Red
4. UCSB A
5. CSUSM A
6. UCSD A
7. Saddleback A
8. Saddleback B
9. Mira Costa Blue
9. UCSB B
11. CSUSM B
12. UCSC
13. CSULB A
14. Mira Costa White
14. Point Loma B
16. LMU
16. SDSU B
18. UCI
19. Golden West
19. UCLA
21. Pepperdine
22. USD
23. CPSLO A
24. UCR
25. CSULB B
26. UCSD B
28. CPSLO B
29. CSULB C

COLLEGE MEN
1. Marty Weinstein
2. Andrew Gahan
3. Hunter Lysaught
4. Chris Smith
5. Nick Olsen

6. Chris Abad

COLLEGE WOMEN
1. Lipoa Kahaleuahi
2. Darlene Connolly
3. Lilly Howard
4. Chelsea Rauhut
5. Sunshine Makarow
6. Allie Brown

COLLEGE LONGBOARD
1. Troy Mothershead
2. Chris Smith
3. Chase Stavron
4. Kevin Osborne
5. Mick Rodgers
6. Jon Hoover

NSSA GOLD COAST CONFERENCE, EVENT #4 • NSSA NORTHWEST CONFERENCE, EVENT #3
MORRO BAY, CALIFORNIA
October 18–19

The NSSA ran two conference contests concurrently at Morro Bay. Conrad Car took his third win of the season and Mini Grom John Mel won his second straight event.

EVENT #4
EXPLORER MEN
1. Conrad Carr
2. Shane Orr
3. Shaun Burns
4. Tanner Kehl
5. Jeremy Carter
6. Britt Galland

EXPLORER JUNIORS
1. Kokoro Tomatsuri
2. Andrew Jacobson
3. Conrad Carr
4. Christian Ramirez
5. Shaun Burns
6. Josh Stone

EXPLORER BOYS
1. Kanoa Igarashi
2. Trevor Thornton
3. Kyle Marre
4. Kadin Panesi
5. Jonah Carter
6. Skylar Lawson

EXPLORER MENEHUENE
1. Kanoa Igarashi
2. Brogie Panesi
3. Nic Hdez
4. Kei Kobayashi
5. Patrick Curren
6. Decker McAllister

EXPLORER MASTERS
1. Chris Keet
2. Eric Knowles
3. John Wander
4. Tim Burrows

5. Kevin Frederick

EXPLORER SENIORS
1. Tim Wyman
2. Kevin Frederick
3. John Wander
4. Mike Lamm
5. Robert Weiner
6. Masaki Kobayashi

EXPLORER WOMEN
1. Mackenzie Kessler
2. Lakey Peterson
3. Catherine Clark
4. Keenan Reeser
5. Alexis Ross
6. Katie Draeger

EXPLORER GIRLS
1. Lakey Peterson
2. Frankie Harrer
3. Danielle Wyman

EXPLORER LONGBOARD
1. Shayne Millhollin
2. Rory Golden
3. JP Garcia
4. Tyler Millhollin
5. Zach Svenson
6. Liam Hession

EVENT #3
OPEN MEN
1. Christian Ramirez
2. Shaun Burns
3. Shaw Kobayashi
4. Jason Hdez

OPEN JUNIORS
1. Kanoa Igarashi
2. Jake Kelley
3. Brogie Panesi
4. Skylar Lawson

OPEN BOYS
1. Kanoa Igarashi
2. Brogie Panesi
3. Kei Kobayashi
4. Nic Hdez

OPEN MINI GROMS
1. John Mel
2. Kei Kobayashi
3. Akea Tolentino

OPEN WOMEN
1. Kirra Kehoe
2. Keenan Reeser
3. Alexis Ross
4. Asia Carpenter

OPEN LONGBOARD
1. Kirra Kehoe
2. Liam Hession

O'NEILL COLD WATER CLASSIC • ASP 4-STAR WQS MEN'S EVENT #40
STEAMER LANE, SANTA CRUZ, CALIFORNIA
October 21–27

Youth overcame experience at the O'Neill Cold Water Classic, as local youngster Nat Young won the last three heats that he surfed, including the final. Displaying a ferocious back-side attack, Young overcame a few local heroes en route to the win, which made it that much more rewarding and satisfying. Despite falling in the semifinals, Micah Byrne went home a happy man with a $10,000 check after winning the Macy's Trifecta Series.

FINAL
1. Nat Young
2. Chris Waring
3. Granger Larsen
4. Sean Moody

SEMIFINAL 1
1. Granger Larsen
2. Chris Waring
3. Micah Byrne
4. Bud Freitas

SEMIFINAL 2
1. Nat Young
2. Sean Moody
3. Randy Bonds
4. Jason Collins

QUARTERFINAL 1
1. Micah Byrne
2. Granger Larsen
3. David Gonsalves
4. Mason Ho

QUARTERFINAL 2
1. Bud Freitas
2. Chris Waring
3. Chad Compton
4. Blake Howard

QUARTERFINAL 3
1. Jason Collins
2. Randy Bonds
3. Matt King
4. Kyle Garson

QUARTERFINAL 4
1. Nat Young
2. Sean Moody
3. Shaun Ward
4. Cory Lopez

OAKLEY PRO JUNIOR • ASP GRADE 3 PRO JUNIOR MEN'S EVENT
STEAMER LANE,
SANTA CRUZ, CALIFORNIA
October 21–27

In 4- to 6-foot surf at Santa Cruz's coveted Steamer Lane, Mason Ho took the Oakley Junior by posting the highest heat total of the event, a near-perfect 19.10, leaving his fellow finalists in the combination situation. And despite an equal 25th-place finish at Steamer Lane, Sebastian Zietz claimed the Macy's Trifecta title and the $7,000 check.

FINAL
1. Mason Ho
2. Jayke Sharp
3. Bruno Rodrigues
4. Matt Pagan

SEMIFINAL 1
1. Mason Ho
2. Bruno Rodrigues
3. Cody Thompson
4. Luke Davis

SEMIFINAL 2
1. Jayke Sharp
2. Matt Pagan
3. Fisher Heverly
4. Austin Smith-Ford

SEMIFINAL 3
1. Austin Smith-Ford

2. Fisher Heverly
3. Nat Young
4. Gabe Garcia

SEMIFINAL 4
1. Jayke Sharp
2. Matt Pagan
3. Heath Joske
4. Michael Dunphy

VOLCOM JELLYFISH SURF SERIES
CASINO PIER, NEW JERSEY
October 18

After postponing the event due to flatness, Mother Nature provided a bit of solid wind swell and mixed in some groundswell for a few slashable peaks for competitors. Sam Hammer was able to destroy a few lip lines on his way to the payday in the Pro-Am. In the Juniors, Jordan Beverly finally found his winning form after numerous appearances at contests.

MEN PRO-AM
1. Sam Hammer
2. Rob Kelly
3. Mike Gleason
4. Ben Graff
5. Matt Keenan
6. Dean Randazzo

JUNIORS
1. Jordan Beverly
2. Michael Ciramella
3. Balaram Stack
4. Tommy Inkken
5. Tim Mindich
6. Corey Frank

GROMS
1. Pat Schmidt
2. Ben Santiago
3. JD Porter
4. Andrew Rooney
5. Stefan Garman
6. Michael Vanaman

GIRLS
1. Kim Kepich
2. Jessica Kwiecinski
3. Jill Kepich
4. Morgan Gore
5. Jessica Swenson
6. Bethanne Wishbow

FREEDOM CALIFORNIA SURF SERIES, CHRISTIAN SURFING FEDERATION
SAN CLEMENTE,
October 8

The San Clemente crew turned out in force, defending home water while placing at least one finalist in each division. In 2- to 4-foot surf, the environment was fun and friendly for the Freedom California Surf Series, with sunny skies and offshore winds.

OPEN MEN
1. Daniel Ward
2. Vincent Duprat
3. Levi Gregory

JUNIORS
1. JD Macfadden
2. Ryan Graves
3. Keyen Bentley

MASTERS
1. Paul Pugliesi

2. Vincent Duprat
3. Anthony Fergeson
OPEN WOMEN
1. Erika Cook
2. Emmy Merrell
3. Erica Tow
LONGBOARD MEN
1. Mike Stone
2. Bert Fernando
3. Shea Roney
SUPER GROMS
1. Colin Deveze
2. Coly Ward
3. Blake Brown
GIRLS
1. Bryan Lutz
2. Kennedi Gheradini
3. Haley Putnam
BOYS
1. Kevin Shulz
2. Spencer Bentley
3. Ryan Graves
FISH STICKS
1. David Nelson
2. Hunter Smith
3. Shea Roney

NSSA SOUTHWEST CONFERENCE OPEN #3
SOUTHSIDE HUNTINGTON BEACH PIER, CALIFORNIA
October 25–26

A late-season southwest swell produced strong 4- to 6-foot surf and a brutal side current for NSSA competitors on the south side of HB Pier. Locals Vance Smith and Kanoa Igarashi won their first heats in their respective divisions and never looked back. At 11 years and 26 days, Igarashi was the youngest NSSA competitor to win an Open Juniors division; he also won the Open Boys.

OPEN MEN
1. Vance Smith
2. Christian Saenz
3. Evan Kane
4. Riley Metcalf
OPEN JUNIORS
1. Kanoa Igarashi
2. Jared Thorne
3. Derek Peters
4. Colin Moran
OPEN BOYS
1. Kanoa Igarashi
2. Nic Hdez
3. Jacob Davis
4. Patrick Curren
5. Jay Christenson
6. Colin Deveze
OPEN MINI GROMS
1. Jake Marshall
2. Griffin Colapinto
3. Tyler Gunter
4. Kei Kobayashi
5. Ryland Rubens
6. Nolan Rapoza
OPEN WOMEN
1. Lakey Peterson
2. Courtney Conlogue
3. Catherine Clark
4. Kaleigh Gilchrist
OPEN MEN LONGBOARD
1. Scott Brandenburg
2. Shaun Thompson
3. Nathan Thompson

PEQUENOS GRANDES SURFERS
PLAYA REVOLCADERO, MEXICO
October 25–26

Around 60 competitors came to the shores of Playa Revolcadero to take part in the second edition of the Revolcadero Historico. Organized by the Assembly of Surfers of Revolcadero, the event also raises awareness for the ecosystem in the area, in particular the future existence of the local turtles.

UNDER 8 BOYS
1. Sebastian Hernandez
2. Emiliano Cruz
3. Dennis Mendoza
4. Jone Pereira
UNDER 11 BOYS
1. Sasha Donnanno
2. Nahum Corzo
3. Melchor Peralta
4. Johny Corzo
UNDER 14 BOYS
1. Vicente Vega
2. Mike Velasco
3. Jimmy Corzo
4. Sasha Donnanno
UNDER 17 GIRLS
1. Pamela Verboonen
2. Asaya Aymara Corzo
3. Maria Amadio
4. Leila Takeda
UNDER 17 BOYS
1. Cristian Evengelista
2. Martin Vazquez
3. Aldahir Cruz
4. Cesar Petroni

RIP CURL GROMSEARCH NATIONAL FINAL, PRESENTED BY BOOST MOBILE
SALT CREEK, CALIFORNIA
November 2

Riding a stream of contest momentum, Santa Cruz's Nat Young followed up his WQS contest win with a victory at the Rip Curl GromSearch National Final. After relinquishing the lead to North Carolina's Fisher Heverly, Young retook the lead in commanding fashion with a 9.33 to follow his 9.0. With the win, Young reserved his spot at the International Rip Curl GromSearch Final to be held at Bells Beach, Australia, in conjunction with the Rip Curl Pro WCT during Easter of 2008. Flying under the radar, Chandler Parr also punched her ticket with a win in the Under 16 Girls.

UNDER 16 BOYS
1. Nat Young
2. Fisher Heverly
3. Conrad Carr
4. Kolohe Andino
UNDER 16 GIRLS
1. Chandler Parr ($500)
2. Nage Melamed
3. Hanna Harrison
4. Catherine Clark
UNDER 14 BOYS
1. Ian Crane
2. Luke Davis

3. Kain Daly
4. Colin Moran
UNDER 12 BOYS
1. Koa Smith
2. Andrew Jacobson
3. Kadin Panesi
4. Taylor Clark

NSSA SOUTHWEST CONFERENCE OPEN #4
OCEANSIDE SOUTH JETTY, SAN DIEGO, CALIFORNIA
November 1–2

Competitors in the fourth stop on the NSSA Southwest circuit were granted more swell than they knew what to do with at Oceanside's South Jetty: a solid southwest swell sent clean, 3- to 5-foot waves for Saturday's preliminary rounds, and then a new west swell arrived, providing good 4-6 foot surf for Sunday. After consecutive runner-up finishes in the Open Men category, Christian Saenz finally took the top spot on the podium.

OPEN MEN
1. Christian Saenz
2. Vance Smith
3. Riley Metcalf
4. Jared Thorne
OPEN JUNIORS
1. Jared Thorne
2. Taylor Thorne
3. Kelly Zaun
4. Carlos Zapata
OPEN BOYS
1. Skip McCullough
2. Kanoa Igarashi
3. Patrick Curren
4. Jay Christenson
5. Nic Hdez
6. Kei Kobayashi
OPEN MINI GROMS
1. Jake Marshall
2. Tyler Gunter
3. Sam Wickwire
4. Griffin Colapinto
5. Nicholas Marshall
6. Ryland Rubens
OPEN WOMEN
1. Taylor Pitz
2. Courtney Conlogue
3. Kaleigh Gilchrist
4. Tara Franz
OPEN LONGBOARD MEN
1. Scott Brandenburg
2. Michael Maddox
3. Shaun Thompson
4. Matt Elias Calles
5. Cody Ulrich

OXBOW WLT • ASP WORLD LONGBOARD TOUR, EVENT #2
SAN ONOFRE, SAN DIEGO, CALIFORNIA
November 5–9

After 12 years of near misses, Bonga Perkins won his second World Longboard title held in classic San Onofre conditions. It came down to a do-or-die final for Perkins and Antoine Delpero, with the winner taking longboarding's top honors. Delpero and Perkins finished second and third respectively at the first stop on the WLT held at An-

glet, France, in May. Semifinalist Ned Snow was also surfing well throughout, staging a number of upsets before falling to Perkins. Snow netted the only perfect 10 of the event in his round 4 heat with ratings leader Harley Ingleby.

FINAL
1. Bonga Perkins
2. Antoine Delpero
SEMIFINAL 1
1. Bonga Perkins
2. Ned Snow
SEMIFINAL 2
1. Antoine Delpero
2. Alex Salazar
QUARTERFINAL 1
1. Bonga Perkins
2. Timothee Creignout
QUARTERFINAL 2
1. Ned Snow
2. Eduardo Bage
QUARTERFINAL 3
1. Antoine Delpero
2. Josh Baxter
QUARTERFINAL 4
1. Alex Salazar
2. Matthew Moir

NSSA SOUTHWEST CONFERENCE EXPLORER SEASON EVENT #4
HUNTINGTON BEACH PIER, CALIFORNIA
November 8–9

An overnight jump in swell had the finals of the NSSA Southwest Explorer fourth stop in pumping 4- to 8-foot waves at HB Pier. In the stellar conditions, the HB locals excelled. Huntington Beach High's Colton Larson found the overhead conditions to his liking on his way to the Explorer Men title.

EXPLORER MEN
1. Colton Larson
2. Brent Bowen
3. Makito Shito
4. Cort Cespedes
EXPLORER JUNIORS
1. Derek Peters
2. Nick Fowler
3. Dale Timm
4. JD Lewis
EXPLORER BOYS
1. Kanoa Igarashi
2. Breydon Taylor
3. Ian Simmons
4. Jake Halstead

Bonga Perkins. Photo ASP Morris © Covered Images.

EXPLORER MENEHUENE
1. Kanoa Igarashi
2. Jake Marshall
3. Jay Christenson
4. Skip McCullough
5. Keone Betanzos
6. Kody Clemmons
EXPLORER MASTERS
1. Neil Bern
2. Rick Takahashi
3. Chris Munsterman
4. Tim Senneff
5. Brett Jordan
6. Tom Matthews
EXPLORER SENIORS
1. Mike Gillard
2. Rick Takahashi
3. Terry Gillard
4. Rusty Phillipy
5. Scott Whitmer
6. Tim Senneff
EXPLORER SUPER SENIORS
1. Randy Fox
2. Rusty Phillipy
3. Mike Gillard
4. Tim Senneff
5. David Winslow
6. Mark Silva
EXPLORER WOMEN
1. Harley Taich
2. Shelby Detmers
3. Natalie Anzivino
4. Erin Hamilton
5. Jordan Hundley
EXPLORER GIRLS
1. Leah Pakpour
2. Melina Smith
3. Harley Taich
4. Paige Ortiz
5. Kylie Loveland
6. Lauren Heinmeyer
EXPLORER LONGBOARD
1. Mike Gillard
2. Terry Gillard
3. Tony Bartovich
3. Conner Morey
5. Lucas Dirkse
6. Brandon Garske
6. Brian Biggins

VOLCOM STONE GREAT WHITE SURF SERIES
STEAMER LANE, SANTA CRUZ, CALIFORNIA
November 8–9

The day prior to the start of the event, Steamer Lane looked like a lake. But the day of the event a swell hit, starting out in the 2- to 4-foot range and building to overhead bombs by the end of the day.

The Pro-Am division tore up the practically empty lineup, sending buckets of water flying on each wave. In the end, the Smith brothers pulled away from the group, with Tyler taking the win.

MEN PRO-AM
1. Tyler Smith
2. Russel Smith
3. Randy Bonds
4. Jesse Columbo
5. Bud Freitas
6. Matt Myers

JUNIORS
1. Nat Young
2. Pete Mueller
3. Shawn Burns
4. Jason Hernandez
5. Noah Wegrich
6. Patrick Shaughnessy

GROMS
1. Andrew Jacobson
2. Kadin Panesi
3. Willie Eaglton
4. Nick Hernandez
5. Seven Adams
6. Brogie Logan

GIRLS
1. Jenny Uselinger
2. Lexi Wilson
3. Mackenzie Kessler
4. Jamilah Star
5. Vanessa Floyd
6. Savannah Shaughnessy

NSSA WEST COAST COLLEGE TEAMS SEASON, EVENT #2
SOUTH MISSION BEACH, SAN DIEGO, CALIFORNIA
November 8–9

After the surf nearly tripled in size overnight, finalists in the NSSA West Coast College event were faced with 8- to 10-foot faces, gusty winds and a racing north-to-south current. In the Men's Shortboard final, Hunter Lysaught's top-to-bottom style was rewarded with solid scores and ultimately the event title.

COLLEGE TEAM PTS
1. CSUSM—A
2. PT LOMA—A
3. UCSD—A
4. SDSU—A
5. UCSB—A
6. Mira Costa—Red
7. Saddleback—A
8. UCSB—B
9. Mira Costa—White
10. Mira Costa—Blue
11. Saddleback—B
12. USD
13. LMU
14. CSUSM—B
15. UCSD—B
16. CPSLO—A
17. Point Loma—B
18. UCSB—C
18. UCLA
20. CSULB—A
21. Pepperdine
22. Golden West
23. UCI
24. Clairmont College
25. SDSU—B
26. CSULB—B
27. CSULB—C
28. CPSLO—B

COLLEGE MEN
1. Hunter Lysaught—PL A
2. Sean Murphy—CSUSM A
3. Mark Everds—UCSD A
4. Kyle Jax—PL A
5. Scott McBride—CSUSM A
6. Court Carroll—MC Blue

COLLEGE WOMEN
1. Lipoa Kahaleuahi—UCSB A
2. Gretchen Wegrich—UCSD A
3. Sunshine Makarow—CSUSM A
4. Chelsea Rauhut—UCSD A
5. Chloe Buckley—MC White
6. Rachel Harris—UCSB A

COLLEGE LONGBOARD
1. Chris Smith—CSUSM A
2. Christian Clark—MC White
3. Troy Mothershead—PL A
4. Chase Stavron—Saddleback B
5. Paul Steinberg—UCSB B
6. Chris Koerner—SDSU A

VOLCOM BEAVERFISH SURF SERIES
NORTH CHESTERMAN'S, TOFINO, BRITISH COLUMBIA
November 8–9

Under heavy winds and rainy skies, the Beaverfish went off in Tofino, BC. The weather didn't faze the locals in the contest, who, after pulling on the 5mm wetsuits, booties, gloves and hoods, left the conditions as an afterthought. In the Groms final, Simon Bauer blasted out of the gates, snagging an 8-point ride before the other finalists even realized the horn had sounded. Bauer led from start to finish, claiming the win.

MEN PRO-AM
1. Peter Devries
2. Sepp Bruhwiler
3. Shannon Brown
4. Noah Cohen
5. Ben Murphy
6. Raph Bruhwiler

JUNIORS
1. Janek Peladeau
2. Frazer Mayor
3. Simon Bauer
4. Ryan Oke
5. James Martin
6. Lance Gauld

GROM
1. Simon Bauer
2. Jack Sanford
3. Angelo Carlazzoli
4. Mitchell Sanderson
5. Kevin Porteous
6. James Martin

GIRLS
1. Catherine Bruhwiler
2. Leah Oke
3. Steph Wightman
4. Shaddy Kariatsumari
5. Carmen Meyer
6. Tai Travis

COSTA DEL MAR PRO CHAMPIONSHIPS, PRESENTED BY THE CITY OF ROSARITO • ASP LQS 1-STAR MEN EVENT
HUNTINGTON BEACH PIER, CALIFORNIA
November 15–16

Taylor Jensen won his second consecutive LQS event in peaky 2- to 4-foot surf at HB Pier. With a number of top talents in town for the Oxbow WLT the previous weekend at San Onofre, the level of surfing throughout the event was stellar. Jensen, who won the last ASP LQS at Huntington Beach, the Honda U.S. Open, started quick in the final, earning a 9.0 en route to a heat total of 16.67 and the win.

FINAL
1. Taylor Jensen
2. Harley Ingleby
3. Kekoa Uemura
4. Tony Silvagni

SEMIFINAL 1
1. Tony Silvagni
2. Harley Ingleby
3. Steve Newton
4. Cole Robbins

SEMIFINAL 2
1. Kekoa Uemura
2. Taylor Jensen
3. Colin McPhillips
4. Ben Skinner

QUARTERFINAL 1
1. Steve Newton
2. Cole Robbins
3. Alexis Deniel
4. Kai Sallas

QUARTERFINAL 2
1. Harley Ingleby
2. Tony Silvagni
3. Troy Mothershead
4. Ned Snow

QUARTERFINAL 3
1. Colin McPhillips
2. Kekoa Uemura
3. Billy Harris
4. Eric Lloy

QUARTERFINAL 4
1. Taylor Jensen
2. Ben Skinner
3. Joe Aaron
4. Josh Baxter

PXM INTERNATIONAL VANS PRO • ASP 3-STAR WQS MEN EVENT
PUERTO ESCONDIDO, OAXACA, MEXICO
November 12–16

Puerto Escondido local Angelo Lozano made it look easy on his way to the PXM Int'l Vans Pro title in powerful 6- to 8-foot walls. Third-place finisher Ryan Turner was also in good form throughout, posting a

Angelo Lozano. Photo Tony Roberts.

perfect 10 and the highest heat score in an earlier heat.

FINALS
1. Angelo Lozano
2. Gabriel Villaran
3. Ryan Turner
4. David Rutherford

SEMIFINAL 1
1. Angelo Lozano
2. Gabriel Villaran
3. Cory Arrambide
4. Matt Mohagen

SEMIFINAL 2
1. Ryan Turner
2. David Rutherford
3. Gabe Garcia
4. Manuel Selman

QUARTERFINAL 1
1. Cory Arrambide
2. Matt Mohagen
3. Dean Brady
4. Rusty Long

QUARTERFINAL 2
1. Angelo Lozano
2. Gabriel Villaran
3. Eric Ramirez
4. Chad Compton

QUARTERFINAL 4
1. David Rutherford
2. Ryan Turner
3. Andre DeMarco
4. Andrew Doheny

QUARTERFINAL 4
1. Manuel Selman
2. Gabe Garcia
3. Brandon Ragenovich
4. Blake Howard

ESA HOLIDAY SURFABOUT
NARRAGANSETT TOWN BEACH, RHODE ISLAND
November 15–16

Held in 4- to 6-foot, near-perfect conditions at the Narragansett Town Beach, locals traversed the challenging conditions en route to a number of solid results. Chuck Barend was the standout of the weekend, winning the Open, Senior Men, and Masters Longboard divisions. For his efforts he was rewarded with the Outstanding Surfer trophy for the event.

MENEHUNES
1. Cob Ingalls

BOYS
1. Matt Nota

GIRLS
1. Mya Kotalac

JUNIOR MEN
1. Ross Ahlborg
2. Chris Orlando
3. James McGraghan
4. Pat Brown
5. Mike Viprino
6. Connor Gammons

MEN
1. Colin Cook
2. Ryan Richer
3. Conrad Ferla

MASTERS
1. Nick Carter

SENIOR MEN
1. Chuck Barend
2. Ron Belanger

SENIOR WOMEN
1. Ana Barend
2. Melanie Kotalac

LEGENDS
1. Peter Pan
2. Janice Causey

OPEN MEN
1. Chuck Barend
2. James McGraghan
3. Chris Orlando
4. Pat Redmond
5. Mike Viprino
6. Nick Carter

OPEN BODYBOARD
1. Pat Redmond
2. Peter Pan

MENEHUNE LONGBOARD
1. Matt Nota

JUNIOR LONGBOARD
1. James McGraghan
2. Chris Orlando
3. Pat Brown

MASTERS LONGBOARD
1. Chuck Barend
2. Ron Belanger
3. Nick Carter

SENIOR WOMEN LONGBOARD
1. Ana Barend
2. Melanie Kotalac
3. Janice Causey

LEGENDS LONGBOARD
1. Peter Pan

14TH ANNUAL QUIKSILVER KING OF THE PEAK
SEBASTIAN INLET, NORTH JETTY, FLORIDA
November 15–16

In 3- to 4-foot surf at Sebastian Inlet, Jacksonville local Cody Thompson went for broke in the one-wave heat score format and put together four Skins before coming face-to-face with his closest challenger. In the end, Thompson prevailed over Asher Nolan with a clean, open barrel and the highest score of the event, 8.33. Cody went on to grab two more Skins and the 2008 title Quiksilver King of the Peak.

RESULTS
1. Cody Thompson
2. Asher Nolan

WSA/HOBIE CHAMPIONSHIP TOUR, EVENT #4
PISMO BEACH PIER, CALIFORNIA
November 9

After conditions transitioned from glassy and summer-like to cold and

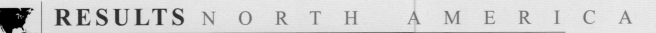
windy, the finals were set to run in challenging, consistent NW wind-swell. In the biggest WSA turnout at Pismo ever, 250 competitors signed up to test their skills in hopes of claiming various division titles.

UNDER 12 BOYS
1. Hunter Johnson
2. Colton Ward
3. Sam Wickwire
4. Corey Colapinto
5. Wil Reid
6. Max Fleming

UNDER 12 GIRLS
1. Sidney Johnson
2. Meah Collins
3. Crystal Dean
4. Frankie Harrer
5. Avalon Johnson
6. Ashley Beeson

UNDER 14 BOYS
1. Kyle Crompton
2. Will Laidlaw
3. Tai Stratton
4. Brandon Hawkins
5. Kevin Schulz
6. Colton Overin

UNDER 16 BOYS
1. Blake Davis
2. Colton Sarlo
3. Sam Zaiser
4. Tony Morelli
5. John White
6. Beau Clarke

UNDER 14 BOYS LONGBOARD
1. Jake Gallagher
2. Dane Petersen
3. Kieran Giffen
4. Dylan Cox
5. Derek Richens
6. Diego Quinonez

UNDER 18 BOYS LONGBOARD
1. Kent Nishiya
2. Bobby Okvist
3. Colton Sarlo
4. Dylan Stratton
5. Theo Lewitt
6. Tanner Swanson

UNDER 14 GIRLS LONGBOARD
1. Rachael Tilly
2. Sidney Johnson,
3. Ashley Beeson

UNDER 18 GIRLS LONGBOARD
1. Rachael Tilly
2. Carly Martin
3. Lisa Tuttle
4. Michelle Bautista Layton

UNDER 14 GIRLS
1. Avalon Johnson
2. Meah Collins
3. Frankie Harrer
4. Kandi Patterson

UNDER 16 GIRLS
1. Frankie Harrer
2. Meah Collins
3. Jessi Duston

UNDER 18 GIRLS
1. Charlotte Dellea
2. Lisa Tuttle
3. Alex Ross
4. Chelsea Byland
5. Madi Swayne
6. Carly Martin

UNDER 18 JUNIOR LONGBOARD
1. David Arganda
2. Ashton Malkin
3. Tony Morelli
4. Trevor Robbins
5. Quaid Birchell
6. Jesse Hinkle

LEGENDS 50+
1. Witt Rowlett
2. Rick Fignetti

3. Jay Boldt
4. Rusty Wink
5. Jim Adrig
6. John Silver

MASTERS 30–39
1. David Nelson
2. Mike Burau
3. Cory Pierce
4. Riley McWilliams
5. Chris Herring
6. Kevin Hamor

MEN 18–29
1. Dane Anderson
2. John Corning
3. James Fazio
4. Chuck Glynn
5. Matthew Jensen
6. Alex Mannix

UNDER 9 MICRO GROM BOYS AND GIRLS LONGBOARD
1. Griffin Foy
2. Malia Faramarzi
3. Trenton Coleman

UNDER 9 MICRO GROM BOYS AND GIRLS SHORTBOARD
1. Michael Tilly
2. Crosby Colapinto
3. Cole Houshmand
4. Griffin Foy
5. Jack Hardley

OPEN MEN LONGBOARD
1. David Arganda
2. Josh Rapozo
3. Jorge Barba
4. Chuck Glynn
5. Yasuyuki Baba

OPEN MEN SHORTBOARD
1. Dane Anderson
2. Sean Johnson
3. Justin Carlson
4. Jake Caughill
5. Steve Weir
6. Colton Sarlo

OPEN WOMEN LONGBOARD
1. Michelle Bautista Layton
2. Morgan Sliff

OPEN WOMEN SHORTBOARD
1. Keenan Reeser
2. Michelle Bautista Layton
3. Dresden Rowlett
4. Chelsea Byland
5. Madi Swayne
6. Morgan Gore

SENIOR MEN 40–49
1. Branton Slowinski
2. Barry Bushman
3. Gabriel Fimbres
4. Mike Dolan
5. Dave Hansberry
6. Raymond Koehler

SENIOR WOMEN LONGBOARD, 35 AND OVER

Oceanside action. Photo Kenny Morris.

1. Carol Malamud
2. Jacque Fait

SENIOR MEN LONGBOARD, 30 AND OLDER
1. Gabriel Fimbres
2. Barry Bushman
3. Jorge Barba
4. Larry Schlick
5. Greg Bolitsky

WOMEN 18+
1. Dresden Rowlett
2. Morgan Gore
3. Heather Carrick
4. Jessica Silver
5. Cybil Oechsle

VOLCOM STONE'S BLOWFISH
SOUTH JETTY, OCEANSIDE, CALIFORNIA
November 15–16

The second stop of the Blow-fish Surf Series went off with 3- to 5-foot peaky, clean conditions with 150 competitors. The Pro-Am division in San Diego is always stacked with top-notch competitors, and Oceanside didn't disappoint with 60 guys battling it out for $500 in cash. Shane Valiere appeared out of nowhere in the final, earning scores that jumped him past the top guys and into the lead.

MEN PRO-AM
1. Shane Valiere
2. Ryan Burch
3. Russel Fawley
4. Josh Buran
5. Drew Irons
6. Justin Quirk

JUNIORS
1. Chase Wilson
2. Jared Cassidy
3. Nick Fowler
4. Max Gardenier
5. Olin Bower
6. JD McFadden

GROMS
1. Kent Nishiya
2. Matt Passaquindicci
3. Kyle Timm
4. Joe Diamond
5. Hunter Johnson
6. Kyle Merrick

GIRLS
1. Jenna Balester
2. Sara Taylor
3. Erika Cook

4. Chelsea Raunhut
5. Darlene Conolly
6. Alissa Lentz

NSSA SOUTHWEST CONFERENCE OPEN #5
CHURCH, SAN CLEMENTE, CALIFORNIA
November 15–16

At the midway point of the 2008-09 season, the 5-star rated event offered valuable points, and there could be no better setting than pristine 2- to 4-foot waves and sunny weather. The contest was a breakout for some and not for others, as several upsets occurred and some of the top seeds were knocked out of the competition early. In the final of the Open Men, familiar names were in the running for the win, but it would be Luke Davis that would prove most capable.

OPEN MEN
1. Luke Davis
2. Ian Crane
3. Conner Coffin
4. Ian Garcia

OPEN JUNIORS
1. Conner Coffin
2. Taylor Thorne
3. Derek Peters
4. Jared Thorne

OPEN BOYS
1. Kanoa Igarashi
2. Jake Marshall
3. Nic Hdez
4. Kei Kobayashi
5. Addy Giddings
6. Colton Ward

OPEN MINI GROMS
1. Jake Marshall
2. Tyler Gunter
3. Kei Kobayashi
4. Ryland Rubens
5. Nolan Rapoza
6. Griffin Colapinto

OPEN WOMEN
1. Chandler Parr
2. Catherine Clark
3. Anise Guzman
4. Taylor Pitz

OPEN LONGBOARD
1. Scott Brandenburg
2. Shaun Thompson
3. Michael Maddox
4. Matt Elias Calles
5. Nathan Thompson

Teddy Navarro. Photo Kenny Morris.

FREEDOM SURF SERIES #3
PISMO BEACH, CALIFORNIA
November 15

Sunny skies, warm offshore winds and solid surf were the conditions of the day, allowing for some fine displays of surfing. In the Men's Open final, everyone was surfing strong, but Paul Pugliesi managed to nab two solid waves, applying his trademark speed and snaps while linking them way down the beach.

BOYS
1. Charlie Fawcett

OPEN WOMEN
1. Kennan Reeser

FISH STICKS
1. Shea Roney

LONGBOARD
1. Bert Fernando

JUNIORS
1. Levi Gregory

OPEN MEN
1. Paul Pugliesi

VOLCOM STONE STARFISH
RIVER JETTIES, NEWPORT BEACH, CALIFORNIA
November 22

The third stop of the Starfish Surf Series kicked off under sunny skies with some insane waves and a huge turnout, until Mother Nature decided to mix things up. A brief whiteout was followed by overcast skies for the rest of the day, but the surf remained rippable. During the back half of the Juniors final, Jared Cassidy came alive, earning two high scores just before the buzzer to steal the win.

MEN PRO-AM
1. Josh Hoyer
2. Brandon Guilemette
3. Michel Flores
4. Brandon Tipton
5. Macy Mullen
6. Max Doucet

JUNIORS
1. Jared Cassidy
2. Christian Saenz
3. Shayne Nelson
4. Chase Wilson
5. Erik Heimstaedt
6. Bobby Okvist

GROMS
1. Taylor Clark
2. Kevin Shultz
3. Dane McCrystal
4. Colin Moran
5. Jack Boyes
6. Tyler Gunter

GIRLS
1. Kaleigh Gilchrist
2. Erica Hosseini
3. Erika Cook
4. Annisa Galindo
5. Leah Pakpour
6. Krystal Shannon

2008–2009 DAYSTAR COPA MANGO TOURNAMENT, CIRCUITO NACIONAL DE SURF
PLAYA JACO, COSTA RICA
November 28–30

In 2- to 4-foot chocolate-colored surf, the finals of the DAYSTAR contest were quite a show for everyone in attendance. Diego Naranjo managed to outlast his fellow finalists and take the win in the Men's Open. With the win, the defending Costa Rican National Champ puts himself in good position to defend and regain his crown.

OPEN MEN
1. Diego Naranjo
2. Jason Torres
3. Olman Morales
4. Federico Pilurzu

JUNIORS (UNDER 18)
1. Carlos Muñoz
2. Ariel Agüero
3. Rudy Jimenez
4. Anthony Fillingam

OPEN WOMEN
1. Lisbeth Vindas
2. Kristin Wilson
3. Nataly Bernold
4. Mariana Samudio

JUNIOR WOMEN (UNDER 18)
1. Lupe Galluccio
2. Nataly Bernold
3. Maia Velarde
4. Elisa Luna

BOYS (UNDER 16)
1. Carlos Muñoz
2. Jordan Hernández
3. Anthony Fillingam
4. Noe Mar McGonagle

GROMMET (UNDER 14)
1. Manuel Mesen
2. Elijah Guy
3. Josué Rodríguez
4. Marta Fillingam

BOYS MINI GROMMET (UNDER 12)
1. Juan Carlos Hernández
2. Andrey López
3. Leonardo Calvo
4. Santana Rosales

GIRLS MINI GROMMET (UNDER 12)
1. Leilani McGonagle
2. Avalon Esterak
3. Cloe Velarde
4. Marta Fillingam

BODYBOARD MEN
1. Richard Marin
2. Joan Mojica
3. Joan Matarrita
4. Donald Berger

MASTERS (OVER 35)
1. Mauro Sergio Oliveira
2. Carlos Velarde
3. Marcelo Matos

4. Tommy Bernof

GRAND MASTERS (OVER 40)
1. Craig Schieber
2. Mike Esterak
3. Carlos Velarde
4. Mario Rodriguez

NOVICES
1. Eduardo Mora
2. Victor Mora
3. Bayron Vargas
4. Henry Peraza

LONGBOARD MEN
1. Martín Pérez
2. Cedric Auffret
3. Anthony Fillingam
4. Adolfo Gómez

NELSCOTT REEF TOW-IN CLASSIC
NELSCOTT REEF, LINCOLN CITY, OREGON
October 1, 2008–March 31, 2009

For the second year in a row, the team of Adam Replogle and Alistair Craft won the 2008 Nelscott Reef Tow-In Classic. After a day of thick fog on Saturday, the field of 16 teams woke up to sunny skies and big surf for the contest on Sunday. Waves were in the 20- to 30-foot range, with calm winds and clear skies. In the first year that the paddle-in division was added to the contest, Kealii Mamala took the win.

2008 TOW-IN RESULTS
1. Adam Replogle & Alistair Craft
2. Jeff Schmucker & Josiah Schmucker
3. Russell Smith & Tyler Smith
4. Zach Wormhoudt & Jake Wormhoudt
5. Brad Gerlach & Mike Parsons
6. Chad Jackson & Jamie Mitchell
7. Tim West & Ion Banner
8. Jeremy Rasmussen & Tom Miller
9. Garrett McNamara & Kealii Mamala
10. Yuri Soledade & Everaldo Pato Texeira
11. Shane Desmond & Tyler Fox
12. Justin Howard & Andre Phillip
13. Jeff Kafka & Benji Darrow
14. Andrew Cotton & Scott Eggers
15. Alec Cooke (Ace Cool) & Ron Barron
16. Mike Parnell & Matt Esnard

2008 PADDLE-IN RESULTS
1. Kealii Mamala
2. Jamie Mitchell
3. Shane Desmond
4. Mike Parsons
5. Gary Linden
6. Justin Howard
7. Chad Jackson
8. Zach Wormhoudt
9. Steve Harnack

PACSUN WSA PRIME SURF SERIES EVENT #3, PRESENTED BY "GOT MILK?"
SOUTH JETTY, OCEANSIDE, CALIFORNIA
December 6

Mother Nature provided perfect shoulder- to head-high peaks with offshore winds, and the competitors gave some stellar surfing performances along with a truckload of gifts for the Marine Corps Toys For Tots program. With some of the top competitors in Hawaii for the North

Andrew Cotton. Photo Richard Hallman/FreelanceImaging.com.

Shore season, the contest was an opportunity for other competitors to gain some ground in the ratings. In the U/14 Boys, Kanoa Igarashi showed a glimmer of the future of the USA Surf Team, wrapping up the win with back-to-back high-scoring rides.

UNDER 18 BOYS
1. Dane Zaun
2. Christian Saenz
3. Christian Arballo
4. Conrad Carr

UNDER 18 GIRLS
1. Courtney Conlogue
2. Chandler Parr
3. Lakey Peterson
4. Tara Franz

UNDER 16 BOYS
1. Derek Peters
2. Ian Crane
3. Kolohe Andino
4. Breyden Taylor

UNDER 16 GIRLS
1. Anise Guzman
2. Emmy Merrill
3. Harley Taich
4. Shelby Detmers

UNDER 14 BOYS
1. Kanoa Igarashi
2. Parker Coffin
3. Jake Marshall
4. Taylor Clark

HO HO SURF OFF, EASTERN SURFING ASSOCIATION (ESA)
NORTH SIDE INDIAN RIVER INLET, DELAWARE
December 6–7

Staying warm was a major part of the competitive strategy at the Ho Ho Surf Off held at Indian River Inlet, as temperatures dipped into the low 40s. With a ticket to the 2009 Regionals in Puerto Rico on the line, the final of the Open Shortboard was a battle. In the end, the lanky goofy-foot Travis Knight distanced himself from Dillon Harrington and took the win.

OPEN SHORTBOARD
1. Travis Knight
2. Dillon Harrington
3. Chris Makibbin
4. Avery Sieg
5. Roy Harrell
6. Jamie Crosby

MENEHUNE SHORTBOARD
1. Shane Moore
2. Jack Fager

3. Simon Hetrick

BOYS SHORTBOARD
1. Brad Flora
2. Avery Sieg
3. Cody Michael
4. Seth Conboy
5. Dallas Harrington
6. Trevor Hanley

JUNIOR MEN SHORTBOARD
1. Dillon Harrington
2. Jamie Crosby
3. Matt Reinhardt
4. Shawn Woolyhan

MEN SHORTBOARD
1. Travis Knight
2. Waldon Remington
3. Roy Harrell
4. Dane Woolyhan

MASTERS SHORTBOARD
1. Chris Makibbin
2. Jack Thomas

SENIOR MEN SHORTBOARD
1. Craig Garfield

JUNIOR WOMEN SHORTBOARD
1. Rachel Harrell
2. Kelly Powell
3. Jenna Landon

WOMEN SHORTBOARD
1. Kelsey Willison

MENEHUNE LONGBOARD
1. Robert Fernandez

MEN LONGBOARD
1. Chris Makibbin

MASTERS LONGBOARD
1. Craig Garfield

WOMEN LONGBOARD
1. Chelsea Remines

OPEN BODYBOARD
1. Craig Chatterton

MENEHUNE BODYBOARD
Bradey Cooling

VOLCOM GOLDFISH SURF SERIES
PISMO PIER, CALIFORNIA
December 2008

Though the forecast called for heavy rains and gnarly winds, the call was made to run the contest anyway. The conditions were as expected, but they backed off over the course of the day, and by the time the Girls final was in the water, the windswells were rather workable. As the final minutes wore down, Rachel Harris unleashed a blistering attack of hacks, following it up with a buzzer-beating wave that solidified the win.

MEN PRO-AM
1. Bobby Morris
2. Nate Tyler
3. Hank Mills
4. Hugh Soderquist
5. Matt Lahg
6. Matt Gallagher

JUNIORS
1. Shaun Burns
2. John Wilson
3. Cody Lewis
4. Elliot Hodges
5. Ian Jenkins
6. Christian Ramirez

GROMS
1. Sam Reagan
2. Kent Nishiya
3. Nick Hdez
4. Mason Reepmaker
5. Vinny Leonelli
6. Joel Scheck

GIRLS
1. Rachel Harris
2. Mackenzie Kessler
3. Amy Covert
4. Ashley Reiley
5. Marissa Kuiken
6. Jill Roberts

NSSA SOUTHWEST CONFERENCE OPEN SEASON #6
SEASIDE REEF, CARDIFF, SAN DIEGO, CALIFORNIA
December 20–21

Youth prevailed big-time at the sixth stop on the NSSA SW Open calendar, with winners of all six categories 15 or younger, including an outstanding victory by Ian Crane in the Open Men division. After a frustrating loss in the Juniors semifinals, Crane stepped his game up in the 2- to 3-foot surf and notched his first Men's win.

OPEN MEN
1. Ian Crane
2. Christian Saenz
3. JD Lewis
4. Doug Van Mierlo

OPEN JUNIORS
1. Kolohe Andino
2. Luke Davis
3. Conner Coffin
4. Taylor Clark

OPEN BOYS
1. Kanoa Igarashi
2. Jake Marshall
3. Jacob Davis
4. Kei Kobayashi
5. Jay Christenson
6. Nic Hdez

OPEN MINI GROM
1. Jake Marshall
2. Tyler Gunter
3. Kei Kobayashi
4. Sam Wickwire
5. Ryland Rubens
6. Griffin Colapinto

OPEN WOMEN
1. Lakey Peterson
2. Courtney Conlogue
3. Chandler Parr
4. Taylor Pitz

OPEN LONGBOARD
1. Matt Elias Calles
2. Michael Maddox
3. Jordan Collins

South America Report

By Reinaldo Andraus

The real roots of South American surfing lie in Peru, the cradle of the sport, with its *caballos de totora*, the ancient means of riding the waves initiated by the fishermen of the north. But in the 1980s and '90s Brazil began to emerge as the surf power, eclipsing its Pacific neighbor. When I began to surf in Sao Paulo, Brazil, in the late 1960s, our first surf pilgrimage was always to Punta Hermosa, Peru, to surf the rock bottom waves before moving on to the reefs of Hawaii. So it is interesting to note that now, after decades of dominance by Brazil, Peru is once again hosting pro surfing events and nurturing great surfers.

It's also interesting to note that in the same year that Brazil held its first surf contest, at Arpoador beach (Rio) in 1965, with international guests Mark Martinson and Dale Stuble dominating the competition, Peru already had a world champion. Felipe Pomar was a star, respected in Hawaii. In his footsteps surfers like Ivo Hanza and Chino Malpartida drew a legacy in Hawaiian waters before any Brazilian surfer became known in the islands.

So it should have been fate that despite the large number of Brazilian surfers tackling the ASP WCT, the first South American champion in the first tier of surfing came from Peru, in the form of Sofia Mulanovich, Women's World Champion in 2004. Sofia, 25, was the one tracking Steph Gilmore closest when the Australian sealed her second WCT title in 2008 at the ripe age of 20, in beautiful waves at Sunset Point. Brazilian charger Silvana Lima, 24, would have stamped Gilmore's ribbon if in the final minutes of the Roxy Pro the salvation wave hadn't shown up for the Aussie girl. Silvana still holds potential to be the first Brazilian WCT champ (man or woman).

On the way to her title Gilmore won, for the second year in a row, the Peruvian event, the Movistar Classic, at Mancora. The contest happened just before the final Hawaiian leg of the women's tour, and Sofia came to her homeland in the lead but couldn't hold the position against the fast and agile girls that tore apart the small left-handers always on offer at that region.

Going back to the beginning of the year, the Hang Loose Pro WQS five star began the season in the "Brazilian Hawaii," Fernando de Noronha, an archipelago where the trade winds blow offshore at the best surfing beaches facing the Northern Hemi swells. Raoni Monteiro, former WCT surfer, took the win, looking on track to make the comeback track to the surfing elite. That didn't happen, as Raoni and almost ten other Brazilian surfers found themselves in the hurting

Silvana Lima. Photo ASP Kirstin © Covered Images.

part of the WQS ratings, just below the cut, by the end of 2008 season.

This was very strange, as Brazilian surfers have a tradition of placing high and even winning the second tier of the ASP Tour. The 2008 season had an all-time record of half a dozen big WQS events in Brazilian waters, all of them won by native surfers, with the exception of the Local Motion Guaruja Surf Pro, taken by Huntington Beach surfer Shaun Ward. If it hadn't been for Jihad Khodr's incredible performance at the Reef Hawaiian Pro, in Haleiwa, Brazil would have a historical first of not qualifying a single surfer through the WQS.

On the other hand, Adriano de Souza had a stellar year, very consistent, with only a place in a final of a World Tour event eluding the talented 21-year-old Guaruja local. Adriano won two WQS events this season, one in Bahia and another in Newcastle. Speculation was big that, had not he been injured just before the Brazilian stop of the World Tour, this could possibly have been his first victory in the highest echelon of surfing.

The Hang Loose Santa Catarina Pro, despite a track record of good surf, has a record of no-shows among the Top 45, including world champions Kelly Slater, Mick Fanning and Andy Irons. But what the event lacked in star power didn't translate to the action in the water, as Australian Bede Durbidge took the chance to jump to runner-up

in the ratings. Brazilians failed to reach the podium, and from the field of 20 seeded into the event, three of them stopped in the quarters.

Heitor Alves was the standout surfer, dropping the jaws of those who endured the rain, and the webcast viewers at home, with an incredible maneuver that was deemed by ASP head judge Perry Hatchett the most outrageous move of the year. Heitor flew over a thick crumbling foam three meters high, spun into the air and landed.

Less than a month after the departure of the World Tour circus from the south of Brazil, Santa Catarina State started to get flooded by unstoppable rains. The Itajai River Valley, just north of Florianopolis, with beautiful trees hanging from the margins, began to rise and rise. The hills around the area collapsed, burying homes. Thousands of people had to be evacuated in a dozen towns. More than a hundred died, were buried or drowned. Global warming is a heavy thing. Brazil is a country that always felt free of big disasters like volcanos, hurricanes and earthquakes, but it is not free of big floods.

In October the region of Pichilemu, in southern Chile, where the legendary wave of Punta Lobos fires perfect lefts, was the stage for the First International Tow-In Championships. The organization was taken by the APT (Association of Professional Towsurfers), Australians Koby Abberton and Ryan Hipwood collected the victors' trophy, with Brazilian teams taking the other three spots on the podium.

The final note goes to the first international tow-in contest held in Brazil, the Red Nose Tow-In Championship, which took place during November in surf over 10 feet at the beach break of Maresias, in Sao Paulo State. Sylvio Mancusi and Alemao de Maresias became the winners in a three-doubles final that included Carlos Burle and Eraldo Gueiros (third) and runner-up team of Everaldo Pato and Yuri Soledade. Several international teams were invited but didn't show up. The call was made five days in advance. Anyway, the action was blistering.

Despite the large number of Brazilian surfers tackling the ASP World Tour, the first South American champion to reach the first tier of surfing came from Peru, in the form of Sofia Mulanovich, Women's World Champion in 2004.

ROXY SURF & ART
MAR DEL PLAYA, HONU BEACH, ARGENTINA
January 5–6

A weekend of good waves, great vibes and the spirit of Roxy abound at Argentina's Honu Beach. Girls of all ages, from the Under 12s to Masters, and across numerous disciplines competed in the friendly conditions, the sun also coming to the party to create two days of camaraderie. Julieta Guateli surfed well against worthy competition to claim the Amateur Juniors title, Laura Fallo doing likewise in the Seniors. Tete Gil trimmed her way to victory in the Longboard division, whilst the Open title went to Joela Jofre.

GROMMETS
1. Josefina Ané
2. Lucía Cosoleto
3. Trinidad Pose
4. Melanie Gonzalvez Lamas

AMATEUR JUNIORS
1. Julieta Guatelli
2. Cruz Araujo
3. Ana Fernández
4. Raquel Corelich

AMATEUR SENIORS
1. Laura Fallo
2. Loly Pose
3. Sole San Martín
4. Evelyn Eisele

LONGBOARD
1. Tete Gil
2. Sofía Guatelli
3. María Paz Usuna
4. Coni Posse

JUNIOR
1. Lucía Cosoleto
2. María Paz Usuna
3. Maia Cherr
4. Coni Pose

BODYBOARD
1. Isabel Pérez
2. Lucía Cosoleto
3. Julieta Gómez Gerbi
4. Coni Pose

MASTERS
1. Victoria Gil
2. Roxana Di Mauro
3. Rocío Gil

TANDEM
1. Fede Goñi & Lucila Rey
2. Lucas Rubiño & Lucía Cosoleto
3. María Paz Usuna & Maia Cherr
4. Lucas Pérsico & Sofía Guatelli

OPEN
1. Joela Jofre
2. Tete Gil
3. Rosario Rillo
4. Verónica Olano

ALAS REEF CLASSIC ARGENTINA
BIOLOGIA MAR DEL PLATA, ARGENTINA
January 11–13

Slim pickings on the wave front made for an interesting competition, surfers being forced to go to great lengths in order to show their best to the judges. Venezuelan Mágnum Martinez came from behind in the two-way final to steal the victory from Mexican Diego Cadena, his two final waves creating his winning score of just 12.66

points. A home win in the Women's final delighted the crowd, Ornella Pellizzari exceeding the talents of her opponents easily and proving her worthiness for a future WQS standing. Venezuela secured one and two in the Junior Pro division, Rafael Pereyra and Francisco Bellorin stepping up to stave off the advances of Leonardo Gianotti and Guillermo Satt, who took third and fourth respectively. And it was an all-Argentine final for the Longboard finals, Daniel Gil taking the trophy to deny the 2007 Latin Champion Martin Perez a first-place start to the year.

OPEN MEN FINAL
1. Mágnum Martinez
2. Diego Cadena

SEMIFINAL 1
1. Mágnum Martinez
2. Rafael Pereyra

SEMIFINAL 2
1. Diego Cadena
2. Moa Suarez

OPEN WOMEN
1. Ornella Pellizzari
2. Sofia Bórquez
3. America Valeria Solé
4. Jessica Anderson

PRO JUNIOR
1. Rafael Pereyra
2. Francisco Bellorin
3. Leonardo Gianotti
4. Guillermo Satt

MEN LONGBOARD
1. Daniel Gil
2. Martin Perez
3. Federico Goñi
4. Leandro Santacroce

VIVA O VERÃO HB SURF PRO-AM ANJUSS
PRAIA BRAVA, BRAZIL
January 20

Brazil's finest turned out for the second stage of the Paranaense de Surf Pro-Am circuit, the ocean providing glassy, if a little murky, three-foot peaks for the contenders. Péricles Demitri stood tall as the definitive victor of the Pro-Am event, a solid three points ahead of his nearest rival, Alessandro Pulga. Pulga did well to scrape a silver medal, with barely more than a point separating second, third and fourth places. Jéssica Bianco slew her rivals, indomitable in the Women's final and likely to remain a strong force on the Brazilian home circuit.

MEN PRO-AM
1. Péricles Demitri
2. Alessandro Pulga
3. Celso Júnior
4. Cesar Teixeira

GROMMETS
1. Alan Borges
2. Wesley Richard
3. Sandriel Foguinho
4. Leonardo Marin

JUNIORS
1. Paulo Derengoski
2. Cesar Teixeira
3. João Marcos
4. Henrique Ricardo

CADETS
1. João Marcos
2. Júnior Sartori

3. Henrique Ricardo
4. Luiz Conceição Sardinha

OPEN WOMEN
1. Jéssica Bianco
2. Andressa Carvalho
3. Camila Prado
4. Vitoria Borges

MASTERS
1. Sandro Piu
2. Tulio Crisanto
3. Gil Cordeiro
4. Claudio Udet

CURITIBA
1. Douglas Nemes
2. Renato Trogue
3. Guto Skavaza
4. Amauri Maia

QUIKSILVER KING OF THE GROMS
MARPLATENSE BIOLOGÍA, PLAYA GRANDE, ARGENTINA
January 21–27

Cordovan wunderkind Mariano Arreyes scored the deuce at Argentina's "Big Beach," Playa Grande, retaining the throne as Quiksilver King of the Groms. Unable to usurp the crowned 2007 champion, Caué Wood, Santiago Muniz and Francisco Usuna had to make do with second to fourth places respectively. Though surfing on his backhand, Arreyes milked the long but crumbling, wind-affected waves to the shore in order to gain maximum points for each ride, the tactic paying dividends, with judges awarding the champion for his persistence. Guillermo Satt ventured in all the way from Chile but was unfortunately denied, the main event's third-place getter, Santiago Muniz, claiming the podium's top spot, relegating Satt to second.

JUNIORS
1. Mariano Arreyes
2. Caué Wood
3. Santiago Muniz
4. Francisco Usuna

UNDER 16 BOYS
1. Santiago Muniz
2. Guillermo Satt
3. Pedro Francistegui
4. Brian Masmut

UNDER 14 BOYS
1. Facundo Arreyes
2. Julián Martínez
3. Brian Masmut
4. Luciano Lallia

UNDER 12 BOYS
1. Facundo Arreyes
2. Lucía Cosoletto
3. Josefina Anee
4. Juan Uhart
5. Nazareno Rodríguez
6. Sebastián Ventura

ALAS REEF CLASSIC PERU MOVISTAR CUP
PLAYA PUNTA ROCAS, PERU
February 8–10

Groomed four-foot waves blessed the ALAS Reef Classic Peru Movistar Cup, competitors reveling in

the conditions and delighting spectators with a display of exceptional surfing. The second installment of the Latin American Surfing Tour culminated in a thrilling, evenly matched final, Costa Rican Diego Naranjo doing battle with Leandro Usuna of Argentina. The lead yo-yoed from one surfer to the other, either capable of taking the win. But when the final horn sounded, it was Naranjo who had the upper hand. Peruvian sensation Analí Gomez continued her good form, this time going one better than previous results with a win in the Women's Open.

OPEN MEN FINAL
1. Diego Naranjo
2. Leandro Usuna

SEMIFINAL 1
1. Diego Naranjo
2. Gary Saavedra

SEMIFINAL 2
1. Leandro Usuna
2. Diego Medina

PRO JUNIOR
1. Leonardo Gianotti
2. Dylan Southworth
3. Maximilian Cross
4. Francisco Bellorin

OPEN WOMEN
1. Analí Gomez
2. Agostina Pellizzari
3. Ornella Pellizzari
4. Sofia Bórquez

MEN LONGBOARD
1. Martin Perez
2. Vincent Delaplace
3. Tamil Martino
4. Patricio Gonzales

REEF CLASSIC EQUADOR ALAS
MONTAÑITA, ECUADOR
February 12–16

A nail-biting climax to the Reef Classic saw an ever-changing lead finalized with just 49 seconds remaining on the clock. Small waves didn't impair the surfers, finalists Gabriel Escudero and Rafael Pereyra drawing everything they could from the minimal swell. Pereya held the advantage leading

into the final stages, but Escudero remained calm and patient, snagging a running wave inside the final minute and using every ounce of his talent and the wave's power to receive a 5.10 score from the judges. This was just enough to capture the lead, and despite a last-ditch attempt form Pereya, Escudero retained the lead and gained the victory. The Pellizari sisters dominated the Women's Open, strong throughout the division and not diminishing in skills into the final. Ornella claimed the win with Agostina a close second, leaving Dominique Barona (EQU), Sofia Borquez (CHI) and Nadja de Col (PERU) to contest for third to fifth positions.

OPEN MEN
1. Gabriel Escudero
2. Rafael Pereyra

OPEN WOMEN
1. Ornella Pellizzari
2. Agostina Pellizzari
3. Dominique Barona
4. Sofia Borquez
5. Nadja de Col

HANG LOOSE PRO • ASP 5-STAR PRIME MEN'S EVENT
FERNANDO DE NORONHA, BRAZIL
February 12–17

Brazil's Raoni Montiero succeeded in taking a win for the host nation in the five-star ASP Hang Loose Pro, holding a lead over North American Gabe Kling. A near-perfect swell was breaking for the event, four-foot pitching waves making for a spectacular display from some former World Tour competitors and numerous aspiring surfers. Barrels abound throughout the contest, allowing for some high-scoring rides from many of the competitors. Montiero opened the final event with a near-nine-point ride, placing Kling in a catch-up position from the outset. Despite a strong semifinal win, Kling couldn't find the waves or the scores needed to overcome his Brazilian counterpart. Another local, Peterson Rosa,

Adriano De Souza. Photo ASP Rowland © Covered Images.

also made a strong impression but for very different reasons, the former World Tour surfer invading the judges' tower in dispute of his heat loss to Gabe Kling. Under the stringent laws of the ASP, Rosa received a US$5,000 fine for the offense, casting a significant, albeit small, shadow on an otherwise positive and exciting event.

FINAL
1. Raoni Monteiro
2. Gabe Kling
SEMIFINAL 1
1. Raoni Monteiro
2. Jonathan Gonzalez
SEMIFINAL 2
1. Gabe Kling
2. Hizunomê Bettero
QUARTERFINAL 1
1. Raoni Monteiro
2. Wilson Nora
QUARTERFINAL 2
1. Jonathan Gonzalez
2. Brett Simpson
QUARTERFINAL 3
1. Hizunomê Bettero
2. Nathaniel Curran
QUARTERFINAL 4
1. Gabe Kling
2. Tim Boal

ALAS REEF CLASSIC REÑACA 2008
REÑACA, CHILE
February 22–24

Surprises, upsets and continually changing leaders infested the Reñaca leg of the Reef Classic, last-minute victories and outsiders frequently being the order of the day. Although a sizeable swell had turned on for the day, the wind was undermining the conditions from early on. Kalle Carranza brought Mexican flair to Chile, coming out on top after a hard fight through the semis and into the final against Venezuelan Francisco Bellorin. Challenging hard, Bellorin presented a very real threat to the victor, but having surfed in and won the Pro Junior division, the young surfer came up short, allowing Carranza the win. The Longboard division was a low-scoring affair, but Argentina's Martin Perez sunk his teeth into the lead and wouldn't let go until the victory was sealed.

OPEN MEN
1. Kalle Carranza
2. Francisco Bellorin
MEN LONGBOARD
1. Martin Perez
2. Patricio Gonzalez
3. Emmanuel Rojas

BILLABONG PRO JUNIOR CHILE • ALAS & ASP GRADE 1 MEN'S PRO JUNIOR / ALAS & ASP GRADE 1 WOMEN'S PRO JUNIOR
PUNTA DE LOBOS, PICHILEMU, CHILE
February 29–March 2

An invasion flooded Chile for the

Billabong Pro Junior, all but two of the male surfers from the quarterfinals onwards being Brazilian. The Brazilians did the courteous thing, though, and brought a plenitude of waves with them, glassy six-foot peaks frequenting the lineup. Ricardo dos Santos was the undisputed standout of the final day of contest, a 9.75 score punctuated with a perfect 10 in his quarterfinal heat against the only remaining local surfer, Manuel Selman. Dos Santos paddled into a beautiful wave, pulling into first one, then another glorious barrel, carving a gouging cutback to register the heat win and his first-ever perfect 10-point score. Brazil also emerged with a smile in the Women's division, Gabriela Leite outsurfing Peruvian Valeria Sole to emerge on top.

MEN FINAL
1. Ricardo dos Santos
2. Alex Ribeiro
SEMIFINAL 1
1. Alex Ribeiro
2. Gabriel Pastori
SEMIFINAL 2
1. Ricardo dos Santos
2. Peterson Crisanto)
QUARTERFINAL 1
1. Gabriel Pastori
2. Alex Lima
QUARTERFINAL 2
1. Alex Ribeiro
2. Veiga
QUARTERFINAL 3
1. Peterson Crisanto
2. Maximiliano Cross
QUARTERFINAL 4
1. Ricardo dos Santos
2. Manuel Selman
WOMEN FINAL
1. Gabriela Leite
2. Valeria Sole
SEMIFINAL 1
1. Gabriela Leite
2. Chantalla Furlanetto
SEMIFINAL 2
1. Valeria Sole
2. Jessica Anderson

CIRCUITO MARESIA BRASILEIRO DE SURF • BRAZILIAN CONFEDERATION OF SURF (CBS)
STELLA MARIS, SALVADOR, BRAZIL
February 29–March 2

Three days of fierce competition brought together teams from across Brazil to fight for their region's reputation in the waves. Sao Paulo was challenged throughout the event but remained strong, winning four of the six divisions and holding a total of ten finals berths. Local favorite, Felipe Toledo was joined by Sao Paulo teammate Edgar Groggia in the finals of the Grommet division, Toledo justifying his status with a first place, Groggia following up in third. In the Boys Junior, the first and third to Sao Paulo were repeated, Nathan Brandi and Miguel Pupo taking the places, Brandi also achieving second in the Cadets, and Jessé Mendes bolstering Sao Paulo's overall position on the team's

table. Camila Cássia went strong for the team, gaining yet another win for Sao Paulo, whilst Team Paraná surfer and event favorite Nathalie Martins lived up to her reputation with a first in the Girls Junior.

OPEN MEN
1. Marco Fernandez
2. Leandro Alberto
3. Luel Felipe
4. Thiago Muller
BOYS JUNIOR
1. Nathan Brandi
2. John Max
3. Miguel Pupo
4. Adriano Santos
CADETS
1. Jessé Mendes
2. Nathan Brandi
3. Santiago Muniz
4. Caio Ibelli
GROMMETS
1. Felipe Toledo
2. Ítalo Ferreira
3. Edgar Groggia
4. Navarrese Matheus
GIRLS JUNIOR
1. Nathalie Martins
2. Greta Sisson
3. Kaena Brandi
4. Barbara Muller

Gabriel Escudero. Photo Emiliano Gatica.

OPEN WOMEN
1. Camila Cássia
2. Michele Desbouillo
3. Kaena Brandi
4. Barbara Muller
TEAM STANDINGS
1. São Paulo
2. Santa Catarina
3. Rio de Janeiro
4. Paraná
4. Rio Grande of North
6. Bahia
7. Ceará
8. Espirito Santo
9. Rio Grande Do Sul
10. Pernambuco

PERUVIAN NATIONAL CHAMPIONSHIP
LA ISLA, PUNTA HERMOSA, PERU
March 1–2

Proving that surfing talent is genetic, Matías Mulanovich emulated in many ways his sister and former ASP World Champion Sofia's powerful maneuvers and winning form. In of-

ten trying though occasionally inspirational conditions, Mulanovich drew together powerful turns and aerial trickery to take this significant win in a matter of hours after his esteemed sister emerged victorious in the first ASP World Tour event of the season at Snapper Rocks, Australia. With sporadic swells reaching up to five feet, contestants had to work hard to gain scoring waves, but Mulanovich's patience and experienced wave selection rewarded him with the points required for the victory. Brissa Malaga came runner-up to Nadja De Col in the first semifinal of the Women's Open but wouldn't let her defeater intimidate her, stepping up her game to win the final heat.

OPEN MEN FINAL
1. Matías Mulanovich
2. Gonzalo "Chendo" Velasco
3. Gustavo Swayne
4. Gabriel Villarán
SEMIFINAL 1
1. Gabriel Villarán
2. Matías Mulanovich
3. Percy Pardo
4. Coco Fernandez
SEMIFINAL 2
1. Gonzalo Velasco
2. Gustavo Swayne
3. Javier Swayne
4. John Urcia
UNDER 18 BOYS FINAL
1. Piero Delucchi
2. Sebastián Rios
3. Nicholas Nugent
4. Franc Portocarrero
SEMIFINAL 1
1. Franc Portocarrero
2. Piero Delucchi
3. Miguel Tudela
4. Mario Almeida
SEMIFINAL 2
1. Sebastián Rios
2. Nicholas Nugent
3. Alessandro Luis
4. Giuliano Giunta
UNDER 16 BOYS
1. Martin Jerí Jr
2. Alessandro Luis
3. Cristóbal De Col
4. Juninho Urcia
MASTERS FINAL
1. Germa'n Aguirre
2. Titi De Col
3. José Carlos de Tramontana
4. Jorge Posso

SEMIFINAL 1
1. Titi De Col
2. José Carlos de Tramontana
3. Martin Jerí
4. Domingo Pianezzi
SEMIFINAL 2
1. Germán Aguirre
2. Jorge Posso
3. Bruno Michilot
4. Eduardo Villarán
MEN LONGBOARD FINAL
1. Piccolo Clemente
2. Tamil Martino
3. Claudius Balducci
4. Juan José Corzo
OPEN WOMEN FINAL
1. Brissa Malaga
2. Nadja De Col
3. Dew Larrañaga
4. Alexia Jerí
SEMIFINAL 1
1. Nadja De Col
2. Brissa Málaga
3. Karen Mendiguetti
SEMIFINAL 2
1. Dew Larrañaga
2. Alexia Jerí
3. Analí Gómez
UNDER 18 LADIES
1. Alexia Jerí
2. Nadja De Col
3. Macarena Vélez
4. Mariángela Zapata

BILLABONG PRO JUNIOR 2008 ASP SOUTH AMERICA JUNIOR TOUR
PRAIA DE TORRES, RIO GRANDE DO SUL, BRAZIL
May 19–21

Blue skies and a highly contestable three- to four-foot swell graced the Praia de Torres for the Brazilian leg of the South America Junior Tour. Host nation Brazil swept the board, from first to equal fifth placings, Alejo Muniz taking each heat one step at a time to eventuate a win. Overcoming the exceptional talents of former Quiksilver King of the Groms and Latin America Pro Junior Champion Wiggolly Dantas amongst a gamut of skilled surfers, Muniz held tight to claim the title. Nathalie Martins surfed with vigor throughout the event, defeating all challengers with calm repose, wrapping up the final with a significant point superfluity.

FINAL STANDINGS
1. Alejo Muniz
2. Magno Pacheco
3. Franklin Serpa
3. Wiggolly Dantas
5. Marco Fernandez
5. Victor Borges
5. Ricardo Wendhausen
5. Alex Ribeiro

THE QUIK PRO ARGENTINA, PRESENTED/DISPLAYED BY SAMSUNG
LA PALOMA ARGENTINA
April 25–27

An event of upsets and surprises

ensued in the Argentinian leg of the Quik Pro, outsiders ousting favorites and former winners coming tantalizingly close to a double win. Former event victor Maxi Suri fell short of retaining his title, despite an exceptional display from the early stages. Also in fine form was Juan Coffer, unfortunate third placer to Suri and eventual champion Agustín Bollini. Bollini missed the prediction list in the lead up to the event, but by the contest's mid-stages he was already being pegged for a finals berth. Despite a solid performance placed by the former champion, it was Bollini who turned tables, taking the win convincingly.

FINAL
1. Agustín Bollini
2. Maxi Siri
SEMIFINAL 1
1. Maxi Siri
2. Juan Coffer
SEMIFINAL 2
1. Agustín Bollini
2. Diego Conti

FTC CONTEST CIRCUITO BAIANO DE SURF UNIVERSITÁRIO 2008
VILLAS DO ATLÂNTICO, LAURO DE FREITAS
June 18

The 2008 installment of the Circuito Baiano de Surf Universitário saw a two-way battle for first place between Charles Costa and current University State Bi-Champion Lucas Guillerme. Guillerme mastered the conditions, gaining the Mahalo Best Wave award with an 8.5 ride early in the event, but couldn't find the same wave in the final, falling frustratingly short in the dying minutes. The lead seesawed for the entire heat between Costa and Guillerme, both surfing evenly and matching scores blow for blow. With eight minutes on the clock, Guillerme held the lead, but the heat wasn't over and Costa returned the volley with a 5.5—just enough to edge him into first place. Despite a manageable 4.76 required by Guillerme, the ocean didn't provide and the former champion had to concede victory.

COLLEGE DIVISION FINAL
1. Charles Costa
2. Lucas Guillerme
3. Vinícius Satyro
4. Flávio Galini
INVITEES DIVISION FINAL
1. Rudá Carvalho
2. Bruno Mateus
3. Marco Fernandez
4. Wheslen Christian
SCHOOL JUNIOR DIVISION FINAL
1. Marco Fernandez
2. Adriano Cambuti
3. Samuel Silva
4. Lucas Silva
MID-SCHOOL DIVISION FINAL
1. Danilo Almeida
2. Demi Brasil
3. José Wilson
4. Ian Costa
GROMMETS SCHOOL DIVISION FINAL
1. Ian Costa

2. Ian Santos
3. Edson Júnior
4. Adauto Filho
MAHALO AIR SHOW WINNER
Ítalo Rosa
MAHALO BEST WAVE WINNER
Lucas Guillerme

HANG LOOSE SURF ATTACK, AMATEUR SÃO PAULO CIRCUIT
ITAMAMBUCA, UBATUBA, SAO PAULO
June 24

Defending his current State Champion status, Miguel Pupo entered the Hang Loose Surf Attack as favorite and didn't fail to deliver. Amassing a grand score of 18.50 from his two waves, Pupo left no doubt that he will again be the one to watch on the São Paulo Circuit and State titles. Thiago Guimarães-surfed well and, had it not been for the resounding talents of Pupo, would have been the heat's standout. São Sebastião's Gabriel Medina was hard-pressed to muster a win in the Under 16 division, needing to create something special in order to make a victory of his heat. Raising the bar, Medina took his game above the lip to the favor of the judges, resulting in a pair of significant scores to make the high spot on the podium. Young Wesley Dantas showed all present that a bright future awaits him, claiming the title in both the Under 12 and Under 10 divisions.

UNDER 18 BOYS
1. Miguel Pupo
2. Thiago Guimarães
3. Filipe Toledo
4. Ian Gouveia
UNDER 16 BOYS
1. Gabriel Medina
2. Thiago Guimarães
3. Kristian Kimmerson
4. Lucas Santos
UNDER 14 BOYS
1. Filipe Toledo
2. Yan Dabecow
3. Wesley Dantas
4. Luan Wood
UNDER 12 BOYS
1. Wesley Dantas
2. Lucas Silveira
3. Edgar Groggia
4. Alex Sandro Santos
UNDER 10 BOYS
1. Wesley Dantas
2. Leo Guimarães
3. Herbert Moreno
4. Victor Mendes

LOCAL MOTION GUARUJÁ SURF PRO • ASP 5-STAR WQS MEN'S EVENT #18
PITANGUEIRAS BEACH, GUARUJA, BRAZIL
June 24–29

As the only non-Brazilian in the quarterfinals, California's Shaun Ward was far from the crowd favorite. But the 25-year-old failed to let the pressure hinder his surf-

ing, steadily knocking out first one then another local challenger to make his way through to the final and victory. Ward had a dicey path through his final heat, opponent Simão Romão, of Rio de Janeiro, surfing the heat's best wave for a mid-seven-point score. But, unable to follow up, Romão had to concede the victory, Ward following up a 6.83 ride with a low 6 points, not fantastic but plenty enough to seal the win. Romão had a positive prequel to his finals performance, denying ASP World Tour surfer Rodrigo Dornelles of an advance. Opening the heat with a 7.33, Dor-

nelles started strong, but Romão came back with two high scores to proceed with ease. With the victory, Ward climbed a huge 47 points up the overall WQS ladder.

FINAL
1. Shaun Ward
2. Simão Romão
SEMIFINAL 1
1. Shaun Ward
2. André Silva
SEMIFINAL 2
1. Simão Romão
2. Rodrigo Dornelles
QUARTERFINAL 1
1. Shaun Ward
2. Tomas Hermes
QUARTERFINAL 2
1. André Silva
2. Marco Polo
QUARTERFINAL 3
1. Simão Romão
2. Adilton Mariano
QUARTERFINAL 4
1. Rodrigo Dornelles
2. Davi do Carmo

BILLABONG SURF ECO FESTIVAL, APRESENTA NOVA SCHIN • ASP 5-STAR WQS MEN'S EVENT #17 / ASP 5-STAR WQS WOMEN'S EVENT #5
PRAIA DO FORTE, BAHIA, BRAZIL
July 17–21

In finals dominated by Brazilians, ASP World Tour surfers Adriano de

Souza and Silvana Lima stood out as the surfers to beat from the get-go. With a collection of talented surfers to overcome through the heats, both victors had their work cut out, but their years of experience paid off when the heats climaxed. De Souza faced fellow countryman Marcelo Trekinho, the young Brazilian doing exceptionally to make the final, having defeated former World Tour surfer Yuri Sodré in the quarterfinal. On his path to the victory, de Souza dispensed with Australian Shaun Cansdell and U.S. surfer, Nathaniel Curran, both highly skilled in their own right. But when the final came,

Alex Ribeiro. Photo Aleko Stergiou.

it was a one-sided affair, de Souza simply too experienced for Trekinho. Conversely, Silvana Lima had a tough battle against Australian teen sensation Sally Fitzgibbons. With swell peaking at the four-foot mark, Lima was under pressure throughout the heat. Leading into the final minute, it was Fitzgibbons who held the upper hand. But a late wave from Lima resulted in a score of 8.5, pulling the Brazilian into the lead and ultimately onto the top spot on the podium.

MEN FINAL
1. Adriano de Souza
2. Marcelo Trekinho
SEMIFINAL 1
1. Adriano de Souza
2. Nathaniel Curran
SEMIFINAL 2
1. Marcelo Trekinho
2. Ricardo Ferreira
QUARTERFINAL 1
1. Adriano de Souza
2. Shaun Cansdell
QUARTERFINAL 2
1. Nathaniel Curran
2. Leandro Bastos
QUARTERFINAL 3
1. Ricardo Ferreira
2. Jihad Kohdr
QUARTERFINAL 4
1. Marcelo Trekinho
2. Yuri Sodré
WOMEN'S FINAL
1. Silvana Lima
2. Sally Fitzgibbons
SEMIFINAL 1
1. Silvana Lima
2. Diana Cristina
SEMIFINAL 2

1. Sally Fitzgibbons
2. Monik Santos

HANG LOOSE SURF ATTACK 2ND STAGE, AMATEUR SÃO PAULO CIRCUIT
PIER MONAGUA BRAZIL
July 19–20

Miguel Pupo again stamped his superiority on the Brazilian Junior Circuit with a convincing win in stage two of the Hang Loose Surf Attack. A back-to-back victory gave Pupo a substantial lead on the series leader board,

almost 800 points above his closest rival, Filipe Toledo. Taking on a barrage of Gustavos, Araújo, Machado and Sanches—all finalists—Pupo again stepped up to the plate with the skills needed to overcome his talented rivals. Gabriel Medina barely missed out on a similar double bill, coming in second to Vitor Valentim in the Under 16 final. But it was Wesley Danta who again impressed, winning the Under 10s, only coming fourth in the Under 12s but excelling to claim the win in the Under 14 division, an exceptional feat for the young man, surfing against competitors up to four years his senior.

UNDER 18 BOYS
1. Miguel Pupo
2. Gustavo Araújo
3. Gustavo Machado
4. Gustavo Sanches
UNDER 16 BOYS
1. Vitor Valentim
2. Gabriel Medina
3. Thiago Guimarães
4. Filipe Toledo
UNDER 14 BOYS
1. Wesley Dantas
2. Igor Moraes
3. Edgar Groggia
4. Luan Wood
UNDER 12 BOYS
1. Edgar Groggia
2. Deivid Silva
3. Filipe Toledo
4. Wesley Dantas
UNDER 10 BOYS
1. Wesley Dantas
2. Herbert Moreno
3. Léo Guimarães
4. David Toledo

FTC CONTEST CIRCUITO BAIANO DE SURF UNIVERSITÁRIO 2008

PIRUÍ, AREMBEPE, CAMAÇARI, BRAZIL
August 31

In a near repeat of the previous event, the second stage of the Circuito Baiano De Surf Universitário saw Lucas Guillerme, Charles Costa and Vinícius Satyro filling the top three places of the FTC Open Men's division. But unlike the opening stage, in which current University State Bi-Champion Lucas Guillerme succumbed to Charles Costa's persistent advances, Guillerme reiterated his two-year dominance of the series. Alexandre Milazzo achieved a perfect 10 to claim the win in the University Bodyboard division over Everton Muniz. But Muniz would get his revenge in the invitee's event, forcing Milazzo into second.

MEN COLLEGE DIVISION
1. Lucas Guillerme
2. Charles Costa
3. Vinícius Satyro
4. Bruno Matheus

WOMEN COLLEGE DIVISION
1. Carine Góes
2. Tiala Fernanda

MEN UNIVERSITY BODYBOARD
1. Alexandre Milazzo
2. Everton Muniz
3. Vinícius Alvin
4. Henrique Milazzo

WOMEN UNIVERSITY BODYBOARD
1. Juliana Dourado
2. Pollyanna Aciole

INVITEES DIVISION
1. Marco Fernandez
2. Valmir Neto
3. Jeferson Oliveira
4. Bruno Matheus

INVITED BODYBOARD
1. Everton Muniz
2. Alexandre Milazzo
3. Vinícius Alvin
4. Henrique Milazzo

SCHOOL JUNIOR DIVISION
1. Marco Fernandez
2. Willy Correa
3. Ian Costa
4. Samuel Lima

MID-SCHOOL DIVISION
1. Danilo Almeida
2. Eduardo Santana
3. Ian Costa
4. Landerson Costa

GROMMETS SCHOOL DIVISION
1. Ian Costa
2. Robério Pereira
3. Ian Santos
4. Adauto Costa

GIRLS SCHOOL DIVISION
1. Priscila Souza
2. Noelane Circenis

EXPRESSION SESSION WINNER
Rudá Carvalho

GATORADE SURF CLASSIC • ASP MEN'S 4-STAR WQS EVENT / ASP MEN'S SOUTH AMERICA PRO TOUR STOP #3

PRAIA DA SAUDADE, SÃO FRANCISCO DO SUL CITY, SANTA CATARINA STATE, BRAZIL
September 6–9

Despite coming up against ASP World Tour surfer Peterson Rosa, Jadson André brought together a wealth of skill and a mature

Raoni Monteiro. Photo ASP Kirstin © Covered Images.

competition outlook to take a significant win in the Gatorade Surf Classic. Claiming one of the most prominent wins of his career, the Brazilian surfer gained significant points from the ASP four-star event, to elevate himself considerably in the WQS standings.

FINAL
1. Jadson André
2. David do Carmo
3. Thomas Hermes
4. Peterson Rosa

SEMIFINAL 1
1. Jadson André
2. David do Carmo
3. Miguel Pupo
4. Guilherme Ferreira

SEMIFINAL 2
1. Peterson Rosa
2. Tomas Hermes
3. Marco Giorgi
4. Márcio Farney

QUARTERFINAL 1
1. Guilherme Ferreira
2. Jadson André
3. Michel Roque
4. Petterson Thomaz

QUARTERFINAL 2
1. Miguel Pupo
2. David do Carmo
3. Caetano Vargas
4. Paulo Moura

QUARTERFINAL 3
1. Márcio Farney
2. Thomas Hermes
3. João Gutemberg
4. Antonio Eudes

QUARTERFINAL 4
1. Peterson Rosa
2. Marco Giorgi
3. Gilmar Silva
4. Thiago de Souza

BILLABONG LADIES PRO • ASP 4-STAR WOMEN'S WQS EVENT

COSTÃO DO SANTINHO, BRAZIL
October 1–4

Rain and small waves hampered the Billabong Ladies Pro held at Brazil's Costão do Santinho, but that didn't stop the competitors from creating an awesome display of surfing for what few crowds stuck it out through the downpours. ASP World Tour veteran Silvana Lima proved why she had landed a spot on the World Tour with a powerful display that gave her a convincing victory over fellow country-woman Tita Tavares. Tavares, a four-time Brazilian National Champion herself, surfed an admirable heat and had, through the former stages, shown that she was a very real threat in taking a fifth national crown. New Zealand's Paige Hareb was the only outsider to get a grip on the event, advancing to the semifinal before being stopped in her tracks by the eventual winner.

WOMEN FINAL
1. Silvana Lima
2. Tita Tavares

SEMIFINAL 1
1. Tita Tavares
2. Jacqueline Silva

SEMIFINAL 2
1. Silvana Lima
2. Paige Hareb

MEN FINAL
1. Alex Ribeiro
2. Alex Lima

WOMEN FINAL
1. Diana Cristina
2. Bethany Hamilton

GATORADE SURF CLASSIC • ASP MEN'S 4-STAR WQS EVENT / ASP MEN'S SOUTH AMERICA PRO TOUR STOP #3

PRAIA DA SAUDADE, SÃO FRANCISCO DO SUL CITY, SANTA CATARINA STATE, BRAZIL
September 6–9

In front of a 6,000-strong home crowd, the ASP Men's Four Star Gatorade Surf Classic crowned a surprise champion in Jadson André. A light offshore groomed four-foot peaks at the Praia Da Saudade, an impressive array of talent gracing the event. Peterson Rosa, as a former ASP World Tour contender, was a firm favorite for the title, his quest for re-qualification on the World Tour no doubt driving him. Certainly in the heats leading up to the final Rosa was the dominant player, surfing through the stages with ease. But, come the final, it was Jadson André who was the man to watch. Current State Champion Miguel Pupo did well to surf confidently into the semis, but again André was to prove the giant-slayer, knocking Pupo back to third. At just 18 years of age, André no doubt made a lasting impression on his peers, but, despite the 875 points gained towards his WQS standing, it looked like taking another year or so for the Brazilian surfer to make the big time.

FINAL
1. Jadson André
2. David do Carmo
3. Thomas Hermes
4. Peterson Rosa

SEMIFINAL 1
1. Jadson André
2. David do Carmo
3. Miguel Pupo
4. Guilherme Ferreira

SEMIFINAL 2
1. Peterson Rosa
2. Tomas Hermes
3. Marco Giorgi
4. Márcio Farney

QUARTERFINAL 1
1. Guilherme Ferreira
2. Jadson André
3. Michel Roque
4. Petterson Thomaz

QUARTERFINAL 2
1. Miguel Pupo
2. David do Carmo
3. Caetano Vargas
4. Paulo Moura

QUARTERFINAL 3
1. Márcio Farney
2. Thomas Hermes
3. João Gutemberg
4. Antonio Eudes

QUARTERFINAL 4
1. Peterson Rosa
2. Marco Giorgi
3. Gilmar Silva
4. Thiago de Souza

BILLABONG GIRLS PRO • ASP WQS WOMEN'S EVENT #11

BARRA DA TIJUCA, RIO DE JANEIRO, BRAZIL
September 8–18

In an almost entirely World Tour-dominated final, Rebecca Woods surfed a blistering heat to take a win over fellow Australians Stephanie Woods and Jessi Miley-Dyer and local hope Tita Tavares. Winning each heat from the quarterfinals onwards, Woods never looked in doubt for a finals berth, but the stage started on Rocky ground for the young Aussie.

Tita Tavares opened the heat in the lead, but with an impressive 8.83 single-wave score, Woods leapt into the lead, an advantage that she maintained to the climax. The sizeable swell allowed the girls the opportunity to unleash a plethora of powerful maneuvers, impressing judges and spectators alike. But it was Woods who took the crowning glory.

FINAL
1. Rebecca Woods
2. Stephanie Gilmore
3. Jessi Miley-Dyer
4. Tita Tavares

SEMIFINAL 1
1. Stephanie Gilmore
2. Tita Tavares
3. Silvana Lima
4. Tais de Almeida

SEMIFINAL 2
1. Rebecca Woods
2. Jessi Miley-Dyer
3. Nicola Atherton
4. Monik Santos

QUARTERFINAL 1
1. Taís de Almeida
2. Silvana Lima
3. Krisna de Souza
4. Valeria Sole

QUARTERFINAL 2
1. Tita Tavares
2. Stephanie Gilmore
3. Melanie Redman
4. Juliana Quint

QUARTERFINAL 3
1. Rebecca Woods
2. Jessi Miley-Dyer
3. Samantha Cornish
4. Layne Beachley

QUARTERFINAL 4
1. Nicola Atherton
2. Monik Santos
3. Serena Brooke
4. Gabriela Teixeira

BILLABONG LADIES PRO • ASP 4-STAR WOMEN'S WQS EVENT

COSTÃO DO SANTINHO, BRAZIL
October 1–4

A day of rain and small waves soon turned into a day of Limas, brother-sister team Silvana and Alex turning on a superb display of surfing in the final stages of the Billabing Ladies Pro and the Brazilian leg of the Billabong Pro Junior. Whilst Silvana blitzed the Ladies event young Alex was pipped at the post by fellow Brazilian Alex Ribiero, having to remain content with a second. Silvana surfed an impeccable heat, opening the event with a seven-point ride, followed by another, both soon to be replaced by a pair of mid-eights. Her opponent, Tita Tavares, was unable to match the World Tour surfer, but the young Brazilian gained vital points towards her World Qualifying Series quest. Hawaiian Bethany Hamilton was again bridesmaid in the Ladies' Pro Junior, local Diana Christina claiming the victory with ease.

LADIES PRO FINAL
1. Silvana Lima
2. Tita Tavares

SEMIFINAL 1
1. Tita Tavares
2. Jacqueline Silva
SEMIFINAL 2
1. Silvana Lima
2. Paige Hareb
PRO JUNIOR MEN
1. Alex Ribeiro
2. Alex Lima
PRO JUNIOR WOMEN
1. Diana Cristina
2. Bethany Hamilton

HANG LOOSE SURF ATTACK • AMATEUR SÃO PAULO CIRCUIT
PRAIA DO TOMBO, GUARUJÁ, BRAZIL
October 16

São Paulo's fourth stage of the Hang Loose Surf Attack brought to light once more the breadth of talent in the region. Surfing with opponents of up to five years his senior, Filipe Toledo proved that age is immaterial. Contesting the heats with confidence beyond his years, Toldeo threatened all he came up against. But the day's premiere event win would go to Gabriel Medina, the leader of the Under 14 ladder at the time, as well as the 3rd place overall in the U/18. Miguel Pupo, who was unable to attend the event, was relegated to 4th place overall by Medina, Lucas Santos and Filipe Toledo, who gained third and fourth respectively.

UNDER 18 BOYS
1. Gabriel Medina
2. Jessé Mendes
3. Lucas Santos
4. Filipe Toledo
UNDER 16 BOYS
1. Caio Ibelli
2. Gabriel Medina
3. Luan Felipe
4. Giovanni Ferreira
UNDER 14 BOYS
1. Deivid Silva
2. Filipe Toledo
3. Yan Daberkow
4. Alexsandro Santos
UNDER 12 BOYS
1. Edgar Groggia
2. Wesley Dantas
3. Igor Moraes
4. Phelipe Chagas
UNDER 10 BOYS
1. Wesley Dantas
2. Herbert Moreno
3. David Toledo
4. Victor Mendes

MARESIA SURF INTERNATIONAL • ASP 6-STAR WQS MEN'S EVENT
ITAJAI, SANTA CATARINA, BRAZIL
October 14–19

In a multi-national finale, Brazil came out on top, with Jano Belo flying the flag for the host nation. Contested in three-foot surf at Itajai, Santa Catarina, the final day of the event was electric, Hawaii, Brazil, Japan and the USA all being repre-

sented in the quarterfinals. Dustin Barca surfed an excellent competition, the Hawaiian unleashing an abundance of tricks and moves, including several barrels, in the penultimate heat. But, come the final, luck prevailed for Belo, Barca being denied the chance, cursed with a drought of significant waves. Masatoshi Ohno (Japan) landed his finest result to date: a third place in a WQS six-star event. Disappointed to make the final, the Japanese surfer was nevertheless happy to take his stand on the podium.

FINAL
Jano Belo
Dustin Barca
SEMIFINAL 1
1. Dustin Barca
2. Masatoshi Ohno
SEMIFINAL 2
1. Jano Belo
2. Marcio Farney
QUARTERFINAL 1
1. Dustin Barca
2. Jadson Andre
QUARTERFINAL 2
1. Masatoshi Ohno
2. Halley Batista
QUARTERFINAL 3
1. Marcio Farney
2. Brett Simpson
QUARTERFINAL 4
1. Jano Belo
2. Adilton Mariano

ONBONGO PRO SURFING • ASP 6-STAR WQS MEN'S EVENT
UBATUBA, SAO PAULO, BRAZIL
October 21–26

Former King of the Groms Wiggolly Dantas scored one of the finest victories of his career thus far, winning the WQS six-star Onbongo Pro Surfing event in Sao Paulo, dispensing with a gamut of fellow countrymen in his path to the final, including former ASP World Tour surfer Raoni Montiero. Dantas was joined by another 18-year-old surfer in the event's final, Jadson André surfing a strong contest to gain a podium placing. Andrés' solid placing in the six-star WQS competition comes just one month after his victory in September's Gatorade Surf Classic, another six-star event. But the near-victory was a bitter loss for the young Brazilian. A win in Brazil's final WQS event of the season would have placed him in 15th place overall, qualifying him for 2009's ASP World Tour. Hizunome Bettero had better luck, his semifinal win elevating him to 13th place on the WQS ladder, enough to give him entry into the tour.

FINAL
1. Wiggolly Dantas
2. Jadson André
SEMIFINAL 1
1. Wiggolly Dantas
2. Hizunome Bettero
SEMIFINAL 2
1. Jadson André
2. Leonardo Neves

QUARTERFINAL 1
1. Wiggolly Dantas
2. Raoni Monteiro
QUARTERFINAL 2
1. Hizunome Bettero
2. Thiago Camarao
QUARTERFINAL 3
1. Leonardo Neves
2. Josh Kerr
QUARTERFINAL 4
1. Jadson André
2. Marcelo Trekinho

APT WORLD CUP TOUR
PUNTA DE LOBOS, PICHILEMU, CHILE
April 15–October 31

After more than six months of wait-

Rebecca Woods. Photo APS Towner © Covered Images.

ing, big-wave destination Punta de Lobos finally turned on, 12- to 15-foot waves crashing onto the dominating cliff face at Pichilemu. Australian duo Koby Abberton and Ryan Hipwood took the top honors in the Association of Professional Towsurfers World Cup event, pulling into some of the biggest, occasionally barreling, waves of the day. Runners up were the Brazilian pairing of Danilo Couto and Rodrigo Resende.

FINAL
1. Koby Abberton/Ryan Hipwood
2. Danilo Couto/ Rodrigo Resende
3. Evarldo Texeira/Yuri Soledad
4. Sylvio Mancusi/Edilson Assuncau
5. Diego Medina/Cristobol Gonzales
6. Grant 'Twiggy' Baker/Reinalso Ibarra
7. Jamie Mitchell/Mark Vissor
8. Scott Chandler/Chuck Patterson

USA VS. BRAZIL GAME CHALLENGE, PRESENTED BY OI NATIONAL SURF LEAGUE
MARESIAS, BRAZIL
November 8–9

Bringing together talents from across generations, the USA vs. Brazil Game Challenge pitted two teams of exceptional talents together in a battle for their respective countries' honors. Team USA seemed to have the event

wrapped up in the first game, staving off threats from the surfers from south of the border to open up a 2.5-point deficit, Shane Beschen, Clay Marzo and Asher Nolan leading the charge. But the tables were turned in the second, Heitor Alves almost singlehandedly bringing his team to victory. Despite some unbelievable surfing from Clay Marzo and Corey Lopez, it was far from enough to redeem the Americans, the Brazilians taking a second win for the series victory.

RESULTS (BEST OF 3)
Brazil 2–USA 1
GAME ONE:
1. USA–79.5
2. Brazil–77
GAME TWO:
1. Brazil–81
2. USA–77.5
GAME THREE:
1. Brazil–81.5
2. USA–78
MVP
Marcelo Trekinho
MOST RADICAL MANOEUVRE
Clay Marzo (power blow tail off-the-top)
TEAM USA:
Tom Curren, Clay Marzo, Shane Beschen, Cory Lopez and Asher Nolan
TEAM BRAZIL:
Marcelo Trekinho, Bruno Santos, Fábio Gouveia, Heitor Alves and Danilo Grillo

LOCAL MOTION SP CONTEST
SÃO PAULO, BRAZIL
December 7

Despite a drop in swell quality and size, the final of the Local Motion SP was a visually spectacular event, with Flavio Boca leading an unprecedented level of surfing. Boca was a consummate professional throughout the event, picking the better waves in the difficult conditions to claim the victory. In the Women's division, Andréa Planas opened the final in a strong position, leading the heat over Juliana Gadelha. But Gadelha was going to prove no easy defeat, advancing into the lead and refusing to relinquish her advantage and taking the win.

OPEN MEN
1. Flavio Boca
2. Mayan Eduardo
3. Marcelo Melo
4. Victor Lage
JUNIORS
1. Erick Proost
2. Caio Rodrigues
3. Guilherme Lopes
4. Pedro Henrique
MEN LONGBOARD
1. Leonardo Paioli
2. Marcelo Melo
3. Danilo Silva
4. Pablo Giachetti
MASTER'S
1. Taciano Parri
2. Flavio Boca
3. Alexander Miranda
4. Beto Schina
OPEN WOMEN
1. Juliana Gadelha
2. Andréa Planas
3. Renata Bosquetti
4. Roberta Costa

CAMPEÕES DO LOCAL MOTION SP CONTEST 08, LOCAL MOTION
EDUCATION CITY, SAO PAOLO
December 17

Brazil's finest young university student surfers congregated on Sao Paolo's beaches for the 2008 Local Motion Championship. Flavio Boca was again a major player in the Open division, taking the win over Eduardo Maia, Marcelo Melo and Victor Lage, second, third- and fourth-place getters respectively. Zone West's Juliana Gadelha was claimant of the Women's title, surfing with style to defeat her talented peers, netting the West's second win of the event. Zone South collected the remainder of the trophies, with Erick Proost winning the Juniors, Taciano Parri the Masters and Leonardo Paioli securing the Longboard division.

OPEN MEN
1. Flavio Boca
2. Eduardo Maia
3. Marcelo Melo
4. Victor Lage
JUNIOR
1. Erick Proost
2. Caio Rodrigues
3. Guilherme Lopes
4. Pedro Henrique
MEN LONGBOARD
1. Leonardo Paioli
2. Marcelo Melo
3. Danilo Silva
4. Paulo Giachetti
MASTER
1. Taciano Parri
2. Flavio Boca
3. Alexandre Miranda
4. Beto Schina
OPEN WOMEN
1. Juliana Gadelha
2. Andréa Planas
3. Renata Bosquetti
4. Roberta Costa

Directory

Pedro Viana Scooby. Photo Alex Laurel.

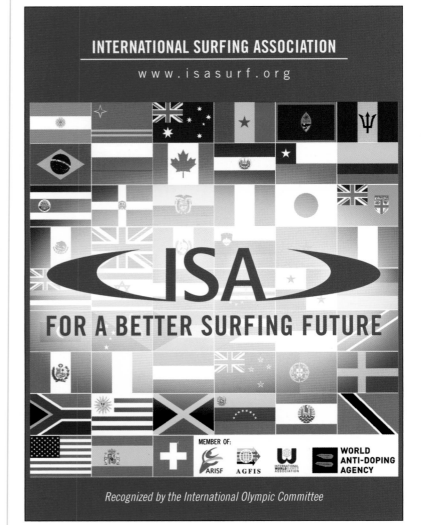

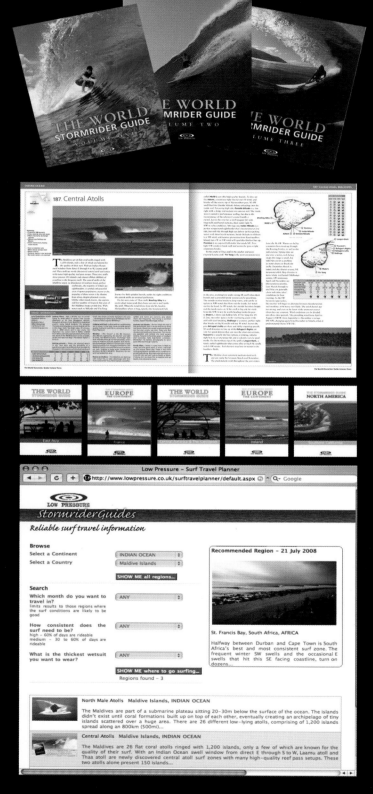

Oakley Icon Ltd.: (+41) 448296100, www.oakley.com

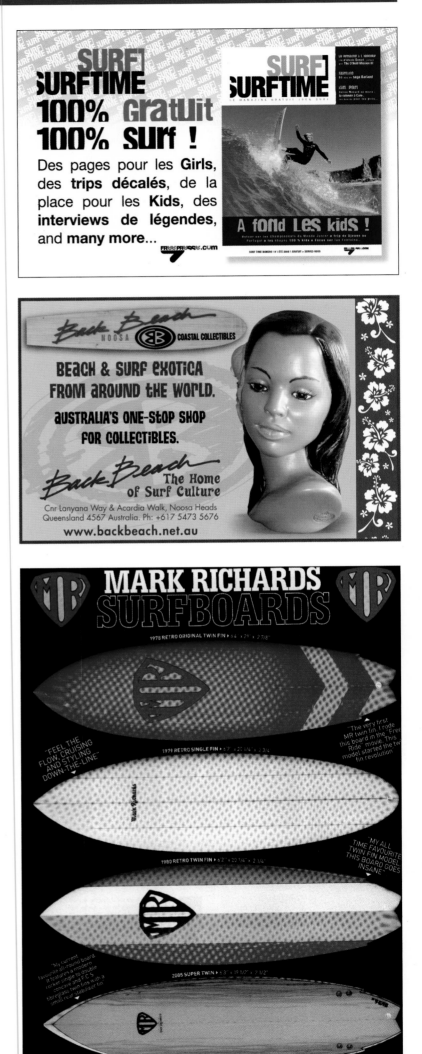

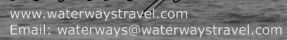

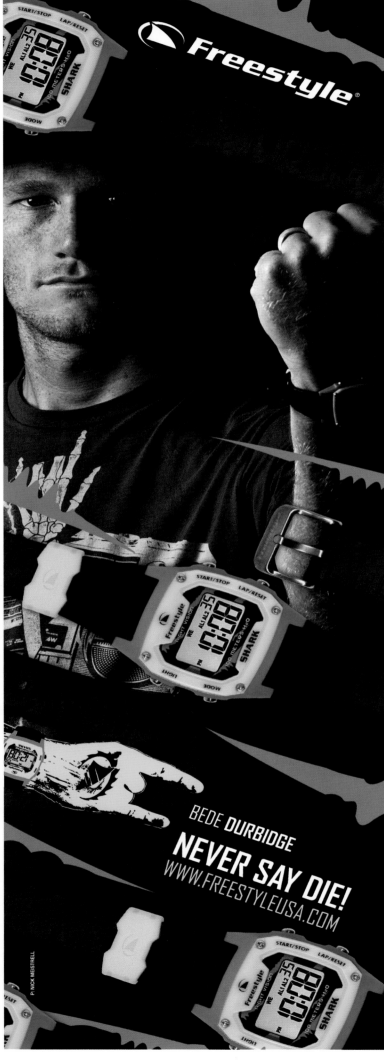

Acknowlegments

Like the website that inspired it, the first *Surfing Yearbook* has been very much a global project, with a vast network of writers, photographers, researchers, editors and designers battling time zones and the tyranny of distance to complete it in timely fashion.

It hasn't been easy, and perhaps those of us who worked on this far-flung team now fully appreciate why such a mammoth project had never been undertaken before. You, the reader, will decide whether the superhuman effort of compilation of this important surfing resource was really worth it, but from my admittedly biased position in the chief editor's chair, I can say that I'm very pleased and proud to have been part of what we hope will become an annual tradition.

In order to get the *Yearbook* off the ground, Surfersvillage founder Bruce Boal and I met in France in October 2006 and basically pooled our vast network of contacts around the surfing world and asked them to help. From global and national governing bodies to lobby groups, environmental activists and individuals who just happened to have their ears to the ground in far-flung outposts of surf, we were inundated with offers of assistance, and in large part they made our idea become a reality.

Specific contributions are credited throughout the book, but here I want to make special mention of some people whose tireless efforts are truly appreciated. Pablo Zannochi from the ISA went way beyond the call of duty to assist, while his boss, ISA president Fernando Aguerre, has been a fervent supporter since the project began. Brodie Carr and Rabbit Bartholomew at the ASP also helped grease the wheels.

When the sheer workload began to seem unbearable, I was assisted in the compilation of news and results by writers whose talents deserved a more intriguing context, but who were happy to join me at the coalface for the dirty work. My sincere thanks to Paul Holmes, Tommy Leitch, Bryan Dickerson and Chasen Marshall.

Bryan Dickerson, who runs the news desk at Surfersvillage from his base in California, has also been a sounding board, photo researcher, copy editor and fact checker throughout this long process, and his breezy can-do attitude and attention to detail has been of huge assistance. The same can be said for France/UK-based Clare McGowan, who came to the *Yearbook* late and played a brilliant catch-up role before taking over the onerous work of photo research. Clare has worked long, hard and uncomplainingly to bring this work to fruition, and we are all in her debt, no one more so than me, the imperfect juggler who sometimes drops a ball, if only for a fleeting second.

Gibbs Smith has developed a reputation as a fine publisher of surf books, and we were delighted when they agreed to become the first publisher of *The Surfing Yearbook*. Editor Madge Baird and designer Kurt Wahlner were a pleasure to work with for their commitment, professionalism and patience with an old Irish seadog and a crusty Antipodean surf mongrel.

Finally, it needs to be said that this book would not be, without the absolute commitment to its publication that Bruce Boal has displayed for more than two years now. It's been a long, hard pregnancy, but Bruce now has a second child he can be proud of.

Phil Jarratt
Noosa Heads, Australia

Monuments. Photo © Mickey Smith.